KAMI·KAZE™

Volume 2

By Shiki Satoshi

HAMBURG // LONDON // LOS ANGELES // TOKYO

Kami-Kaze Vol. 2
Created by Shiki Satoshi

Translation - Ray Yoshimoto
English Adaptation - Jerome Halligan
Copy Editor - Peter Ahlstrom
Retouch and Lettering - Mike Graniel
Production Artist - Jihye "Sophia" Hong
Cover Design - James Lee

Editor - Luis Reyes
Digital Imaging Manager - Chris Buford
Managing Editor - Lindsey Johnston
Editor-in-Chief - Rob Tokar
VP of Production - Ron Klamert
Publisher and E.I.C. - Mike Kiley
President and C.O.O. - John Parker
C.E.O. and Chief Creative Officer - Stuart Levy

A TOKYOPOP Manga

TOKYOPOP Inc.
5900 Wilshire Blvd. Suite 2000
Los Angeles, CA 90036

E-mail: info@TOKYOPOP.com
Come visit us online at www.TOKYOPOP.com

ISBN: 1-59532-925-0

First TOKYOPOP printing: June 2006
10 9 8 7 6 5 4 3 2 1
Printed in the USA

KAMI·KAZE ™

Imprisoned for a thousand years, the 88 beasts seek resurrection from their world so that they can unleash their wrath upon present-day Japan. And a band of young warriors would love nothing more than to let loose these beasts so that they can feast upon the human world. The only thing these warriors needed was the blood from the Girl of Water, who was lost in the human world— without any memory of who she is and what kind of power she possesses. When they finally catch up with her, at the high school that she attends, all manner of mayhem is released on the school, especially when Ishigami shows up, a powerful warrior himself who is trying to prevent the resurrection of the 88 beasts by protecting the Girl of Mizu (water), the young Mikogami Misao. He fails and Mikogami is captured but not before Ishigami throws to her his mystical stone that may serve to protect her.

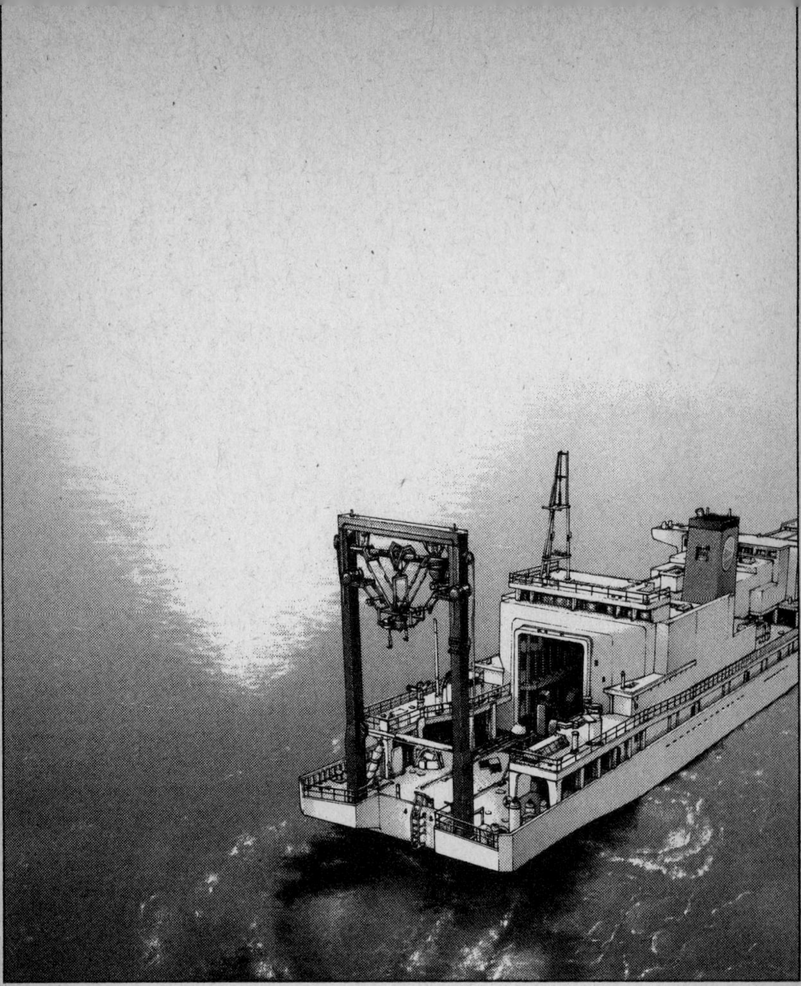
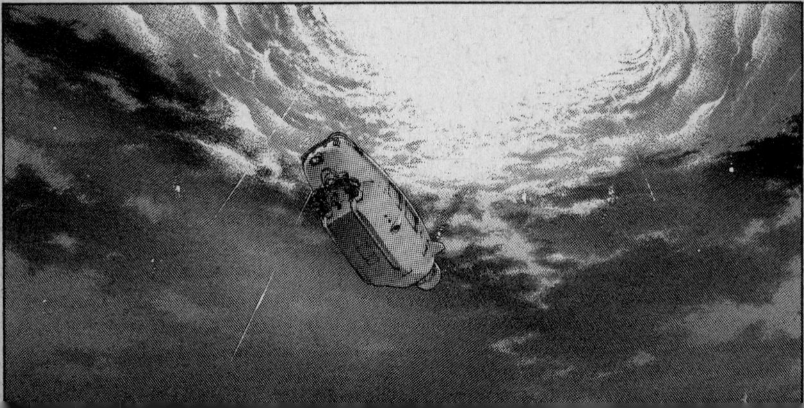

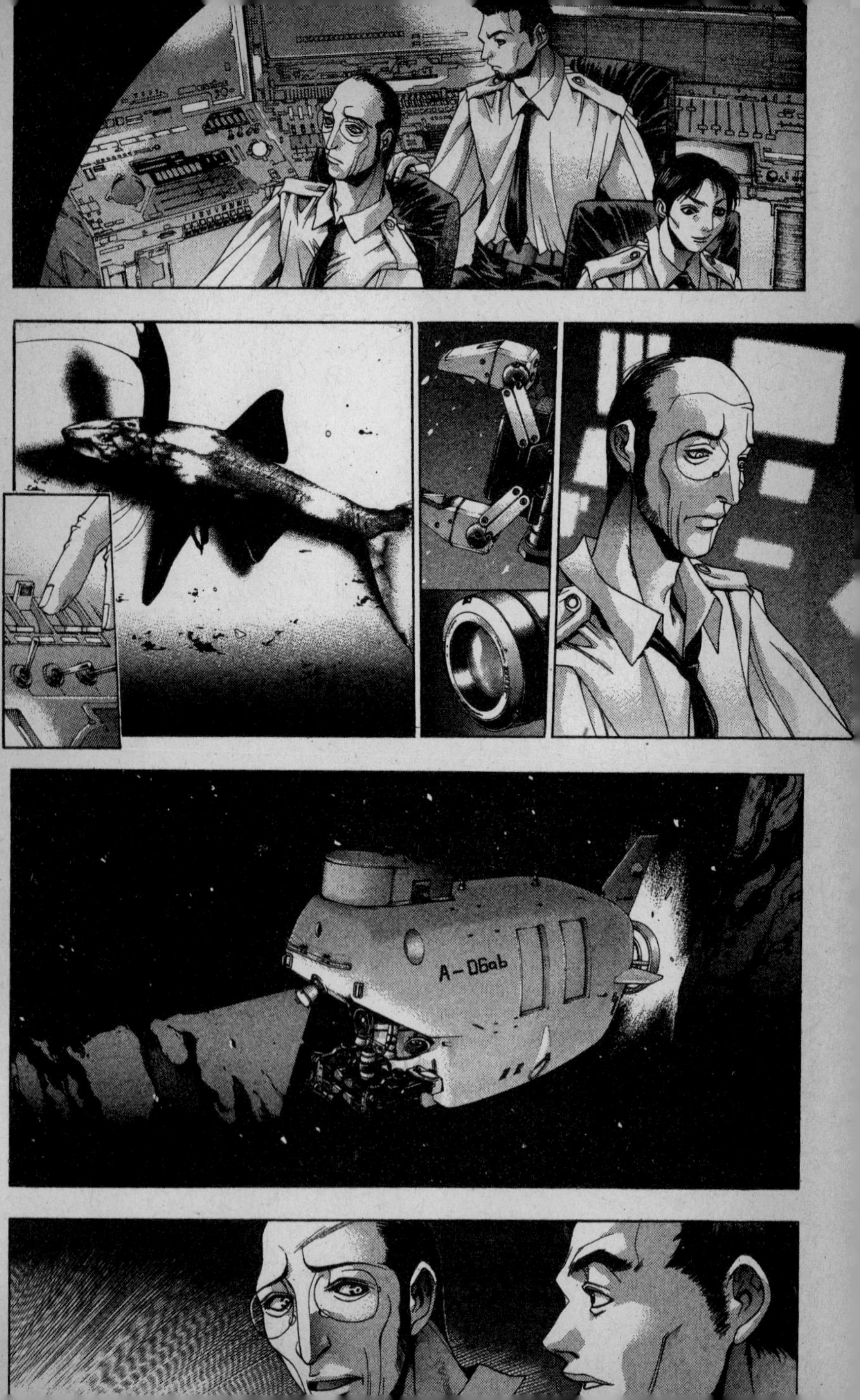
A-D6ab

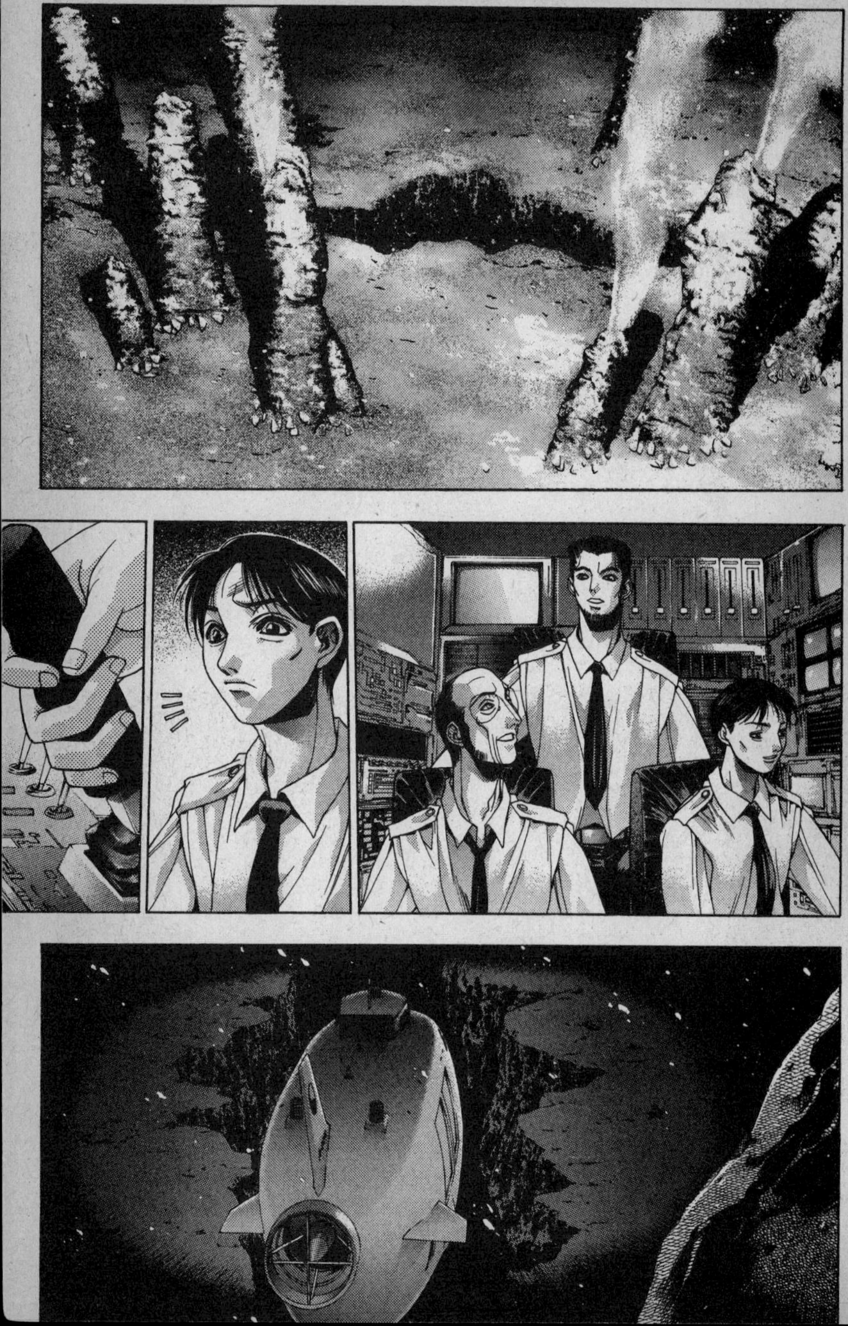

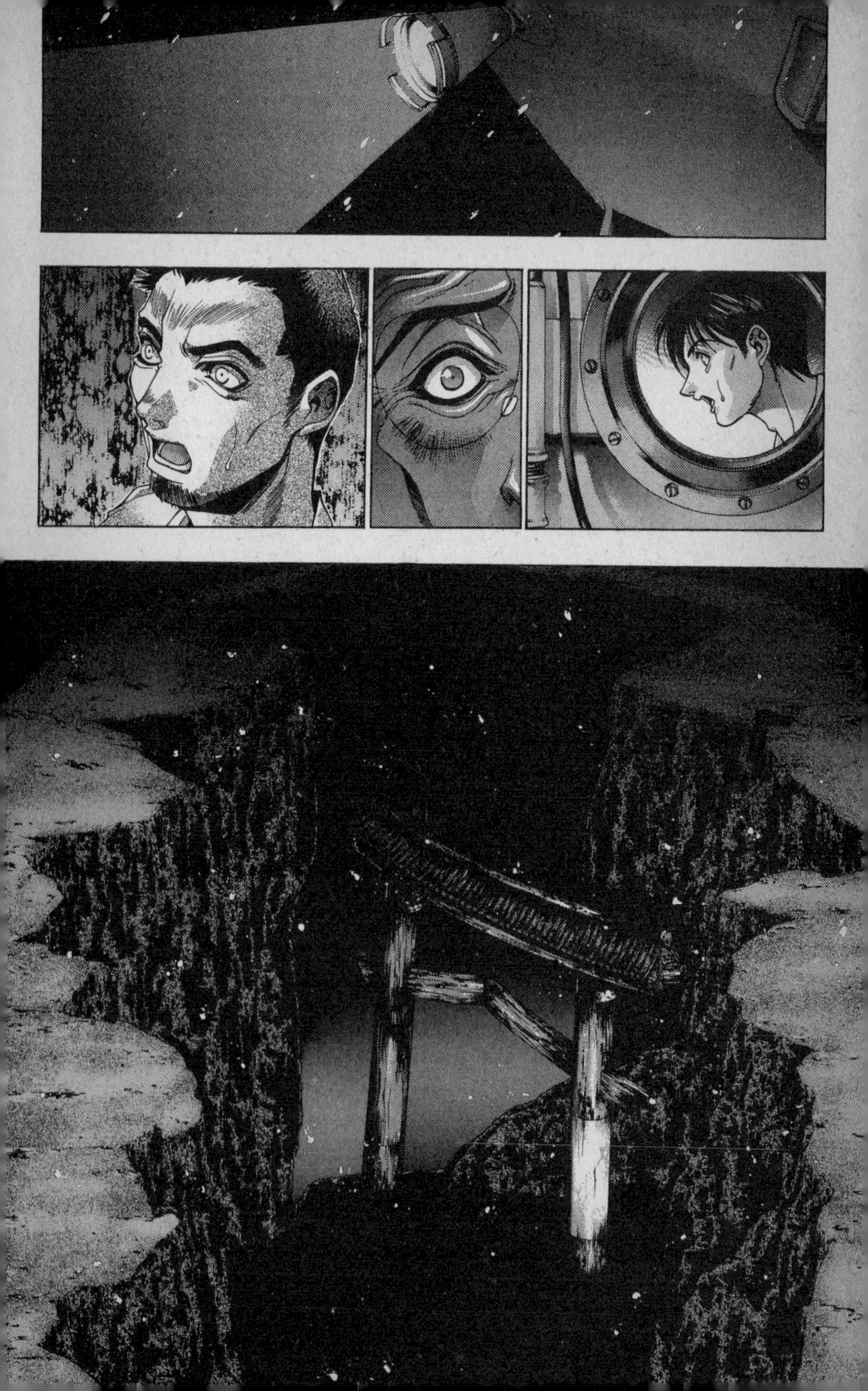

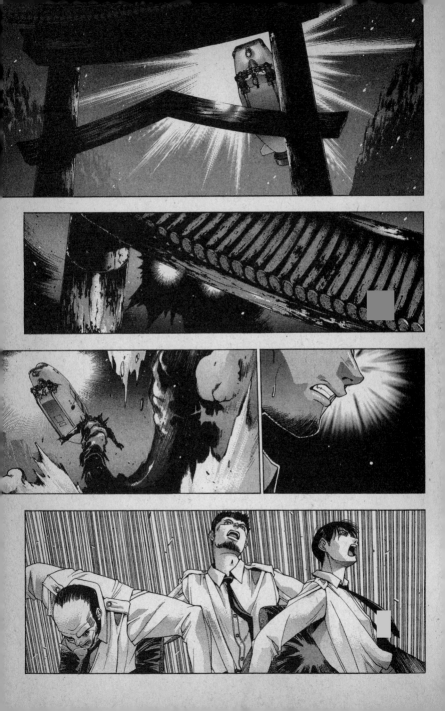

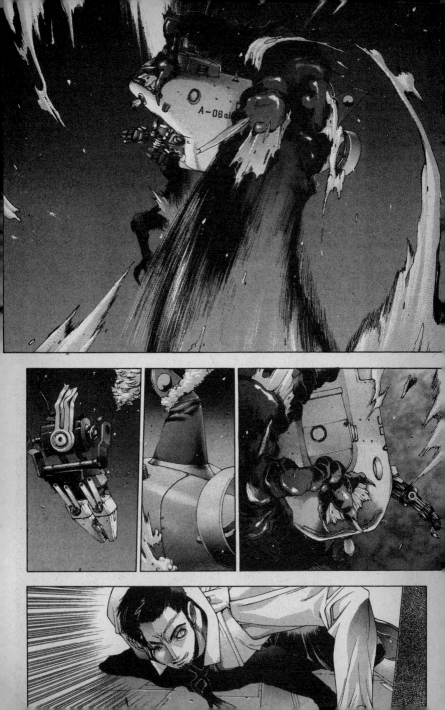

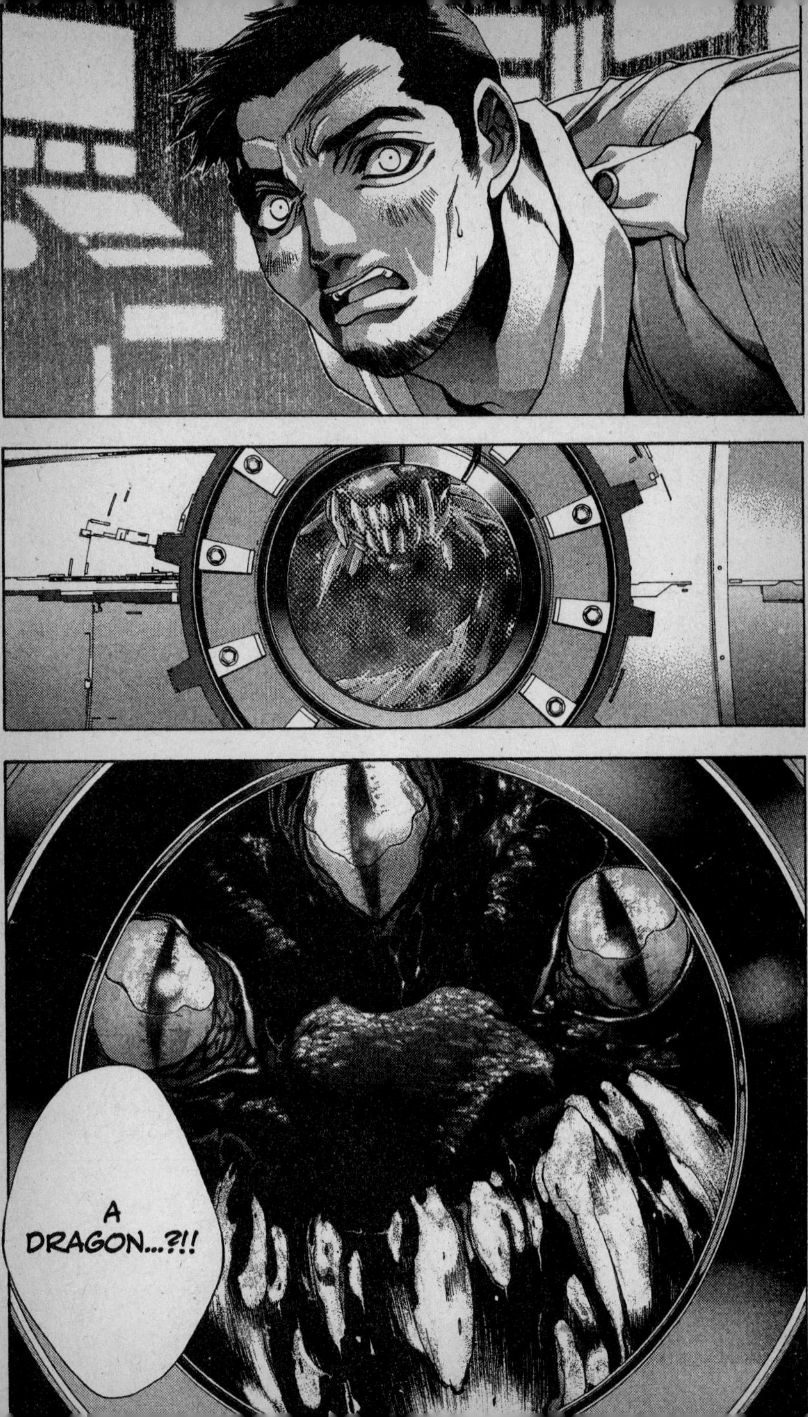
A DRAGON...?!!

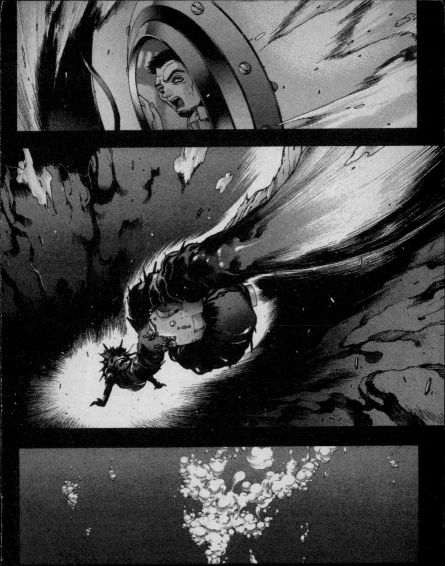

HOW...

...AWFUL.

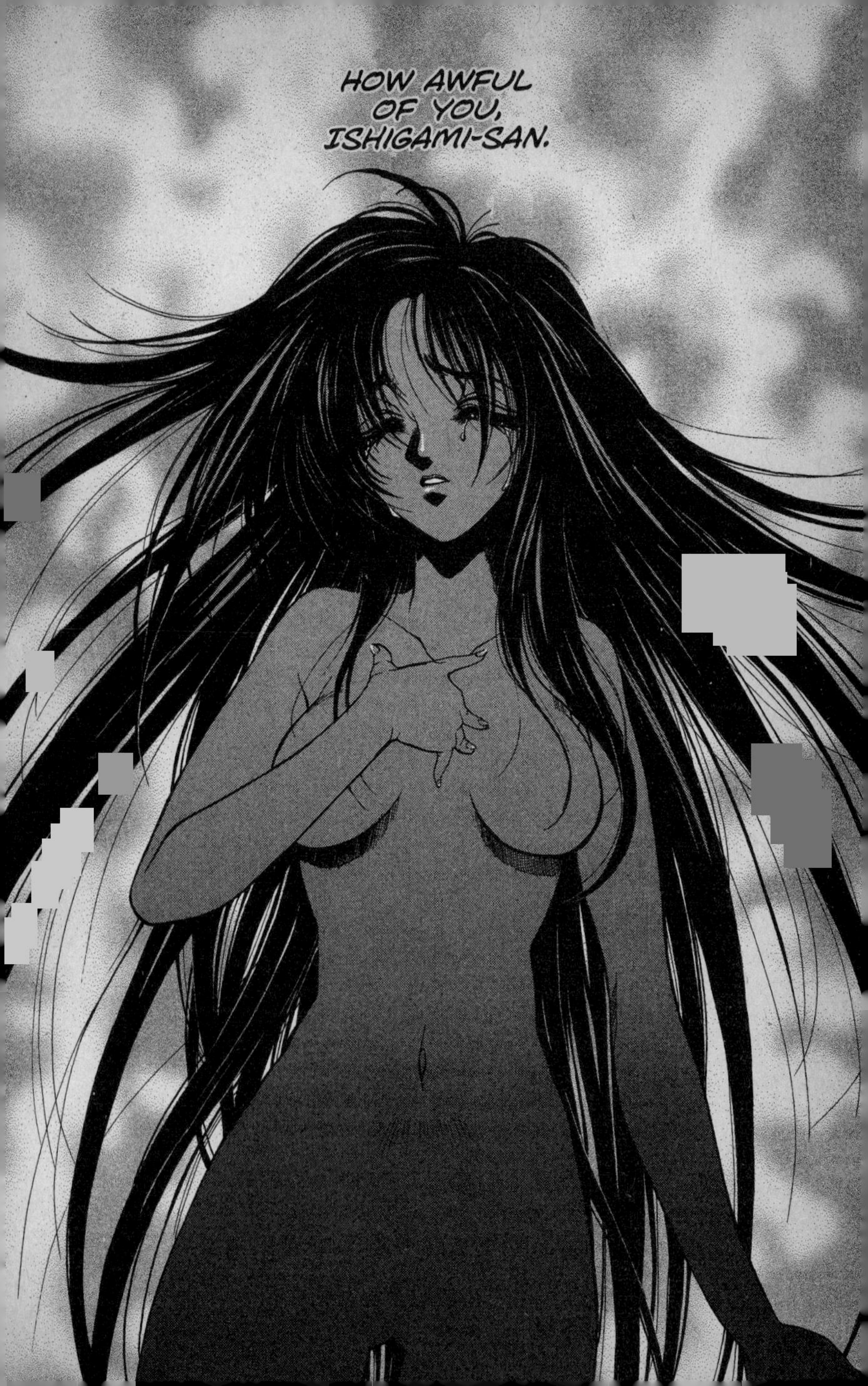
HOW AWFUL OF YOU, ISHIGAMI-SAN.

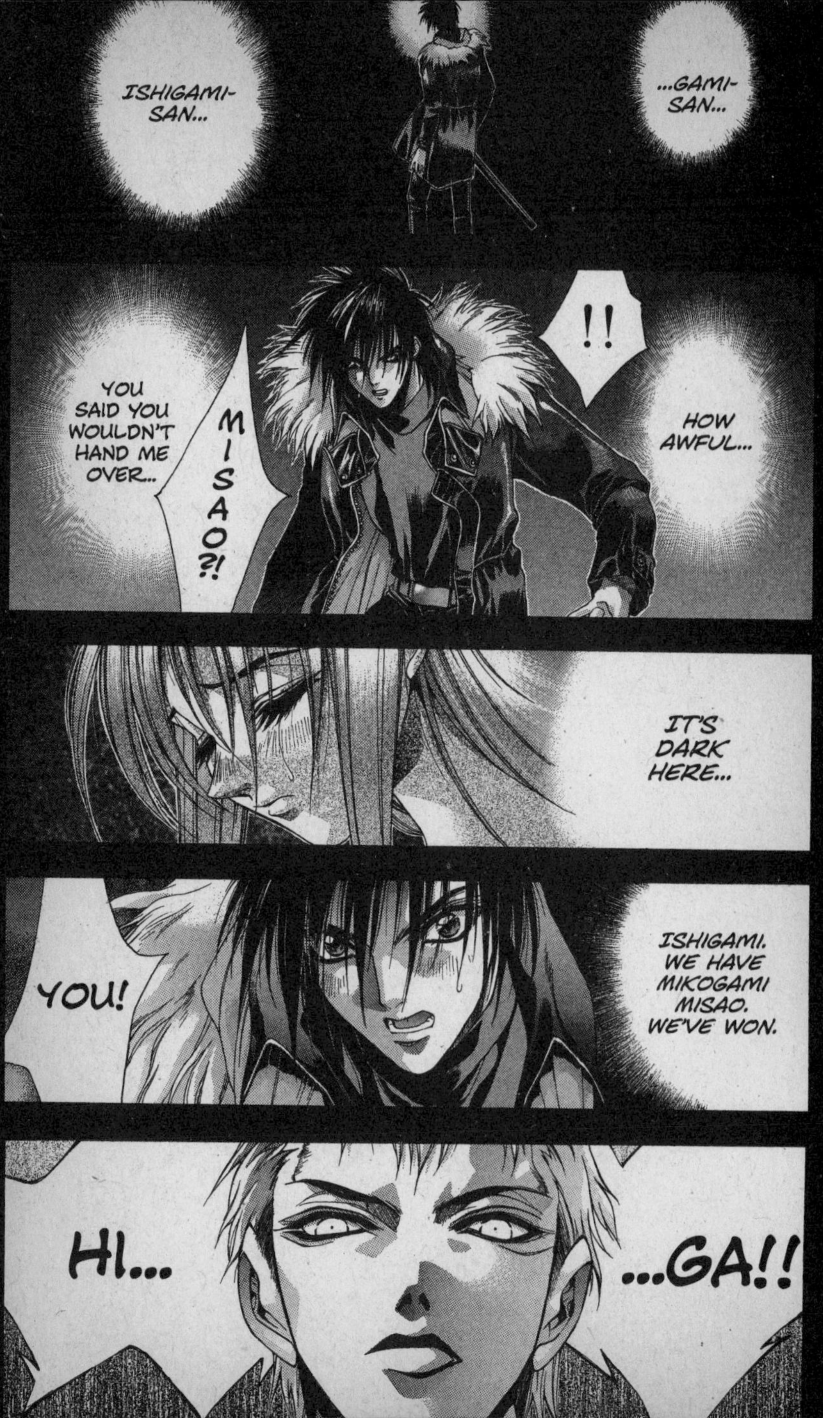

...GAMI-SAN...
ISHIGAMI-SAN...
!!
HOW AWFUL...
MISAO?!
YOU SAID YOU WOULDN'T HAND ME OVER...
IT'S DARK HERE...
ISHIGAMI. WE HAVE MIKOGAMI MISAO. WE'VE WON.
YOU!
HI...
...GA!!

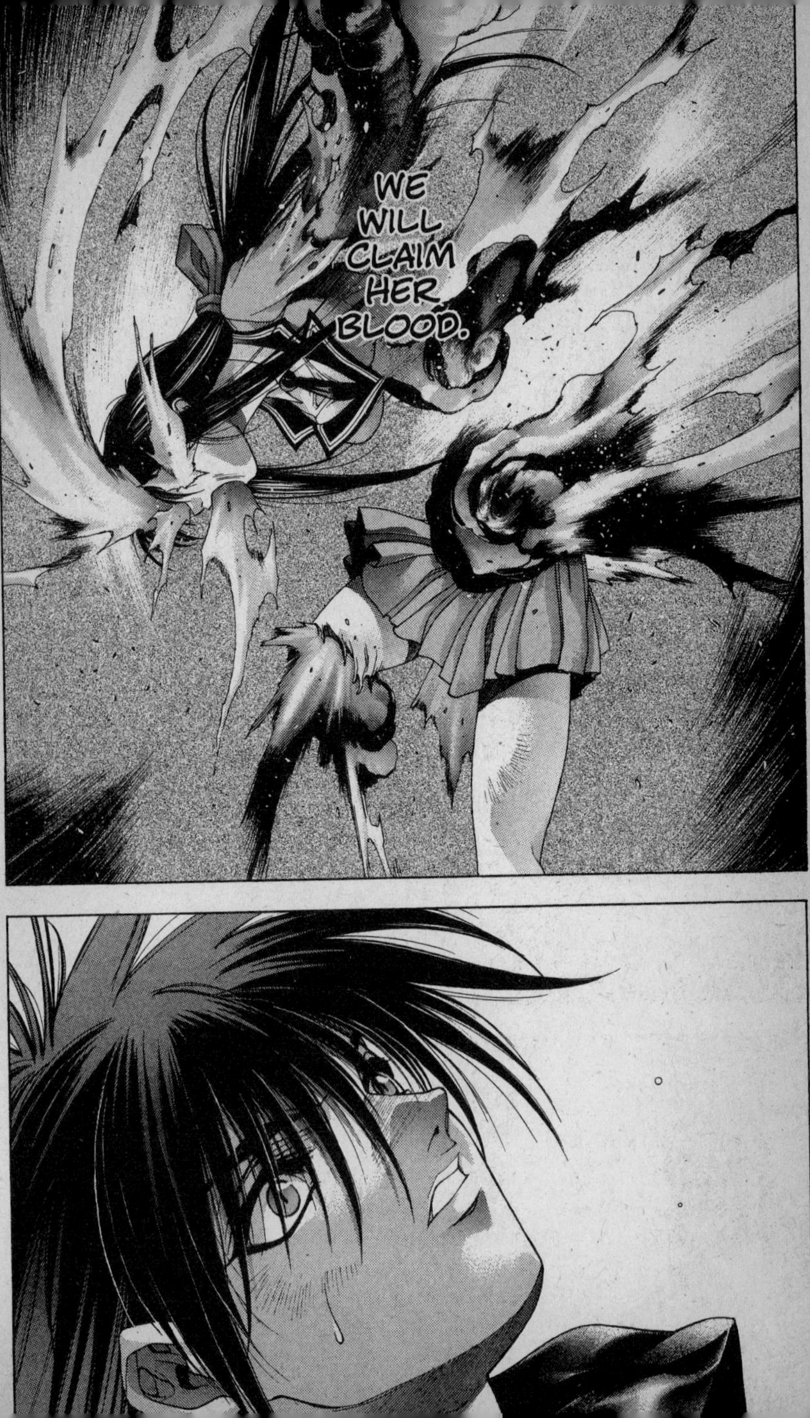
WE WILL CLAIM HER BLOOD.

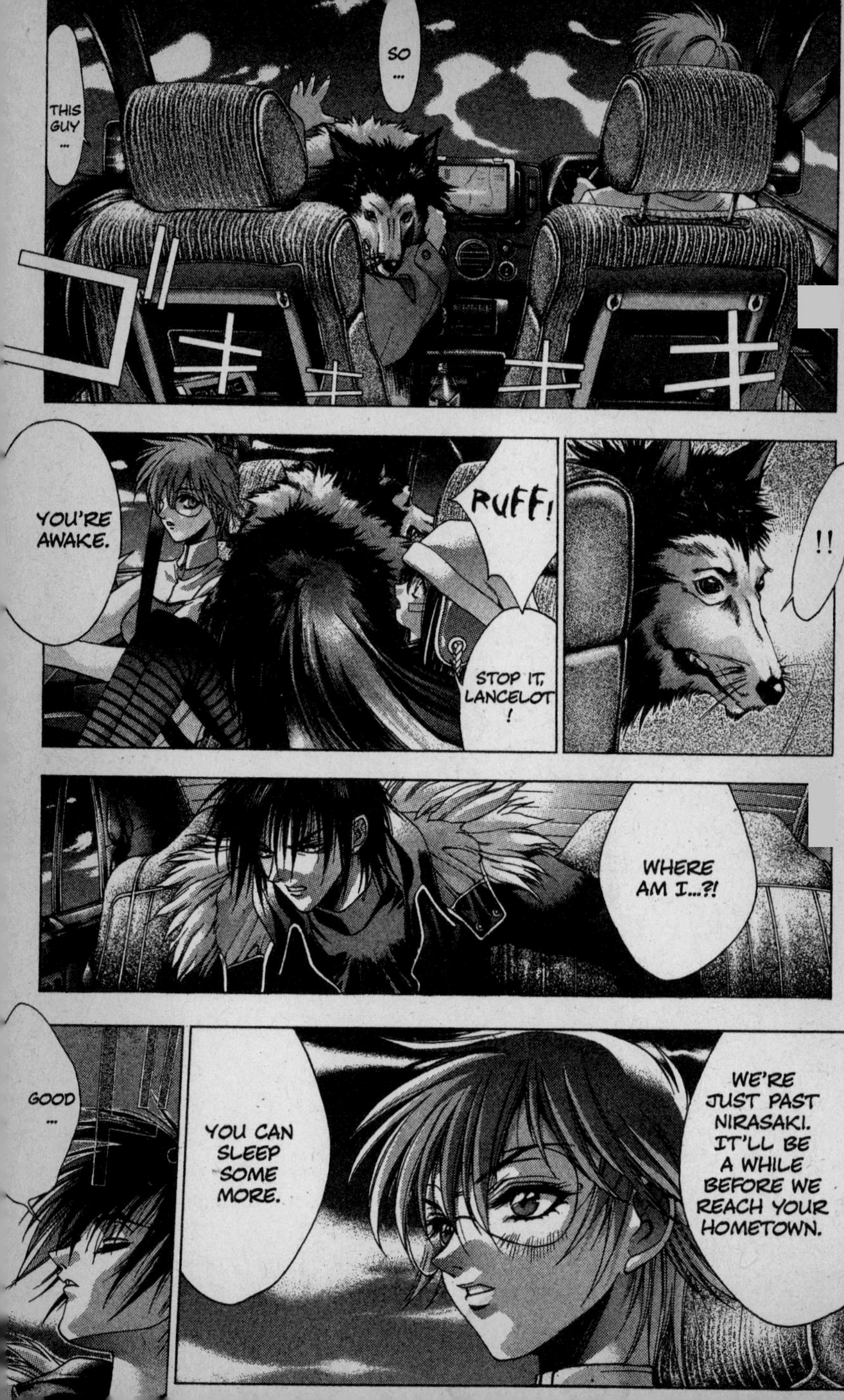
SO ...
THIS GUY ...
!!
RUFF!
STOP IT, LANCELOT!
YOU'RE AWAKE.
WHERE AM I...?!
WE'RE JUST PAST NIRASAKI. IT'LL BE A WHILE BEFORE WE REACH YOUR HOMETOWN.
YOU CAN SLEEP SOME MORE.
GOOD ...

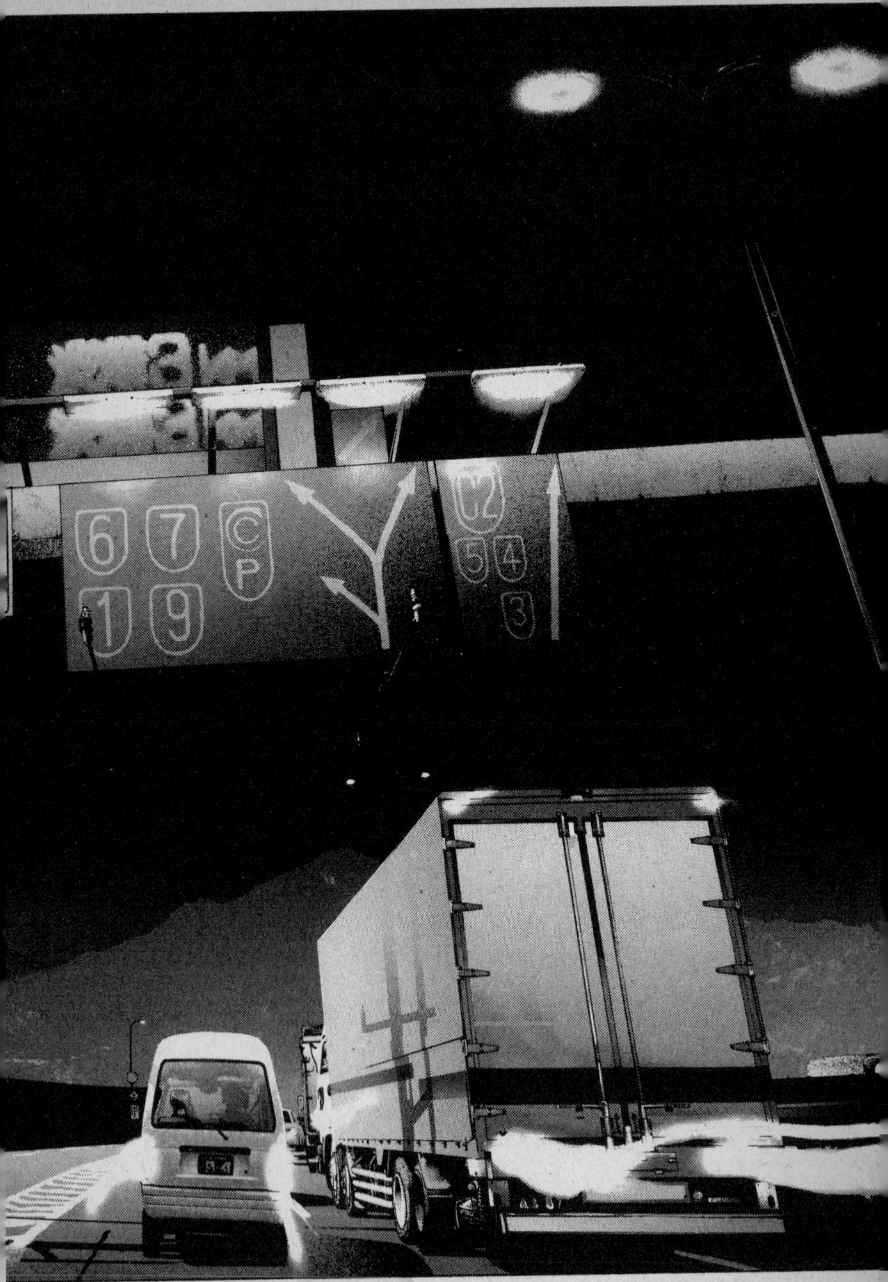
6 7 C P
1 9
C2
5 4
3

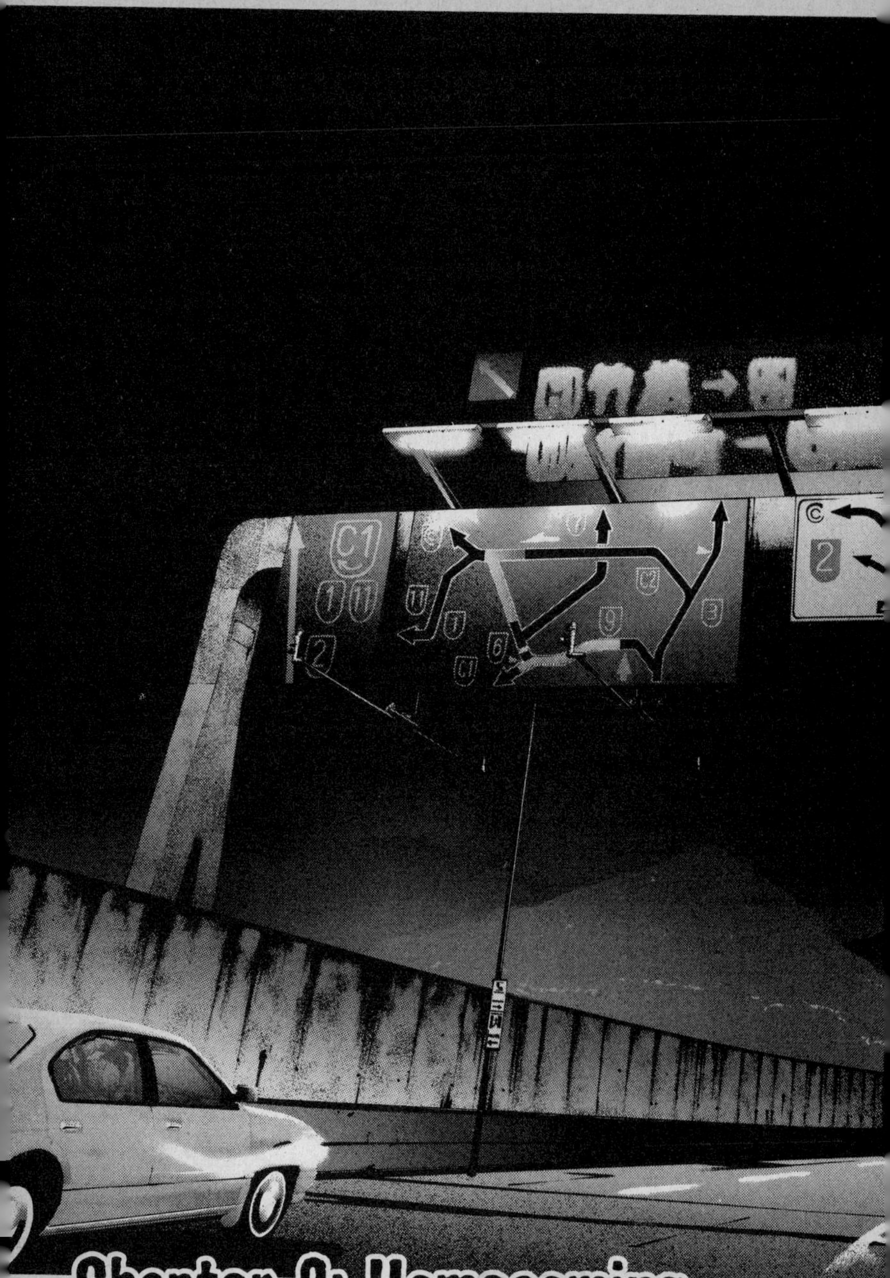

Chapter 8: Homecoming

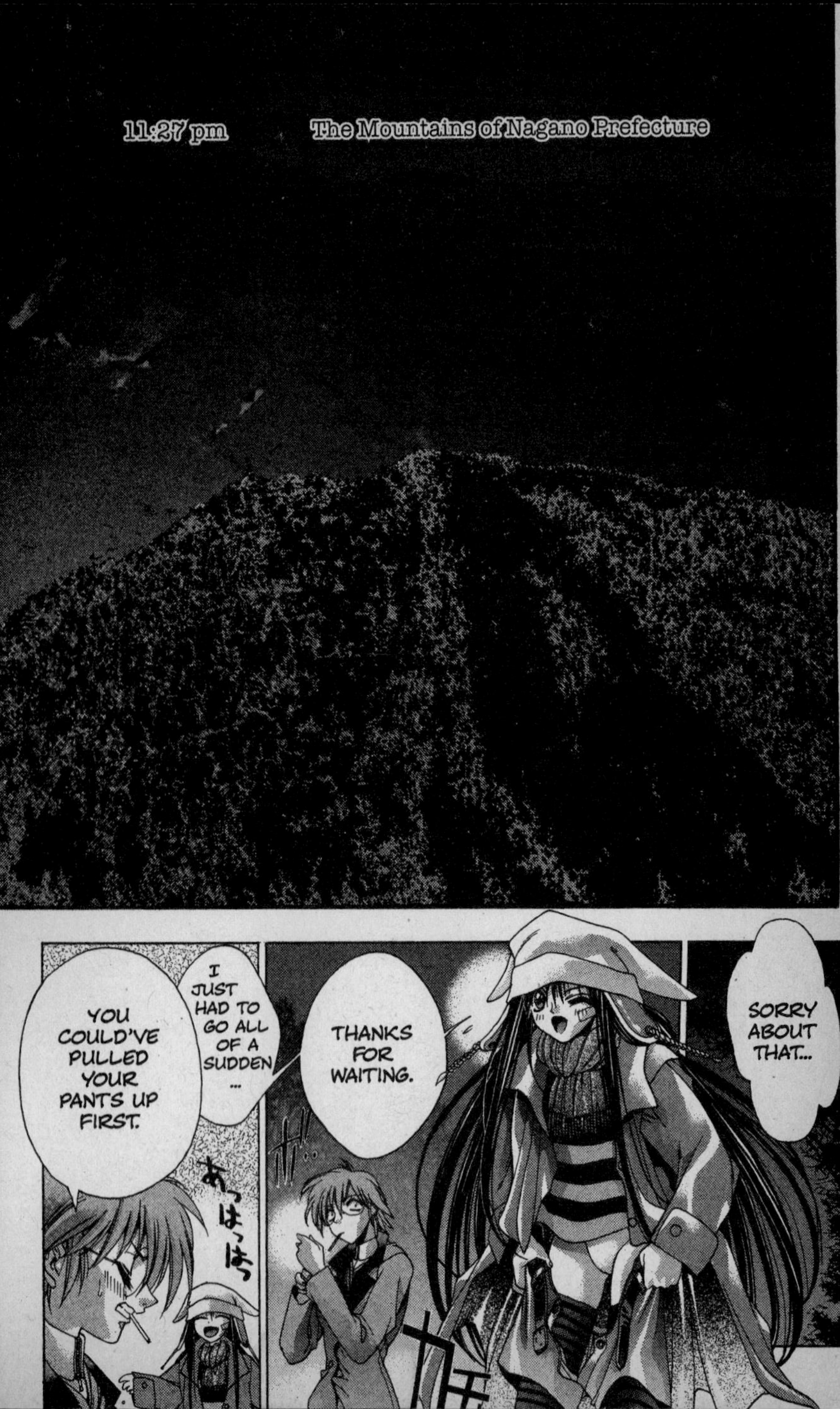

11:27 pm
The Mountains of Nagano Prefecture
SORRY ABOUT THAT...
THANKS FOR WAITING.
I JUST HAD TO GO ALL OF A SUDDEN...
YOU COULD'VE PULLED YOUR PANTS UP FIRST.
あっはっは

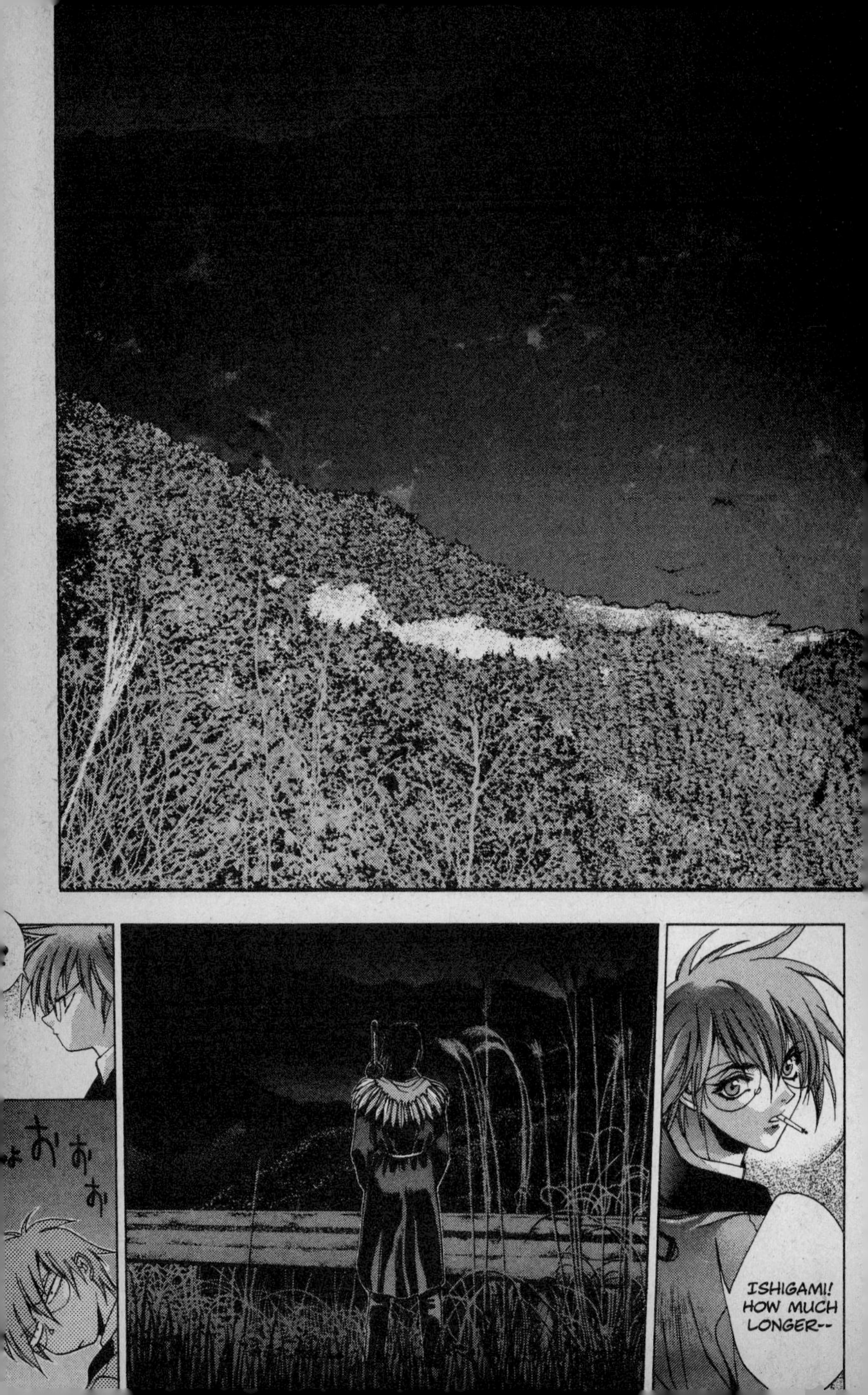
ISHIGAMI! HOW MUCH LONGER--
おおお

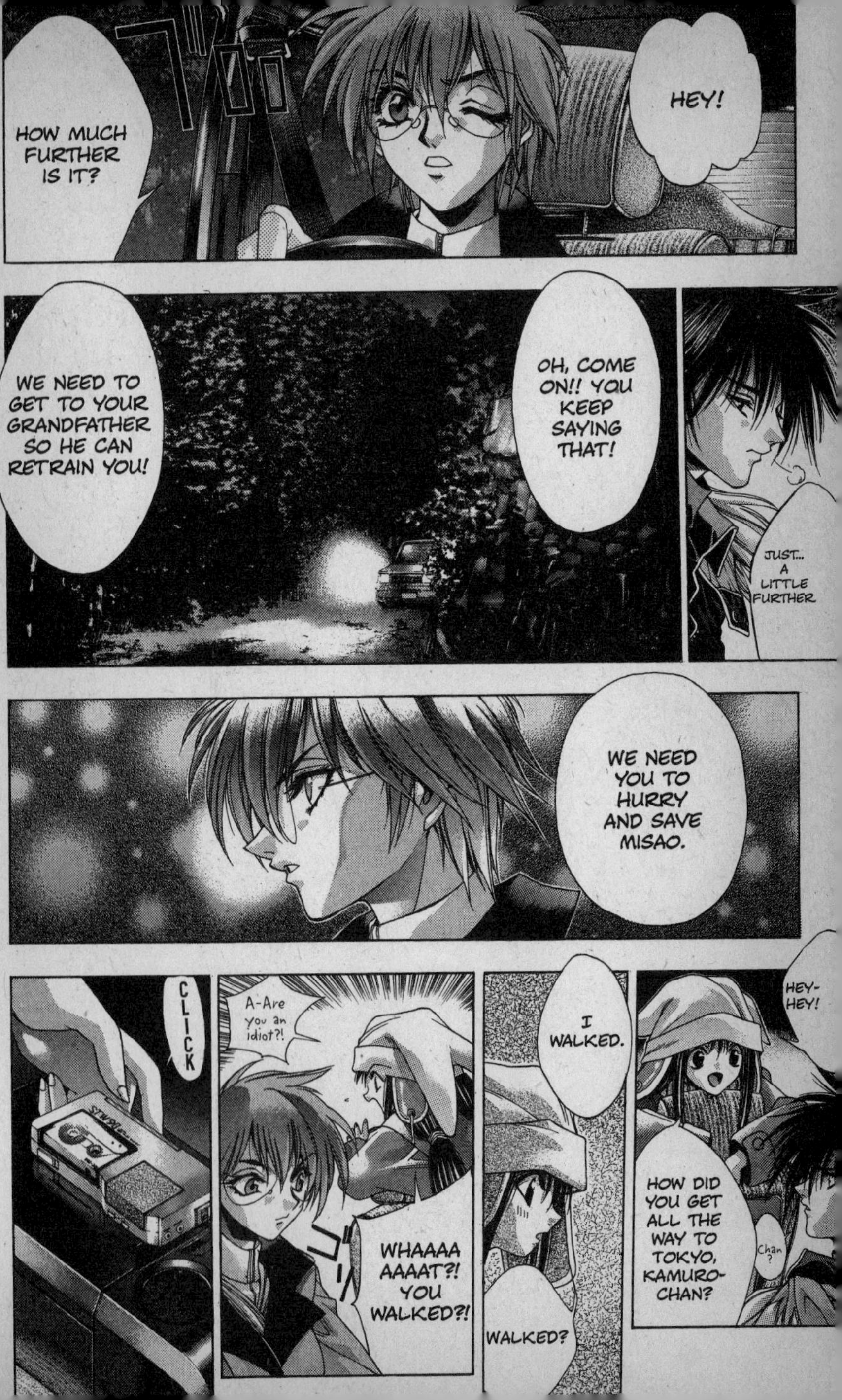
HEY!
HOW MUCH FURTHER IS IT?
JUST... A LITTLE FURTHER
OH, COME ON!! YOU KEEP SAYING THAT!
WE NEED TO GET TO YOUR GRANDFATHER SO HE CAN RETRAIN YOU!
WE NEED YOU TO HURRY AND SAVE MISAO.
HEY-HEY!
HOW DID YOU GET ALL THE WAY TO TOKYO, KAMURO-CHAN?
Chan?
I WALKED.
WALKED?
A-Are you an idiot?!
WHAAAA AAAAT?! YOU WALKED?!
CLICK

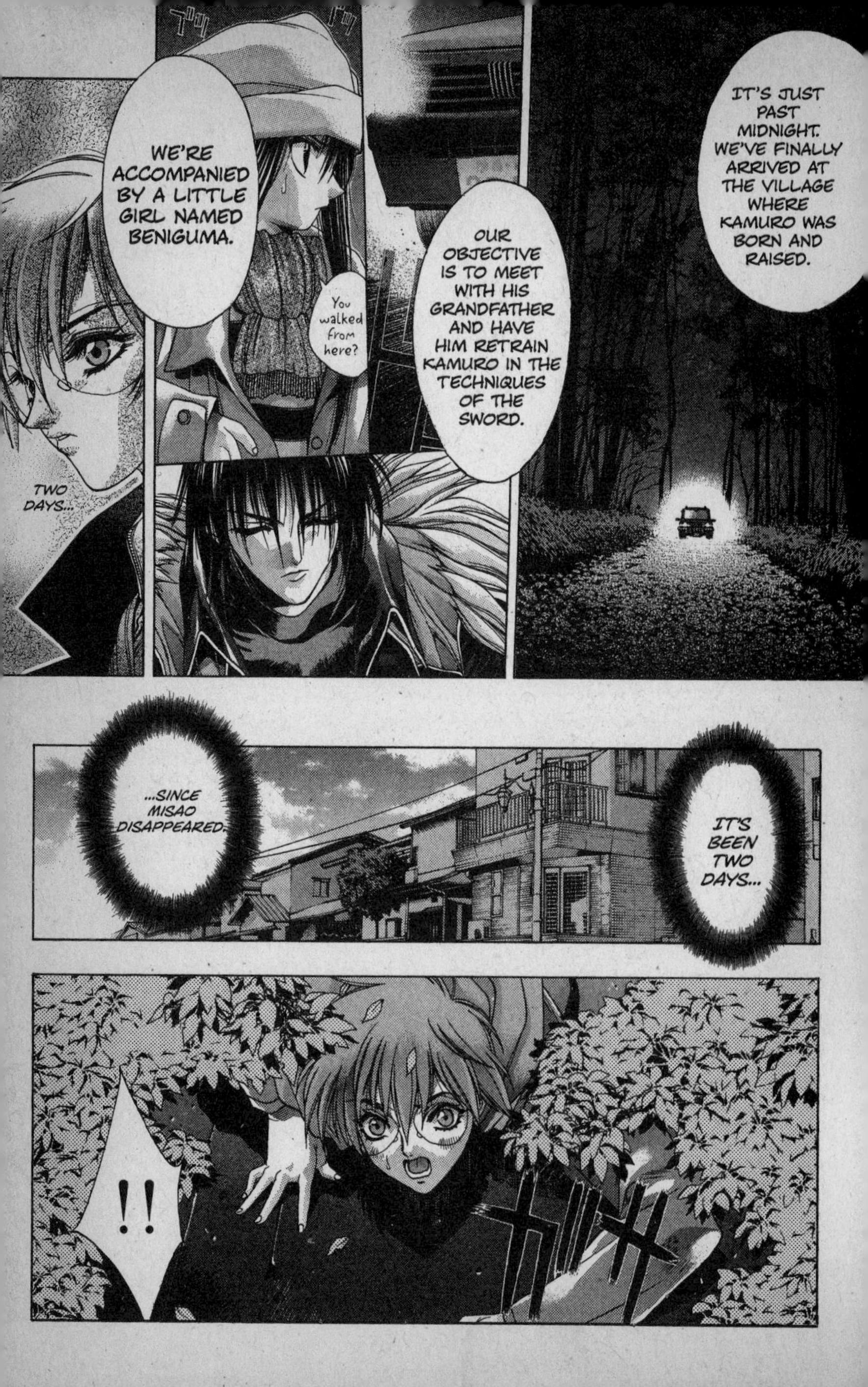
IT'S JUST PAST MIDNIGHT. WE'VE FINALLY ARRIVED AT THE VILLAGE WHERE KAMURO WAS BORN AND RAISED.
OUR OBJECTIVE IS TO MEET WITH HIS GRANDFATHER AND HAVE HIM RETRAIN KAMURO IN THE TECHNIQUES OF THE SWORD.
WE'RE ACCOMPANIED BY A LITTLE GIRL NAMED BENIGUMA.
You walked from here?
TWO DAYS...
IT'S BEEN TWO DAYS...
...SINCE MISAO DISAPPEARED.
!!

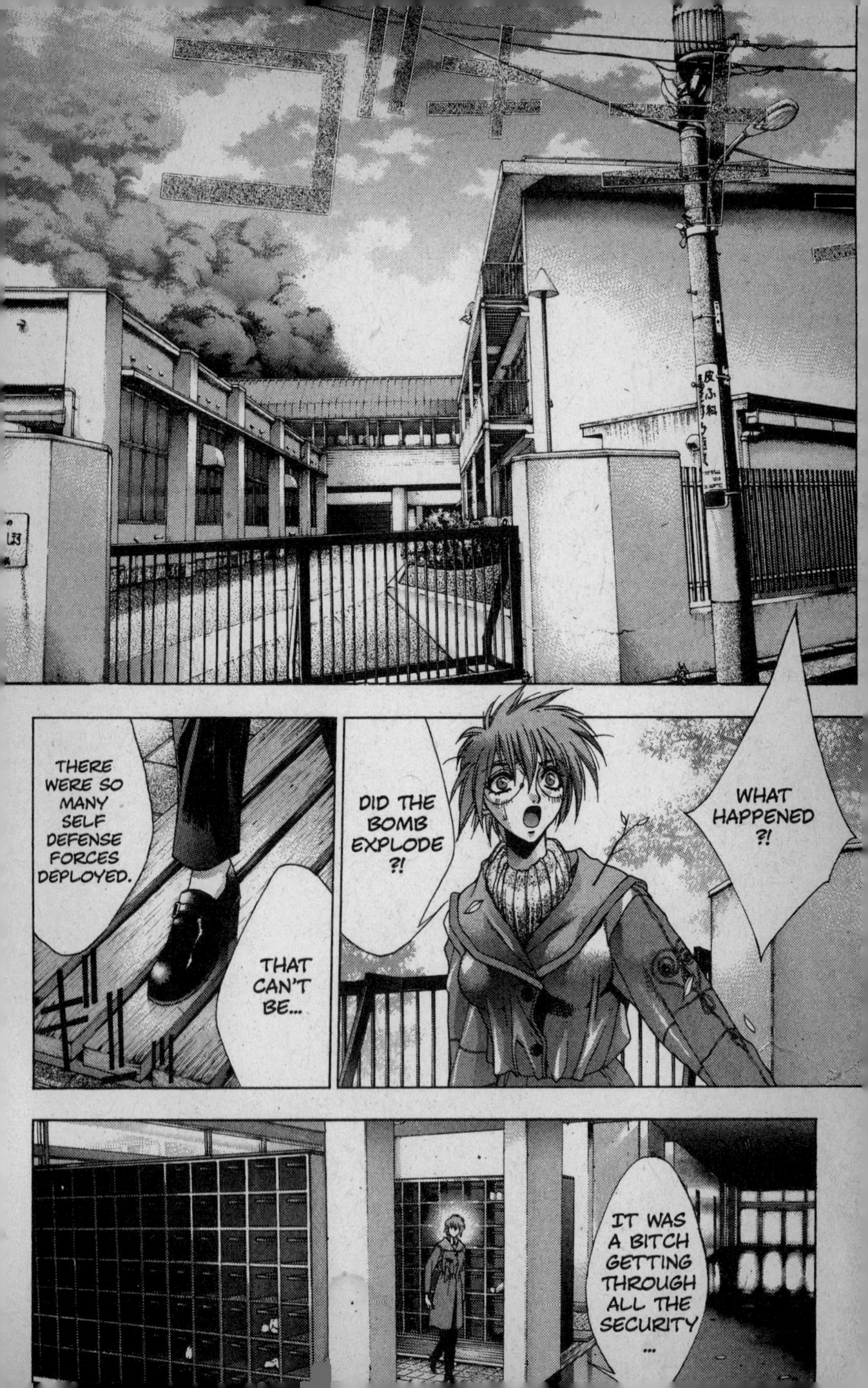
WHAT HAPPENED ?!
DID THE BOMB EXPLODE ?!
THERE WERE SO MANY SELF DEFENSE FORCES DEPLOYED.
THAT CAN'T BE...
IT WAS A BITCH GETTING THROUGH ALL THE SECURITY ...

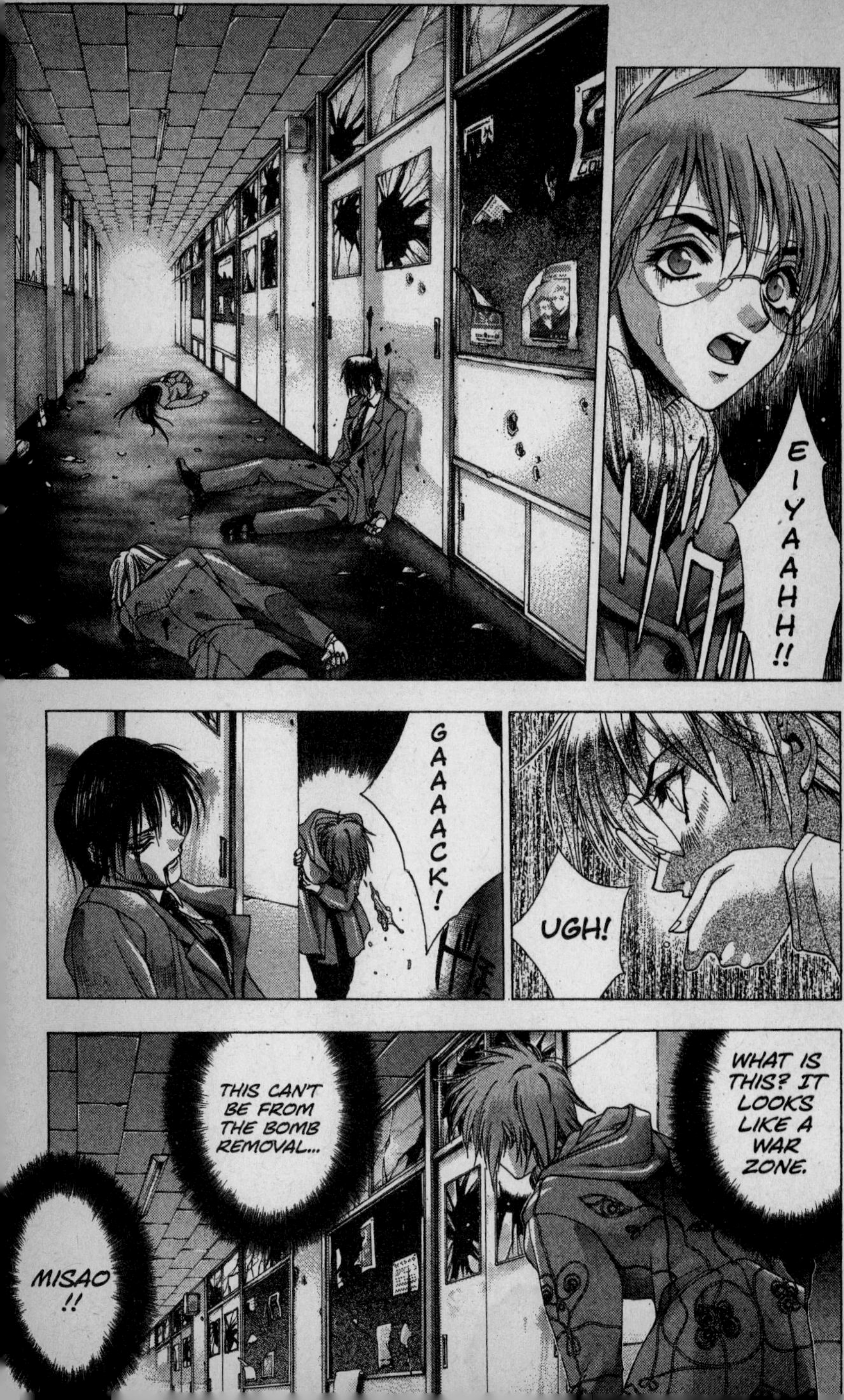
EIYAAAHH!!
UGH!
GAAAACK!
WHAT IS THIS? IT LOOKS LIKE A WAR ZONE.
THIS CAN'T BE FROM THE BOMB REMOVAL...
MISAO!!

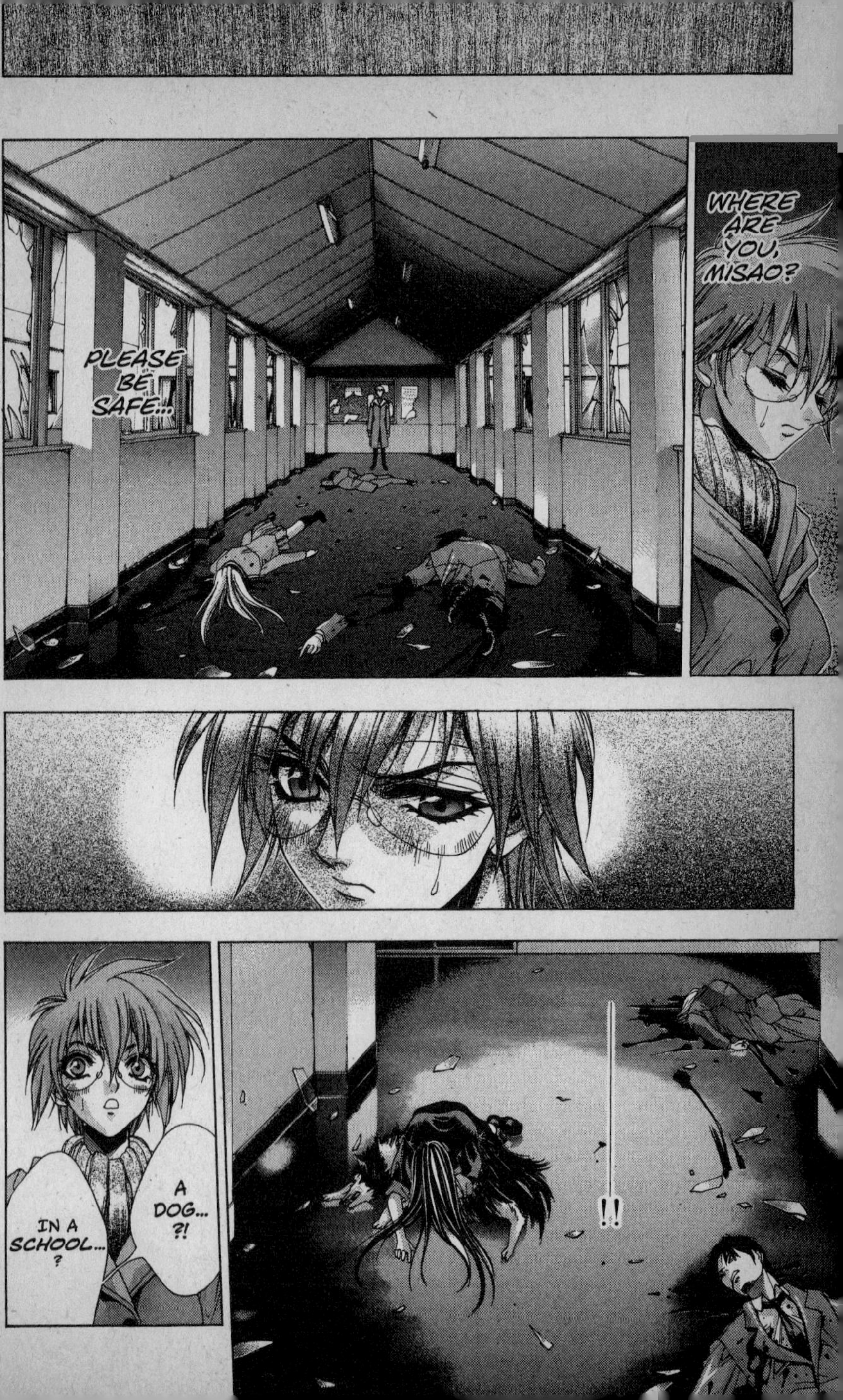
WHERE ARE YOU, MISAO?
PLEASE BE SAFE...
!!
A DOG... ?!
IN A SCHOOL... ?

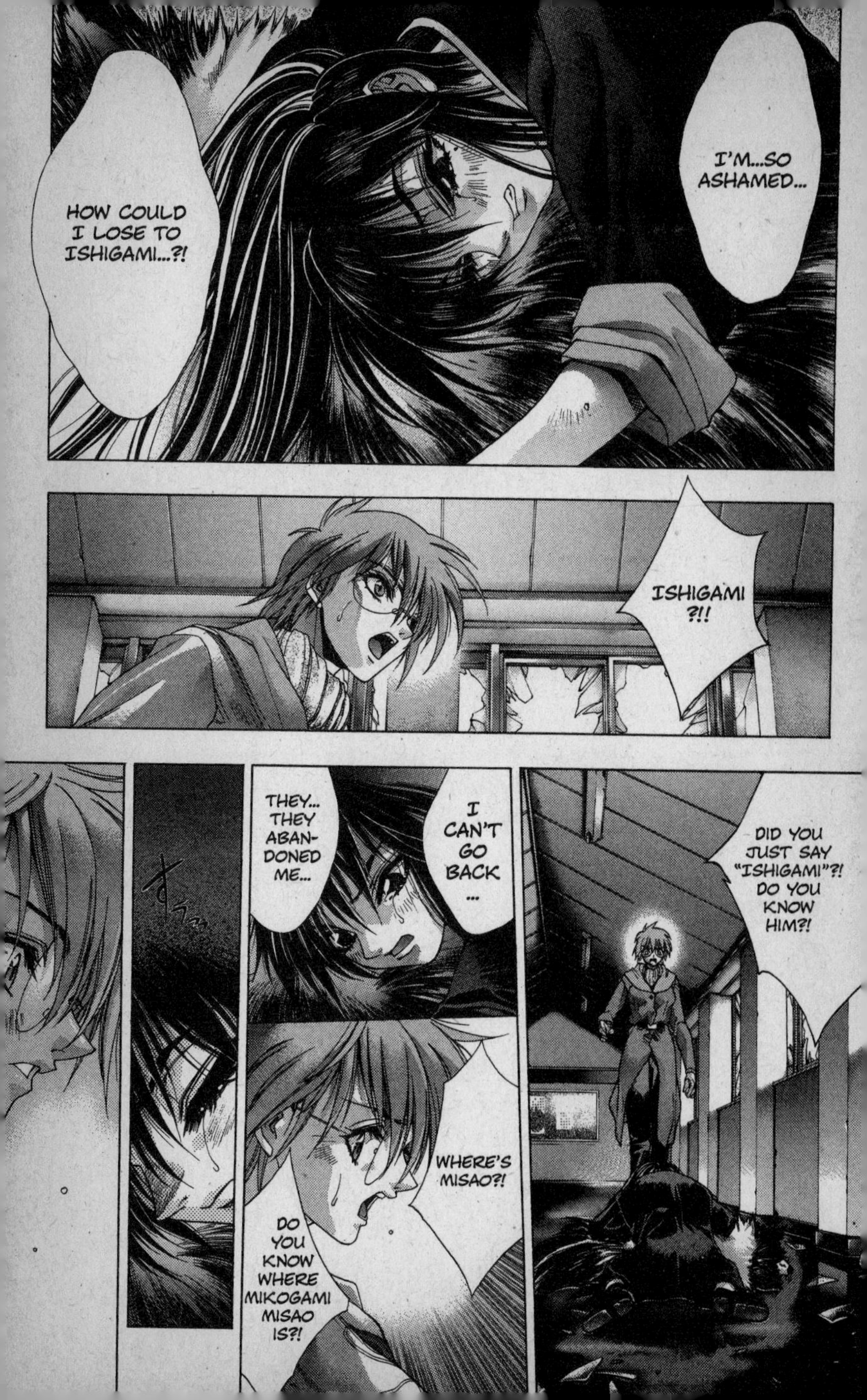
I'M...SO ASHAMED...
HOW COULD I LOSE TO ISHIGAMI...?!
ISHIGAMI ?!!
DID YOU JUST SAY "ISHIGAMI"?! DO YOU KNOW HIM?!
I CAN'T GO BACK ...
THEY... THEY ABANDONED ME...
WHERE'S MISAO?!
DO YOU KNOW WHERE MIKOGAMI MISAO IS?!

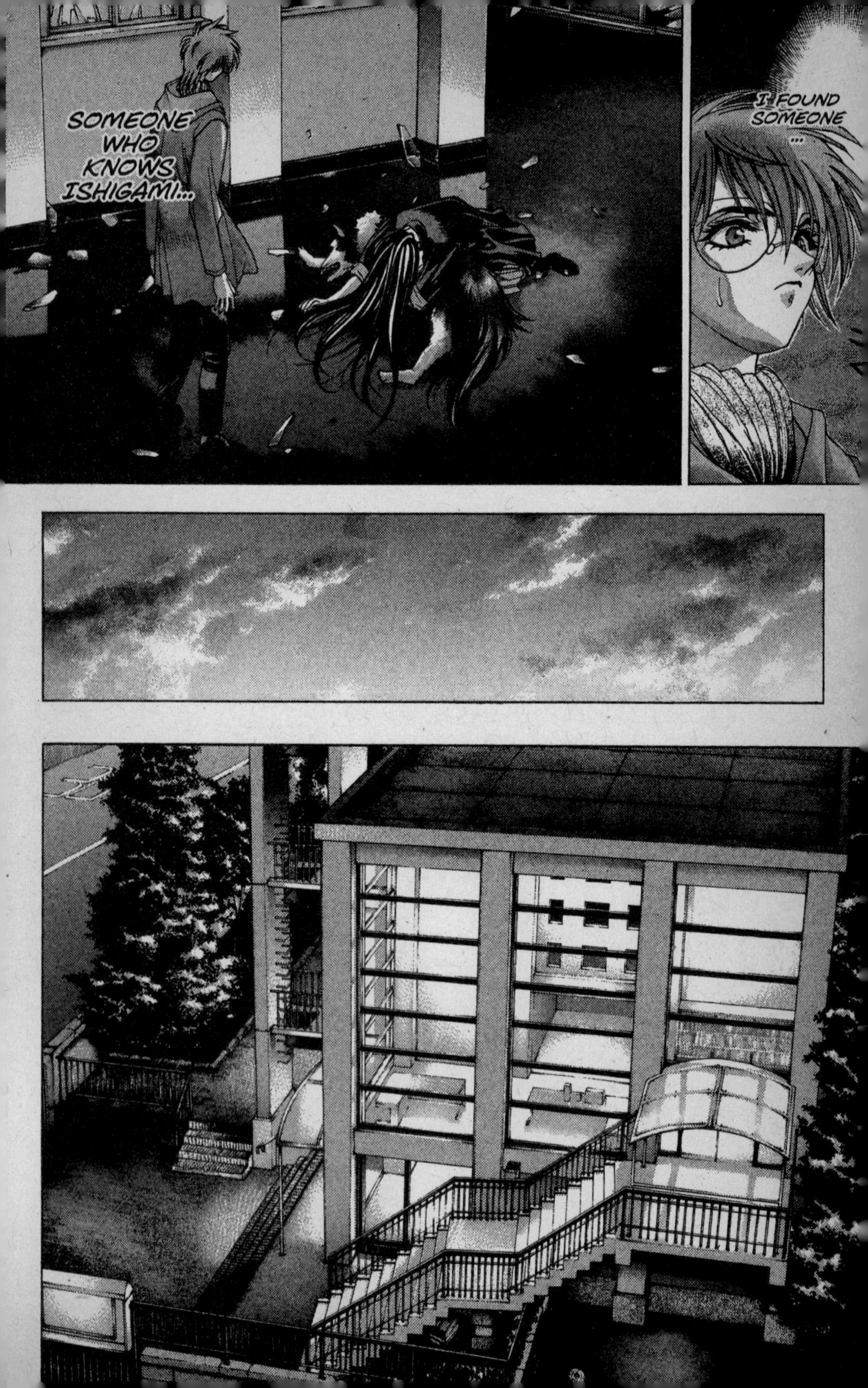
I FOUND SOMEONE ...
SOMEONE WHO KNOWS ISHIGAMI...

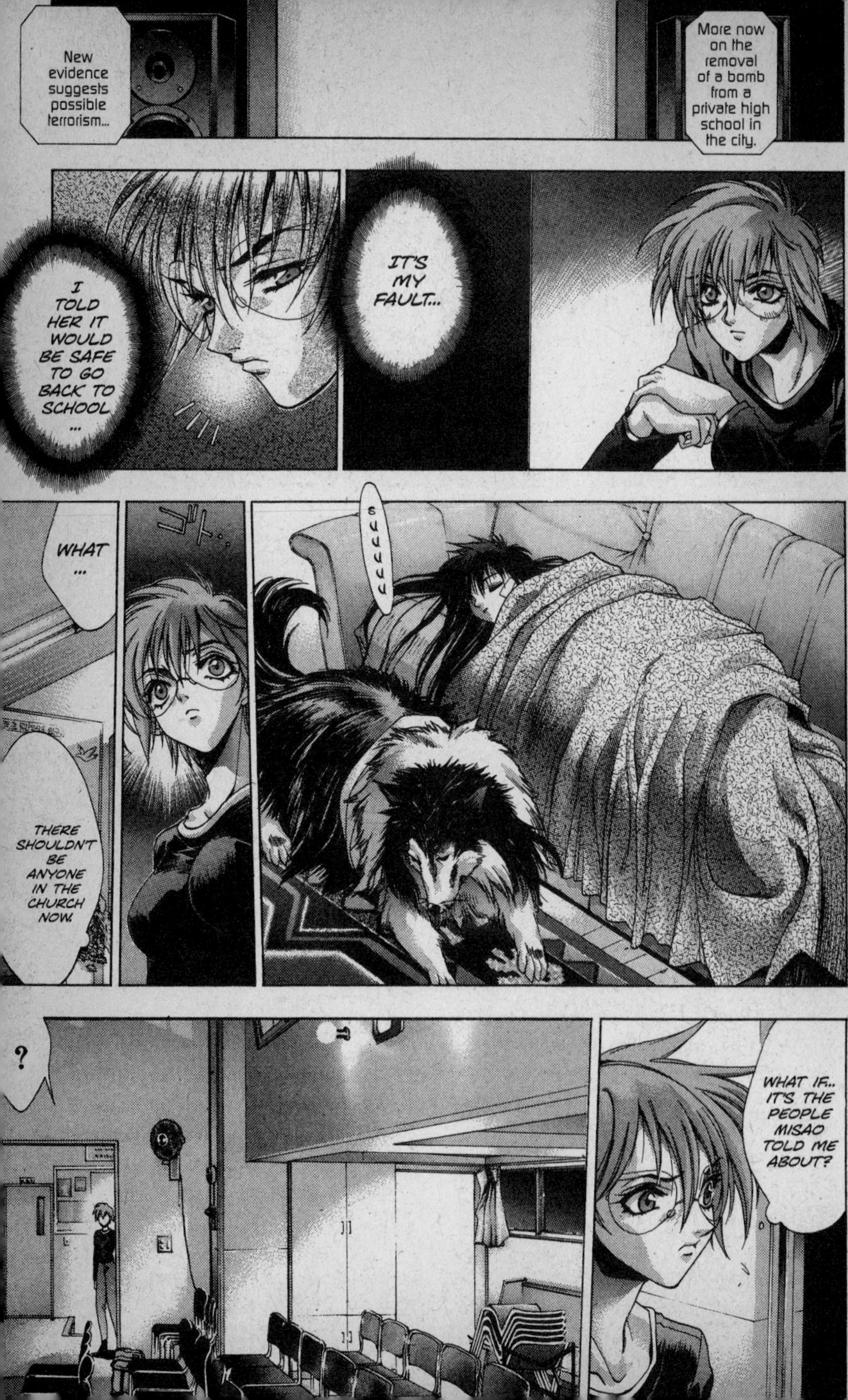
More now on the removal of a bomb from a private high school in the city.
New evidence suggests possible terrorism...
IT'S MY FAULT...
I TOLD HER IT WOULD BE SAFE TO GO BACK TO SCHOOL ...
SUUUUU
ゴト…
WHAT ...
THERE SHOULDN'T BE ANYONE IN THE CHURCH NOW.
WHAT IF... IT'S THE PEOPLE MISAO TOLD ME ABOUT?
?

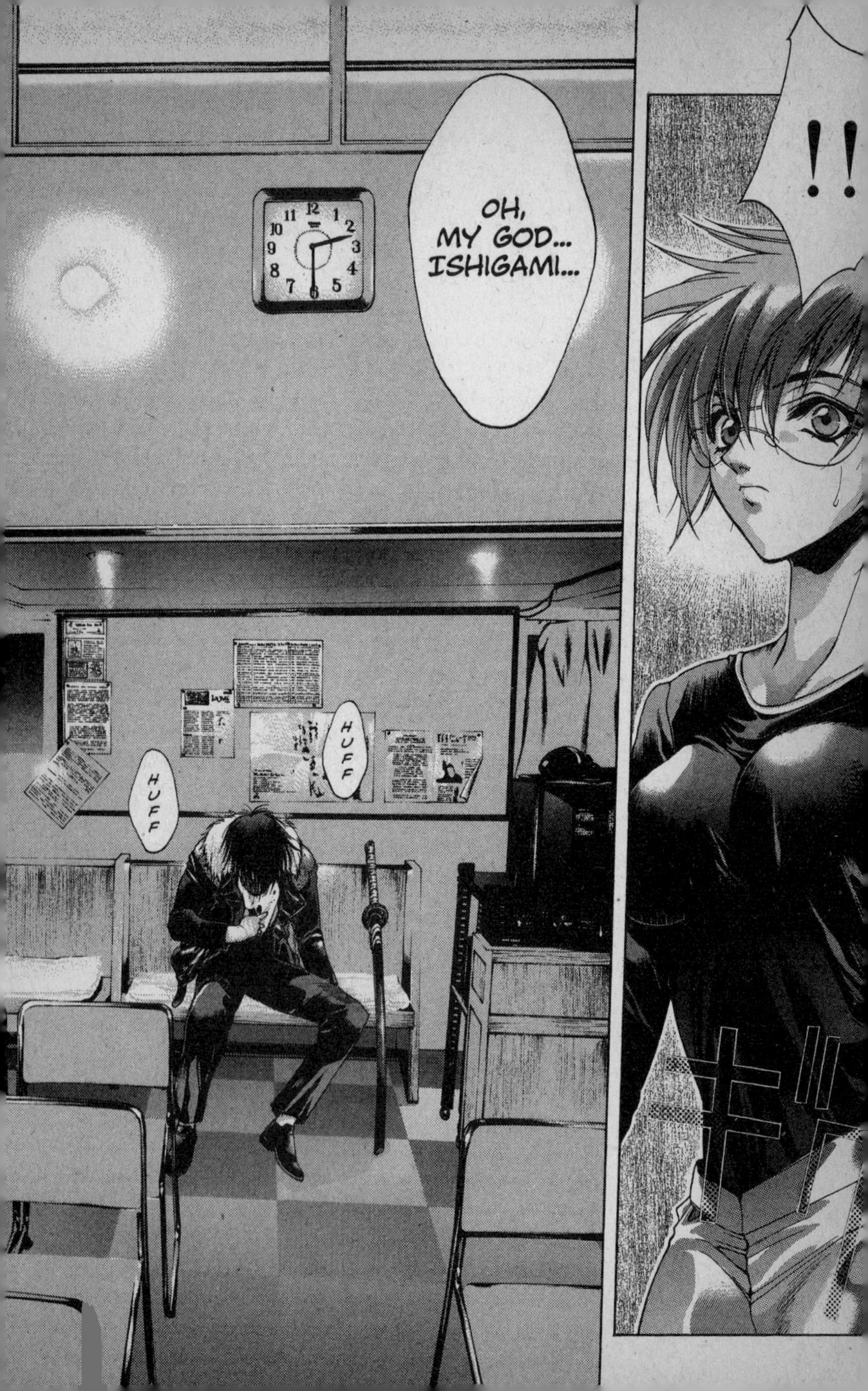
!!
OH, MY GOD... ISHIGAMI...
HUFF
HUFF

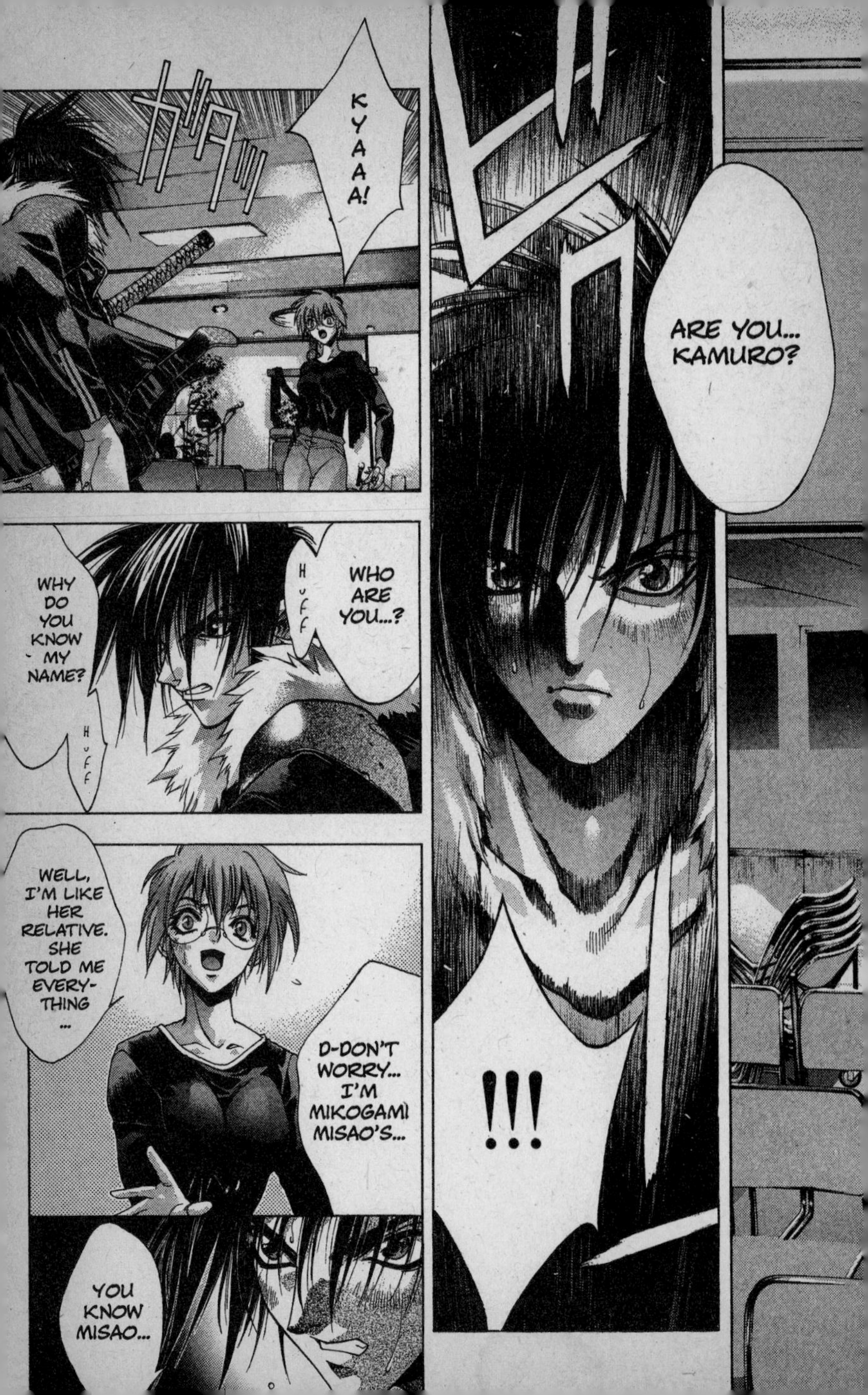
ARE YOU... KAMURO?
!!!
KYAAAA!
WHO ARE YOU...?
HUFF
WHY DO YOU KNOW MY NAME?
HUFF
D-DON'T WORRY... I'M MIKOGAMI MISAO'S...
WELL, I'M LIKE HER RELATIVE. SHE TOLD ME EVERYTHING...
YOU KNOW MISAO...

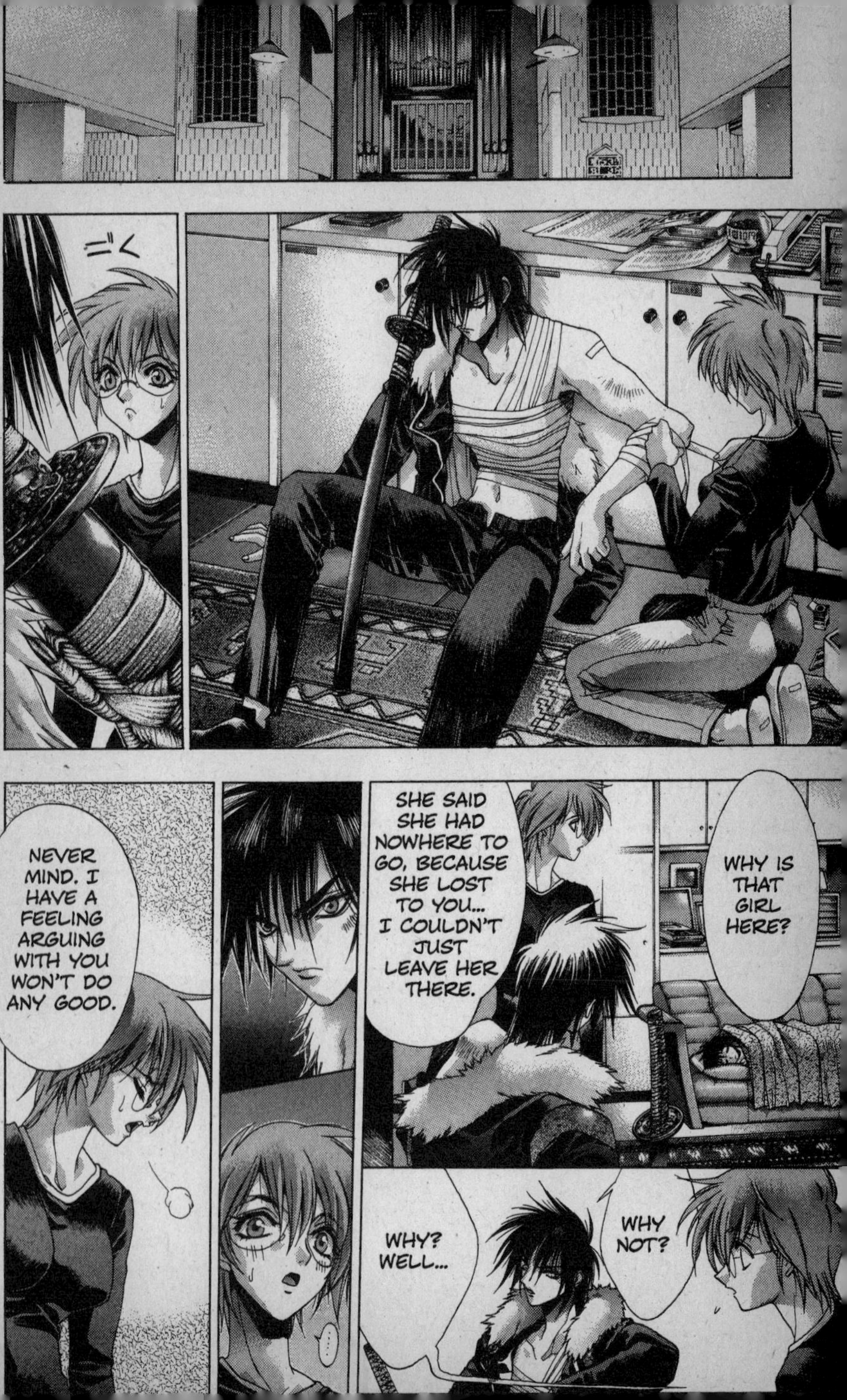
ごく
WHY IS THAT GIRL HERE?
SHE SAID SHE HAD NOWHERE TO GO, BECAUSE SHE LOST TO YOU... I COULDN'T JUST LEAVE HER THERE.
WHY NOT?
WHY? WELL...
...
NEVER MIND. I HAVE A FEELING ARGUING WITH YOU WON'T DO ANY GOOD.

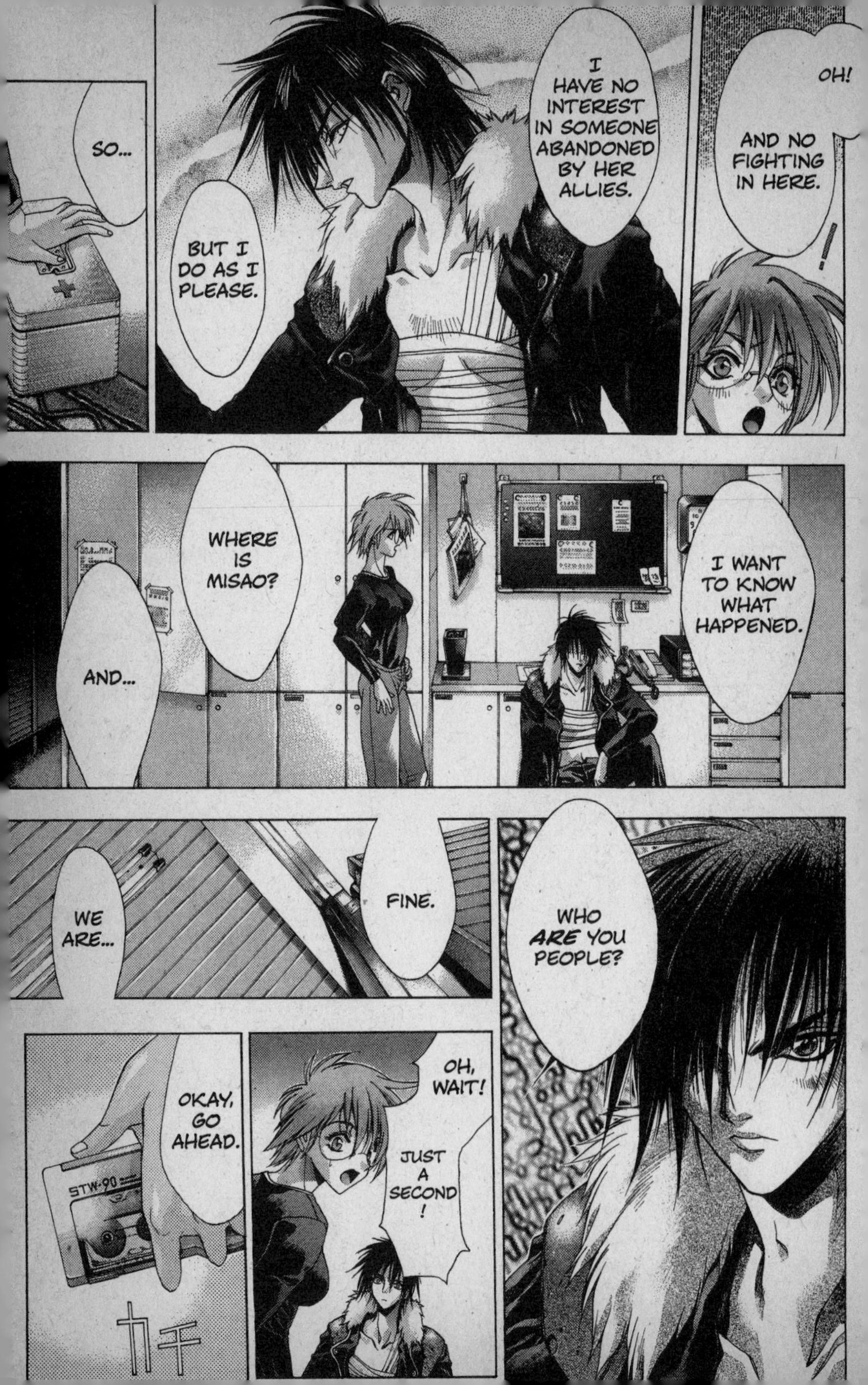
OH!
AND NO FIGHTING IN HERE.
I HAVE NO INTEREST IN SOMEONE ABANDONED BY HER ALLIES.
BUT I DO AS I PLEASE.
SO...
I WANT TO KNOW WHAT HAPPENED.
WHERE IS MISAO?
AND...
WHO *ARE* YOU PEOPLE?
FINE.
WE ARE...
OH, WAIT!
JUST A SECOND!
OKAY, GO AHEAD.
STW-90
カチ

IN ANCIENT TIMES, A WORLD OF ORDER AND PEACE WAS ACHIEVED THROUGH A NATURAL PHILOSOPHY KNOWN AS **AMANARIMICHI**. THAT PHILOSOPHY STATES THAT THE WORLD IS COMPRISED OF THE FIVE ELEMENTS: UTSUHO (SKY), HANI (EARTH), KAZE (WIND), HO (FIRE), AND MIZU (WATER). ALL THINGS IN NATURE COME FROM THE FIVE ELEMENTS, AND ALL THINGS WILL EVENTUALLY RETURN TO THEM.

OF COURSE, HUMANS WERE ALSO BORN FROM AND WOULD RETURN TO THE CYCLE OF THE FIVE ELEMENTS, AND WERE NOT INDEPENDENT OF THIS NATURAL LAW. IN THE WORLD VIEW OF AMANARIMICHI, THERE IS NO DIFFERENCE IN STATUS BETWEEN HUMANS AND OTHER PLANTS AND ANIMALS. HUMANS ARE MERELY A PORTION OF NATURE, NOTHING MORE.

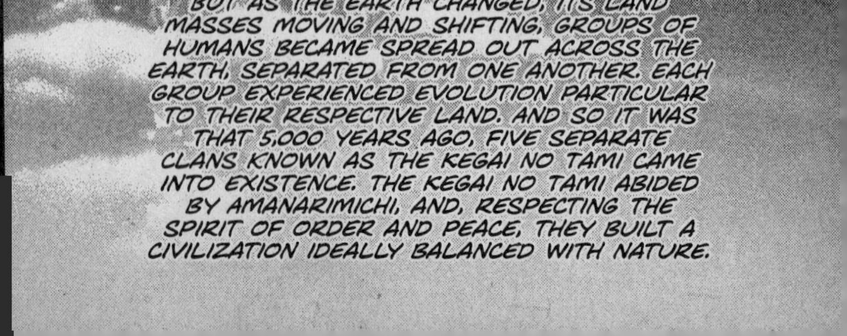

HUMANS, WHO ARE THE PROPER DESCENDANTS OF THE GODS IN HEAVEN, WERE ORIGINALLY ALL ONE SPECIES OF THE HANI CLAN, OR EARTH PEOPLE. BUT AS THE EARTH CHANGED, ITS LAND MASSES MOVING AND SHIFTING, GROUPS OF HUMANS BECAME SPREAD OUT ACROSS THE EARTH, SEPARATED FROM ONE ANOTHER. EACH GROUP EXPERIENCED EVOLUTION PARTICULAR TO THEIR RESPECTIVE LAND. AND SO IT WAS THAT 5,000 YEARS AGO, FIVE SEPARATE CLANS KNOWN AS THE KEGAI NO TAMI CAME INTO EXISTENCE. THE KEGAI NO TAMI ABIDED BY AMANARIMICHI, AND, RESPECTING THE SPIRIT OF ORDER AND PEACE, THEY BUILT A CIVILIZATION IDEALLY BALANCED WITH NATURE.

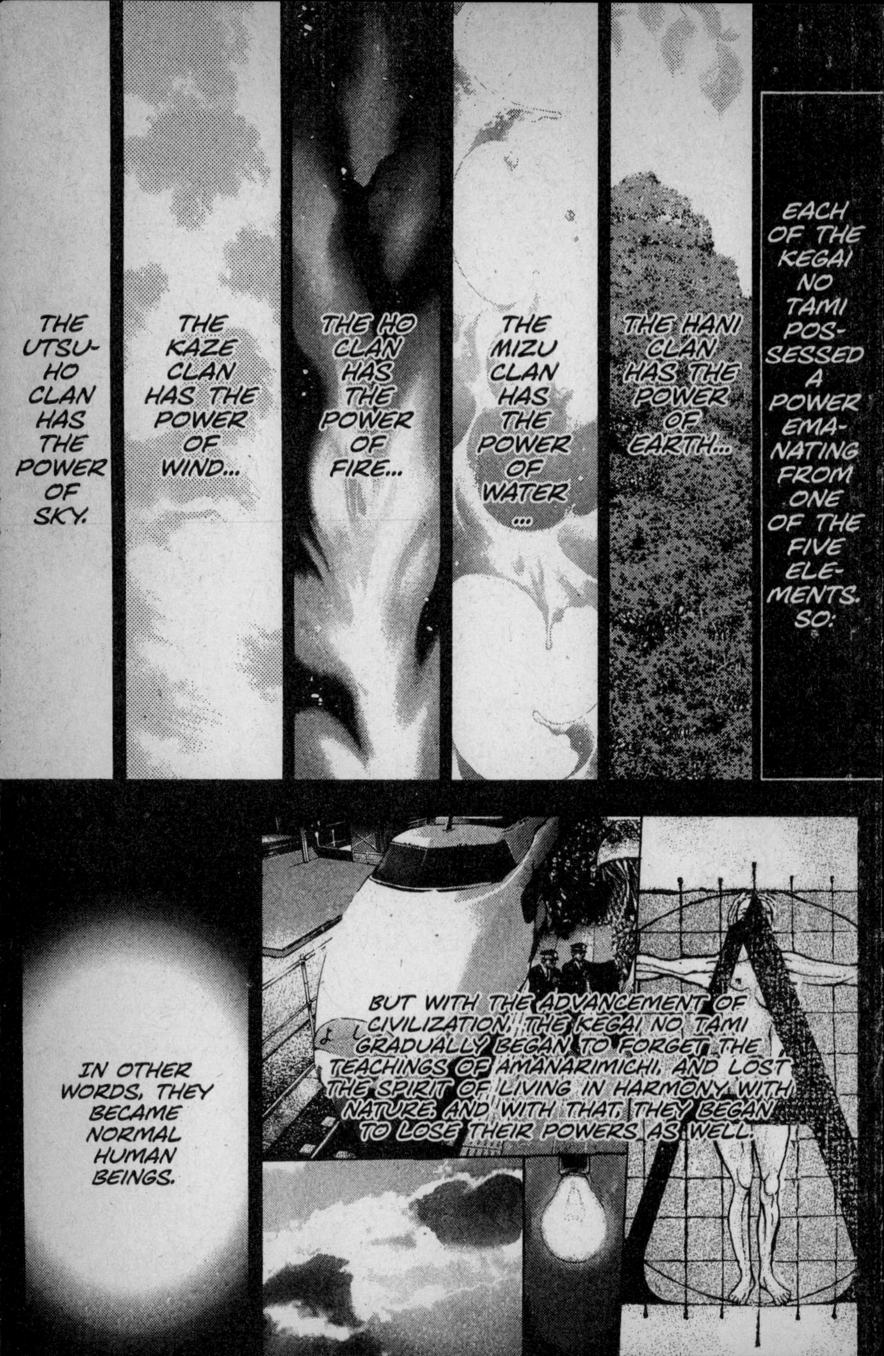
EACH OF THE KEGAI NO TAMI POSSESSED A POWER EMANATING FROM ONE OF THE FIVE ELEMENTS. SO:
THE HANI CLAN HAS THE POWER OF EARTH...
THE MIZU CLAN HAS THE POWER OF WATER...
THE HO CLAN HAS THE POWER OF FIRE...
THE KAZE CLAN HAS THE POWER OF WIND...
THE UTSUHO CLAN HAS THE POWER OF SKY.
BUT WITH THE ADVANCEMENT OF CIVILIZATION, THE KEGAI NO TAMI GRADUALLY BEGAN TO FORGET THE TEACHINGS OF AMANARIMICHI, AND LOST THE SPIRIT OF LIVING IN HARMONY WITH NATURE. AND WITH THAT, THEY BEGAN TO LOSE THEIR POWERS AS WELL.
IN OTHER WORDS, THEY BECAME NORMAL HUMAN BEINGS.

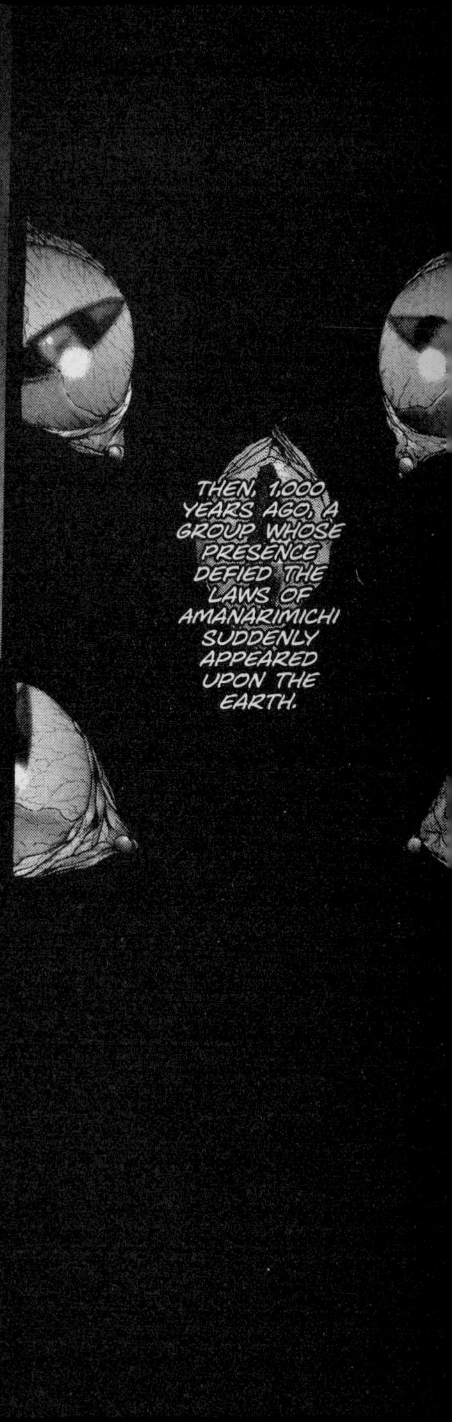
THEN, 1,000 YEARS AGO, A GROUP WHOSE PRESENCE DEFIED THE LAWS OF AMANARIMICHI SUDDENLY APPEARED UPON THE EARTH.
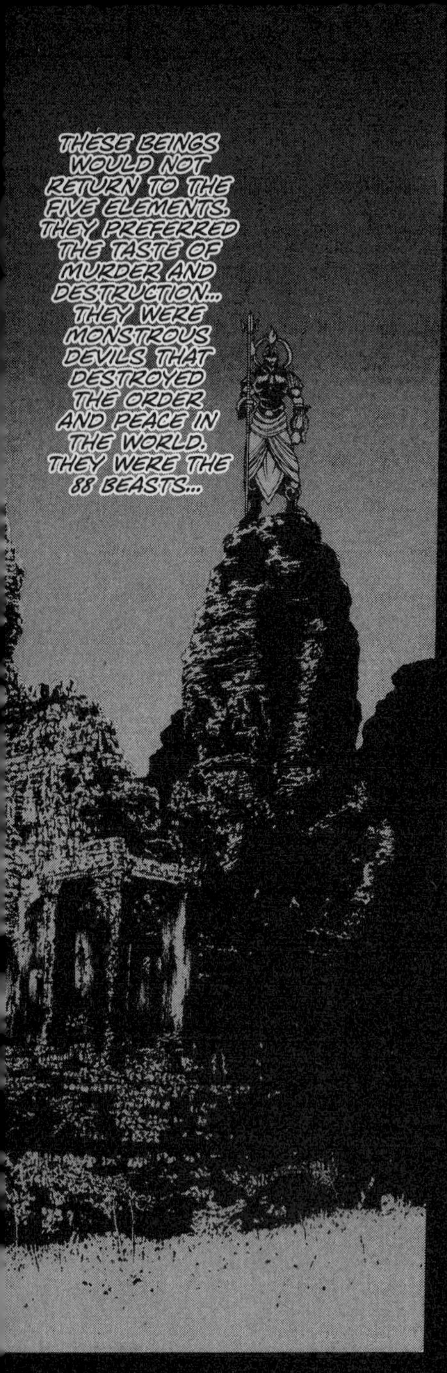
THESE BEINGS WOULD NOT RETURN TO THE FIVE ELEMENTS. THEY PREFERRED THE TASTE OF MURDER AND DESTRUCTION... THEY WERE MONSTROUS DEVILS THAT DESTROYED THE ORDER AND PEACE IN THE WORLD. THEY WERE THE 88 BEASTS...

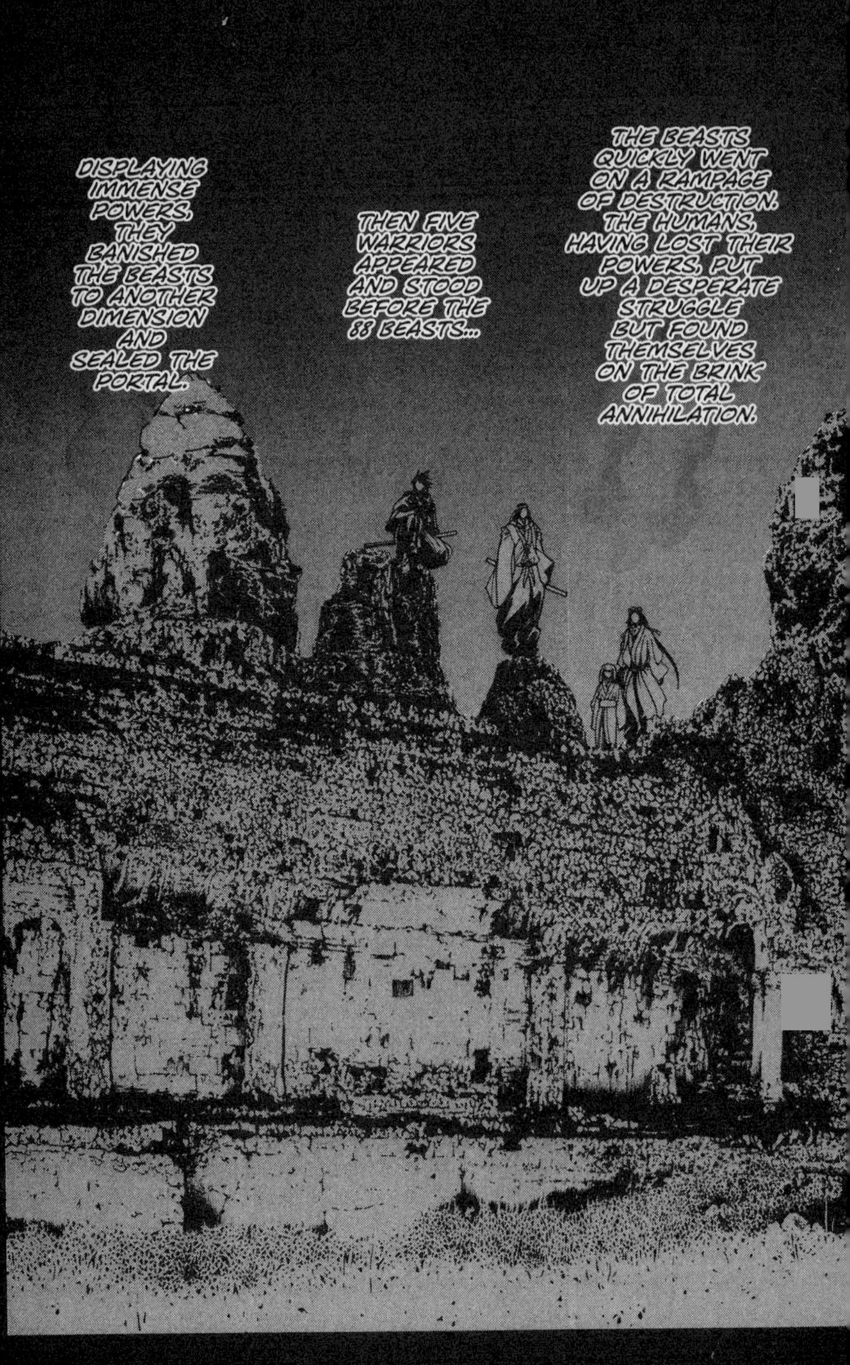
THE BEASTS QUICKLY WENT ON A RAMPAGE OF DESTRUCTION. THE HUMANS, HAVING LOST THEIR POWERS, PUT UP A DESPERATE STRUGGLE BUT FOUND THEMSELVES ON THE BRINK OF TOTAL ANNIHILATION.
THEN FIVE WARRIORS APPEARED AND STOOD BEFORE THE 88 BEASTS...
DISPLAYING IMMENSE POWERS, THEY BANISHED THE BEASTS TO ANOTHER DIMENSION AND SEALED THE PORTAL.

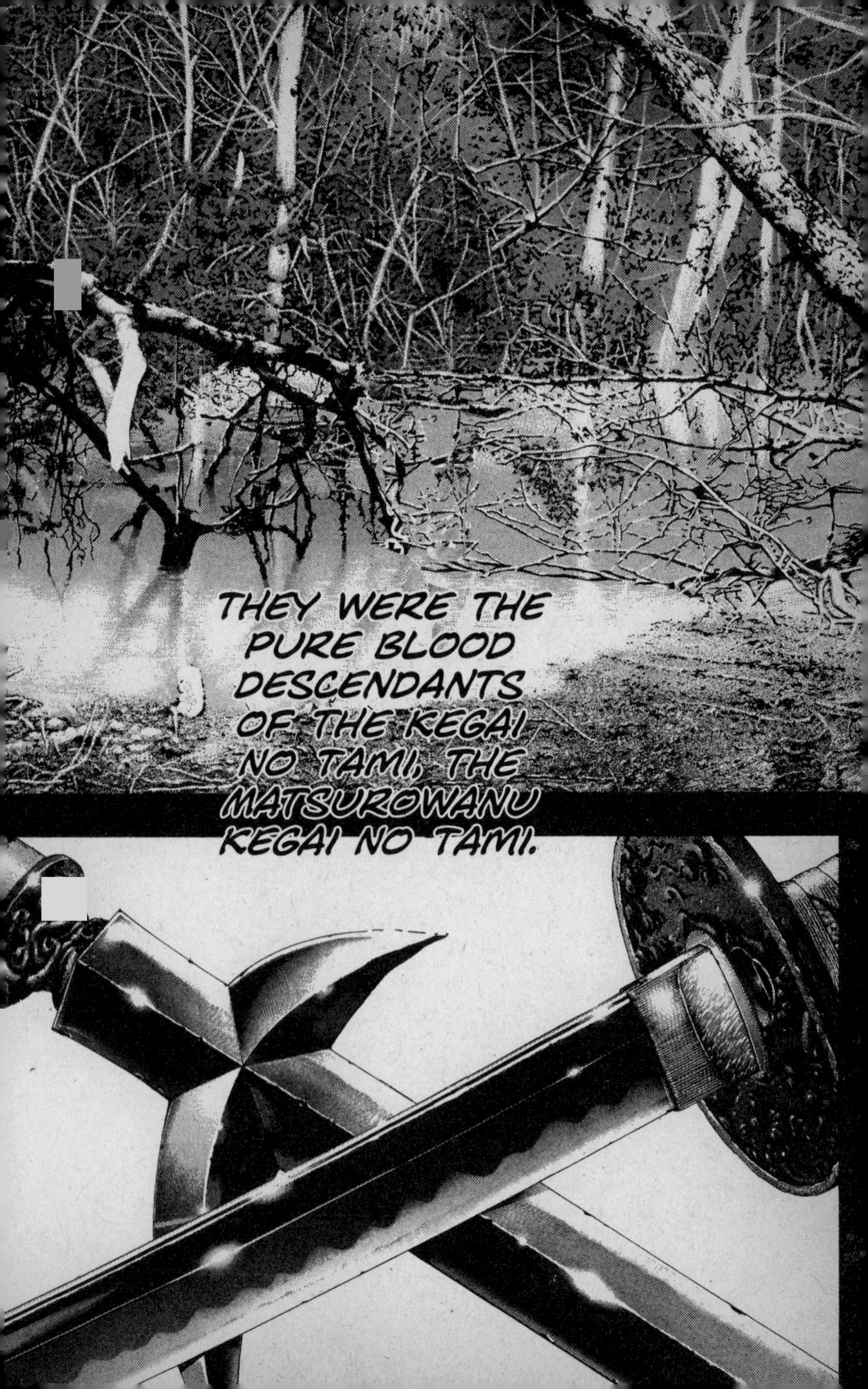
THEY WERE THE PURE BLOOD DESCENDANTS OF THE KEGAI NO TAMI, THE MATSUROWANU KEGAI NO TAMI.

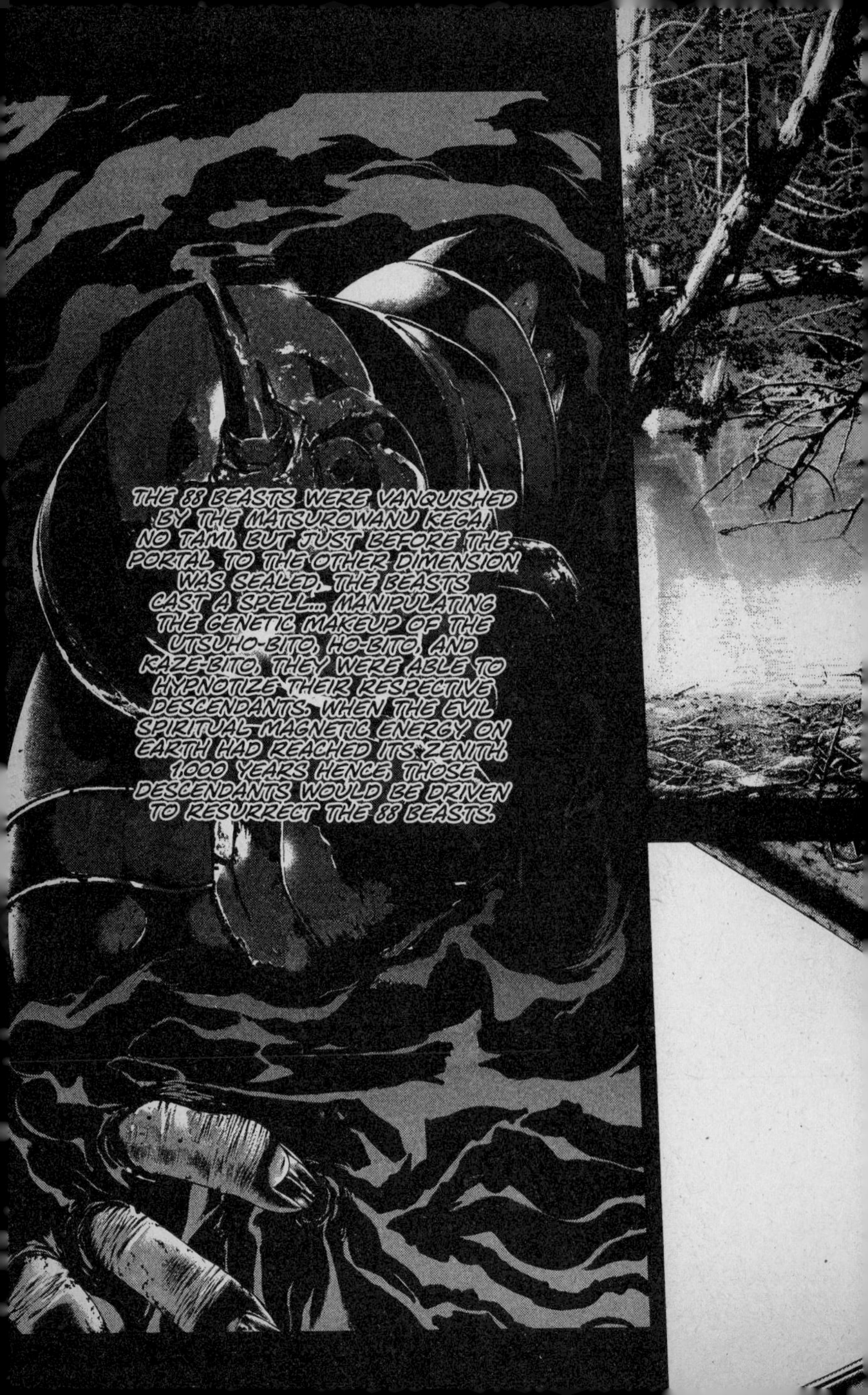
THE 88 BEASTS WERE VANQUISHED BY THE MATSUROWANU KEGAI NO TAMI, BUT JUST BEFORE THE PORTAL TO THE OTHER DIMENSION WAS SEALED, THE BEASTS CAST A SPELL... MANIPULATING THE GENETIC MAKEUP OF THE UTSUHO-BITO, HO-BITO, AND KAZE-BITO, THEY WERE ABLE TO HYPNOTIZE THEIR RESPECTIVE DESCENDANTS. WHEN THE EVIL SPIRITUAL MAGNETIC ENERGY ON EARTH HAD REACHED ITS ZENITH, 1,000 YEARS HENCE, THOSE DESCENDANTS WOULD BE DRIVEN TO RESURRECT THE 88 BEASTS.

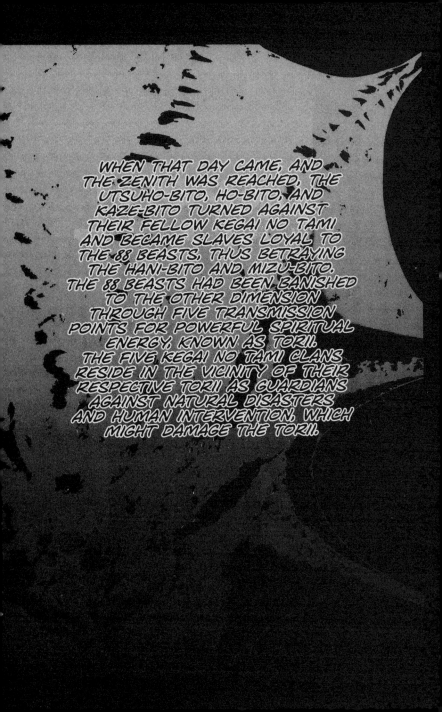

WHEN THAT DAY CAME, AND
THE ZENITH WAS REACHED, THE
UTSUHO-BITO, HO-BITO, AND
KAZE-BITO TURNED AGAINST
THEIR FELLOW KEGAI NO TAMI
AND BECAME SLAVES LOYAL TO
THE 88 BEASTS, THUS BETRAYING
THE HANI-BITO AND MIZU-BITO.
THE 88 BEASTS HAD BEEN BANISHED
TO THE OTHER DIMENSION
THROUGH FIVE TRANSMISSION
POINTS FOR POWERFUL SPIRITUAL
ENERGY, KNOWN AS TORII.
THE FIVE KEGAI NO TAMI CLANS
RESIDE IN THE VICINITY OF THEIR
RESPECTIVE TORII AS GUARDIANS
AGAINST NATURAL DISASTERS
AND HUMAN INTERVENTION, WHICH
MIGHT DAMAGE THE TORII.

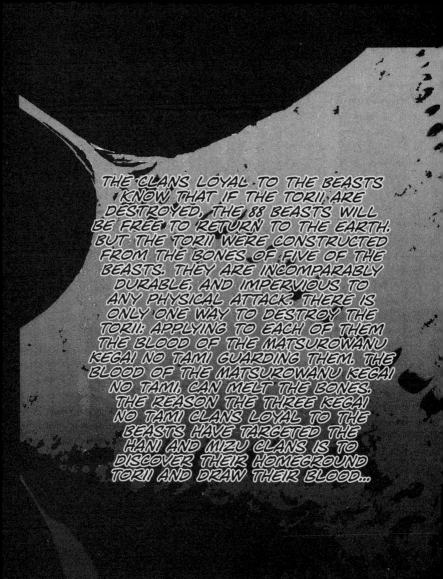

THE CLANS LOYAL TO THE BEASTS KNOW THAT IF THE TORII ARE DESTROYED, THE 88 BEASTS WILL BE FREE TO RETURN TO THE EARTH. BUT THE TORII WERE CONSTRUCTED FROM THE BONES OF FIVE OF THE BEASTS. THEY ARE INCOMPARABLY DURABLE, AND IMPERVIOUS TO ANY PHYSICAL ATTACK. THERE IS ONLY ONE WAY TO DESTROY THE TORII: APPLYING TO EACH OF THEM THE BLOOD OF THE MATSUROWANU KEGAI NO TAMI GUARDING THEM. THE BLOOD OF THE MATSUROWANU KEGAI NO TAMI, CAN MELT THE BONES. THE REASON THE THREE KEGAI NO TAMI CLANS LOYAL TO THE BEASTS HAVE TARGETED THE HANI AND MIZU CLANS IS TO DISCOVER THEIR HOMEGROUND TORII AND DRAW THEIR BLOOD...

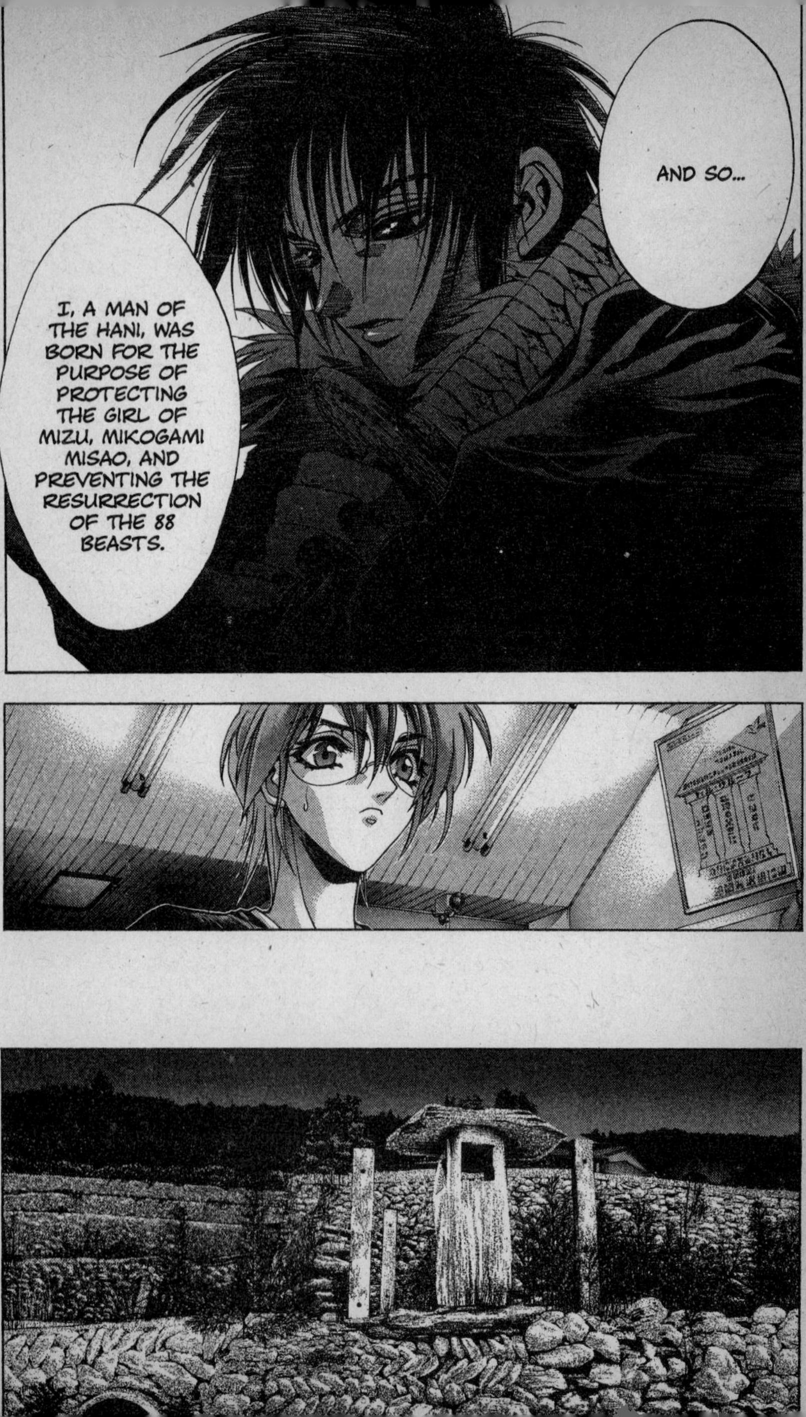
AND SO...
I, A MAN OF THE HANI, WAS BORN FOR THE PURPOSE OF PROTECTING THE GIRL OF MIZU, MIKOGAMI MISAO, AND PREVENTING THE RESURRECTION OF THE 88 BEASTS.

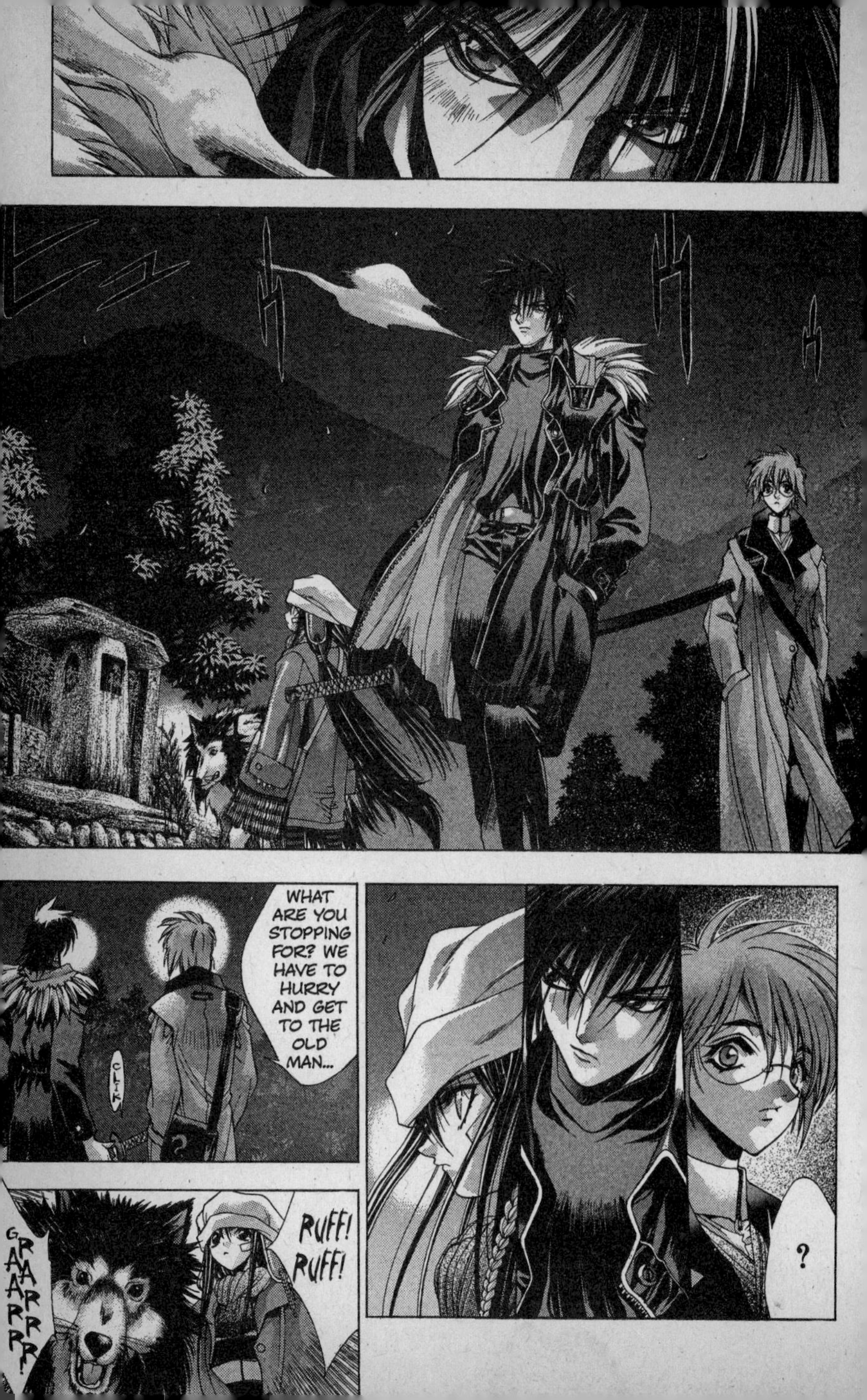
?
WHAT ARE YOU STOPPING FOR? WE HAVE TO HURRY AND GET TO THE OLD MAN...
CLIK
RUFF! RUFF!
GRAAAARRRRR!

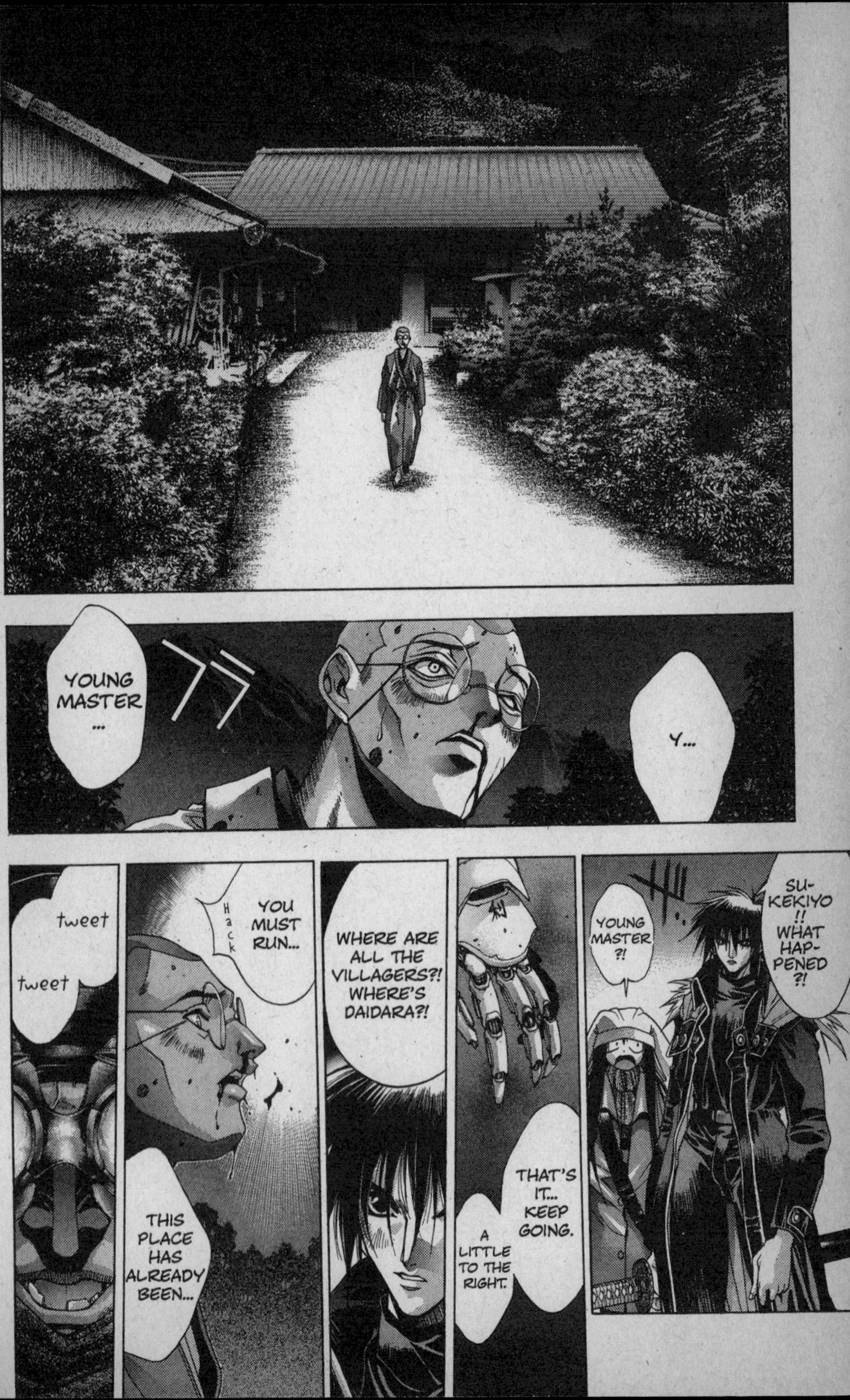
Y...
YOUNG MASTER ...
SU-KEKIYO!! WHAT HAP-PENED?!
YOUNG MASTER?!
THAT'S IT... KEEP GOING.
A LITTLE TO THE RIGHT.
WHERE ARE ALL THE VILLAGERS?! WHERE'S DAIDARA?!
YOU MUST RUN...
Hack
THIS PLACE HAS ALREADY BEEN...
tweet
tweet

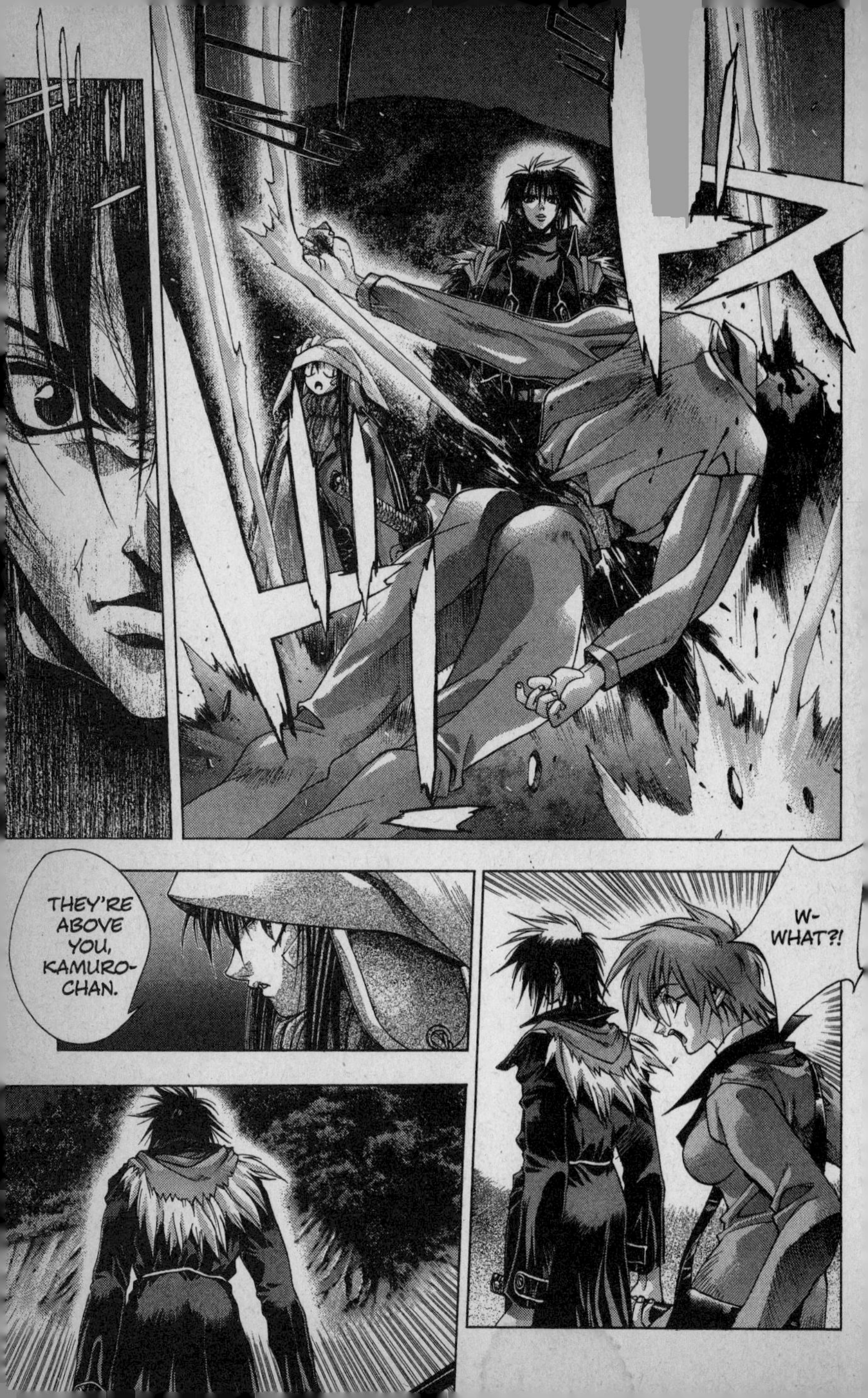

W- WHAT?!
THEY'RE ABOVE YOU, KAMURO-CHAN.

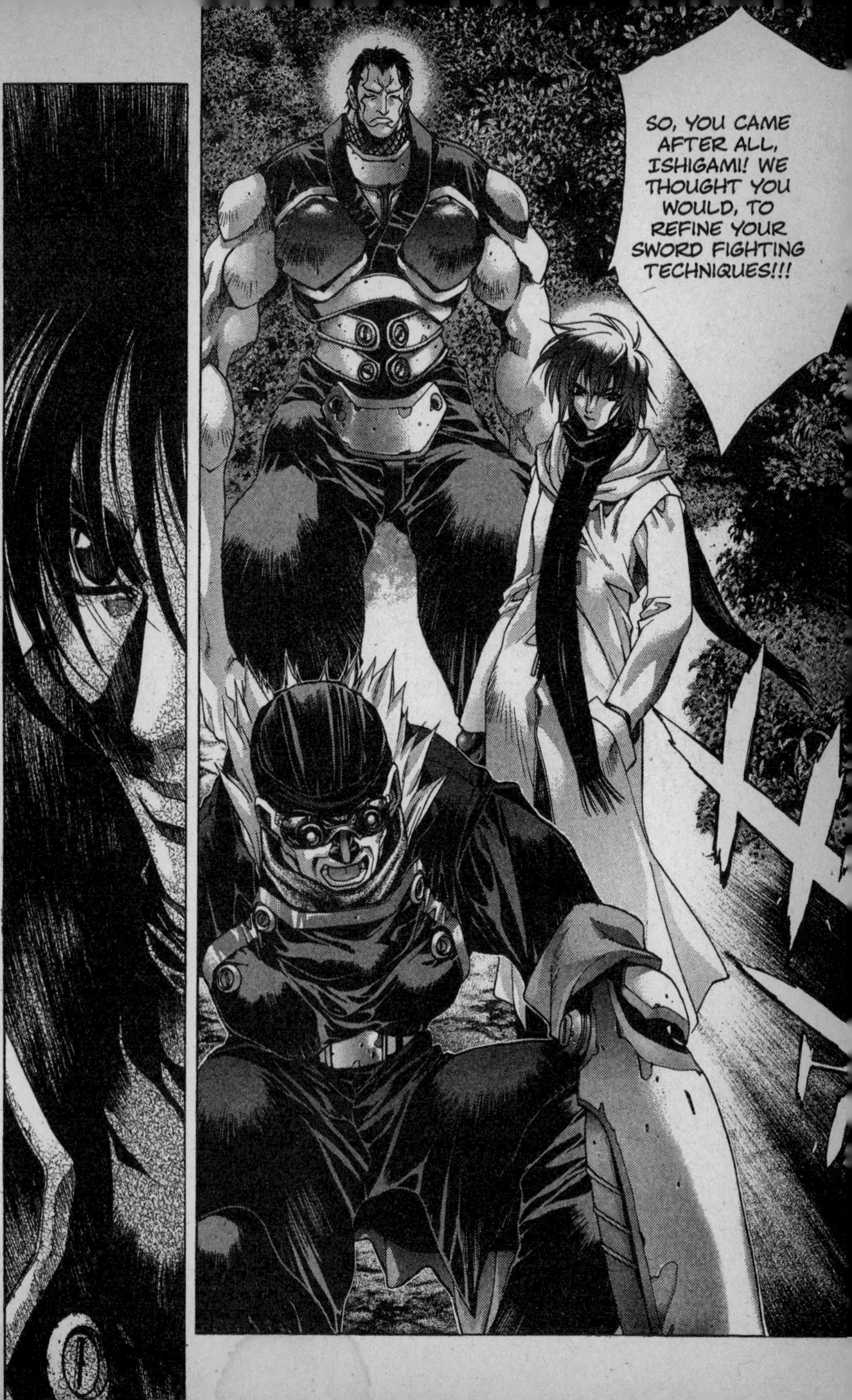
SO, YOU CAME AFTER ALL, ISHIGAMI! WE THOUGHT YOU WOULD, TO REFINE YOUR SWORD FIGHTING TECHNIQUES!!!

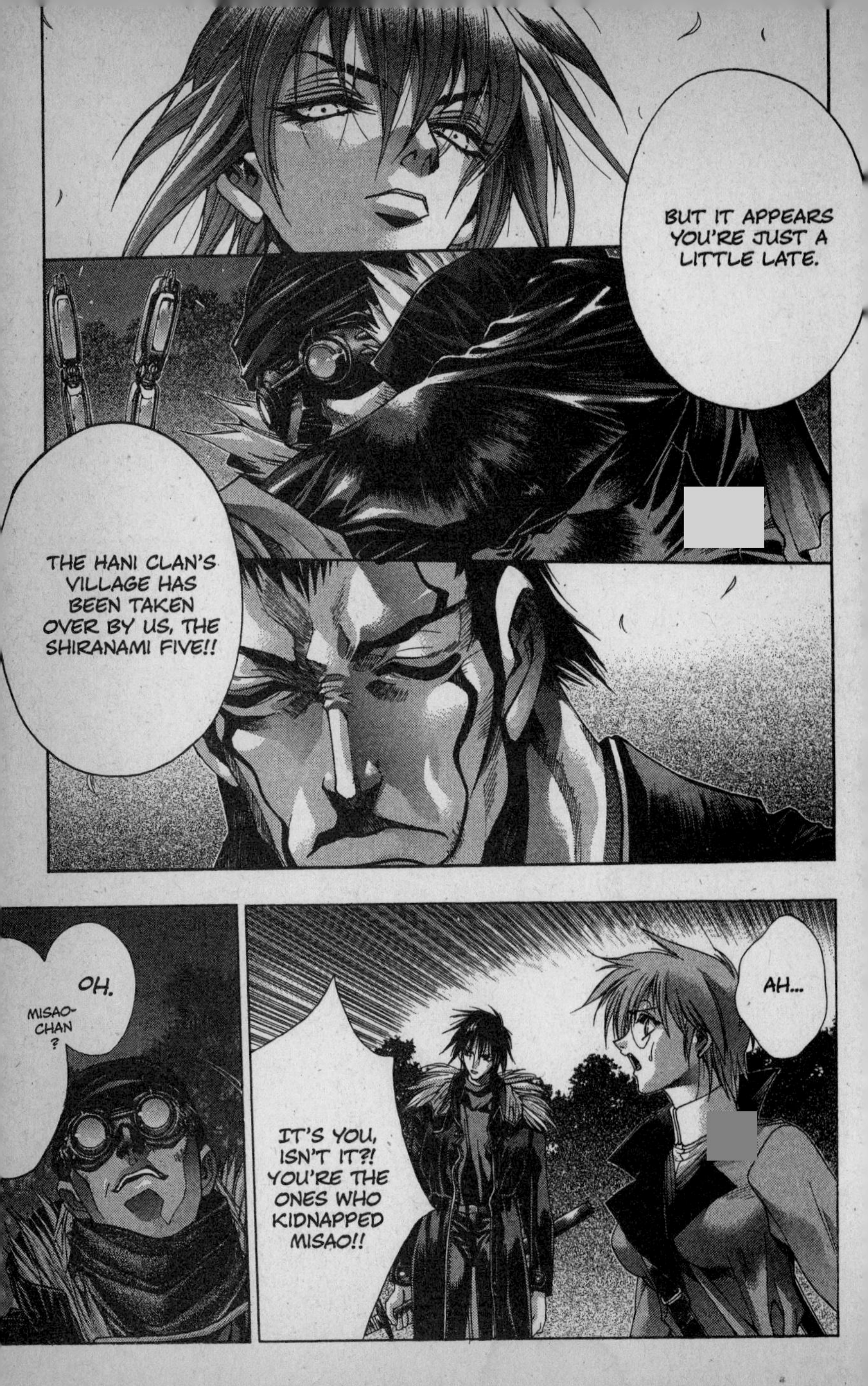
BUT IT APPEARS YOU'RE JUST A LITTLE LATE.
THE HANI CLAN'S VILLAGE HAS BEEN TAKEN OVER BY US, THE SHIRANAMI FIVE!!
AH...
IT'S YOU, ISN'T IT?! YOU'RE THE ONES WHO KIDNAPPED MISAO!!
OH.
MISAO-CHAN?

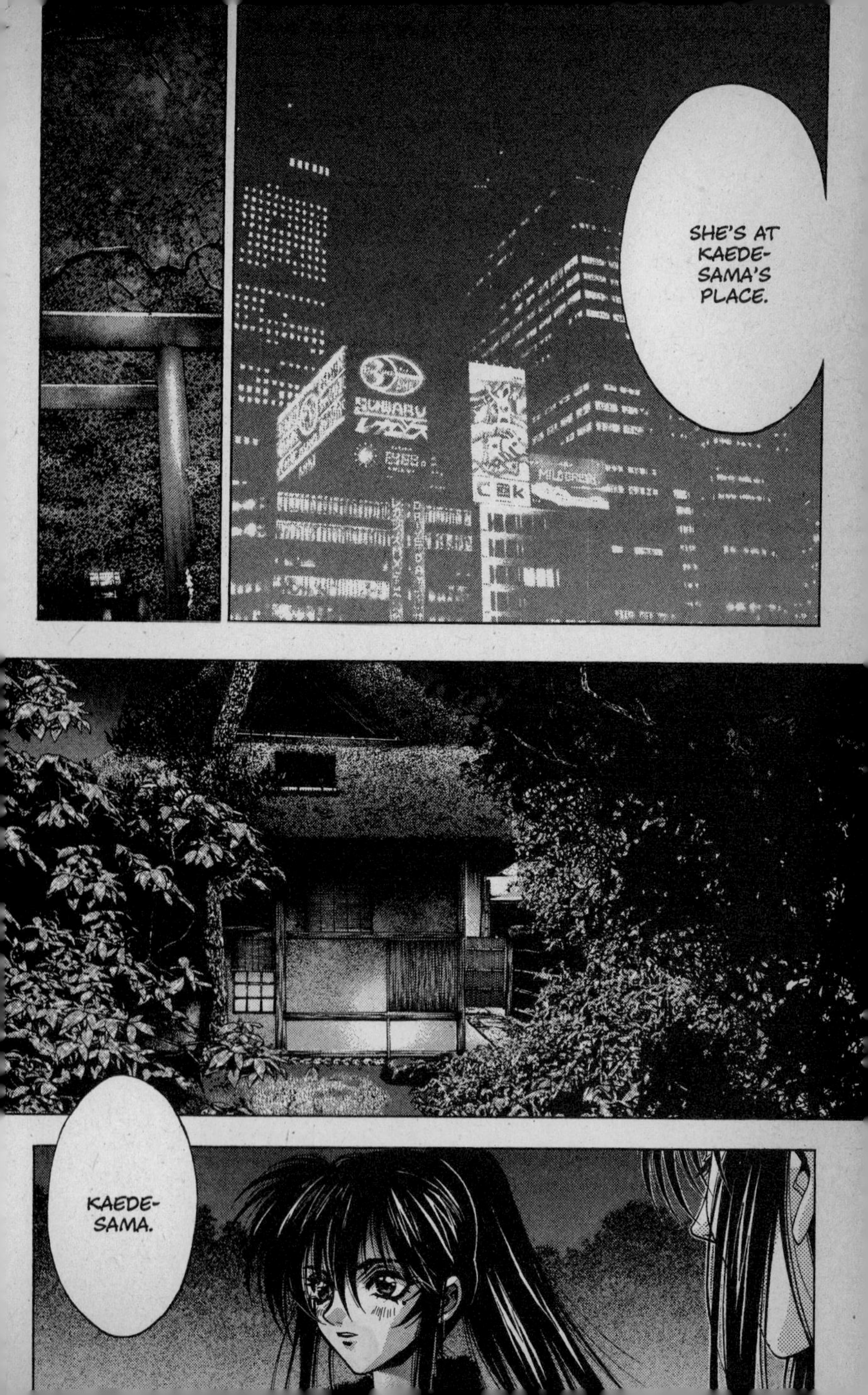
SHE'S AT KAEDE-SAMA'S PLACE.
KAEDE-SAMA.

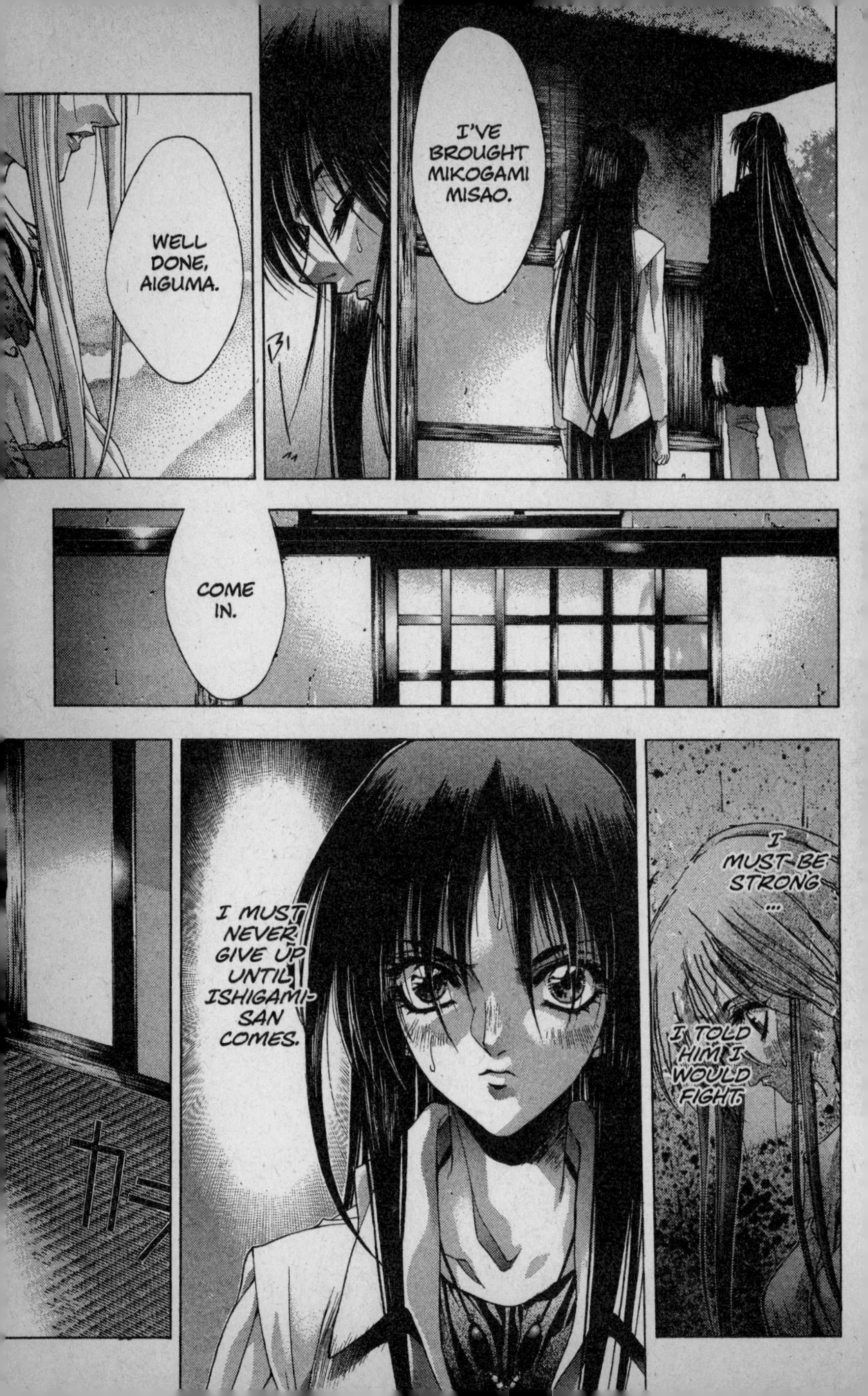
I'VE BROUGHT MIKOGAMI MISAO.
WELL DONE, AIGUMA.
COME IN.
I MUST BE STRONG...
I TOLD HIM I WOULD FIGHT.
I MUST NEVER GIVE UP UNTIL ISHIGAMI-SAN COMES.

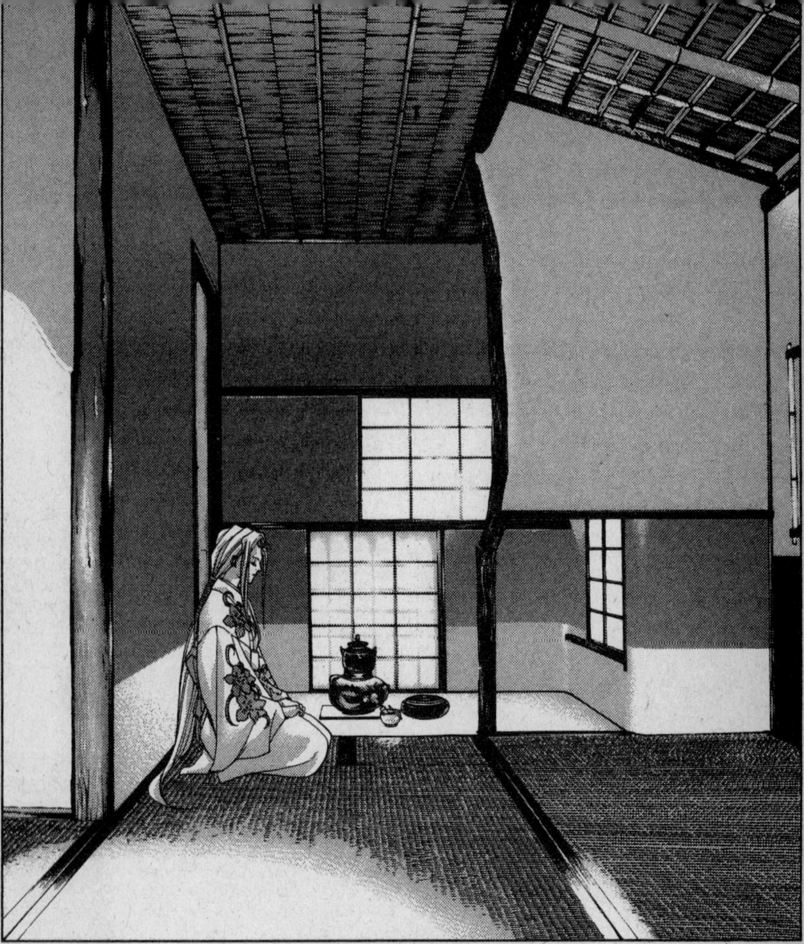

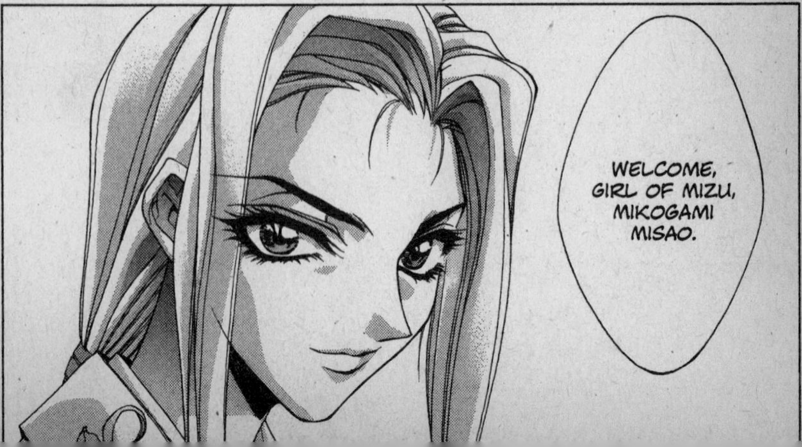
WELCOME, GIRL OF MIZU, MIKOGAMI MISAO.

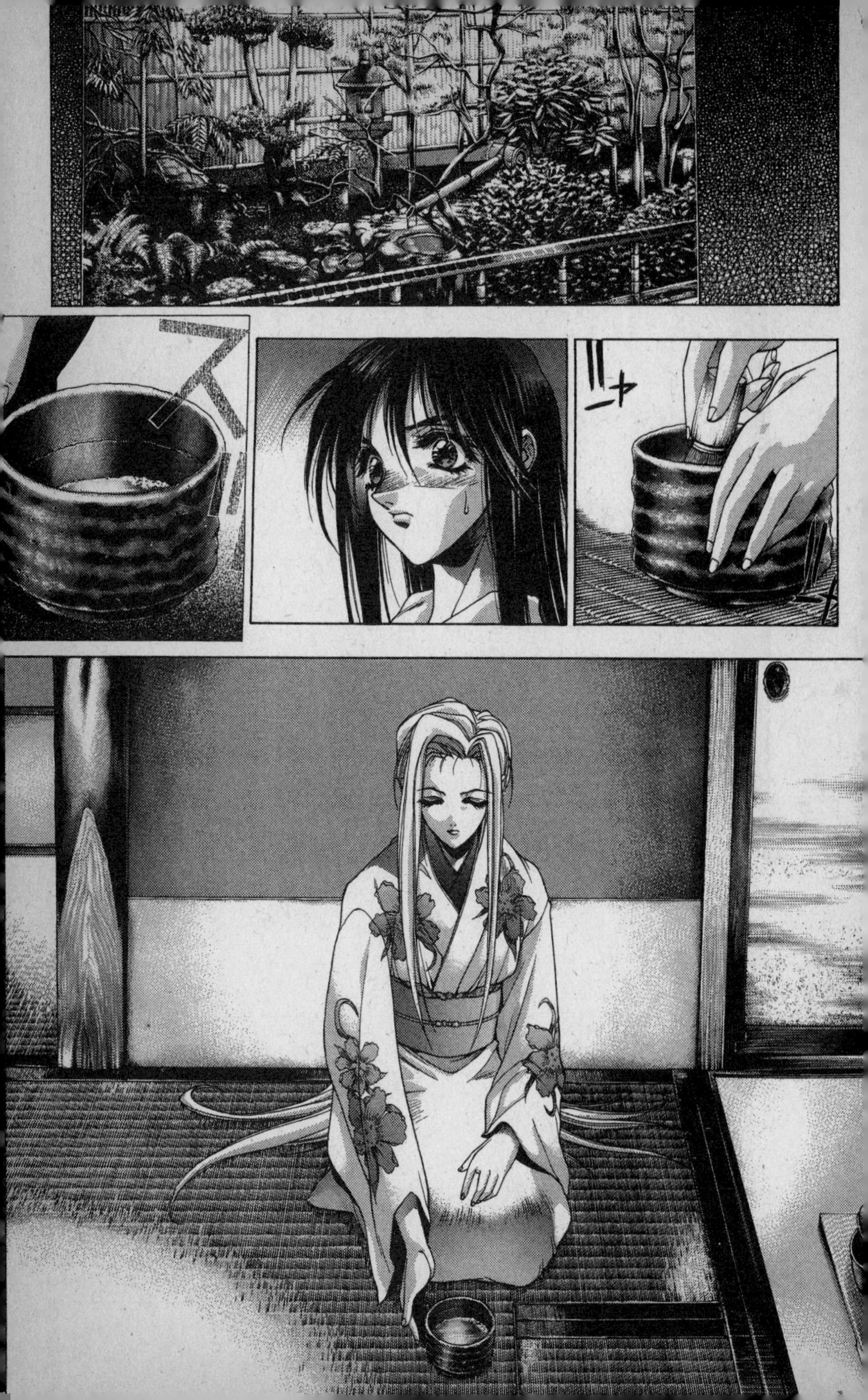

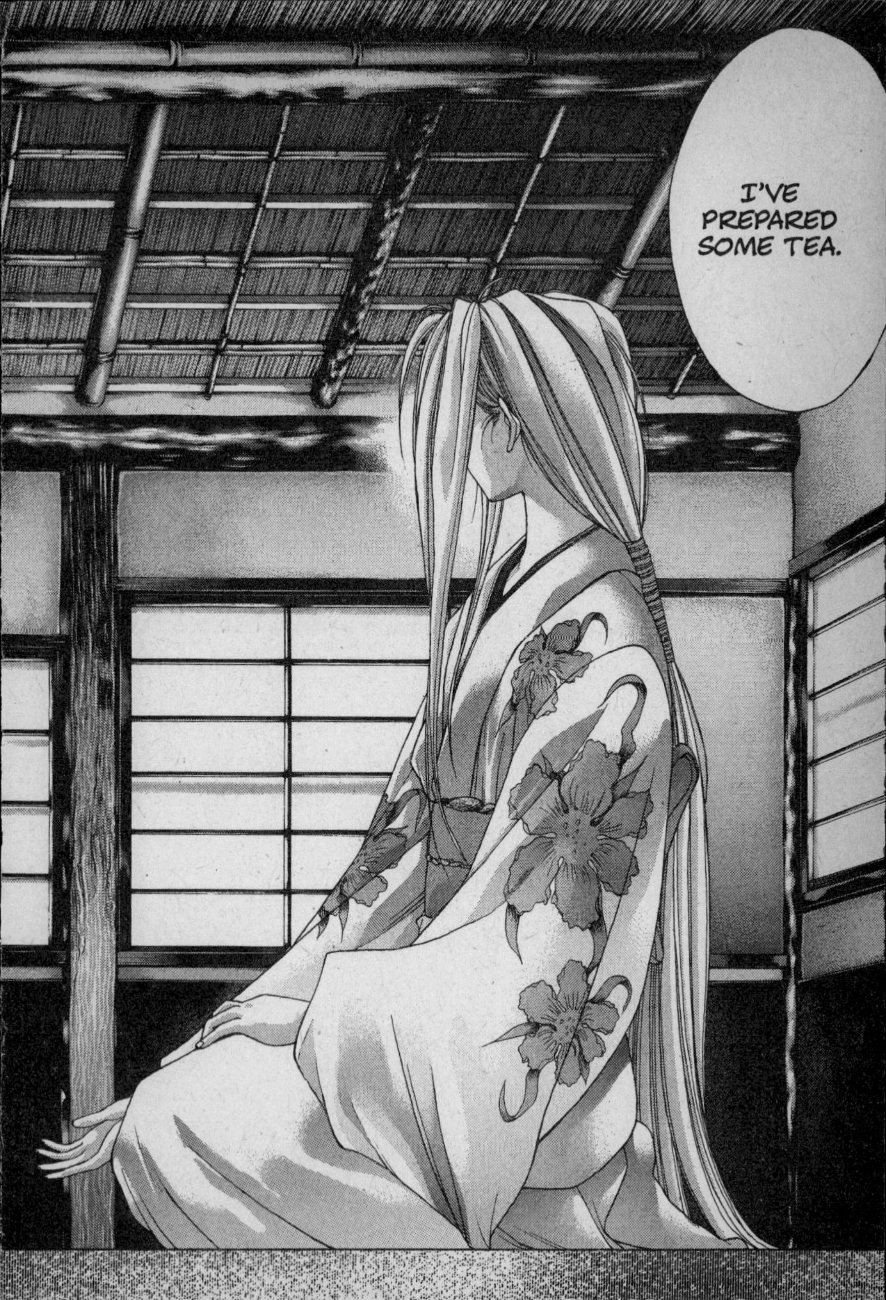
I'VE PREPARED SOME TEA.

Chapter 9: Kaede

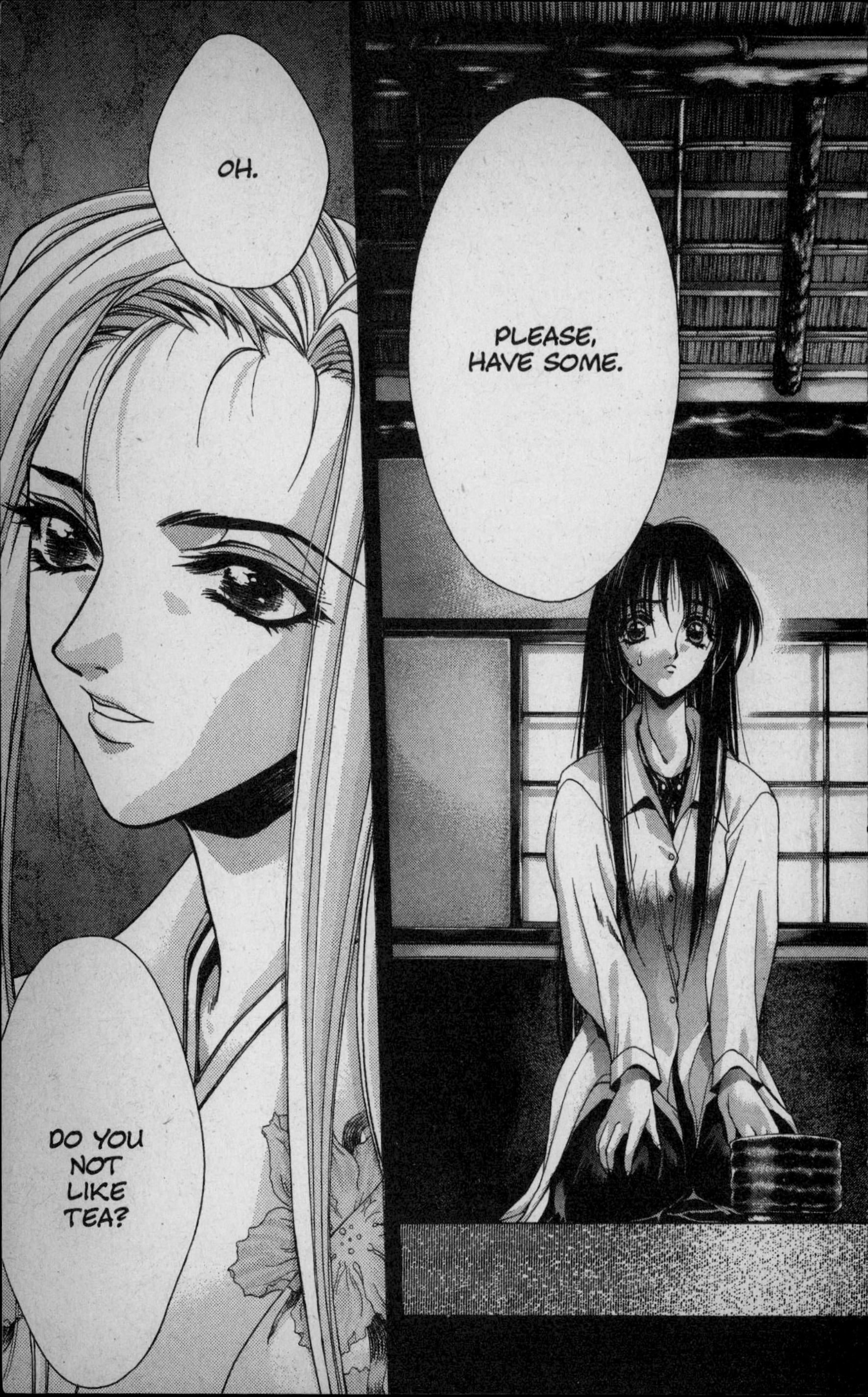
PLEASE, HAVE SOME.
OH.
DO YOU NOT LIKE TEA?

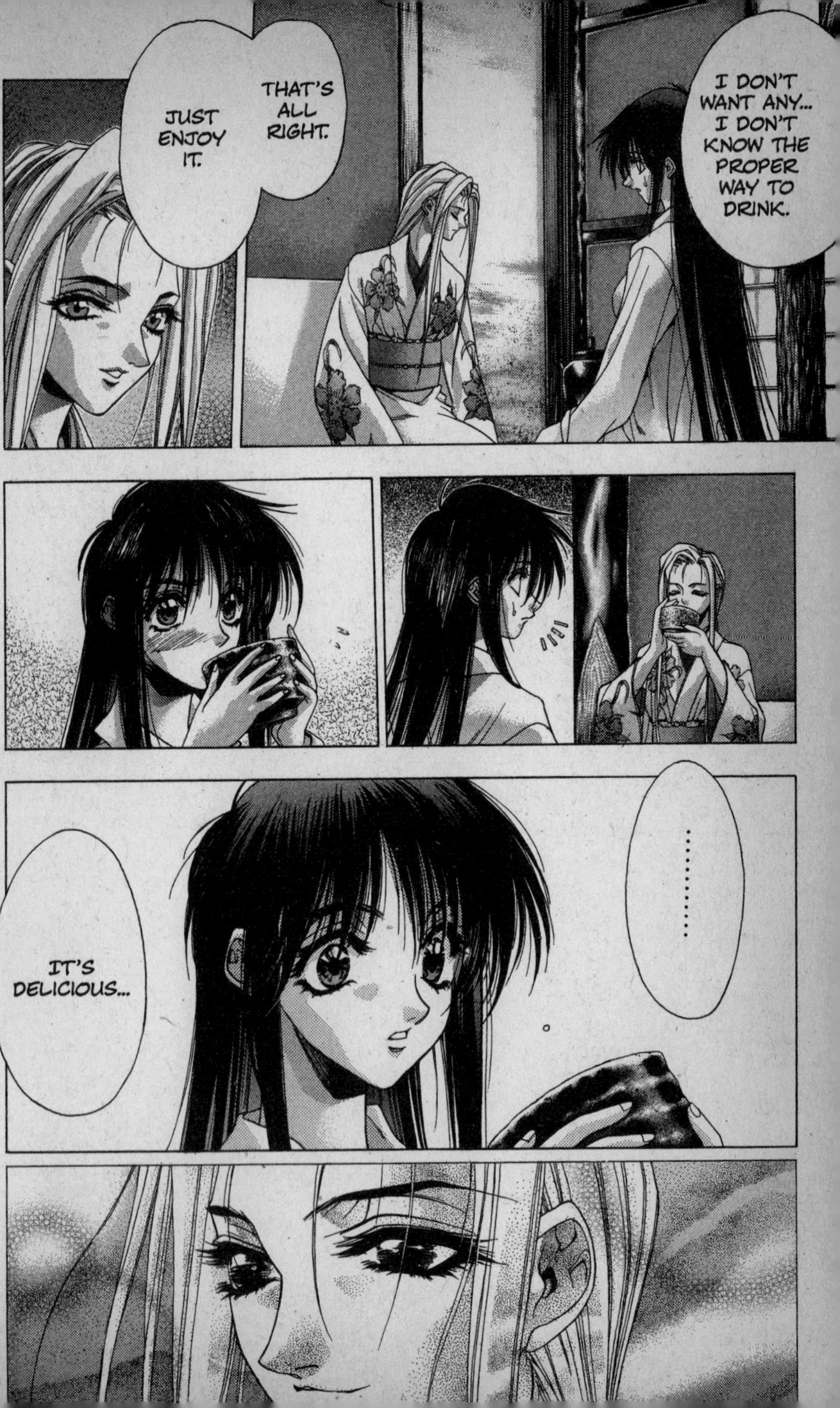

I DON'T WANT ANY... I DON'T KNOW THE PROPER WAY TO DRINK.
THAT'S ALL RIGHT.
JUST ENJOY IT.
......
IT'S DELICIOUS...

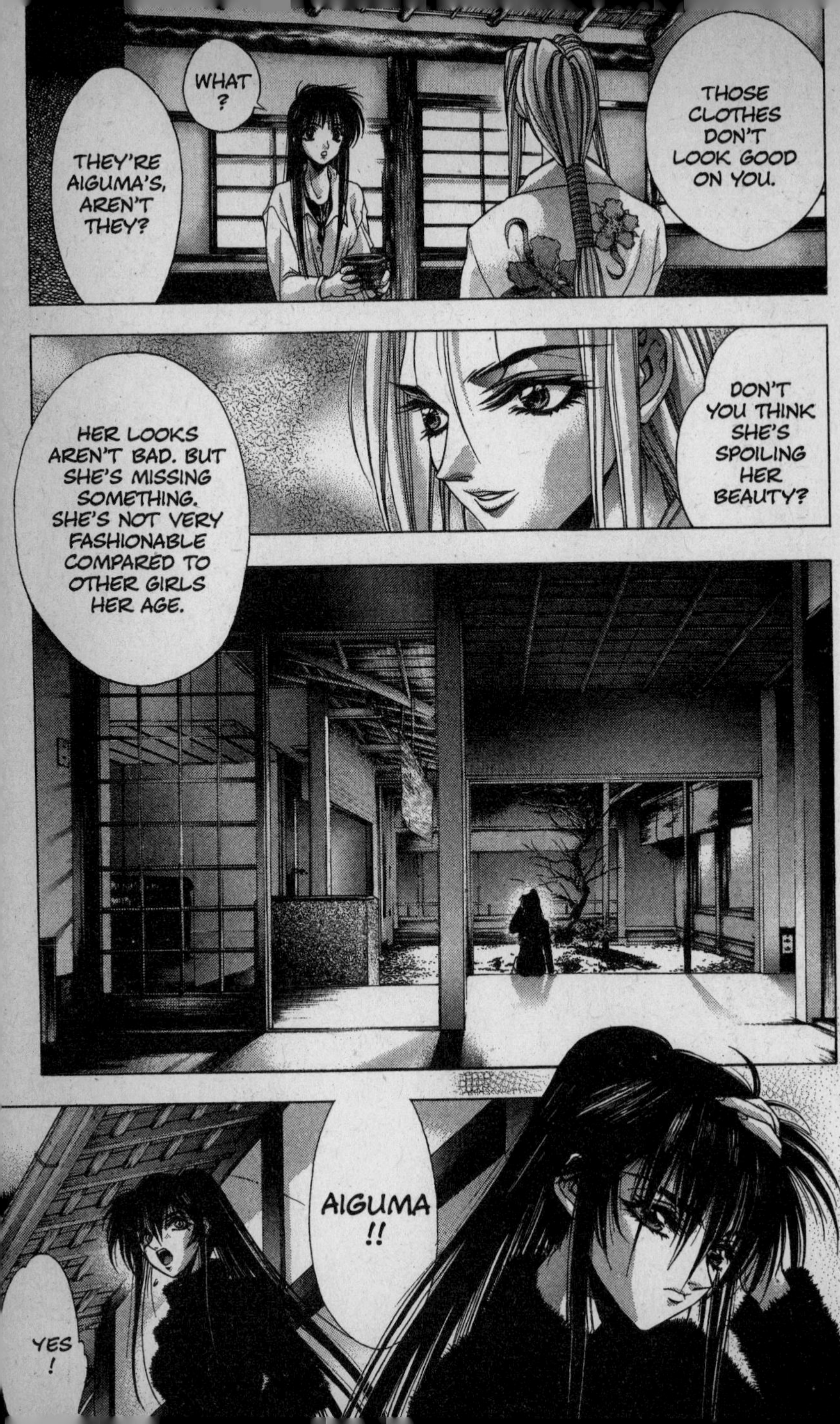
THOSE CLOTHES DON'T LOOK GOOD ON YOU.
WHAT?
THEY'RE AIGUMA'S, AREN'T THEY?
DON'T YOU THINK SHE'S SPOILING HER BEAUTY?
HER LOOKS AREN'T BAD. BUT SHE'S MISSING SOMETHING. SHE'S NOT VERY FASHIONABLE COMPARED TO OTHER GIRLS HER AGE.
AIGUMA!!
YES!

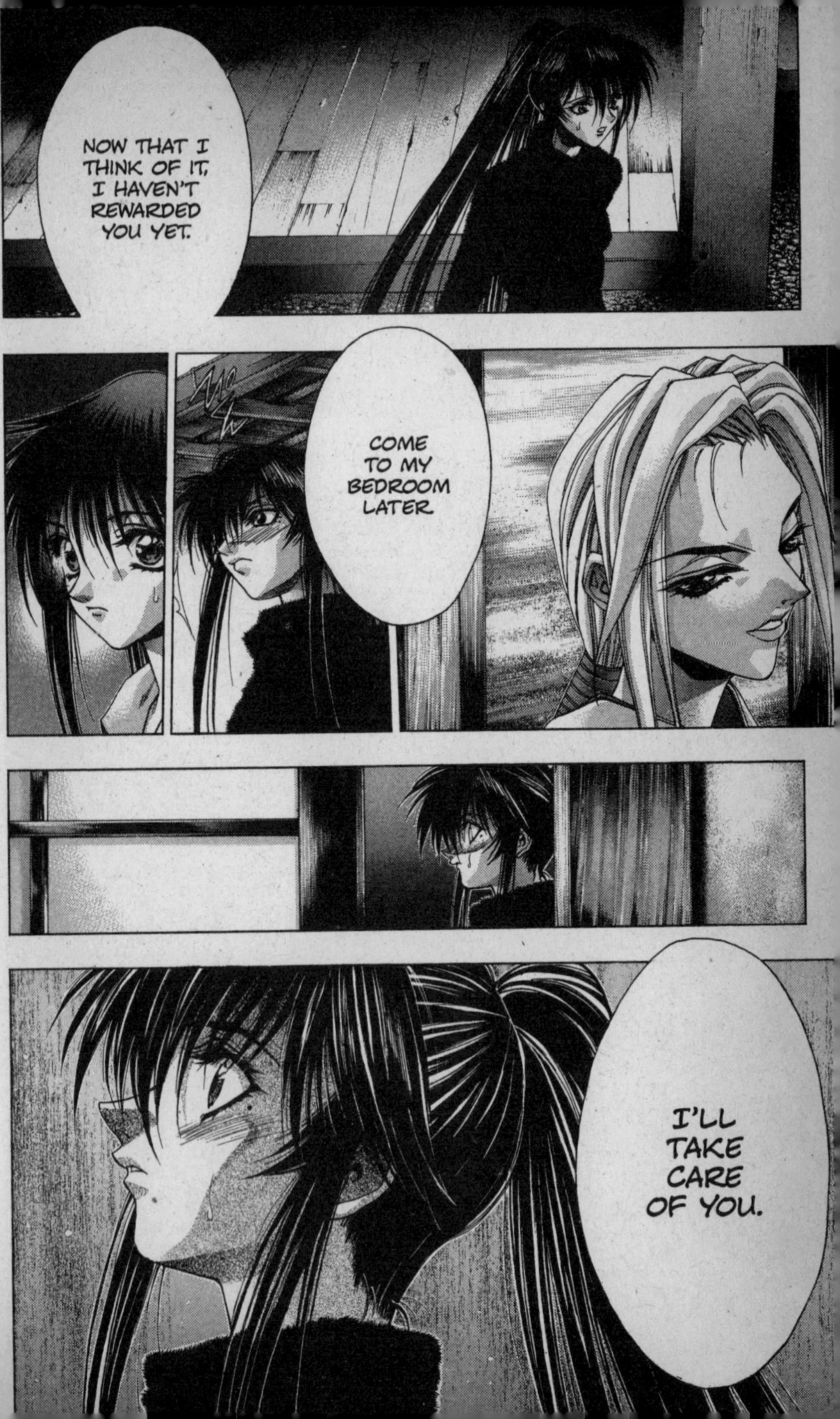
NOW THAT I THINK OF IT, I HAVEN'T REWARDED YOU YET.
COME TO MY BEDROOM LATER
I'LL TAKE CARE OF YOU.

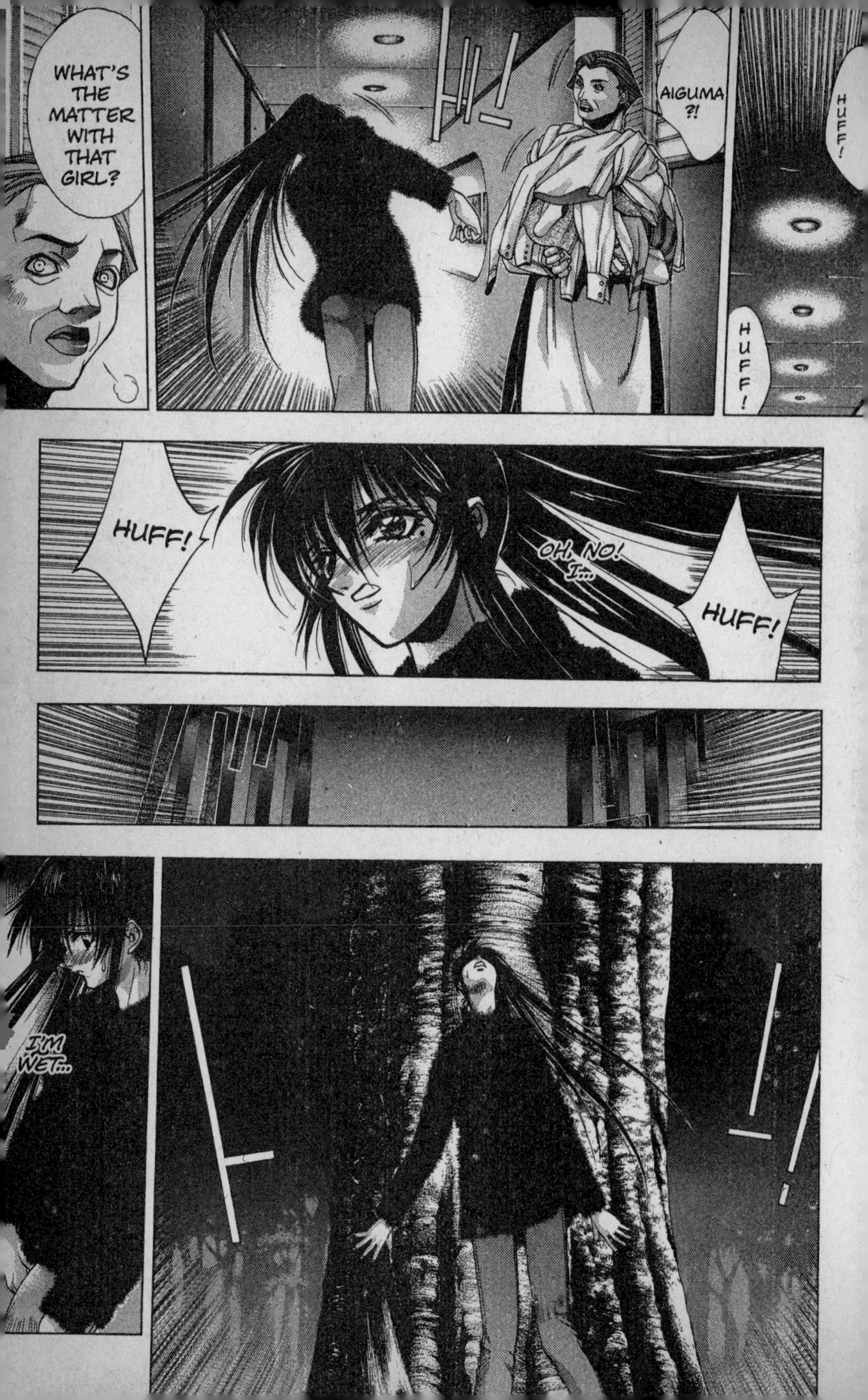
HUFF!
HUFF!
AIGUMA ?!
WHAT'S THE MATTER WITH THAT GIRL?
HUFF!
OH, NO! I...
HUFF!
I'M WET...

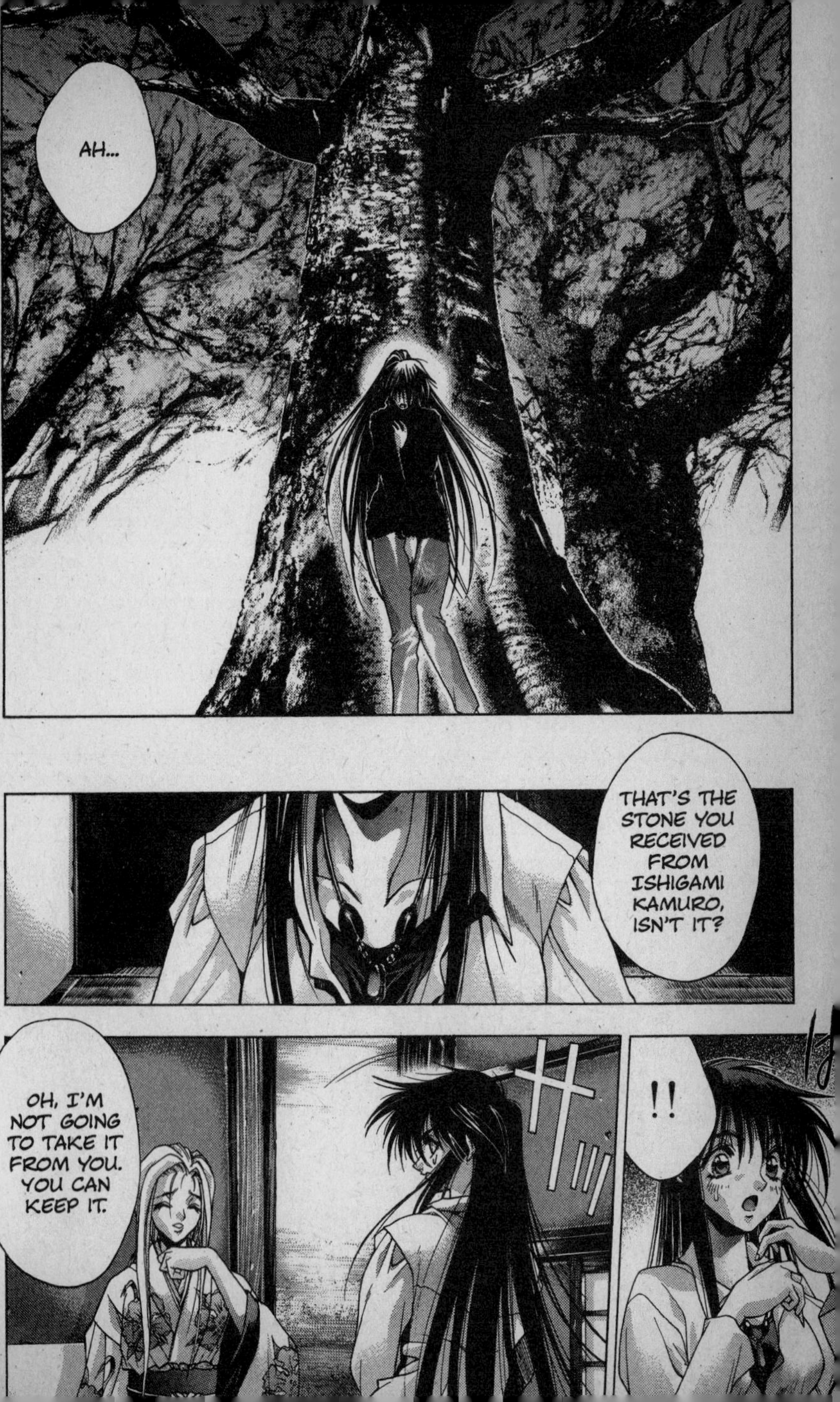
AH...
THAT'S THE STONE YOU RECEIVED FROM ISHIGAMI KAMURO, ISN'T IT?
!!
OH, I'M NOT GOING TO TAKE IT FROM YOU. YOU CAN KEEP IT.

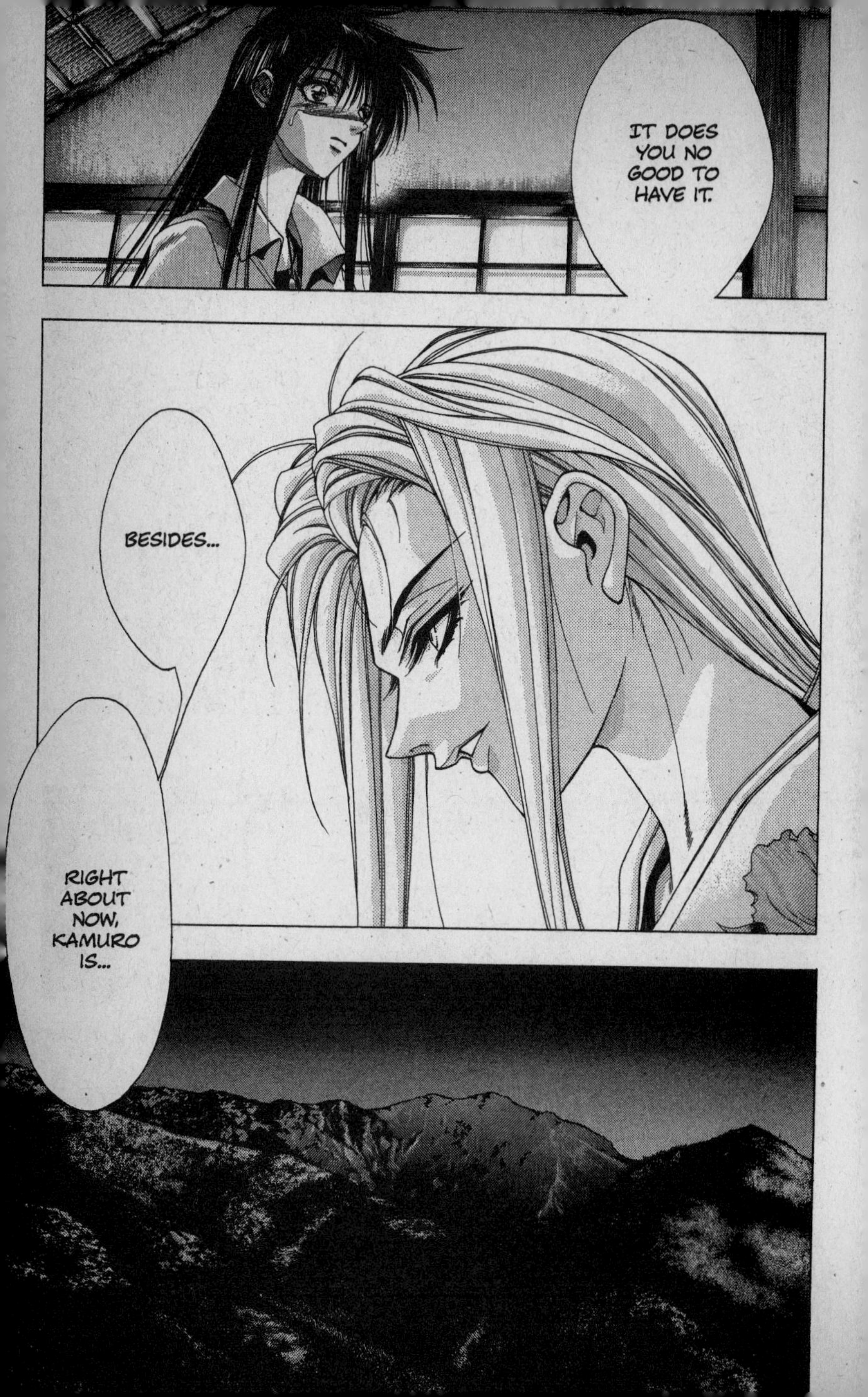
IT DOES YOU NO GOOD TO HAVE IT.
BESIDES...
RIGHT ABOUT NOW, KAMURO IS...

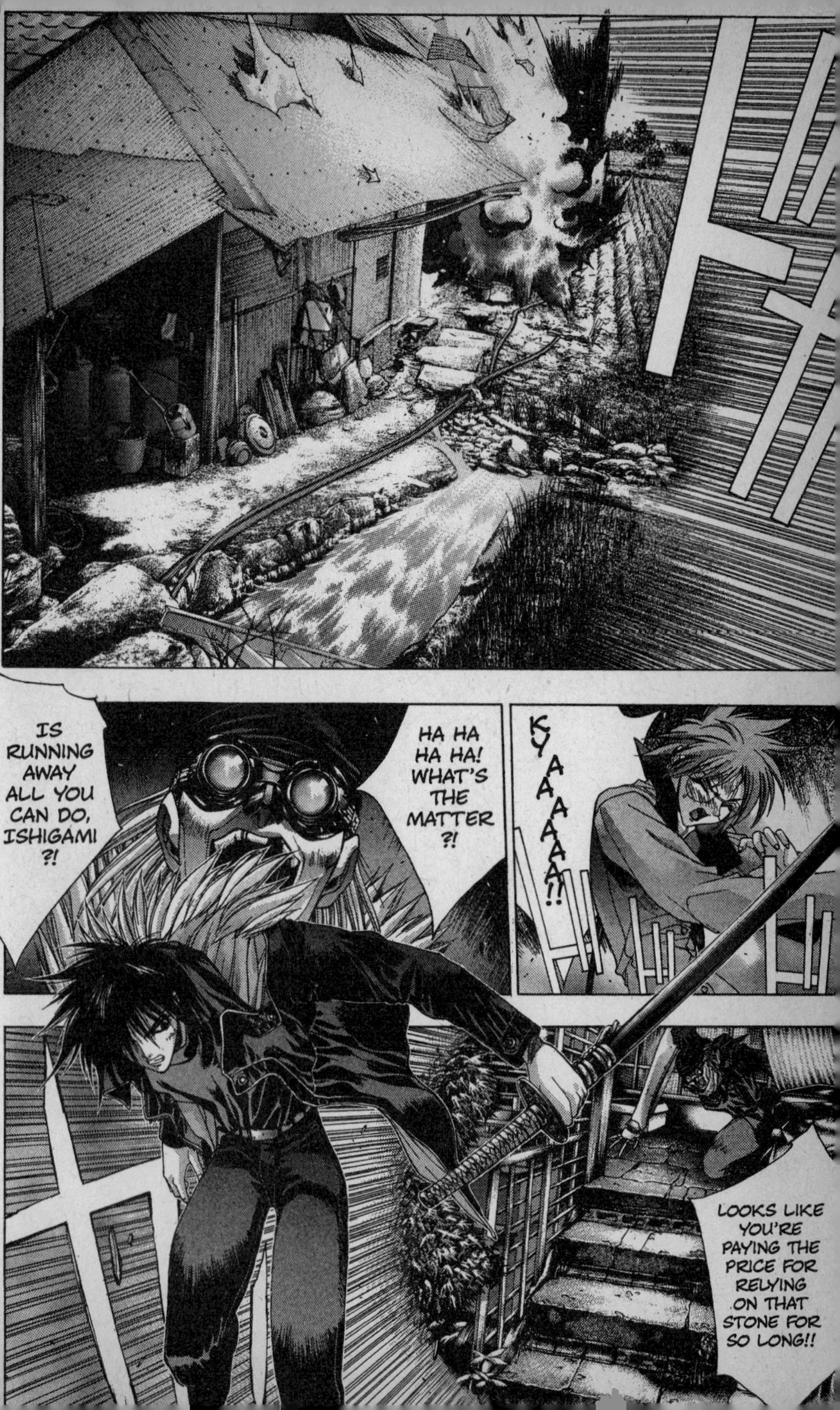
KYAAAAAA!!
HA HA HA HA! WHAT'S THE MATTER ?!
IS RUNNING AWAY ALL YOU CAN DO, ISHIGAMI ?!
LOOKS LIKE YOU'RE PAYING THE PRICE FOR RELYING ON THAT STONE FOR SO LONG!!

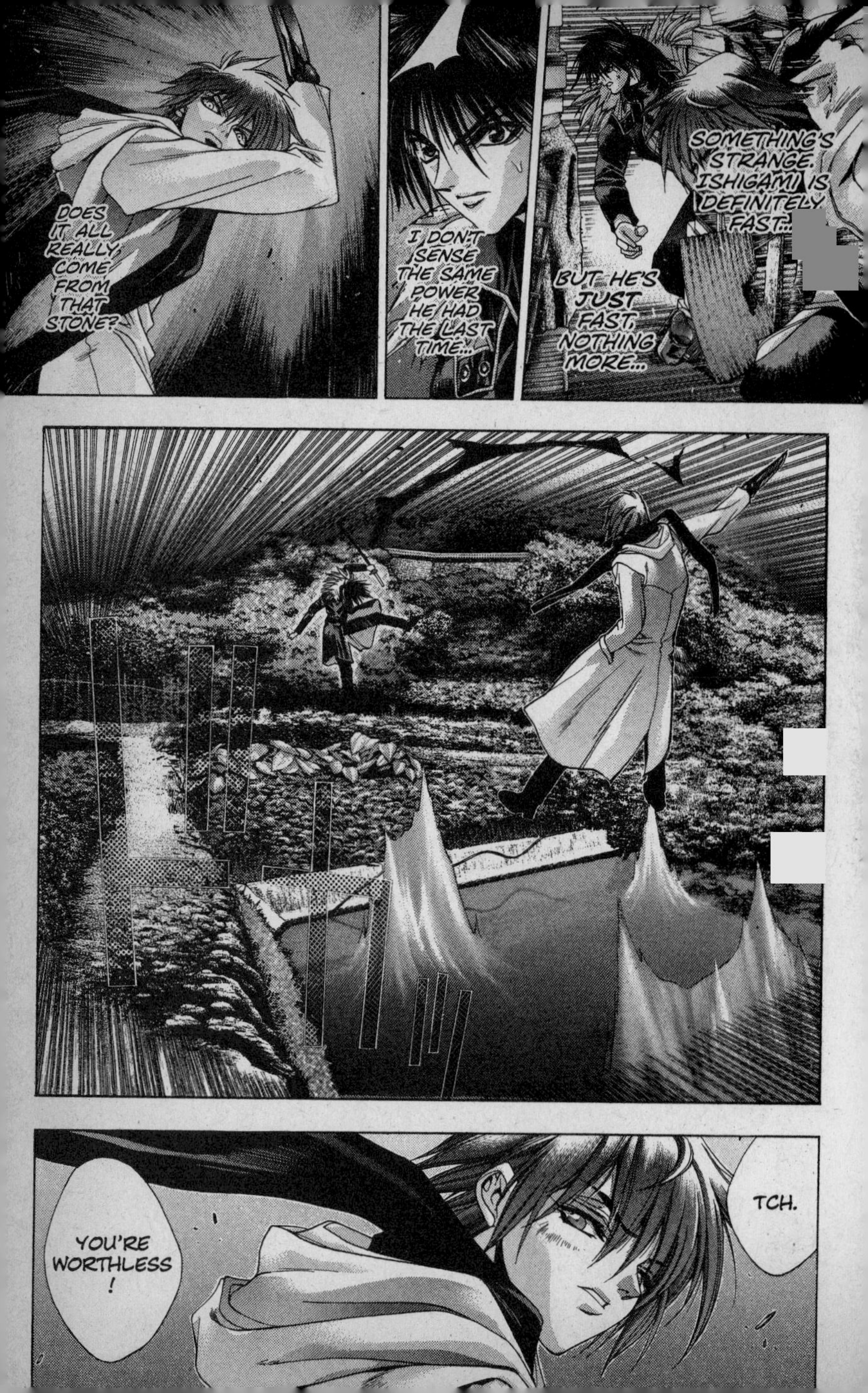
SOMETHING'S STRANGE. ISHIGAMI IS DEFINITELY FAST...
BUT HE'S JUST FAST, NOTHING MORE...
I DON'T SENSE THE SAME POWER HE HAD THE LAST TIME...
DOES IT ALL REALLY COME FROM THAT STONE?
TCH.
YOU'RE WORTHLESS!

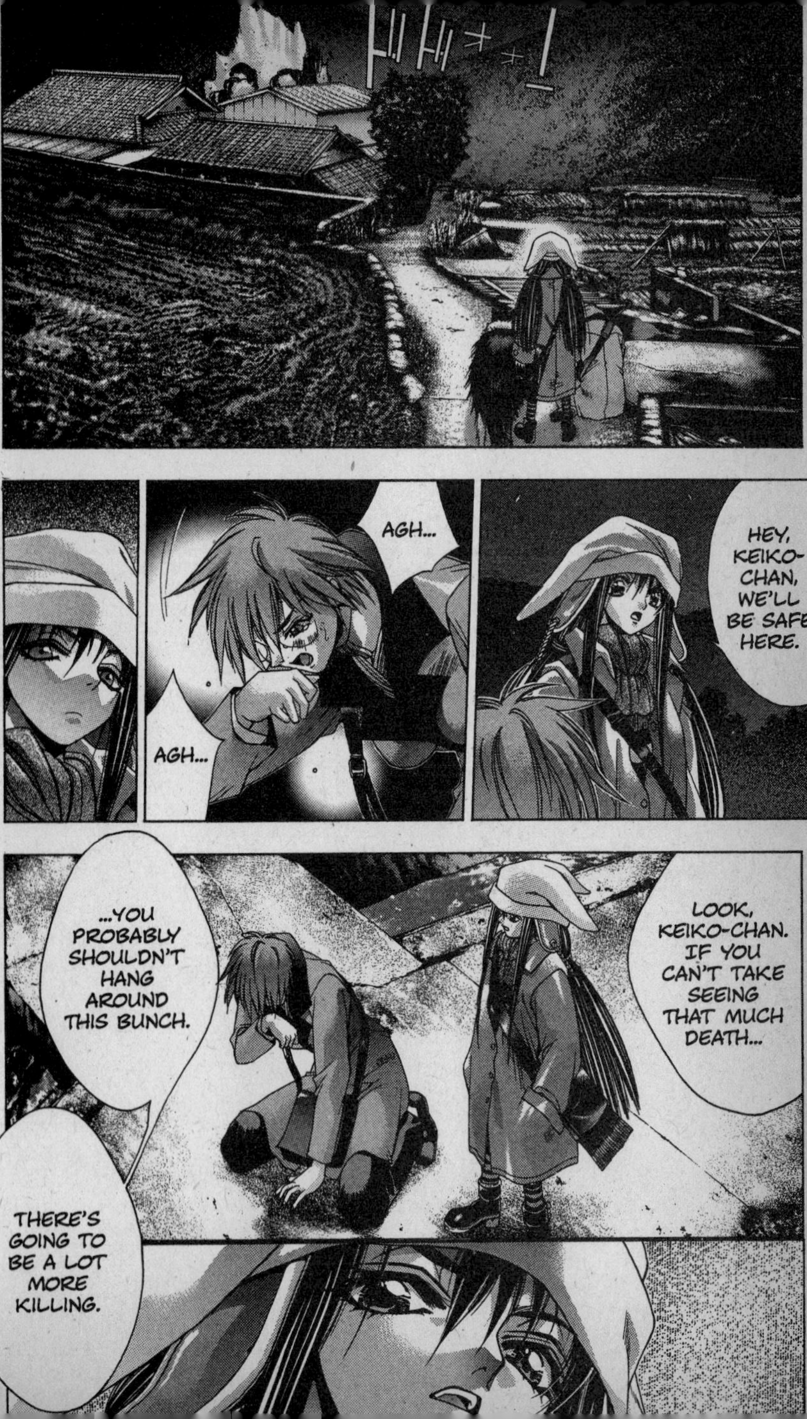
HEY, KEIKO-CHAN, WE'LL BE SAFE HERE.
AGH...
AGH...
LOOK, KEIKO-CHAN. IF YOU CAN'T TAKE SEEING THAT MUCH DEATH...
...YOU PROBABLY SHOULDN'T HANG AROUND THIS BUNCH.
THERE'S GOING TO BE A LOT MORE KILLING.

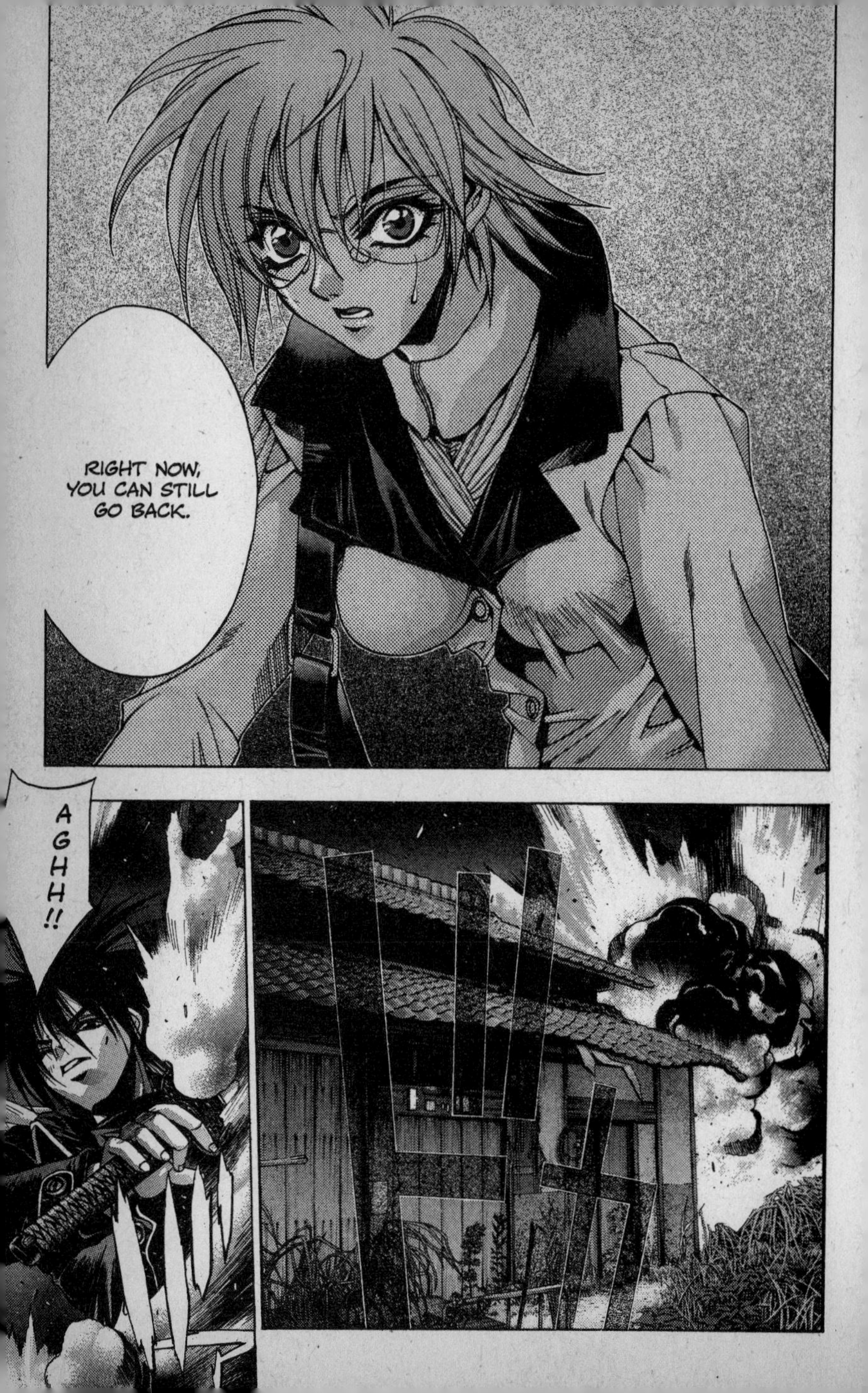
RIGHT NOW, YOU CAN STILL GO BACK.
AGHH!!

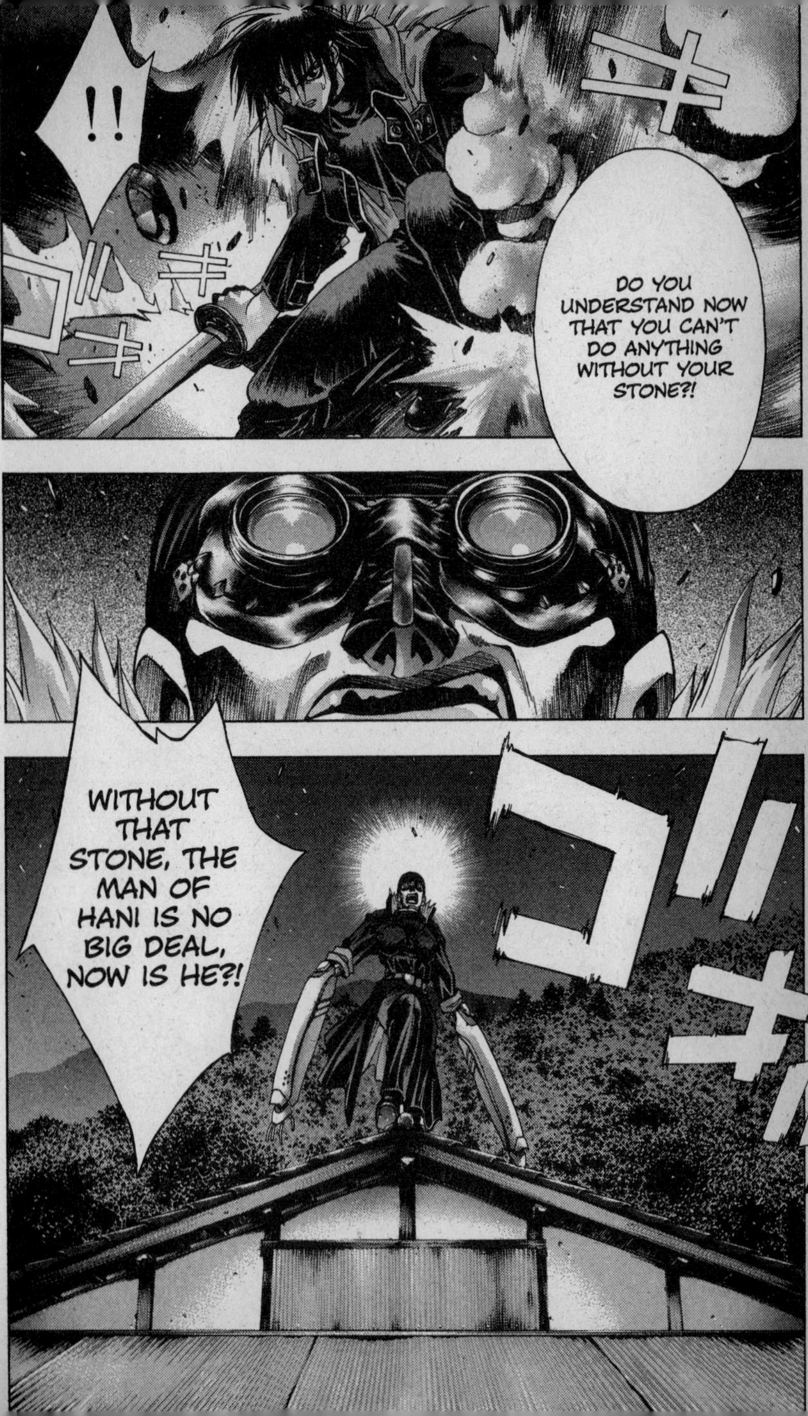
DO YOU UNDERSTAND NOW THAT YOU CAN'T DO ANYTHING WITHOUT YOUR STONE?!
!!
WITHOUT THAT STONE, THE MAN OF HANI IS NO BIG DEAL, NOW IS HE?!

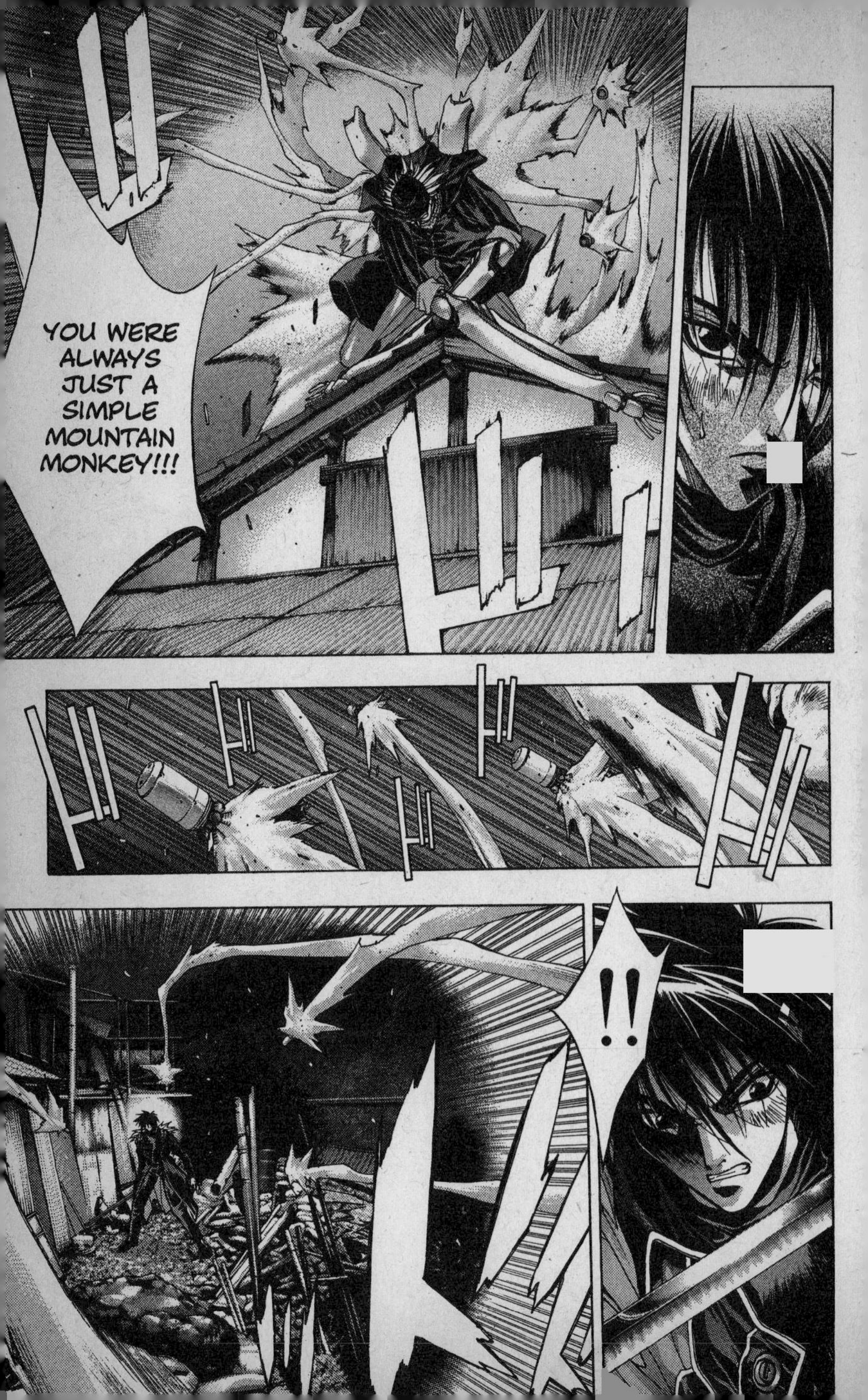
YOU WERE ALWAYS JUST A SIMPLE MOUNTAIN MONKEY!!!
!!

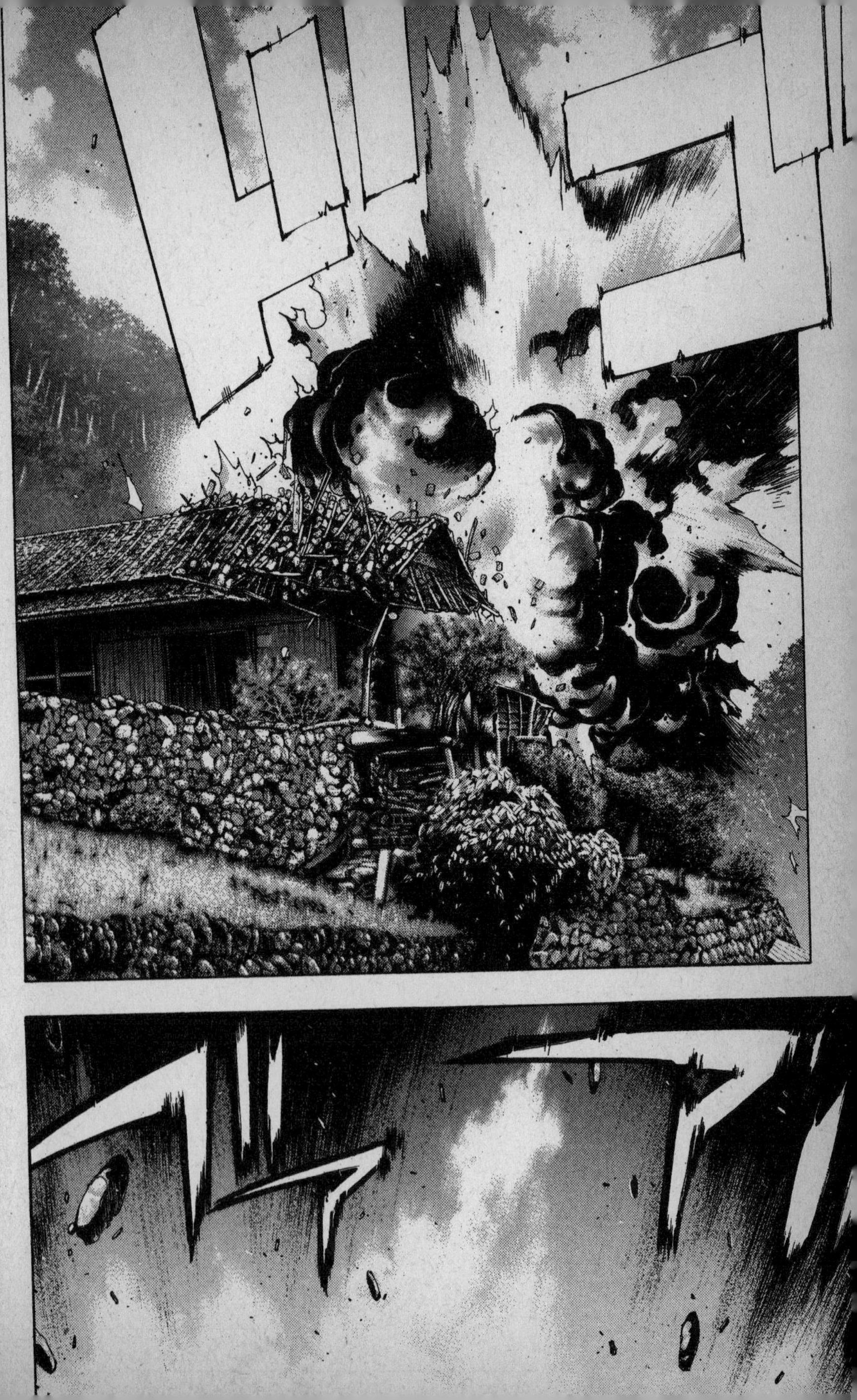

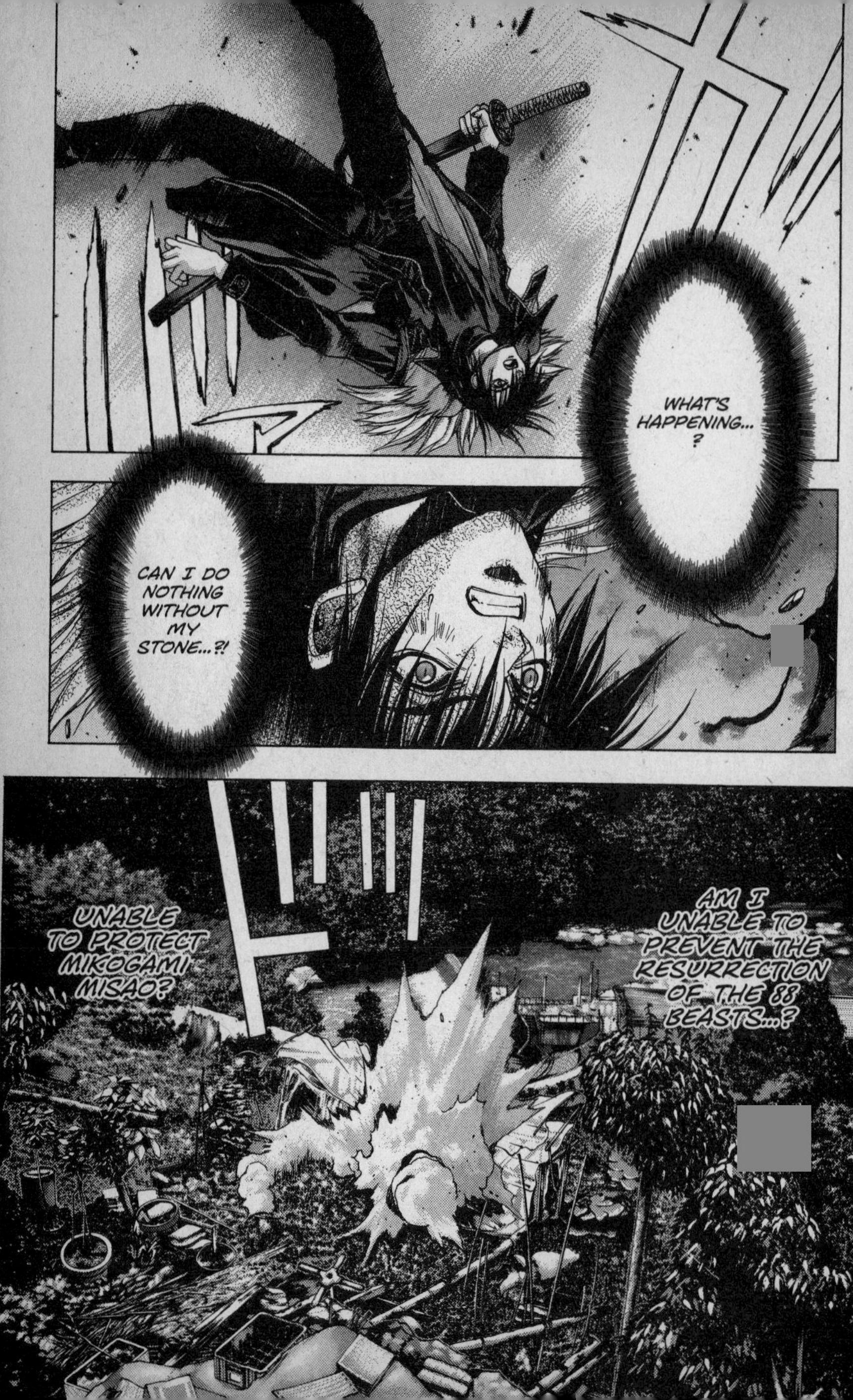
WHAT'S HAPPENING...?
CAN I DO NOTHING WITHOUT MY STONE...?!
AM I UNABLE TO PREVENT THE RESURRECTION OF THE 88 BEASTS...?
UNABLE TO PROTECT MIKOGAMI MISAO?

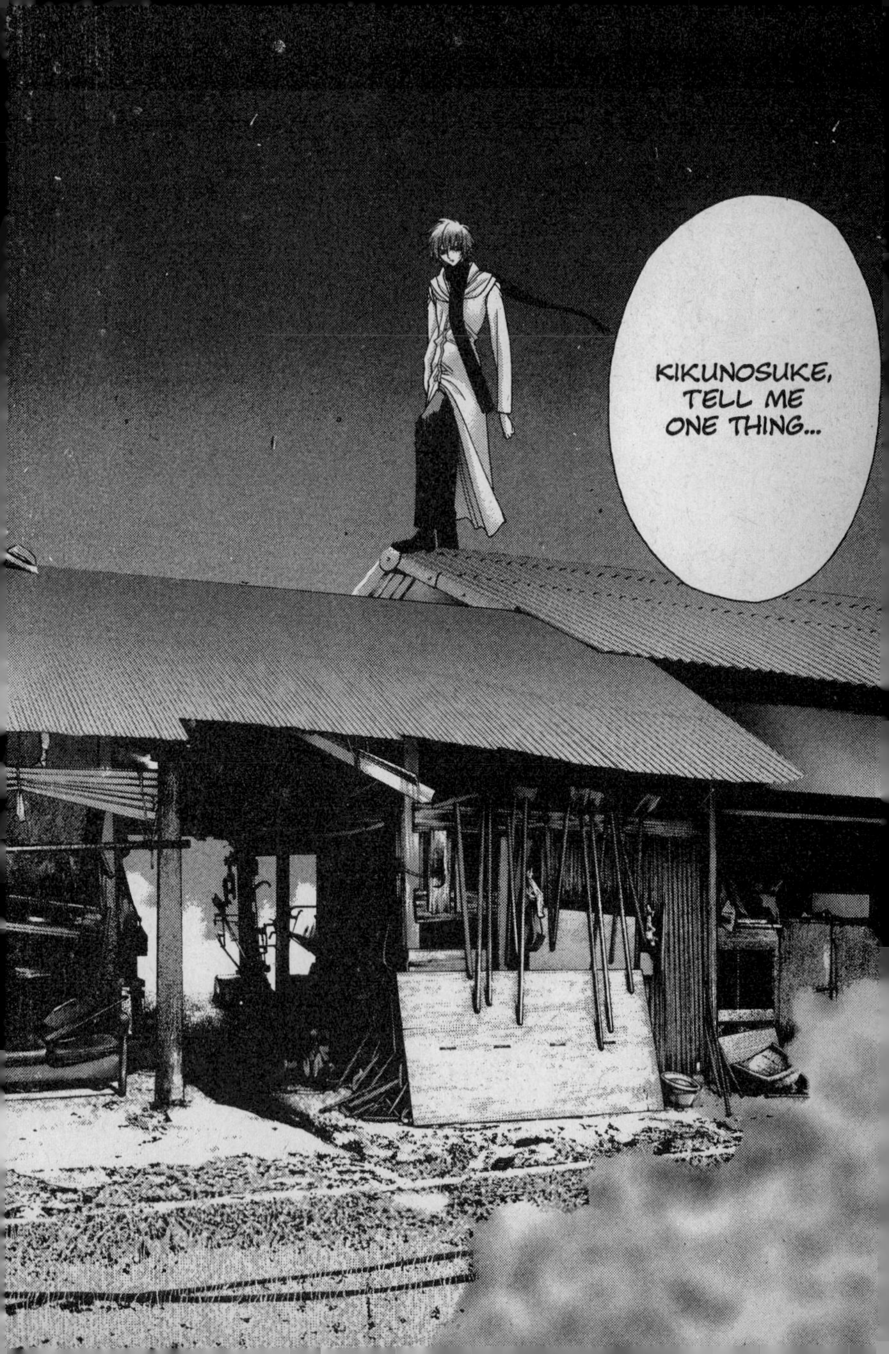
KIKUNOSUKE, TELL ME ONE THING...

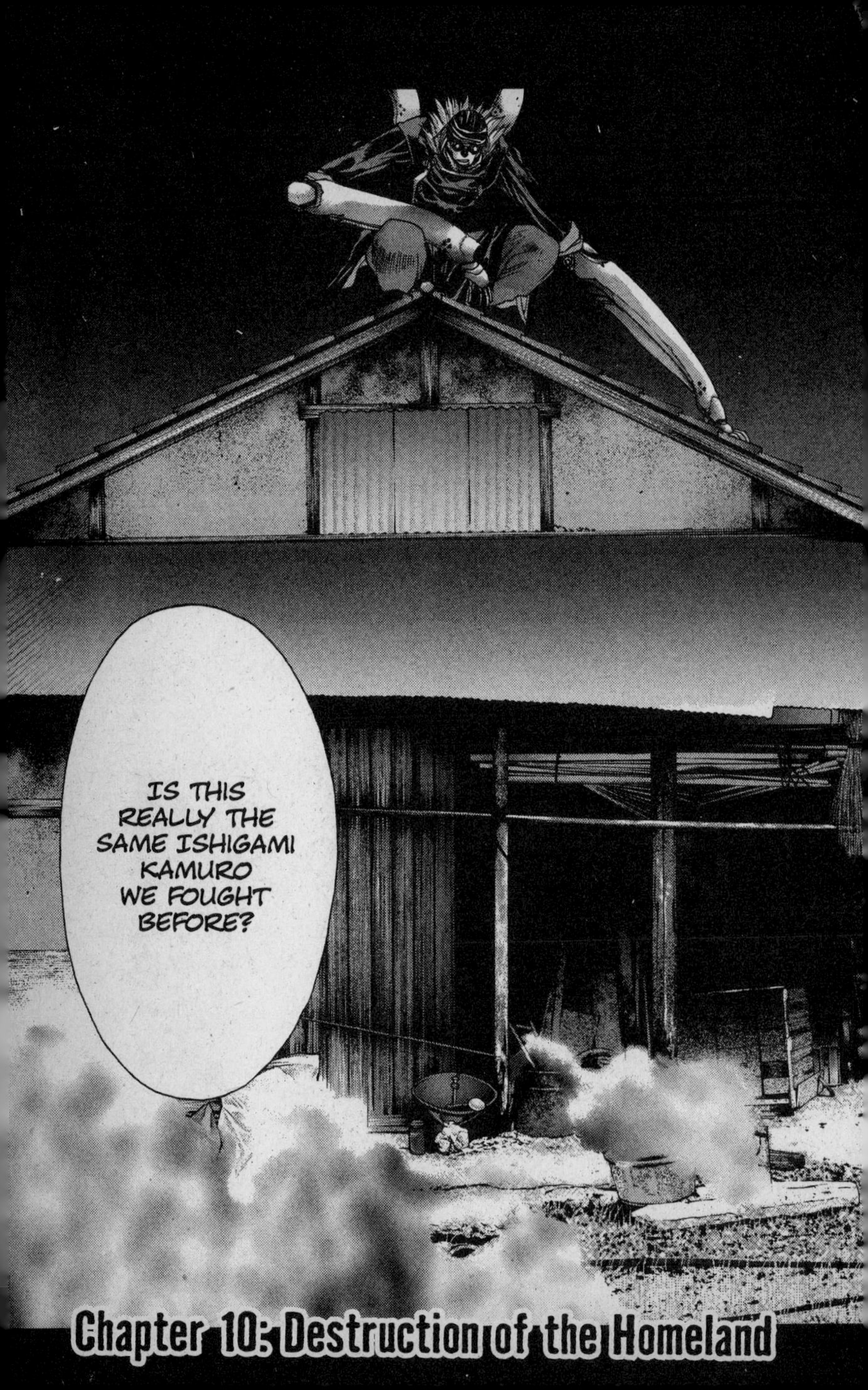
IS THIS REALLY THE SAME ISHIGAMI KAMURO WE FOUGHT BEFORE?

Chapter 10: Destruction of the Homeland

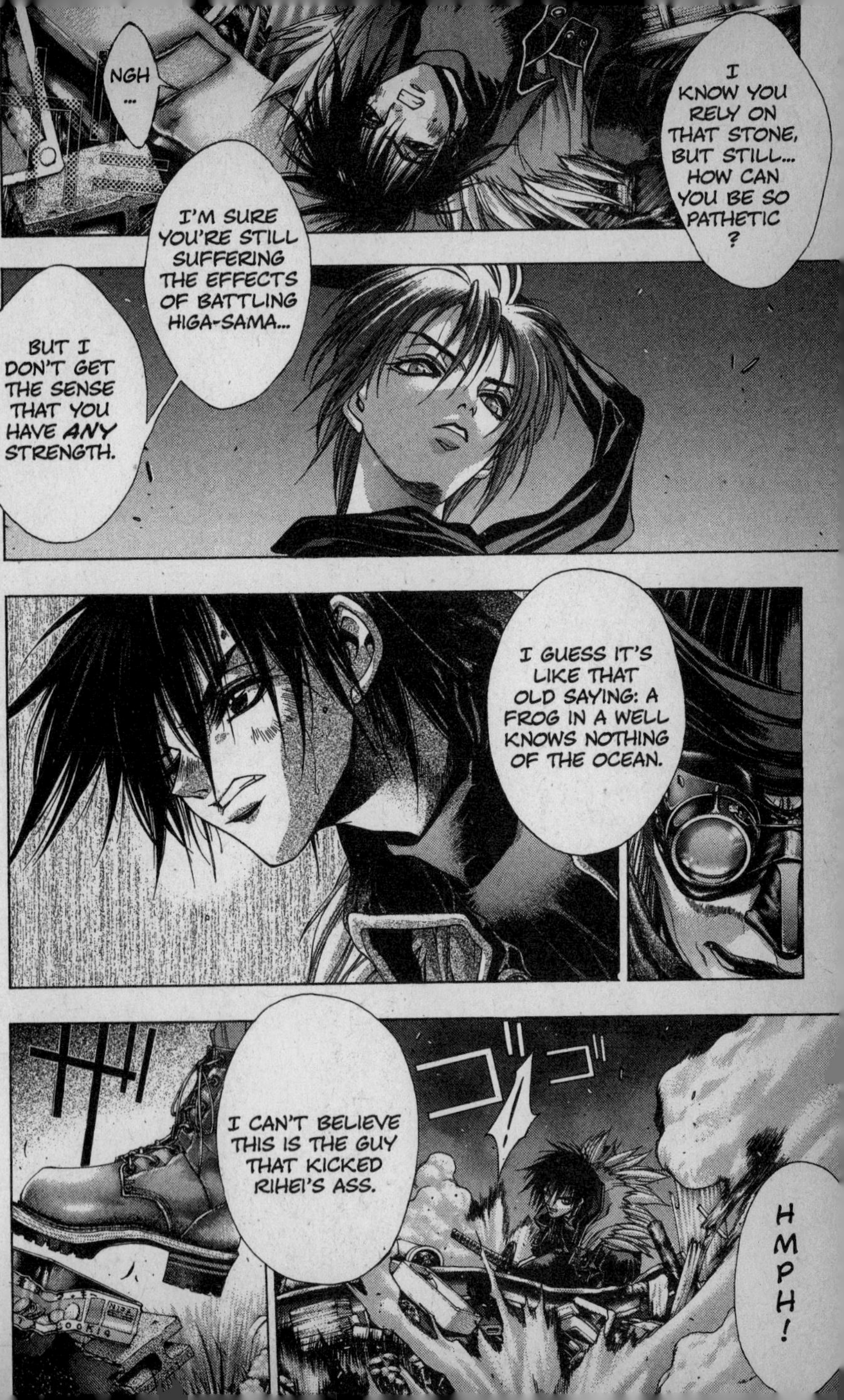
I KNOW YOU RELY ON THAT STONE, BUT STILL... HOW CAN YOU BE SO PATHETIC?
NGH...
I'M SURE YOU'RE STILL SUFFERING THE EFFECTS OF BATTLING HIGA-SAMA...
BUT I DON'T GET THE SENSE THAT YOU HAVE ANY STRENGTH.
I GUESS IT'S LIKE THAT OLD SAYING: A FROG IN A WELL KNOWS NOTHING OF THE OCEAN.
HMPH!
I CAN'T BELIEVE THIS IS THE GUY THAT KICKED RIHEI'S ASS.

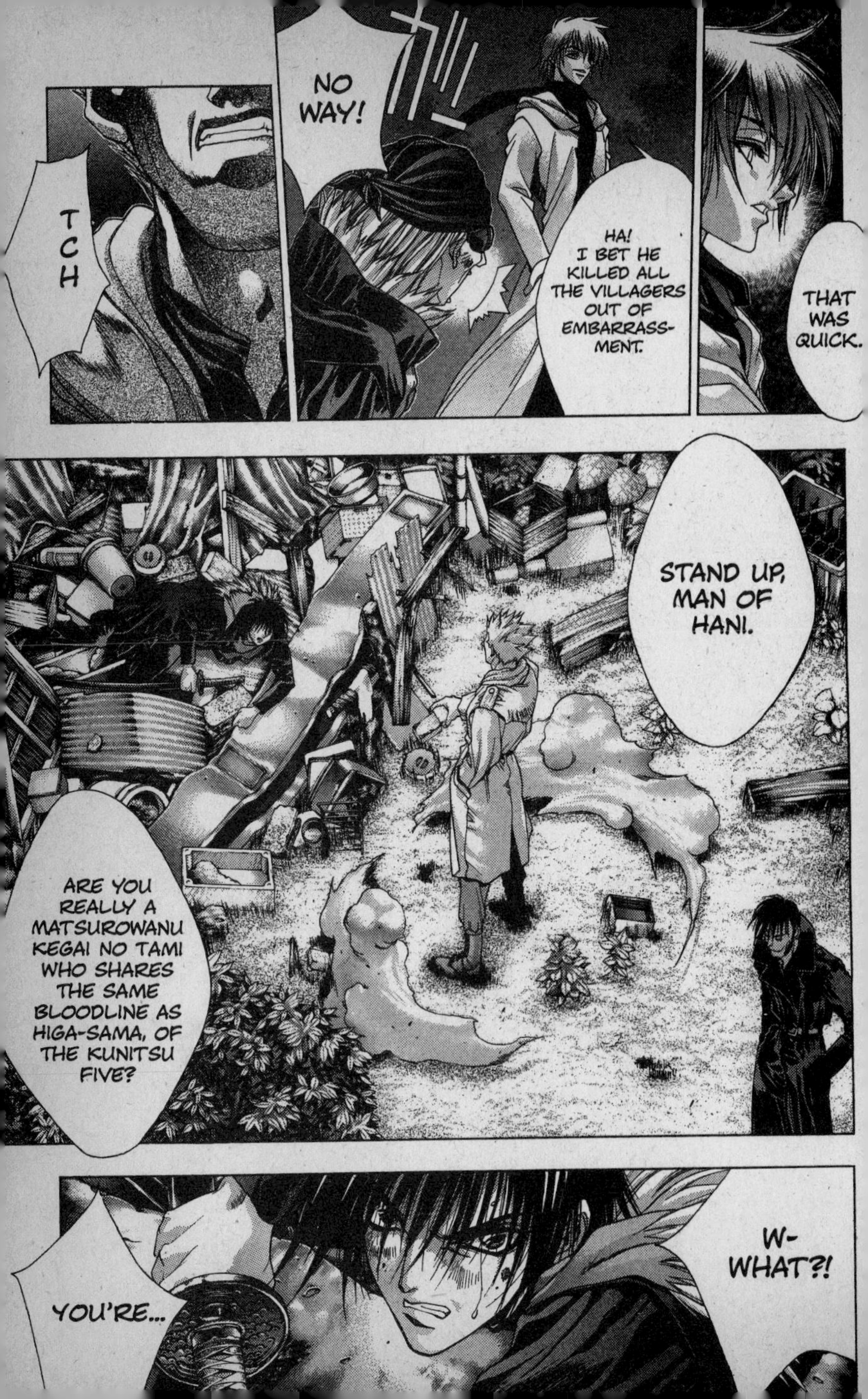
THAT WAS QUICK.
HA! I BET HE KILLED ALL THE VILLAGERS OUT OF EMBARRASS-MENT.
NO WAY!
TCH
STAND UP, MAN OF HANI.
ARE YOU REALLY A MATSUROWANU KEGAI NO TAMI WHO SHARES THE SAME BLOODLINE AS HIGA-SAMA, OF THE KUNITSU FIVE?
W-WHAT?!
YOU'RE...

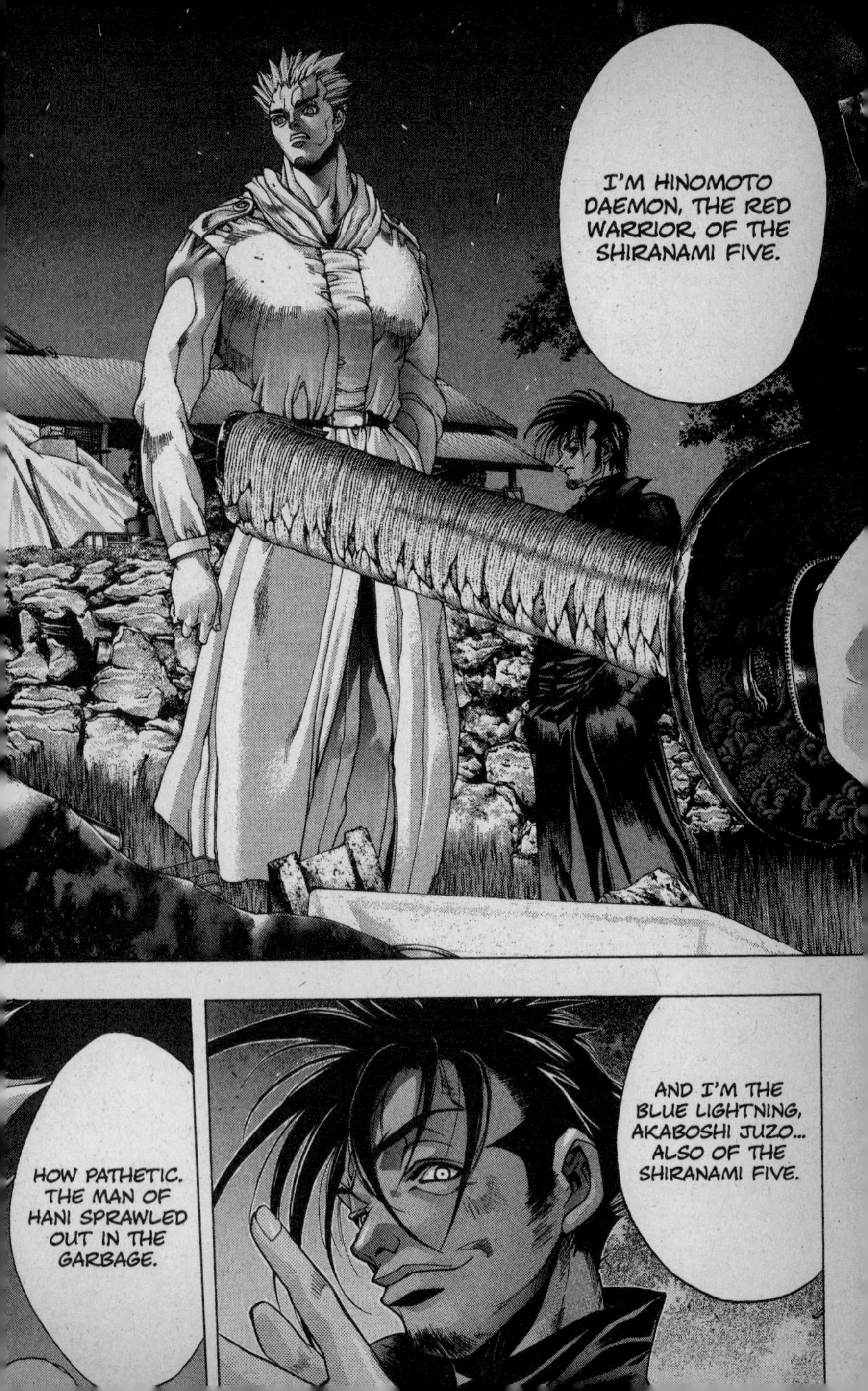
I'M HINOMOTO DAEMON, THE RED WARRIOR, OF THE SHIRANAMI FIVE.
AND I'M THE BLUE LIGHTNING, AKABOSHI JUZO... ALSO OF THE SHIRANAMI FIVE.
HOW PATHETIC. THE MAN OF HANI SPRAWLED OUT IN THE GARBAGE.

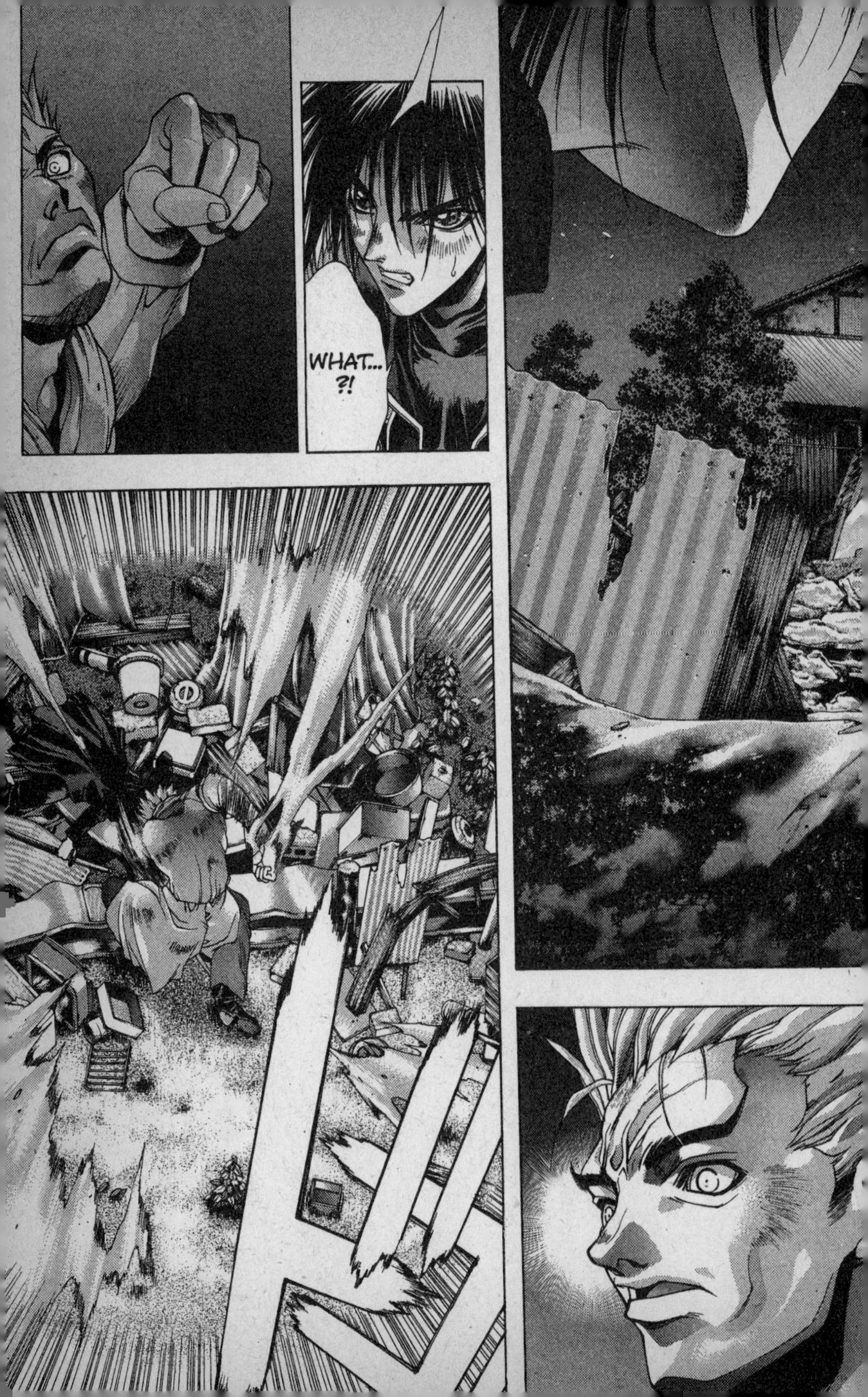
WHAT... ?!

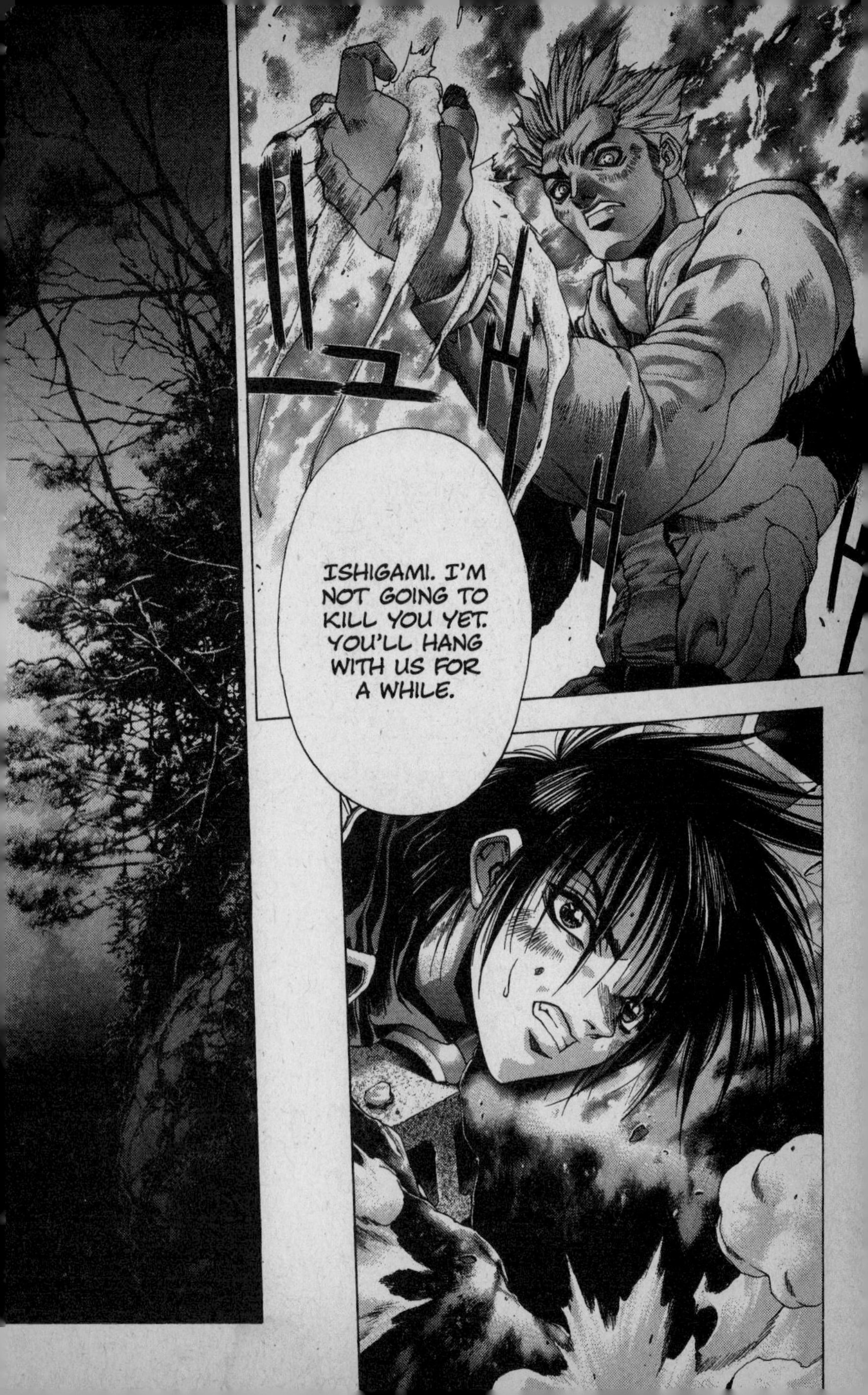
ISHIGAMI. I'M NOT GOING TO KILL YOU YET. YOU'LL HANG WITH US FOR A WHILE.

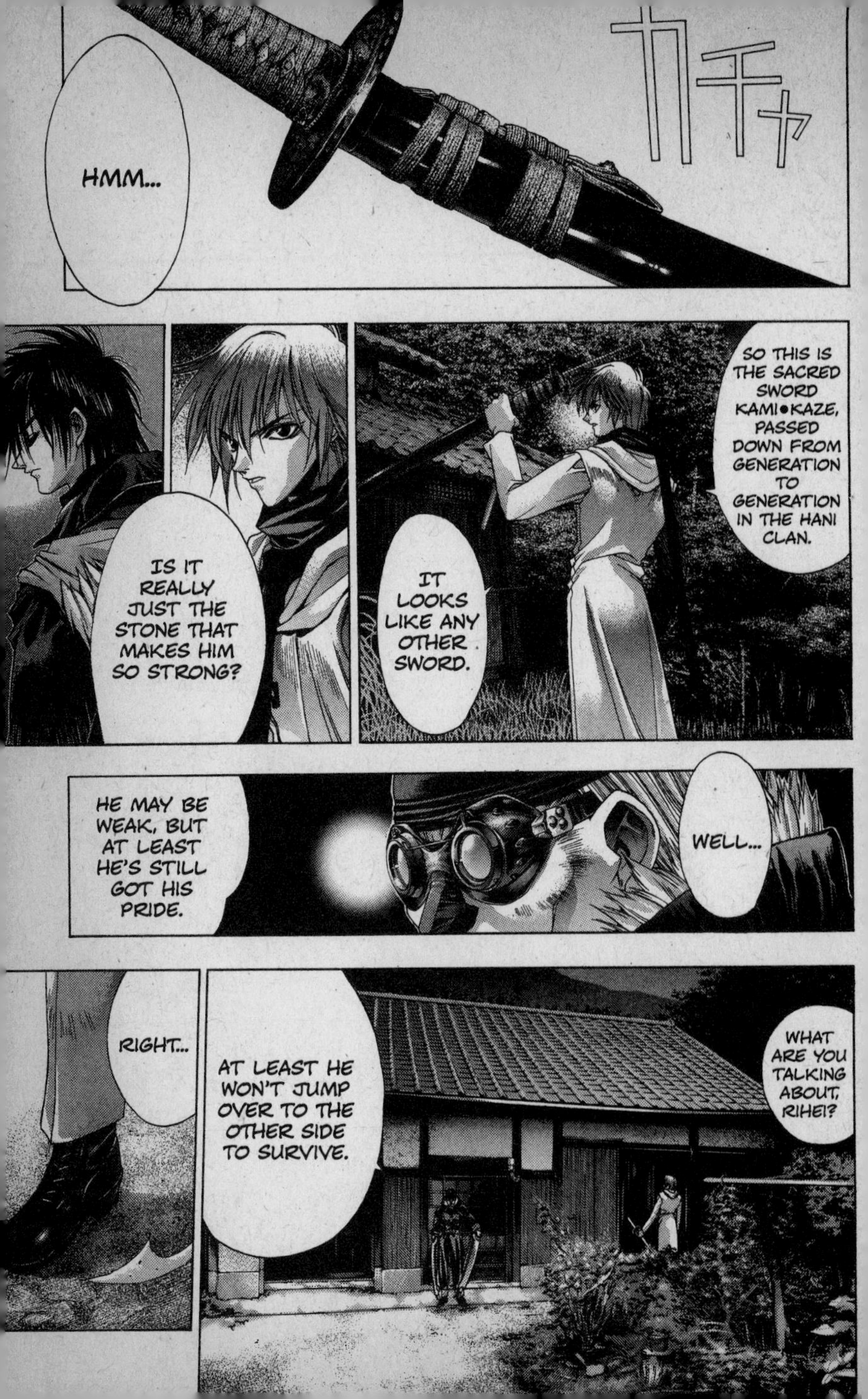
カチャ
HMM...
SO THIS IS THE SACRED SWORD KAMI•KAZE, PASSED DOWN FROM GENERATION TO GENERATION IN THE HANI CLAN.
IT LOOKS LIKE ANY OTHER SWORD.
IS IT REALLY JUST THE STONE THAT MAKES HIM SO STRONG?
WELL...
HE MAY BE WEAK, BUT AT LEAST HE'S STILL GOT HIS PRIDE.
WHAT ARE YOU TALKING ABOUT, RIHEI?
AT LEAST HE WON'T JUMP OVER TO THE OTHER SIDE TO SURVIVE.
RIGHT...

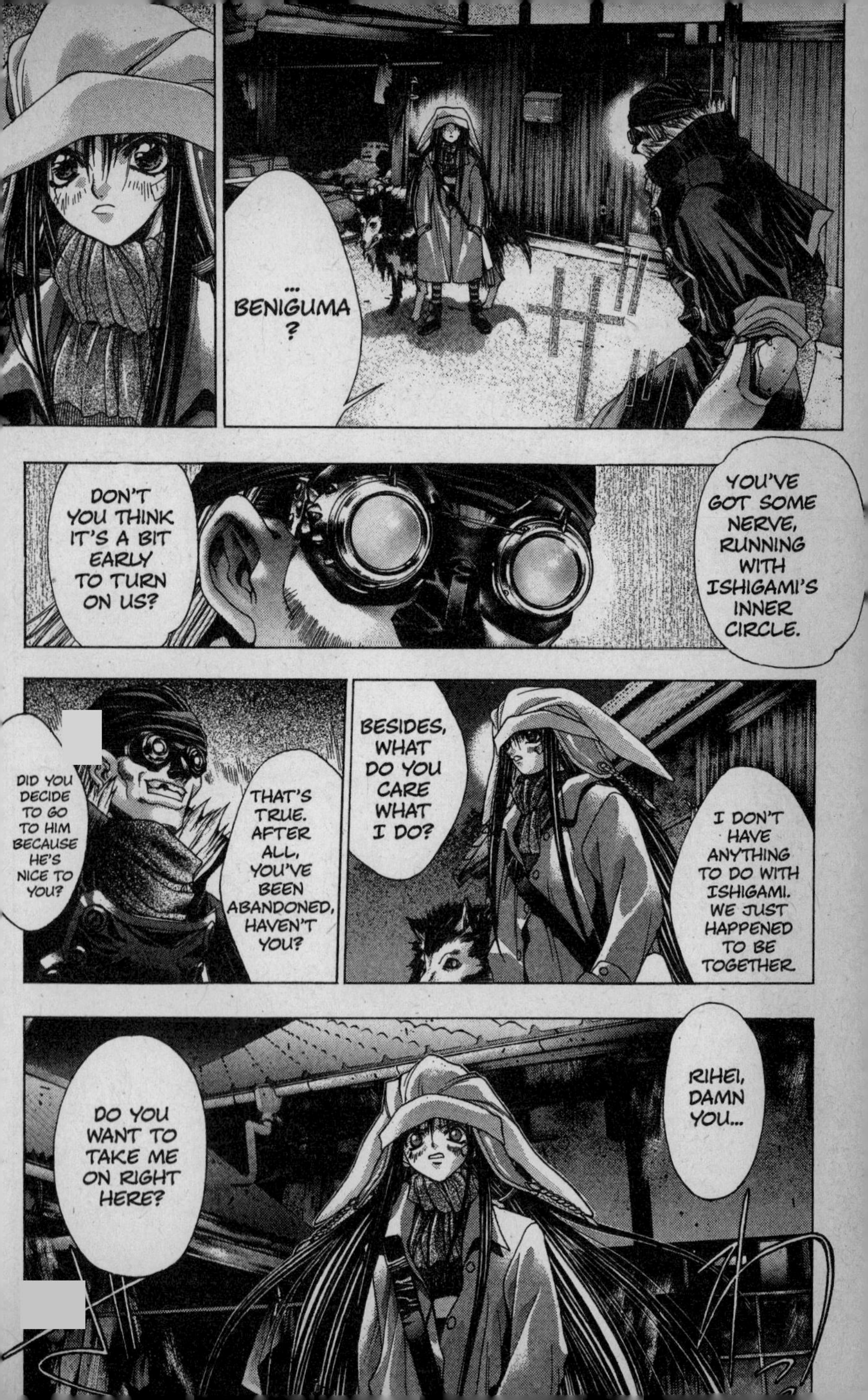
... BENIGUMA ?
YOU'VE GOT SOME NERVE, RUNNING WITH ISHIGAMI'S INNER CIRCLE.
DON'T YOU THINK IT'S A BIT EARLY TO TURN ON US?
I DON'T HAVE ANYTHING TO DO WITH ISHIGAMI. WE JUST HAPPENED TO BE TOGETHER.
BESIDES, WHAT DO YOU CARE WHAT I DO?
THAT'S TRUE. AFTER ALL, YOU'VE BEEN ABANDONED, HAVEN'T YOU?
DID YOU DECIDE TO GO TO HIM BECAUSE HE'S NICE TO YOU?
RIHEI, DAMN YOU...
DO YOU WANT TO TAKE ME ON RIGHT HERE?

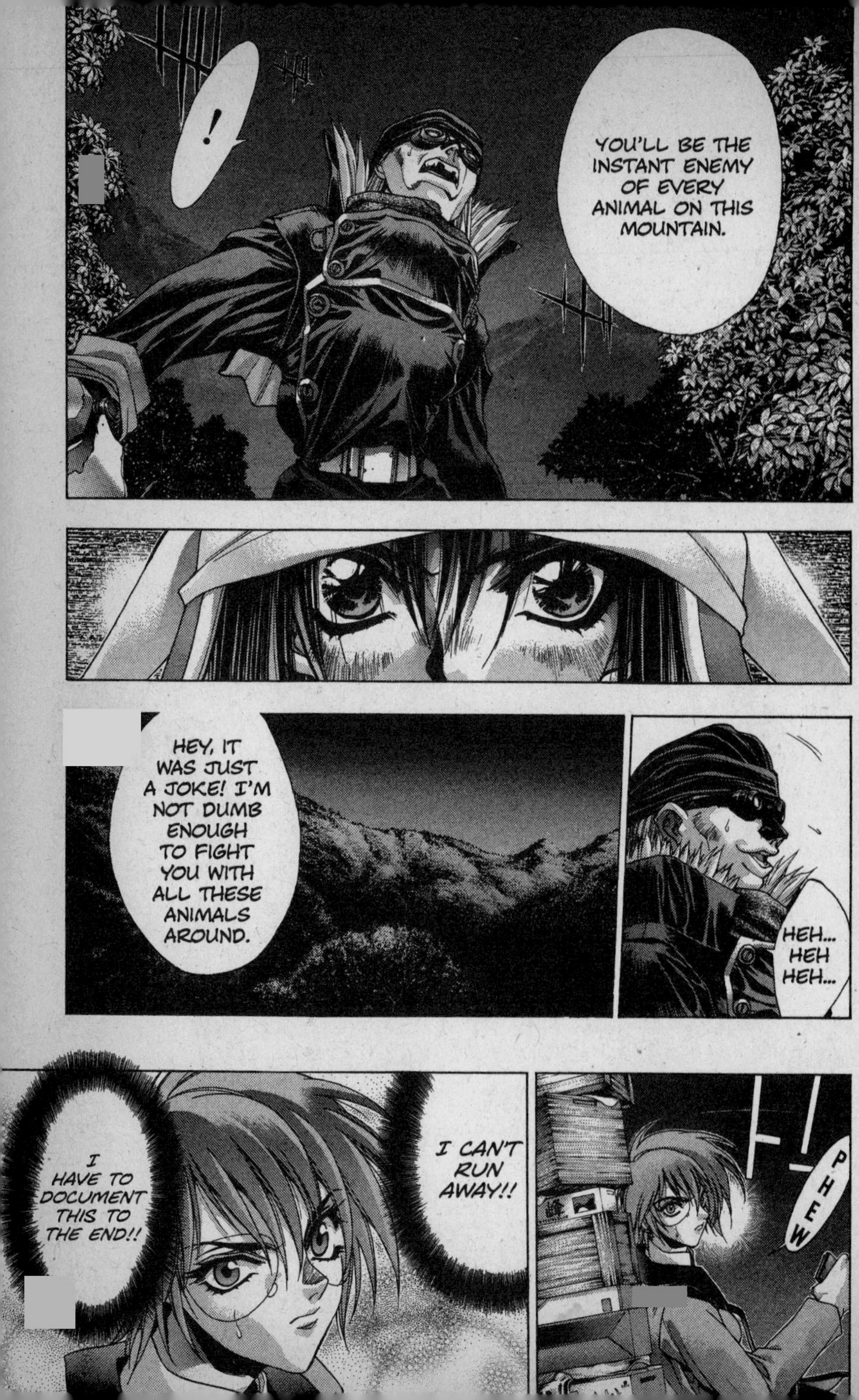
YOU'LL BE THE INSTANT ENEMY OF EVERY ANIMAL ON THIS MOUNTAIN.
!
HEH... HEH HEH...
HEY, IT WAS JUST A JOKE! I'M NOT DUMB ENOUGH TO FIGHT YOU WITH ALL THESE ANIMALS AROUND.
PHEW
I CAN'T RUN AWAY!!
I HAVE TO DOCUMENT THIS TO THE END!!

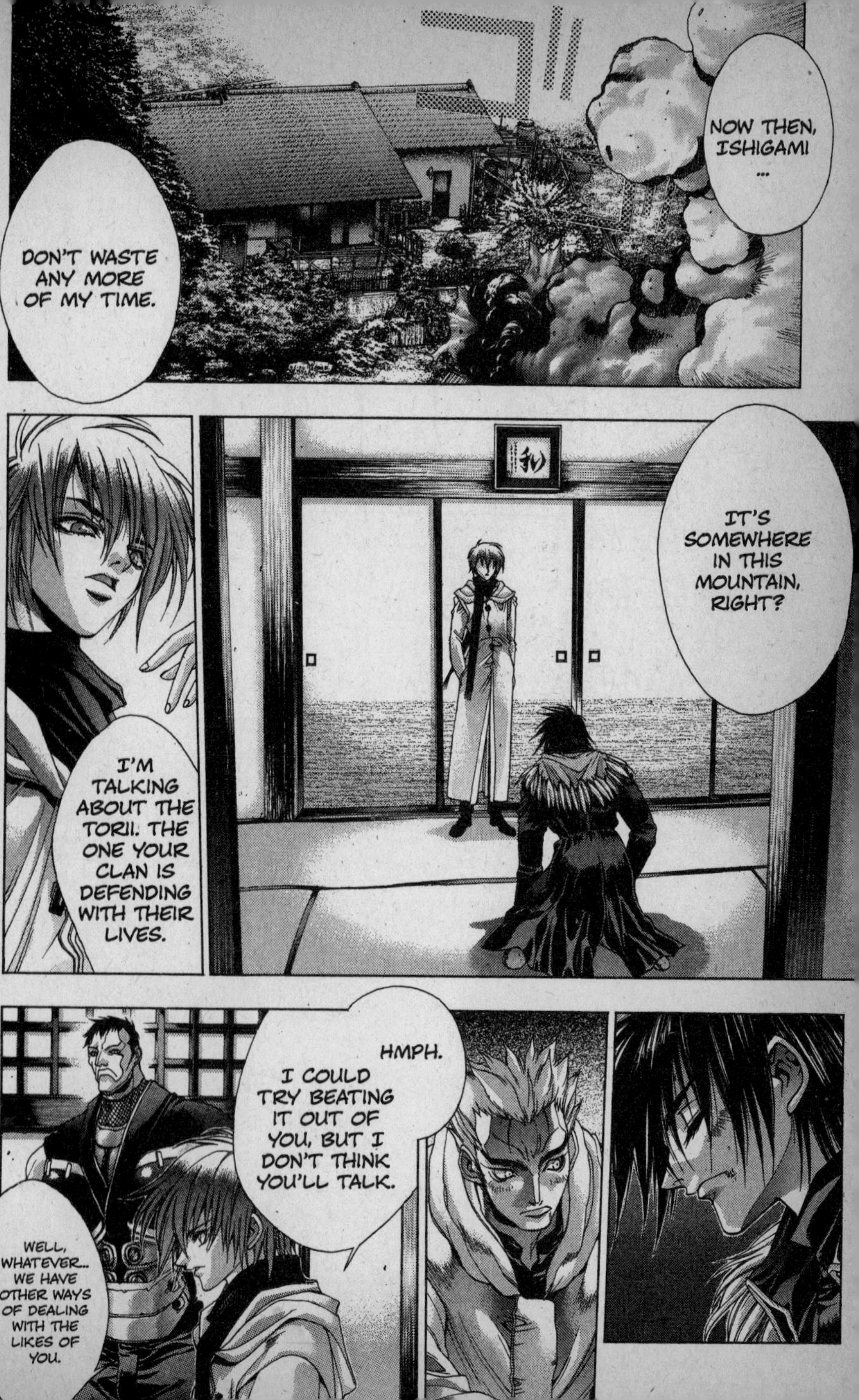
NOW THEN, ISHIGAMI ...
DON'T WASTE ANY MORE OF MY TIME.
IT'S SOMEWHERE IN THIS MOUNTAIN, RIGHT?
I'M TALKING ABOUT THE TORII. THE ONE YOUR CLAN IS DEFENDING WITH THEIR LIVES.
HMPH.
I COULD TRY BEATING IT OUT OF YOU, BUT I DON'T THINK YOU'LL TALK.
WELL, WHATEVER... WE HAVE OTHER WAYS OF DEALING WITH THE LIKES OF YOU.

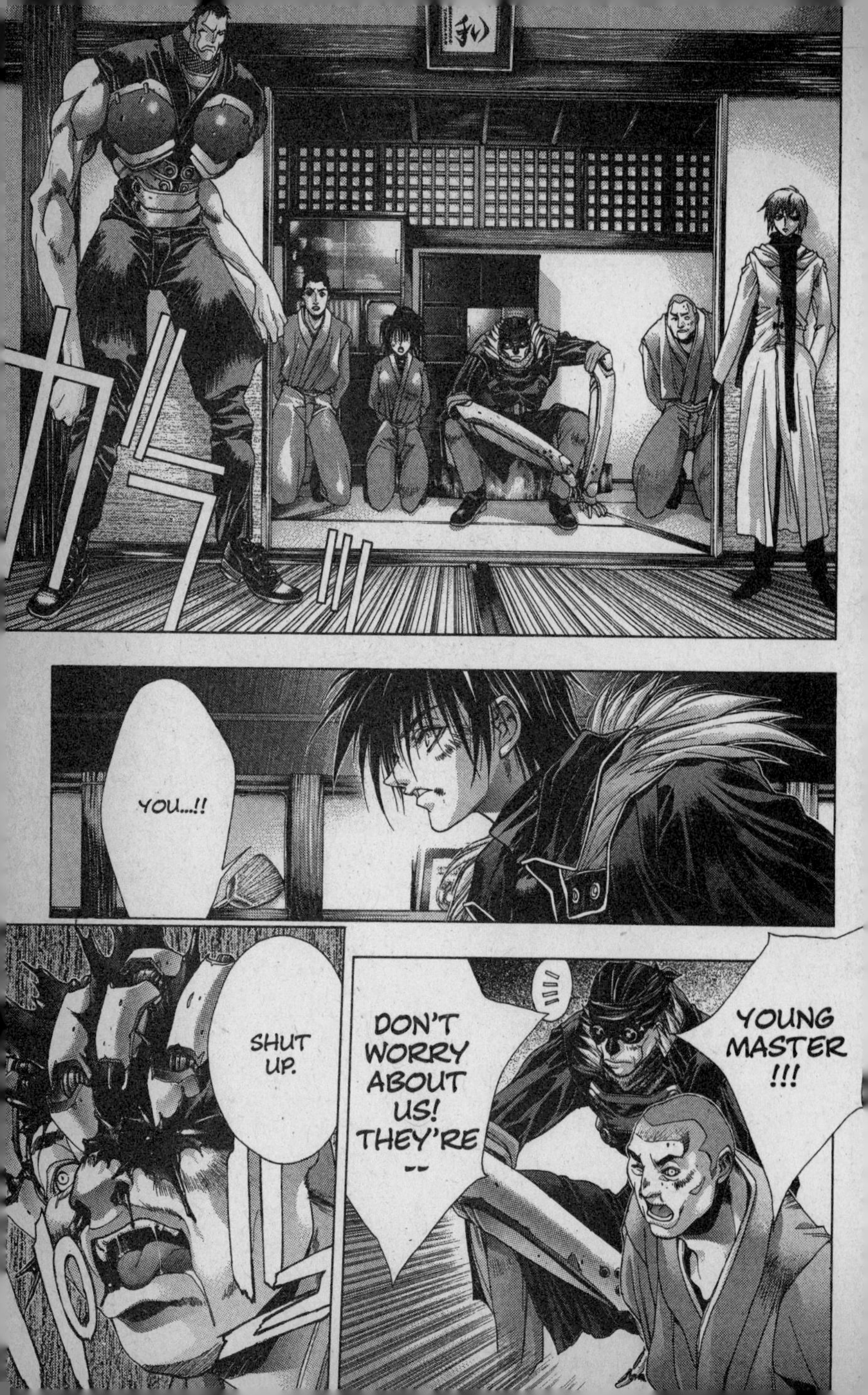
YOU...!!
YOUNG MASTER !!!
!!
DON'T WORRY ABOUT US! THEY'RE --
SHUT UP.

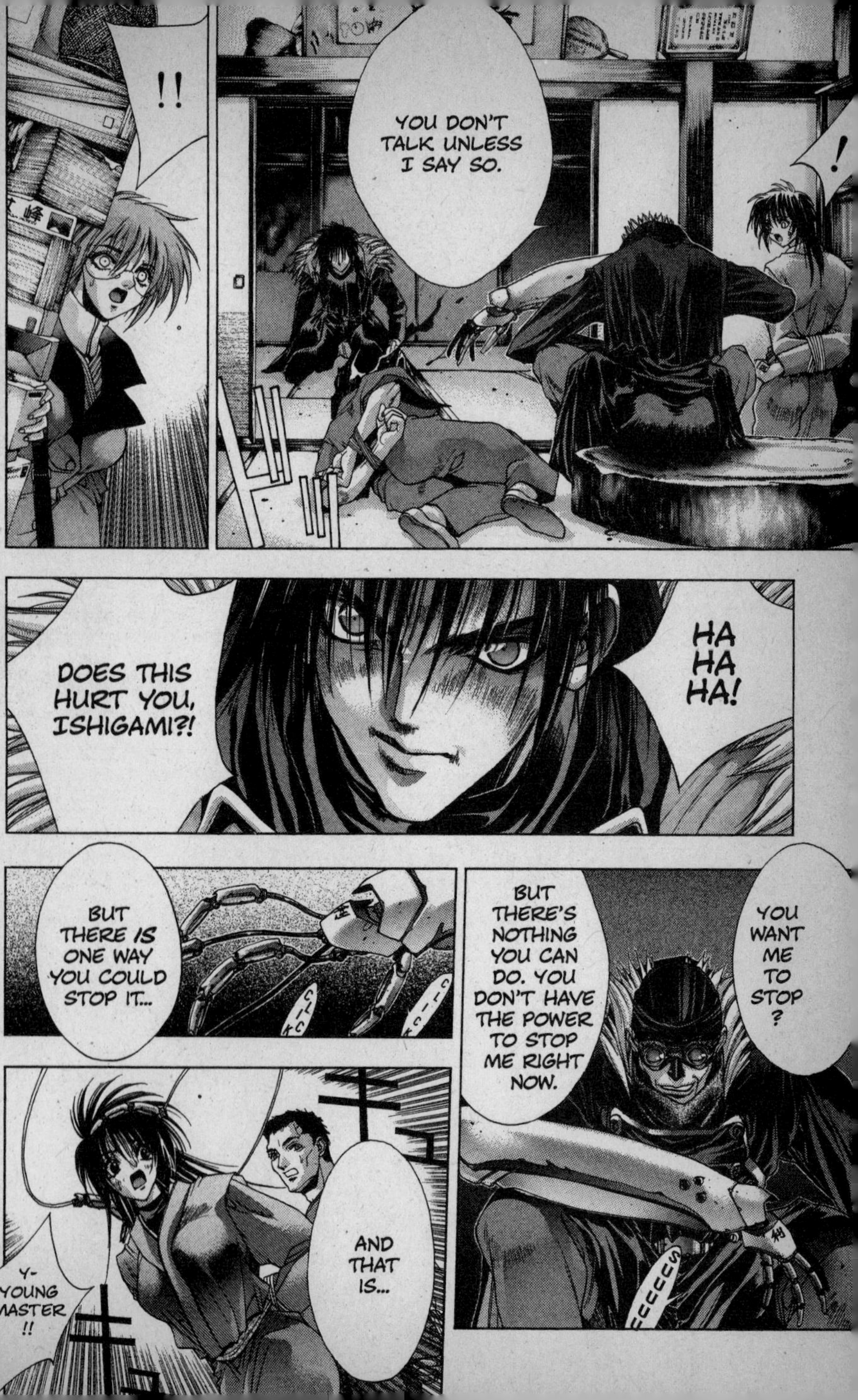
!
YOU DON'T TALK UNLESS I SAY SO.
!!
HA HA HA!
DOES THIS HURT YOU, ISHIGAMI?!
YOU WANT ME TO STOP?
BUT THERE'S NOTHING YOU CAN DO. YOU DON'T HAVE THE POWER TO STOP ME RIGHT NOW.
BUT THERE IS ONE WAY YOU COULD STOP IT...
CLICK
CLICK
AND THAT IS...
Y-YOUNG MASTER !!

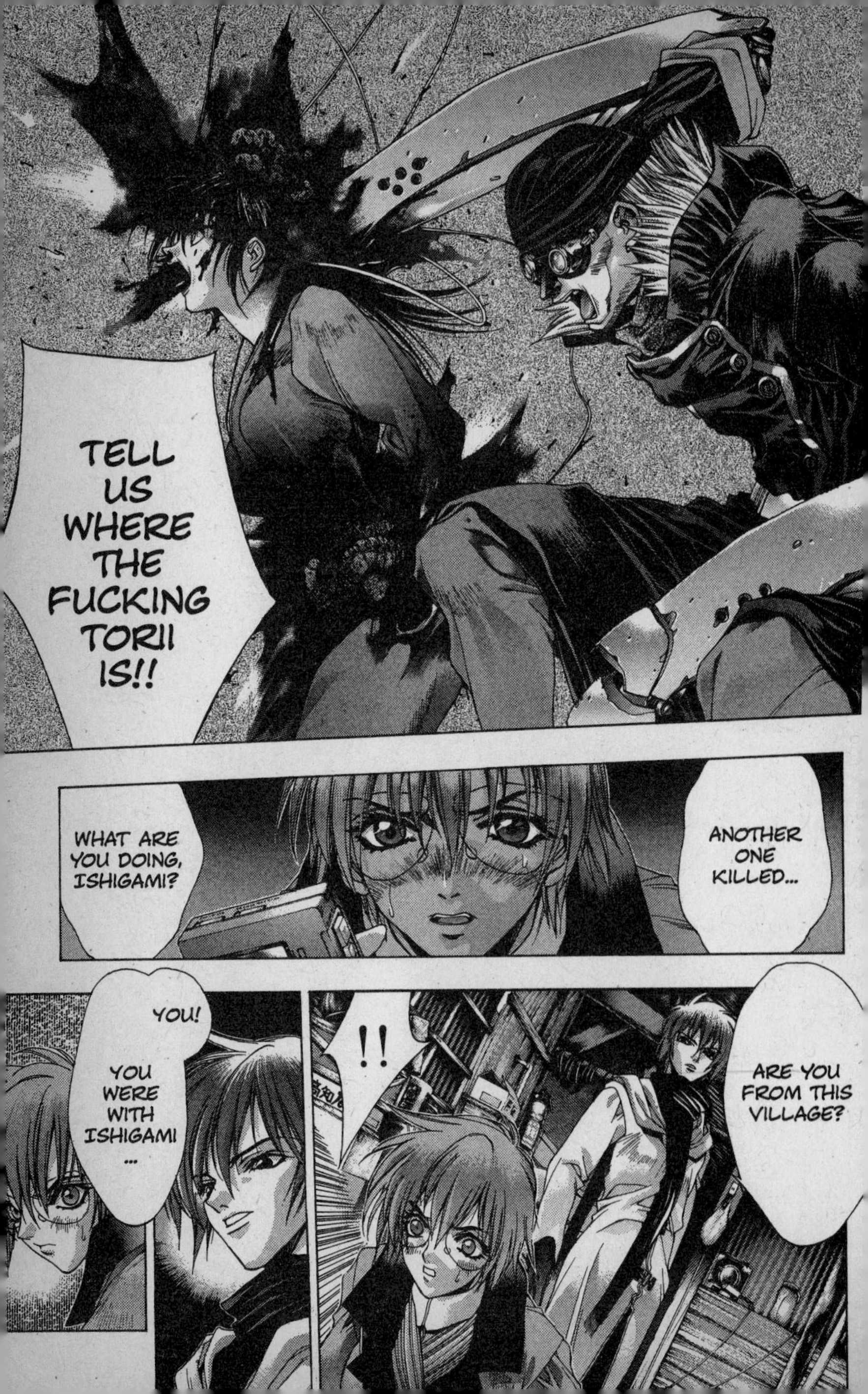
TELL US WHERE THE FUCKING TORII IS!!
ANOTHER ONE KILLED...
WHAT ARE YOU DOING, ISHIGAMI?
ARE YOU FROM THIS VILLAGE?
!!
YOU!
YOU WERE WITH ISHIGAMI ...

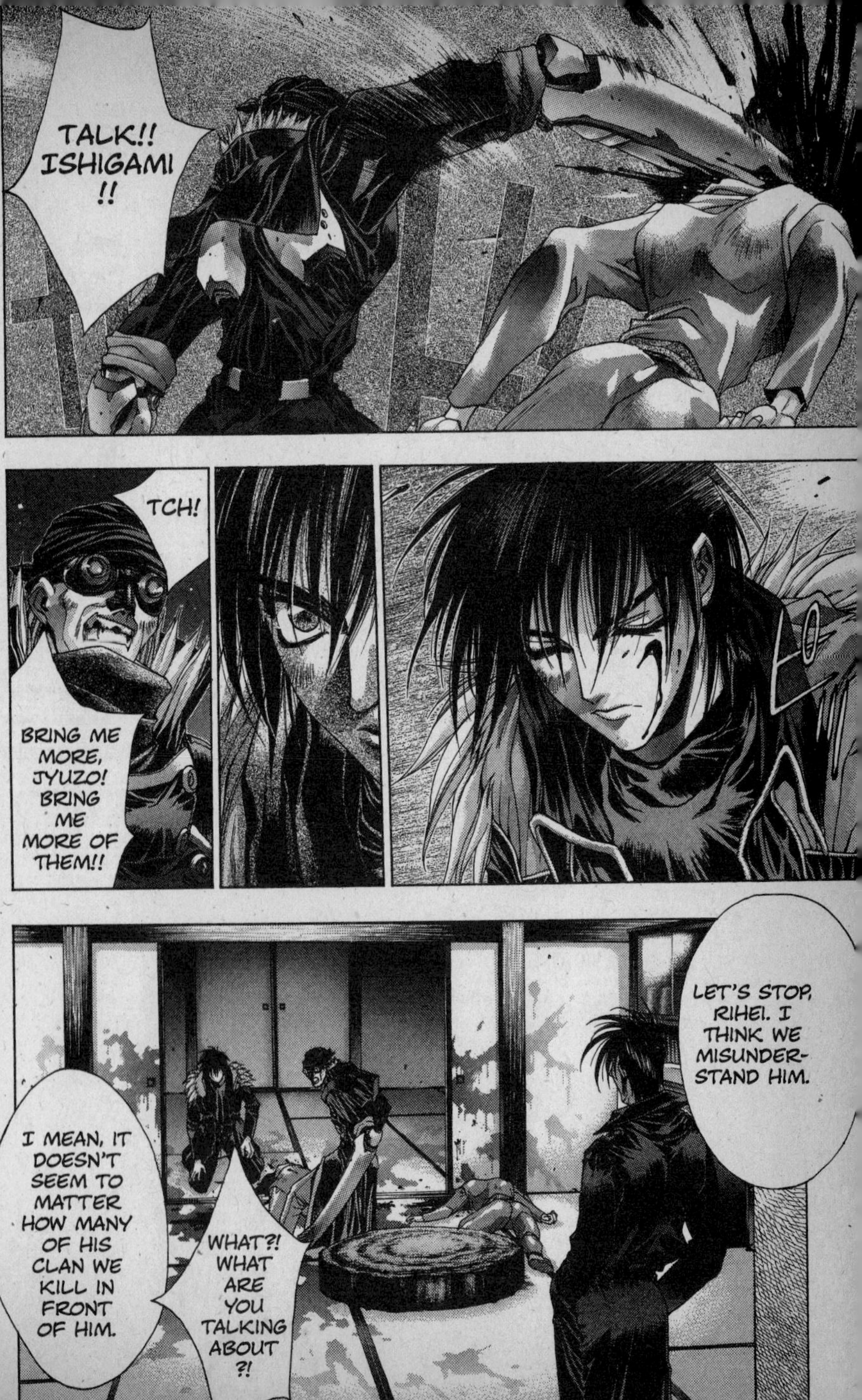
TALK!! ISHIGAMI !!
TCH!
BRING ME MORE, JYUZO! BRING ME MORE OF THEM!!
LET'S STOP, RIHEI. I THINK WE MISUNDER-STAND HIM.
WHAT?! WHAT ARE YOU TALKING ABOUT ?!
I MEAN, IT DOESN'T SEEM TO MATTER HOW MANY OF HIS CLAN WE KILL IN FRONT OF HIM.

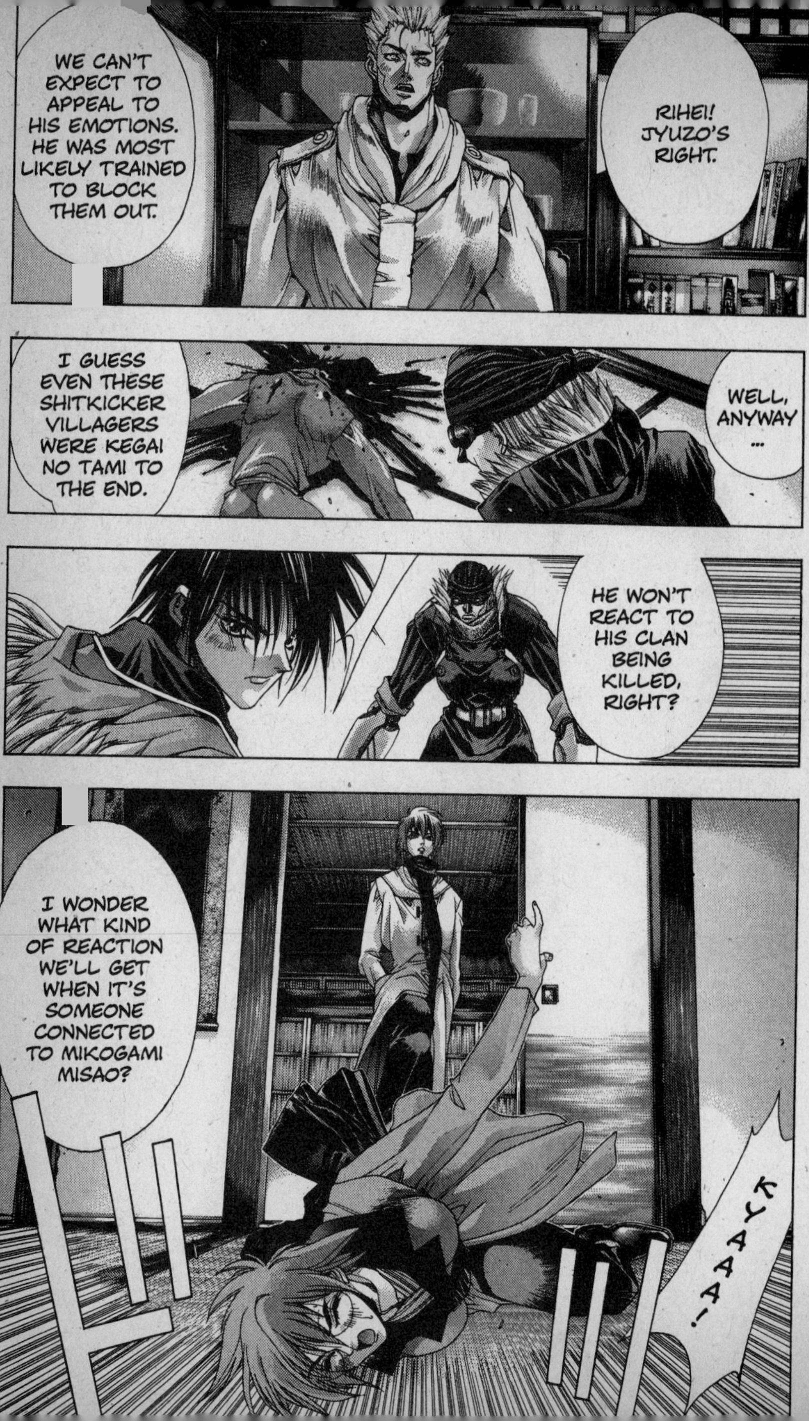
RIHEI! JYUZO'S RIGHT.
WE CAN'T EXPECT TO APPEAL TO HIS EMOTIONS. HE WAS MOST LIKELY TRAINED TO BLOCK THEM OUT.
WELL, ANYWAY ...
I GUESS EVEN THESE SHITKICKER VILLAGERS WERE KEGAI NO TAMI TO THE END.
HE WON'T REACT TO HIS CLAN BEING KILLED, RIGHT?
I WONDER WHAT KIND OF REACTION WE'LL GET WHEN IT'S SOMEONE CONNECTED TO MIKOGAMI MISAO?
KYAAAA!

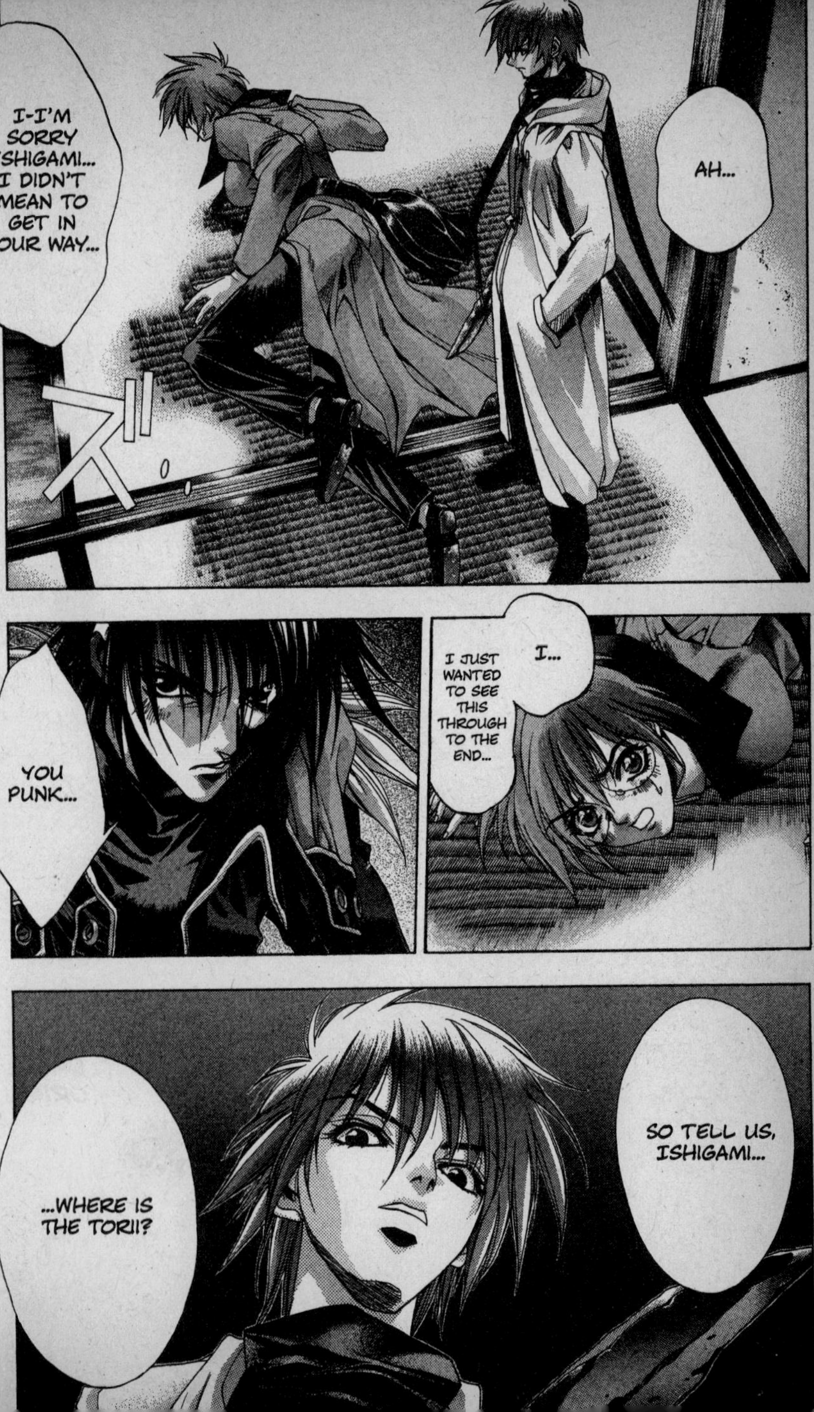
AH...
I-I'M SORRY ISHIGAMI... I DIDN'T MEAN TO GET IN YOUR WAY...
ズ
I...
I JUST WANTED TO SEE THIS THROUGH TO THE END...
YOU PUNK...
SO TELL US, ISHIGAMI...
...WHERE IS THE TORII?

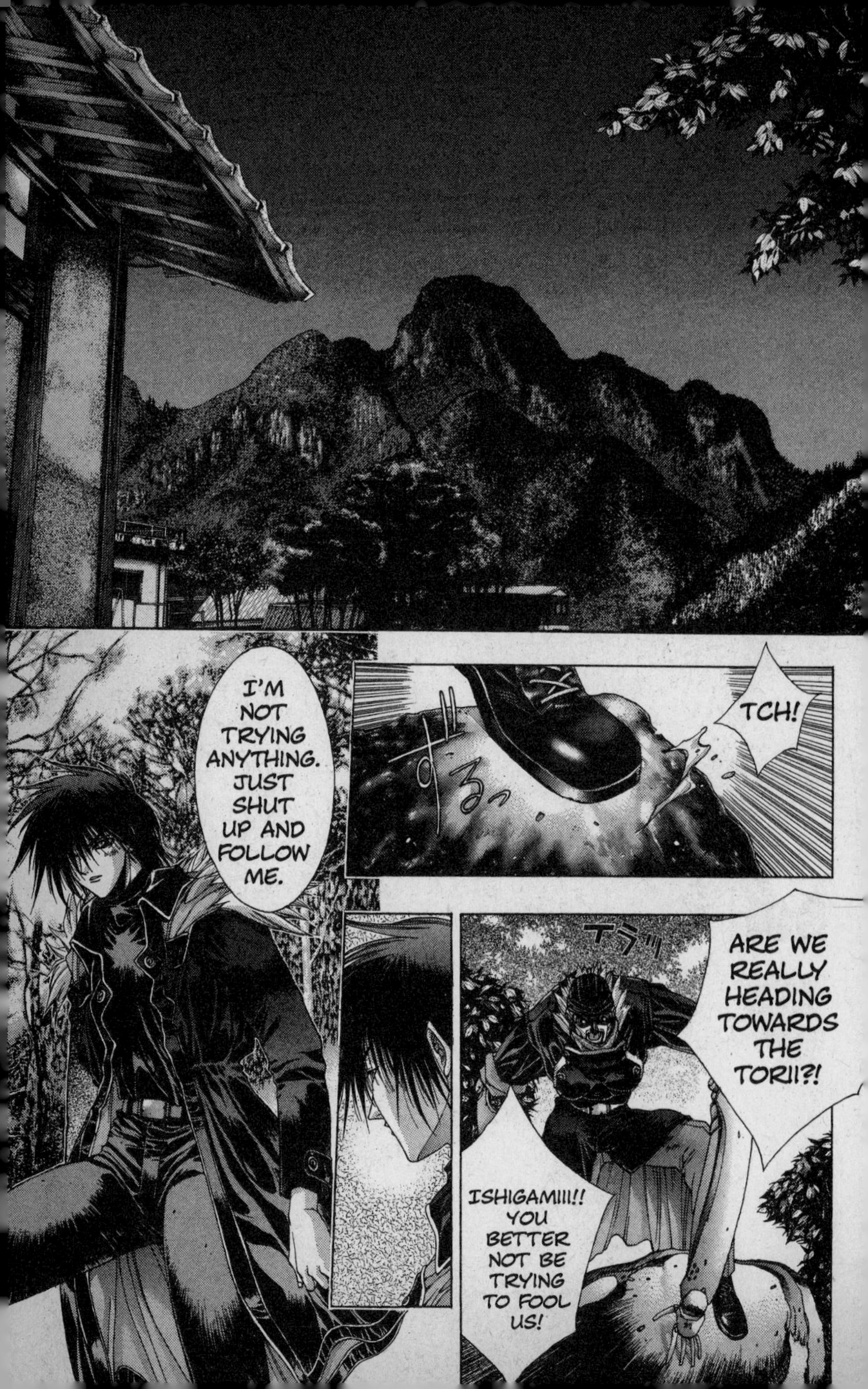
TCH!
ARE WE REALLY HEADING TOWARDS THE TORII?!
ISHIGAMIII!! YOU BETTER NOT BE TRYING TO FOOL US!
I'M NOT TRYING ANYTHING. JUST SHUT UP AND FOLLOW ME.

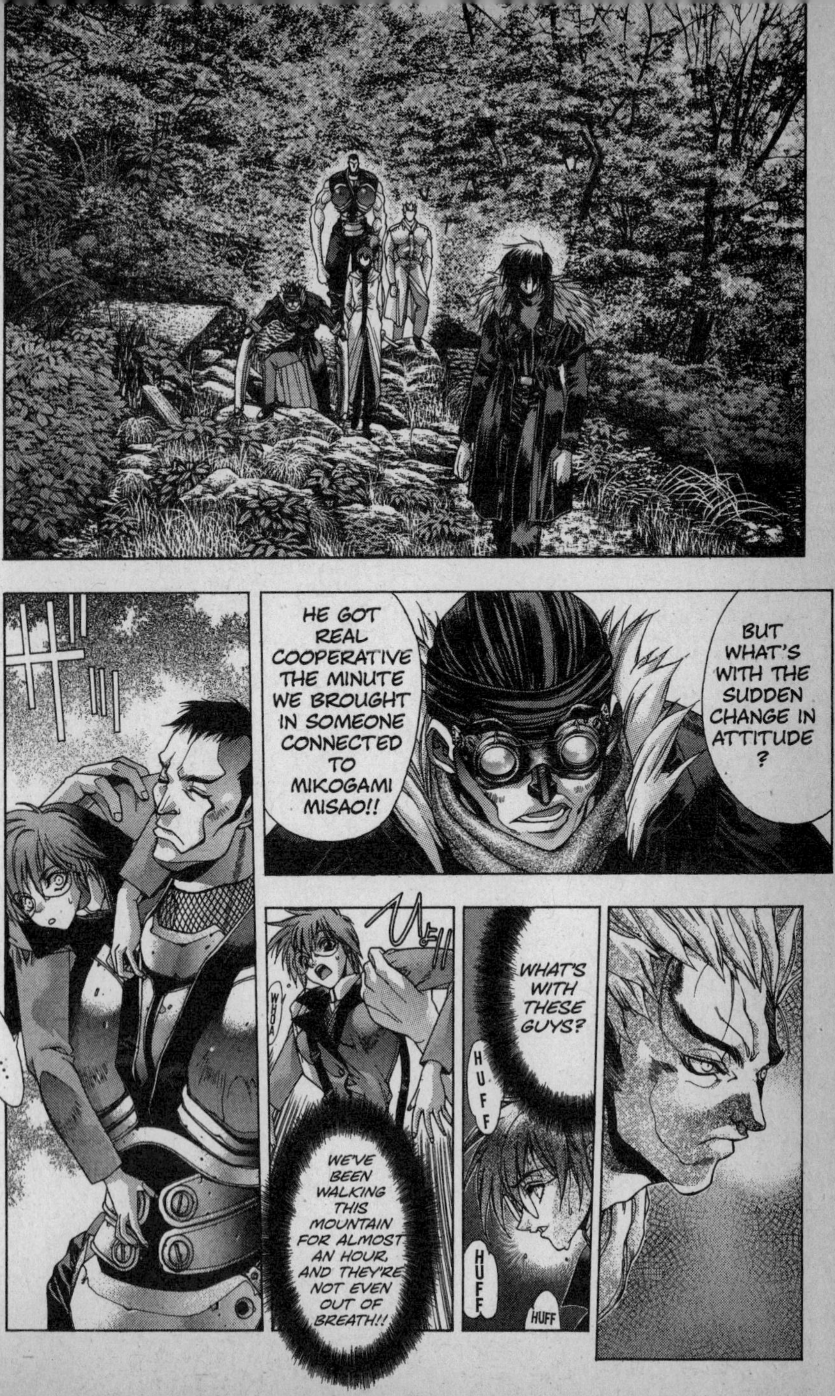
BUT WHAT'S WITH THE SUDDEN CHANGE IN ATTITUDE?
HE GOT REAL COOPERATIVE THE MINUTE WE BROUGHT IN SOMEONE CONNECTED TO MIKOGAMI MISAO!!
WHAT'S WITH THESE GUYS?
HUFF
HUFF
HUFF
WHOA
WE'VE BEEN WALKING THIS MOUNTAIN FOR ALMOST AN HOUR, AND THEY'RE NOT EVEN OUT OF BREATH!!
......

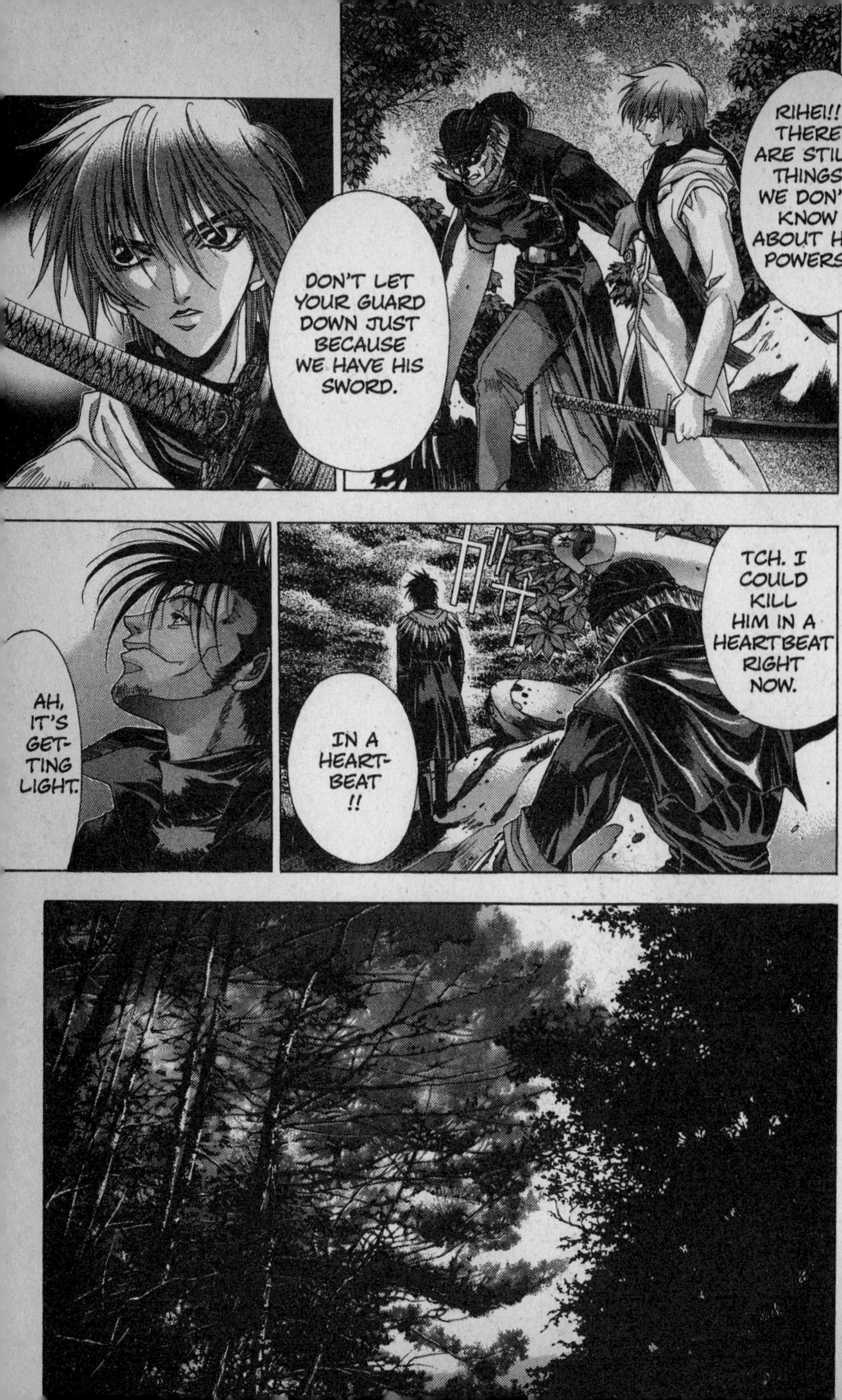
RIHEI!! THERE ARE STILL THINGS WE DON'T KNOW ABOUT HIS POWERS.
DON'T LET YOUR GUARD DOWN JUST BECAUSE WE HAVE HIS SWORD.
TCH. I COULD KILL HIM IN A HEARTBEAT RIGHT NOW.
IN A HEART-BEAT !!
AH, IT'S GET-TING LIGHT.

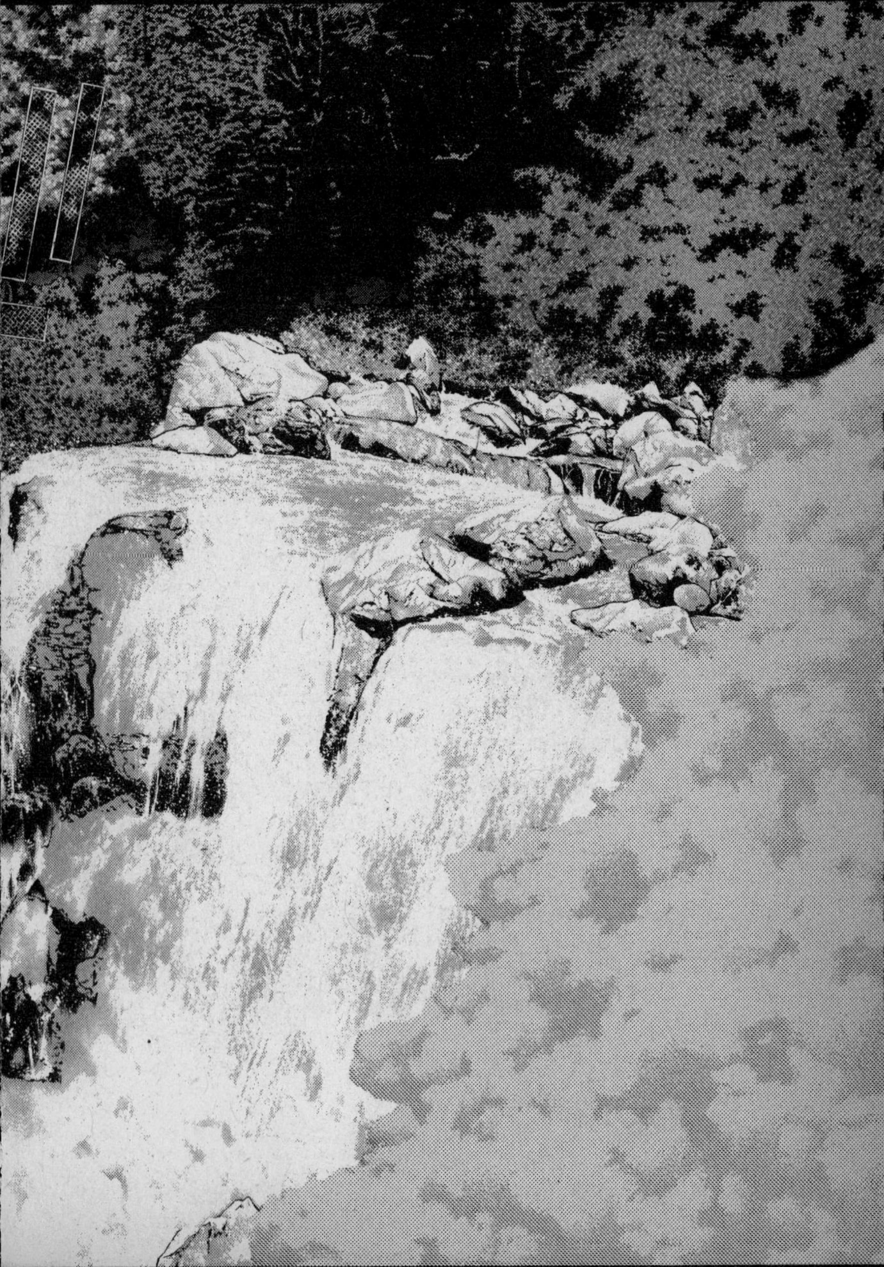

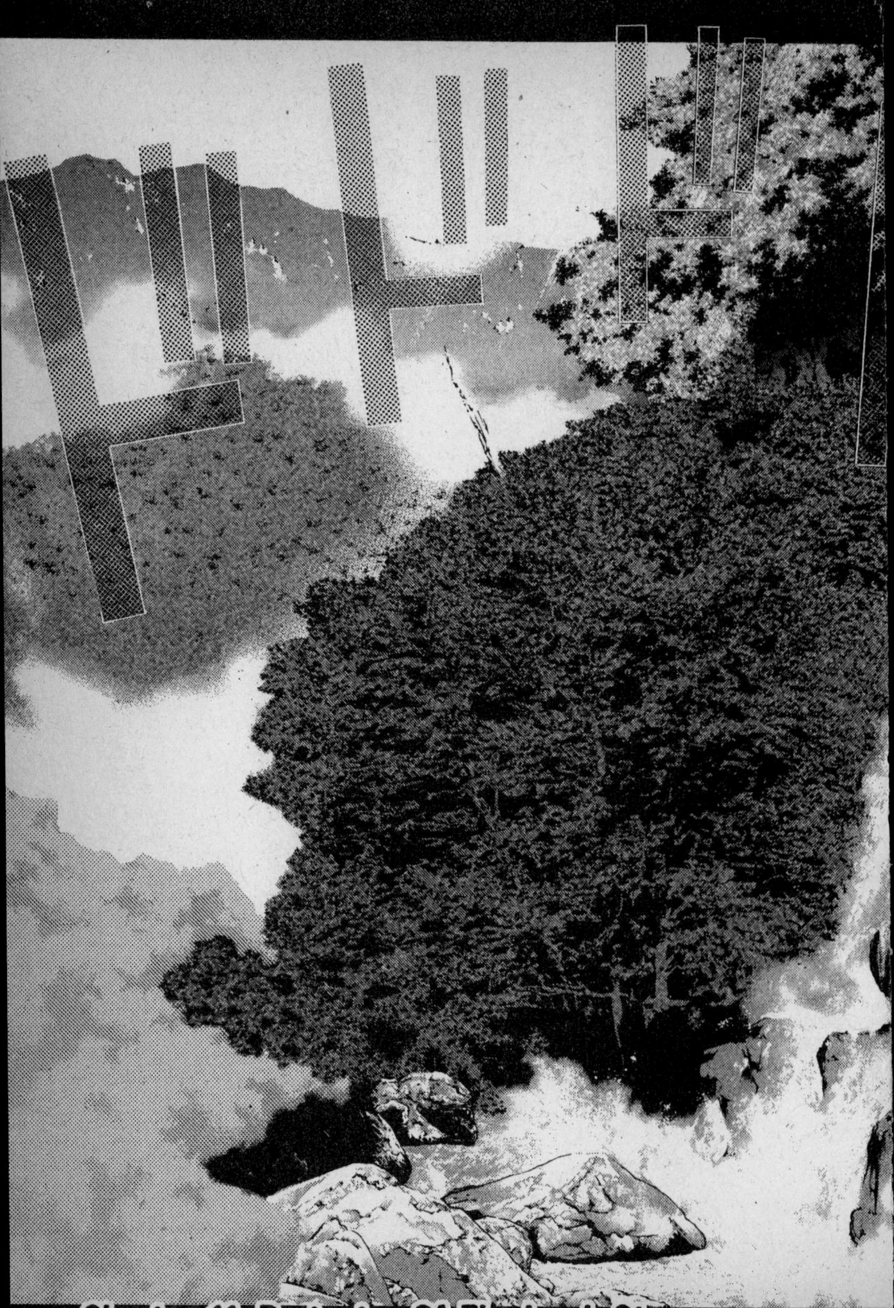
ドドド

Chapter 11: Protector Of The Land, Otsuwa-sama

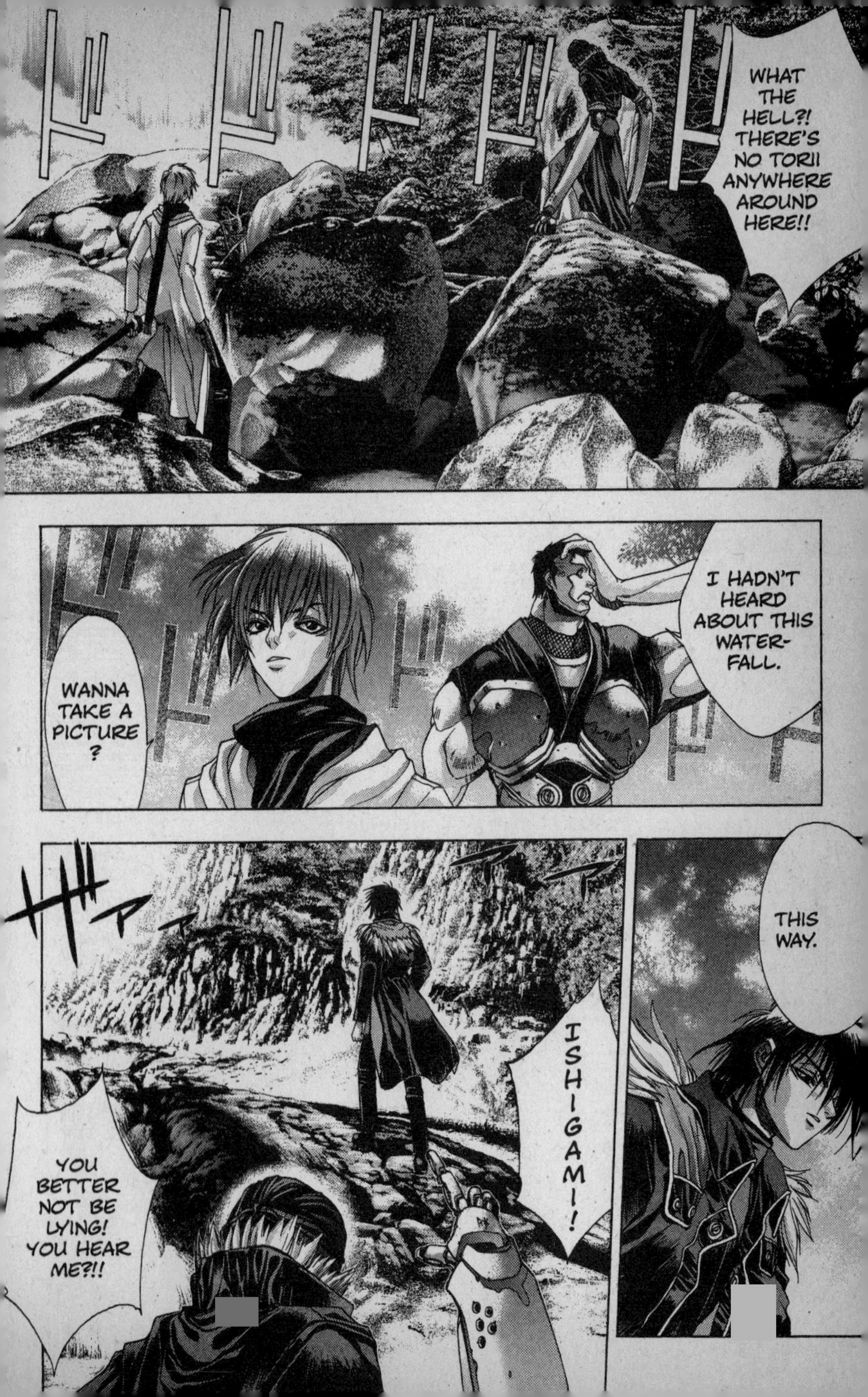
WHAT THE HELL?! THERE'S NO TORII ANYWHERE AROUND HERE!!
I HADN'T HEARD ABOUT THIS WATER-FALL.
WANNA TAKE A PICTURE ?
THIS WAY.
ISHIGAMI!
YOU BETTER NOT BE LYING! YOU HEAR ME?!!

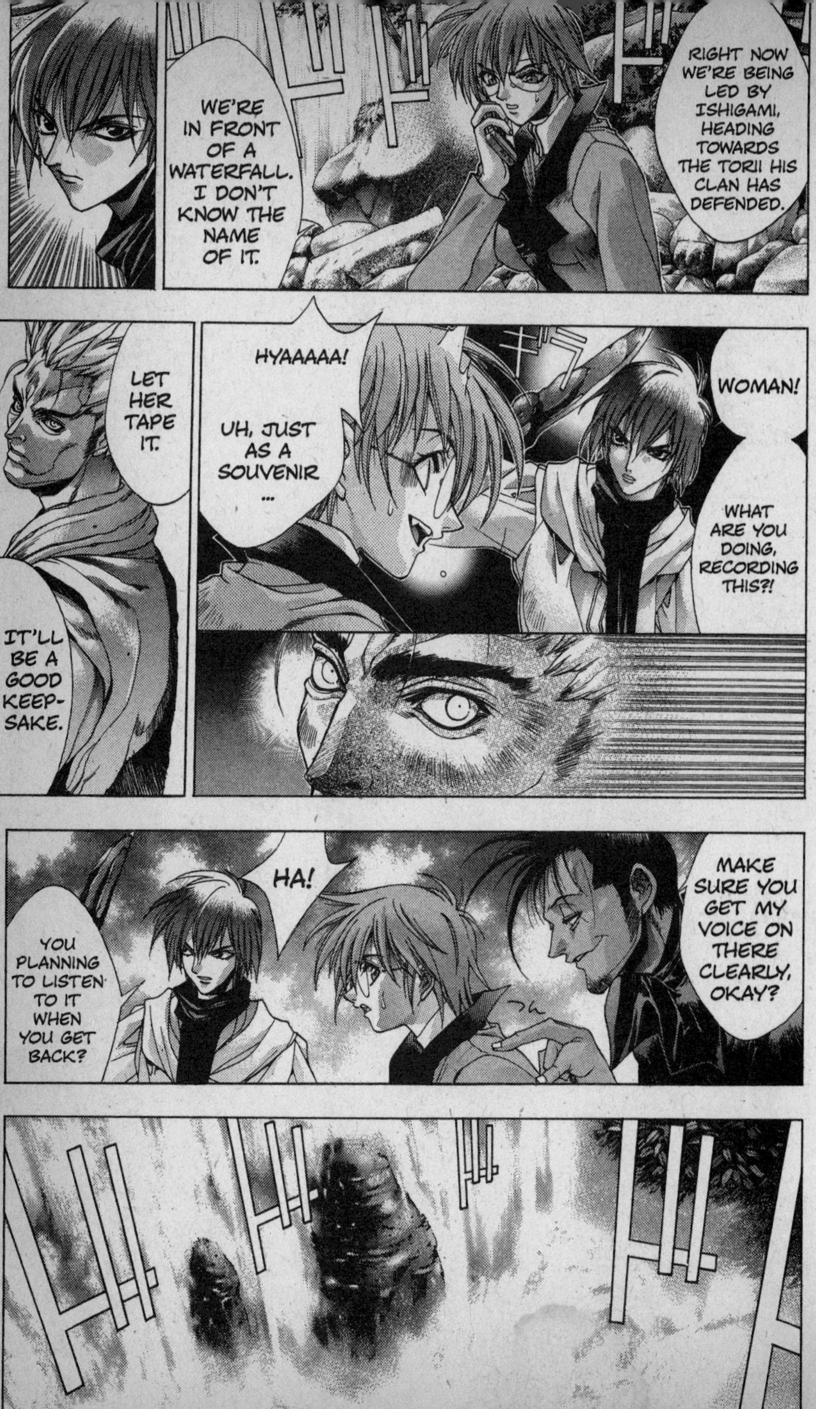
RIGHT NOW WE'RE BEING LED BY ISHIGAMI, HEADING TOWARDS THE TORII HIS CLAN HAS DEFENDED.
WE'RE IN FRONT OF A WATERFALL. I DON'T KNOW THE NAME OF IT.
WOMAN!
WHAT ARE YOU DOING, RECORDING THIS?!
HYAAAAA!
UH, JUST AS A SOUVENIR ...
LET HER TAPE IT.
IT'LL BE A GOOD KEEP-SAKE.
MAKE SURE YOU GET MY VOICE ON THERE CLEARLY, OKAY?
HA!
YOU PLANNING TO LISTEN TO IT WHEN YOU GET BACK?

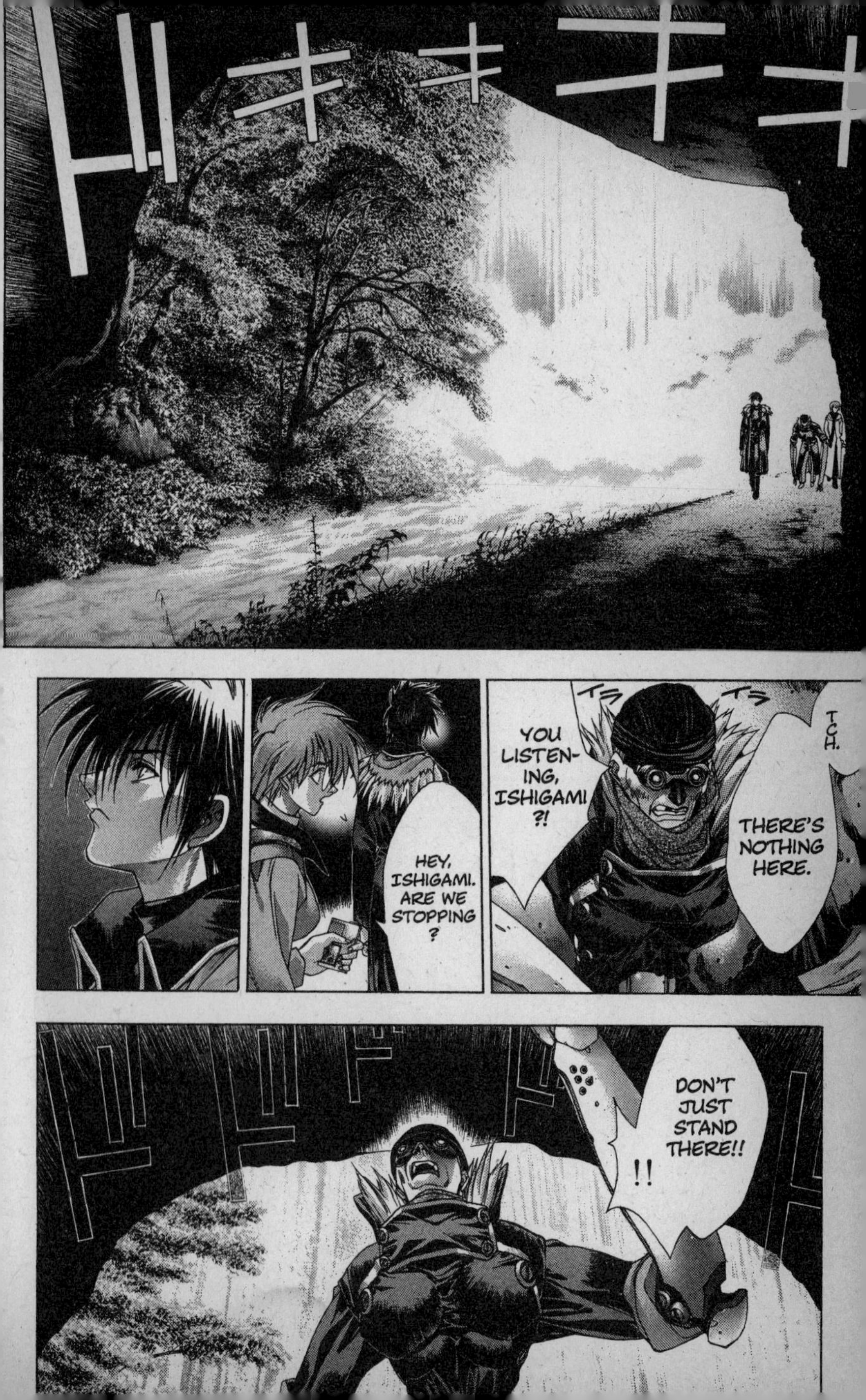
TCH.
THERE'S NOTHING HERE.
YOU LISTENING, ISHIGAMI?!
HEY, ISHIGAMI. ARE WE STOPPING?
DON'T JUST STAND THERE!!
!!

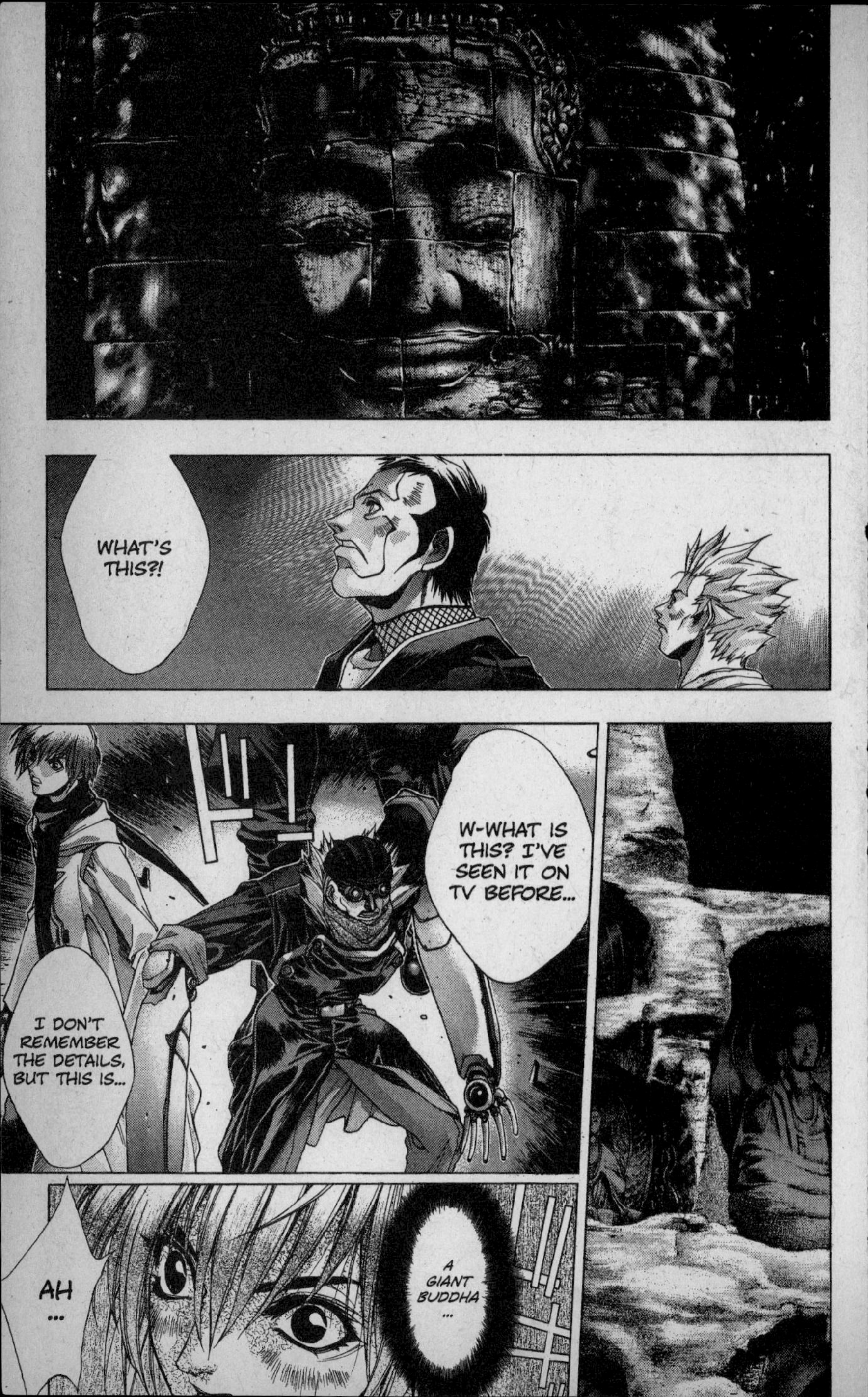
WHAT'S THIS?!
W-WHAT IS THIS? I'VE SEEN IT ON TV BEFORE...
I DON'T REMEMBER THE DETAILS, BUT THIS IS...
A GIANT BUDDHA...
AH...

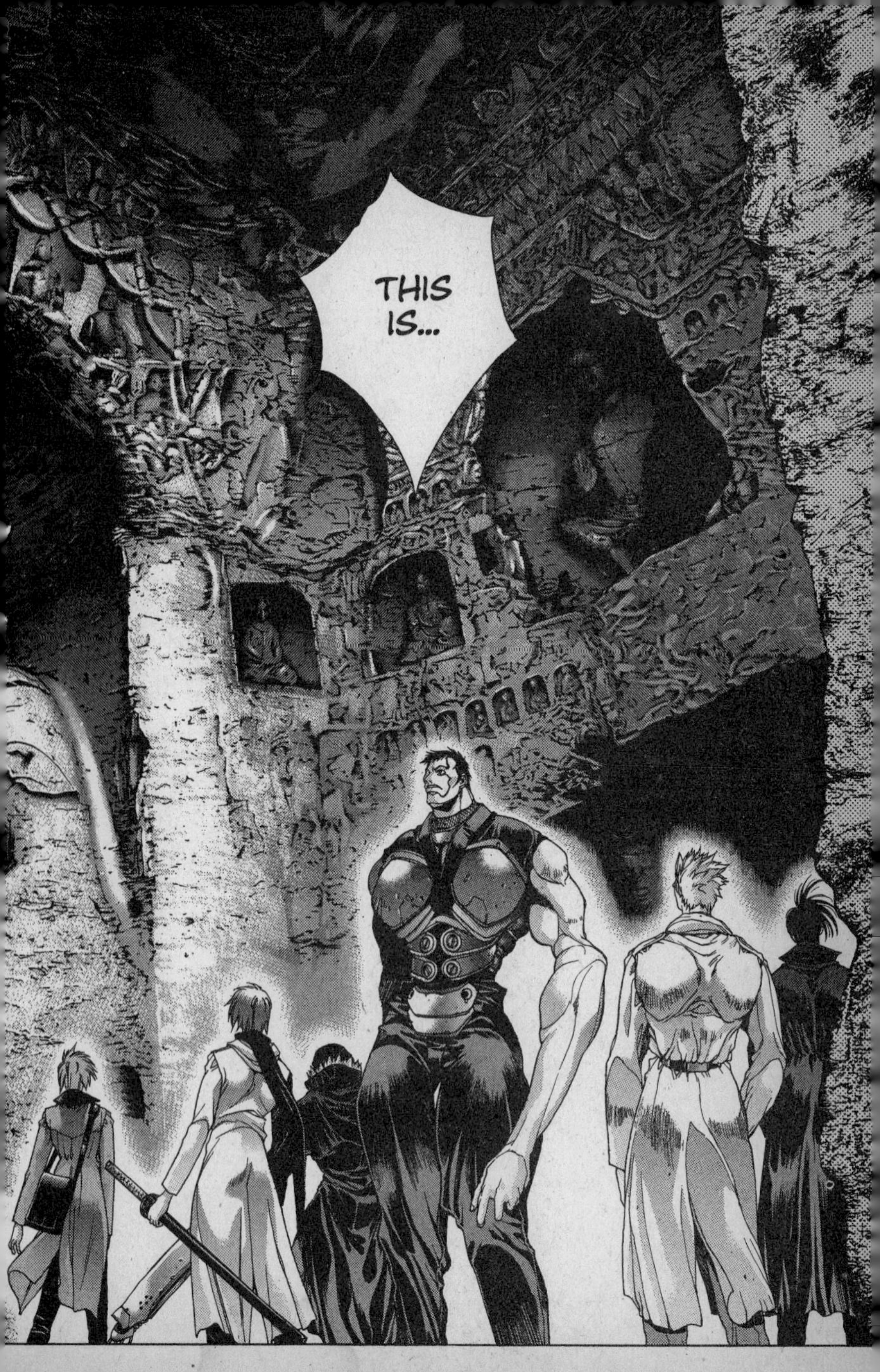
THIS IS...

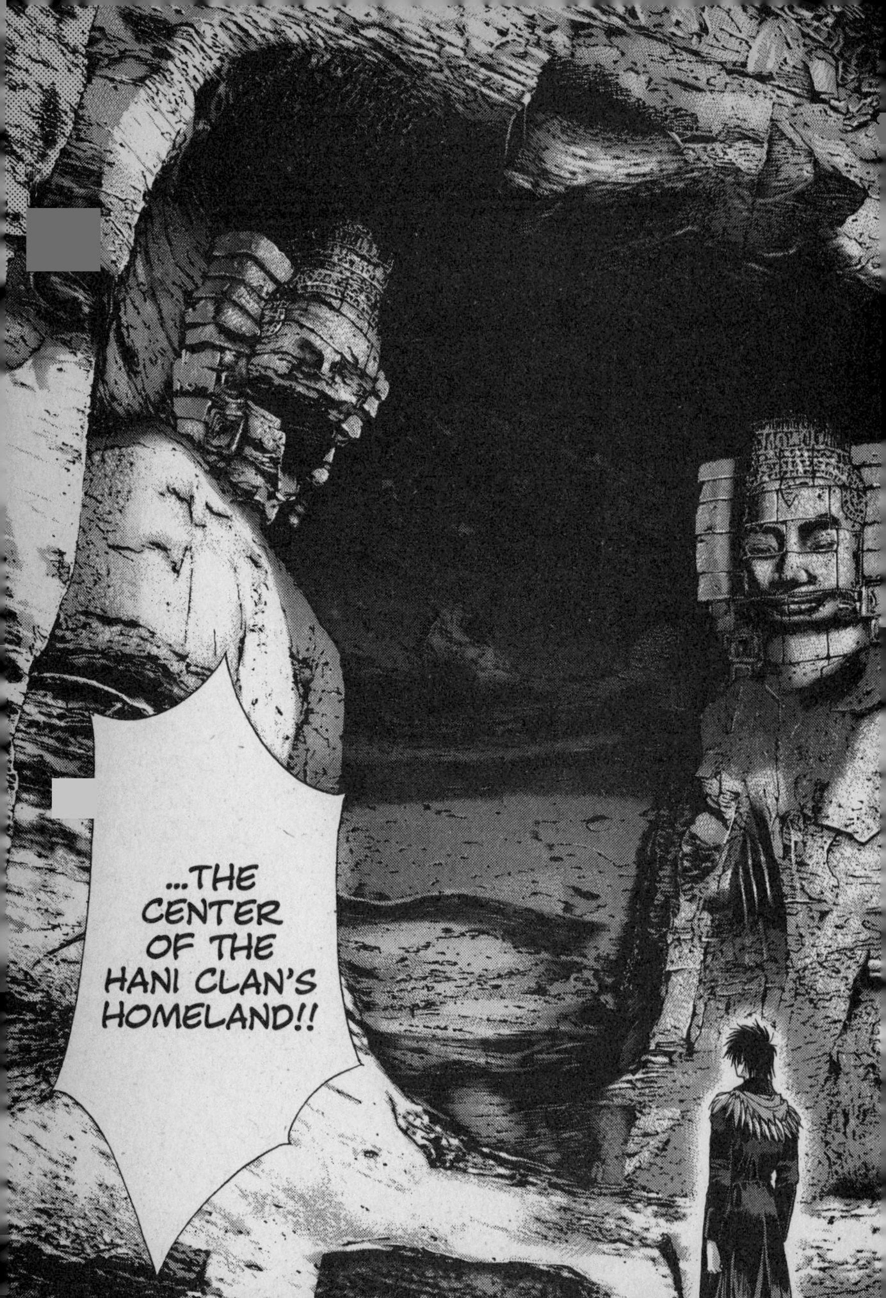
...THE CENTER OF THE HANI CLAN'S HOMELAND!!

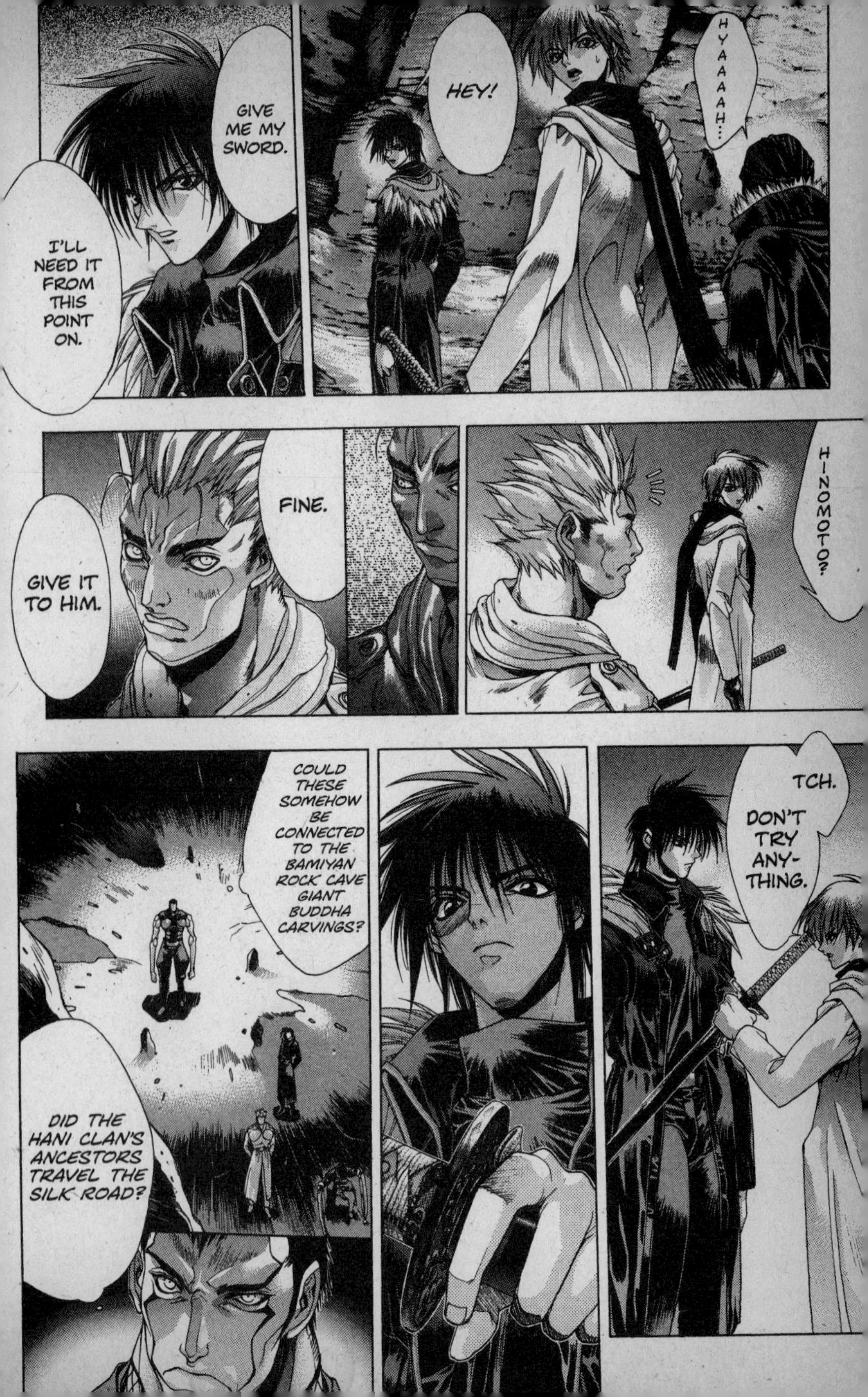
HYAAAAH...
HEY!
GIVE ME MY SWORD.
I'LL NEED IT FROM THIS POINT ON.
HINOMOTO?
FINE.
GIVE IT TO HIM.
TCH.
DON'T TRY ANYTHING.
COULD THESE SOMEHOW BE CONNECTED TO THE BAMIYAN ROCK CAVE GIANT BUDDHA CARVINGS?
DID THE HANI CLAN'S ANCESTORS TRAVEL THE SILK ROAD?

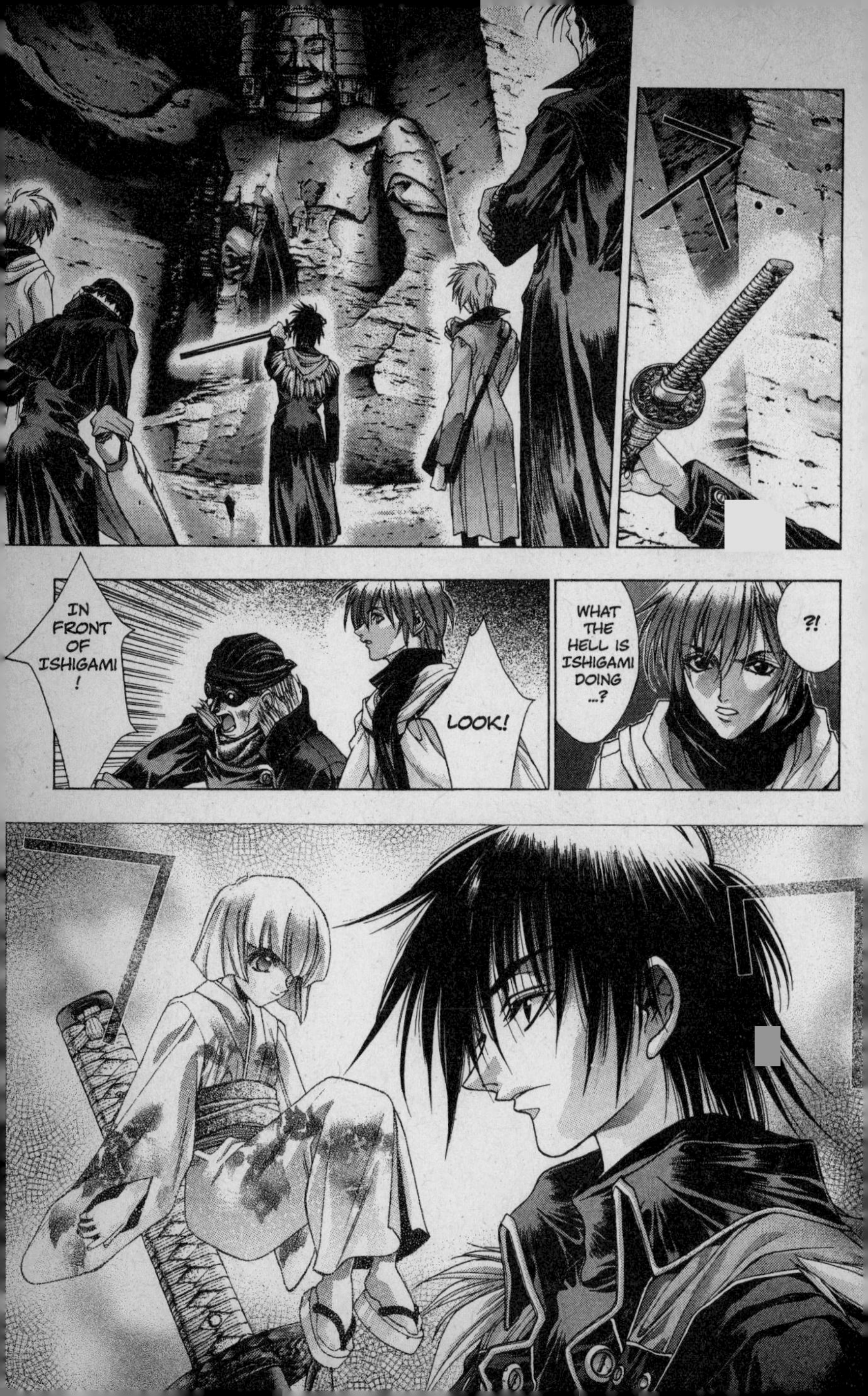
?!
WHAT THE HELL IS ISHIGAMI DOING ...?
LOOK!
IN FRONT OF ISHIGAMI!

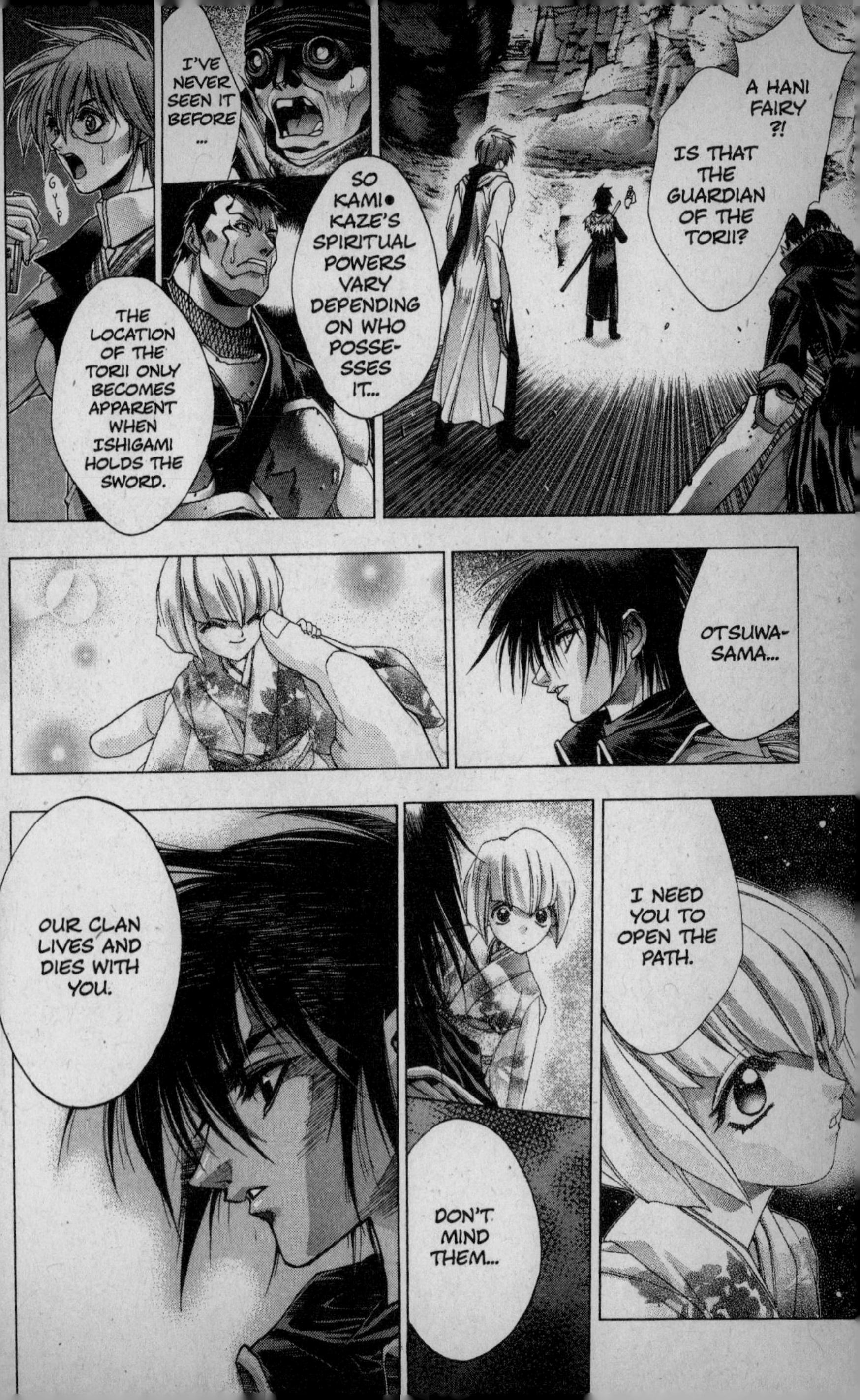
A HANI FAIRY ?!
IS THAT THE GUARDIAN OF THE TORII?
I'VE NEVER SEEN IT BEFORE ...
SO KAMI•KAZE'S SPIRITUAL POWERS VARY DEPENDING ON WHO POSSESSES IT...
THE LOCATION OF THE TORII ONLY BECOMES APPARENT WHEN ISHIGAMI HOLDS THE SWORD.
GYLP
OTSUWA-SAMA...
I NEED YOU TO OPEN THE PATH.
DON'T MIND THEM...
OUR CLAN LIVES AND DIES WITH YOU.

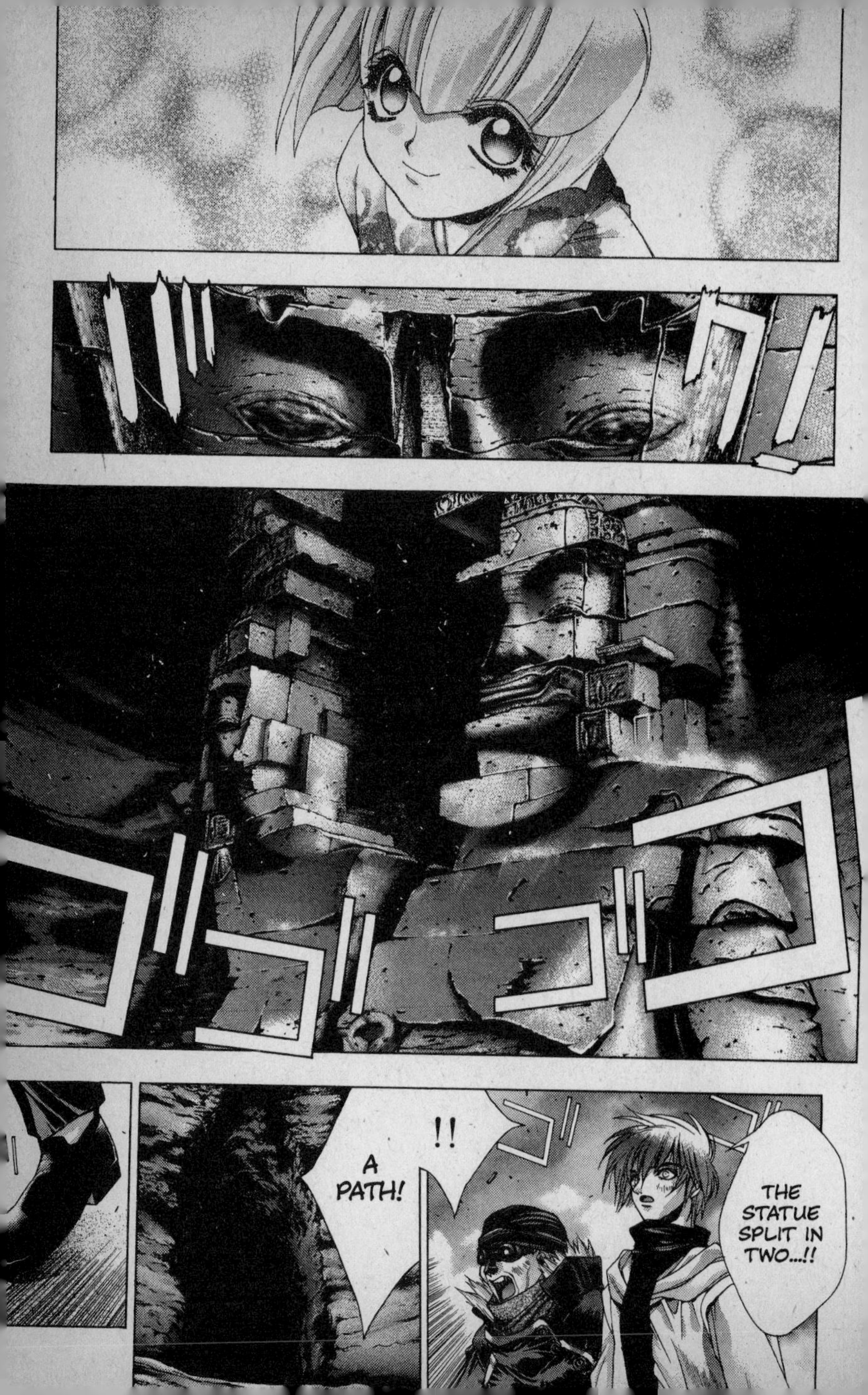
THE STATUE SPLIT IN TWO...!!
!!
A PATH!

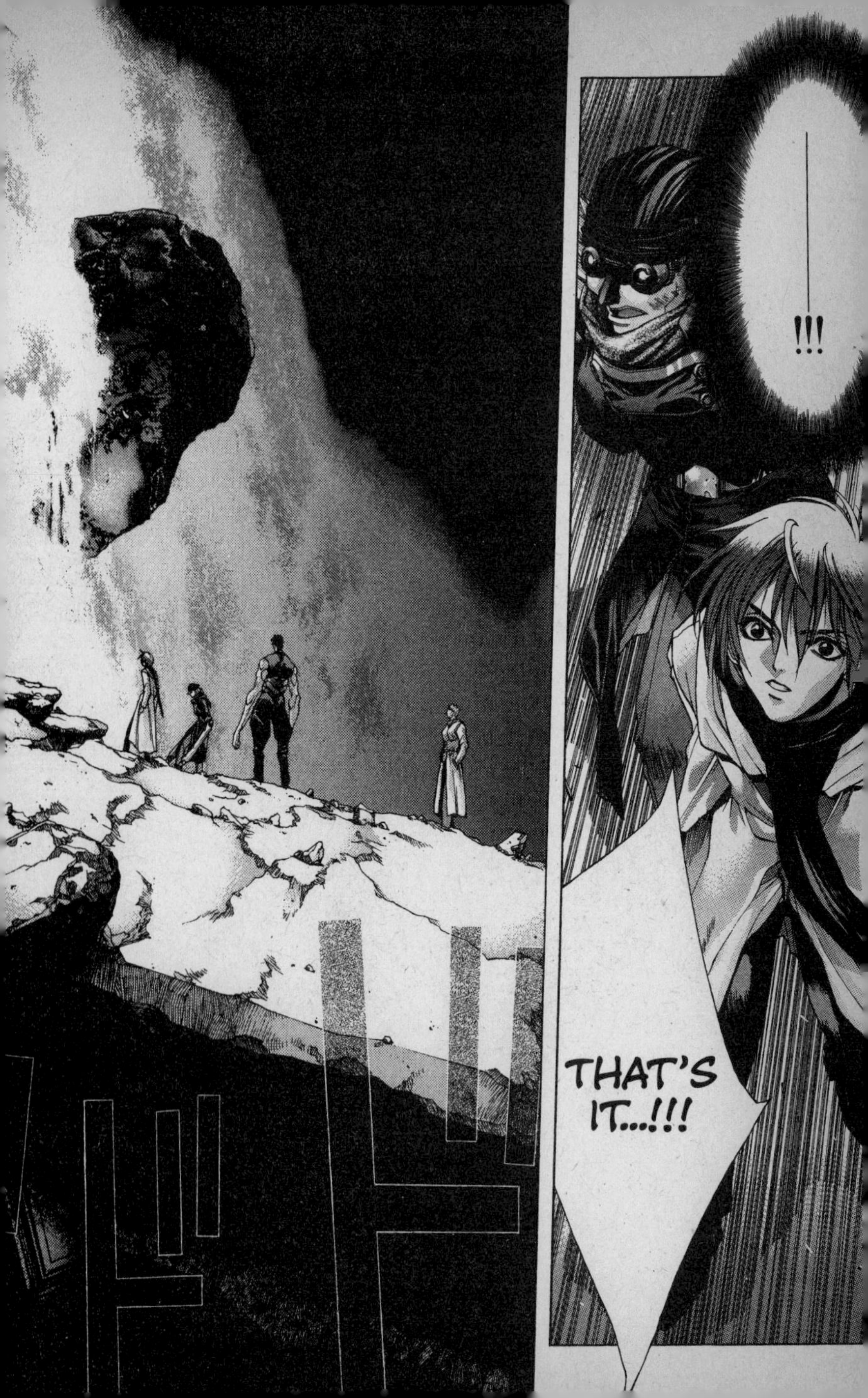

——!!!
THAT'S IT...!!!

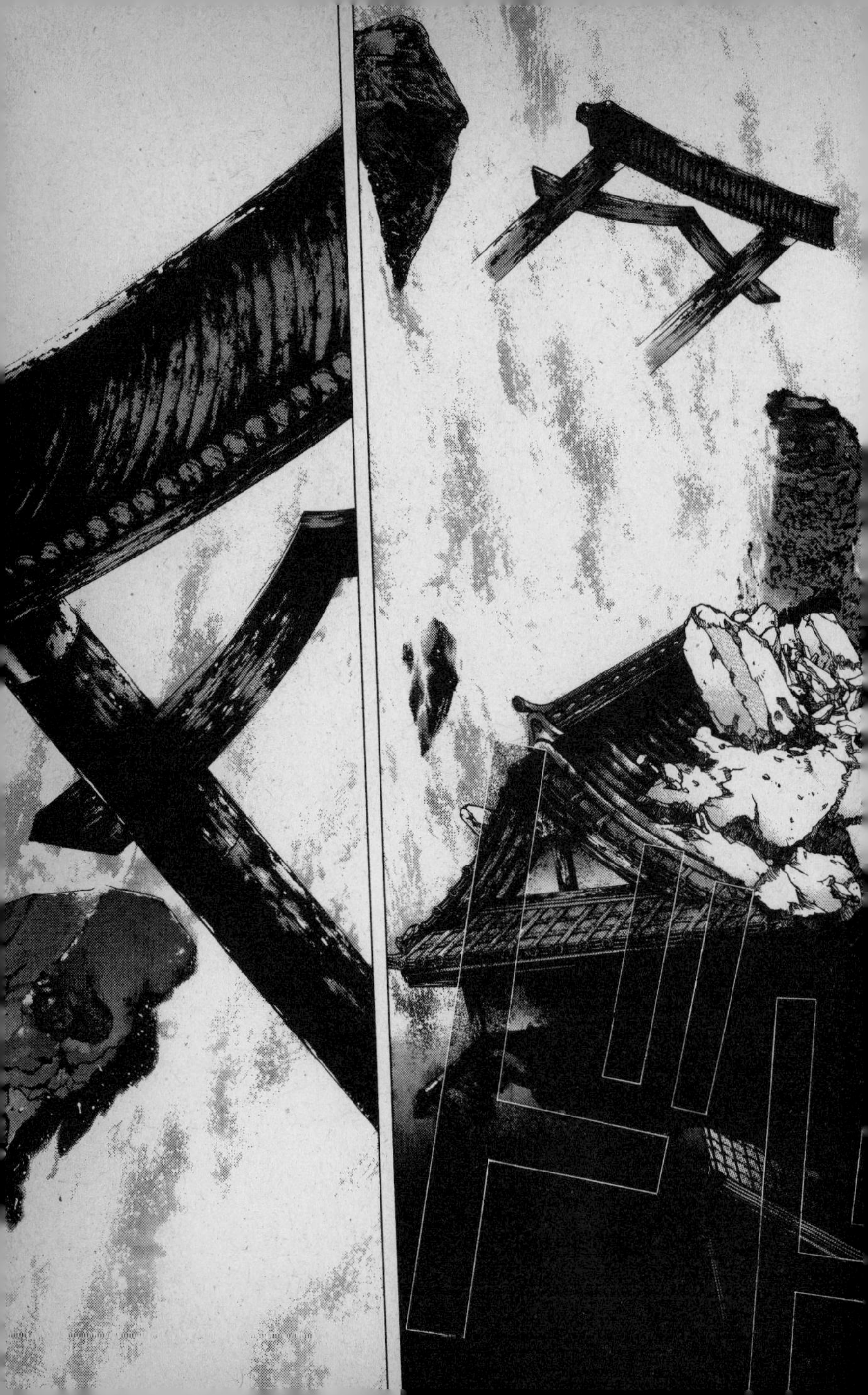

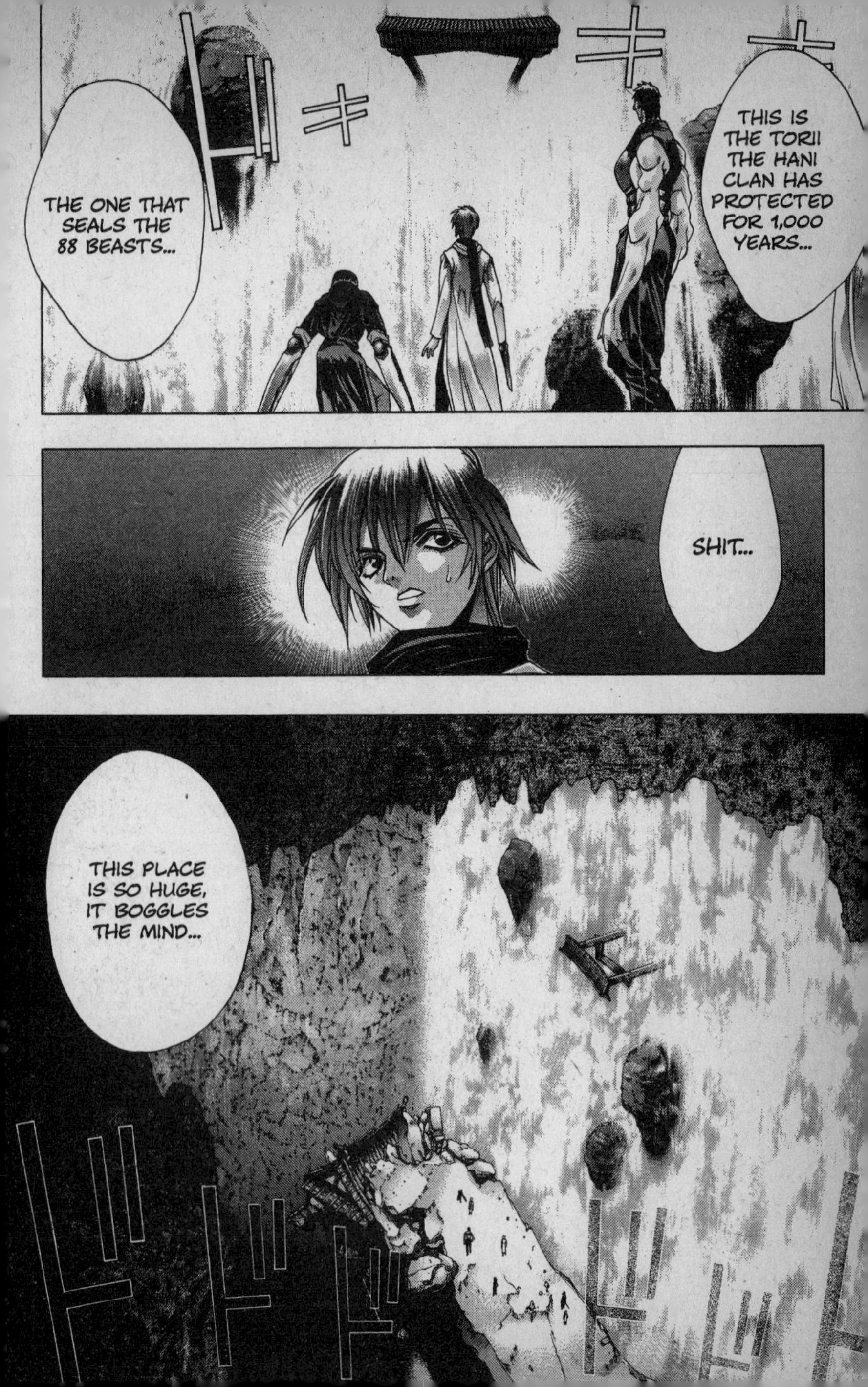
THIS IS THE TORII THE HANI CLAN HAS PROTECTED FOR 1,000 YEARS...
THE ONE THAT SEALS THE 88 BEASTS...
SHIT...
THIS PLACE IS SO HUGE, IT BOGGLES THE MIND...

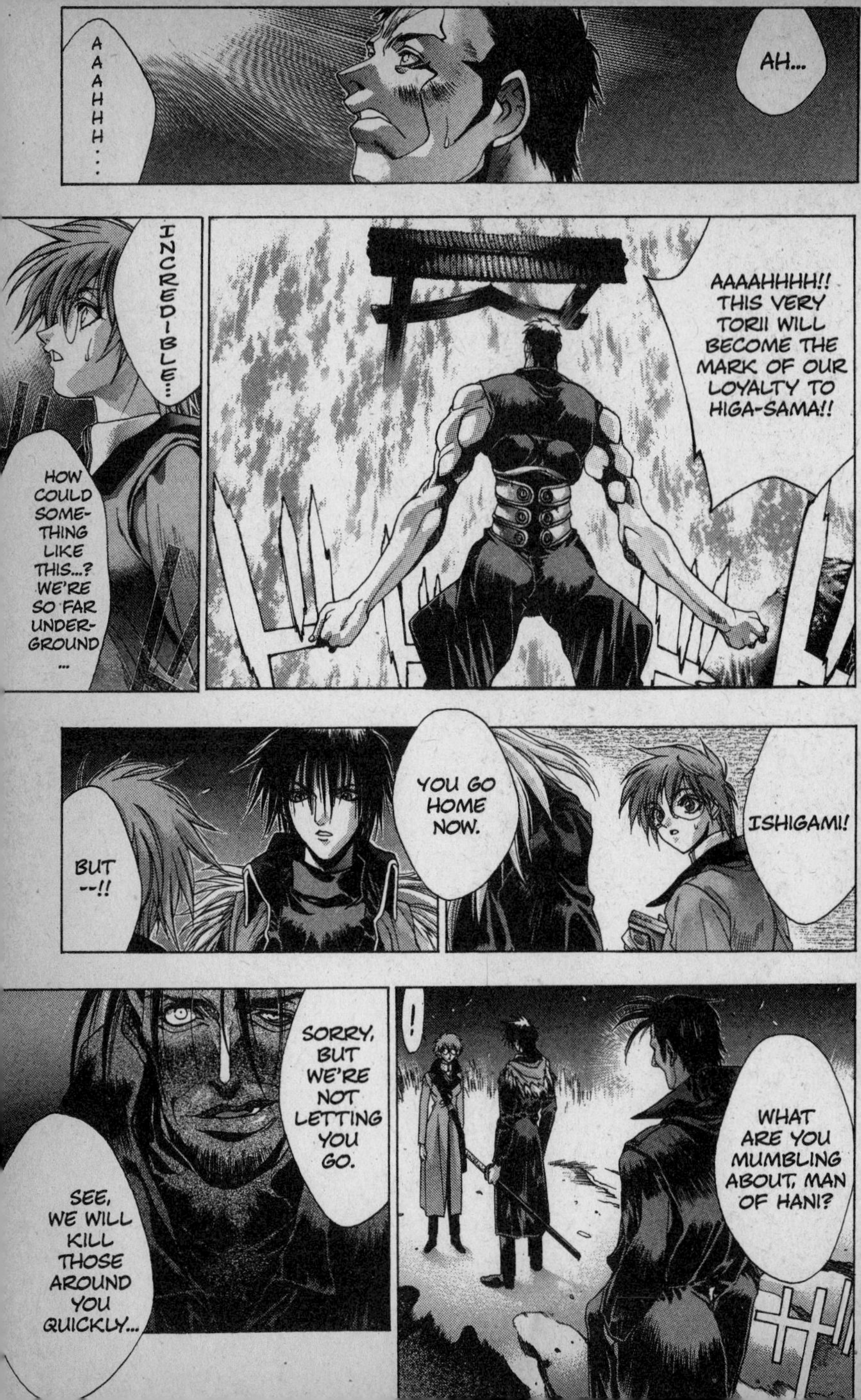
AH...
AAAHHH...
AAAAHHHH!! THIS VERY TORII WILL BECOME THE MARK OF OUR LOYALTY TO HIGA-SAMA!!
INCREDIBLE...
HOW COULD SOMETHING LIKE THIS...? WE'RE SO FAR UNDERGROUND...
ISHIGAMI!
YOU GO HOME NOW.
BUT --!!
!
WHAT ARE YOU MUMBLING ABOUT, MAN OF HANI?
SORRY, BUT WE'RE NOT LETTING YOU GO.
SEE, WE WILL KILL THOSE AROUND YOU QUICKLY...

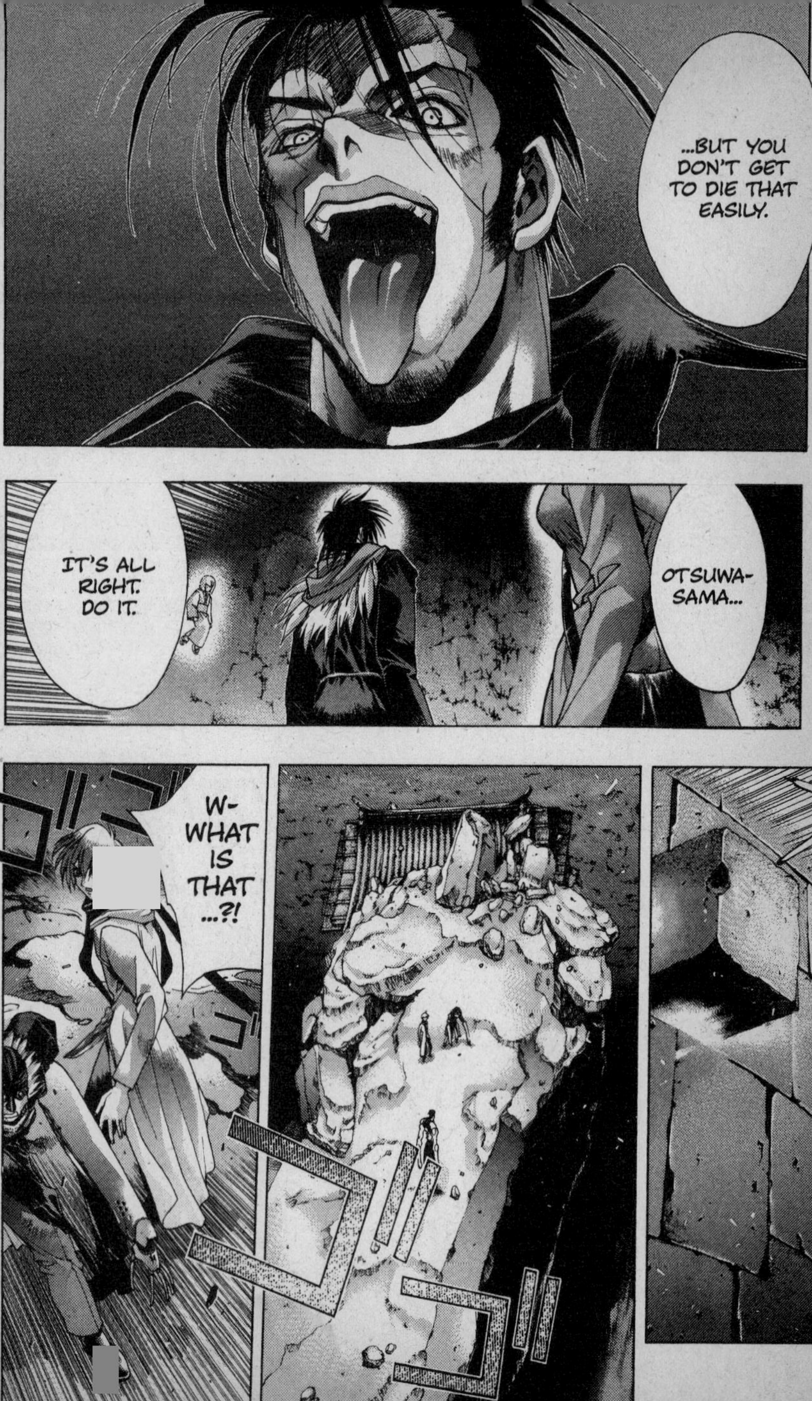
...BUT YOU DON'T GET TO DIE THAT EASILY.
OTSUWA-SAMA...
IT'S ALL RIGHT. DO IT.
W-WHAT IS THAT ...?!

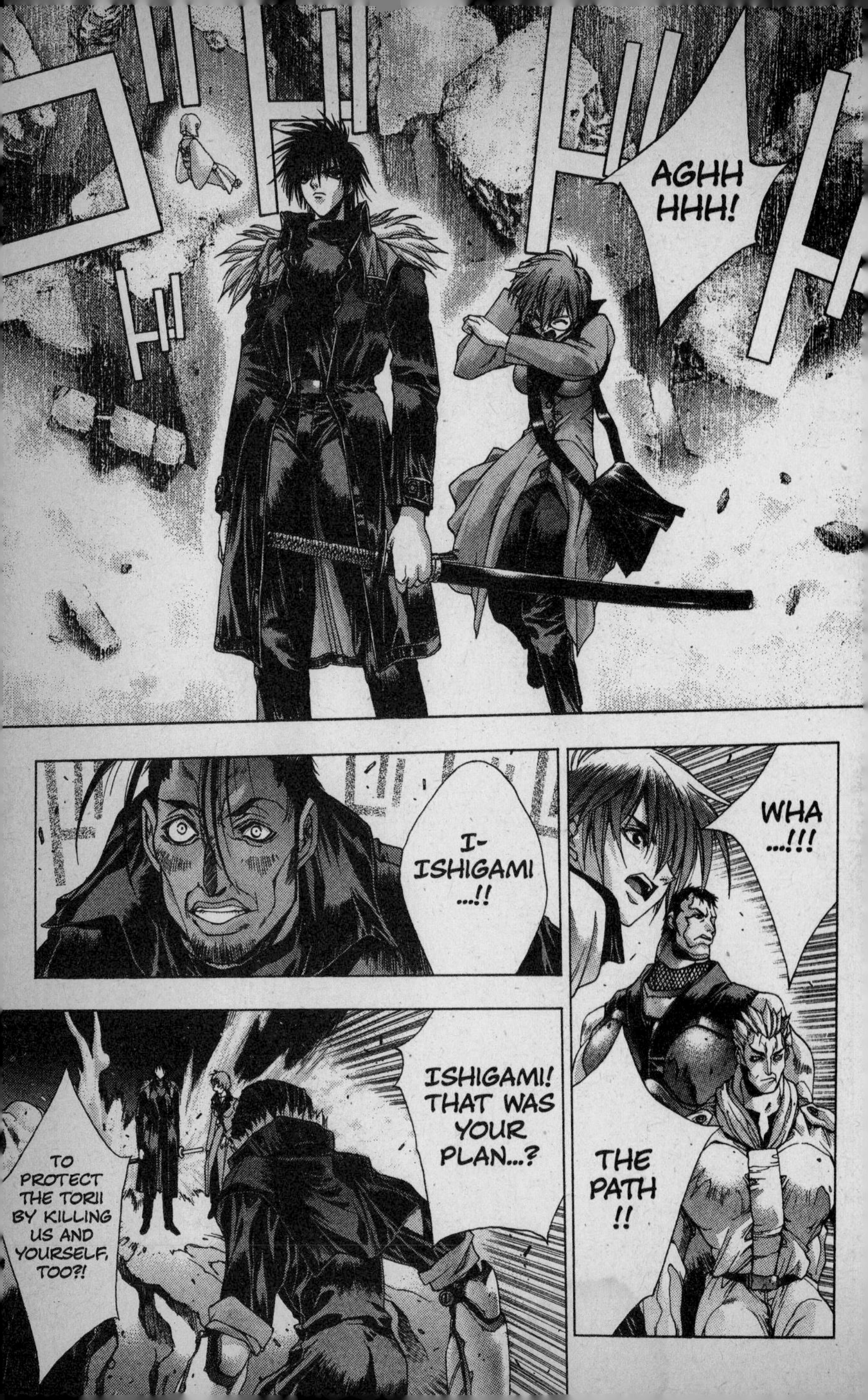
AGHH HHH!
WHA ...!!!
THE PATH !!
I-ISHIGAMI ...!!
ISHIGAMI! THAT WAS YOUR PLAN...?
TO PROTECT THE TORII BY KILLING US AND YOURSELF, TOO?!

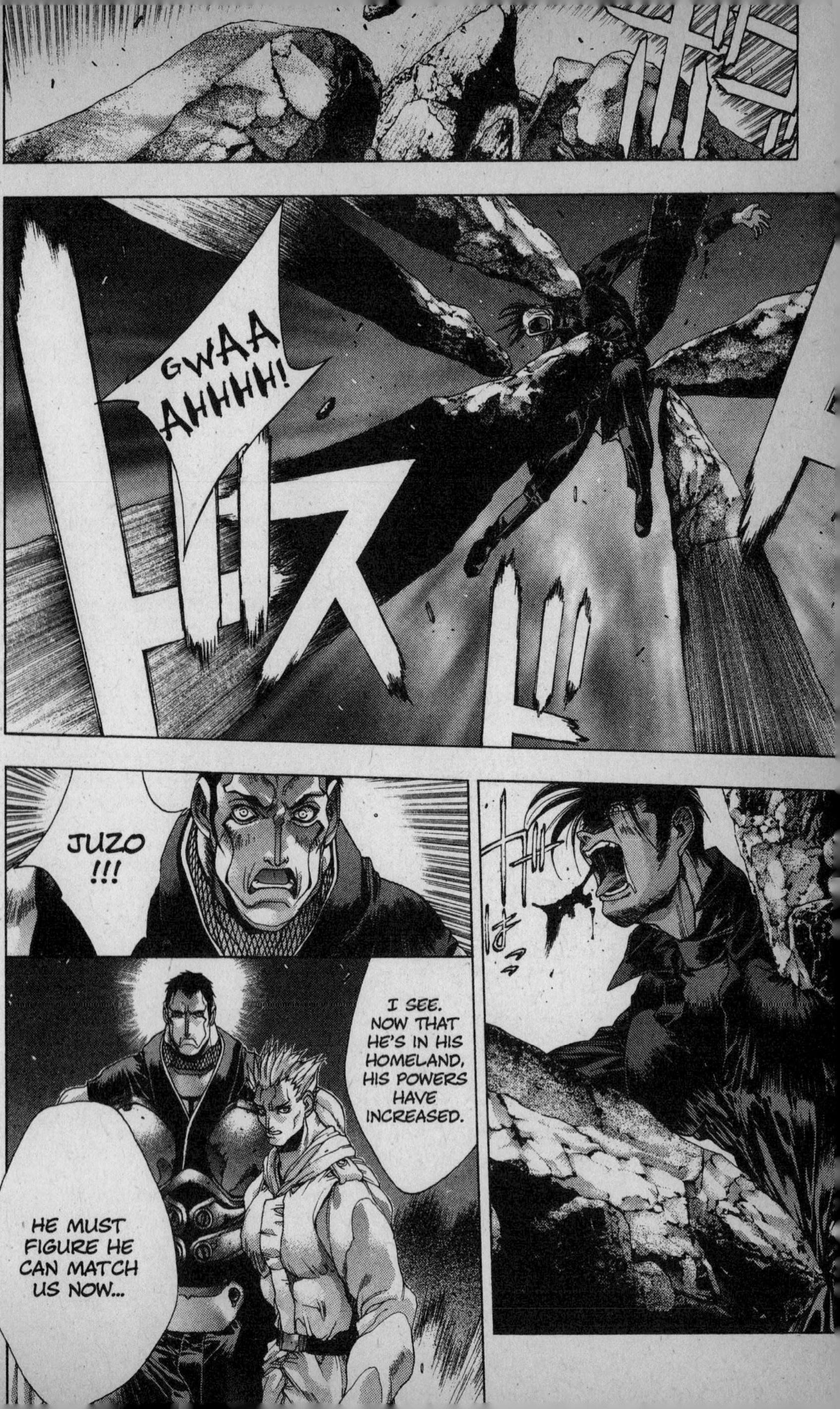
GWAA AHHHH!
JUZO !!!
I SEE. NOW THAT HE'S IN HIS HOMELAND, HIS POWERS HAVE INCREASED.
HE MUST FIGURE HE CAN MATCH US NOW...

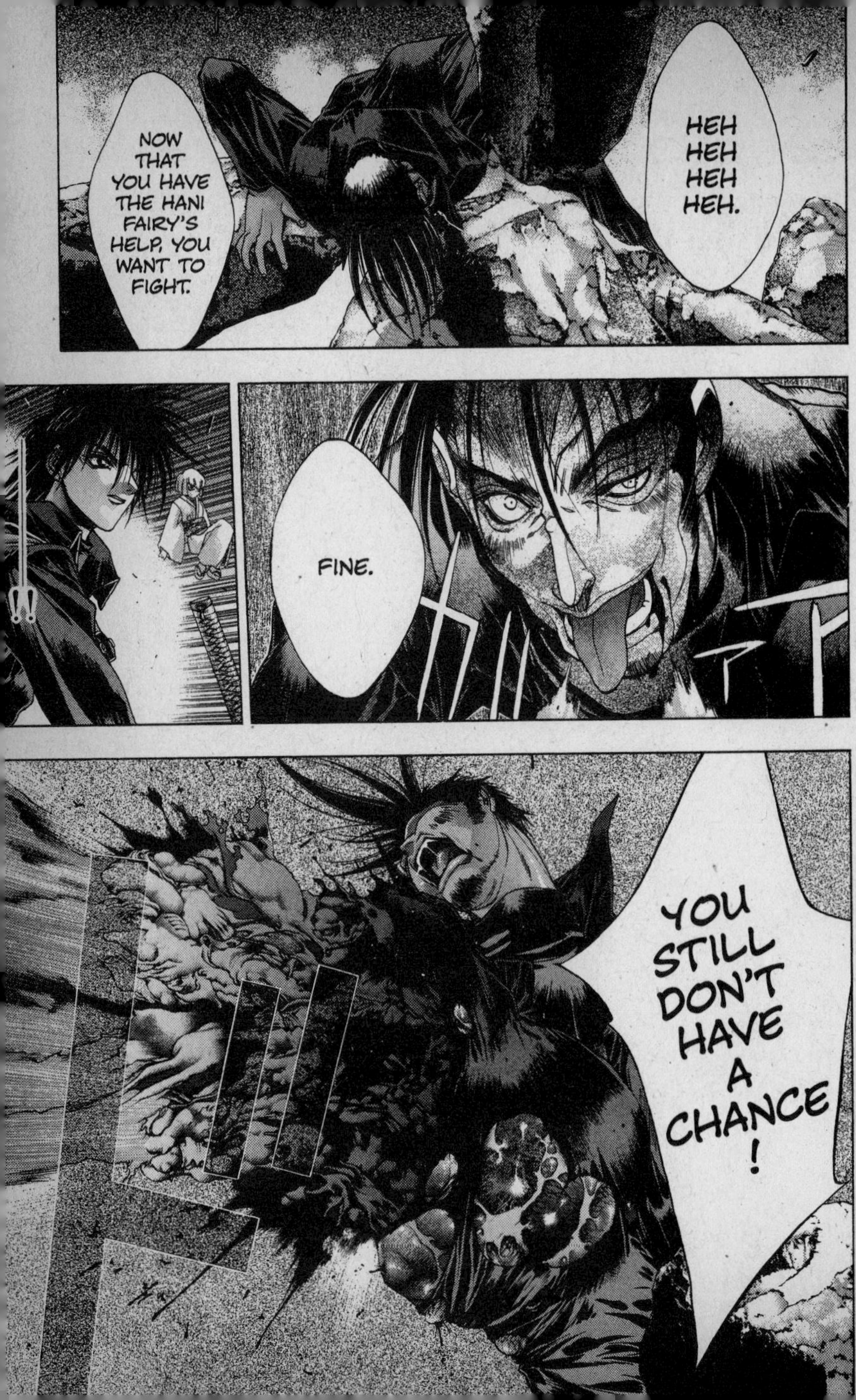
HEH HEH HEH HEH.
NOW THAT YOU HAVE THE HANI FAIRY'S HELP, YOU WANT TO FIGHT.
FINE.
!!
YOU STILL DON'T HAVE A CHANCE!

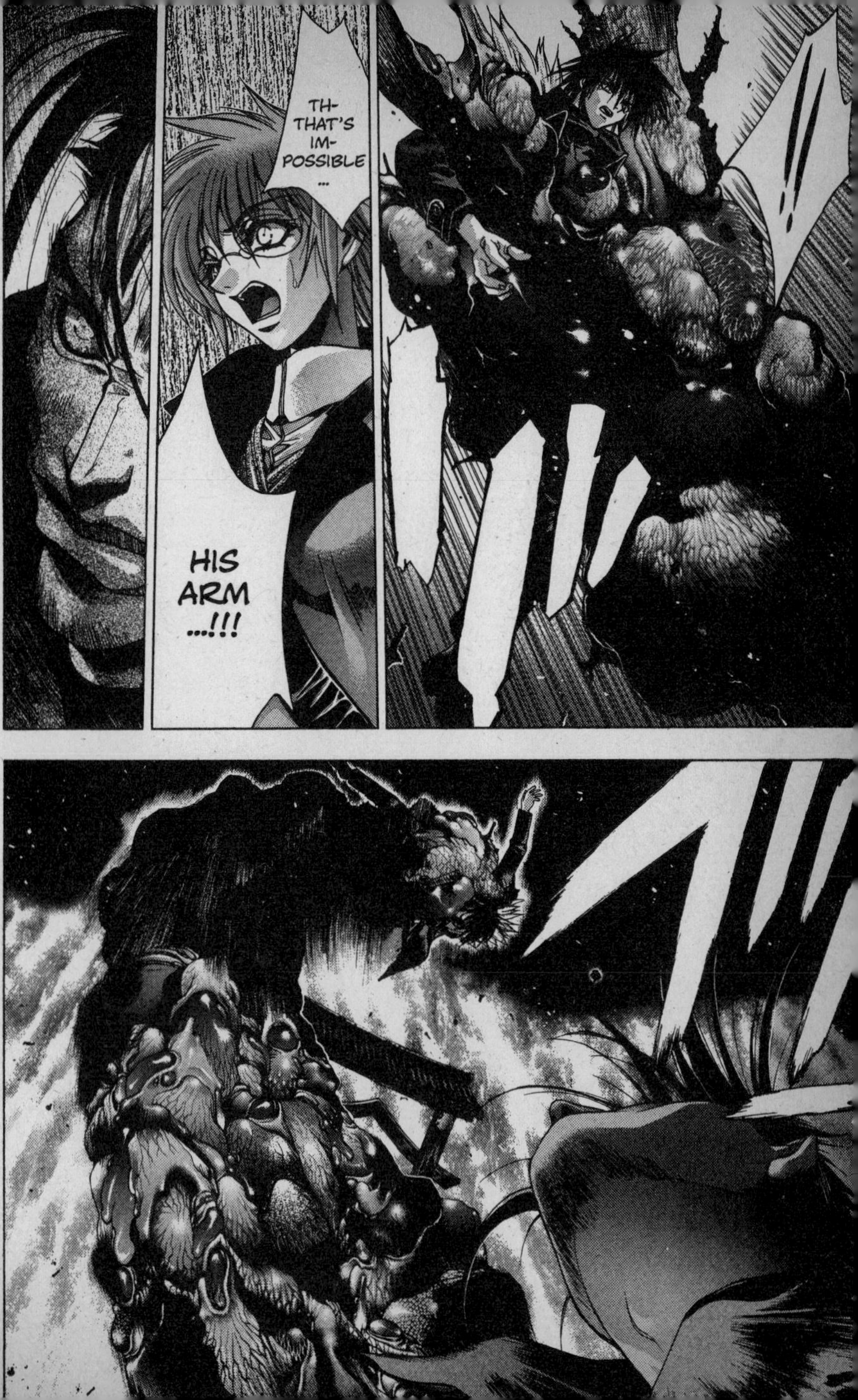
!!
TH-THAT'S IM-POSSIBLE ...
HIS ARM ...!!!

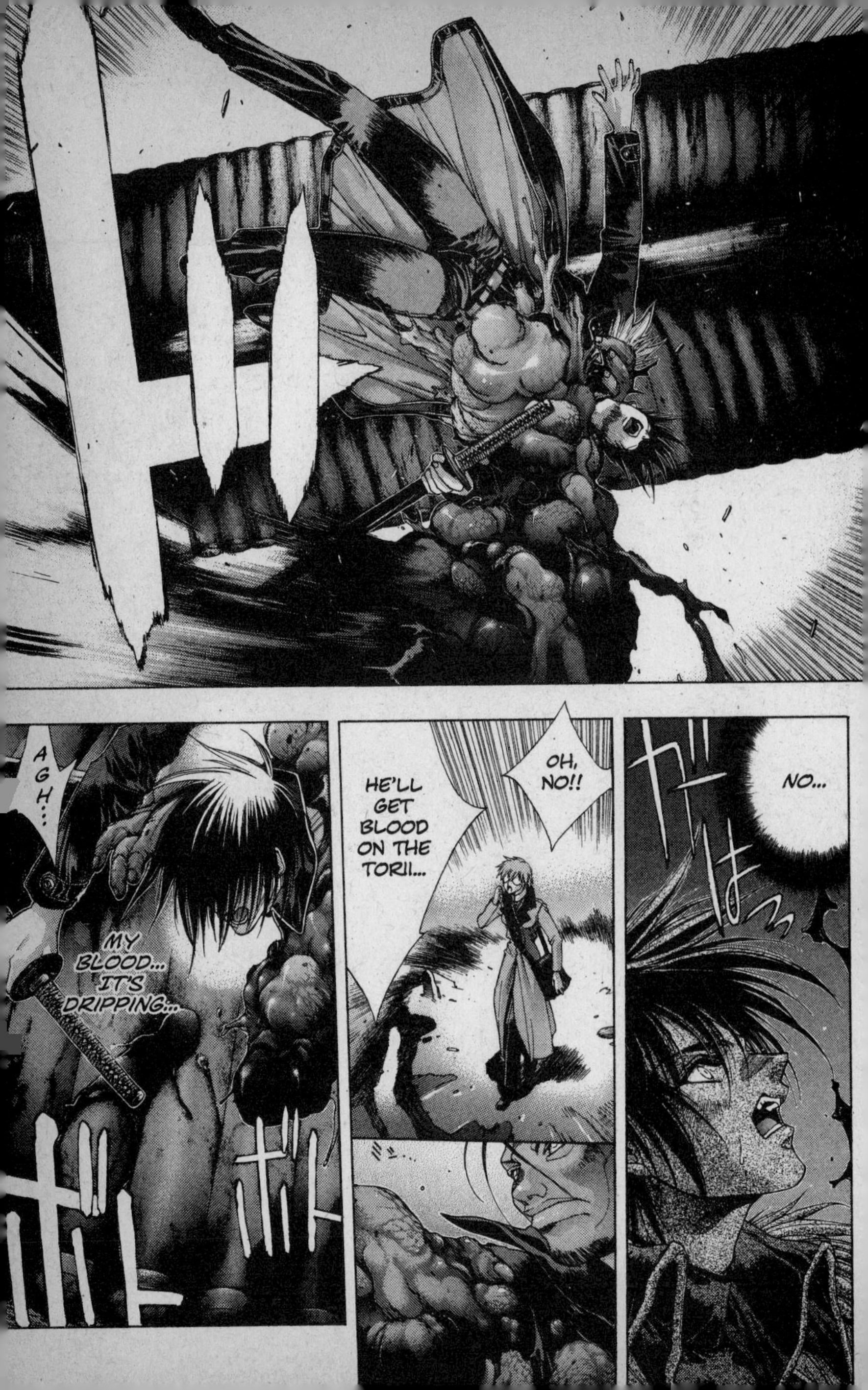
NO...
OH, NO!!
HE'LL GET BLOOD ON THE TORII...
AGH...
MY BLOOD... IT'S DRIPPING...

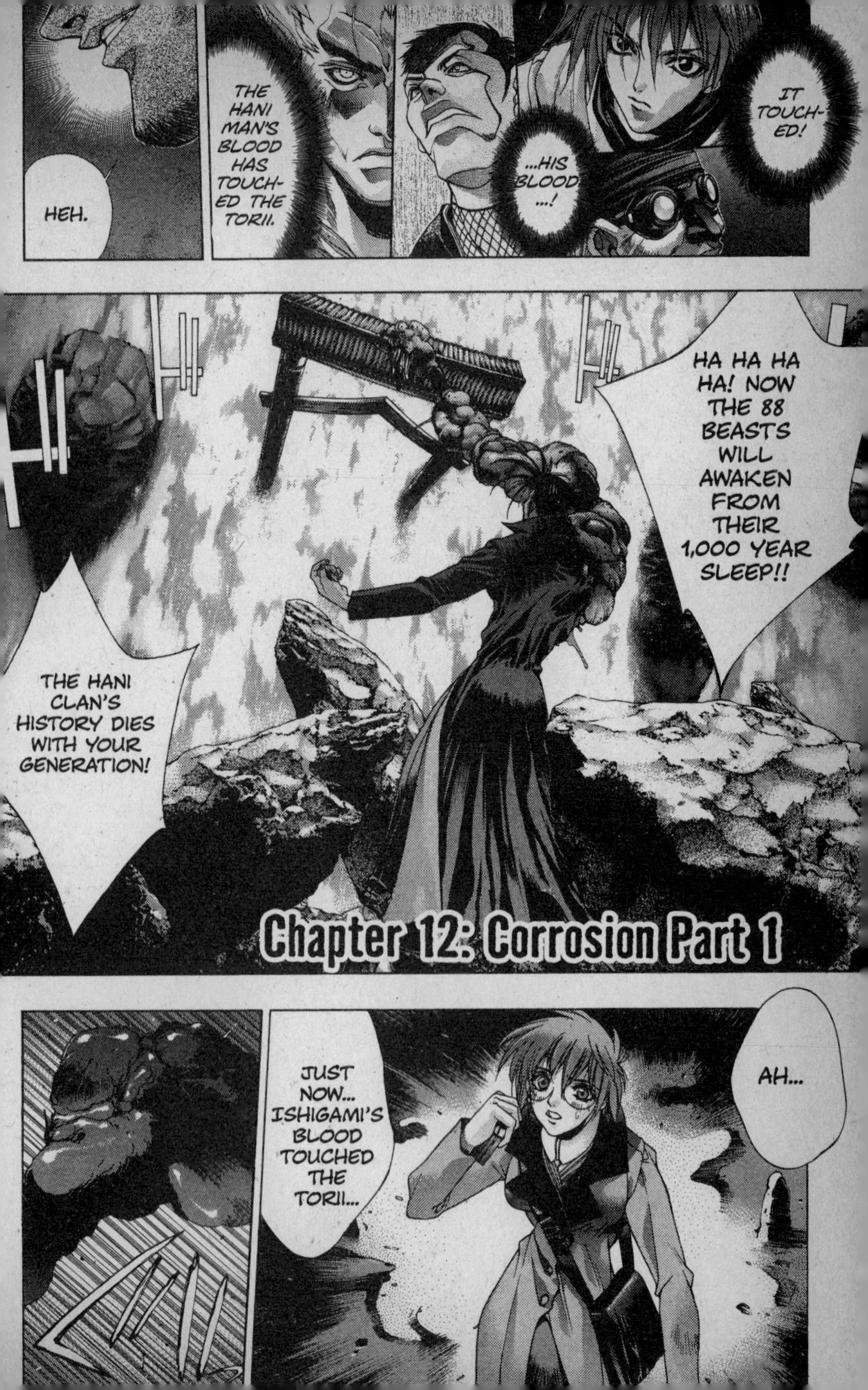
IT TOUCH-ED!
...HIS BLOOD ...!
THE HANI MAN'S BLOOD HAS TOUCH-ED THE TORII.
HEH.
HA HA HA HA! NOW THE 88 BEASTS WILL AWAKEN FROM THEIR 1,000 YEAR SLEEP!!
THE HANI CLAN'S HISTORY DIES WITH YOUR GENERATION!
Chapter 12: Corrosion Part 1
AH...
JUST NOW... ISHIGAMI'S BLOOD TOUCHED THE TORII...

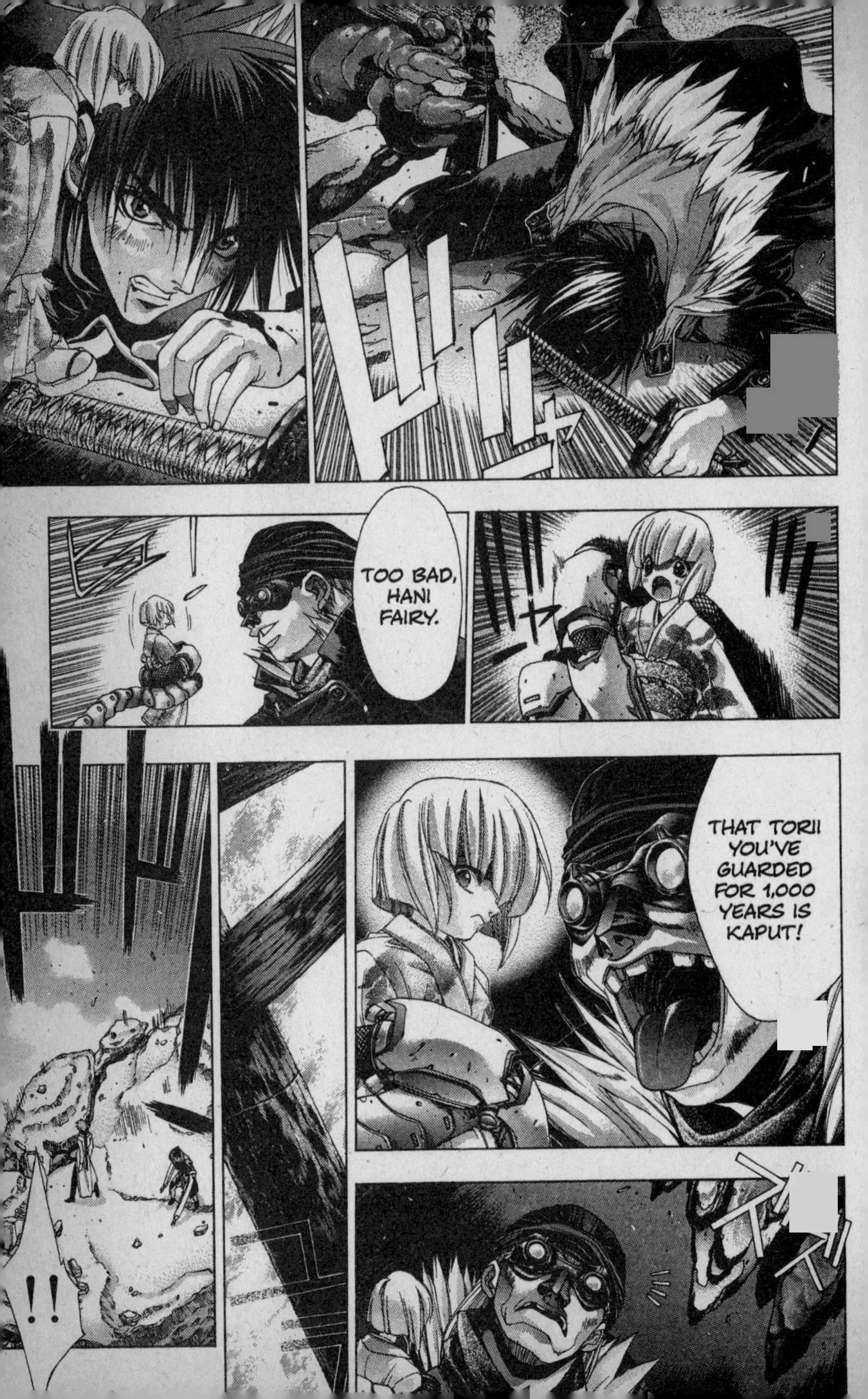
TOO BAD, HANI FAIRY.
THAT TORII YOU'VE GUARDED FOR 1,000 YEARS IS KAPUT!
!!

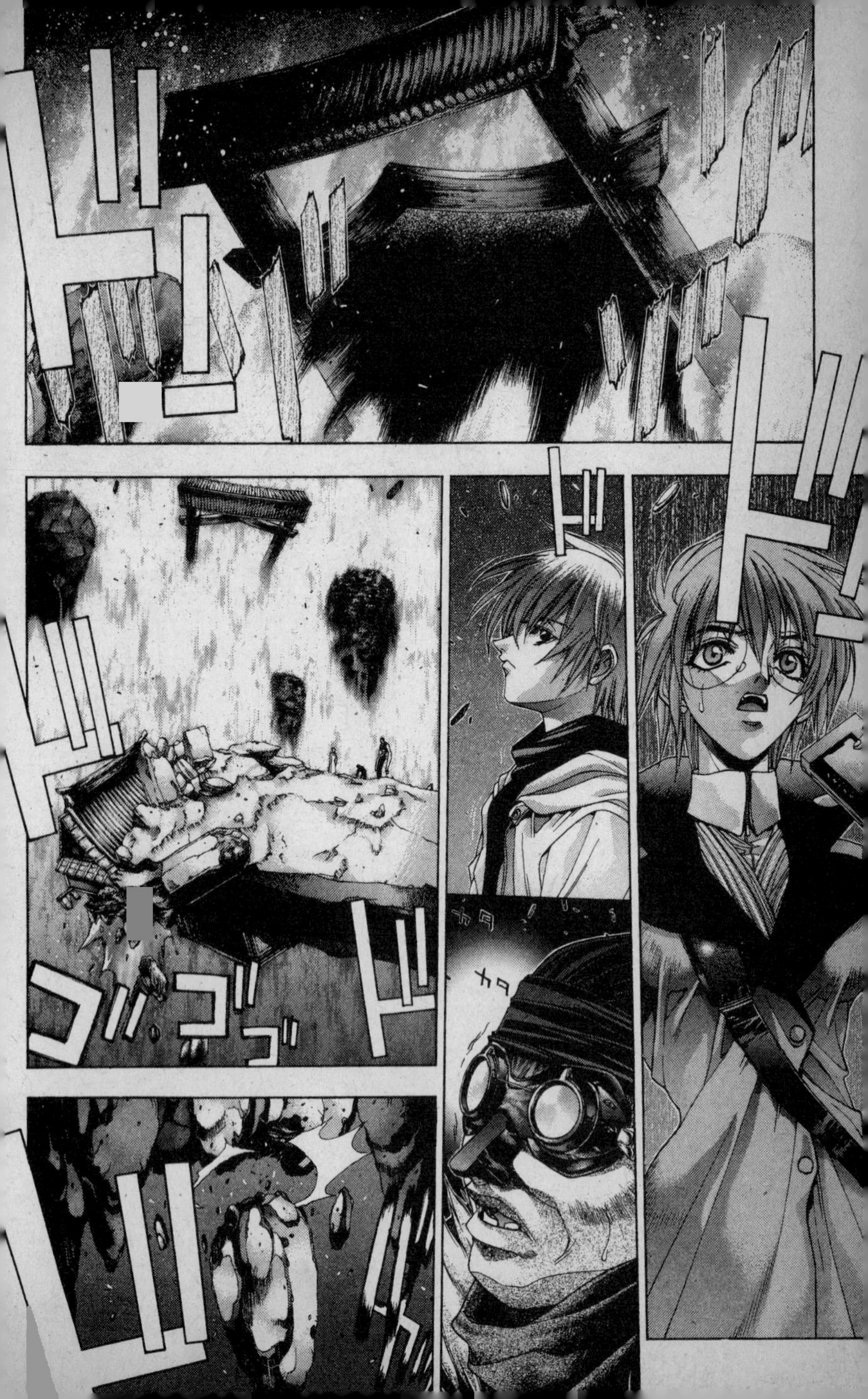

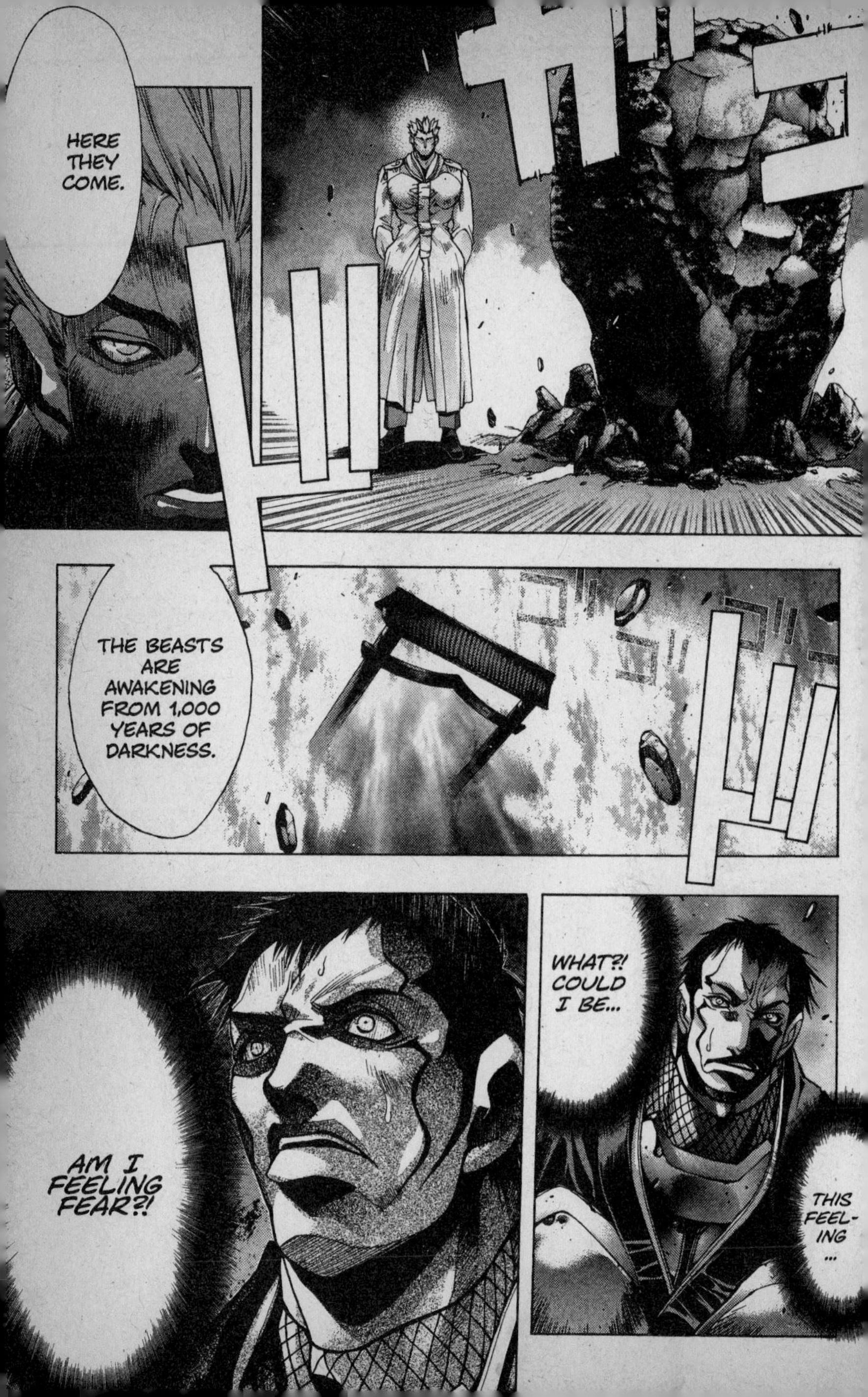
HERE THEY COME.
THE BEASTS ARE AWAKENING FROM 1,000 YEARS OF DARKNESS.
WHAT?! COULD I BE...
THIS FEEL-ING ...
AM I FEELING FEAR?!

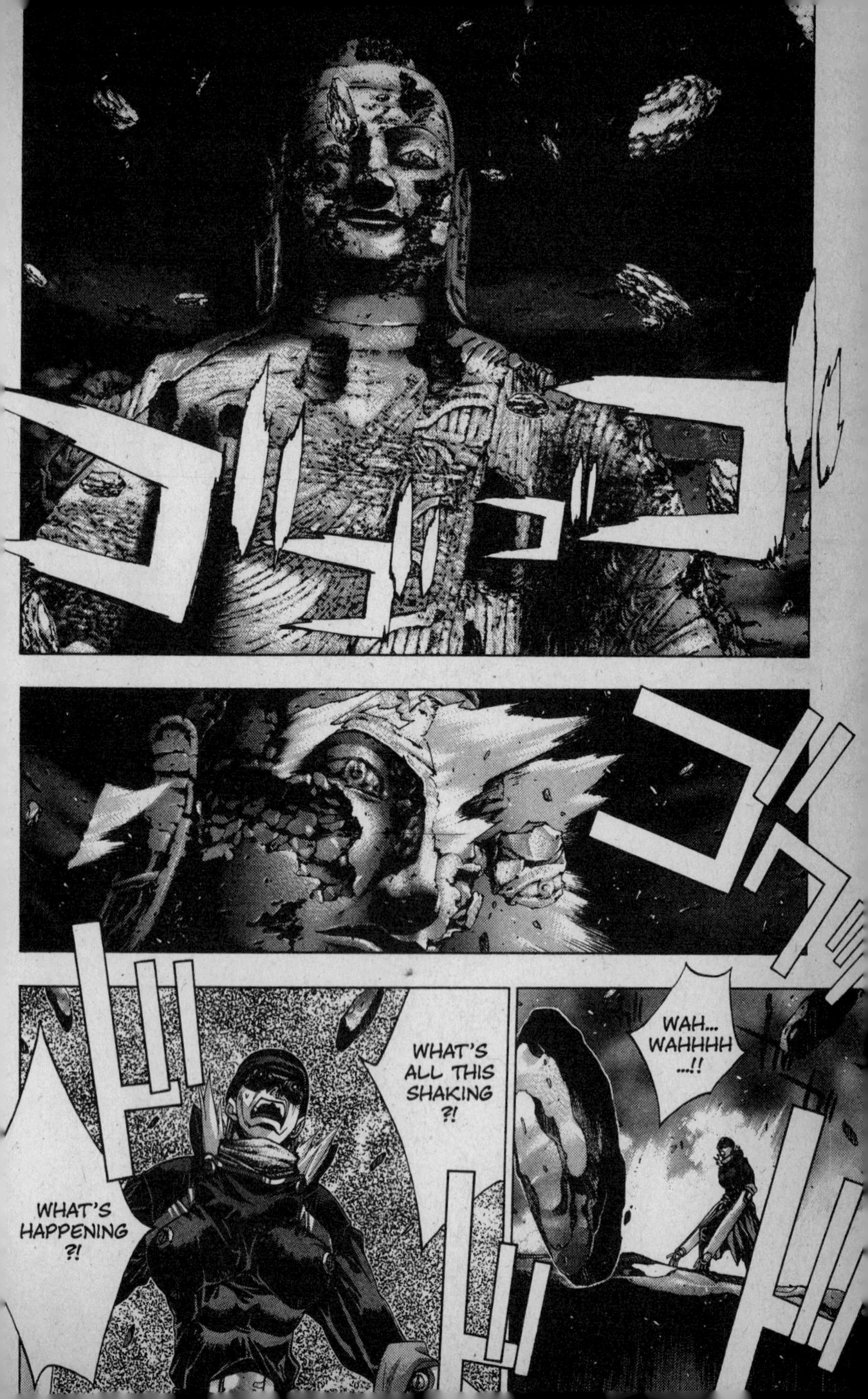
WAH... WAHHHH ...!!
WHAT'S ALL THIS SHAKING ?!
WHAT'S HAPPENING ?!

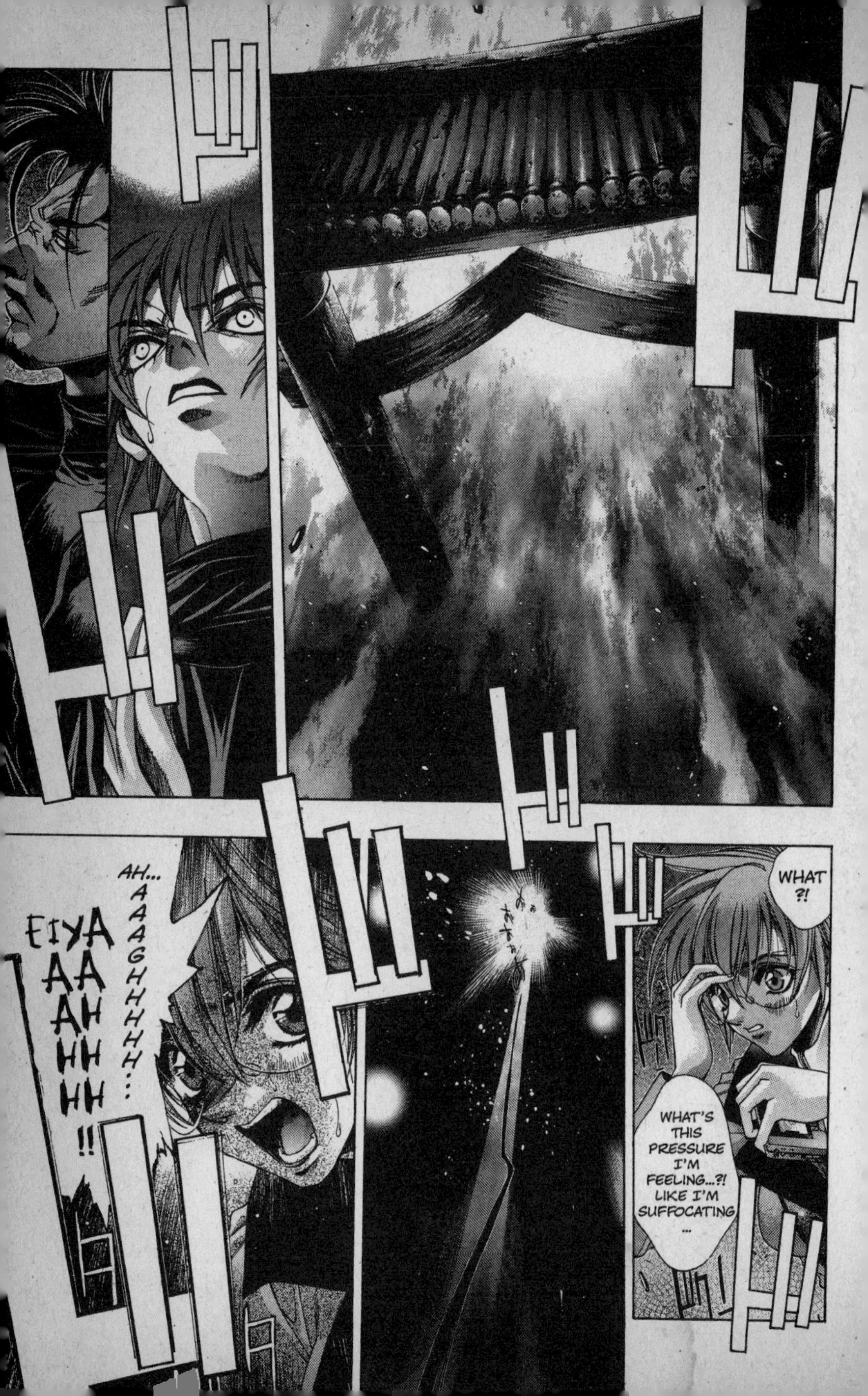
WHAT ?!
WHAT'S THIS PRESSURE I'M FEELING...?! LIKE I'M SUFFOCATING ...
AH... AAAAGHHHHHH...
EIYAAAAHHHHHH!!

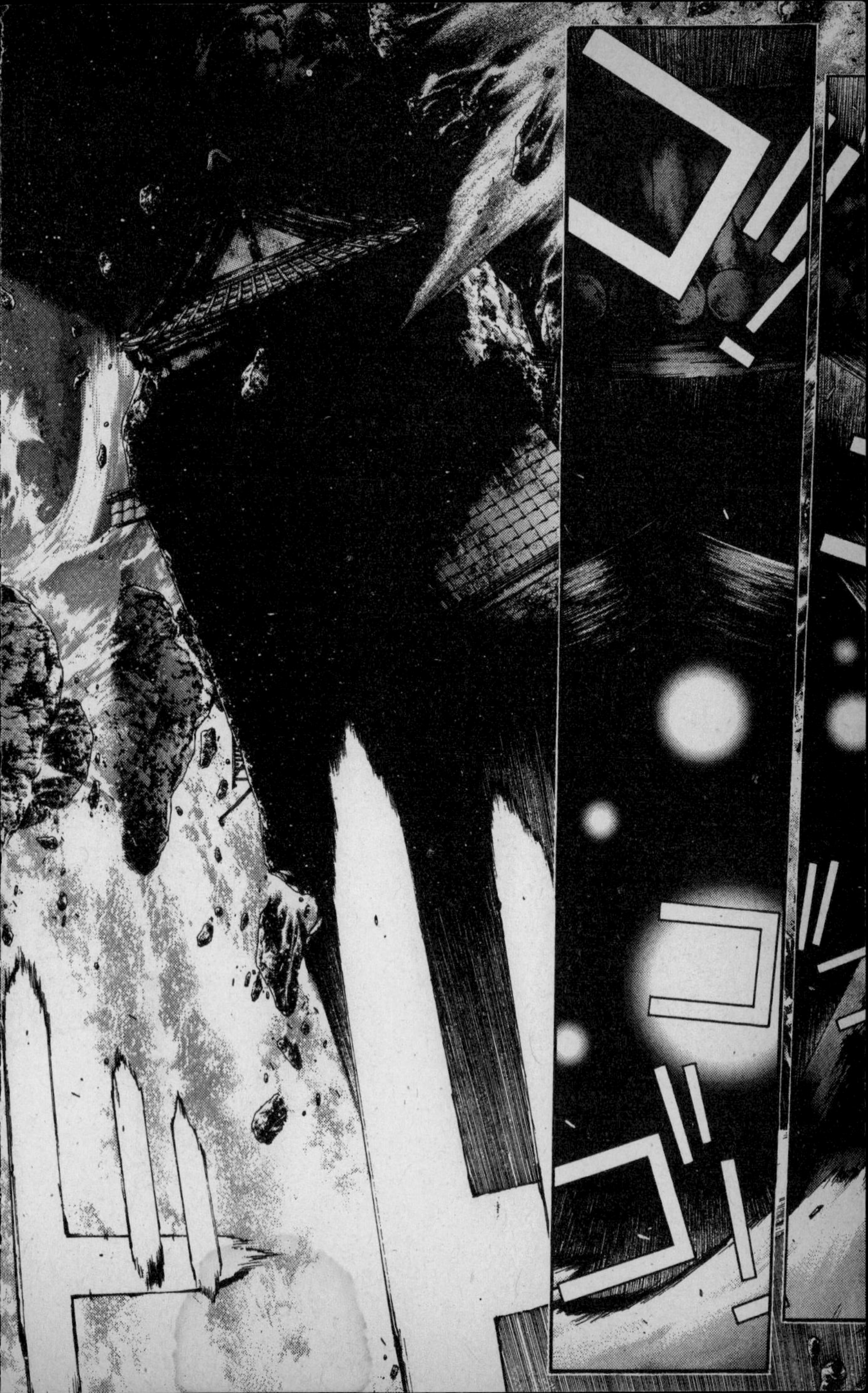
ゴゴゴ

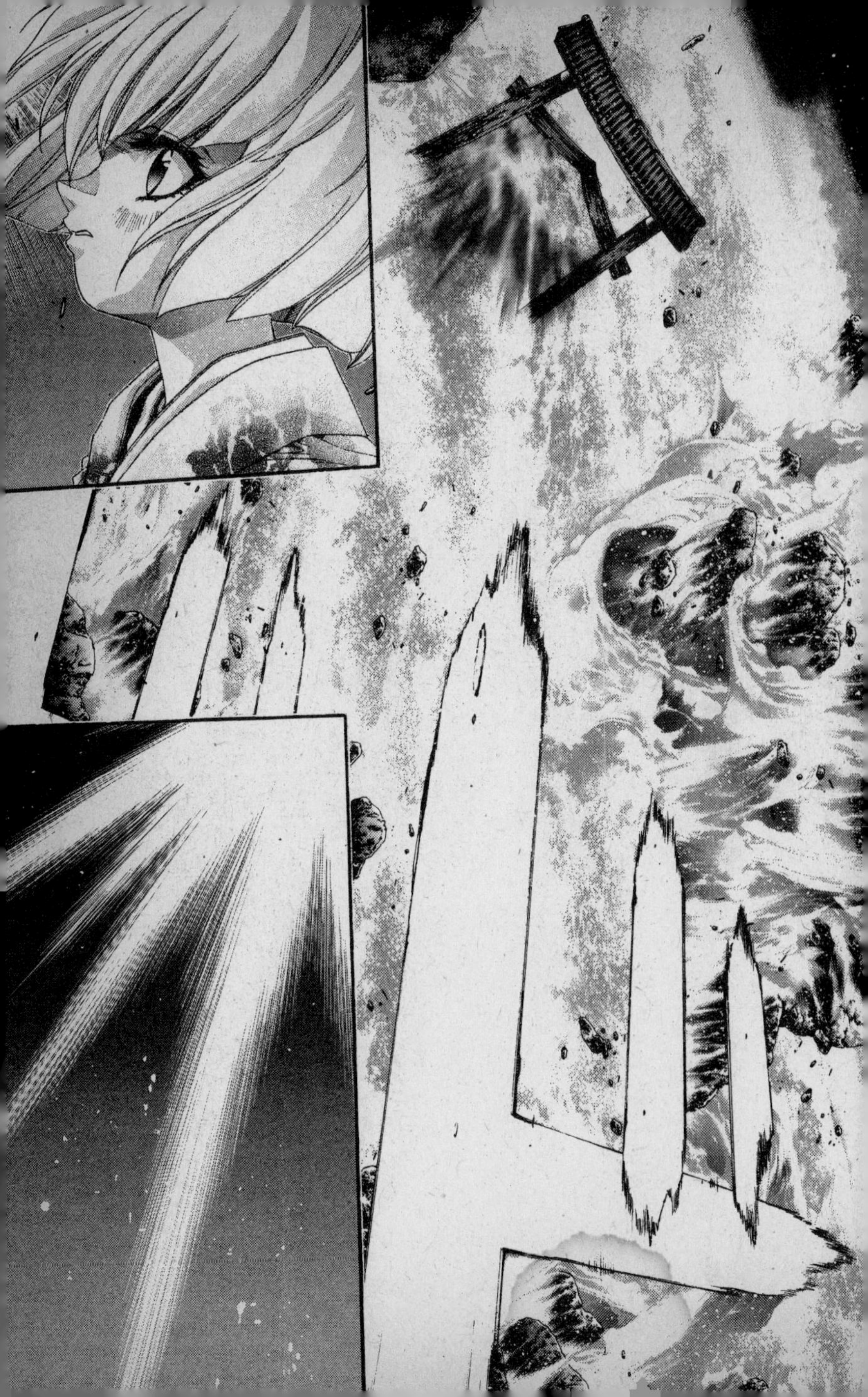

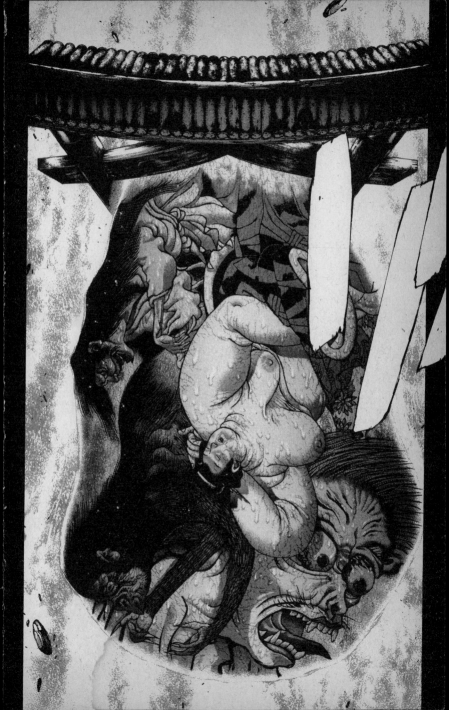

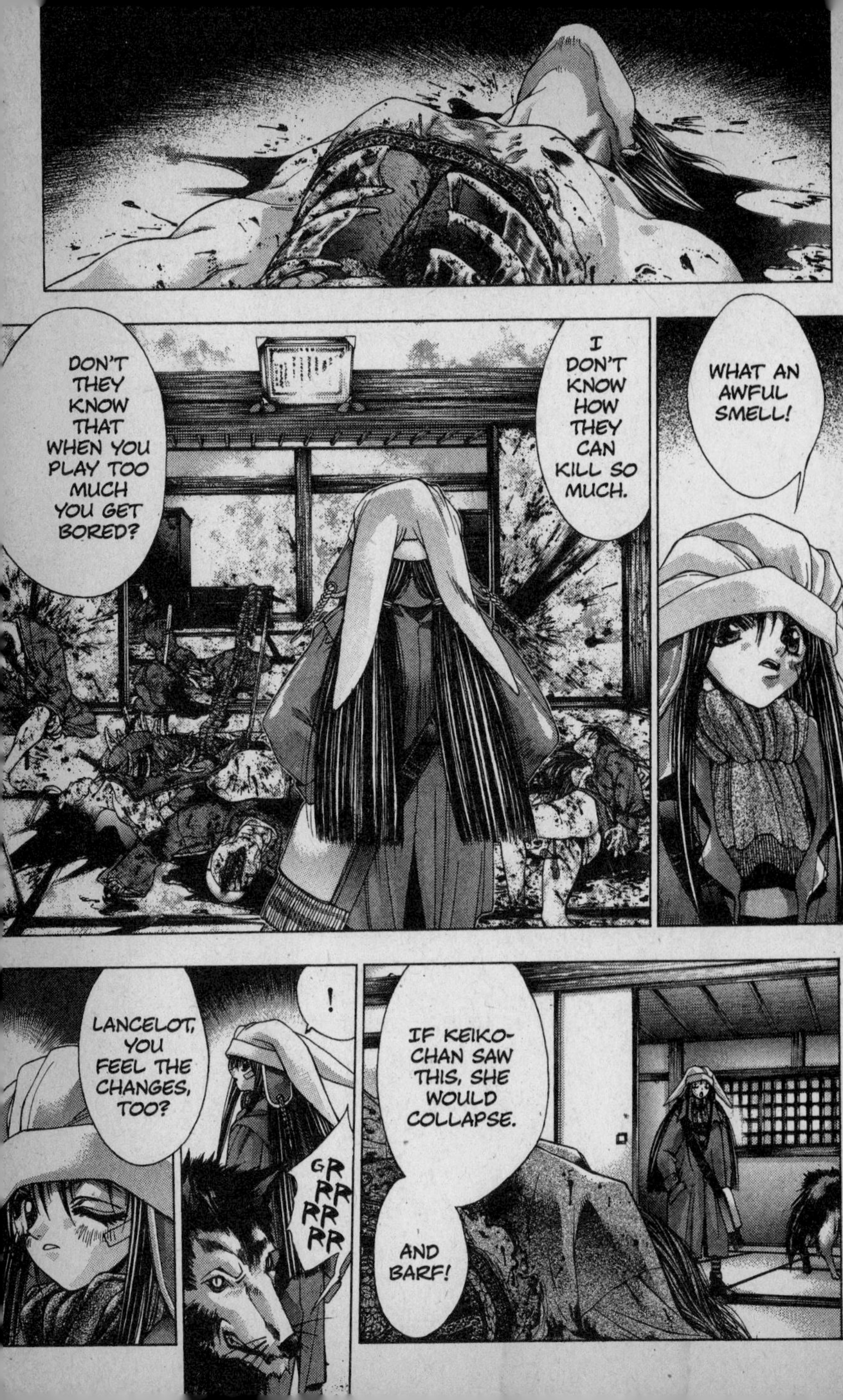
WHAT AN AWFUL SMELL!
I DON'T KNOW HOW THEY CAN KILL SO MUCH.
DON'T THEY KNOW THAT WHEN YOU PLAY TOO MUCH YOU GET BORED?
IF KEIKO-CHAN SAW THIS, SHE WOULD COLLAPSE.
AND BARF!
!
LANCELOT, YOU FEEL THE CHANGES, TOO?
GRRRRRRRR

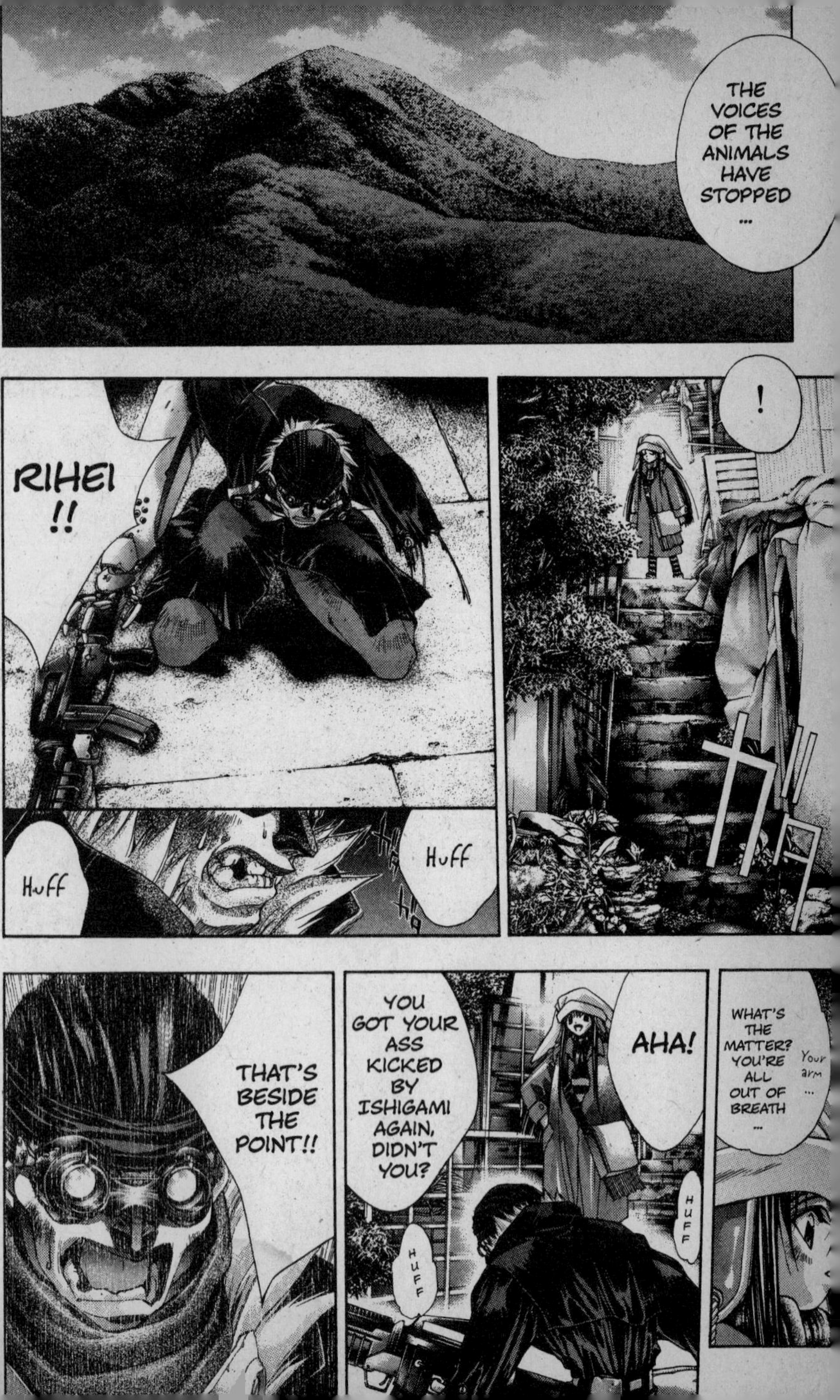
THE VOICES OF THE ANIMALS HAVE STOPPED ...
!
RIHEI !!
Huff
Huff
WHAT'S THE MATTER? YOU'RE ALL OUT OF BREATH ...
Your arm ...
AHA!
HUFF
YOU GOT YOUR ASS KICKED BY ISHIGAMI AGAIN, DIDN'T YOU?
HUFF
THAT'S BESIDE THE POINT!!

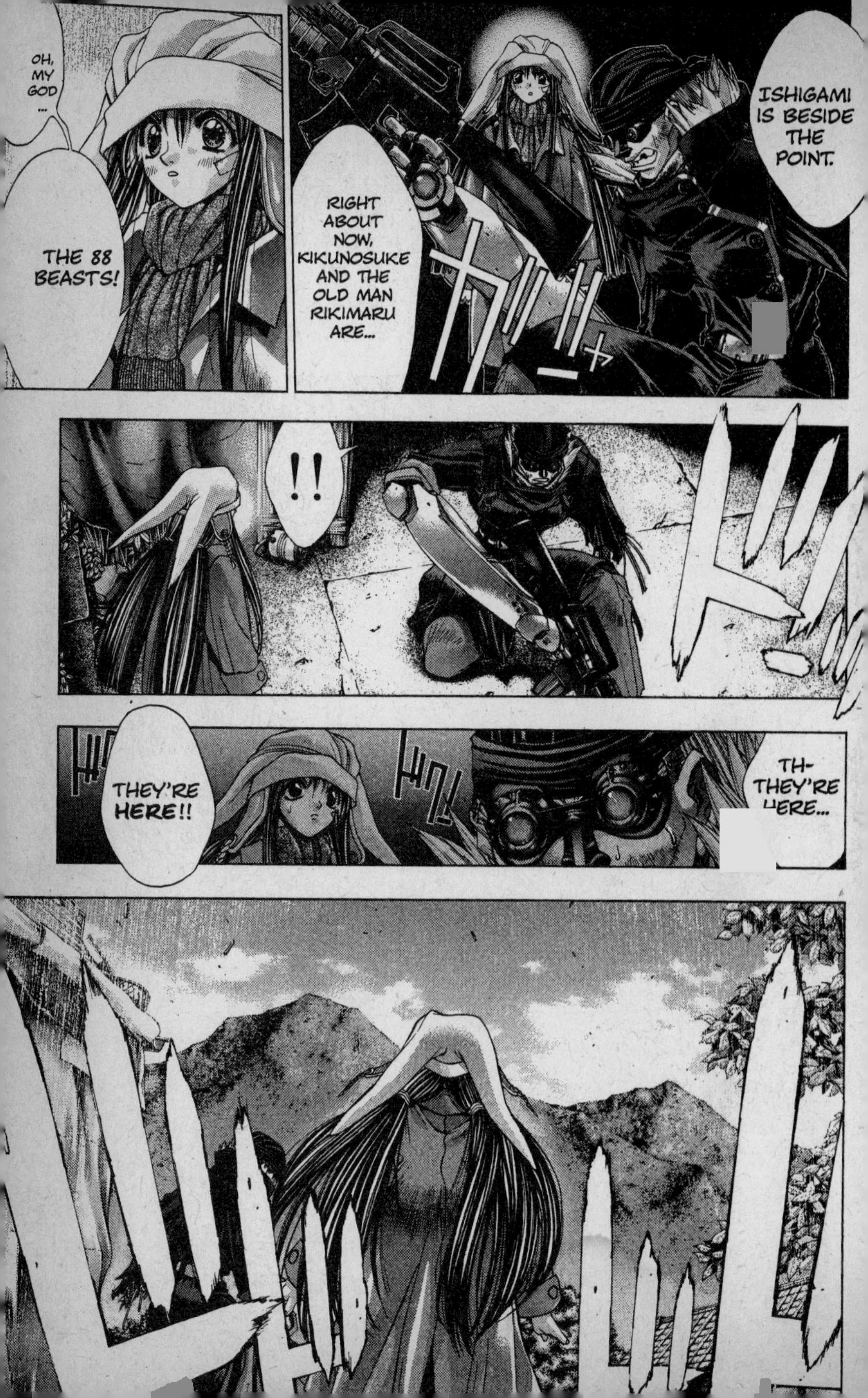
ISHIGAMI IS BESIDE THE POINT.
RIGHT ABOUT NOW, KIKUNOSUKE AND THE OLD MAN RIKIMARU ARE...
OH, MY GOD ...
THE 88 BEASTS!
!!
TH-THEY'RE HERE...
THEY'RE HERE!!

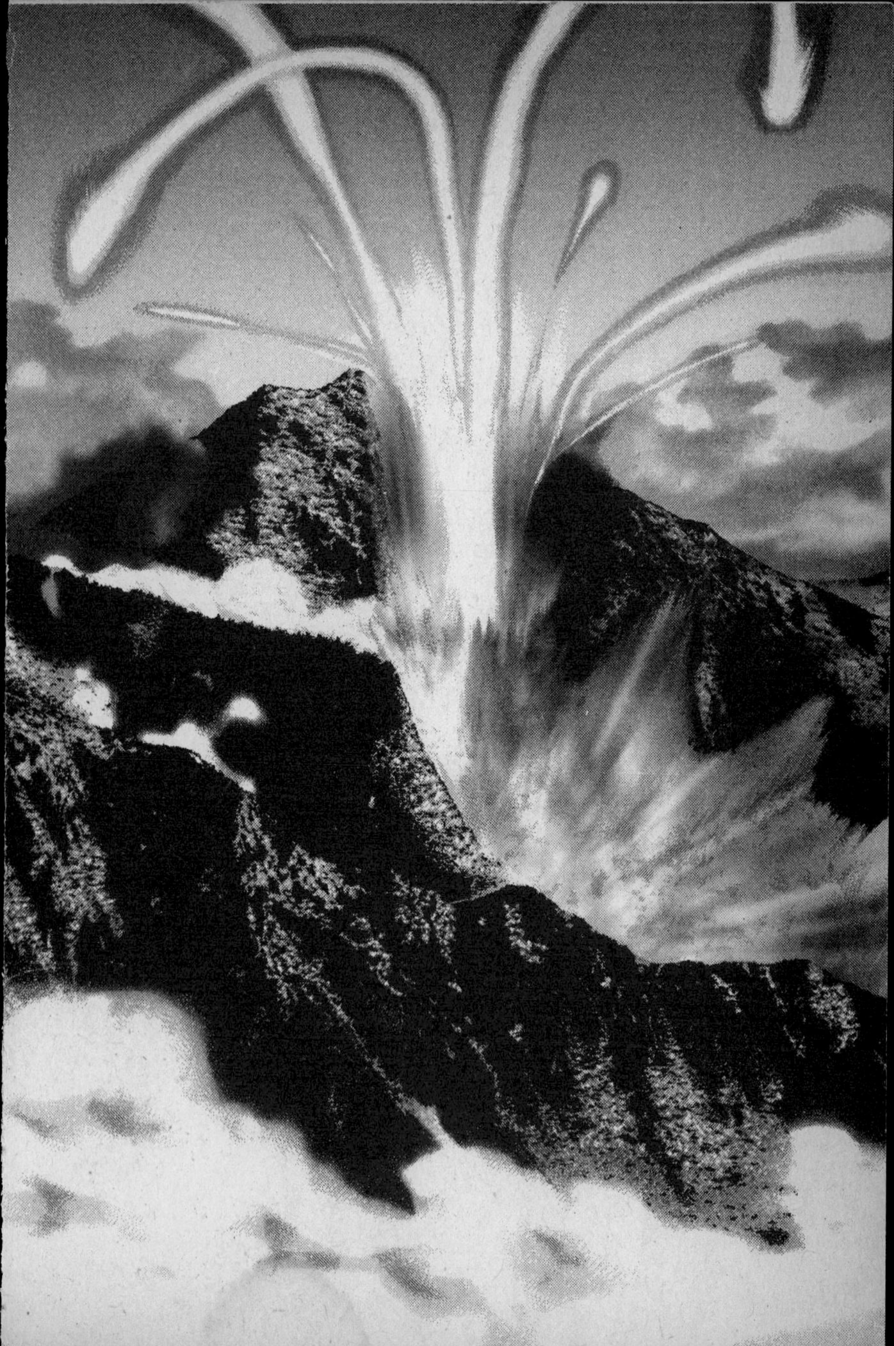

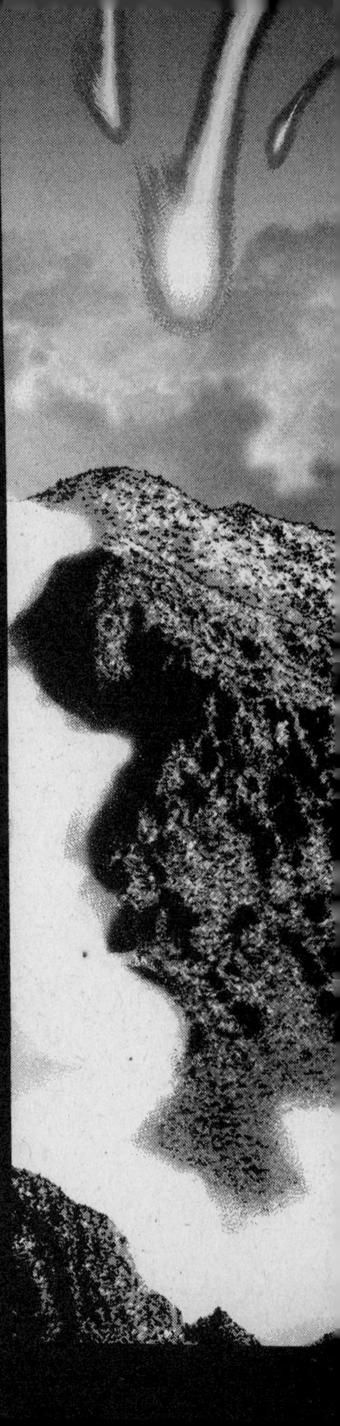
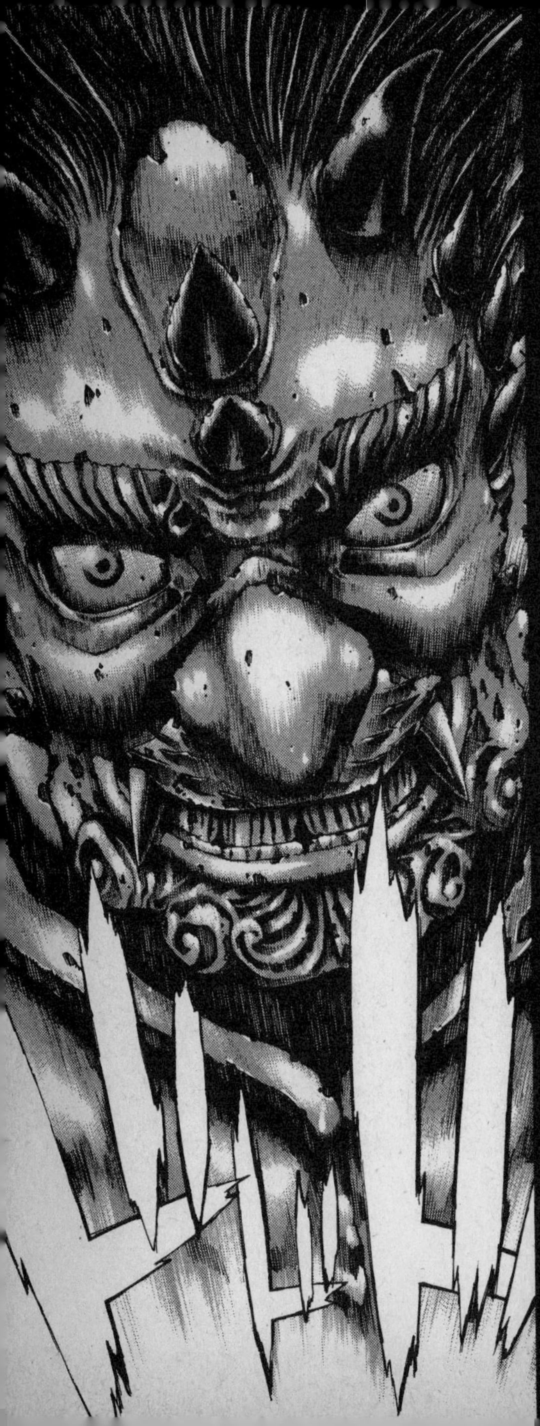

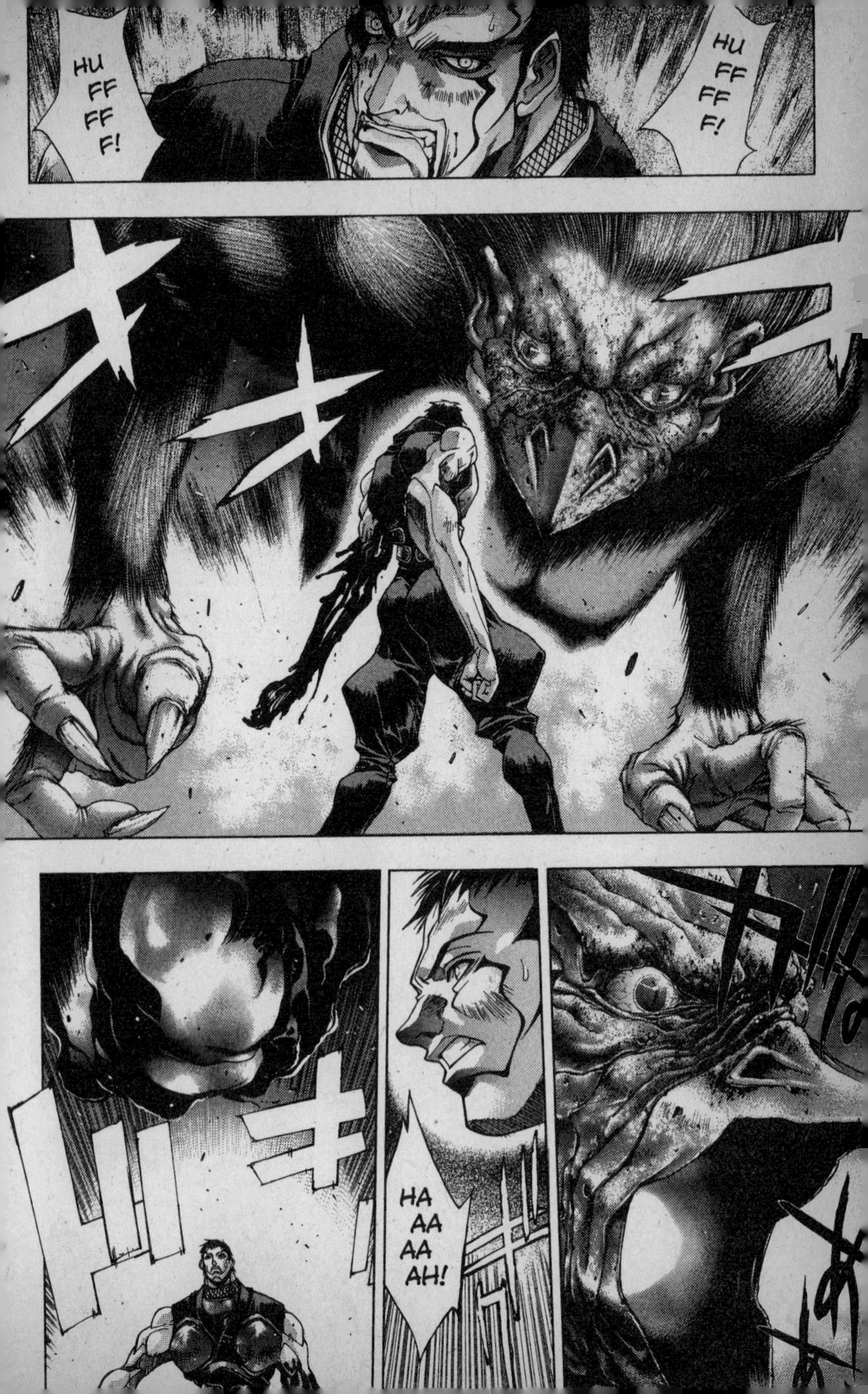
HU FF FF F!
HU FF FF F!
HA AA AA AH!

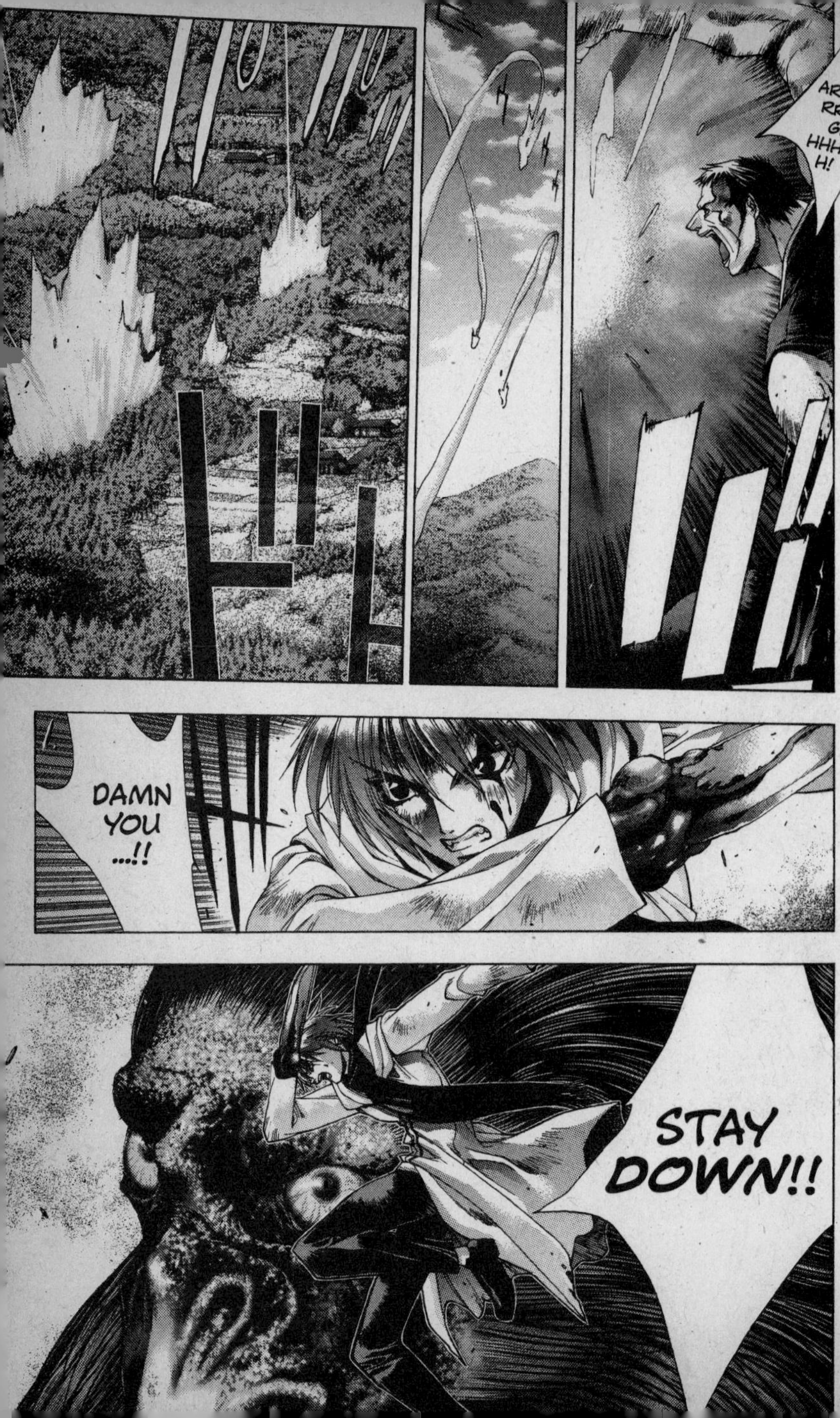
ARR
RRR
GHH
HHH
H!
DAMN
YOU
...!!
STAY
DOWN!!

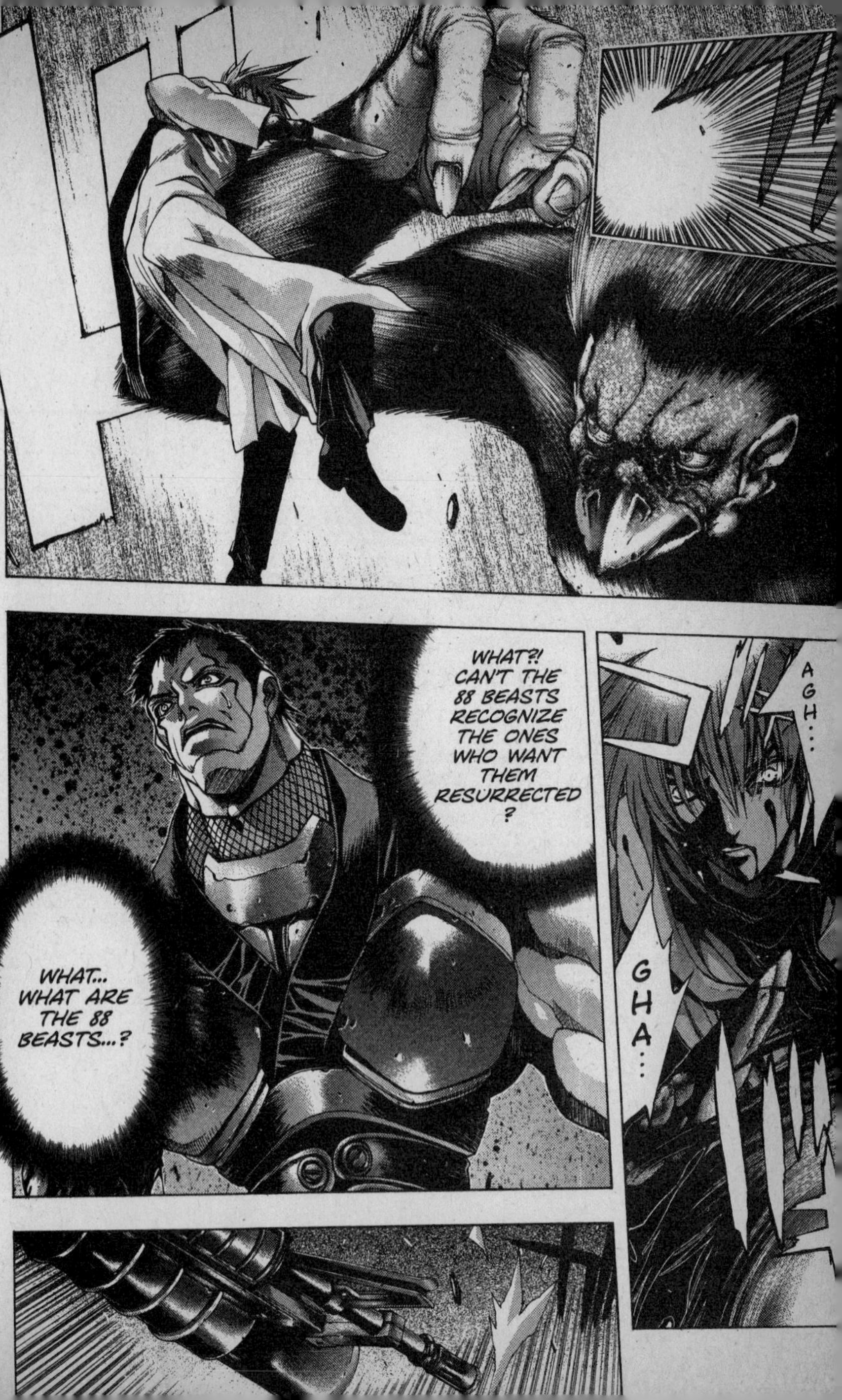
AGH...
GHA...
WHAT?! CAN'T THE 88 BEASTS RECOGNIZE THE ONES WHO WANT THEM RESURRECTED?
WHAT... WHAT ARE THE 88 BEASTS...?

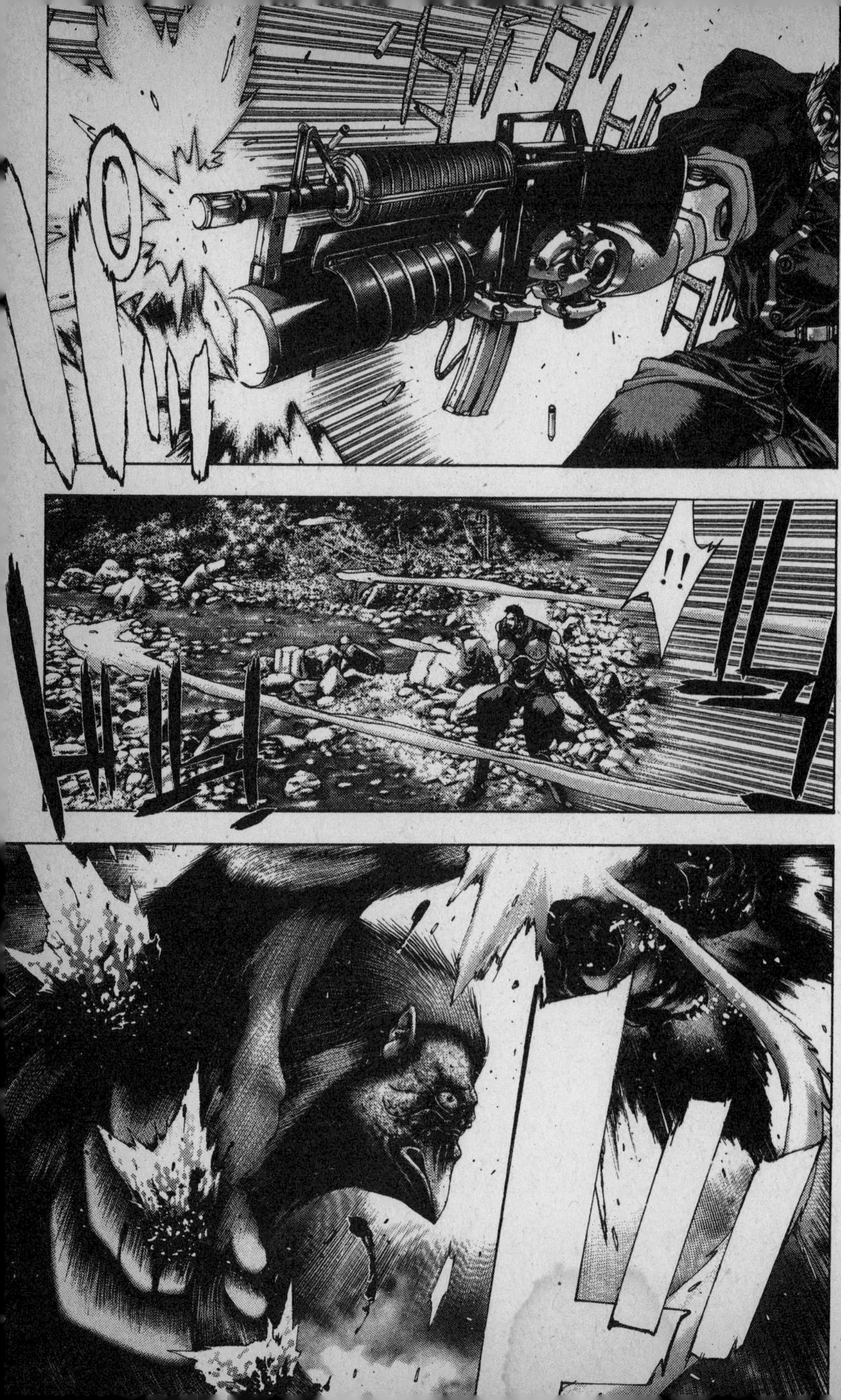
!!

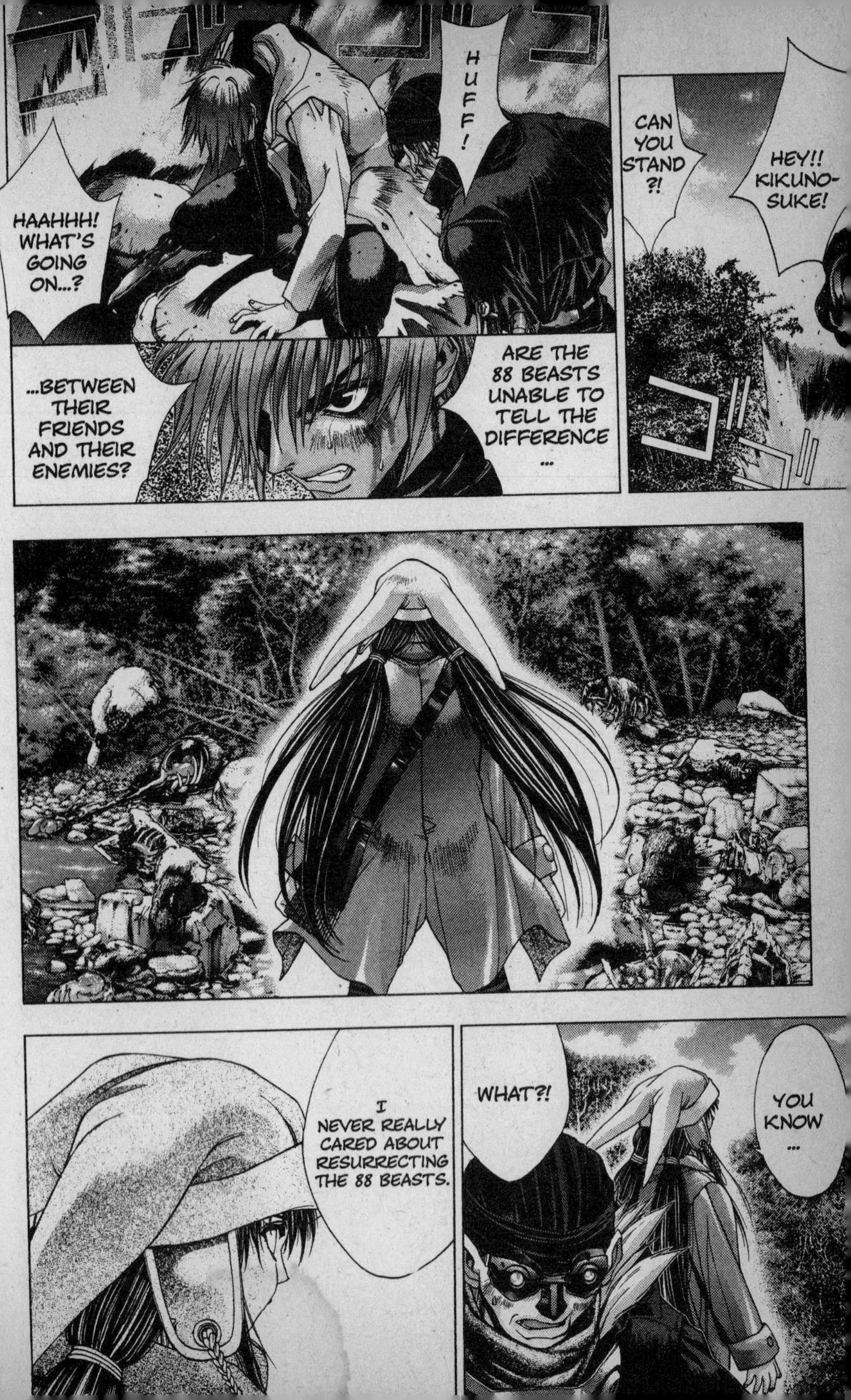
HEY!! KIKUNO-SUKE!
CAN YOU STAND ?!
HUFF!
HAAHHH! WHAT'S GOING ON...?
ARE THE 88 BEASTS UNABLE TO TELL THE DIFFERENCE ...
...BETWEEN THEIR FRIENDS AND THEIR ENEMIES?
YOU KNOW ...
WHAT?!
I NEVER REALLY CARED ABOUT RESURRECTING THE 88 BEASTS.

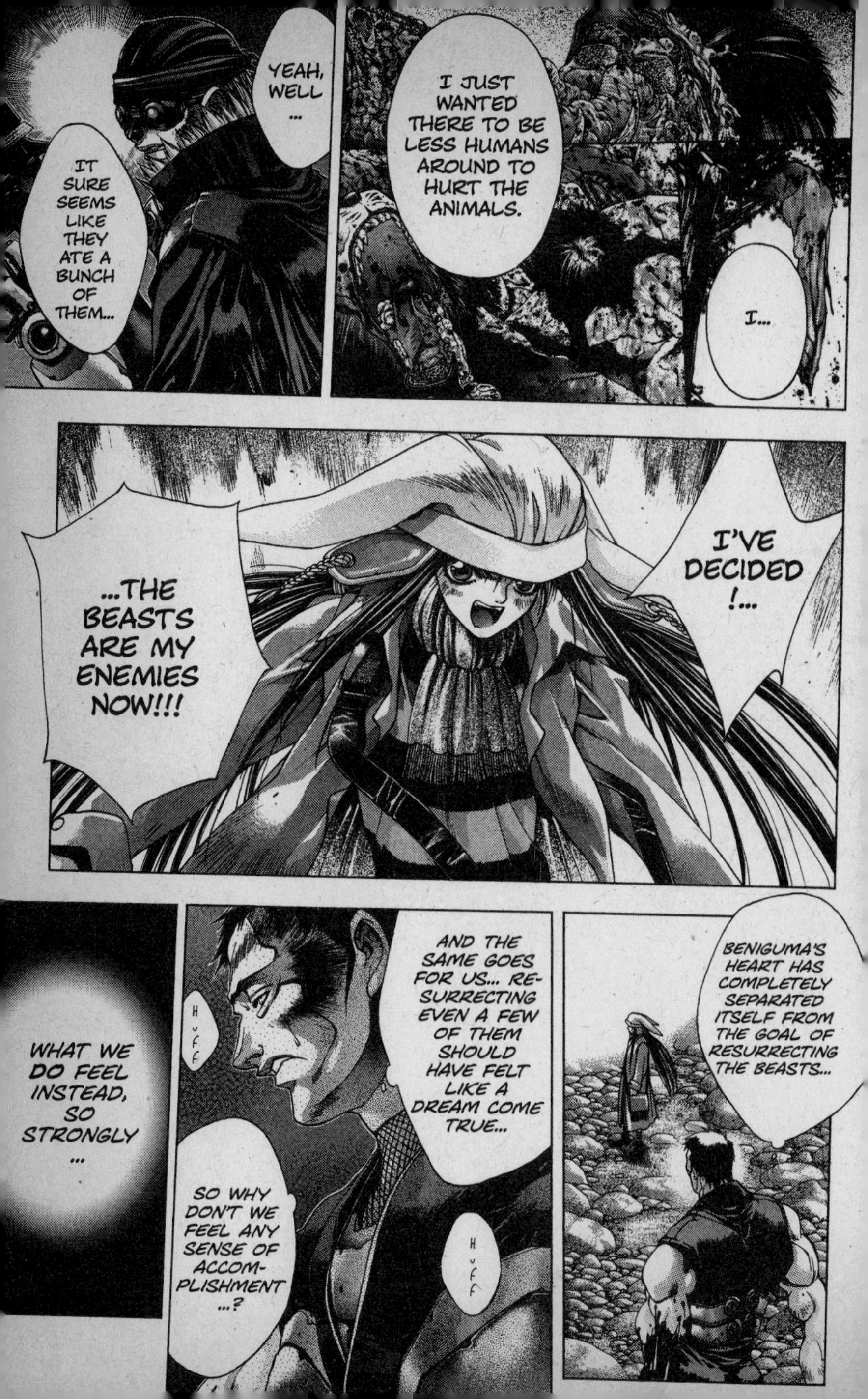
I...
I JUST WANTED THERE TO BE LESS HUMANS AROUND TO HURT THE ANIMALS.
YEAH, WELL...
IT SURE SEEMS LIKE THEY ATE A BUNCH OF THEM...
I'VE DECIDED!...
...THE BEASTS ARE MY ENEMIES NOW!!!
BENIGUMA'S HEART HAS COMPLETELY SEPARATED ITSELF FROM THE GOAL OF RESURRECTING THE BEASTS...
AND THE SAME GOES FOR US... RE-SURRECTING EVEN A FEW OF THEM SHOULD HAVE FELT LIKE A DREAM COME TRUE...
Huff
SO WHY DON'T WE FEEL ANY SENSE OF ACCOM-PLISHMENT...?
Huff
WHAT WE DO FEEL INSTEAD, SO STRONGLY...

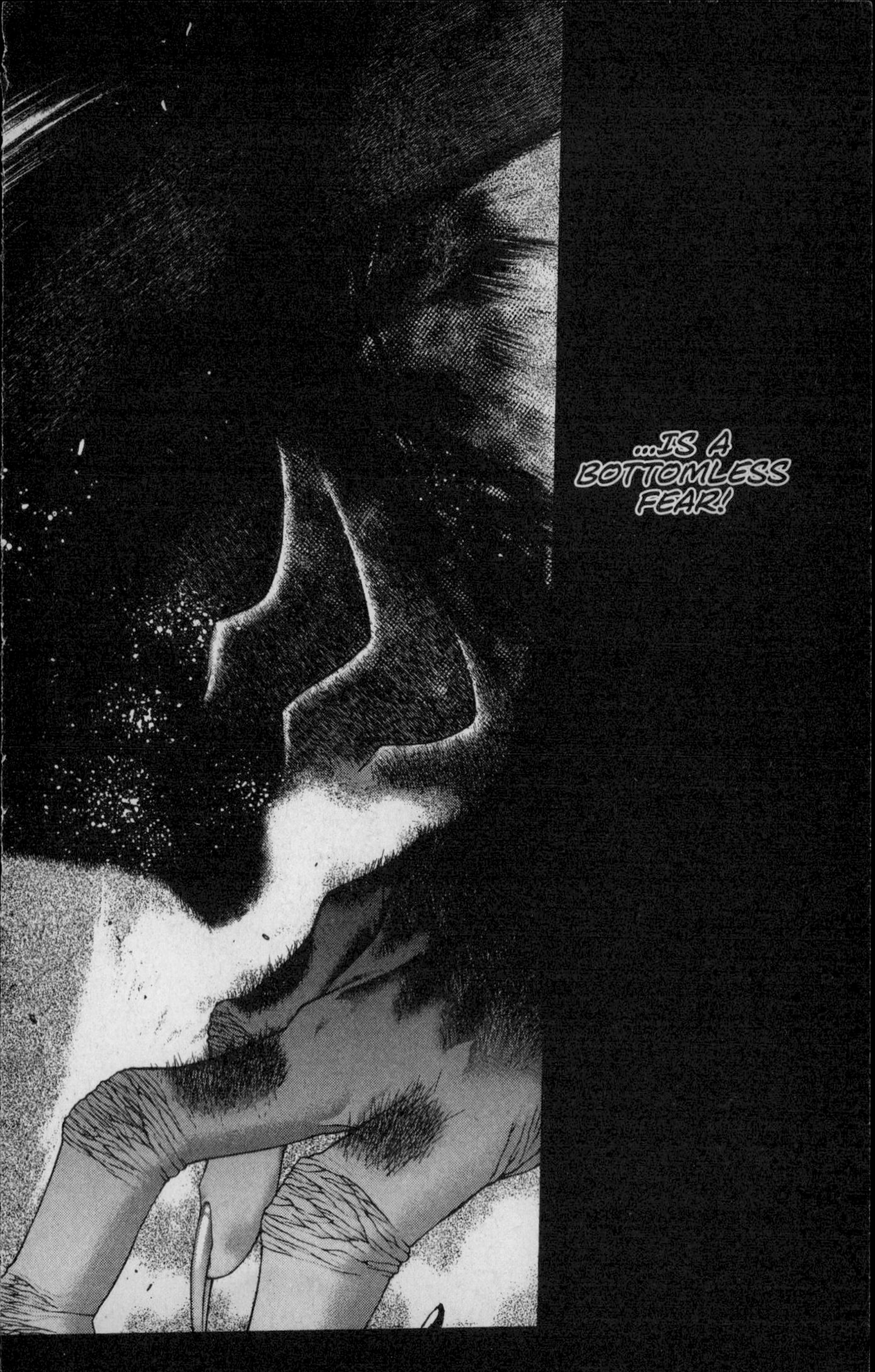
...IS A BOTTOMLESS FEAR!

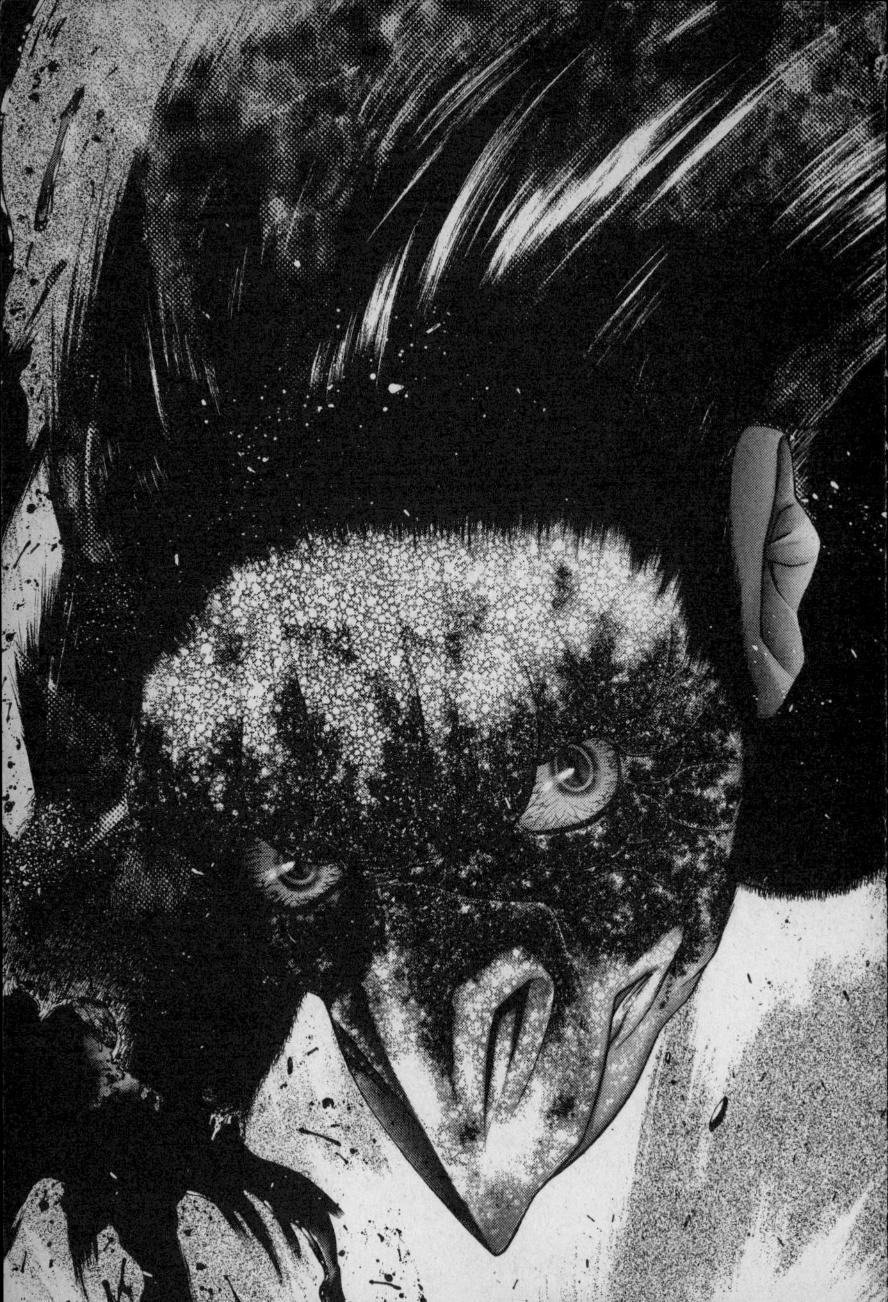

Chapter 13: Corrosion Part 2

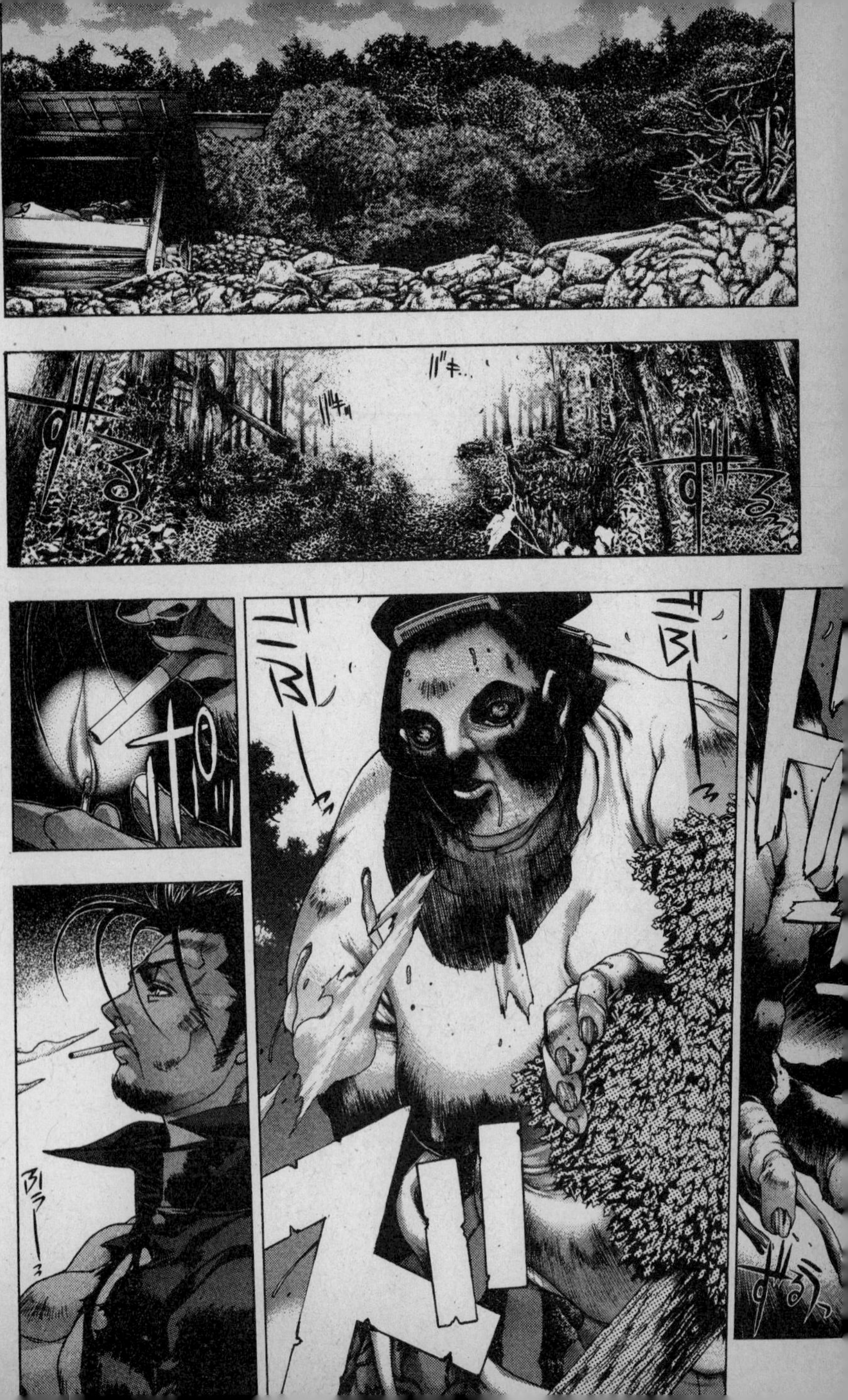
パキ...

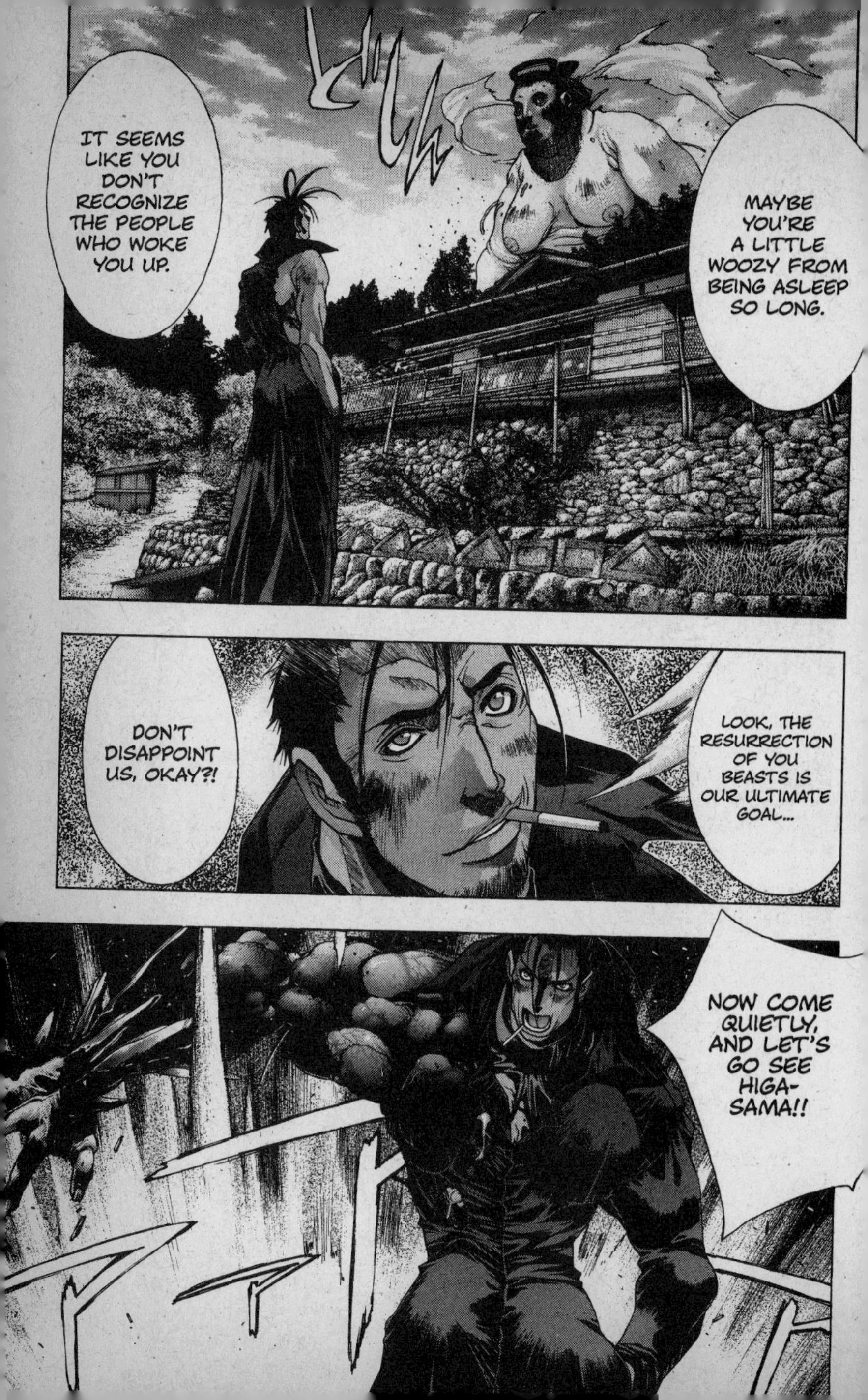
MAYBE YOU'RE A LITTLE WOOZY FROM BEING ASLEEP SO LONG.
IT SEEMS LIKE YOU DON'T RECOGNIZE THE PEOPLE WHO WOKE YOU UP.
LOOK, THE RESURRECTION OF YOU BEASTS IS OUR ULTIMATE GOAL...
DON'T DISAPPOINT US, OKAY?!
NOW COME QUIETLY, AND LET'S GO SEE HIGA-SAMA!!

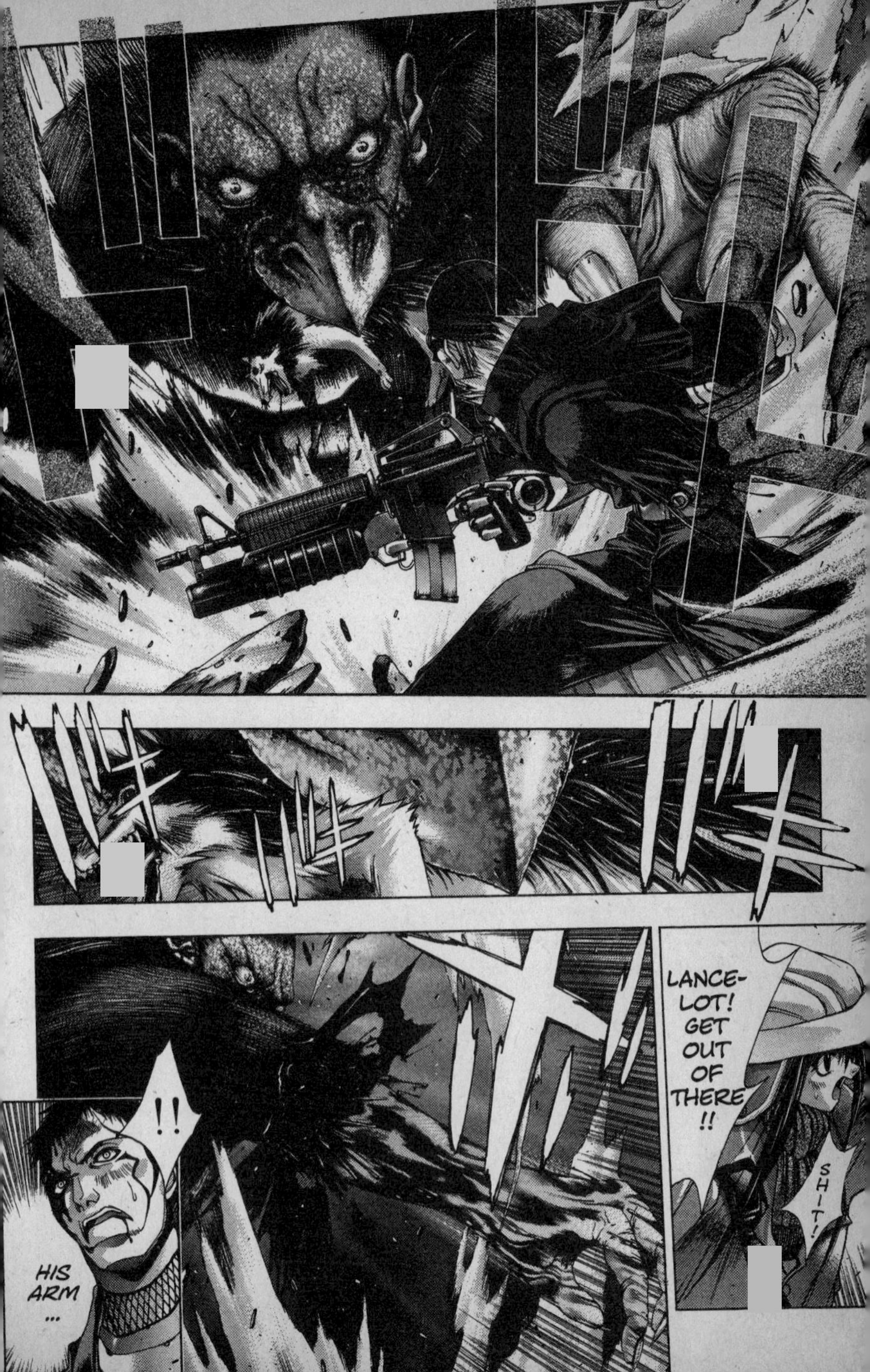
LANCE-LOT! GET OUT OF THERE!!
SHIT!
!!
HIS ARM ...

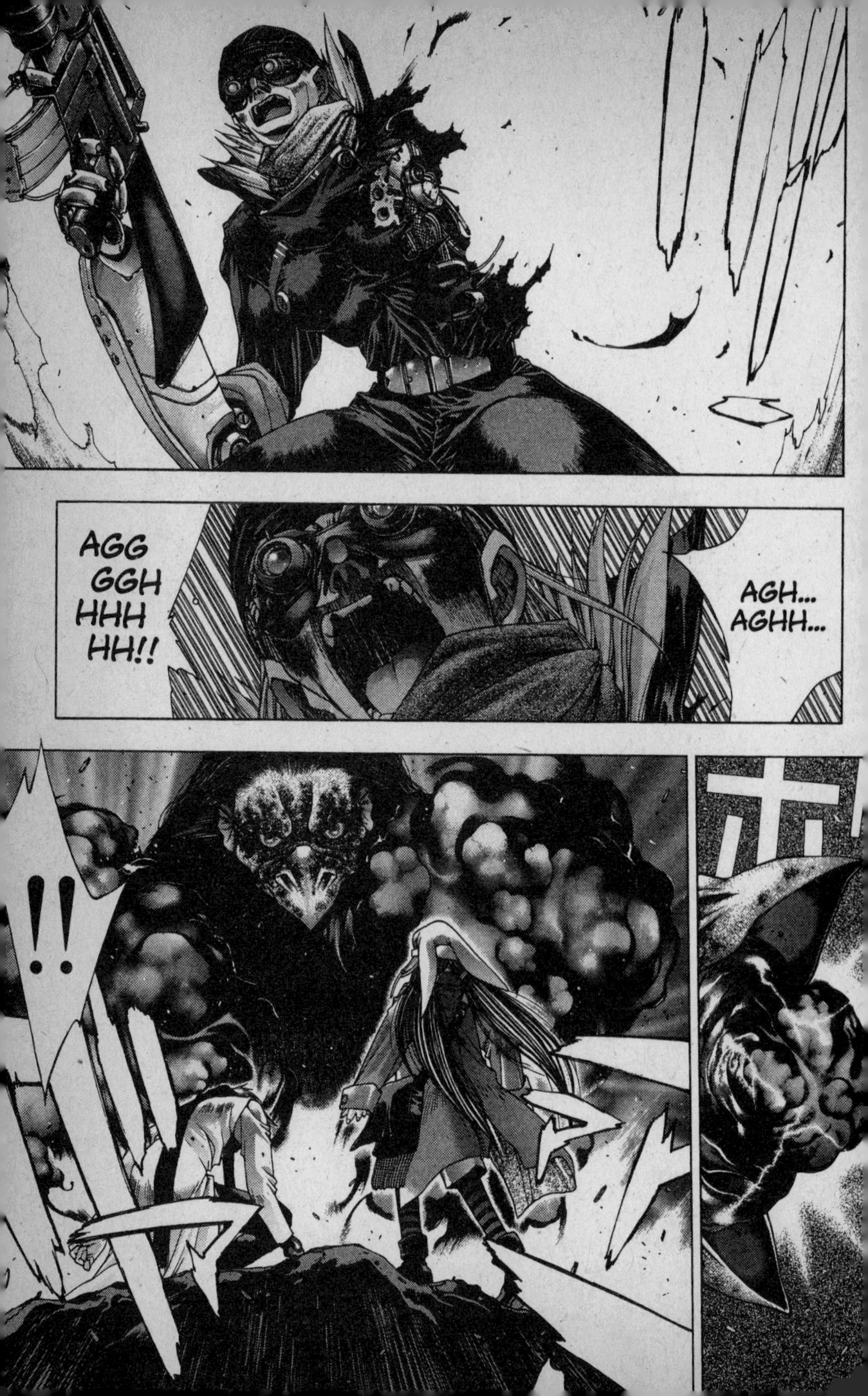
AGH... AGHH...
AGGGGHHHHHH!!
!!

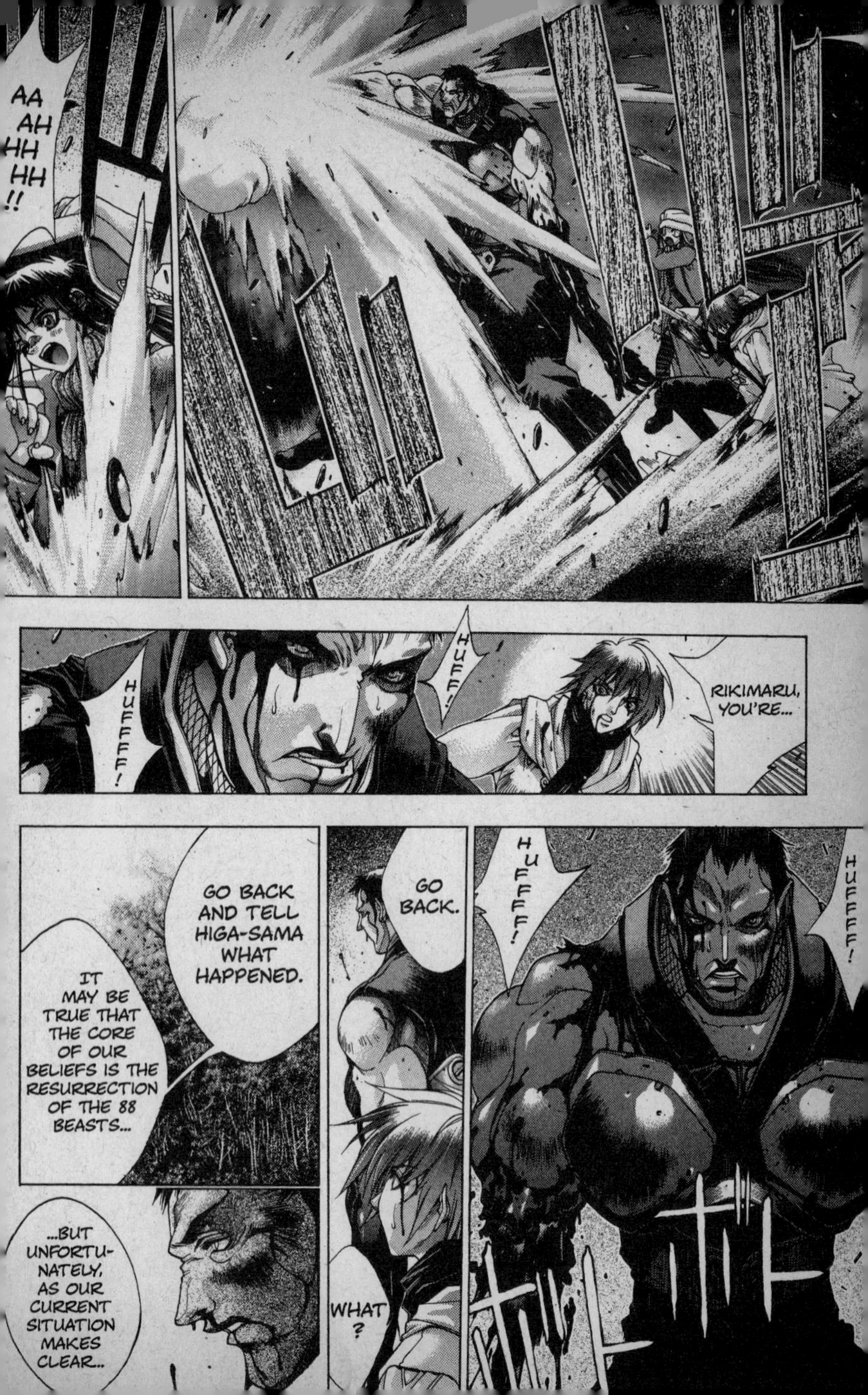
AAAHHHHH!!
RIKIMARU, YOU'RE...
HUFF!
HUFFFFF!
HUFFFFFF!
HUFFFF!
GO BACK.
WHAT?
GO BACK AND TELL HIGA-SAMA WHAT HAPPENED.
IT MAY BE TRUE THAT THE CORE OF OUR BELIEFS IS THE RESURRECTION OF THE 88 BEASTS...
...BUT UNFORTUNATELY, AS OUR CURRENT SITUATION MAKES CLEAR...

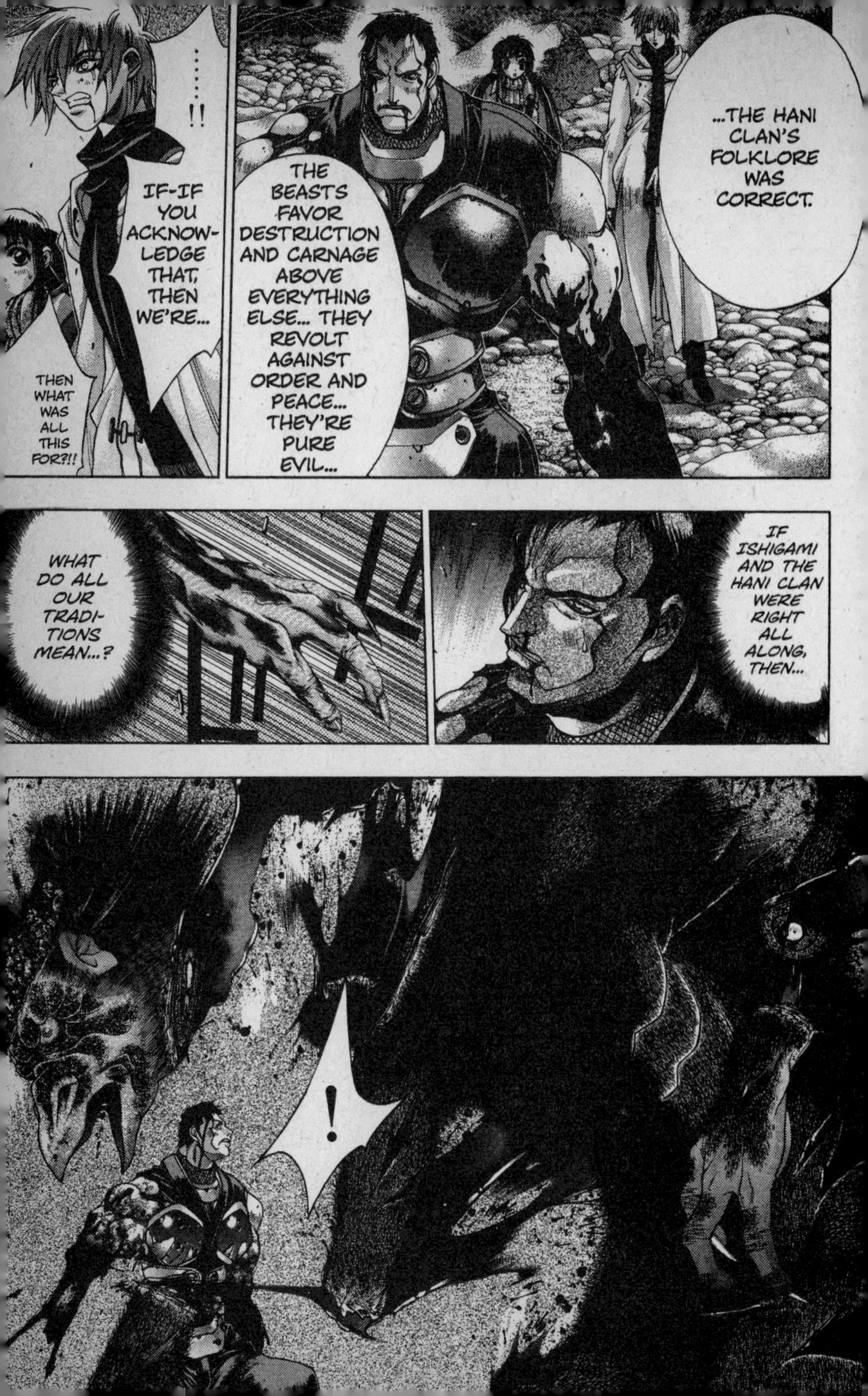
...THE HANI CLAN'S FOLKLORE WAS CORRECT.
THE BEASTS FAVOR DESTRUCTION AND CARNAGE ABOVE EVERYTHING ELSE... THEY REVOLT AGAINST ORDER AND PEACE... THEY'RE PURE EVIL...
......
!!
IF-IF YOU ACKNOWLEDGE THAT, THEN WE'RE...
THEN WHAT WAS ALL THIS FOR?!!
IF ISHIGAMI AND THE HANI CLAN WERE RIGHT ALL ALONG, THEN...
WHAT DO ALL OUR TRADITIONS MEAN...?
!

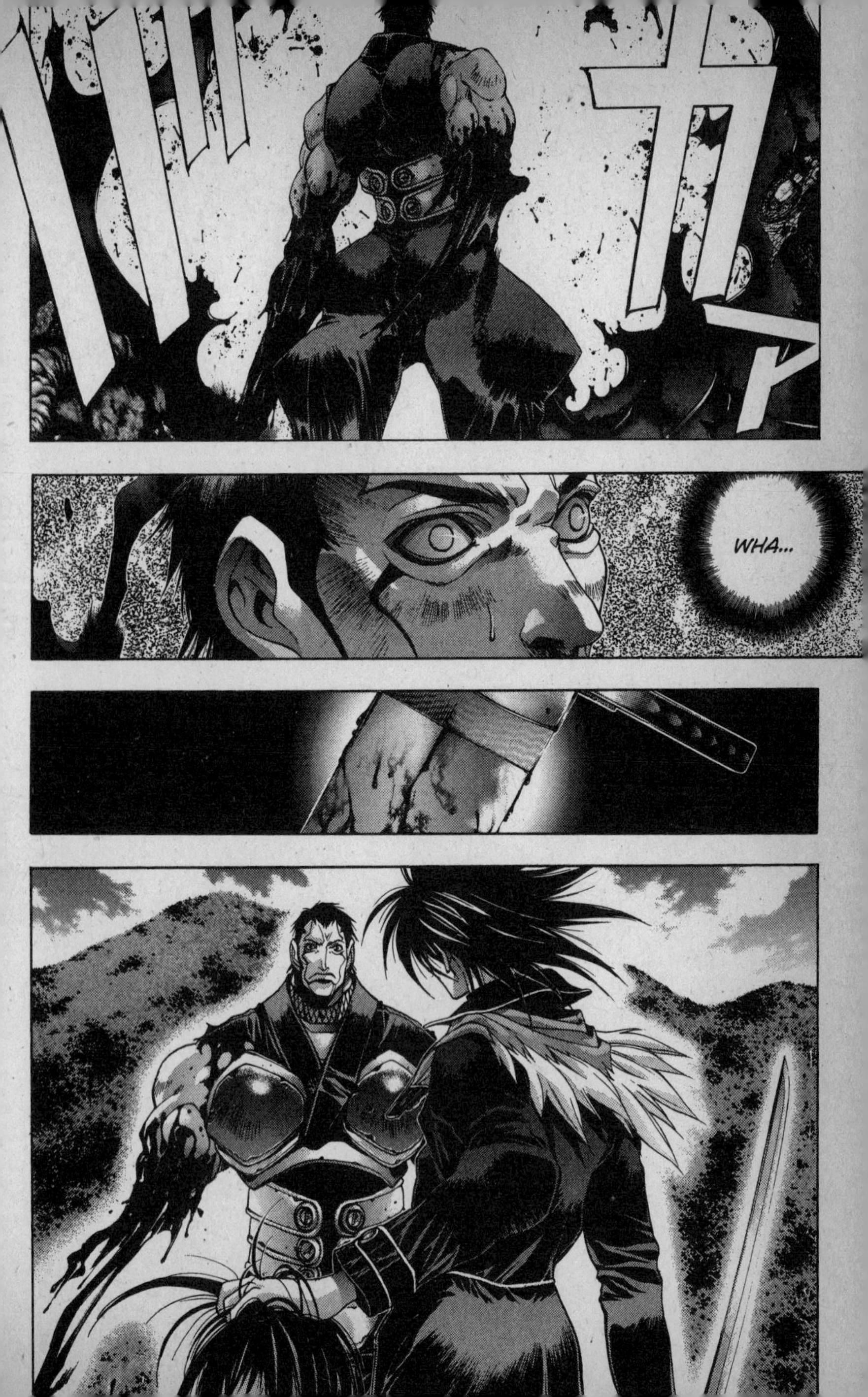
WHA...

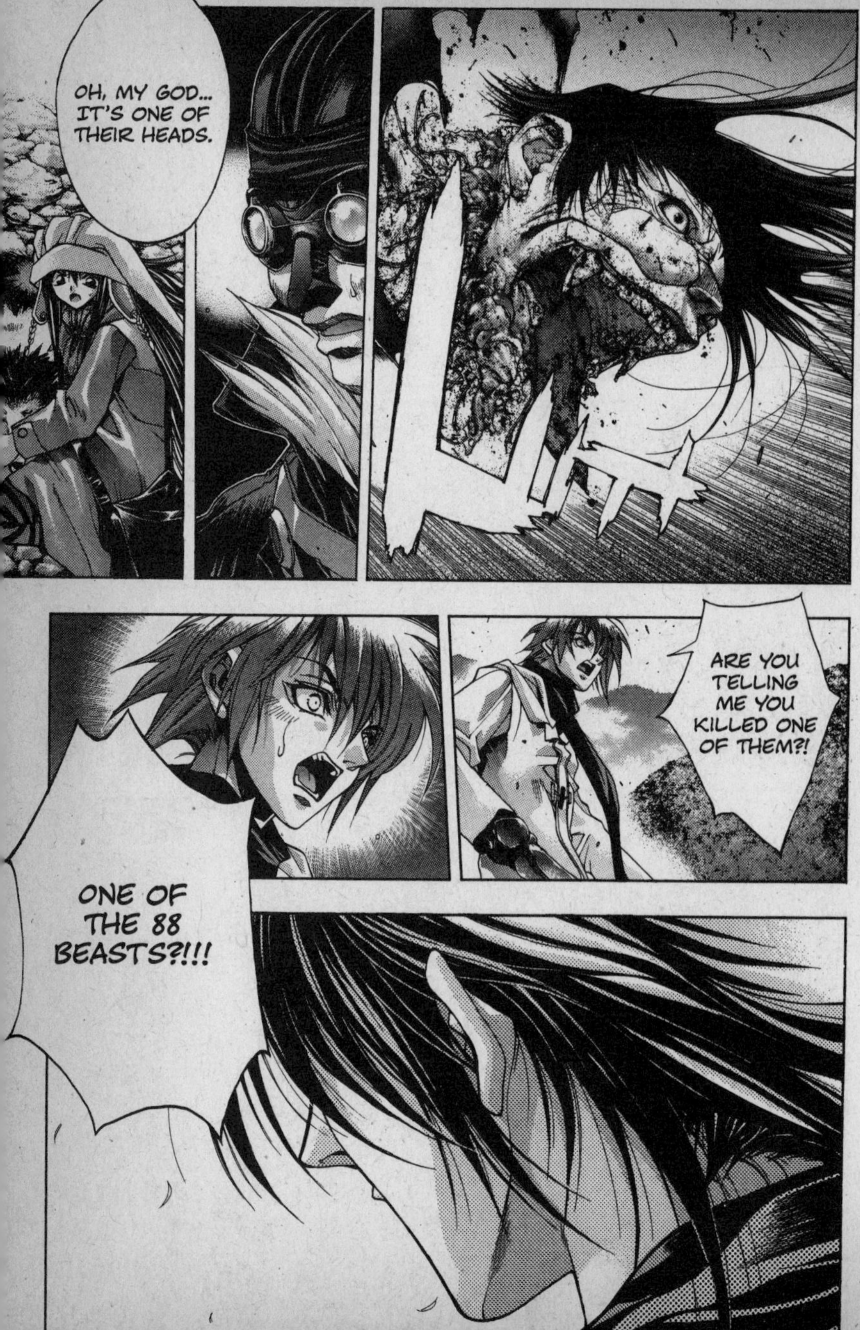
OH, MY GOD... IT'S ONE OF THEIR HEADS.
ARE YOU TELLING ME YOU KILLED ONE OF THEM?!
ONE OF THE 88 BEASTS?!!!

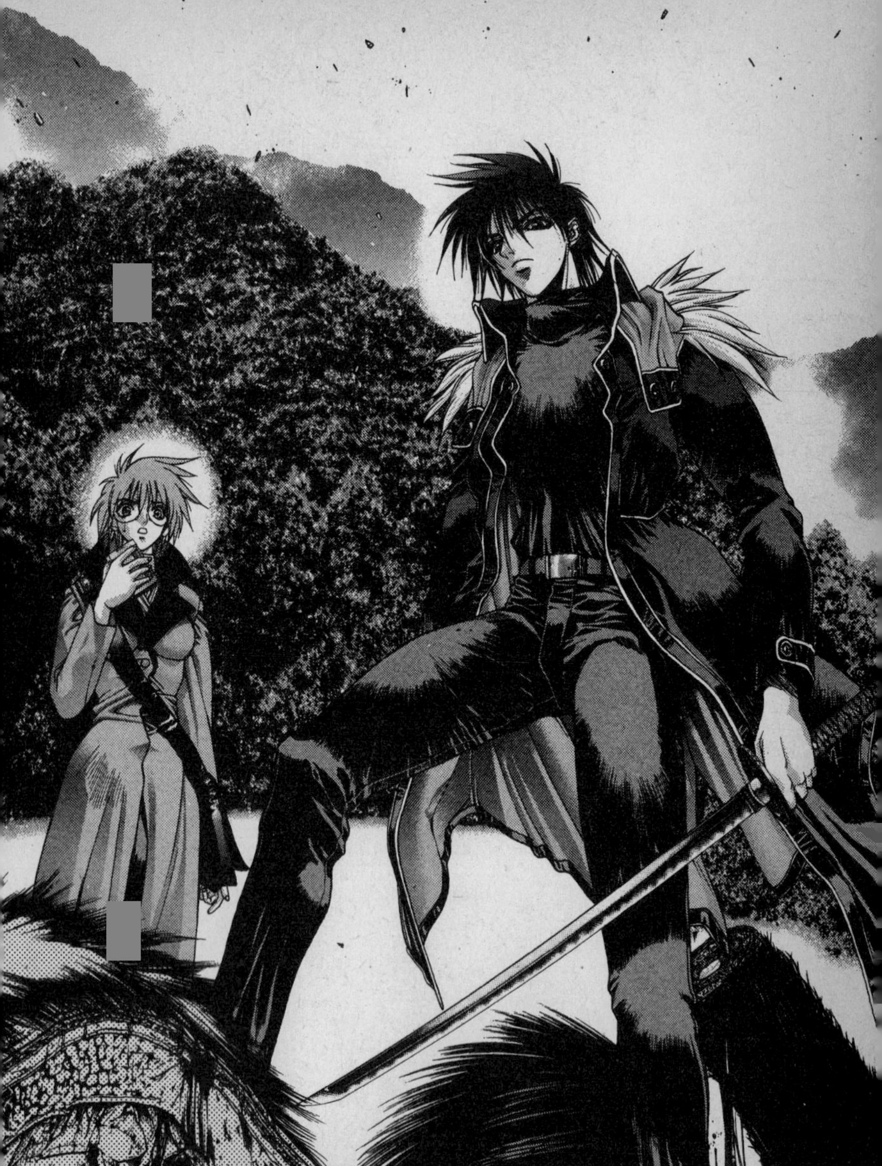

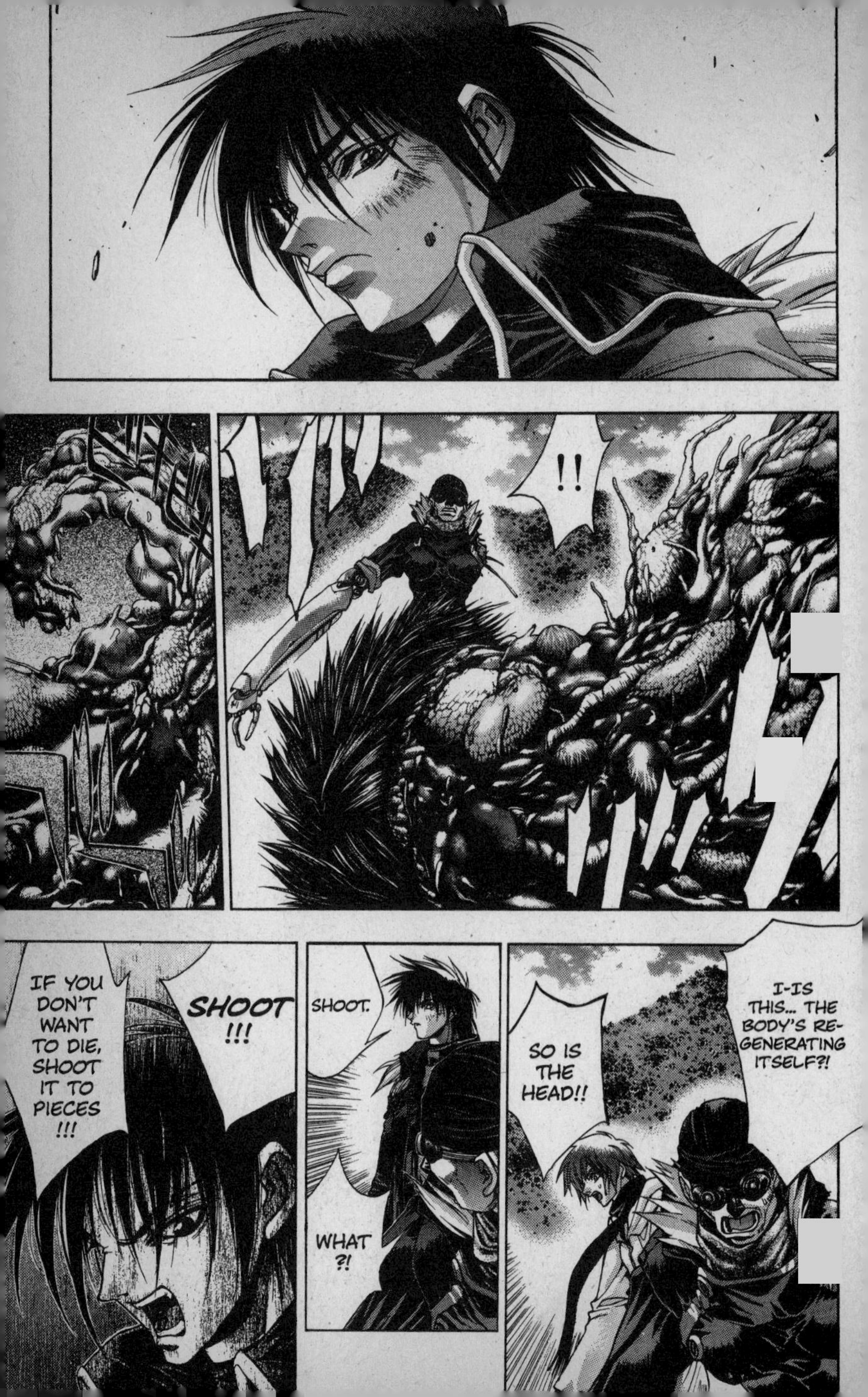

!!
I-IS THIS... THE BODY'S REGENERATING ITSELF?!
SO IS THE HEAD!!
SHOOT.
WHAT ?!
SHOOT !!!
IF YOU DON'T WANT TO DIE, SHOOT IT TO PIECES !!!

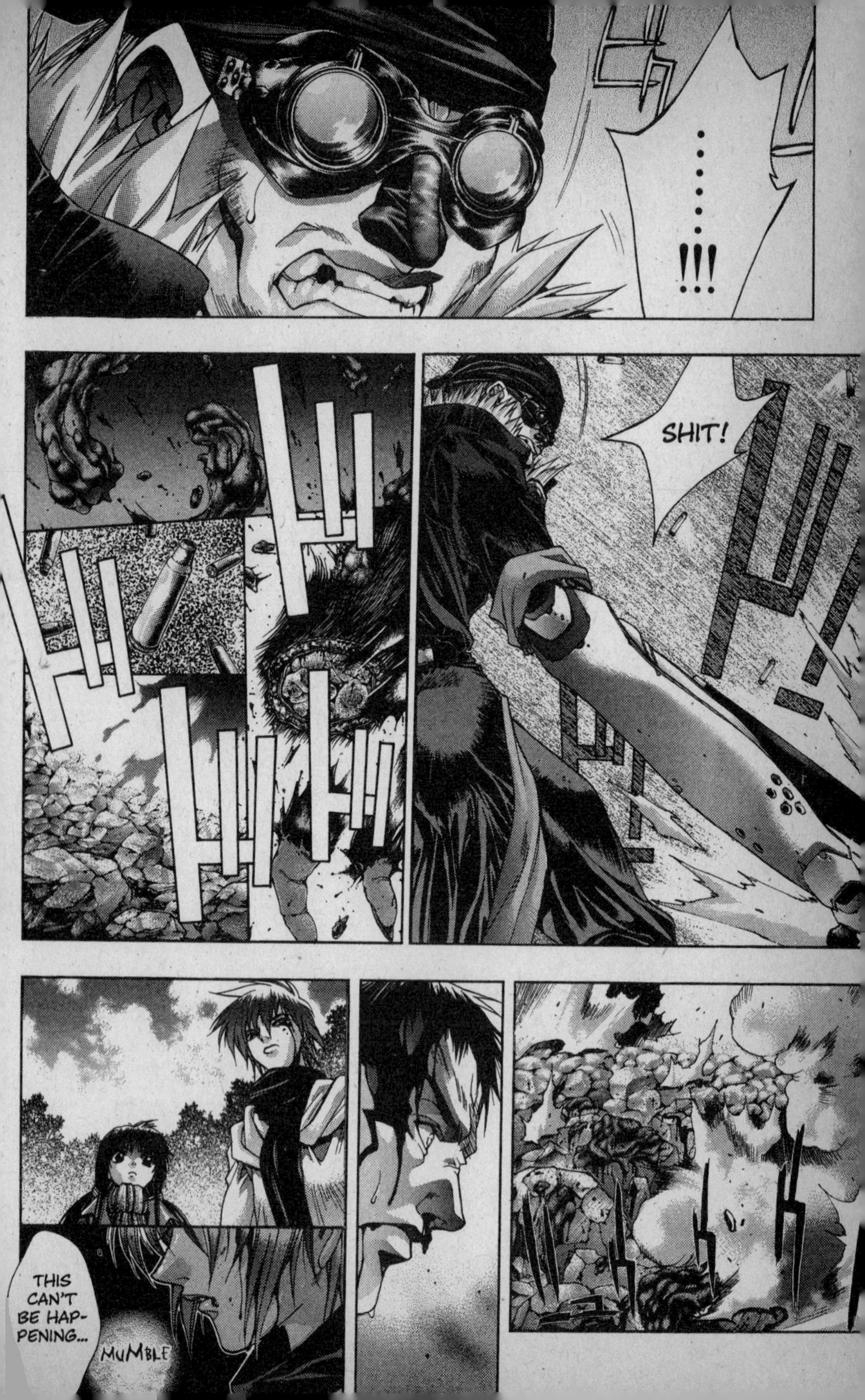
......
!!!
SHIT!
THIS CAN'T BE HAP-PENING...
MUMBLE

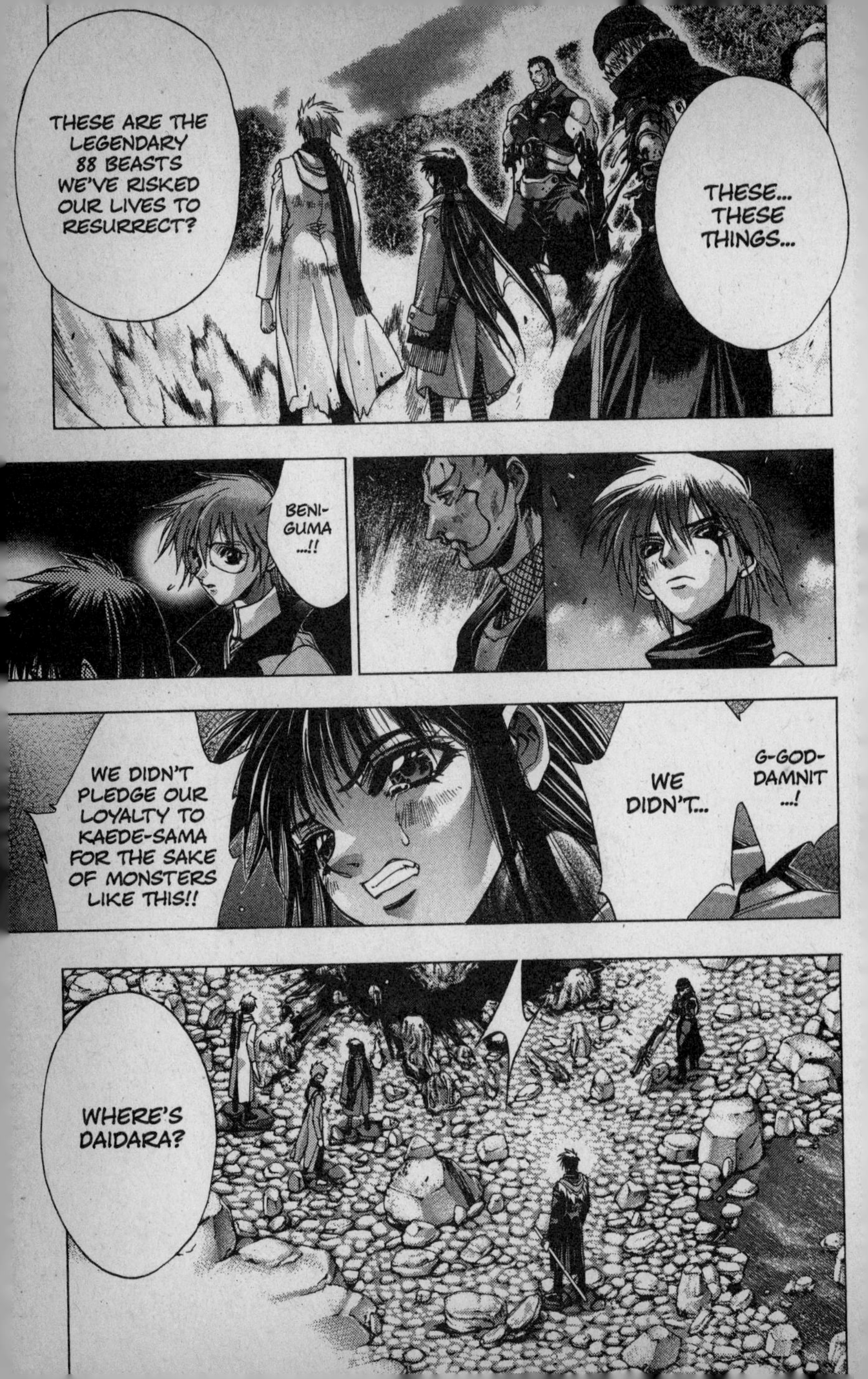
THESE... THESE THINGS...
THESE ARE THE LEGENDARY 88 BEASTS WE'VE RISKED OUR LIVES TO RESURRECT?
BENI-GUMA ...!!
G-GOD-DAMNIT ...!
WE DIDN'T...
WE DIDN'T PLEDGE OUR LOYALTY TO KAEDE-SAMA FOR THE SAKE OF MONSTERS LIKE THIS!!
WHERE'S DAIDARA?

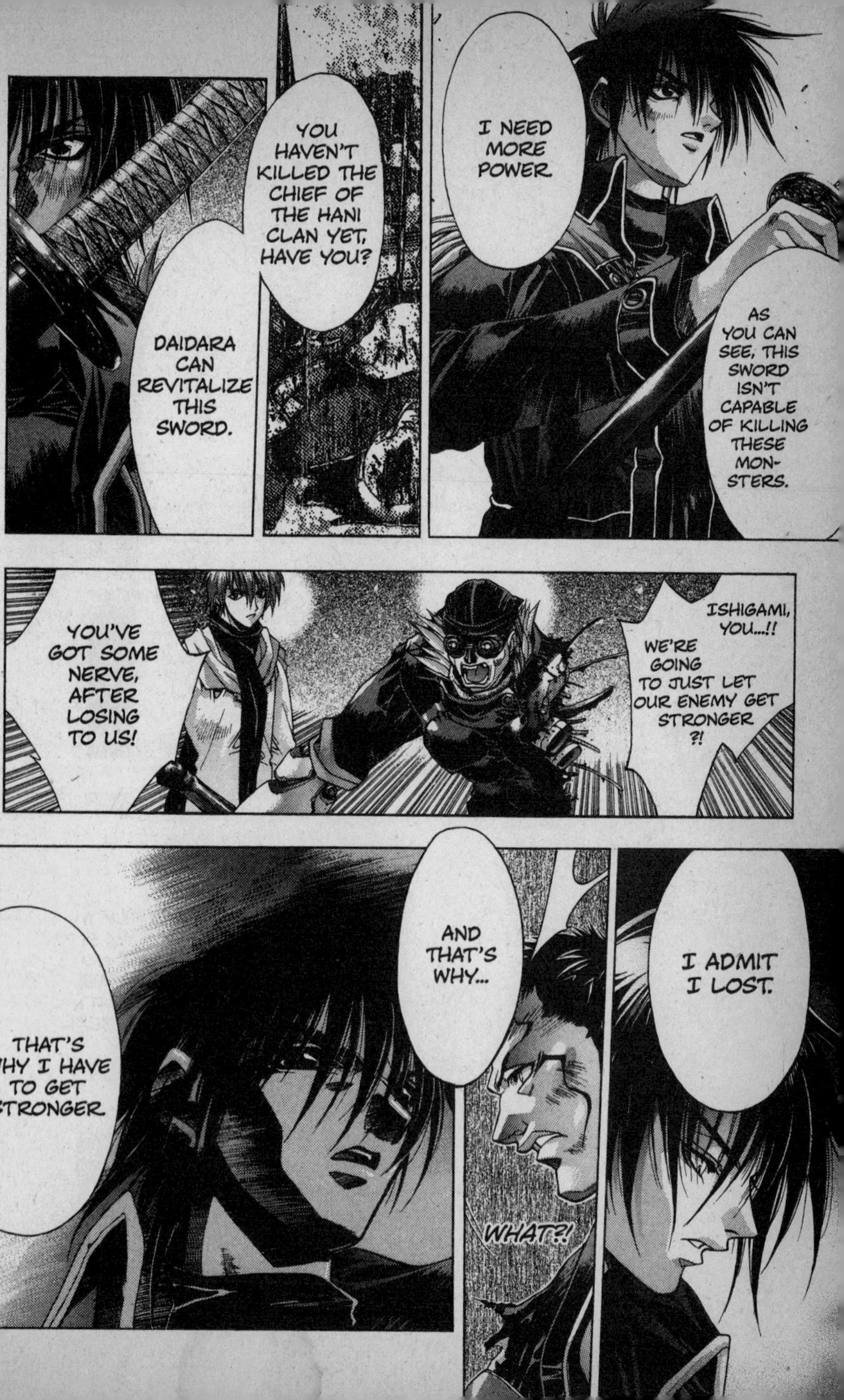
I NEED MORE POWER.
AS YOU CAN SEE, THIS SWORD ISN'T CAPABLE OF KILLING THESE MONSTERS.
YOU HAVEN'T KILLED THE CHIEF OF THE HANI CLAN YET, HAVE YOU?
DAIDARA CAN REVITALIZE THIS SWORD.
ISHIGAMI, YOU...!!
WE'RE GOING TO JUST LET OUR ENEMY GET STRONGER?!
YOU'VE GOT SOME NERVE, AFTER LOSING TO US!
I ADMIT I LOST.
AND THAT'S WHY...
WHAT?!
THAT'S WHY I HAVE TO GET STRONGER.

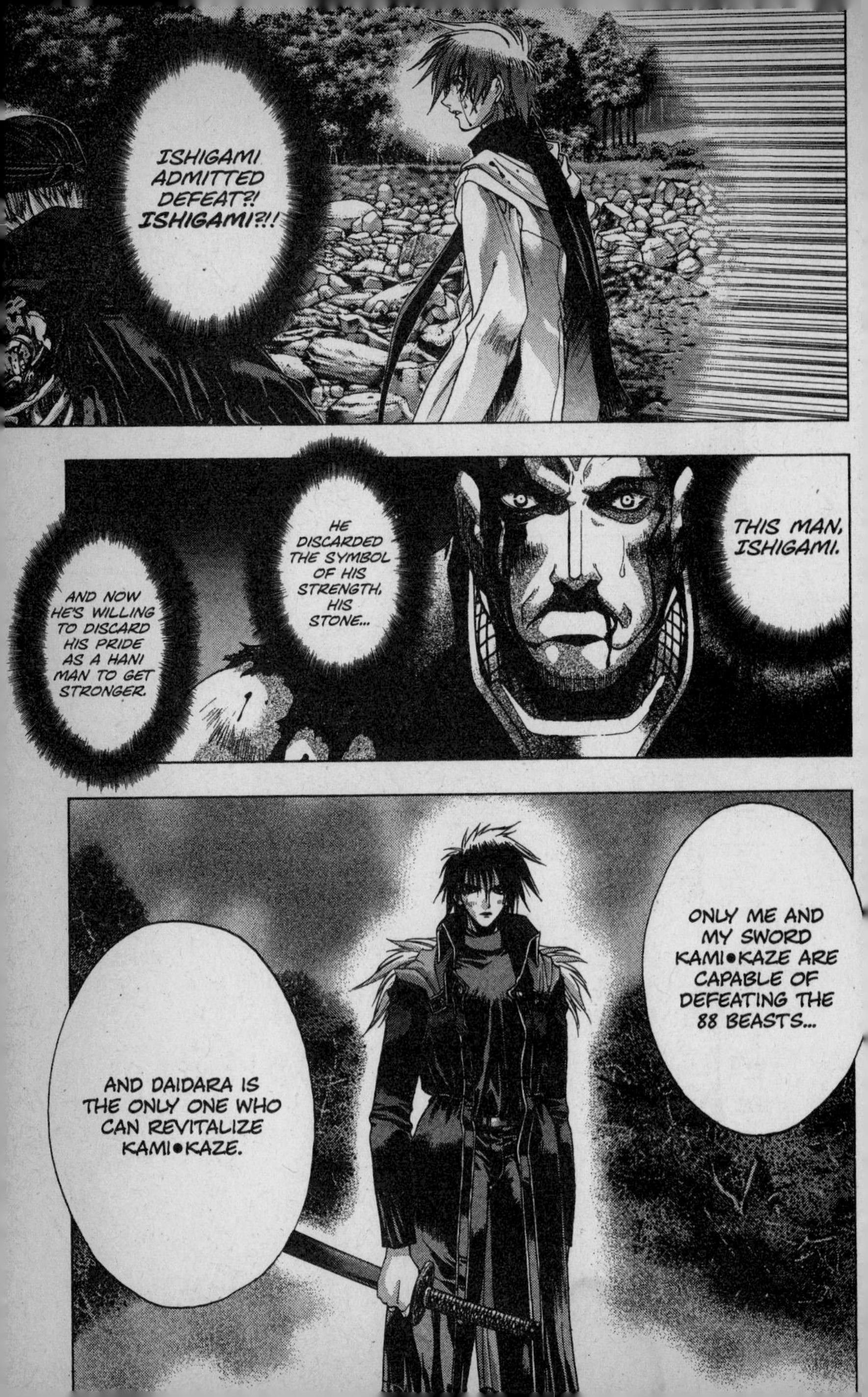
ISHIGAMI ADMITTED DEFEAT?! ISHIGAMI?!!
THIS MAN, ISHIGAMI.
HE DISCARDED THE SYMBOL OF HIS STRENGTH, HIS STONE...
AND NOW HE'S WILLING TO DISCARD HIS PRIDE AS A HANI MAN TO GET STRONGER.
ONLY ME AND MY SWORD KAMI•KAZE ARE CAPABLE OF DEFEATING THE 88 BEASTS...
AND DAIDARA IS THE ONLY ONE WHO CAN REVITALIZE KAMI•KAZE.

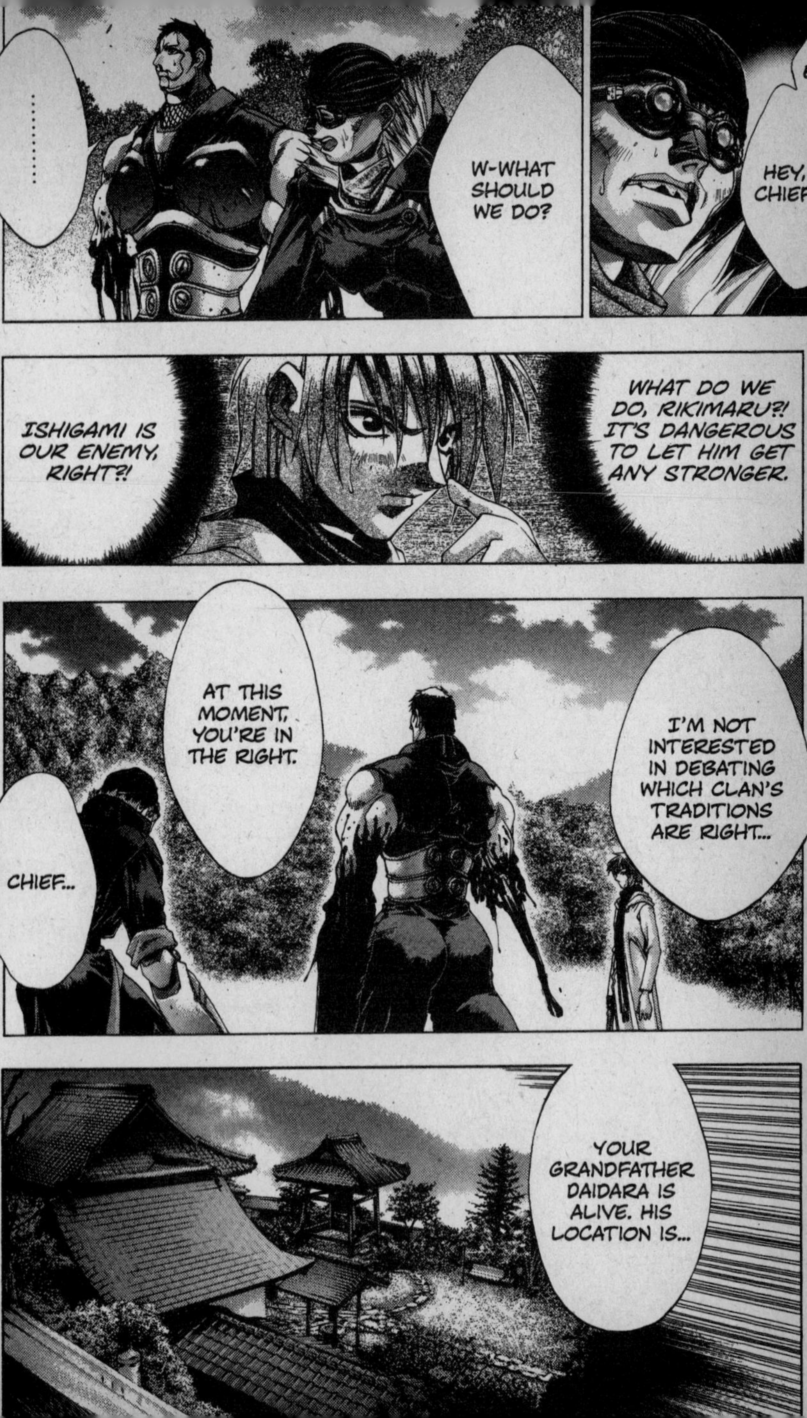
ER ...
HEY, CHIEF.
W-WHAT SHOULD WE DO?
....
WHAT DO WE DO, RIKIMARU?! IT'S DANGEROUS TO LET HIM GET ANY STRONGER.
ISHIGAMI IS OUR ENEMY, RIGHT?!
I'M NOT INTERESTED IN DEBATING WHICH CLAN'S TRADITIONS ARE RIGHT...
AT THIS MOMENT, YOU'RE IN THE RIGHT.
CHIEF...
YOUR GRANDFATHER DAIDARA IS ALIVE. HIS LOCATION IS...

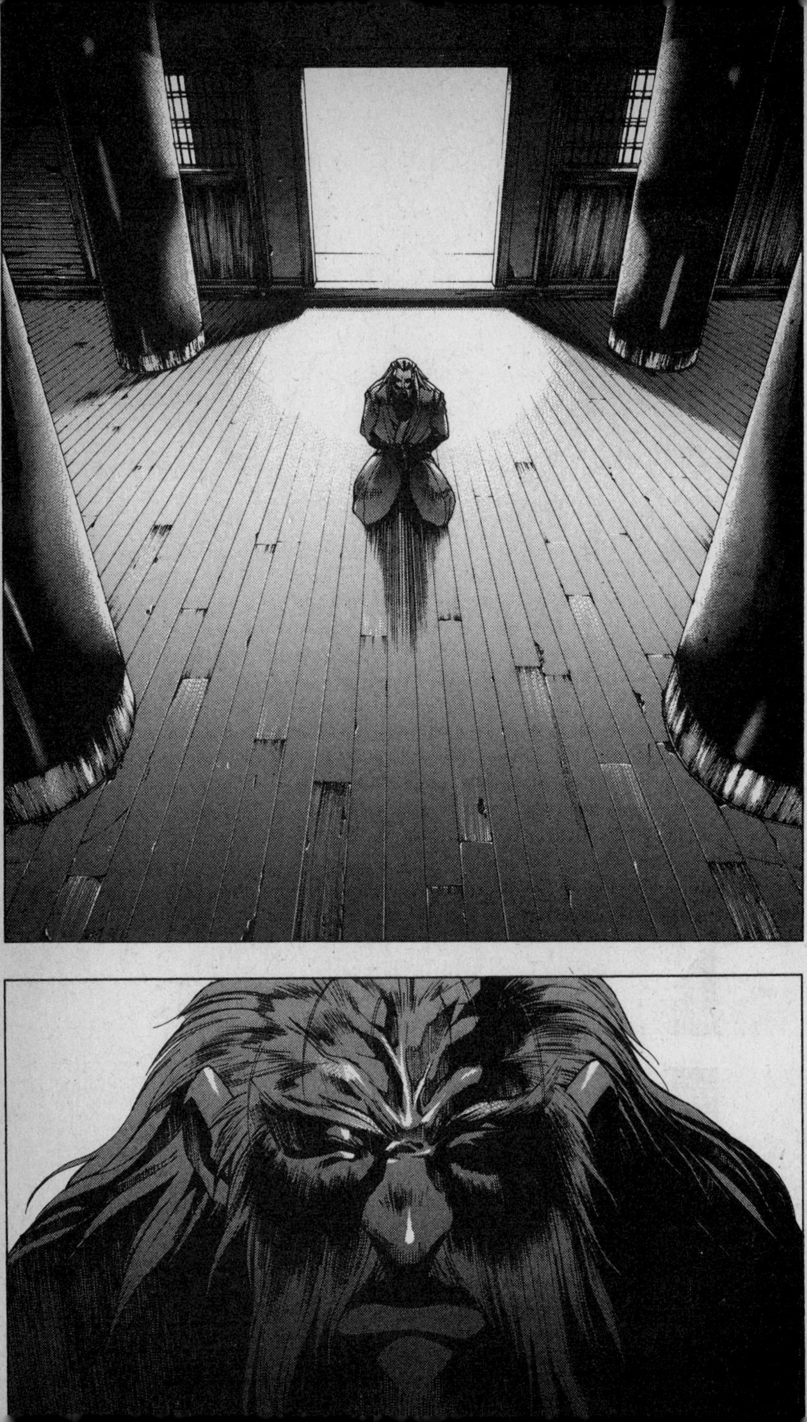

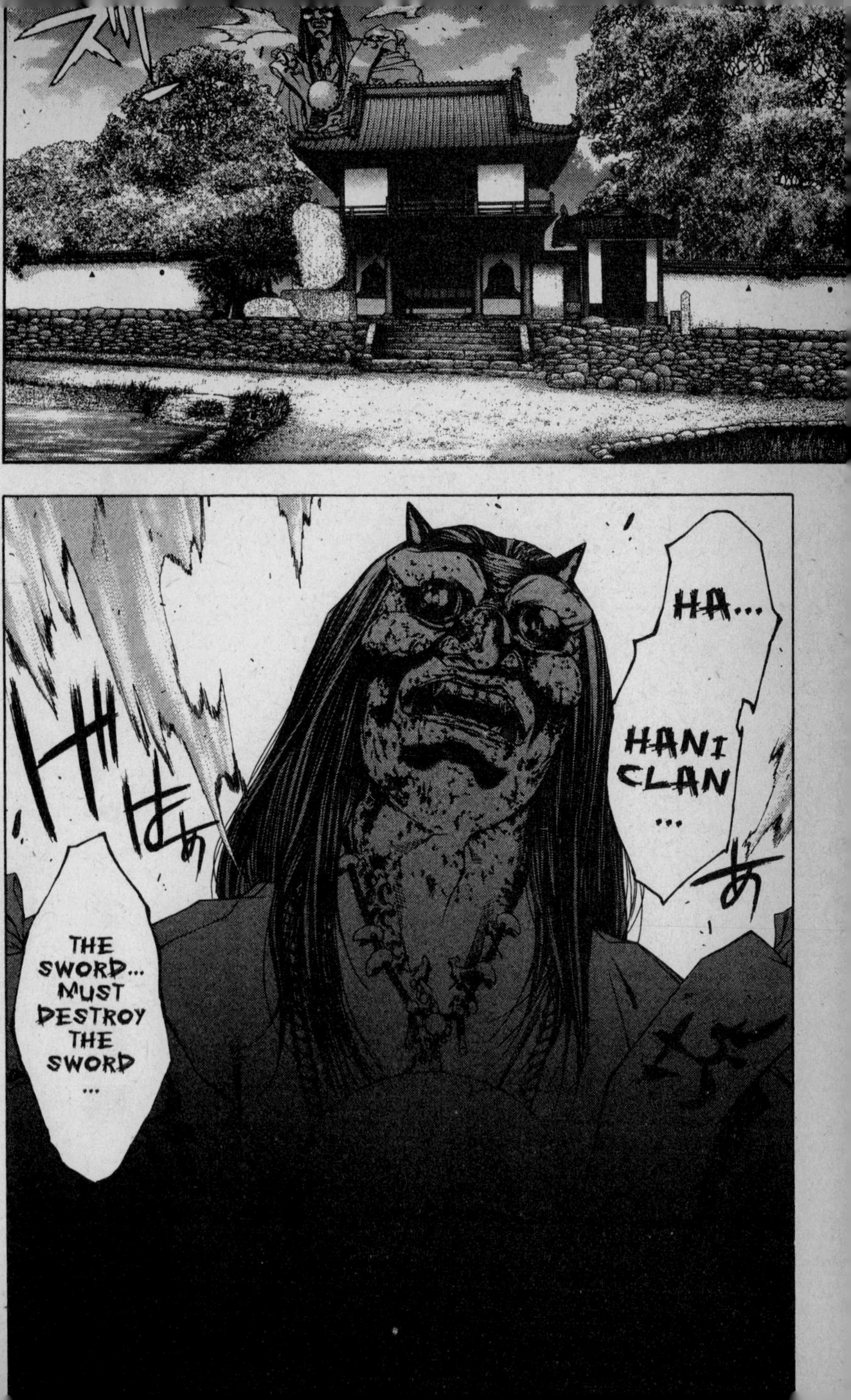
ズリ
HA...
HANI CLAN ...
あ
はあ
THE SWORD... MUST DESTROY THE SWORD ...

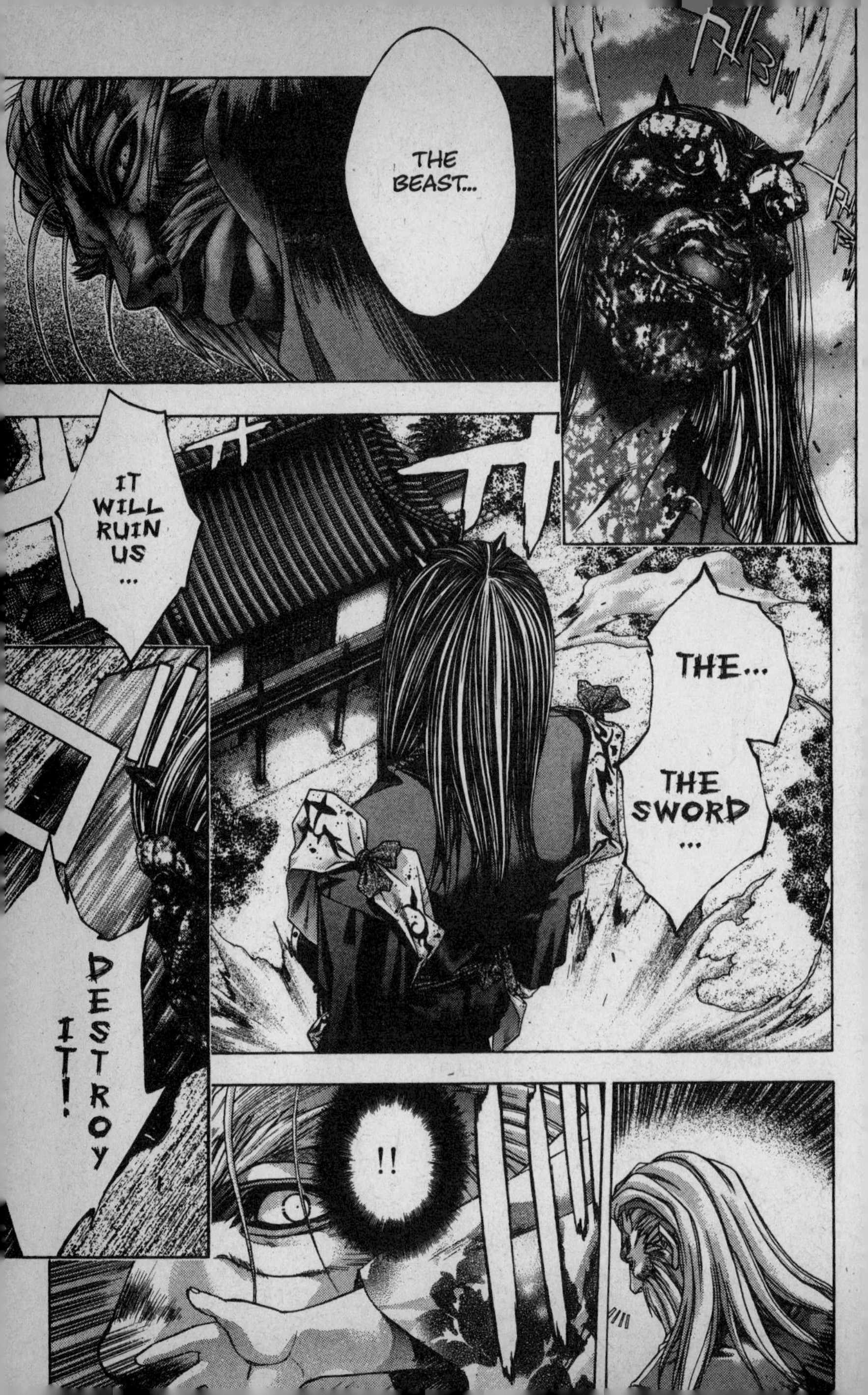
THE BEAST...
IT WILL RUIN US...
THE... THE SWORD...
DESTROY IT!
!!

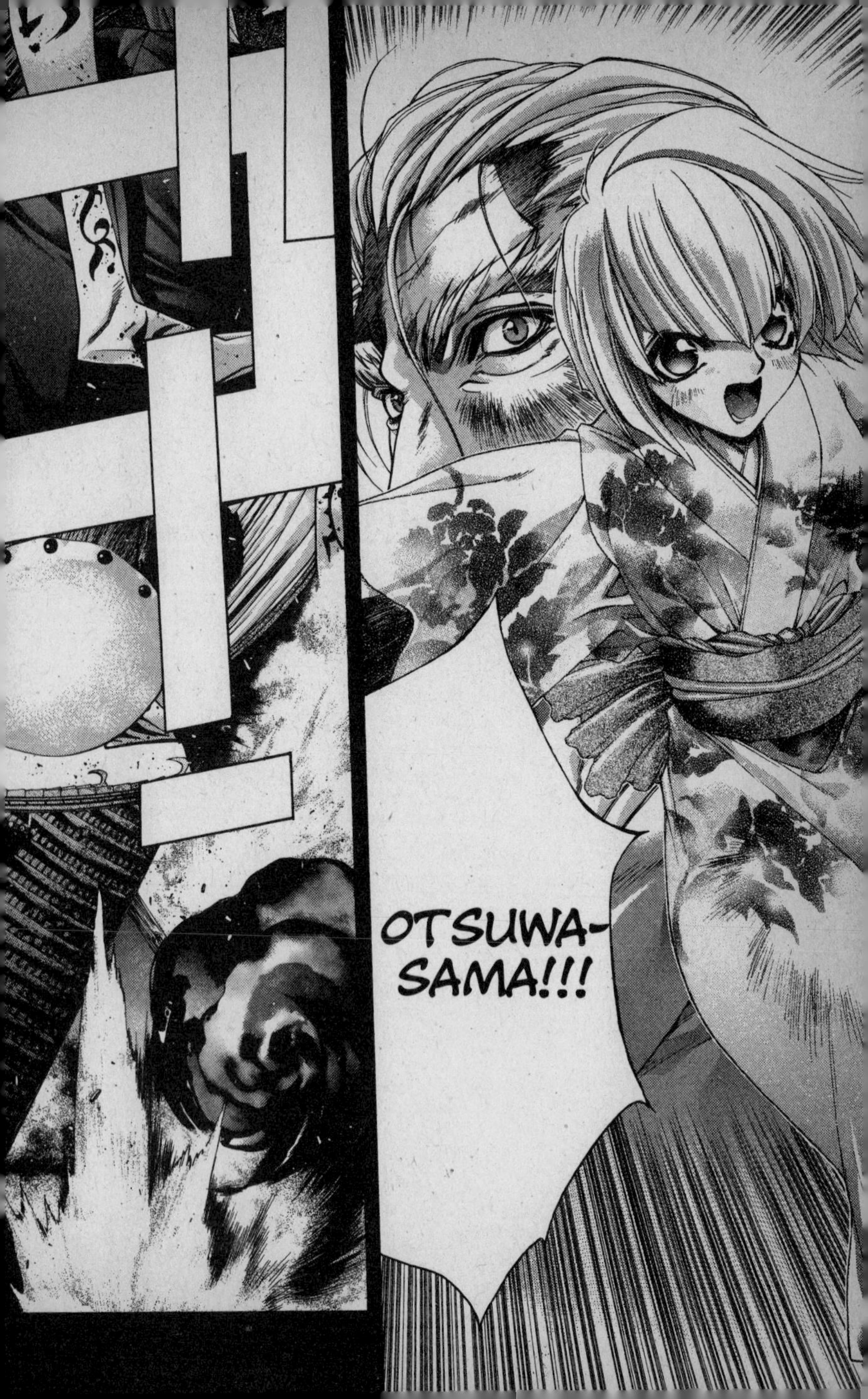
OTSUWA-SAMA!!!

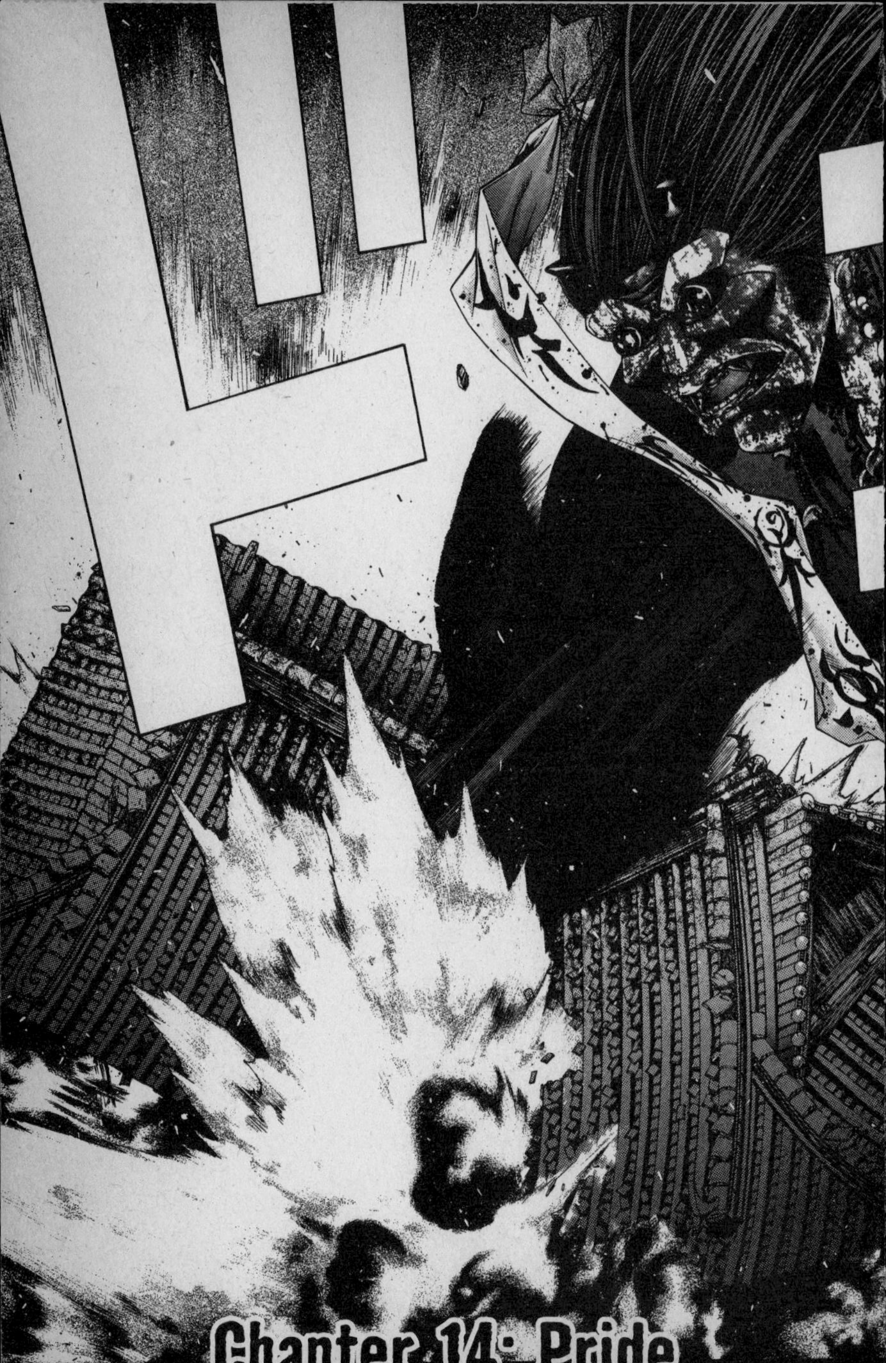

Chapter 14: Pride

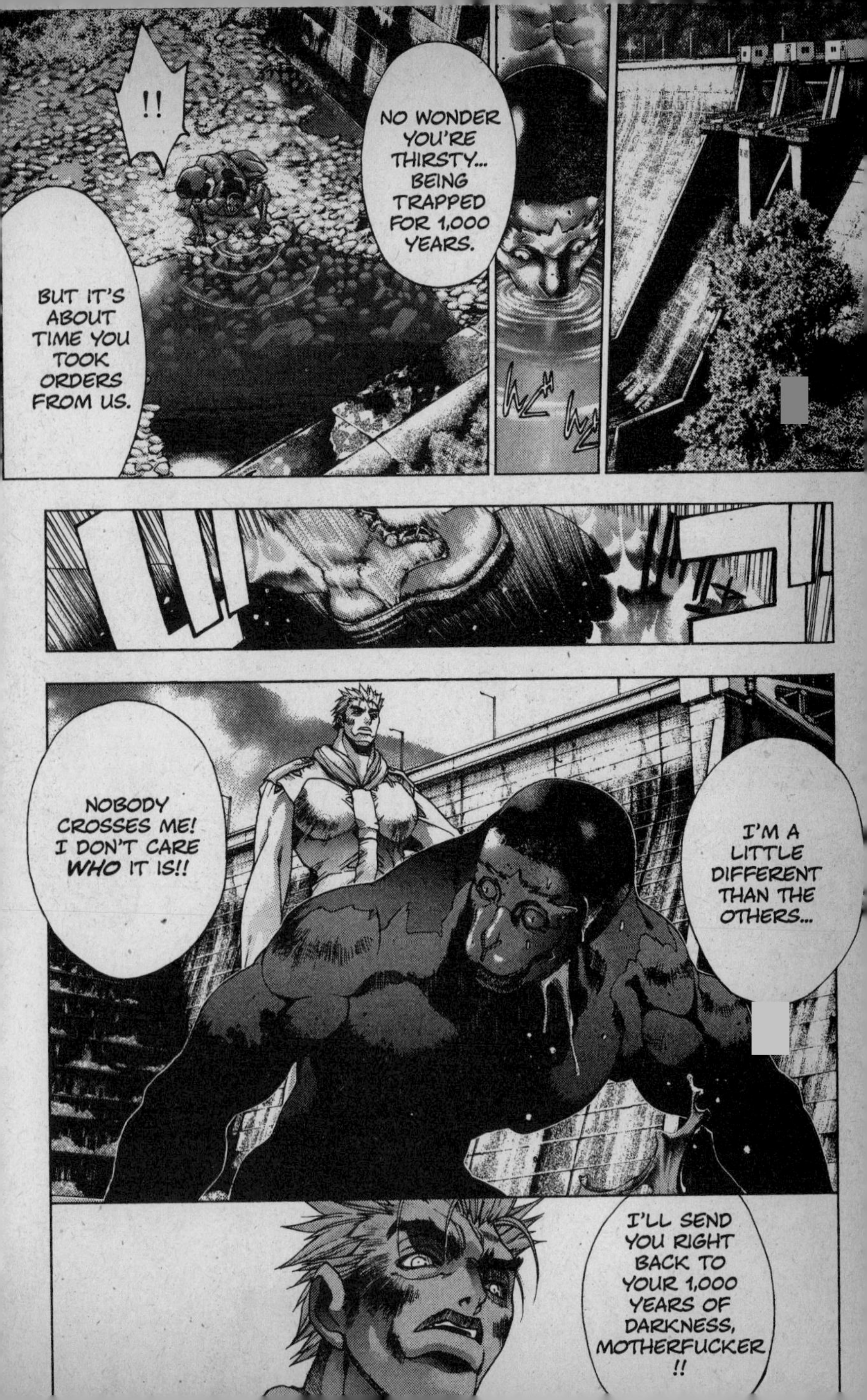
NO WONDER YOU'RE THIRSTY... BEING TRAPPED FOR 1,000 YEARS.
!!
BUT IT'S ABOUT TIME YOU TOOK ORDERS FROM US.
I'M A LITTLE DIFFERENT THAN THE OTHERS...
NOBODY CROSSES ME! I DON'T CARE *WHO* IT IS!!
I'LL SEND YOU RIGHT BACK TO YOUR 1,000 YEARS OF DARKNESS, MOTHERFUCKER !!

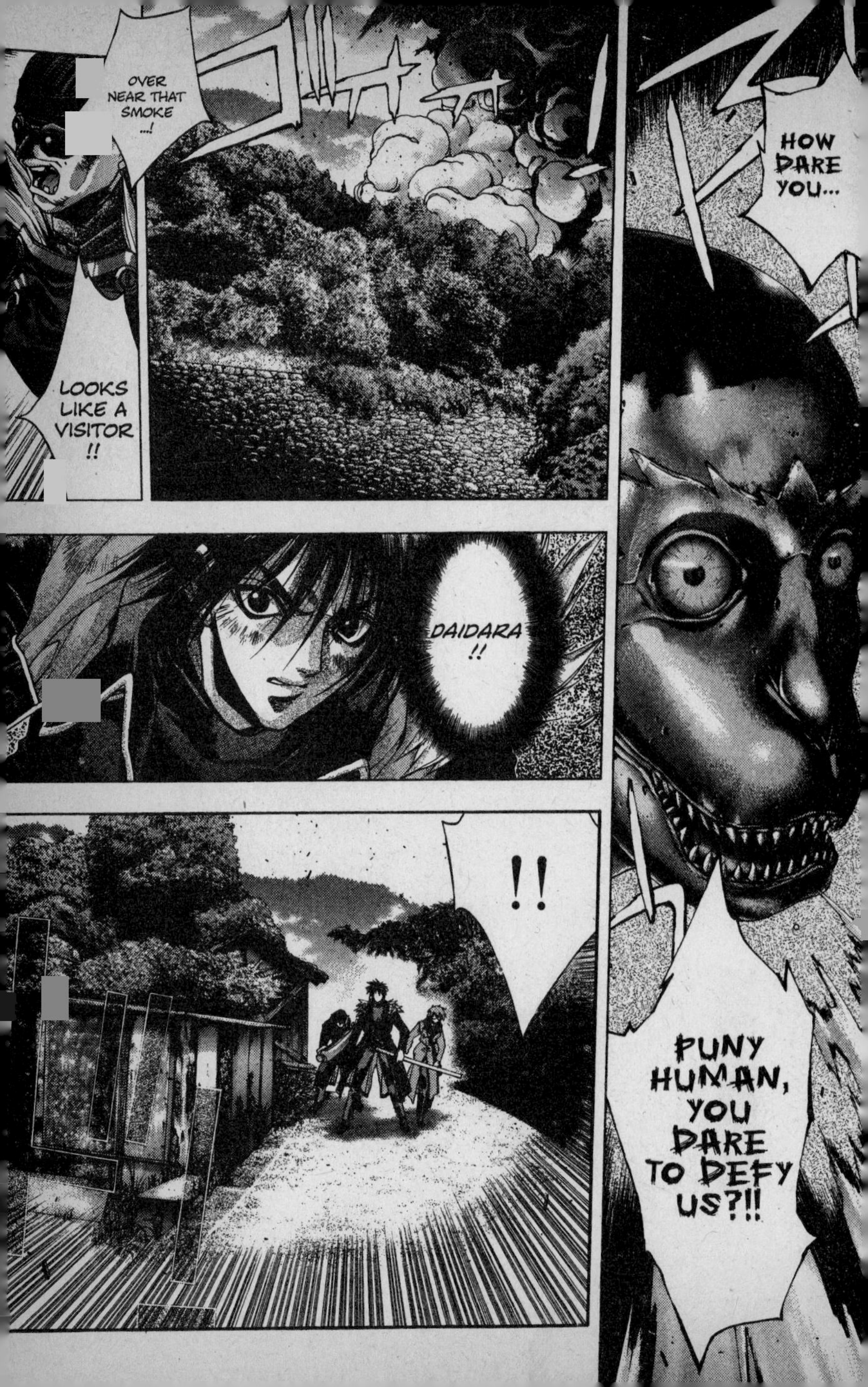
HOW DARE YOU...
PUNY HUMAN, YOU DARE TO DEFY US?!!
OVER NEAR THAT SMOKE ...!
LOOKS LIKE A VISITOR !!
DAIDARA !!
!!

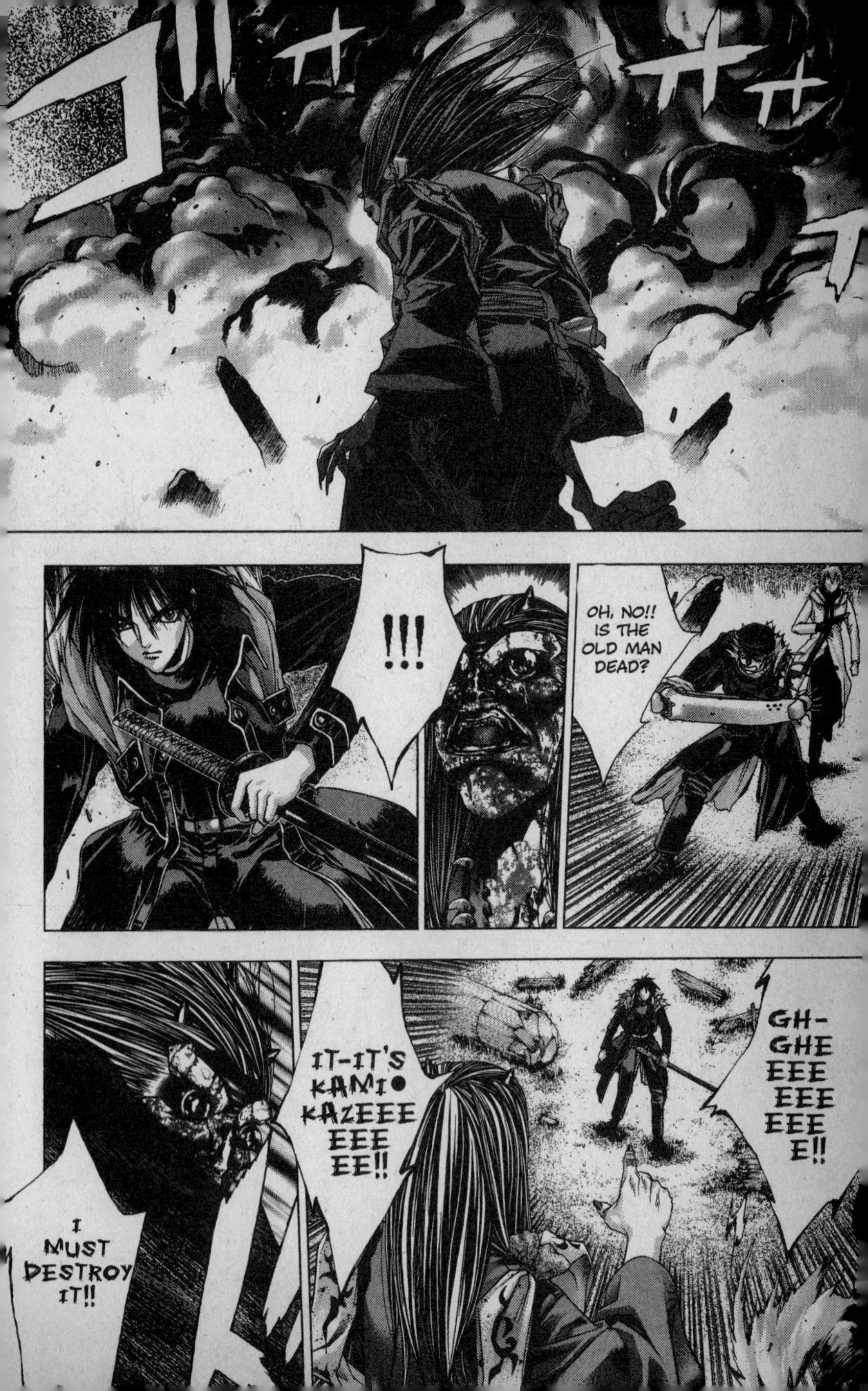
OH, NO!! IS THE OLD MAN DEAD?
!!!
GH-GHEEEEEEEEEEEE!!
IT-IT'S KAMI•KAZEEEEEEEEE!!
I MUST DESTROY IT!!

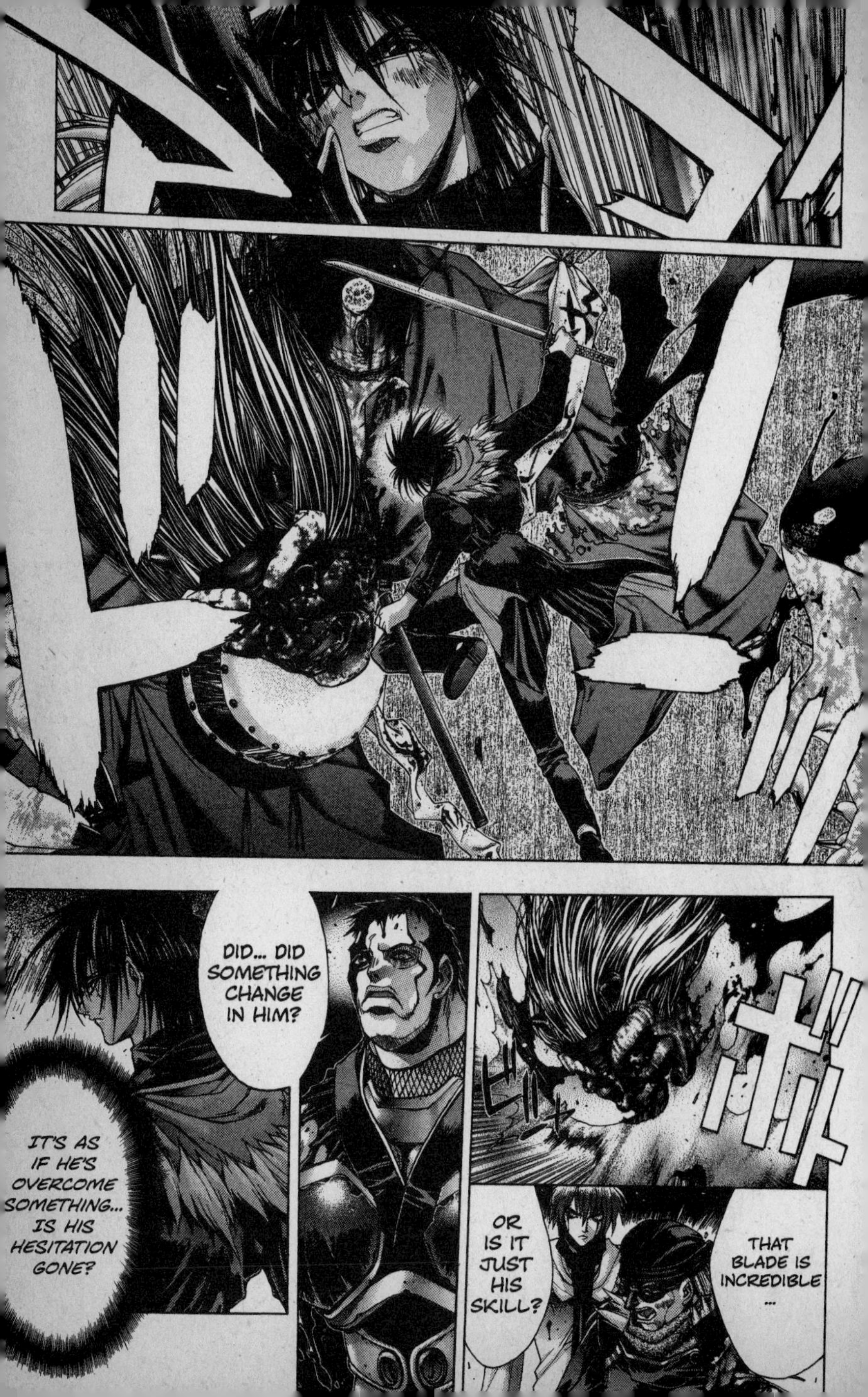
THAT BLADE IS INCREDIBLE ...
OR IS IT JUST HIS SKILL?
DID... DID SOMETHING CHANGE IN HIM?
IT'S AS IF HE'S OVERCOME SOMETHING... IS HIS HESITATION GONE?

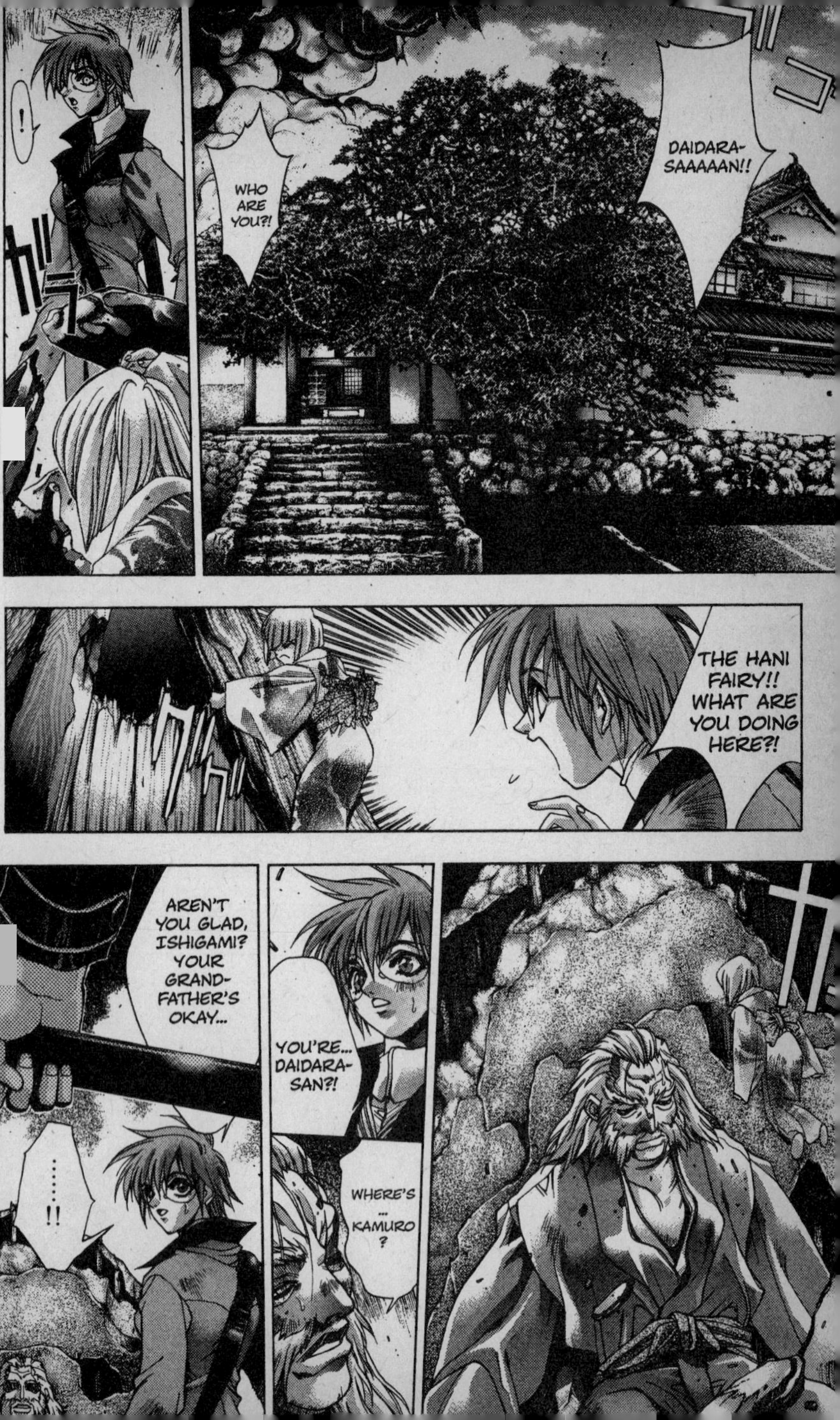
DAIDARA-SAAAAAN!!
WHO ARE YOU?!
!
THE HANI FAIRY!! WHAT ARE YOU DOING HERE?!
YOU'RE... DAIDARA-SAN?!
WHERE'S ... KAMURO?
AREN'T YOU GLAD, ISHIGAMI? YOUR GRAND-FATHER'S OKAY...
......!!

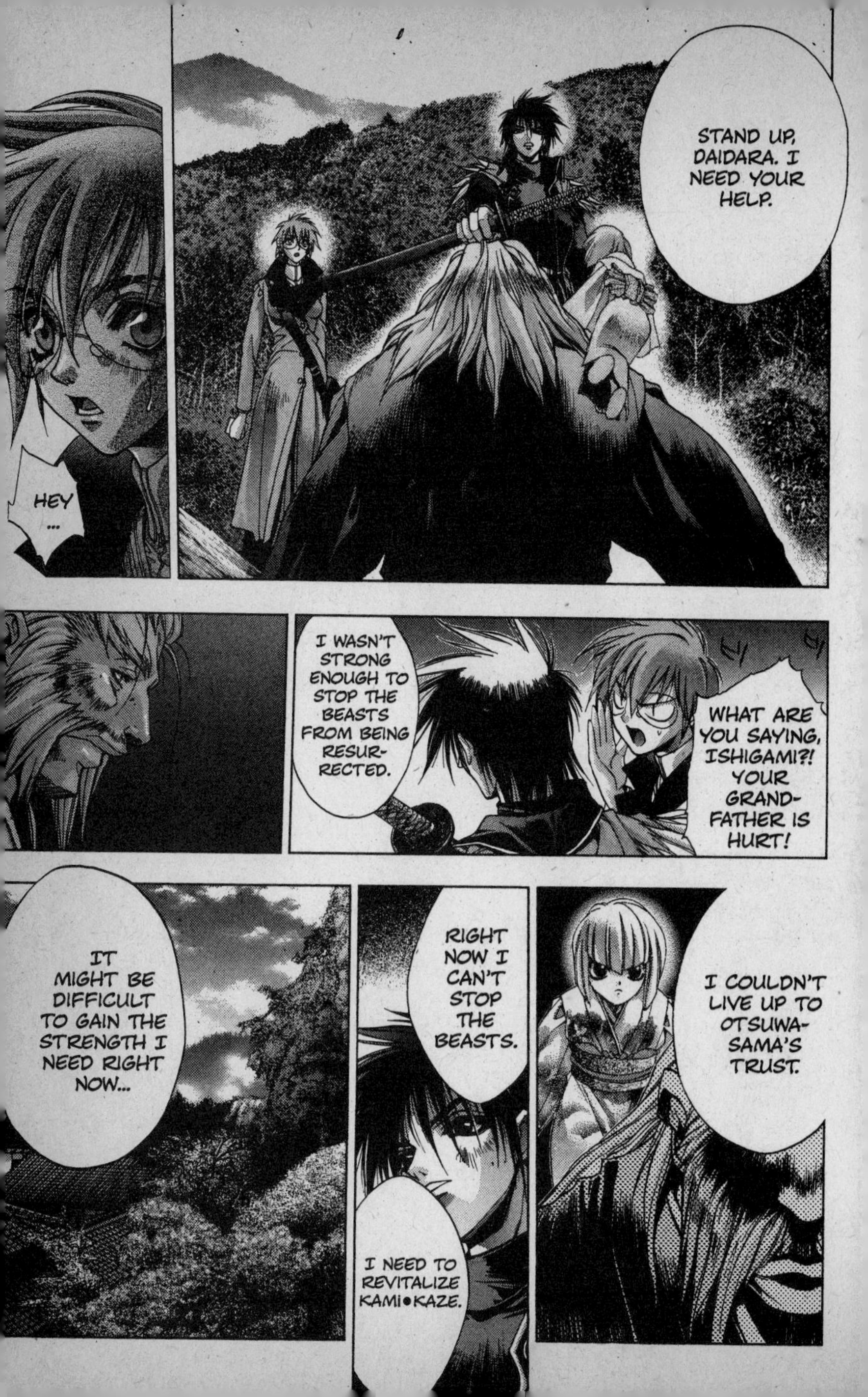
STAND UP, DAIDARA. I NEED YOUR HELP.
HEY ...
WHAT ARE YOU SAYING, ISHIGAMI?! YOUR GRANDFATHER IS HURT!
I WASN'T STRONG ENOUGH TO STOP THE BEASTS FROM BEING RESURRECTED.
I COULDN'T LIVE UP TO OTSUWA-SAMA'S TRUST.
RIGHT NOW I CAN'T STOP THE BEASTS.
I NEED TO REVITALIZE KAMI•KAZE.
IT MIGHT BE DIFFICULT TO GAIN THE STRENGTH I NEED RIGHT NOW...

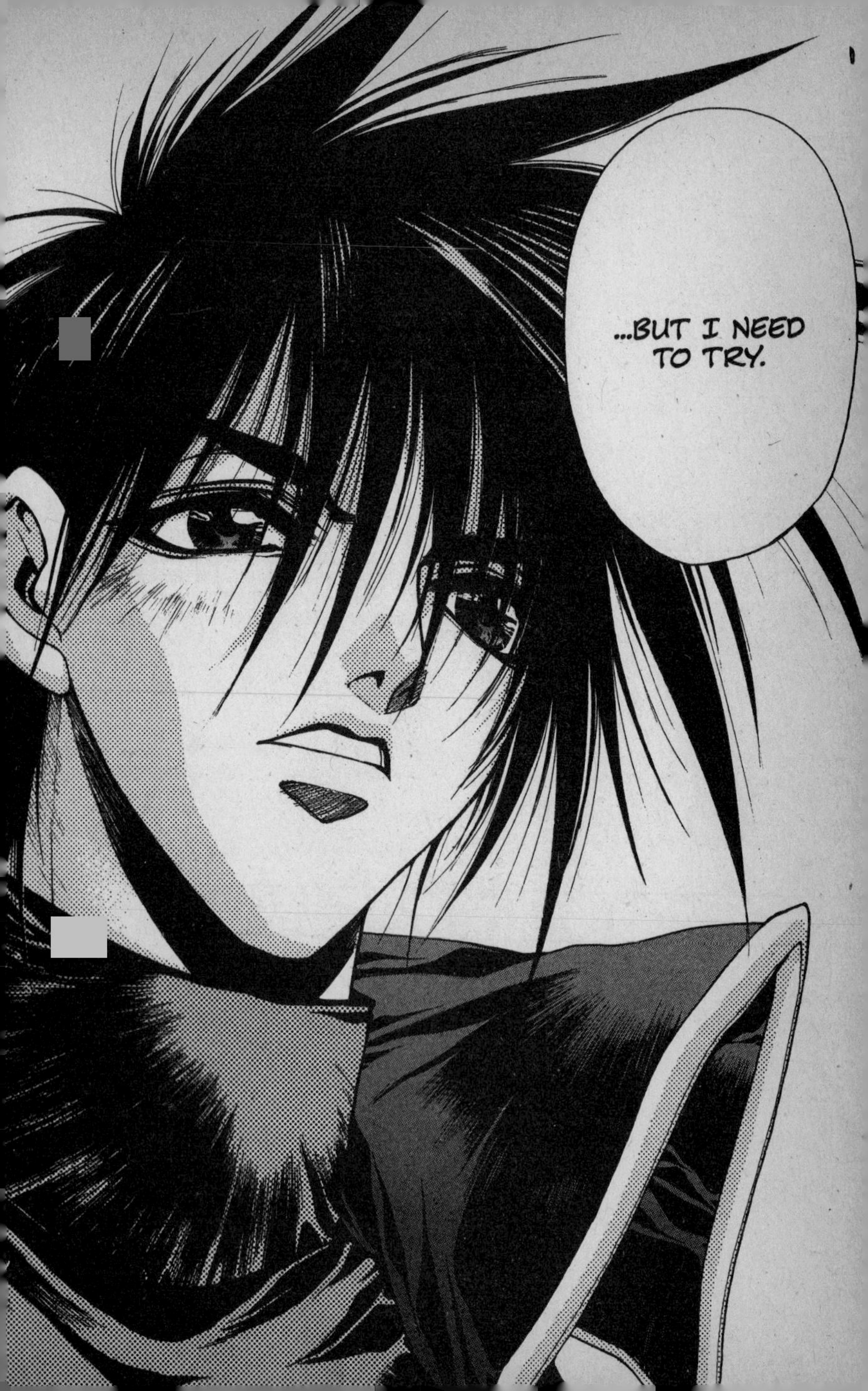
...BUT I NEED TO TRY.

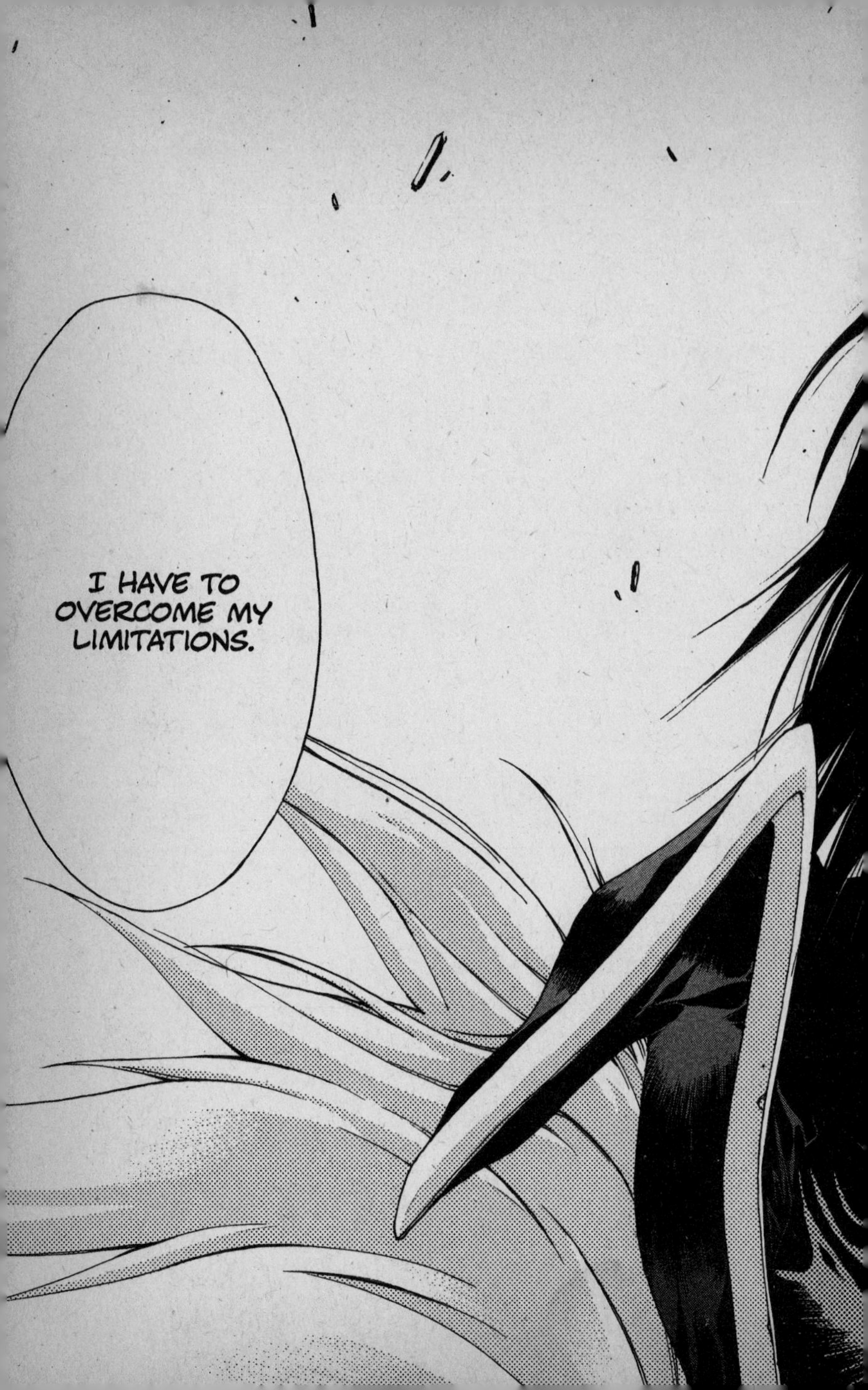
I HAVE TO OVERCOME MY LIMITATIONS.

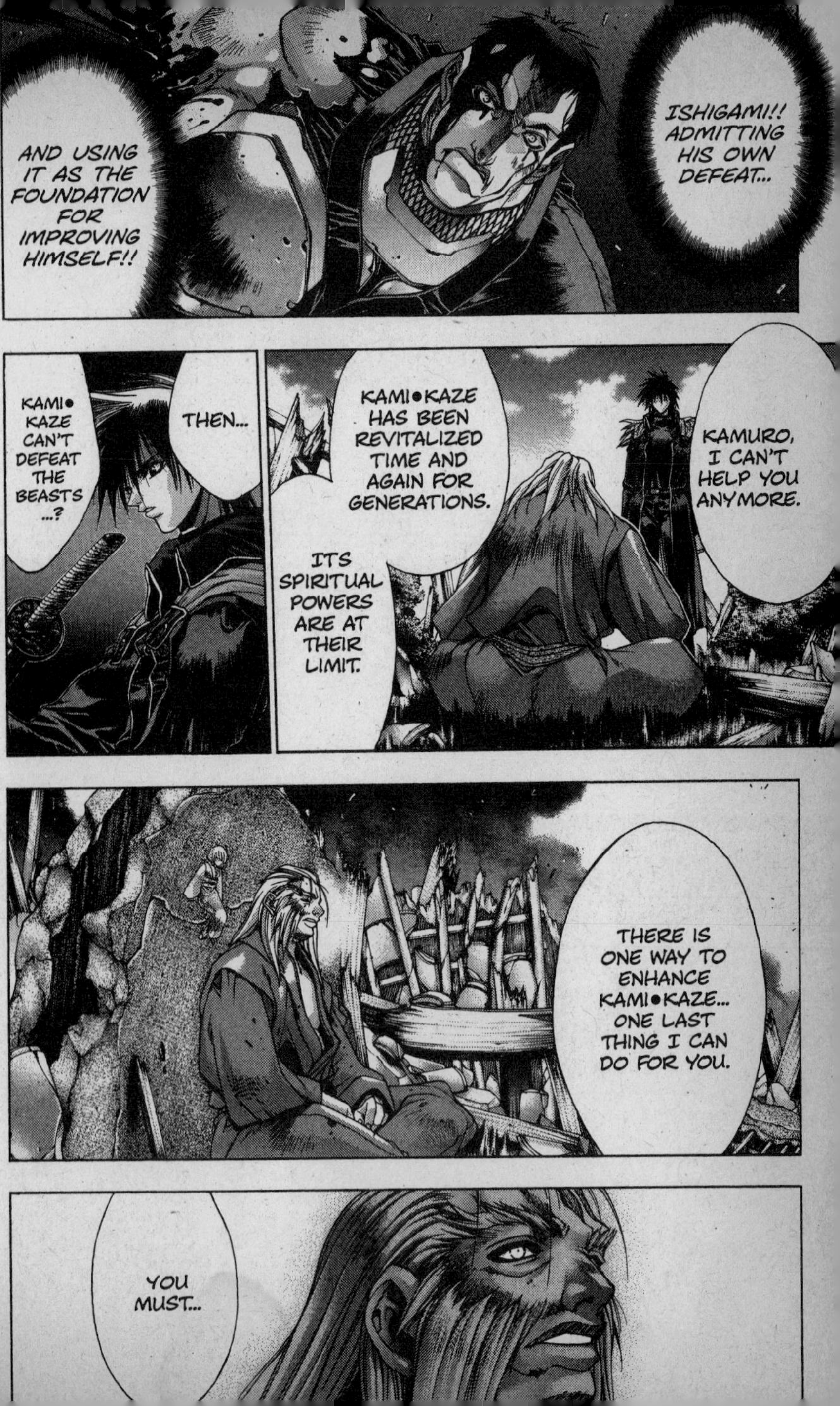
ISHIGAMI!! ADMITTING HIS OWN DEFEAT...
AND USING IT AS THE FOUNDATION FOR IMPROVING HIMSELF!!
KAMURO, I CAN'T HELP YOU ANYMORE.
KAMI•KAZE HAS BEEN REVITALIZED TIME AND AGAIN FOR GENERATIONS.
ITS SPIRITUAL POWERS ARE AT THEIR LIMIT.
THEN...
KAMI• KAZE CAN'T DEFEAT THE BEASTS ...?
THERE IS ONE WAY TO ENHANCE KAMI•KAZE... ONE LAST THING I CAN DO FOR YOU.
YOU MUST...

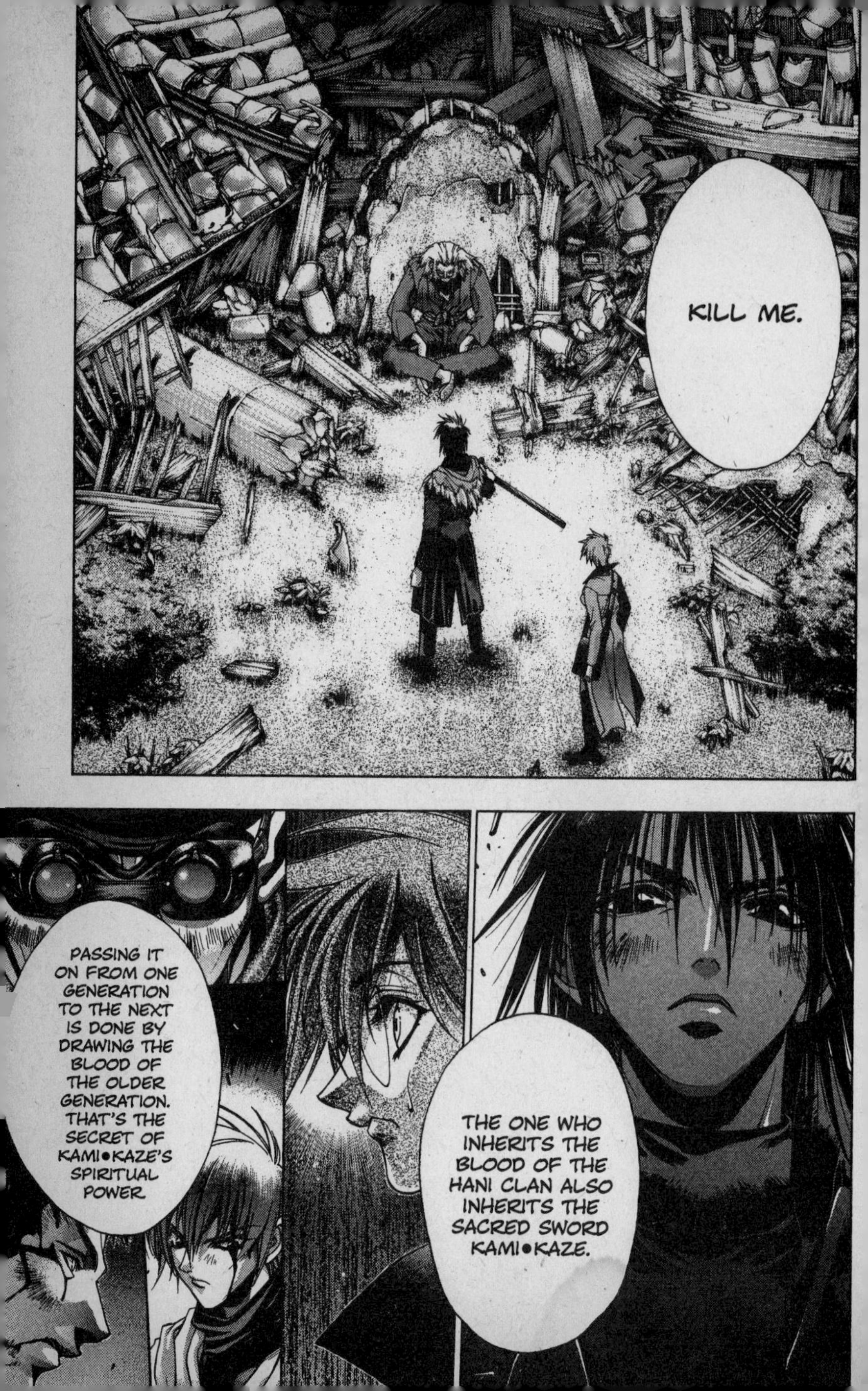
KILL ME.
THE ONE WHO INHERITS THE BLOOD OF THE HANI CLAN ALSO INHERITS THE SACRED SWORD KAMI•KAZE.
PASSING IT ON FROM ONE GENERATION TO THE NEXT IS DONE BY DRAWING THE BLOOD OF THE OLDER GENERATION. THAT'S THE SECRET OF KAMI•KAZE'S SPIRITUAL POWER

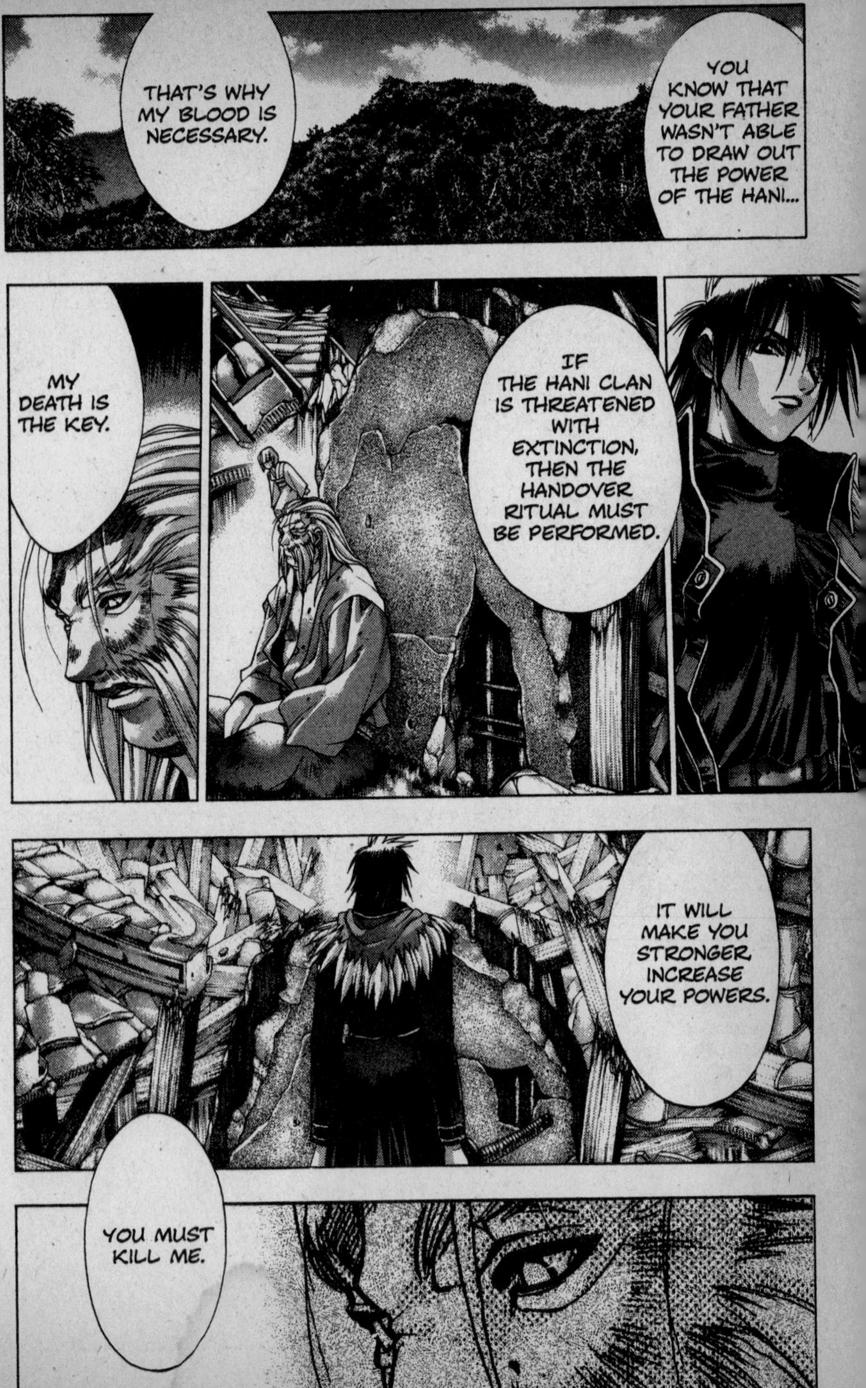
YOU KNOW THAT YOUR FATHER WASN'T ABLE TO DRAW OUT THE POWER OF THE HANI...
THAT'S WHY MY BLOOD IS NECESSARY.
IF THE HANI CLAN IS THREATENED WITH EXTINCTION, THEN THE HANDOVER RITUAL MUST BE PERFORMED.
MY DEATH IS THE KEY.
IT WILL MAKE YOU STRONGER, INCREASE YOUR POWERS.
YOU MUST KILL ME.

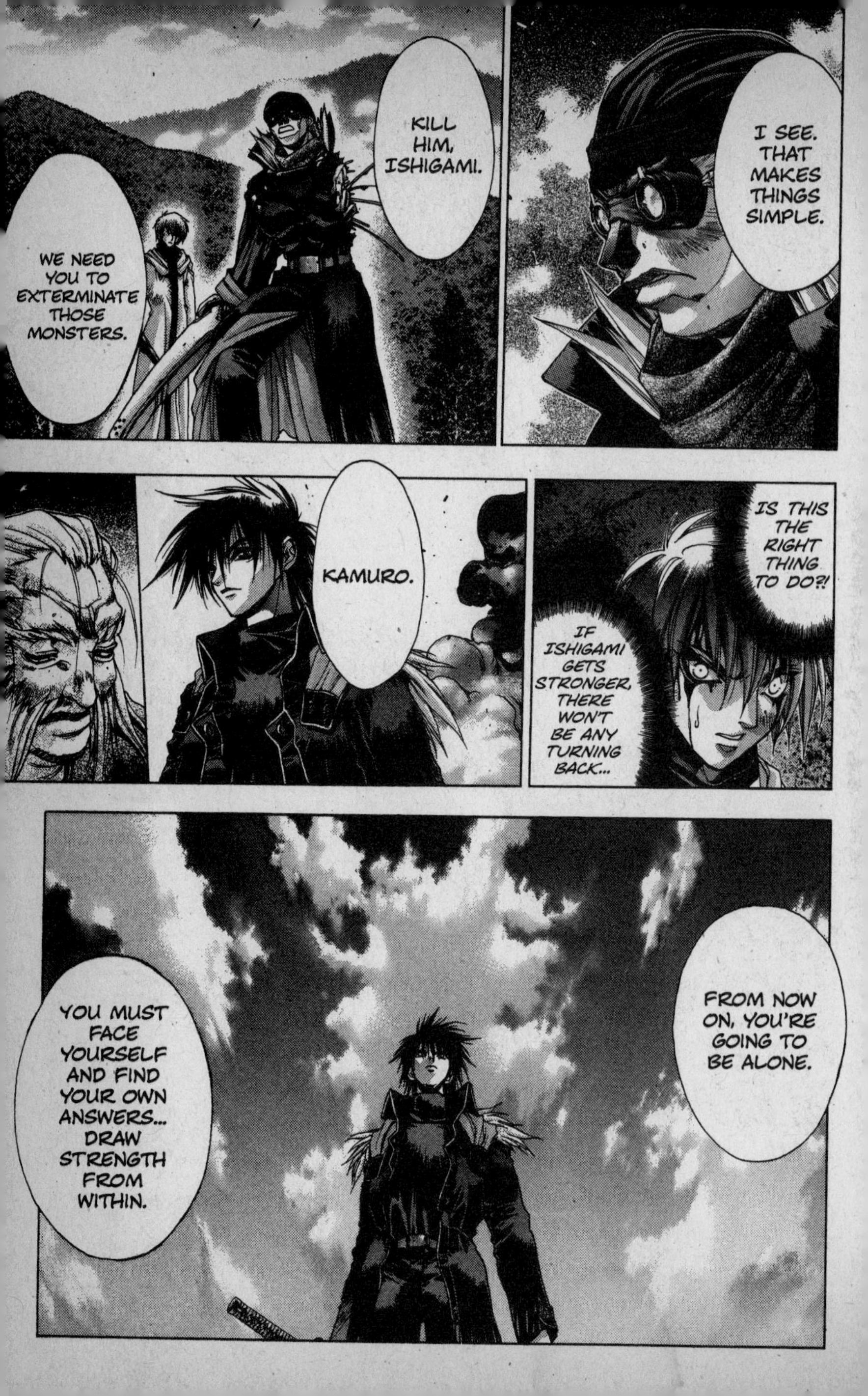
I SEE. THAT MAKES THINGS SIMPLE.
KILL HIM, ISHIGAMI.
WE NEED YOU TO EXTERMINATE THOSE MONSTERS.
IS THIS THE RIGHT THING TO DO?!
IF ISHIGAMI GETS STRONGER, THERE WON'T BE ANY TURNING BACK...
KAMURO.
FROM NOW ON, YOU'RE GOING TO BE ALONE.
YOU MUST FACE YOURSELF AND FIND YOUR OWN ANSWERS... DRAW STRENGTH FROM WITHIN.

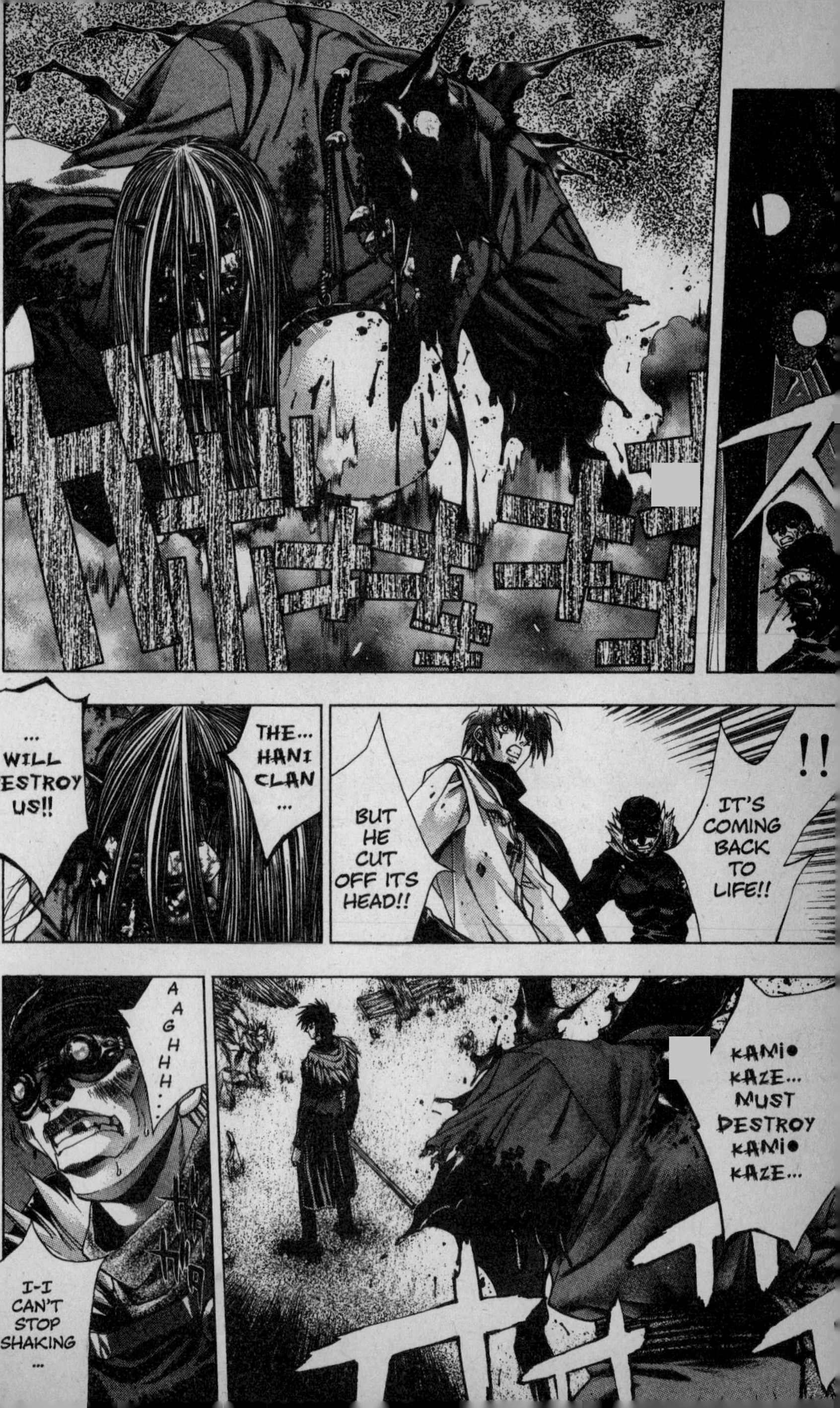
!!
IT'S COMING BACK TO LIFE!!
BUT HE CUT OFF ITS HEAD!!
THE... HANI CLAN ...
... WILL DESTROY US!!
KAMIO KAZE... MUST DESTROY KAMIO KAZE...
AAGHHH...
I-I CAN'T STOP SHAKING ...

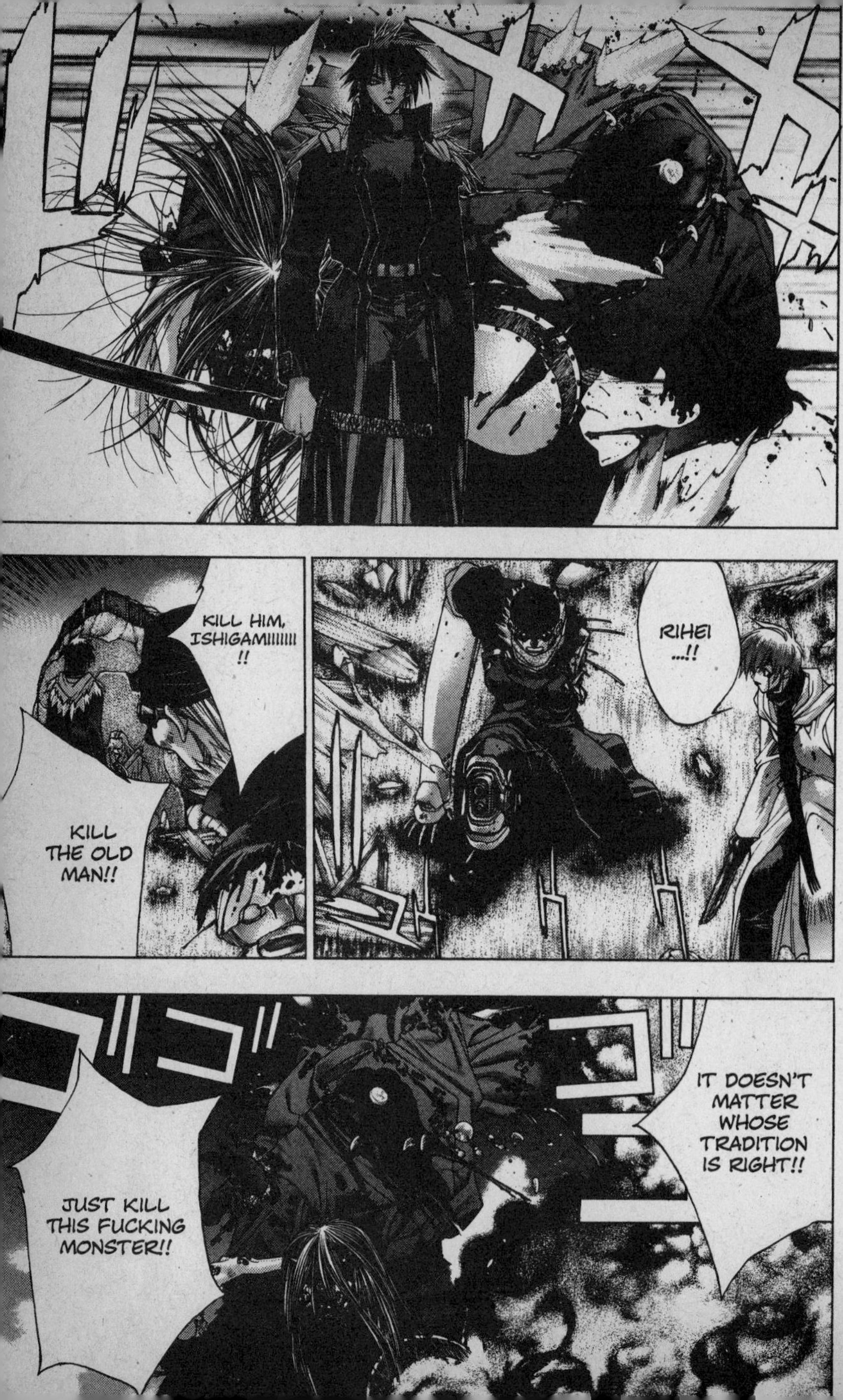
RIHEI ...!!
KILL HIM, ISHIGAMIIIIIII !!
KILL THE OLD MAN!!
IT DOESN'T MATTER WHOSE TRADITION IS RIGHT!!
JUST KILL THIS FUCKING MONSTER!!

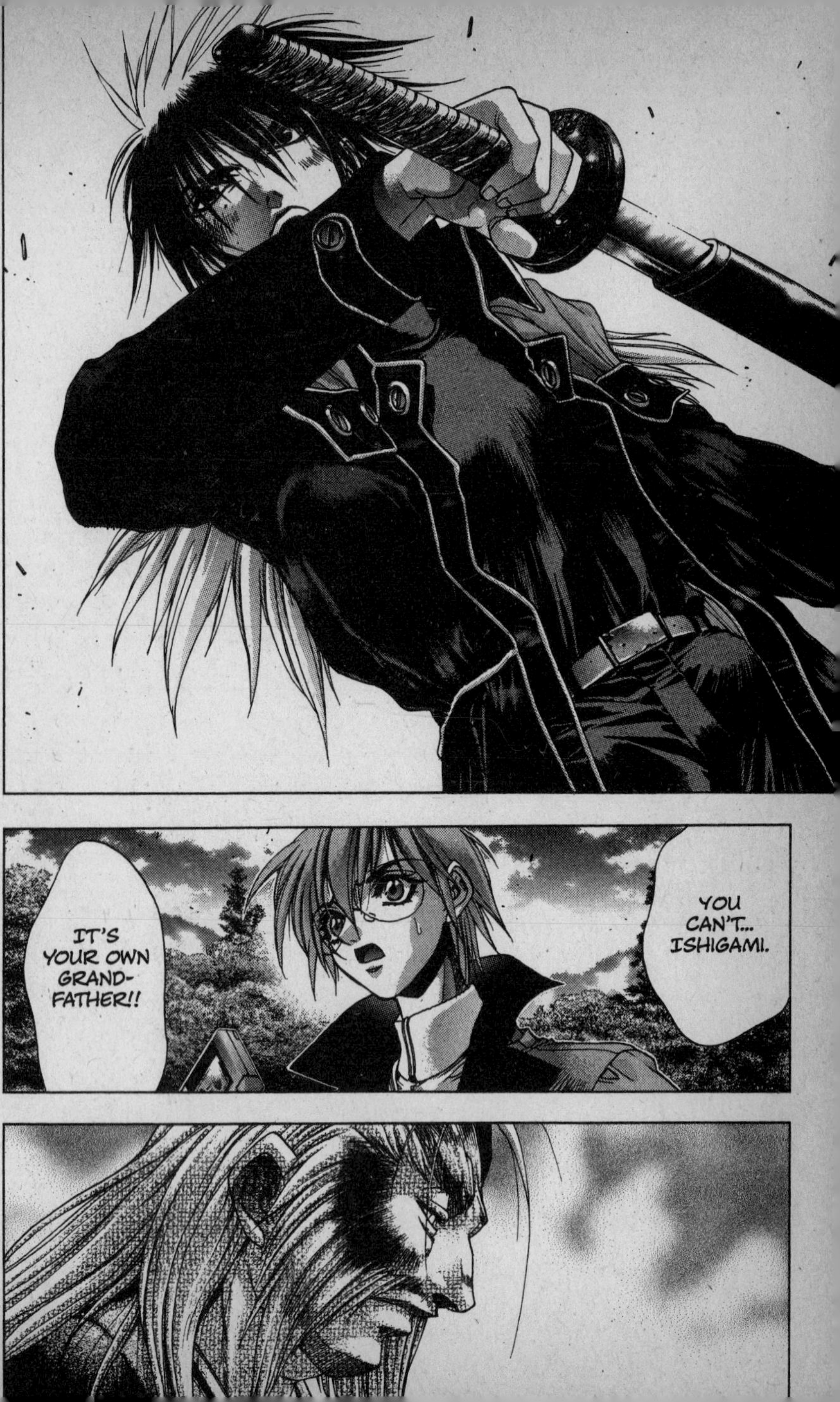
YOU CAN'T... ISHIGAMI.
IT'S YOUR OWN GRAND-FATHER!!

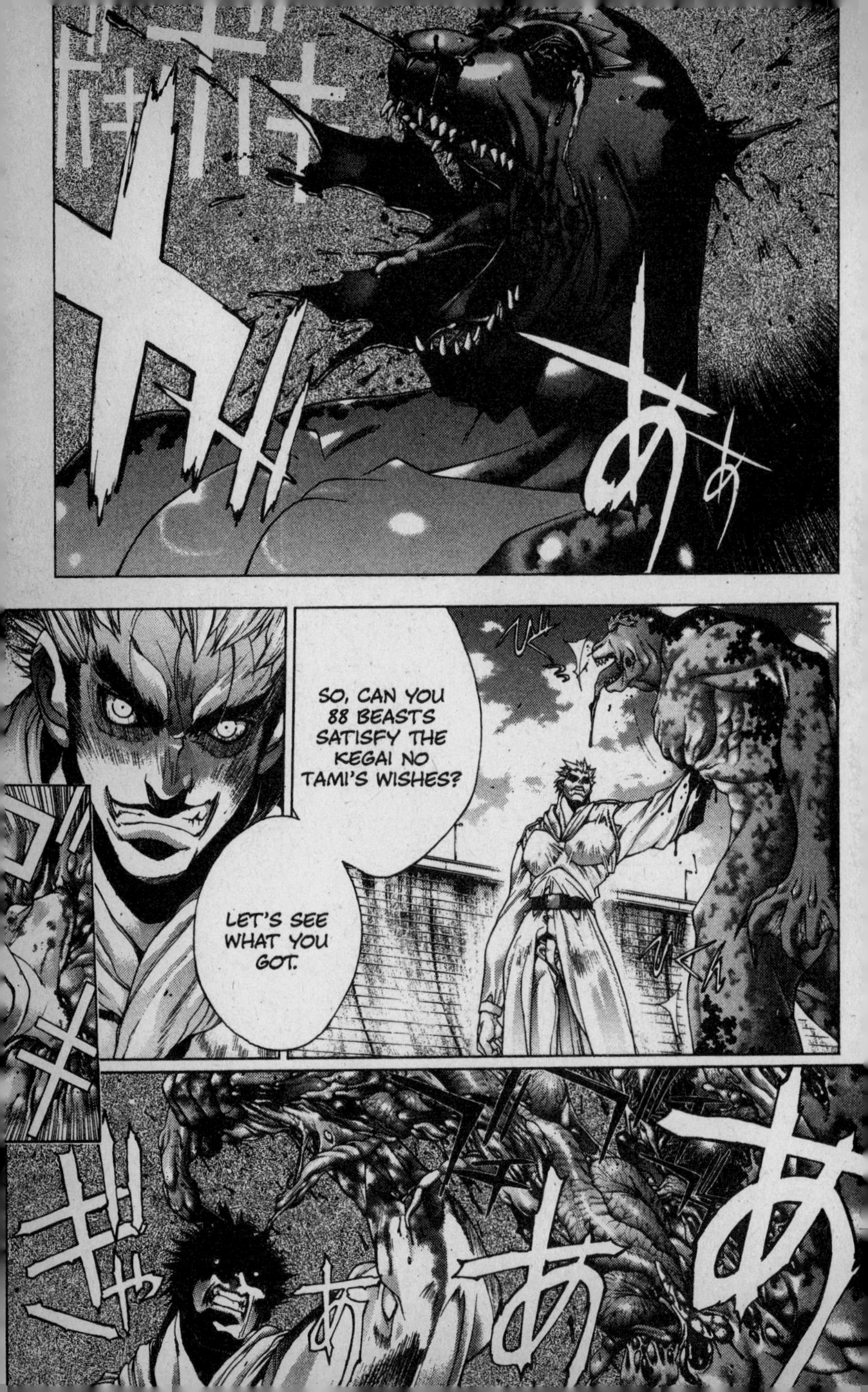
SO, CAN YOU 88 BEASTS SATISFY THE KEGAI NO TAMI'S WISHES?
LET'S SEE WHAT YOU GOT.

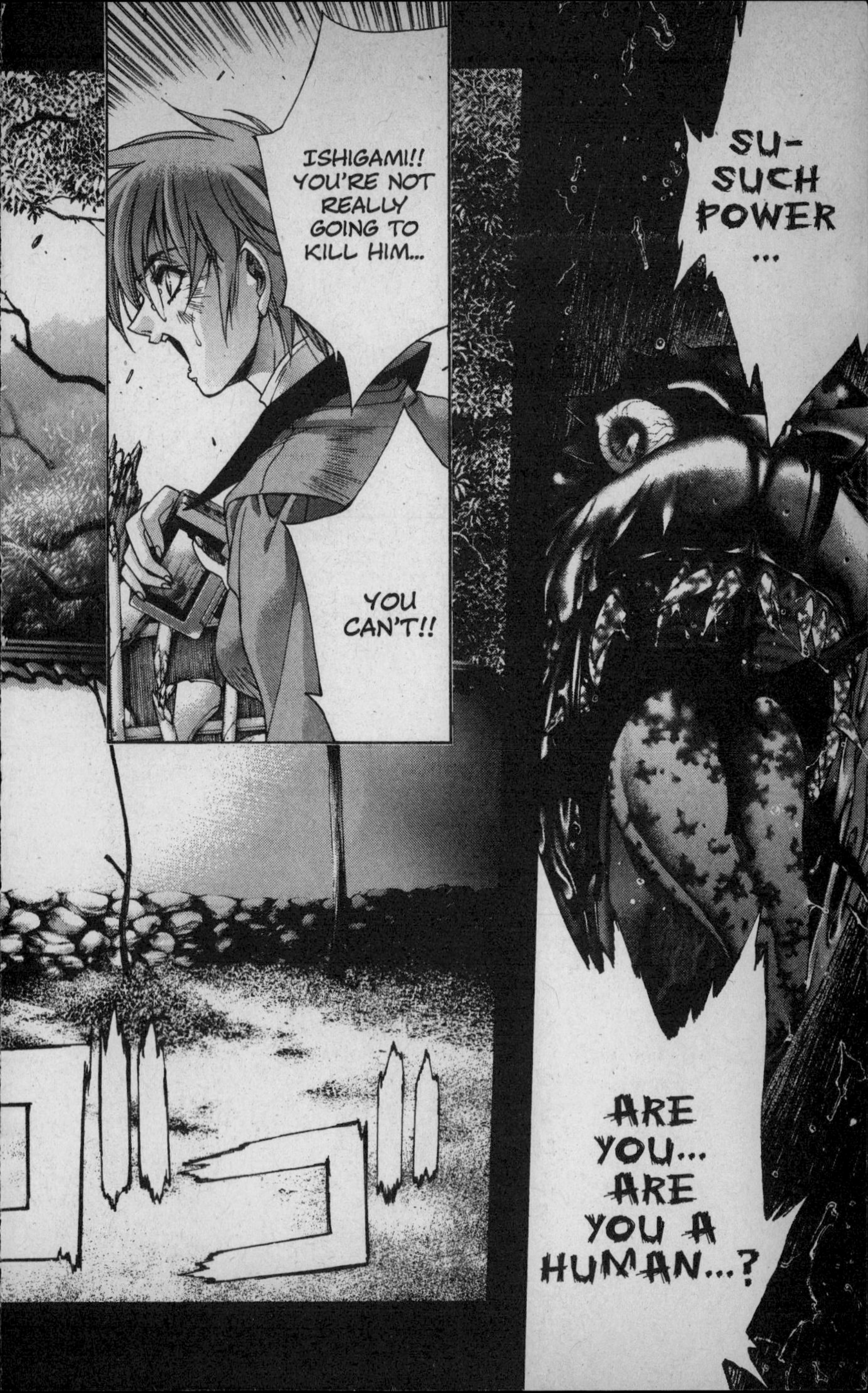
SU-SUCH POWER...
ARE YOU... ARE YOU A HUMAN...?
ISHIGAMI!! YOU'RE NOT REALLY GOING TO KILL HIM...
YOU CAN'T!!

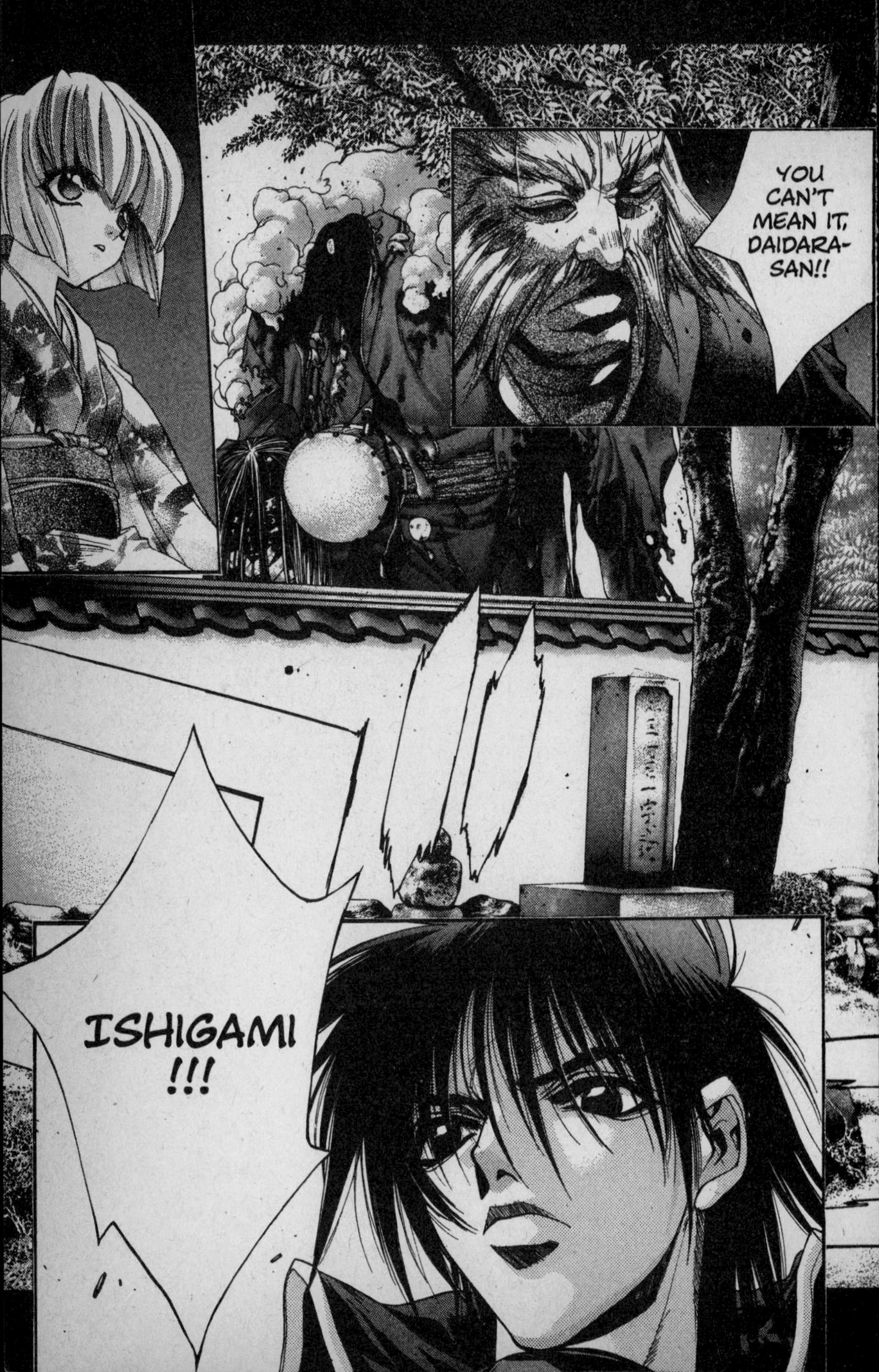
YOU CAN'T MEAN IT, DAIDARA-SAN!!
ISHIGAMI !!!

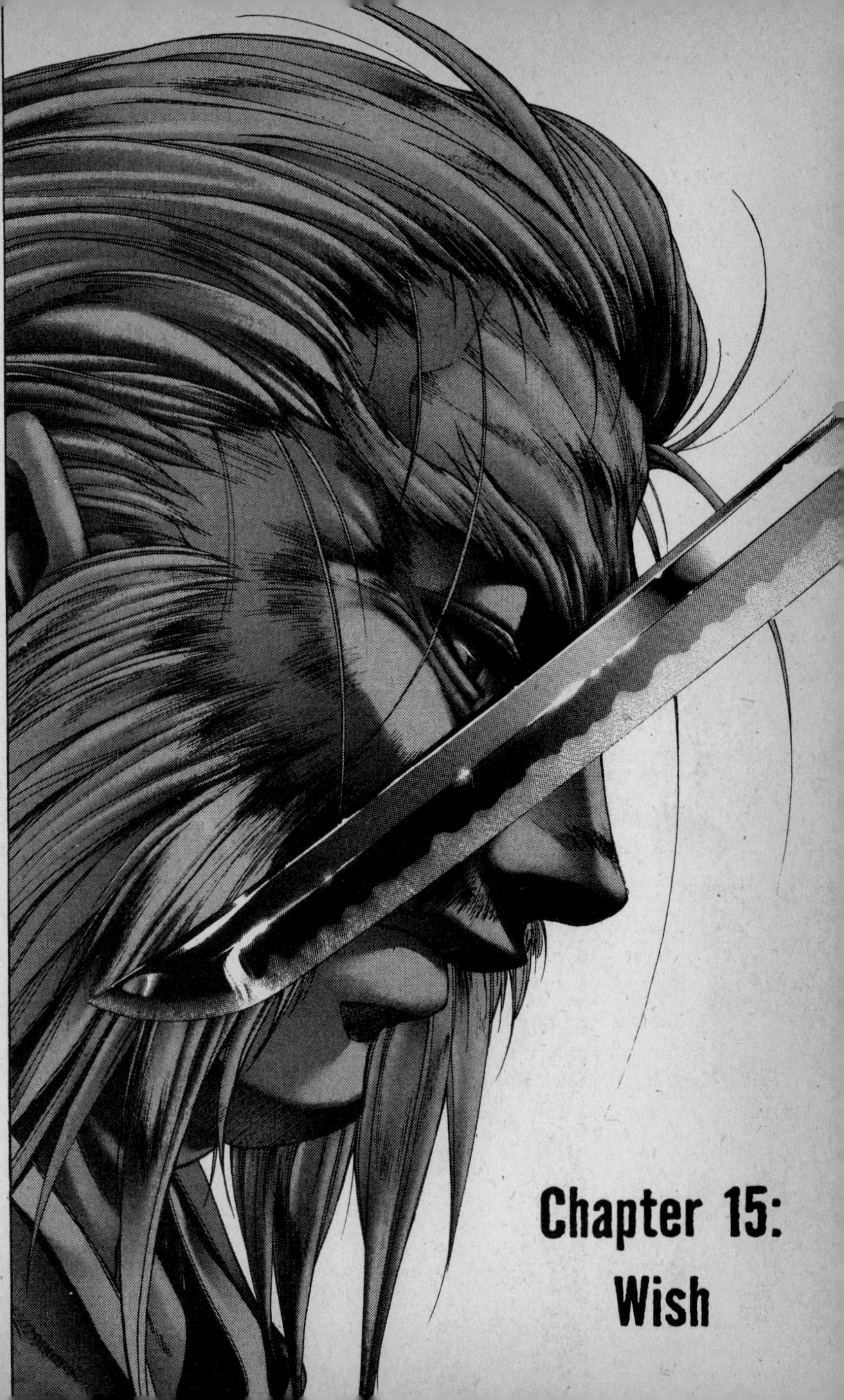

Chapter 15: Wish

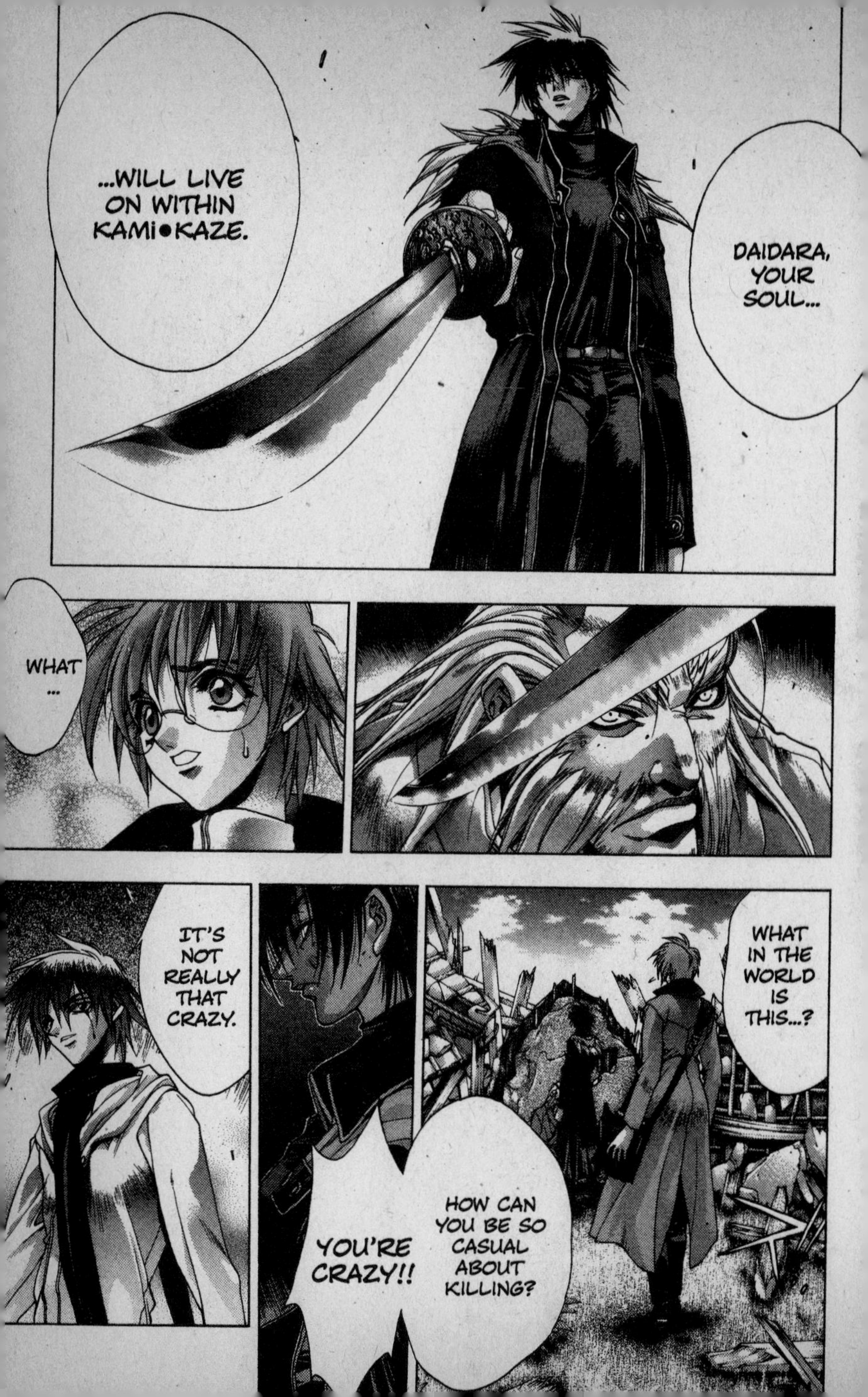
DAIDARA, YOUR SOUL...
...WILL LIVE ON WITHIN KAMI•KAZE.
WHAT ...
WHAT IN THE WORLD IS THIS...?
HOW CAN YOU BE SO CASUAL ABOUT KILLING?
YOU'RE CRAZY!!
IT'S NOT REALLY THAT CRAZY.

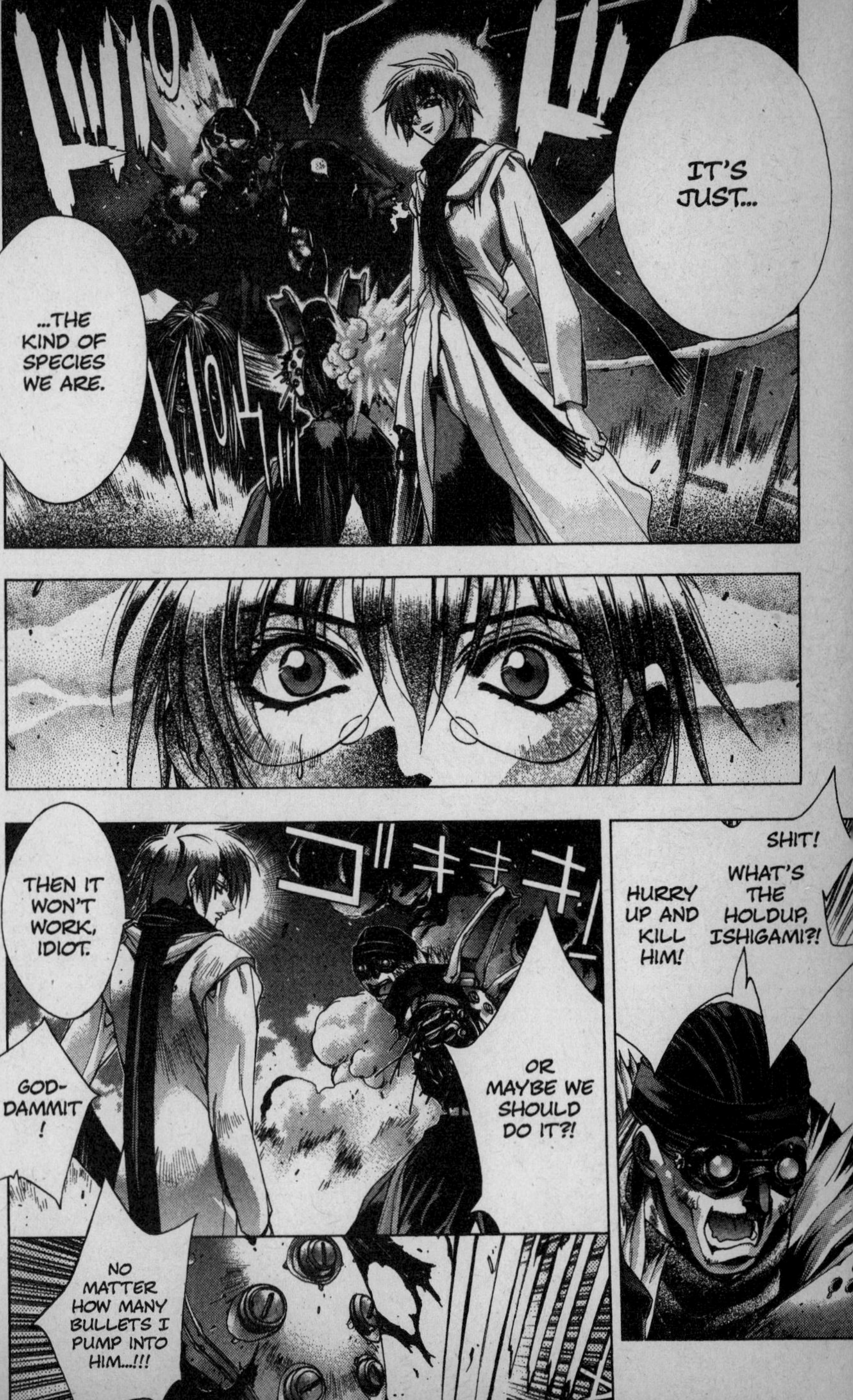
IT'S JUST...
...THE KIND OF SPECIES WE ARE.
SHIT!
WHAT'S THE HOLDUP, ISHIGAMI?!
HURRY UP AND KILL HIM!
OR MAYBE WE SHOULD DO IT?!
THEN IT WON'T WORK, IDIOT.
GOD-DAMMIT!
NO MATTER HOW MANY BULLETS I PUMP INTO HIM...!!!

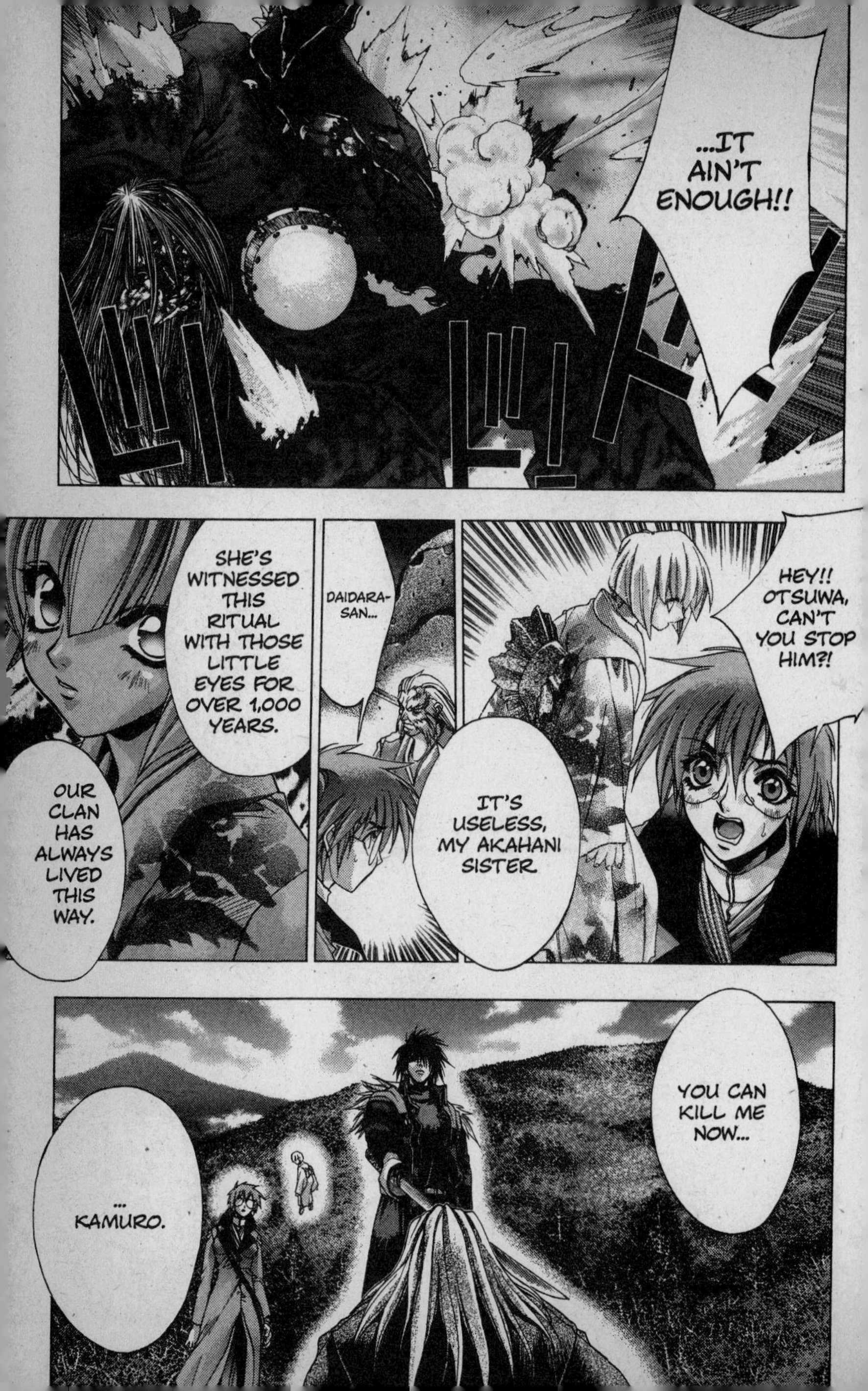
...IT AIN'T ENOUGH!!
HEY!! OTSUWA, CAN'T YOU STOP HIM?!
IT'S USELESS, MY AKAHANI SISTER
DAIDARA-SAN...
SHE'S WITNESSED THIS RITUAL WITH THOSE LITTLE EYES FOR OVER 1,000 YEARS.
OUR CLAN HAS ALWAYS LIVED THIS WAY.
YOU CAN KILL ME NOW...
... KAMURO.

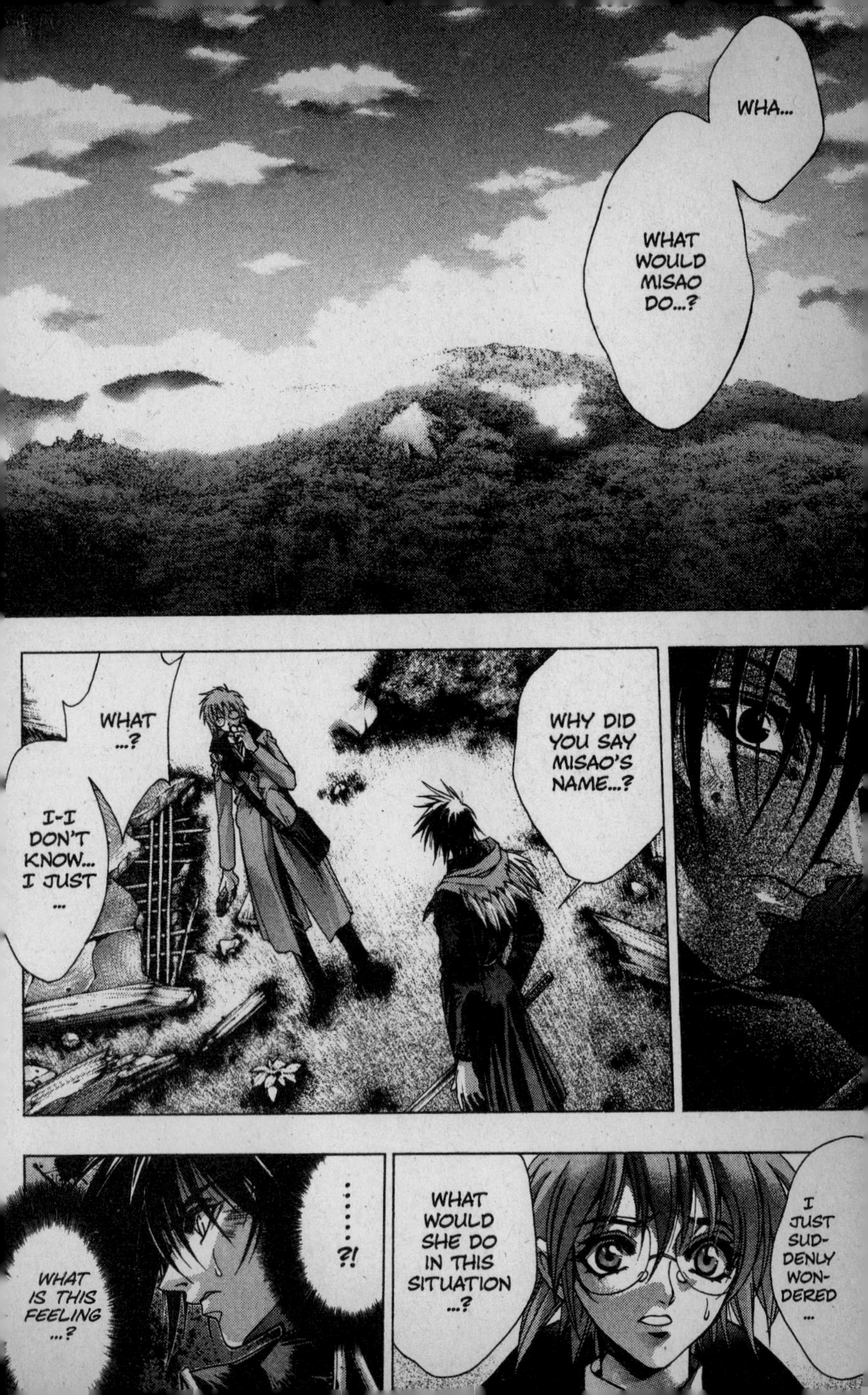
WHA...
WHAT WOULD MISAO DO...?
WHY DID YOU SAY MISAO'S NAME...?
WHAT ...?
I-I DON'T KNOW... I JUST ...
I JUST SUDDENLY WONDERED ...
WHAT WOULD SHE DO IN THIS SITUATION ...?
......?!
WHAT IS THIS FEELING ...?

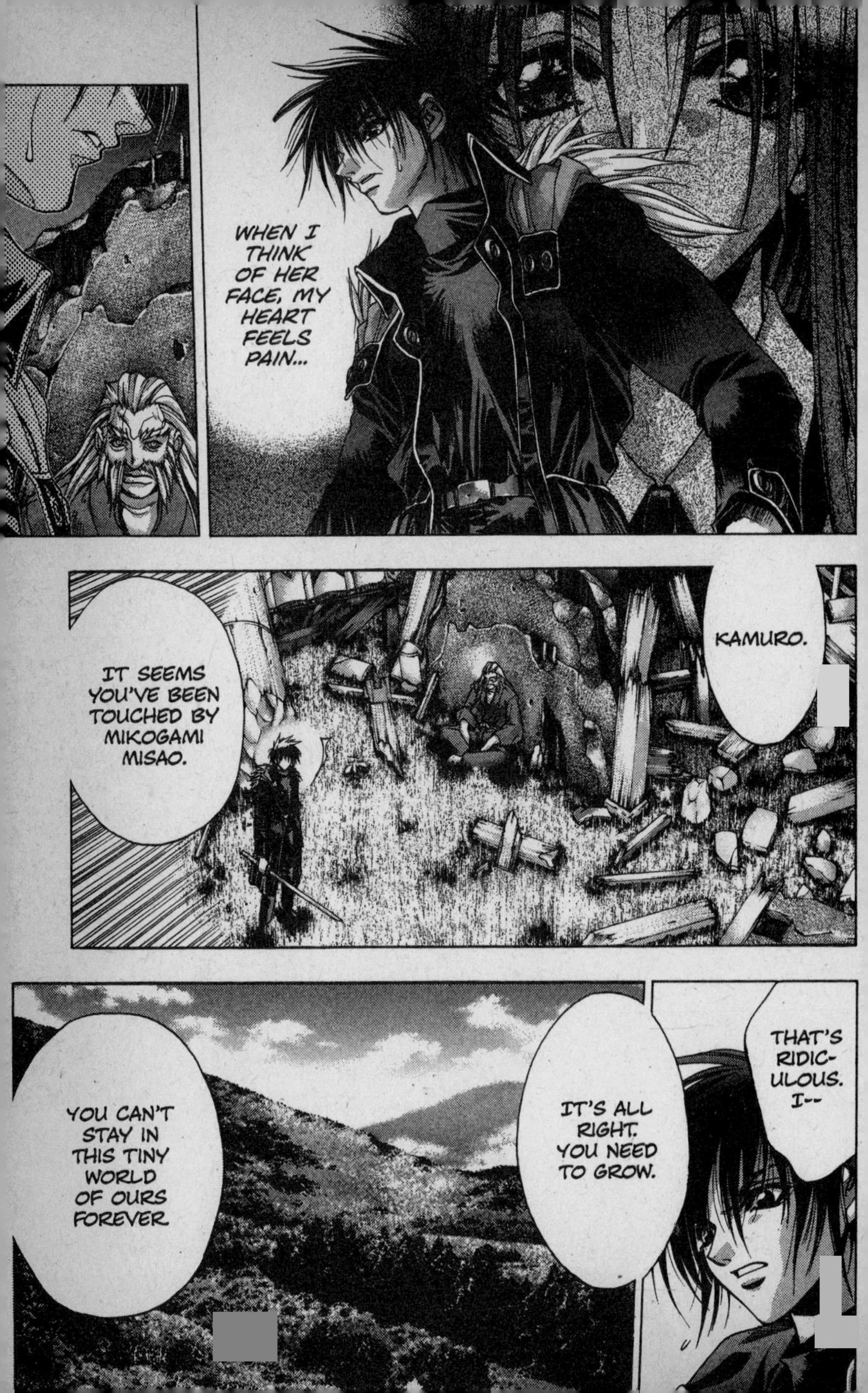
WHEN I THINK OF HER FACE, MY HEART FEELS PAIN...
KAMURO.
IT SEEMS YOU'VE BEEN TOUCHED BY MIKOGAMI MISAO.
THAT'S RIDICULOUS. I--
IT'S ALL RIGHT. YOU NEED TO GROW.
YOU CAN'T STAY IN THIS TINY WORLD OF OURS FOREVER

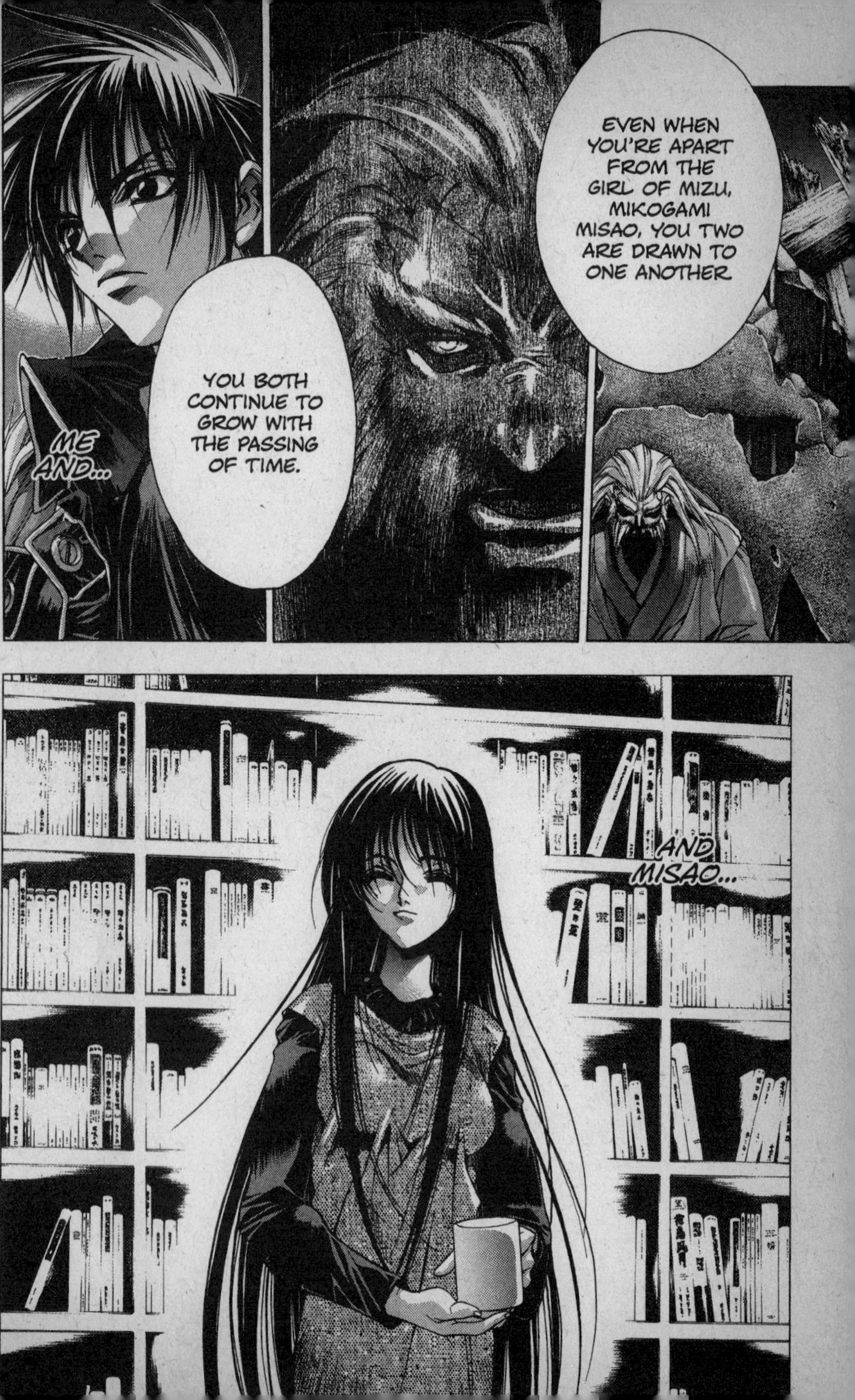
EVEN WHEN YOU'RE APART FROM THE GIRL OF MIZU, MIKOGAMI MISAO, YOU TWO ARE DRAWN TO ONE ANOTHER
YOU BOTH CONTINUE TO GROW WITH THE PASSING OF TIME.
ME AND...
AND MISAO...

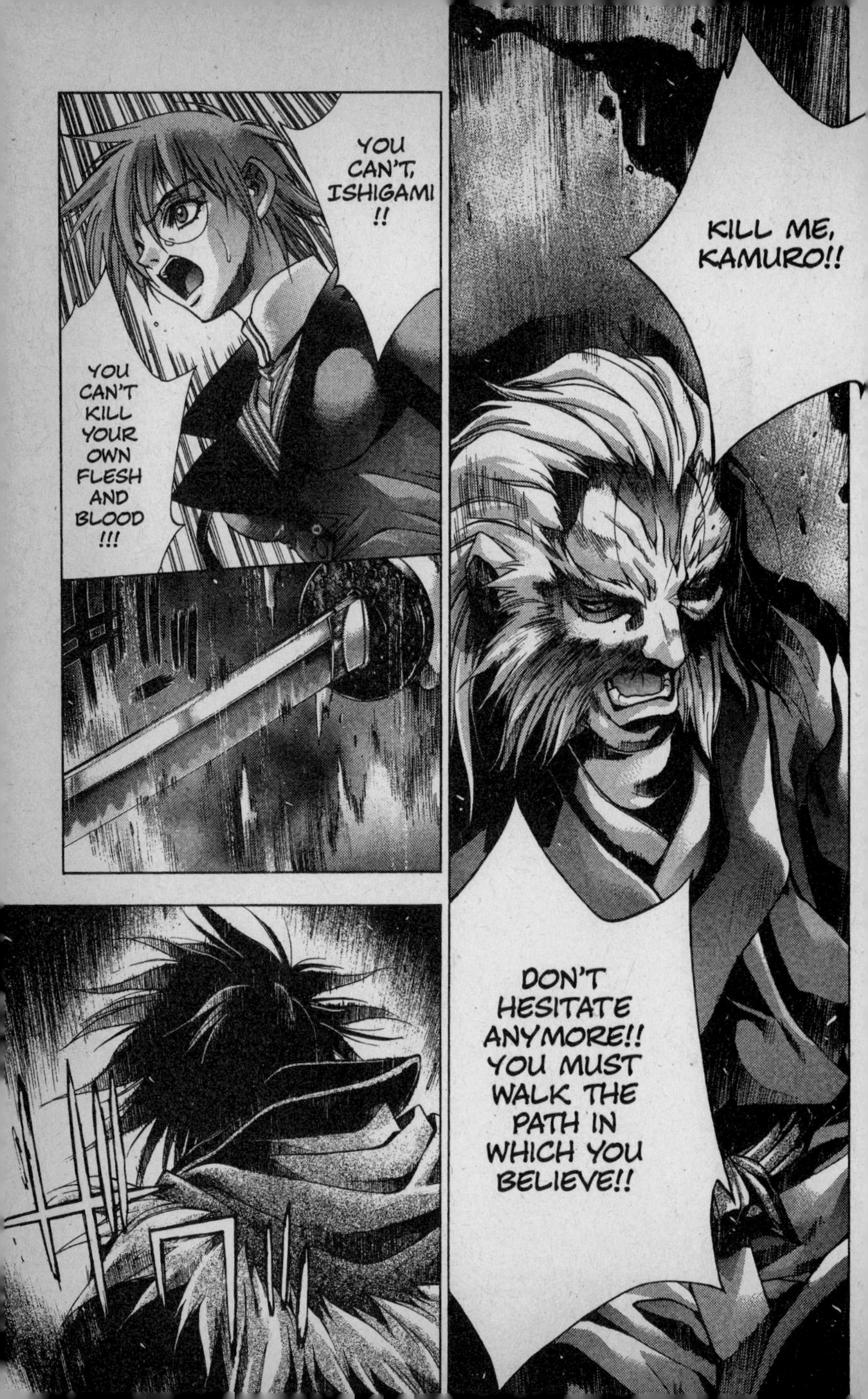
KILL ME, KAMURO!!
DON'T HESITATE ANYMORE!! YOU MUST WALK THE PATH IN WHICH YOU BELIEVE!!
YOU CAN'T, ISHIGAMI !!
YOU CAN'T KILL YOUR OWN FLESH AND BLOOD !!!

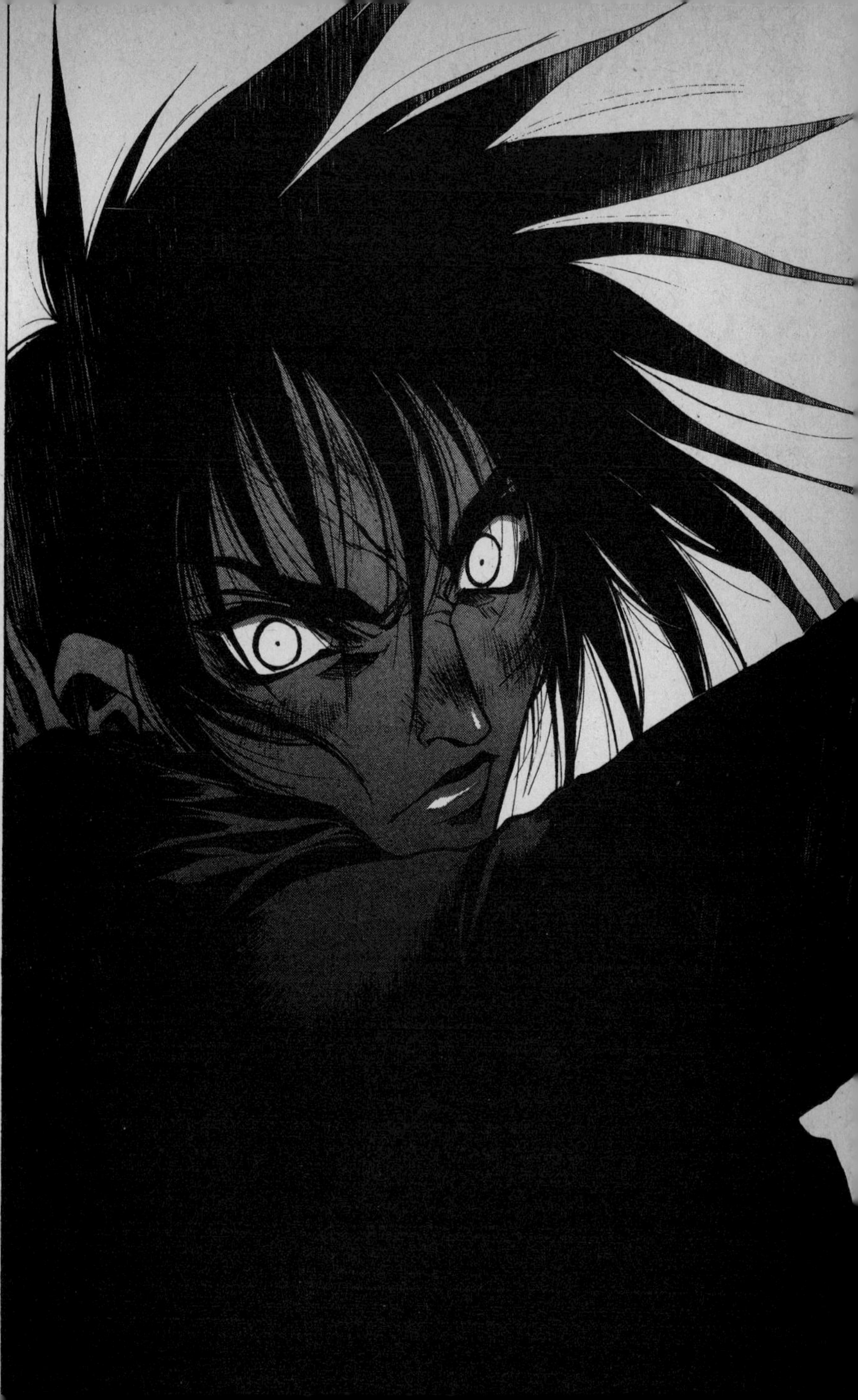

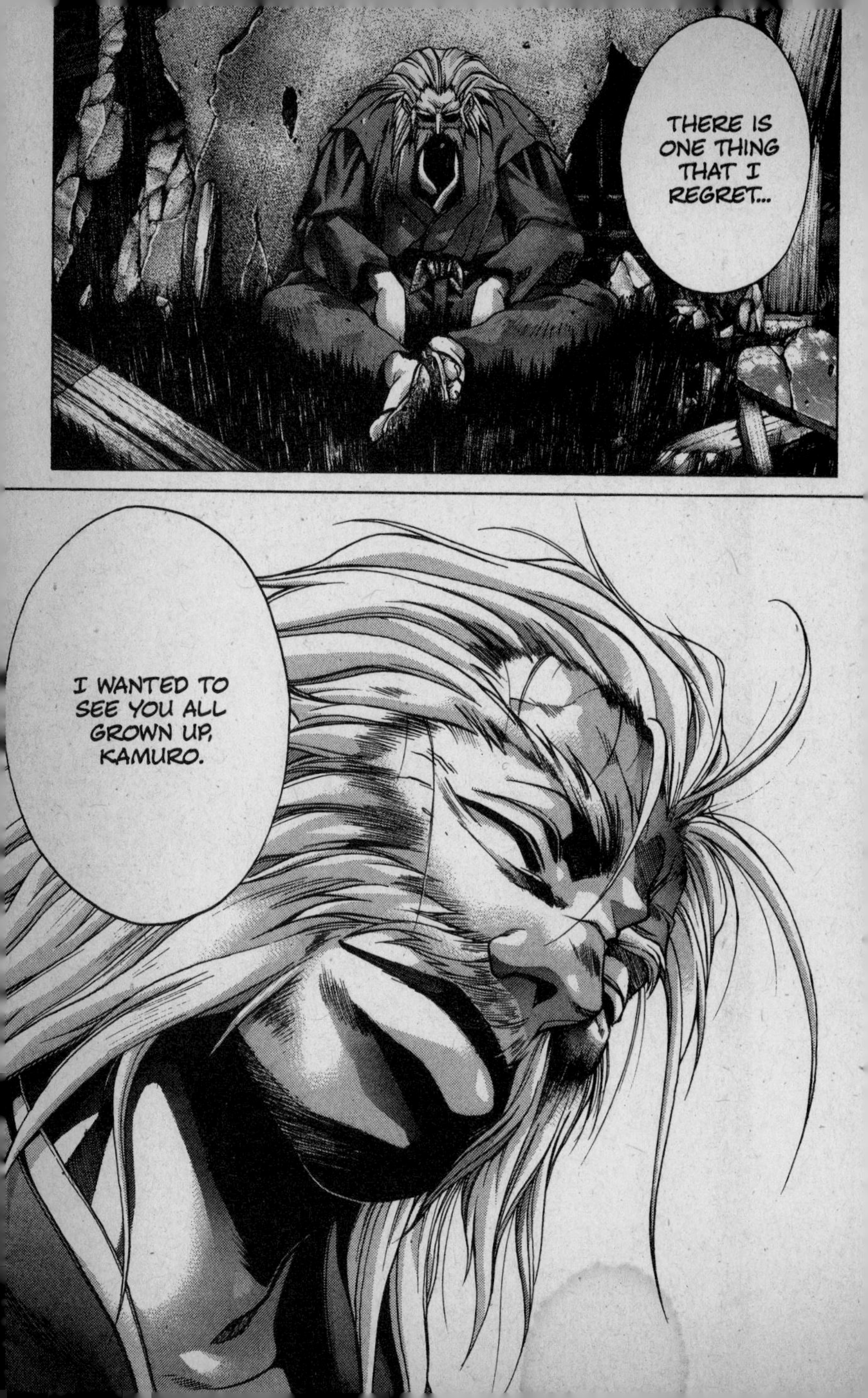
THERE IS ONE THING THAT I REGRET...
I WANTED TO SEE YOU ALL GROWN UP, KAMURO.

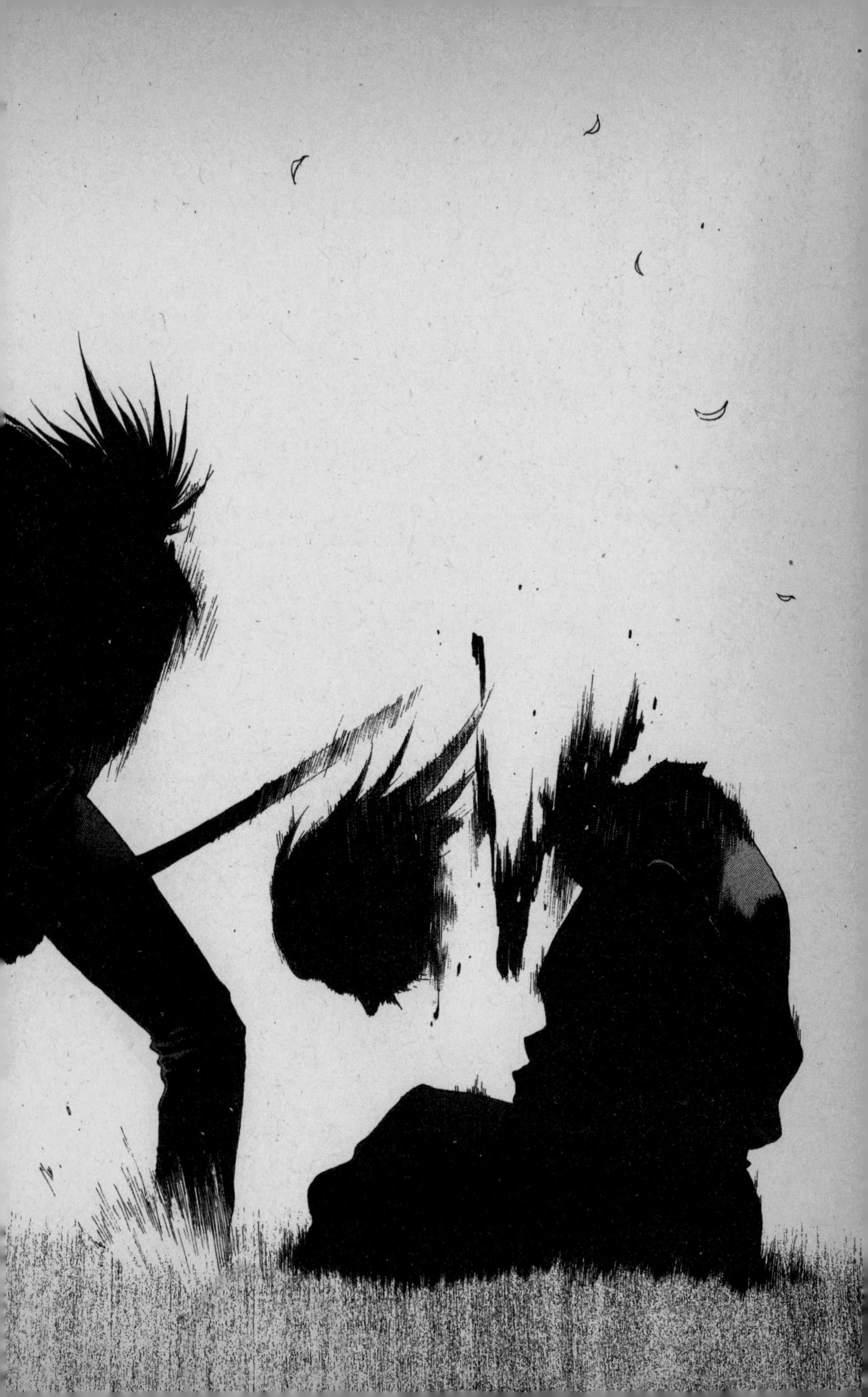

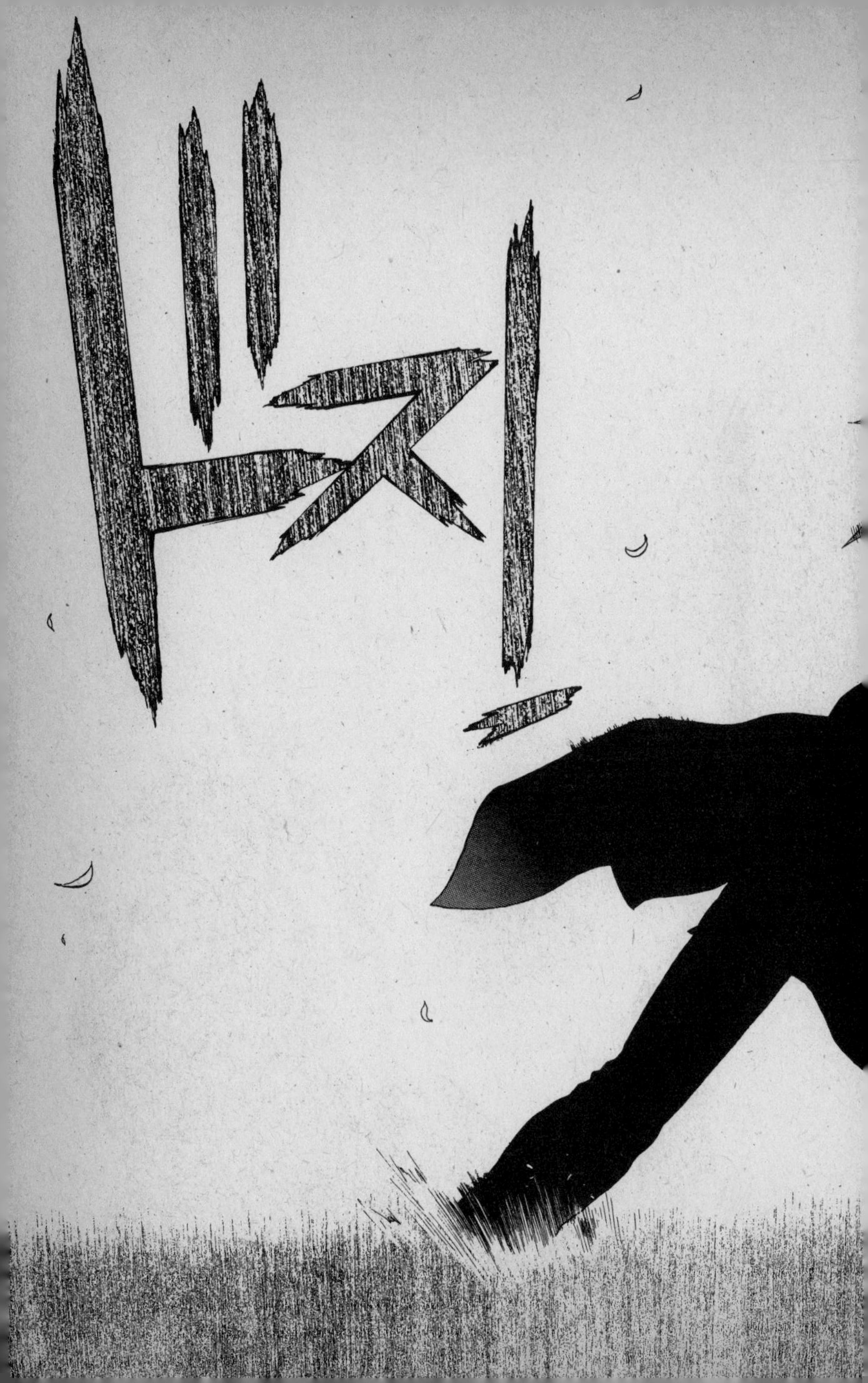
ドズッ

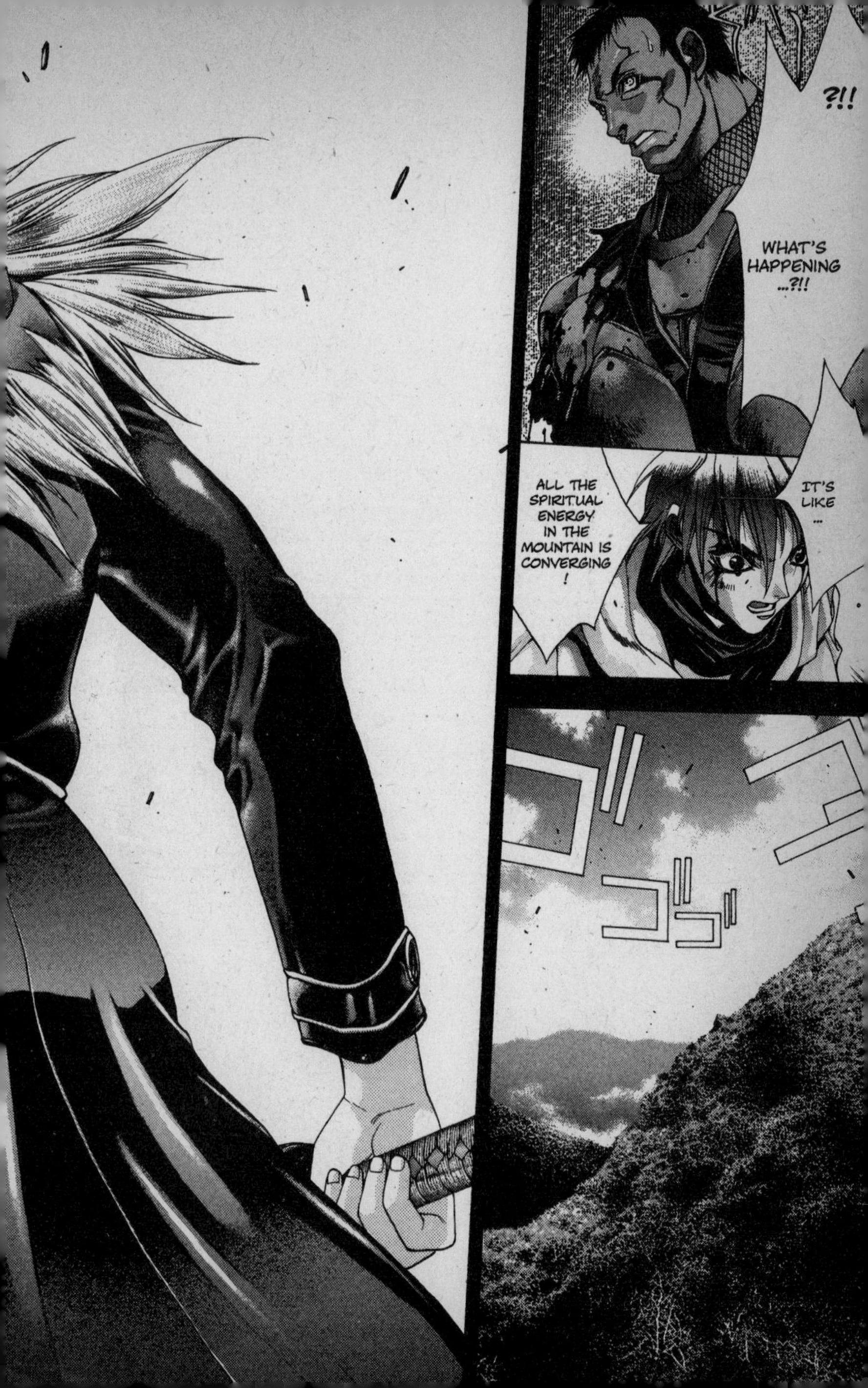

?!!
WHAT'S HAPPENING ...?!!
IT'S LIKE ...
ALL THE SPIRITUAL ENERGY IN THE MOUNTAIN IS CONVERGING !

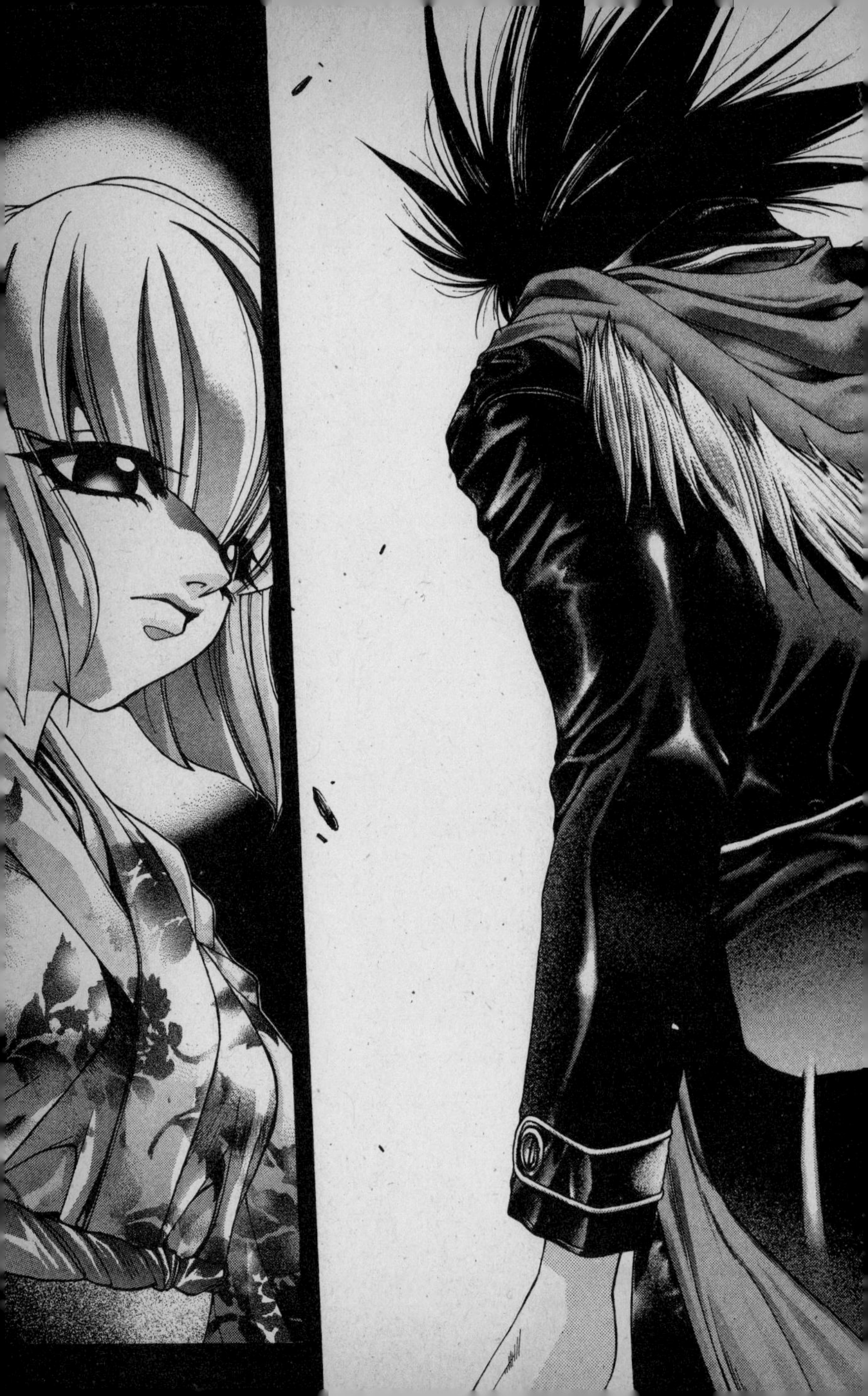

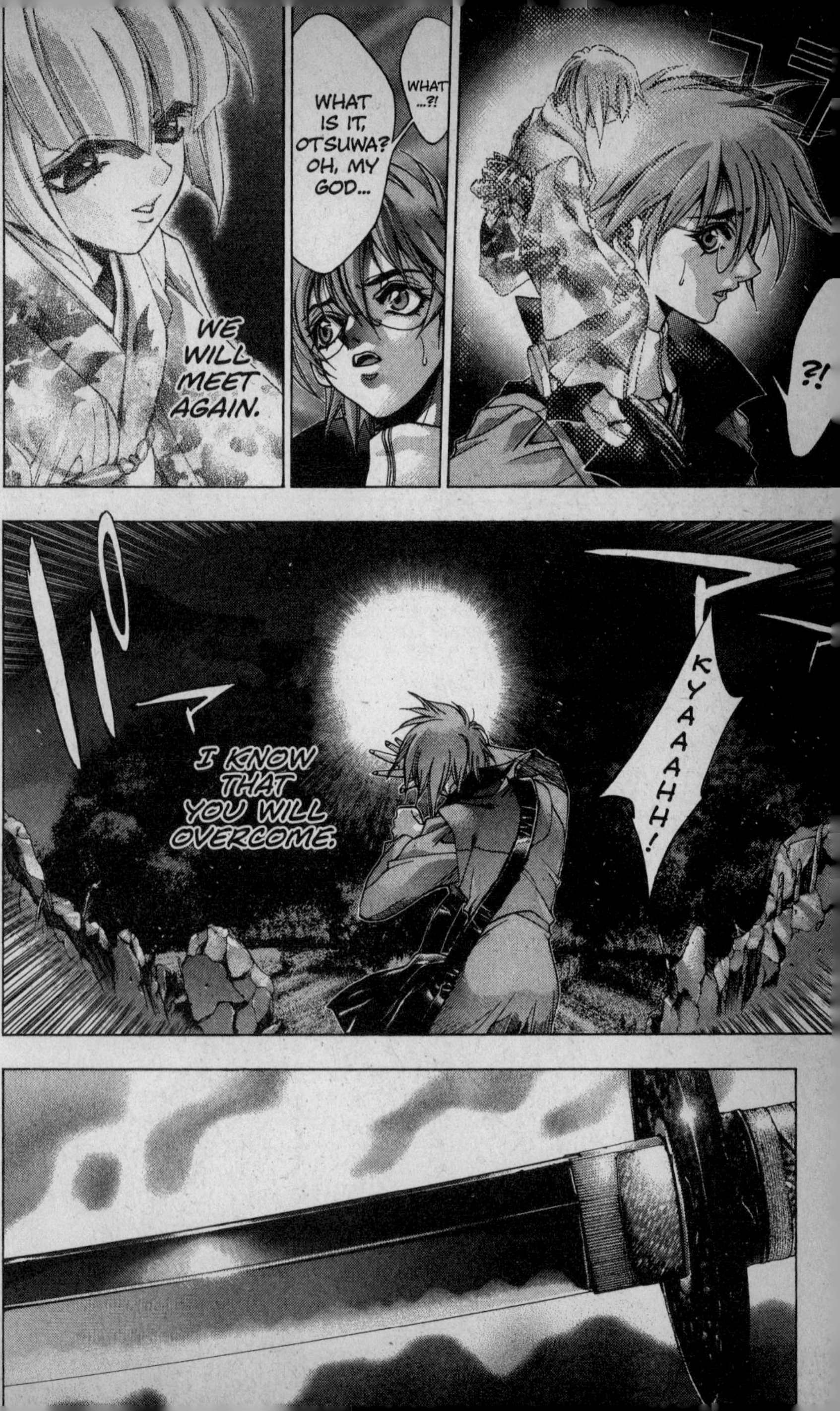
?!
WHAT ...?!
WHAT IS IT, OTSUWA? OH, MY GOD...
WE WILL MEET AGAIN.
KYAAAAHH!
I KNOW THAT YOU WILL OVERCOME.

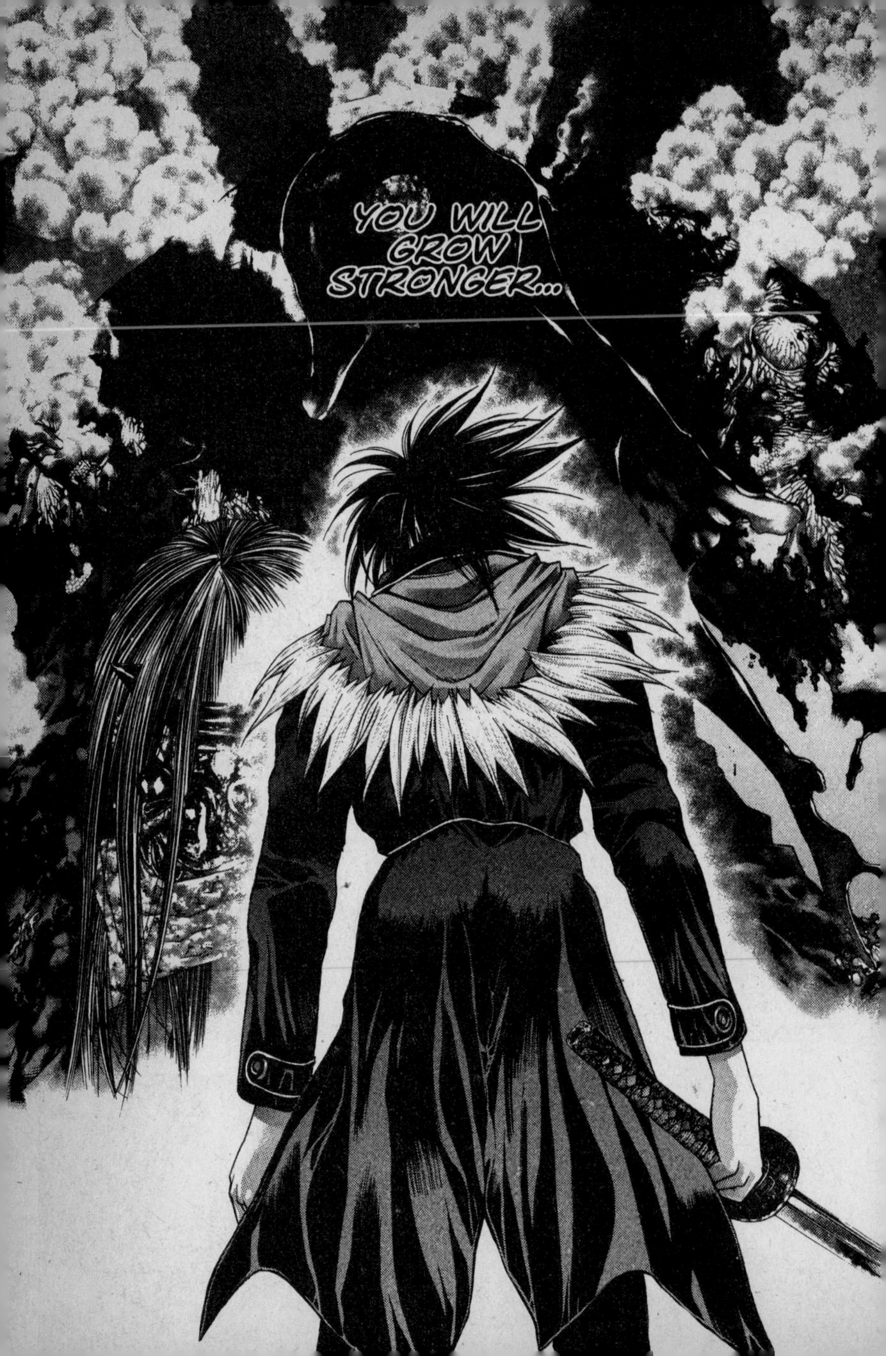
YOU WILL GROW STRONGER...

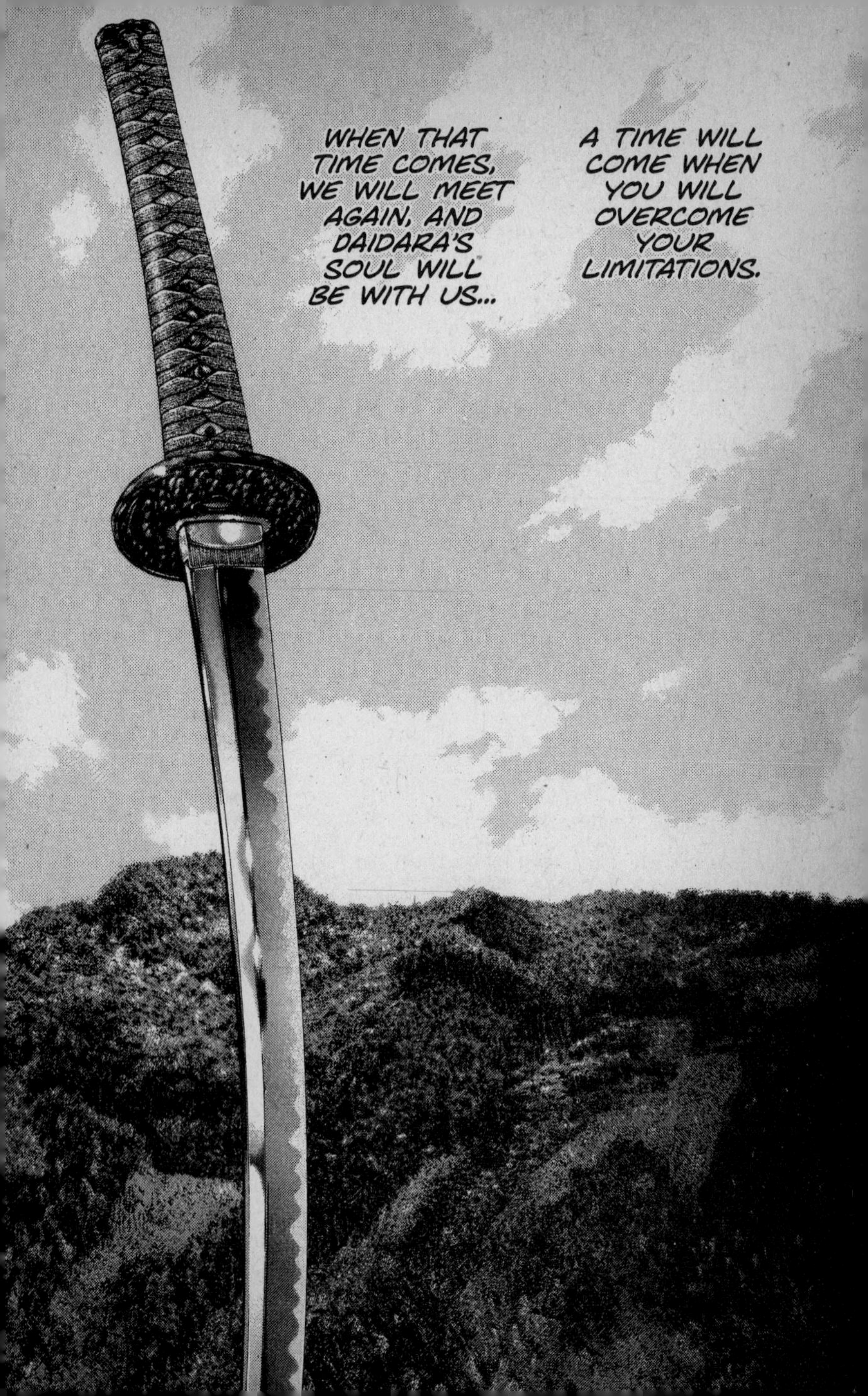
A TIME WILL COME WHEN YOU WILL OVERCOME YOUR LIMITATIONS.
WHEN THAT TIME COMES, WE WILL MEET AGAIN, AND DAIDARA'S SOUL WILL BE WITH US...

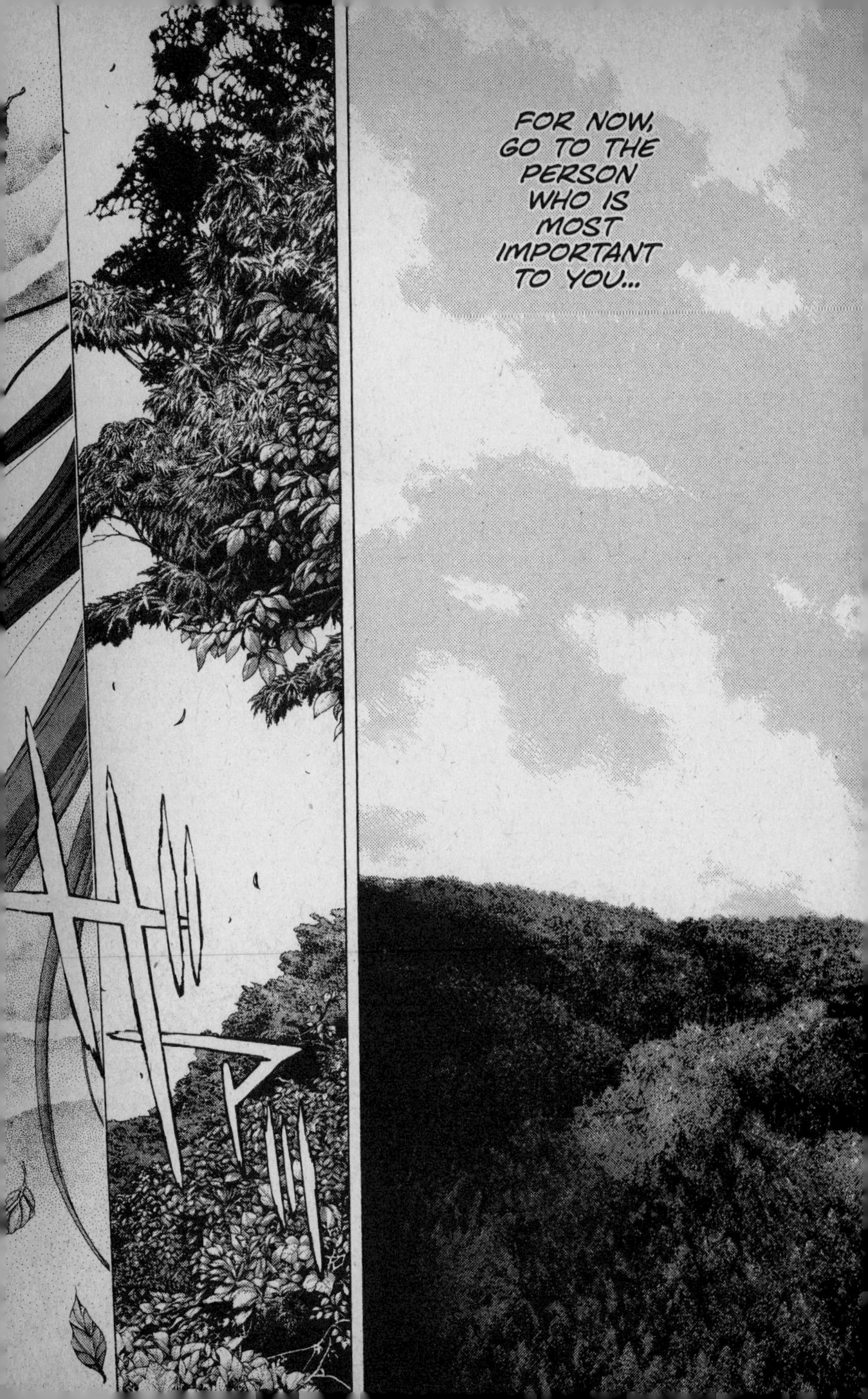
FOR NOW, GO TO THE PERSON WHO IS MOST IMPORTANT TO YOU...

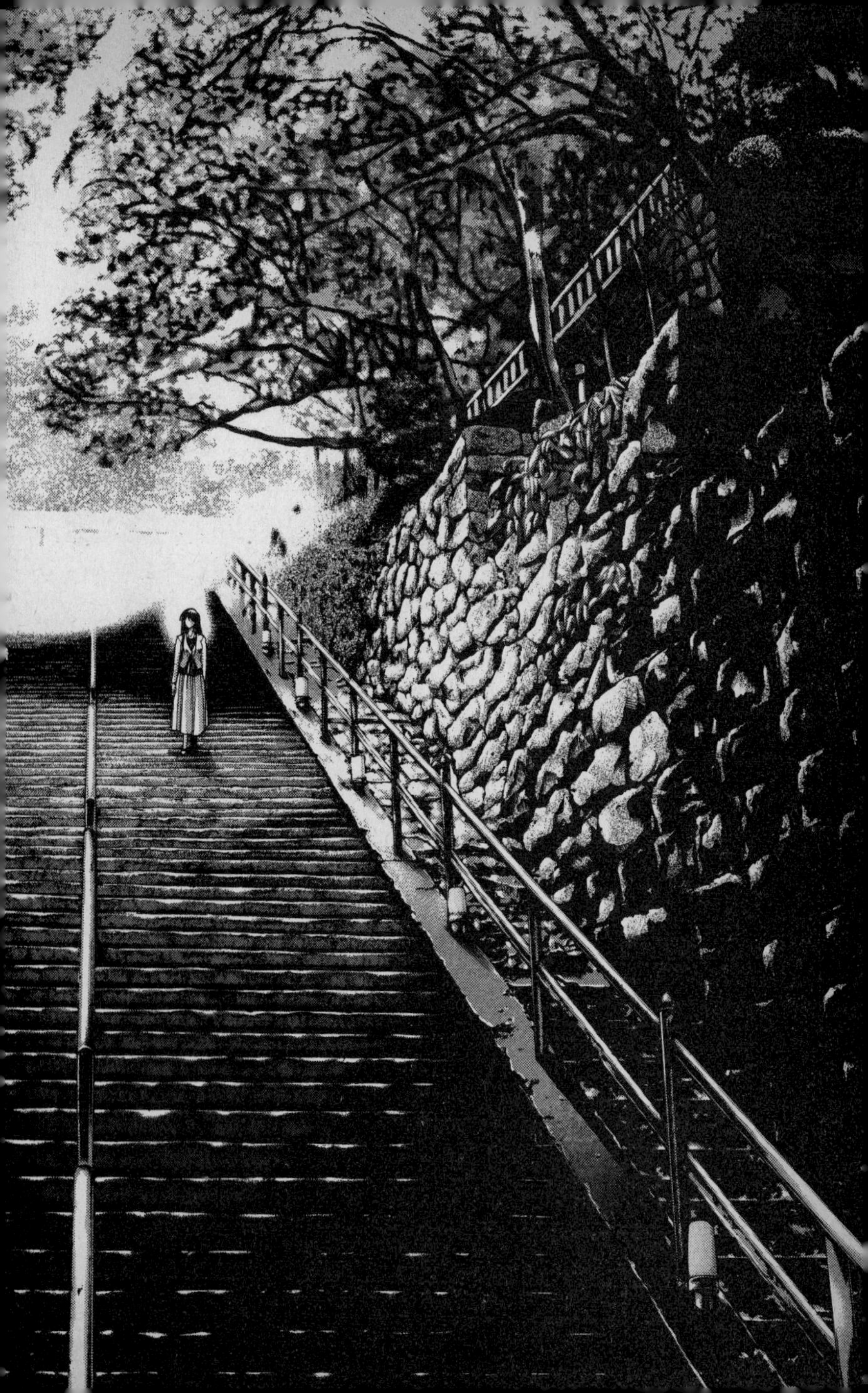

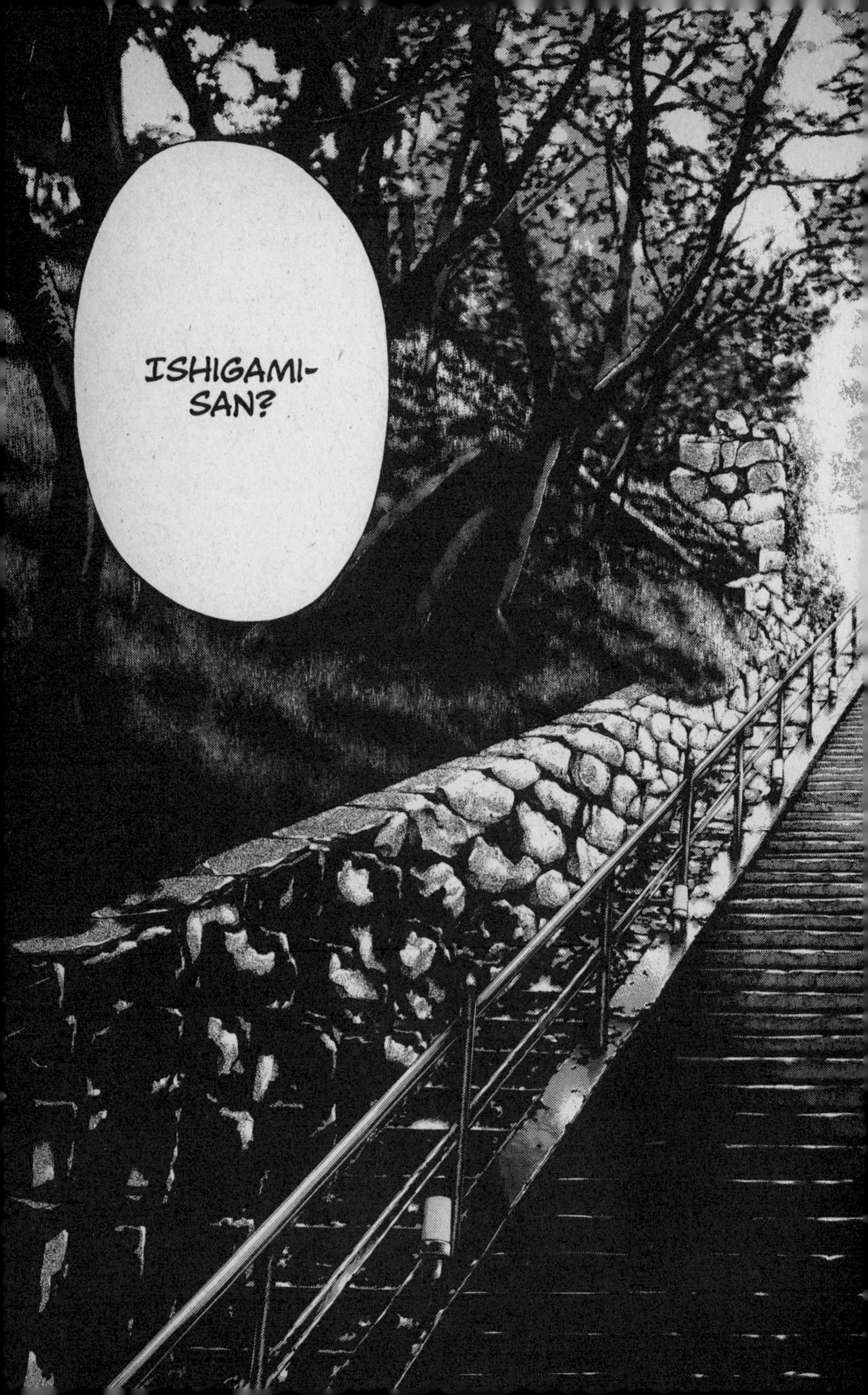
ISHIGAMI-SAN?

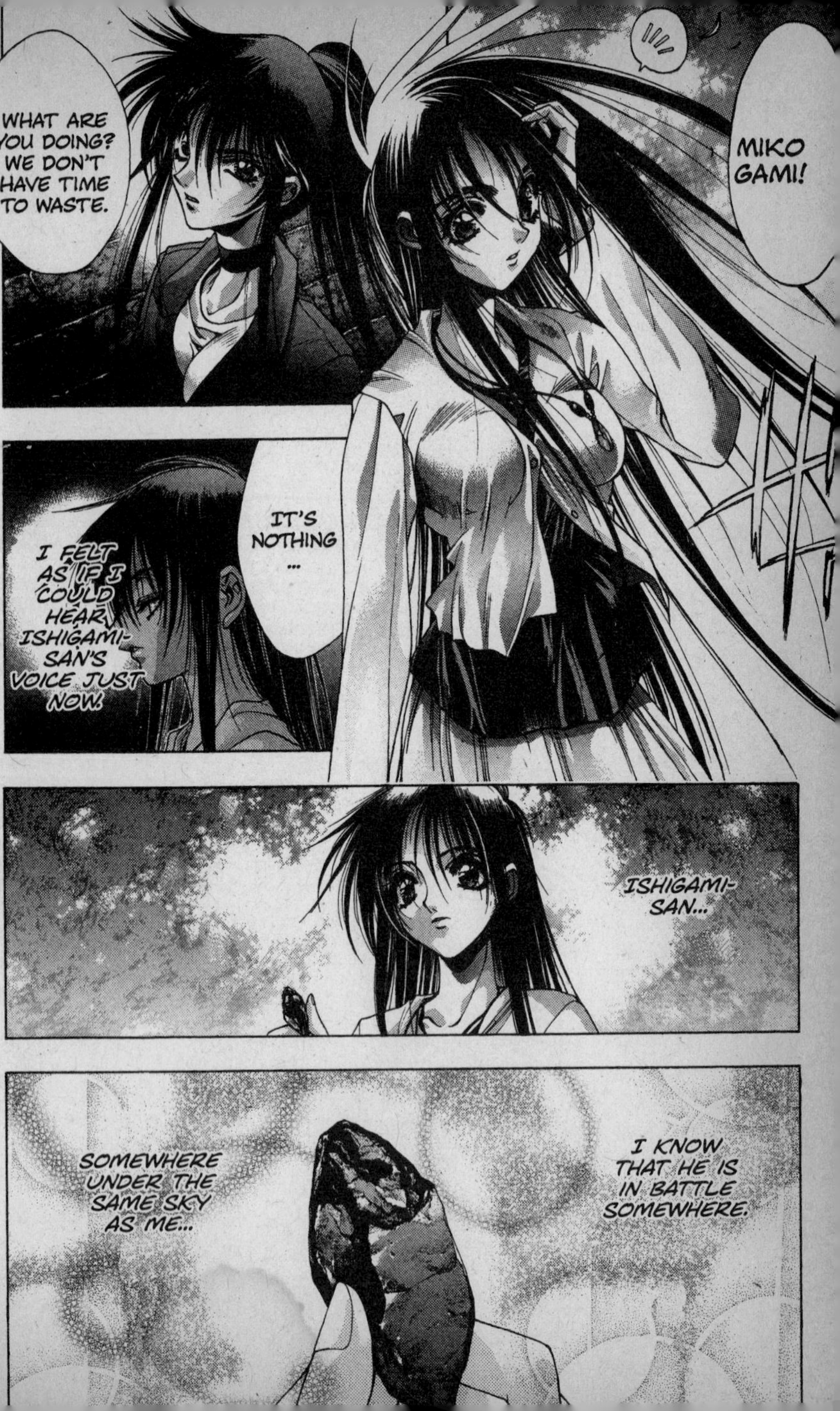
MIKO GAMI!
WHAT ARE YOU DOING? WE DON'T HAVE TIME TO WASTE.
IT'S NOTHING ...
I FELT AS IF I COULD HEAR ISHIGAMI-SAN'S VOICE JUST NOW.
ISHIGAMI-SAN...
I KNOW THAT HE IS IN BATTLE SOMEWHERE.
SOMEWHERE UNDER THE SAME SKY AS ME...

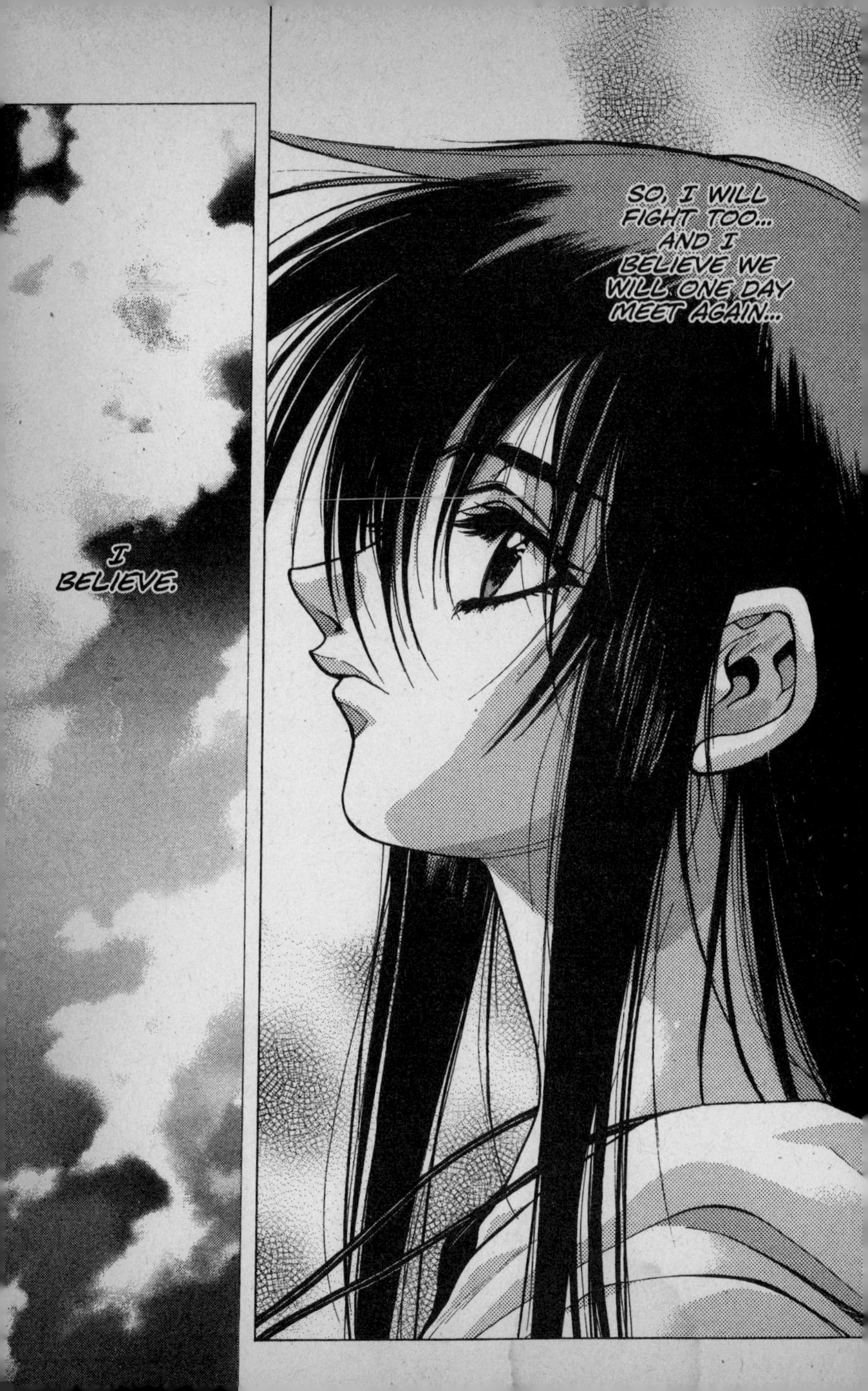
SO, I WILL FIGHT TOO... AND I BELIEVE WE WILL ONE DAY MEET AGAIN...
I BELIEVE.

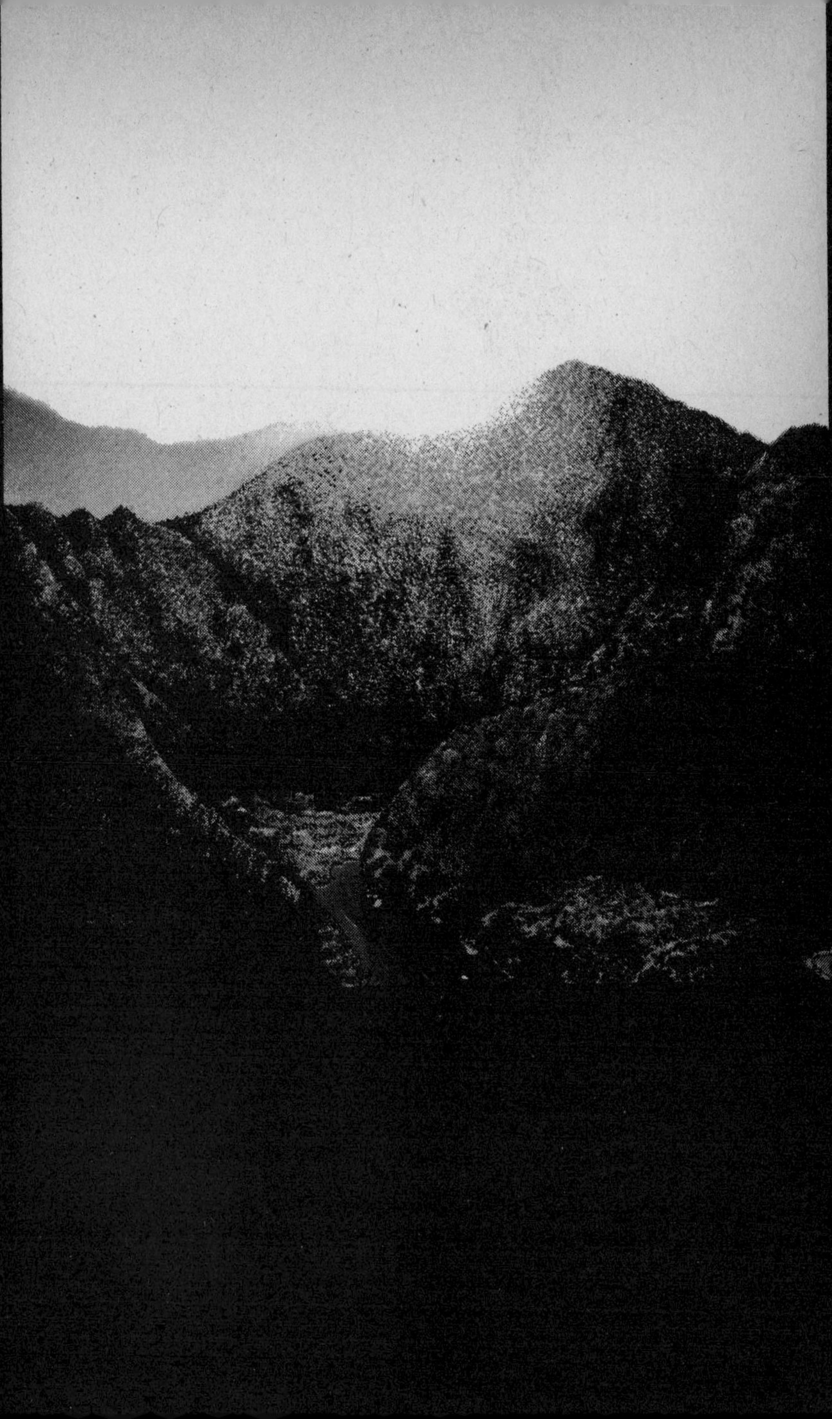

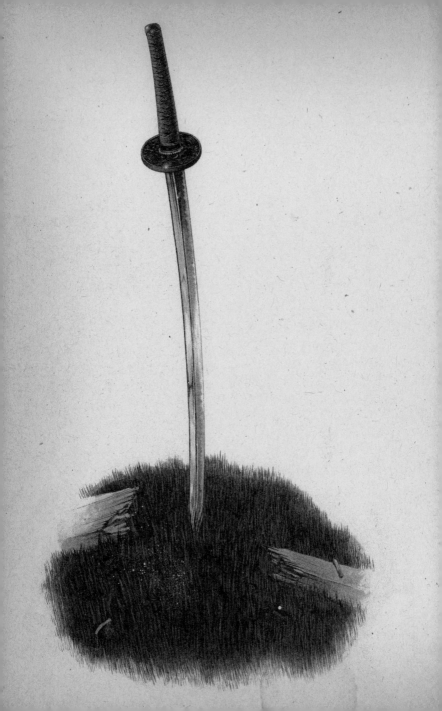

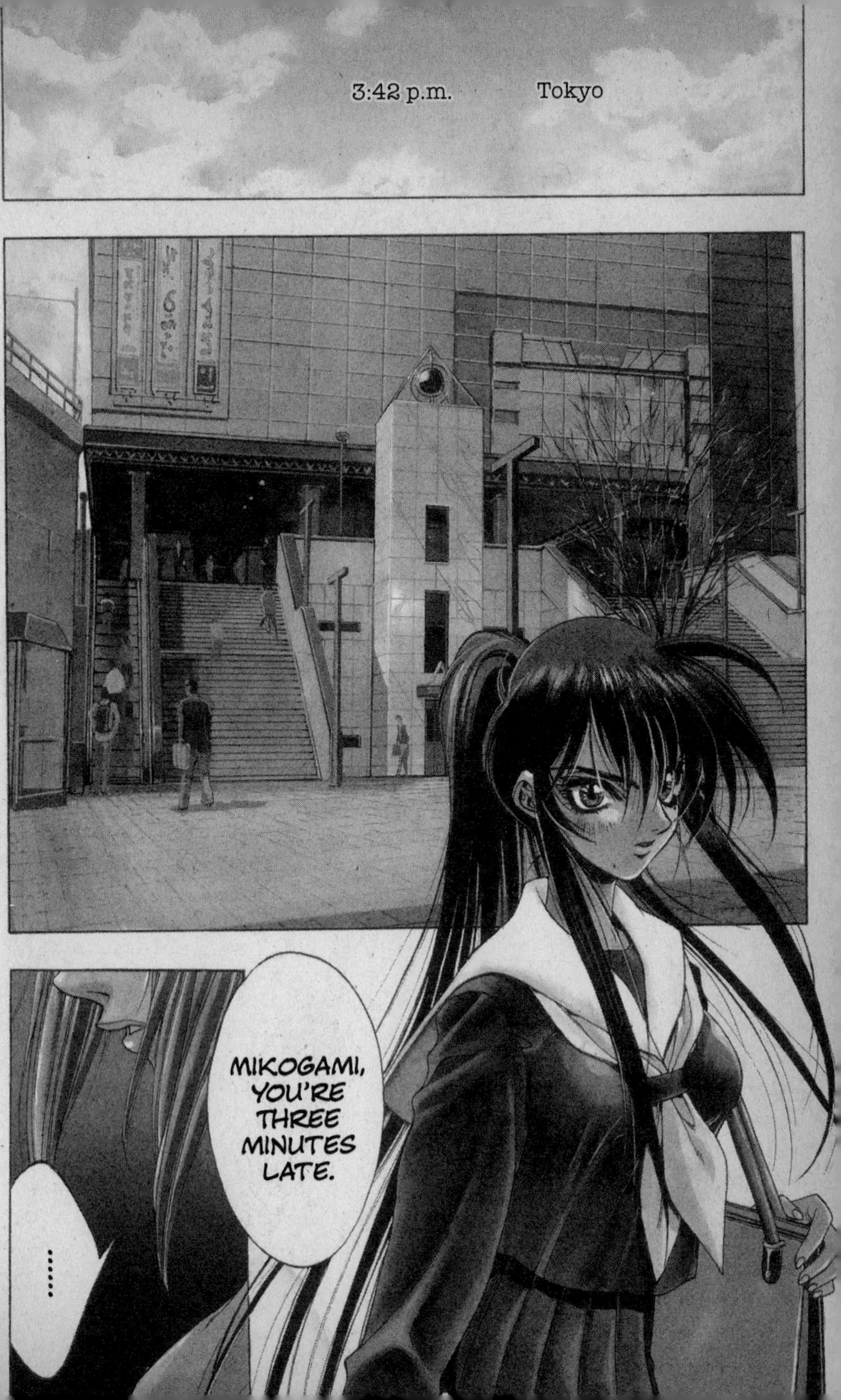
3:42 p.m. Tokyo
MIKOGAMI, YOU'RE THREE MINUTES LATE.
......

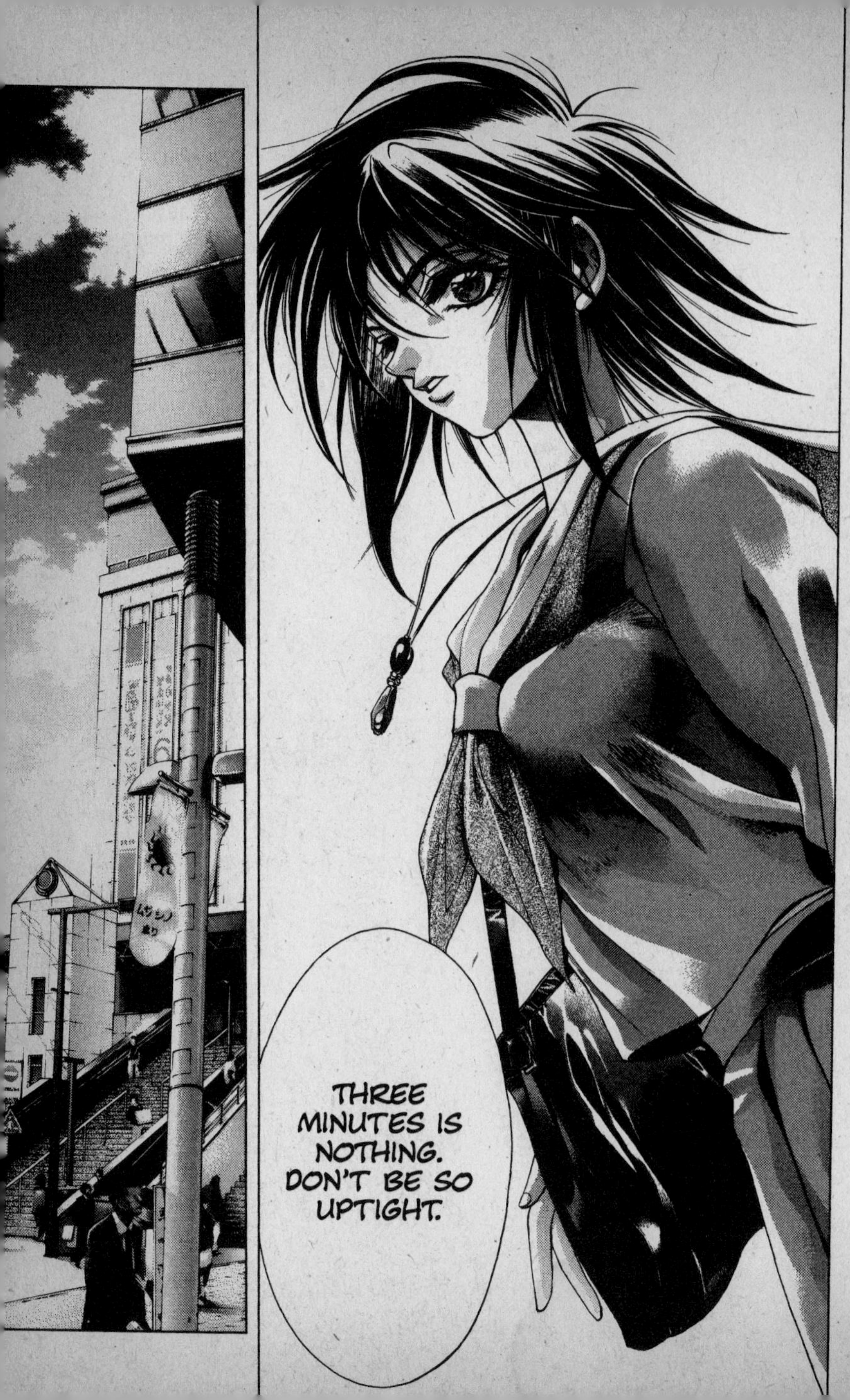
THREE MINUTES IS NOTHING. DON'T BE SO UPTIGHT.

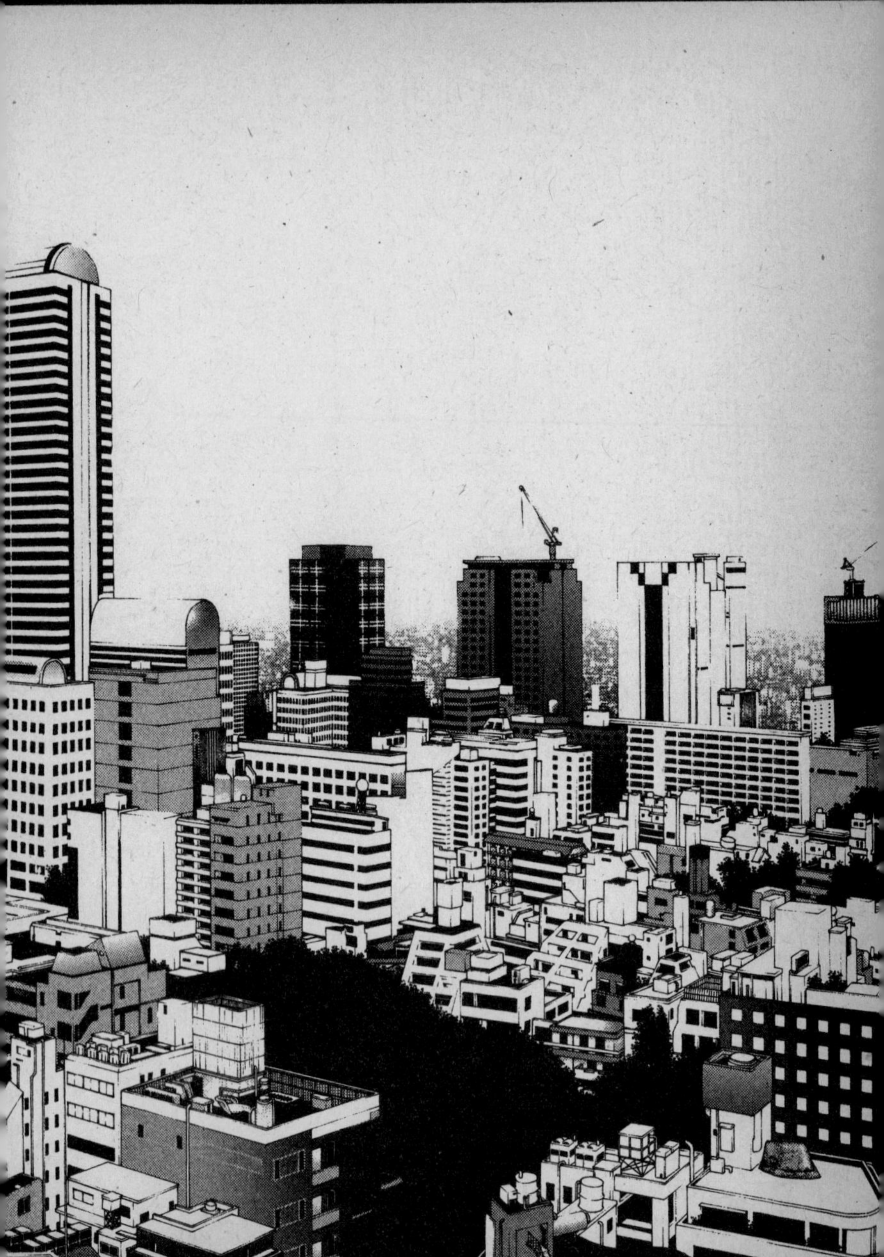

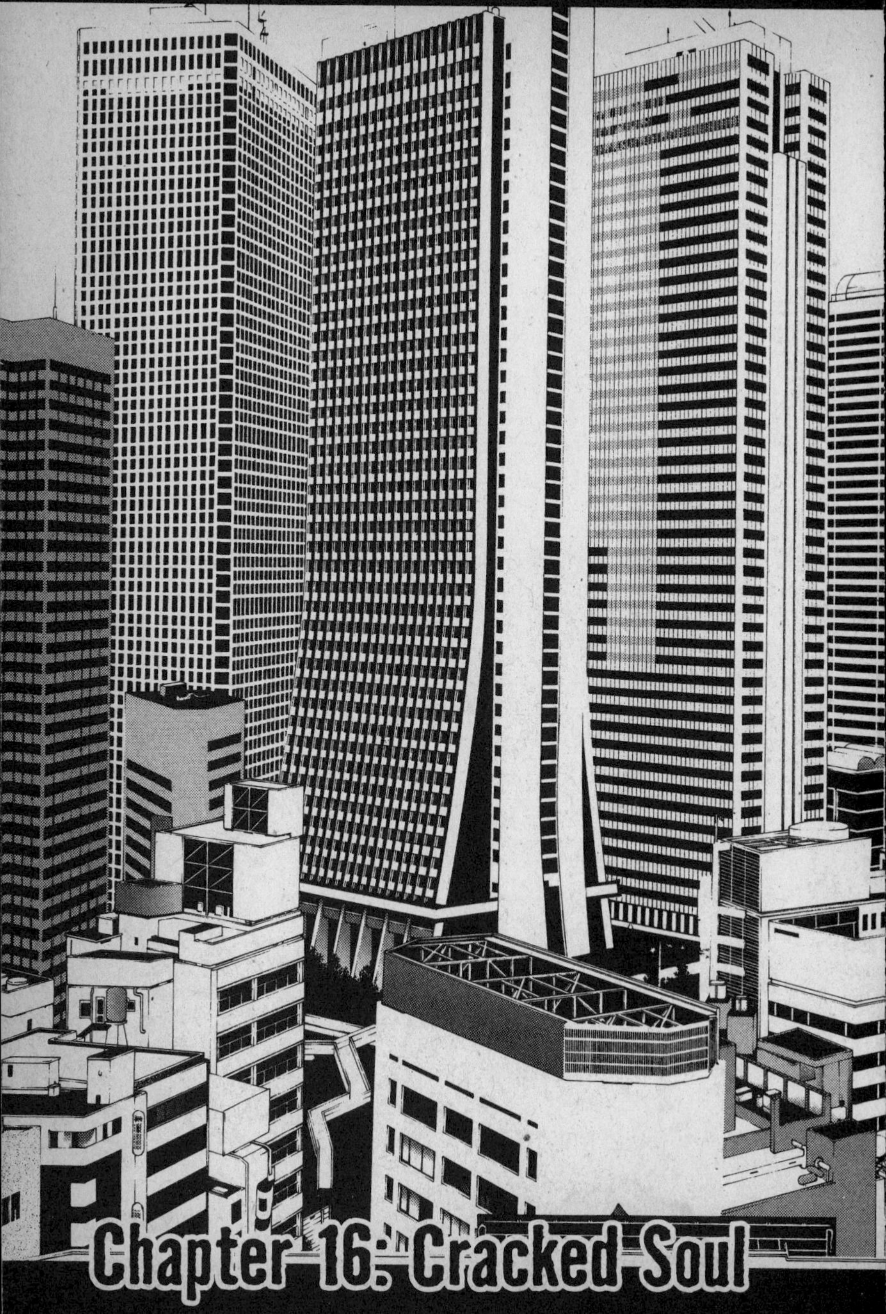
Chapter 16: Cracked Soul

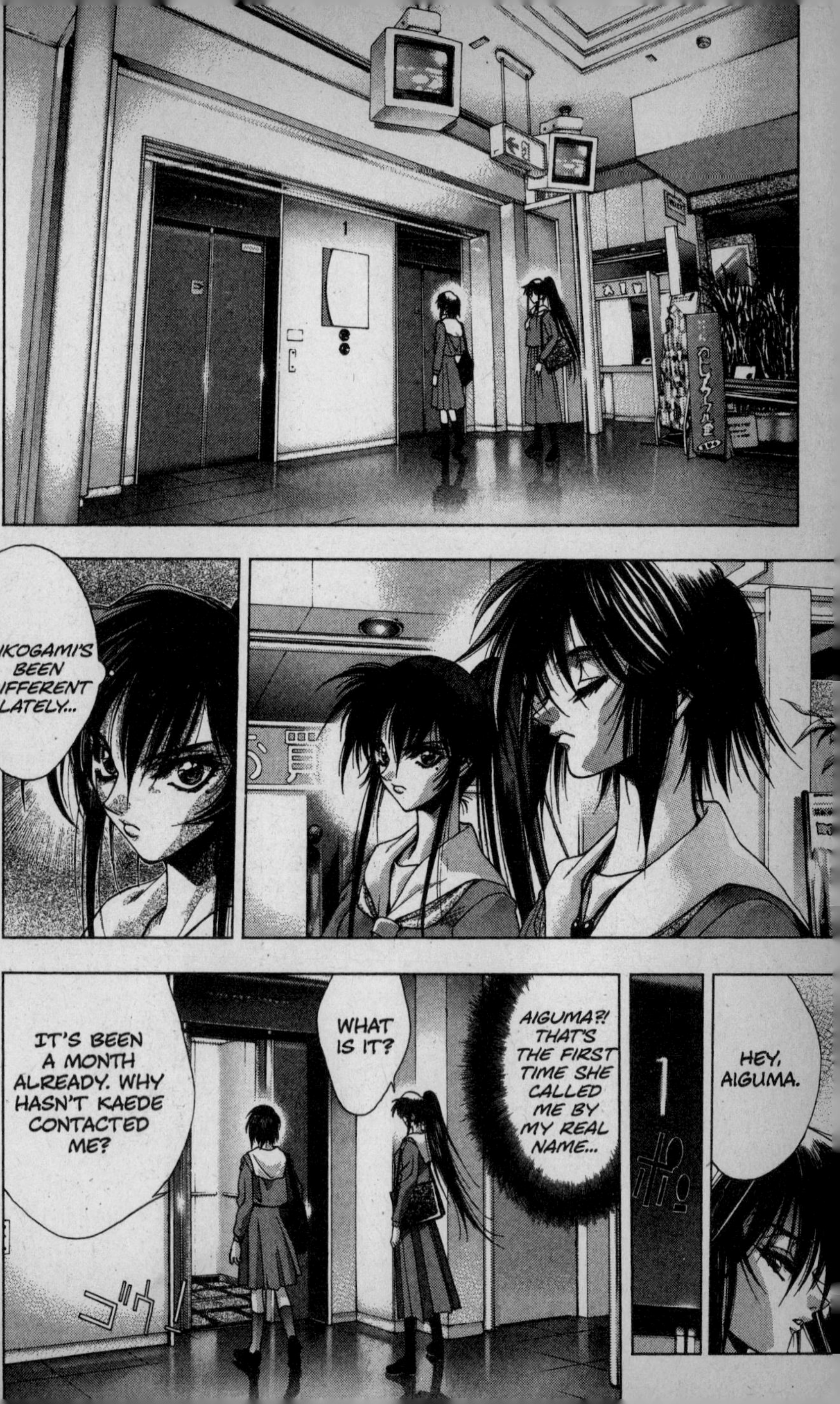
MIKOGAMI'S BEEN DIFFERENT LATELY...
HEY, AIGUMA.
AIGUMA?! THAT'S THE FIRST TIME SHE CALLED ME BY MY REAL NAME...
WHAT IS IT?
IT'S BEEN A MONTH ALREADY. WHY HASN'T KAEDE CONTACTED ME?

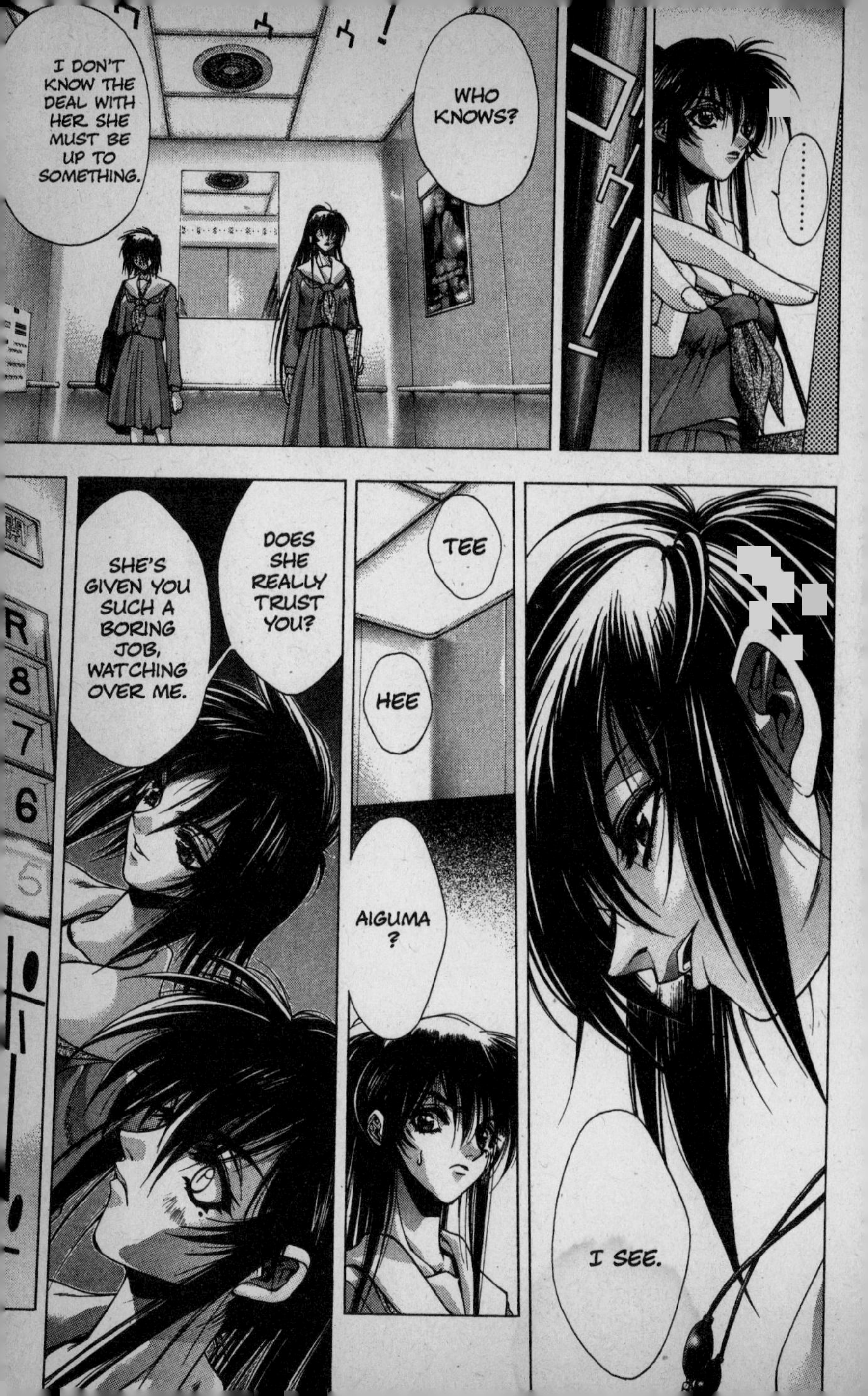
......
WHO KNOWS?
I DON'T KNOW THE DEAL WITH HER. SHE MUST BE UP TO SOMETHING.
I SEE.
TEE
HEE
AIGUMA?
DOES SHE REALLY TRUST YOU?
SHE'S GIVEN YOU SUCH A BORING JOB, WATCHING OVER ME.

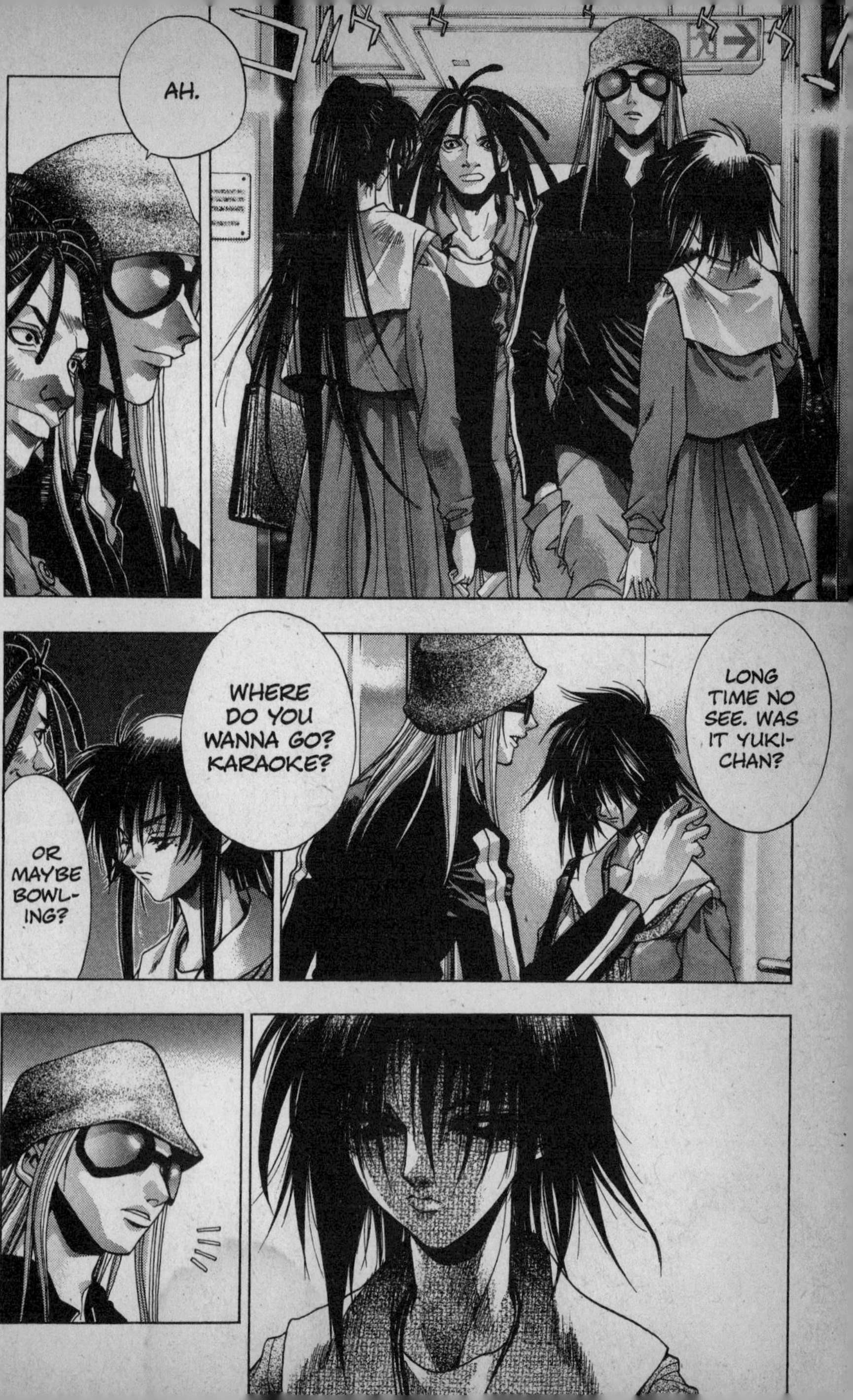
AH.
LONG TIME NO SEE. WAS IT YUKI-CHAN?
WHERE DO YOU WANNA GO? KARAOKE?
OR MAYBE BOWLING?

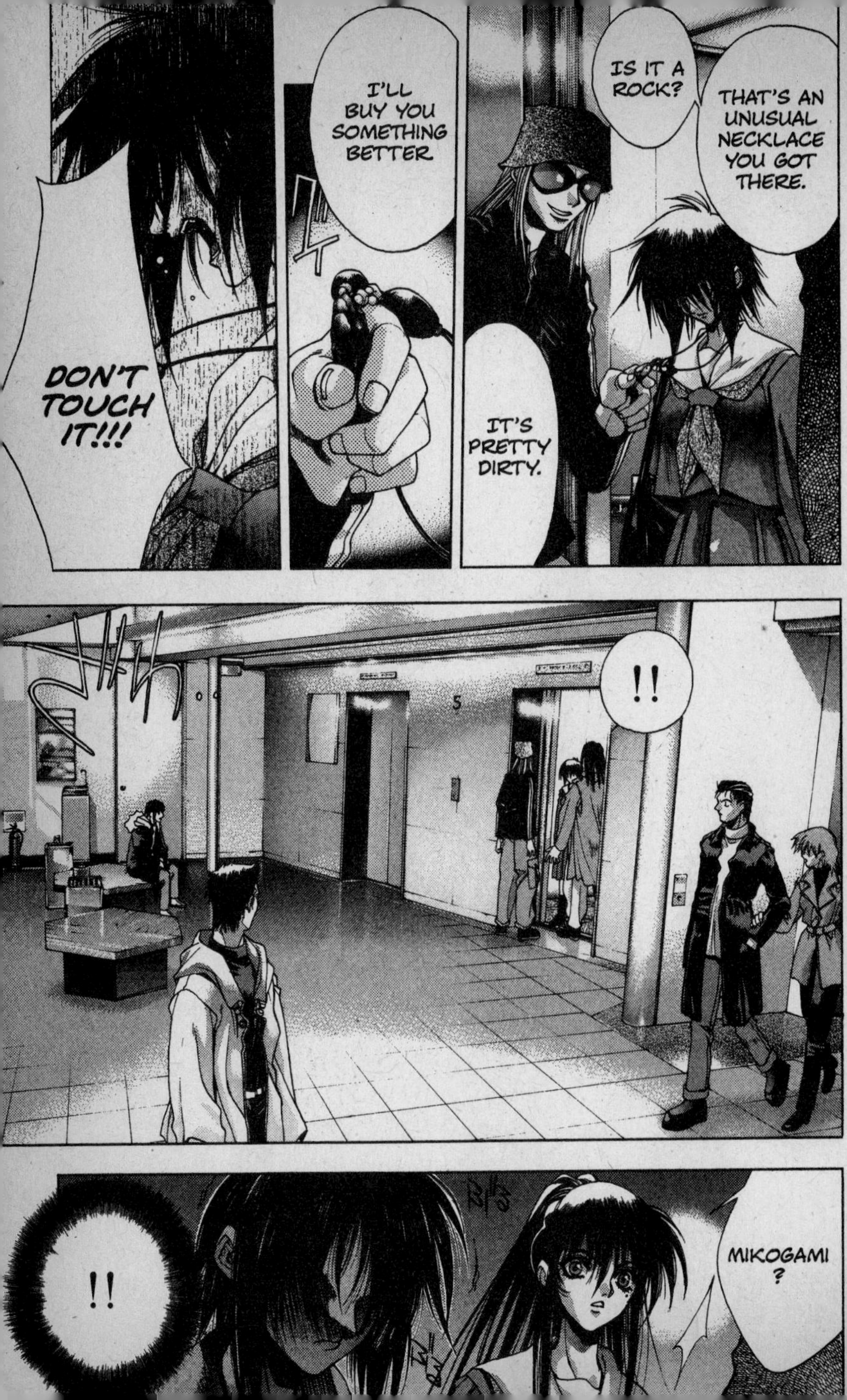
THAT'S AN UNUSUAL NECKLACE YOU GOT THERE.
IS IT A ROCK?
IT'S PRETTY DIRTY.
I'LL BUY YOU SOMETHING BETTER
DON'T TOUCH IT!!!
!!
MIKOGAMI ?
!!

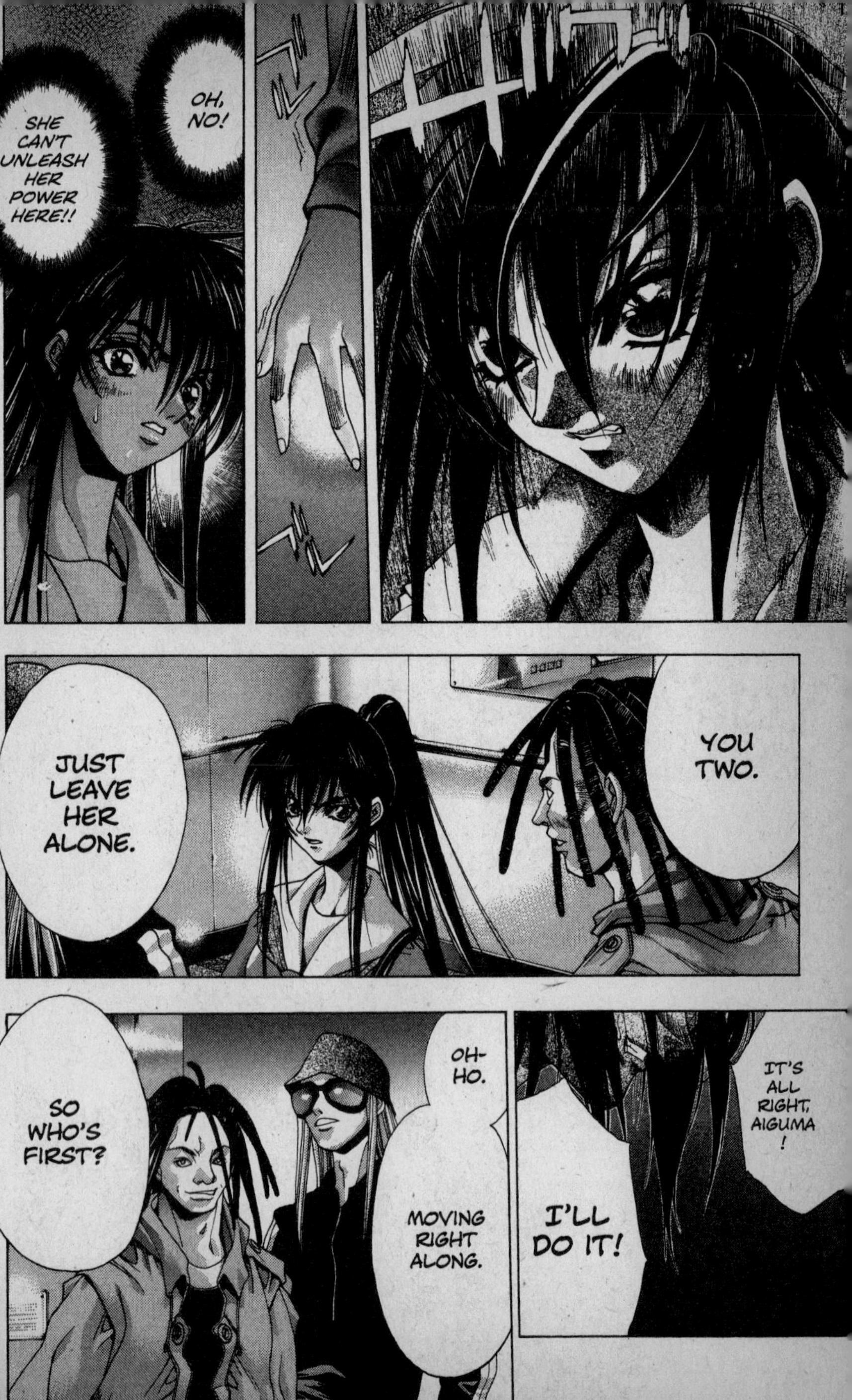
OH, NO!
SHE CAN'T UNLEASH HER POWER HERE!!
YOU TWO.
JUST LEAVE HER ALONE.
IT'S ALL RIGHT, AIGUMA!
I'LL DO IT!
OH-HO.
MOVING RIGHT ALONG.
SO WHO'S FIRST?

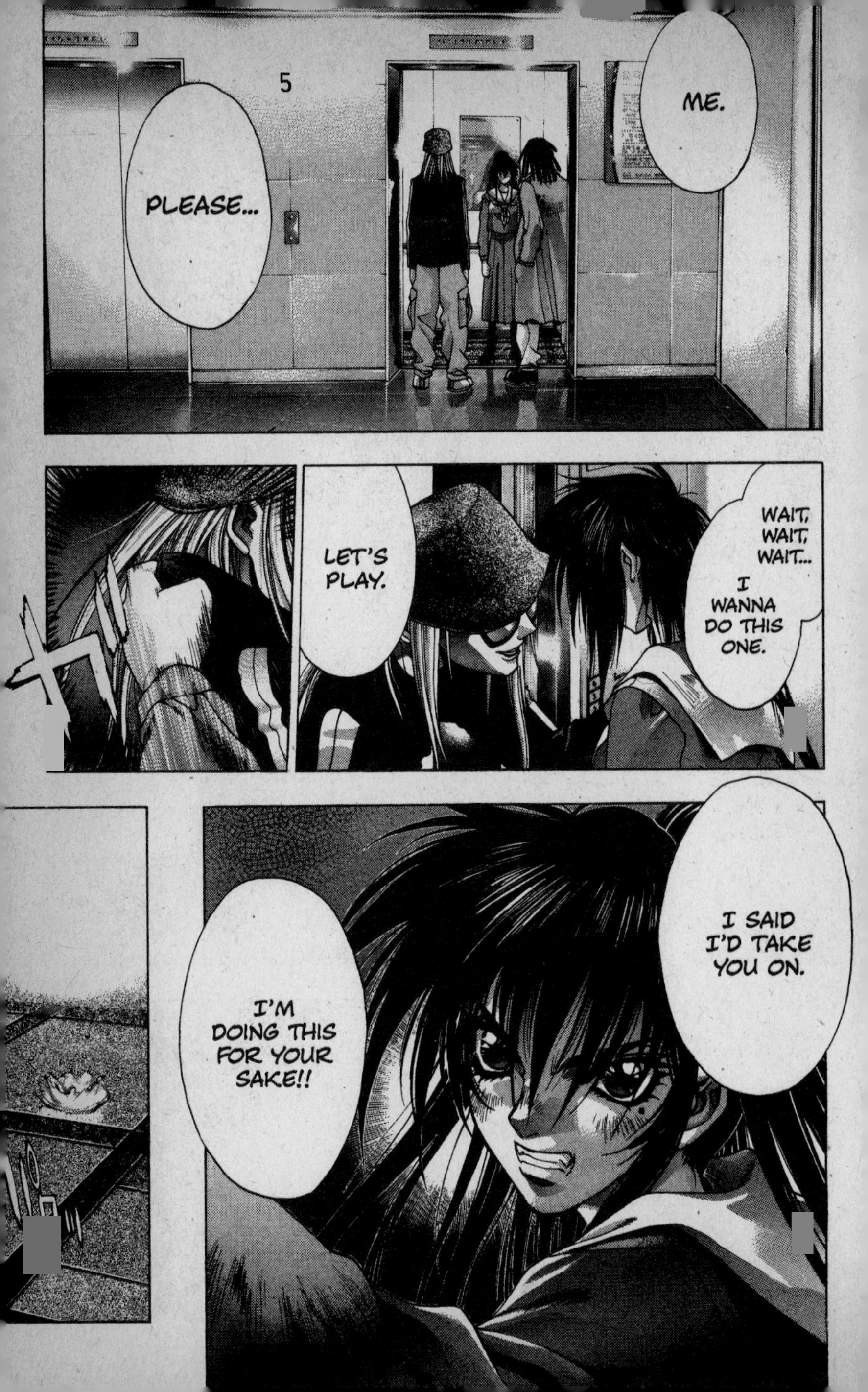
ME.
5
PLEASE...
WAIT, WAIT, WAIT... I WANNA DO THIS ONE.
LET'S PLAY.
I SAID I'D TAKE YOU ON.
I'M DOING THIS FOR YOUR SAKE!!

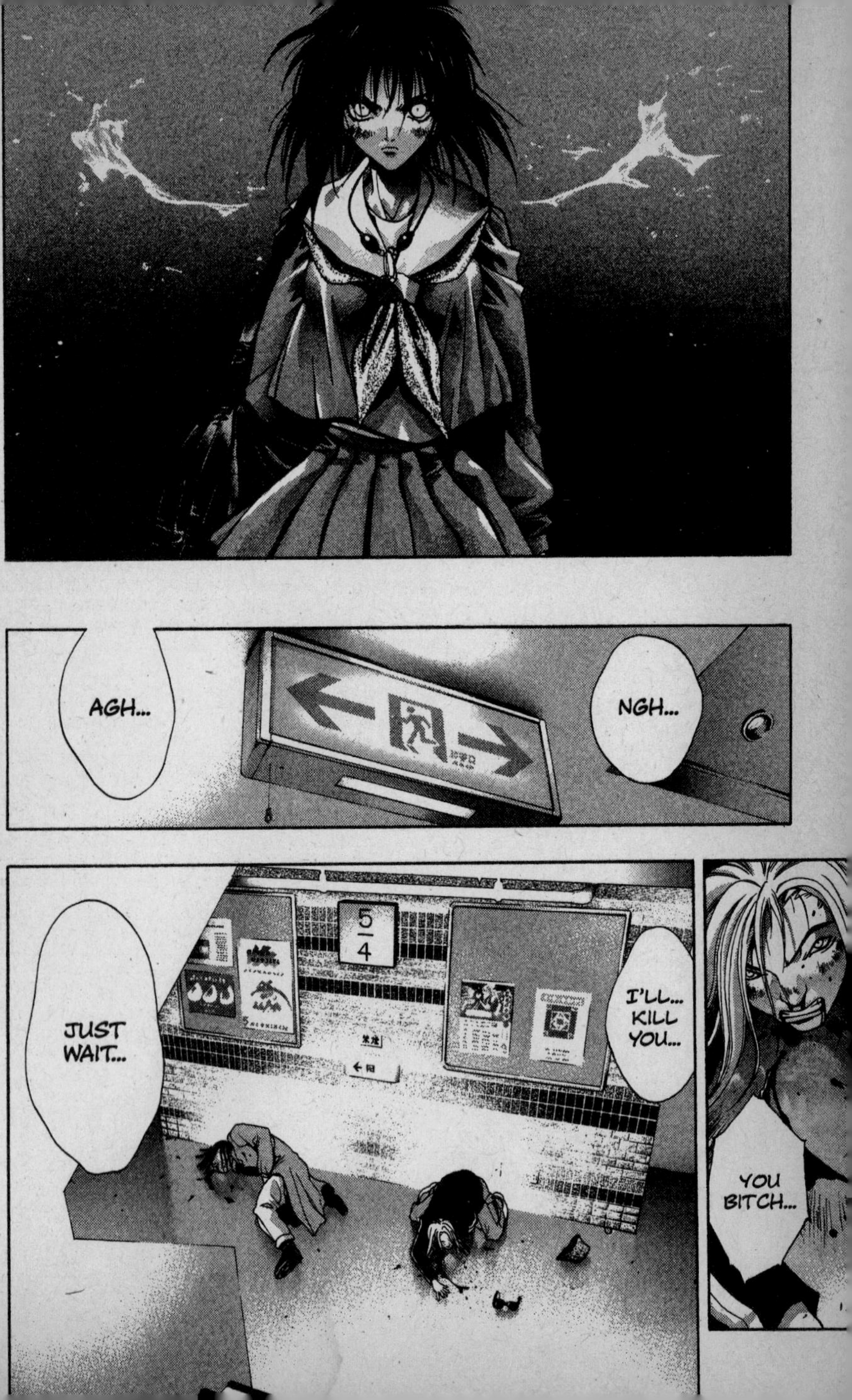
NGH...
AGH...
YOU BITCH...
I'LL... KILL YOU...
JUST WAIT...

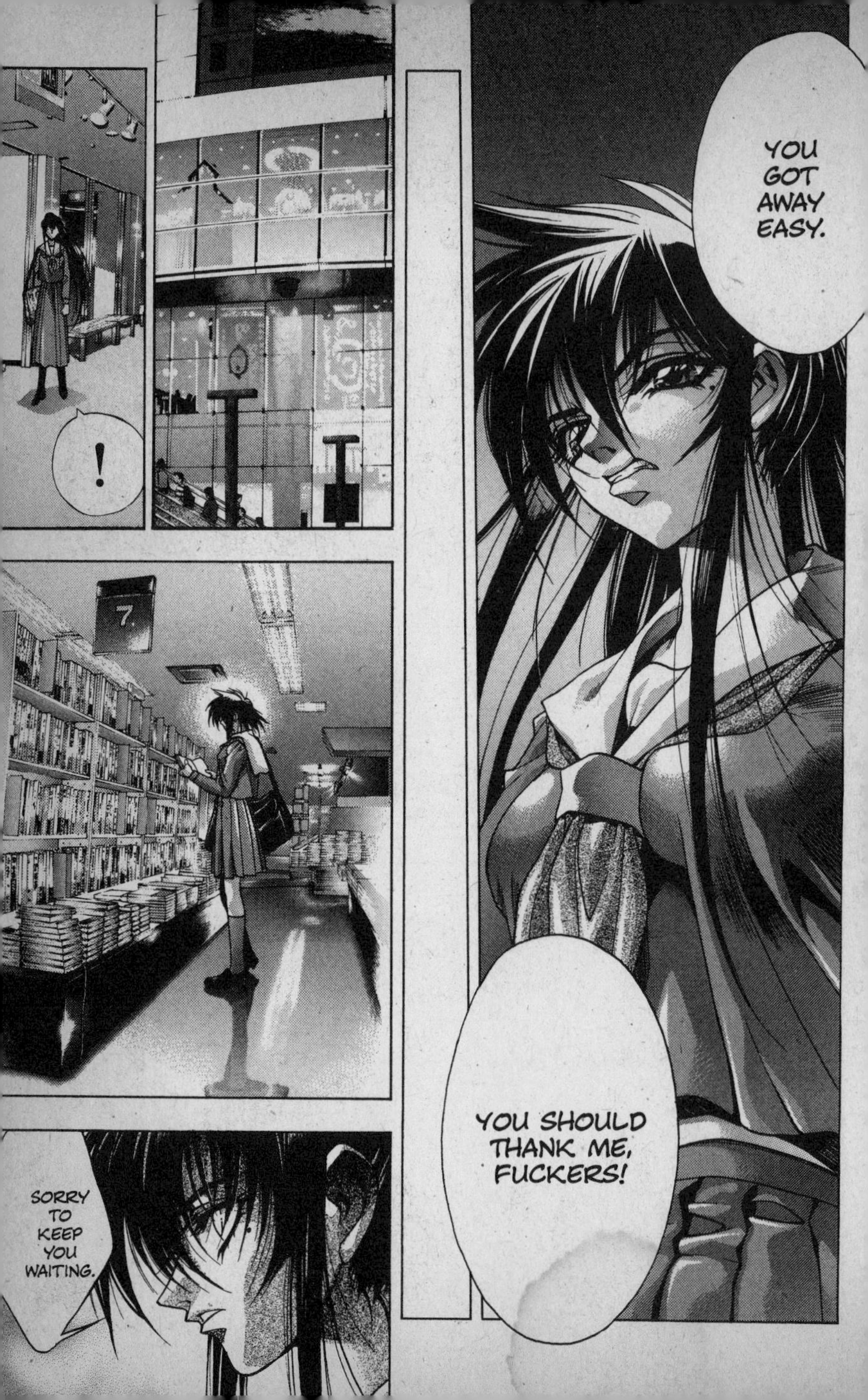
YOU GOT AWAY EASY.
YOU SHOULD THANK ME, FUCKERS!
!
SORRY TO KEEP YOU WAITING.

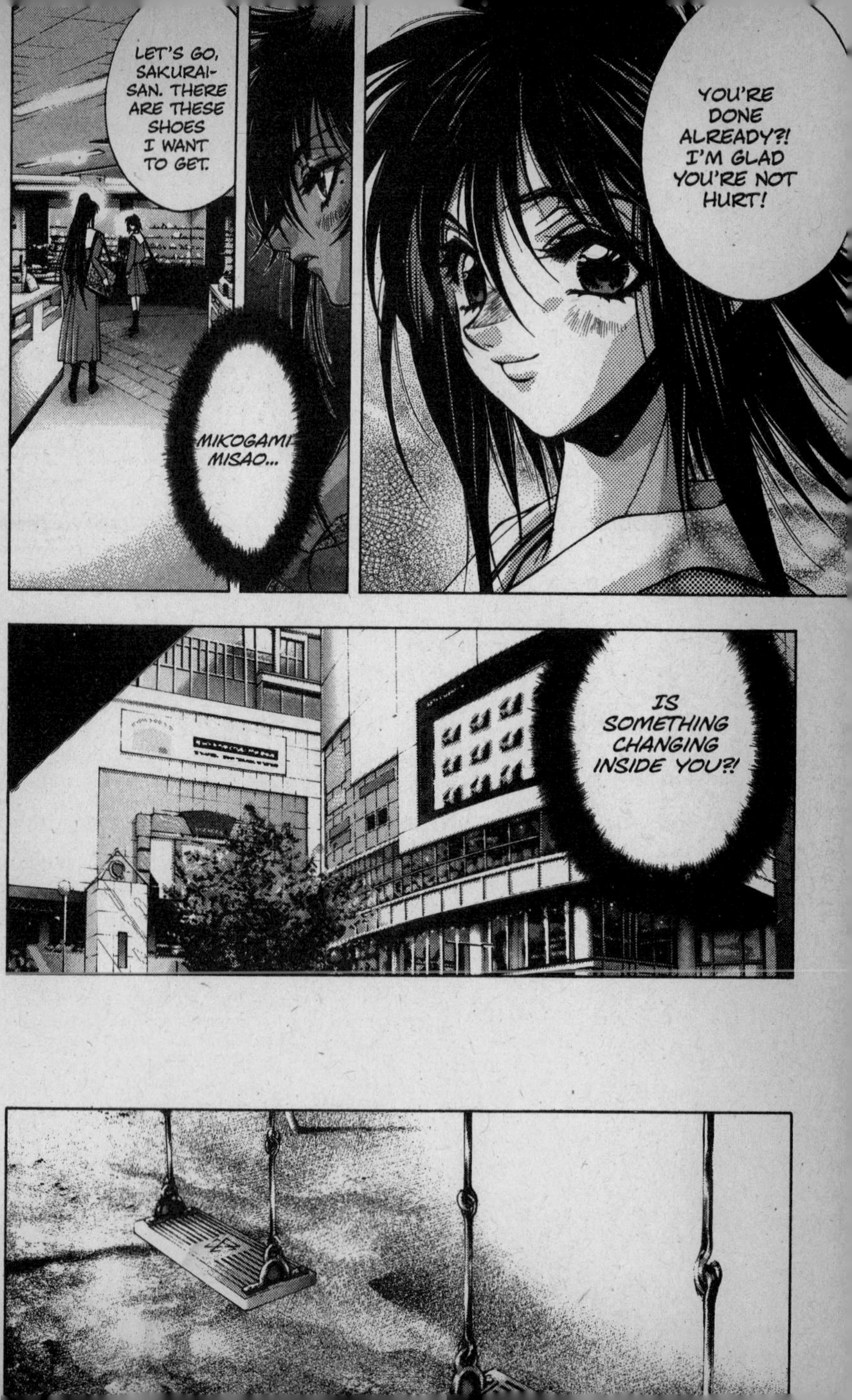
YOU'RE DONE ALREADY?! I'M GLAD YOU'RE NOT HURT!
LET'S GO, SAKURAI-SAN. THERE ARE THESE SHOES I WANT TO GET.
MIKOGAMI MISAO...
IS SOMETHING CHANGING INSIDE YOU?!

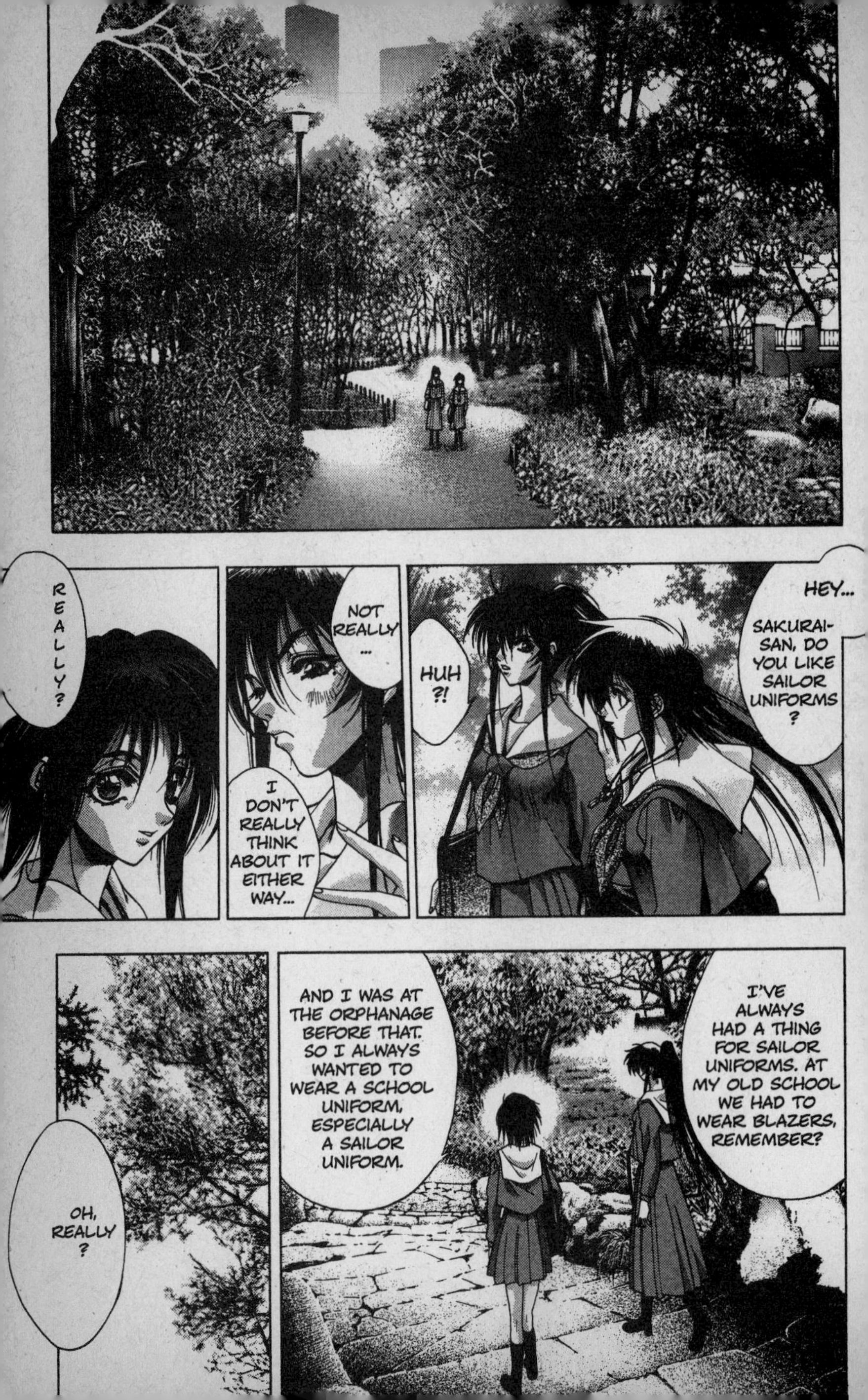
HEY...
SAKURAI-SAN, DO YOU LIKE SAILOR UNIFORMS?
HUH?!
NOT REALLY...
I DON'T REALLY THINK ABOUT IT EITHER WAY...
REALLY?
I'VE ALWAYS HAD A THING FOR SAILOR UNIFORMS. AT MY OLD SCHOOL WE HAD TO WEAR BLAZERS, REMEMBER?
AND I WAS AT THE ORPHANAGE BEFORE THAT. SO I ALWAYS WANTED TO WEAR A SCHOOL UNIFORM, ESPECIALLY A SAILOR UNIFORM.
OH, REALLY?

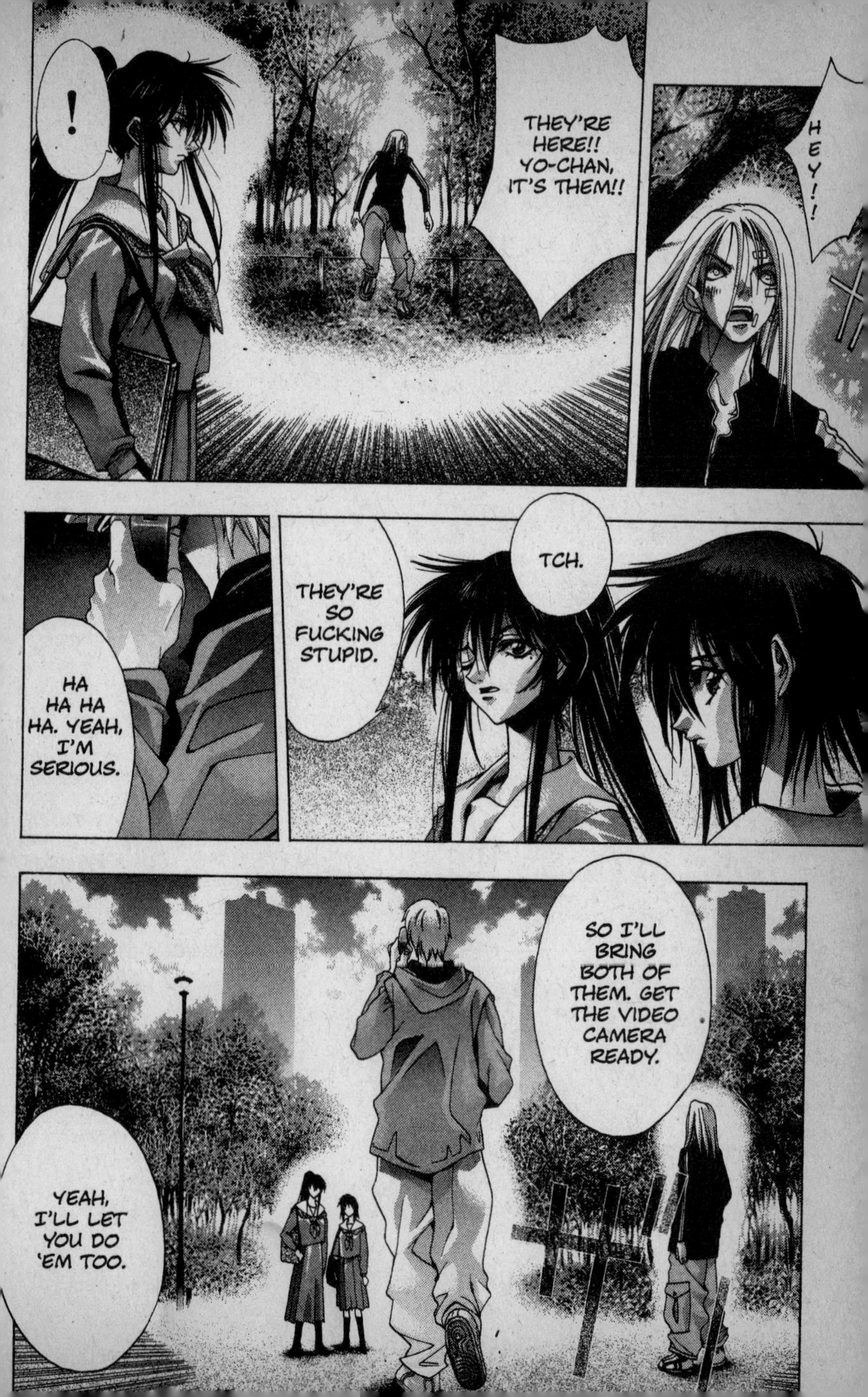
HEY!!
THEY'RE HERE!! YO-CHAN, IT'S THEM!!
!
TCH.
THEY'RE SO FUCKING STUPID.
HA HA HA HA. YEAH, I'M SERIOUS.
SO I'LL BRING BOTH OF THEM. GET THE VIDEO CAMERA READY.
YEAH, I'LL LET YOU DO 'EM TOO.

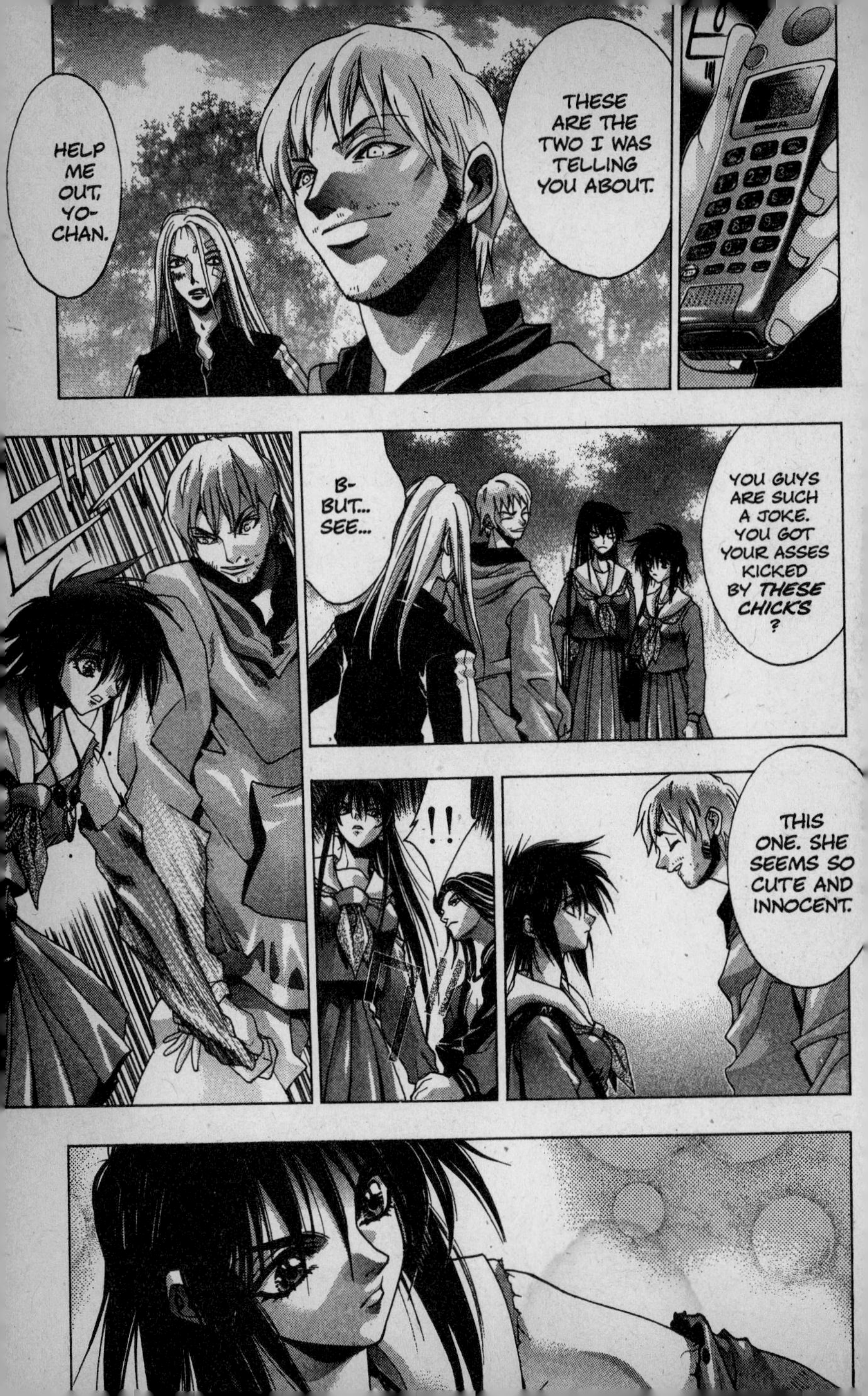
THESE ARE THE TWO I WAS TELLING YOU ABOUT.
HELP ME OUT, YO-CHAN.
YOU GUYS ARE SUCH A JOKE. YOU GOT YOUR ASSES KICKED BY THESE CHICKS ?
B-BUT... SEE...
THIS ONE. SHE SEEMS SO CUTE AND INNOCENT.
!!

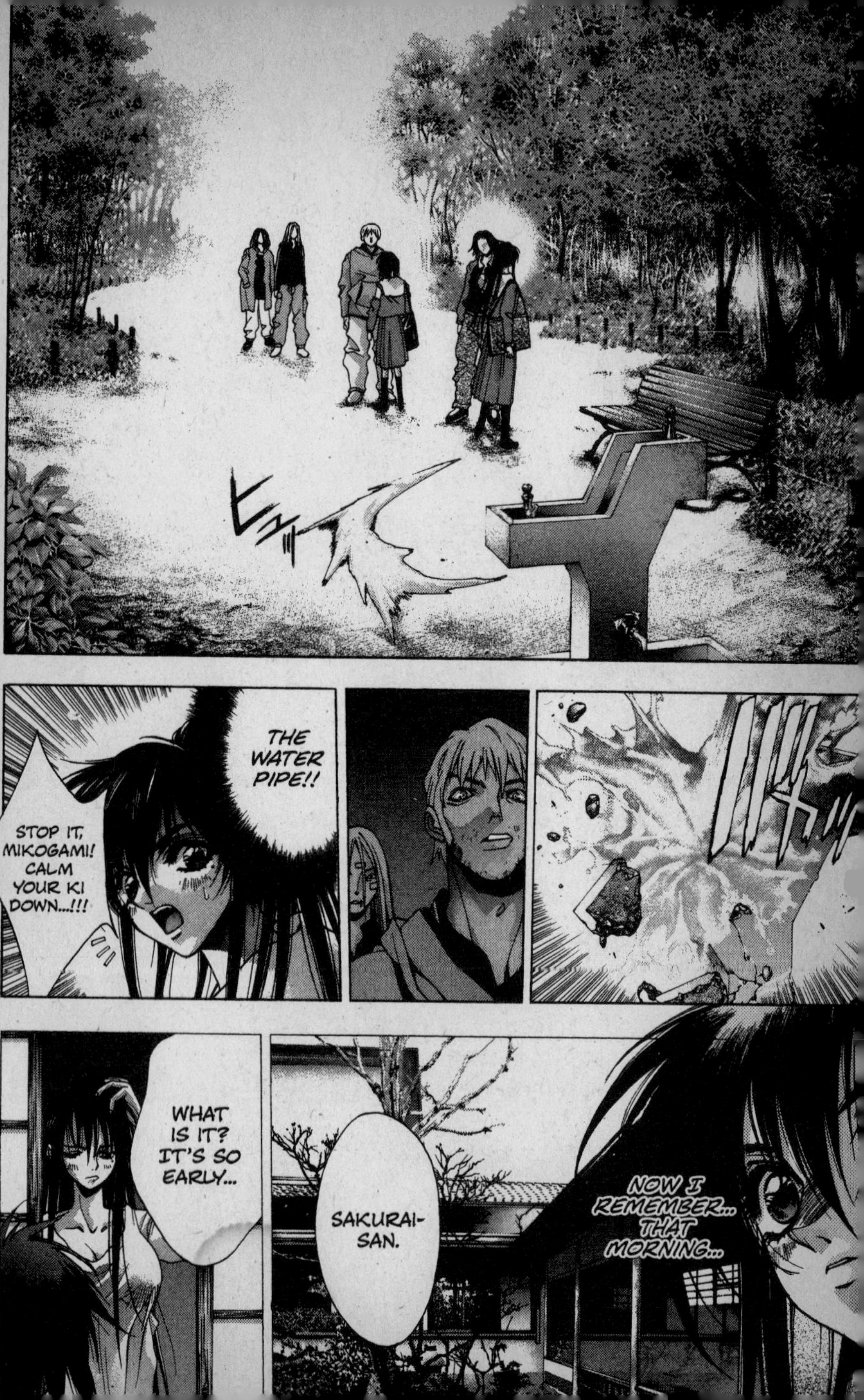
THE WATER PIPE!!
STOP IT, MIKOGAMI! CALM YOUR KI DOWN...!!!
NOW I REMEMBER... THAT MORNING...
SAKURAI-SAN.
WHAT IS IT? IT'S SO EARLY...

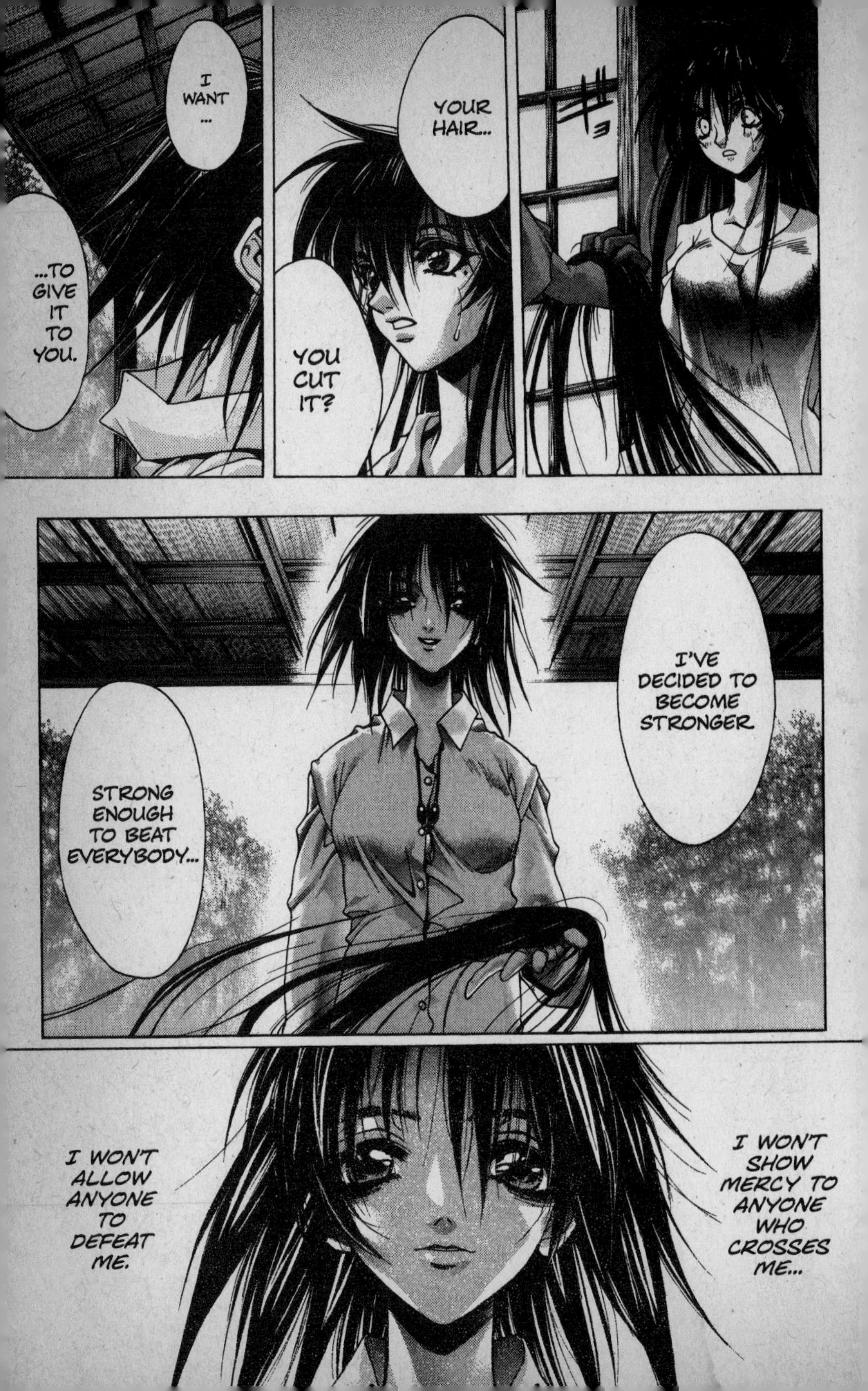
YOUR HAIR...
YOU CUT IT?
I WANT ...
...TO GIVE IT TO YOU.
I'VE DECIDED TO BECOME STRONGER
STRONG ENOUGH TO BEAT EVERYBODY...
I WON'T SHOW MERCY TO ANYONE WHO CROSSES ME...
I WON'T ALLOW ANYONE TO DEFEAT ME.

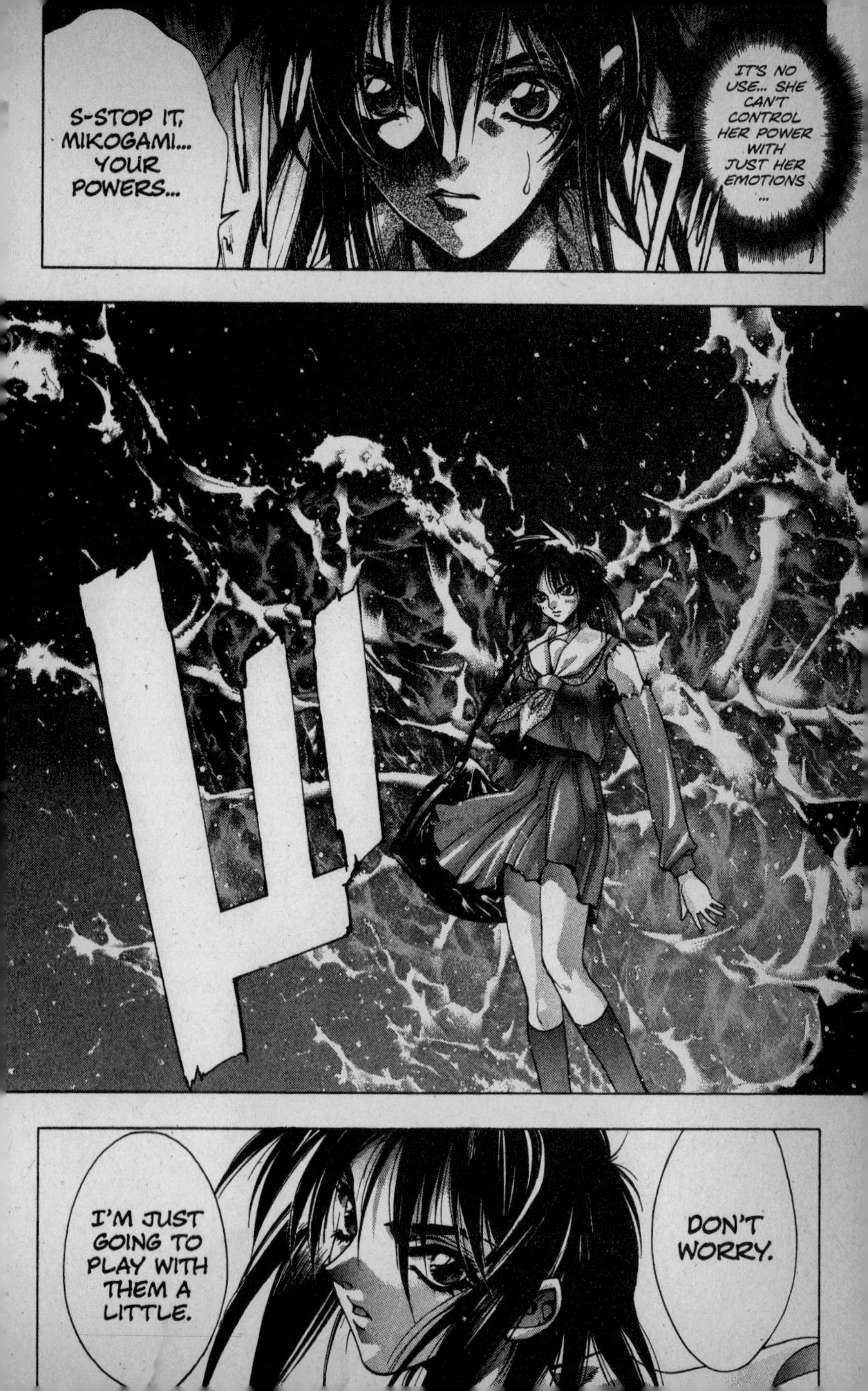
IT'S NO USE... SHE CAN'T CONTROL HER POWER WITH JUST HER EMOTIONS...
S-STOP IT, MIKOGAMI... YOUR POWERS...
DON'T WORRY.
I'M JUST GOING TO PLAY WITH THEM A LITTLE.

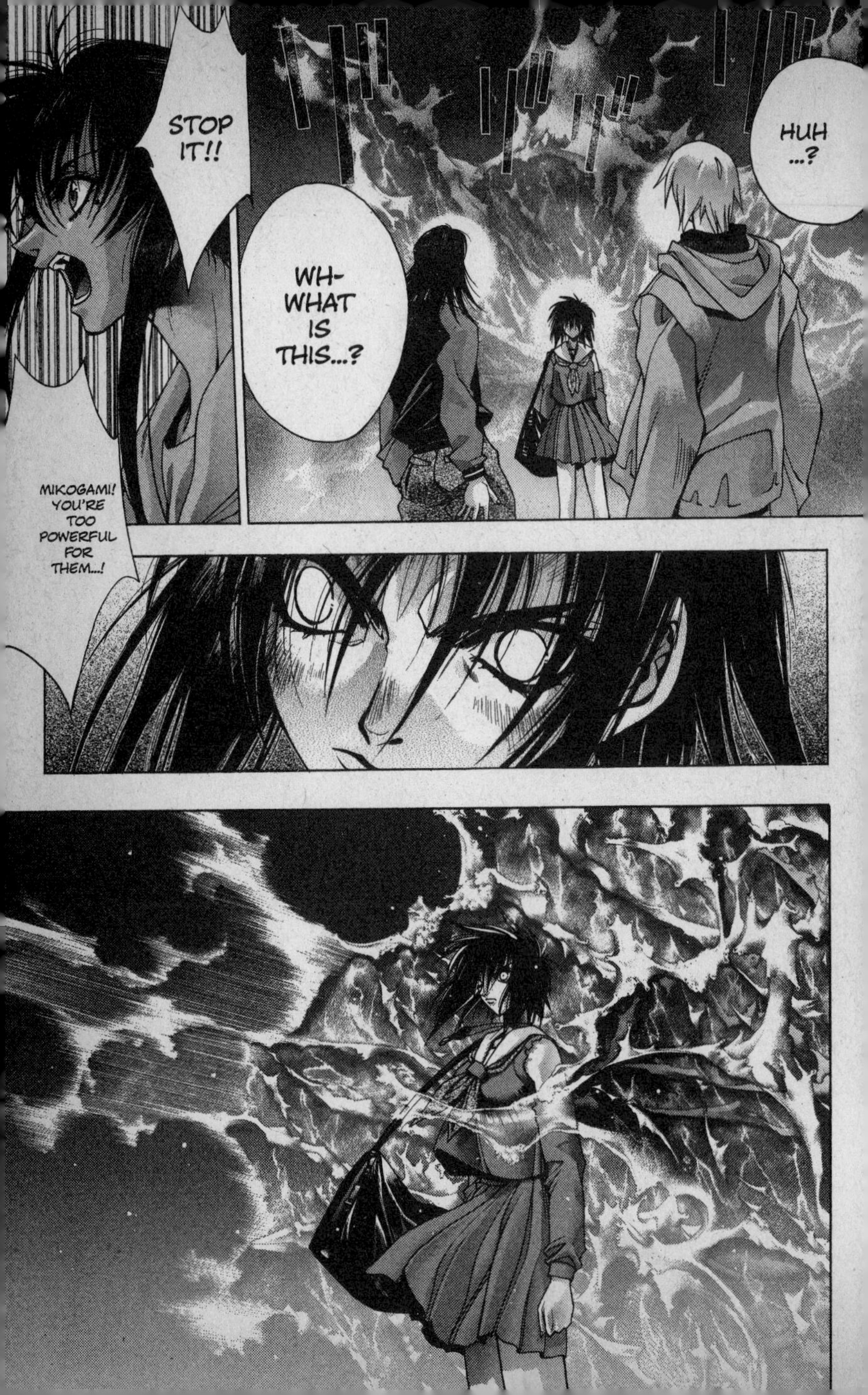
HUH ...?
WH- WHAT IS THIS...?
STOP IT!!
MIKOGAMI! YOU'RE TOO POWERFUL FOR THEM...!

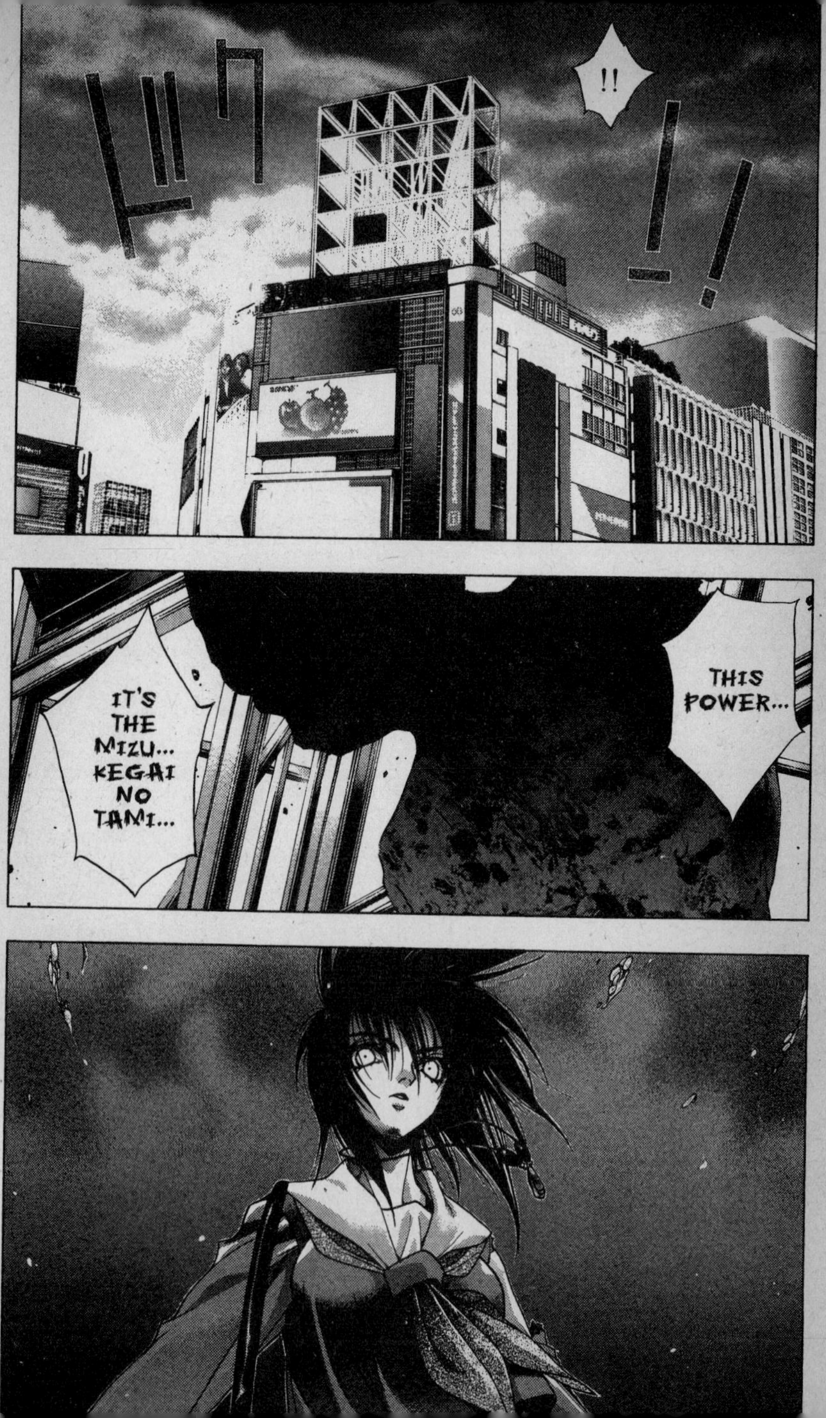
!!
THIS POWER...
IT'S THE MIZU... KEGAI NO TAMI...

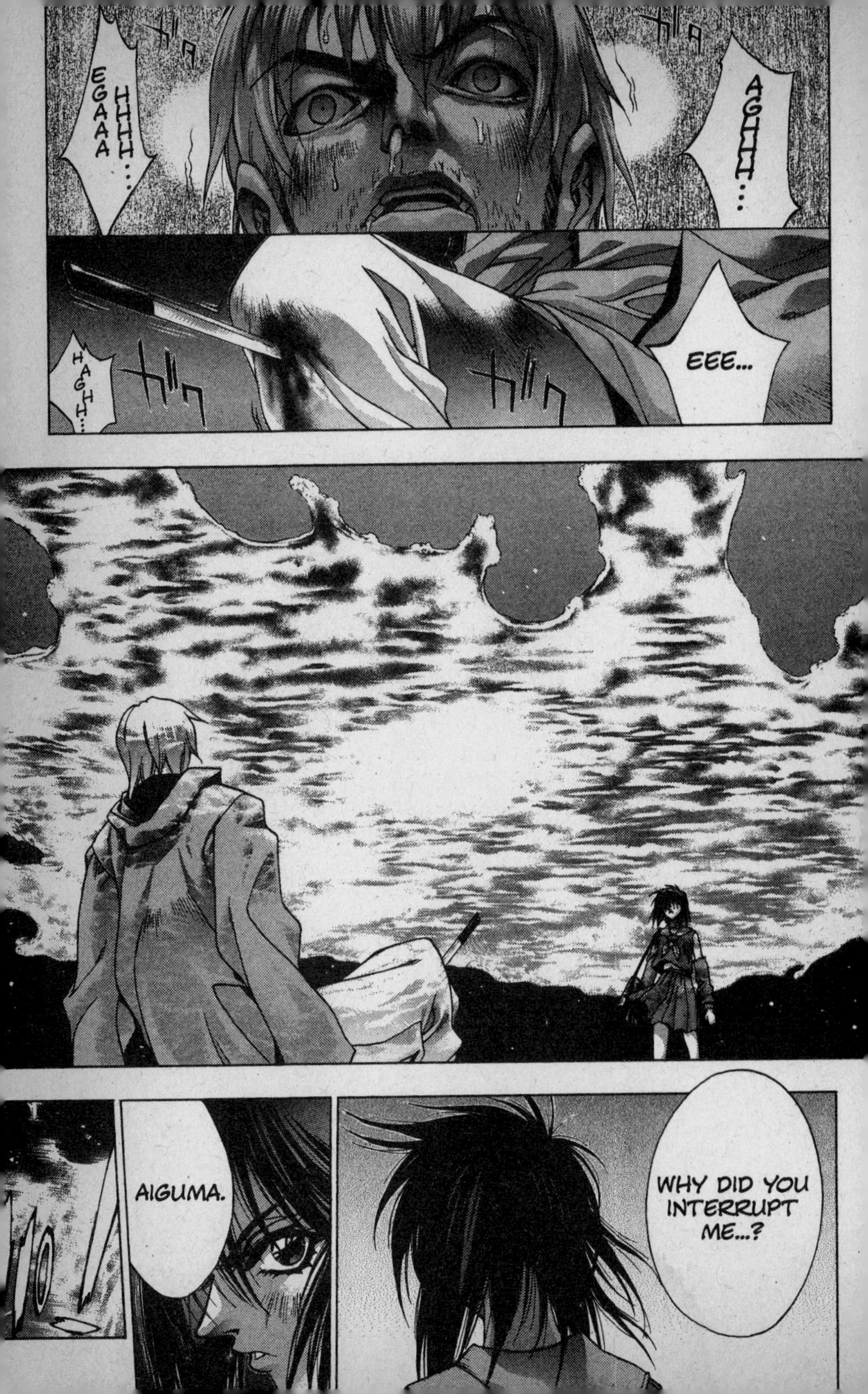
AGUUUH...
EGAAAA HHHH...
EEE...
HAGHH...
WHY DID YOU INTERRUPT ME...?
AIGUMA.

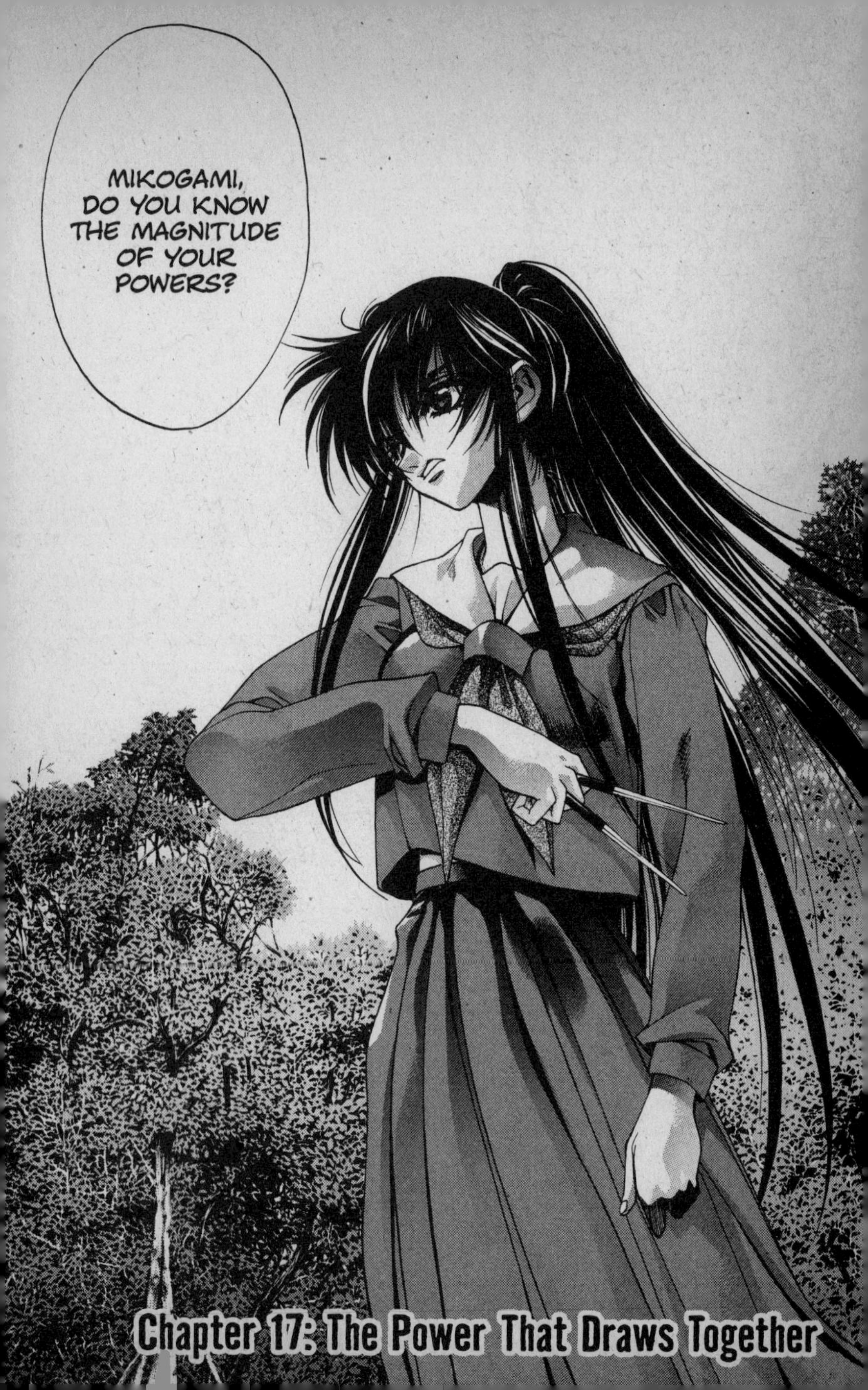
MIKOGAMI, DO YOU KNOW THE MAGNITUDE OF YOUR POWERS?

Chapter 17: The Power That Draws Together

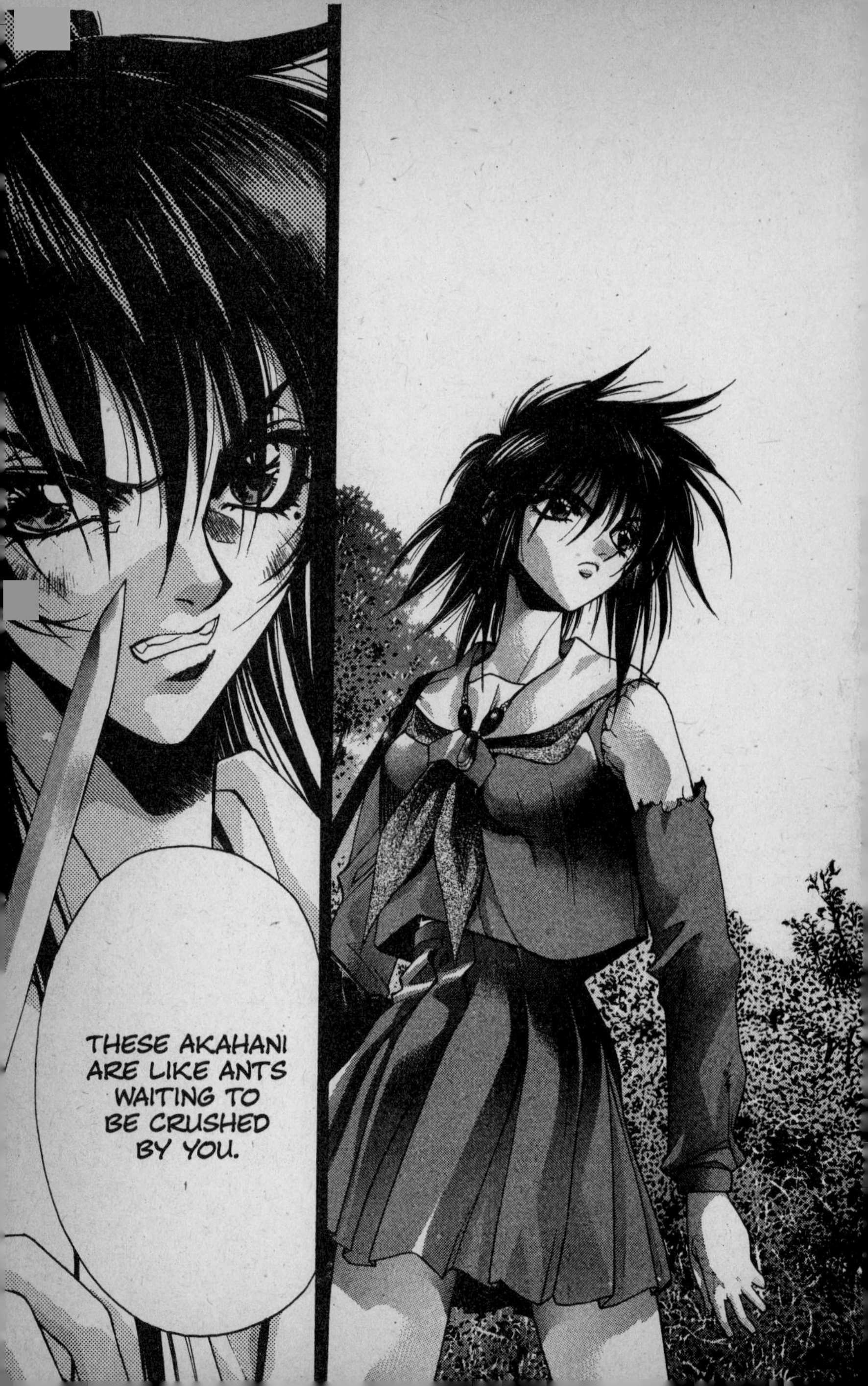
THESE AKAHANI ARE LIKE ANTS WAITING TO BE CRUSHED BY YOU.

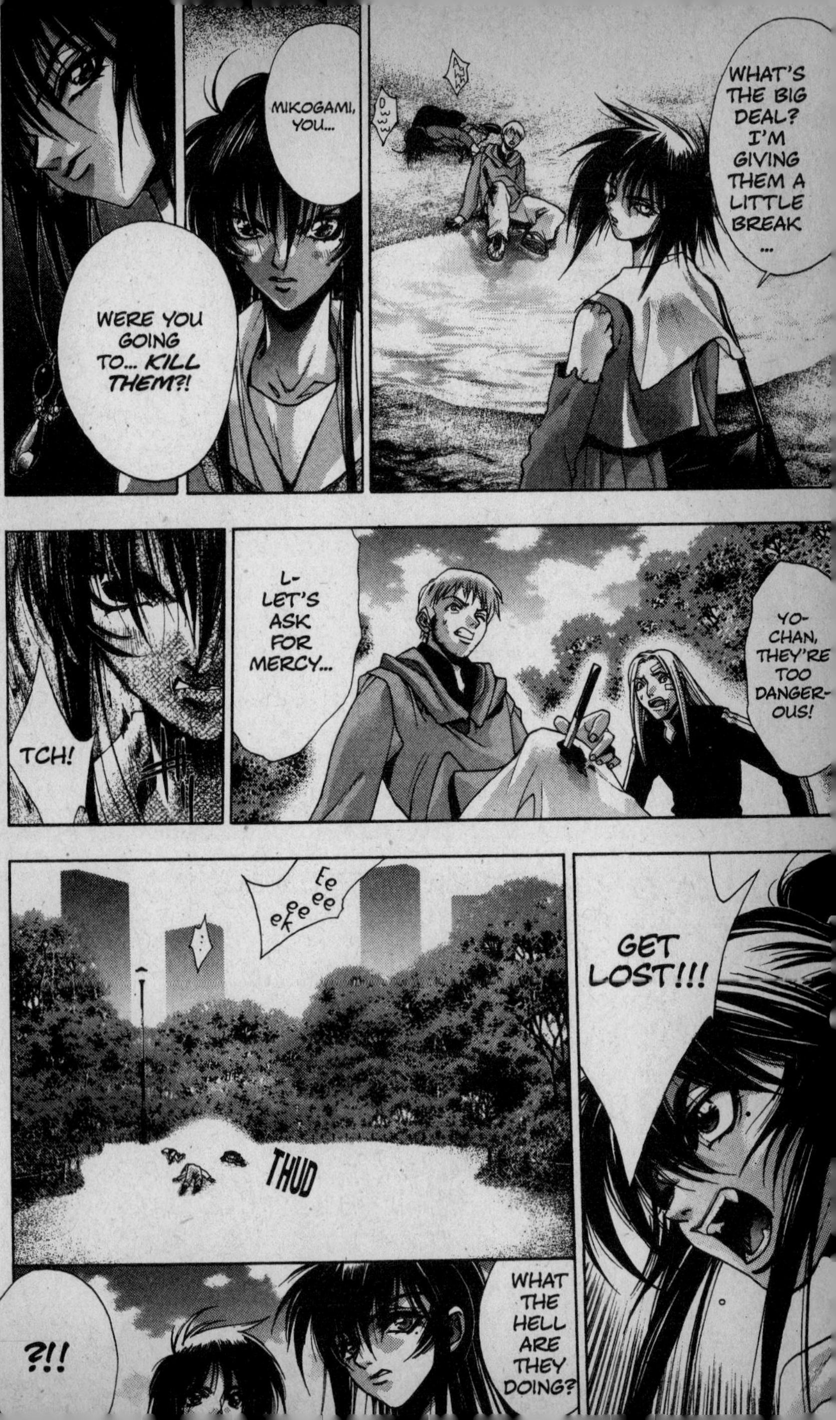
WHAT'S THE BIG DEAL? I'M GIVING THEM A LITTLE BREAK ...
Aghhh
Owww
MIKOGAMI, YOU...
WERE YOU GOING TO... KILL THEM?!
YO-CHAN, THEY'RE TOO DANGER-OUS!
L-LET'S ASK FOR MERCY...
TCH!
GET LOST!!!
Eeeeeek
...
THUD
WHAT THE HELL ARE THEY DOING?
?!!

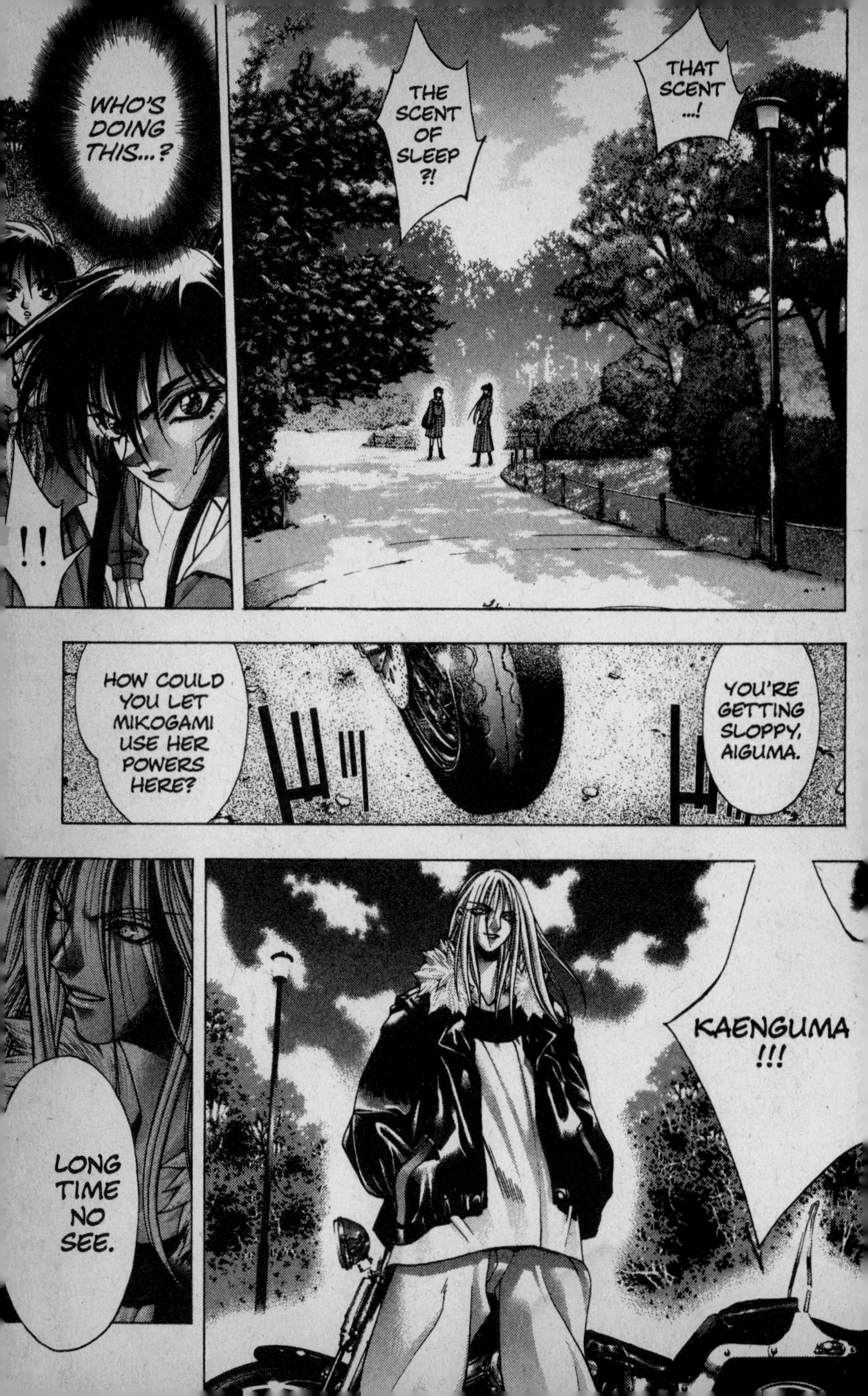
THAT SCENT ...!
THE SCENT OF SLEEP ?!
WHO'S DOING THIS...?
!!
YOU'RE GETTING SLOPPY, AIGUMA.
HOW COULD YOU LET MIKOGAMI USE HER POWERS HERE?
KAENGUMA !!!
LONG TIME NO SEE.

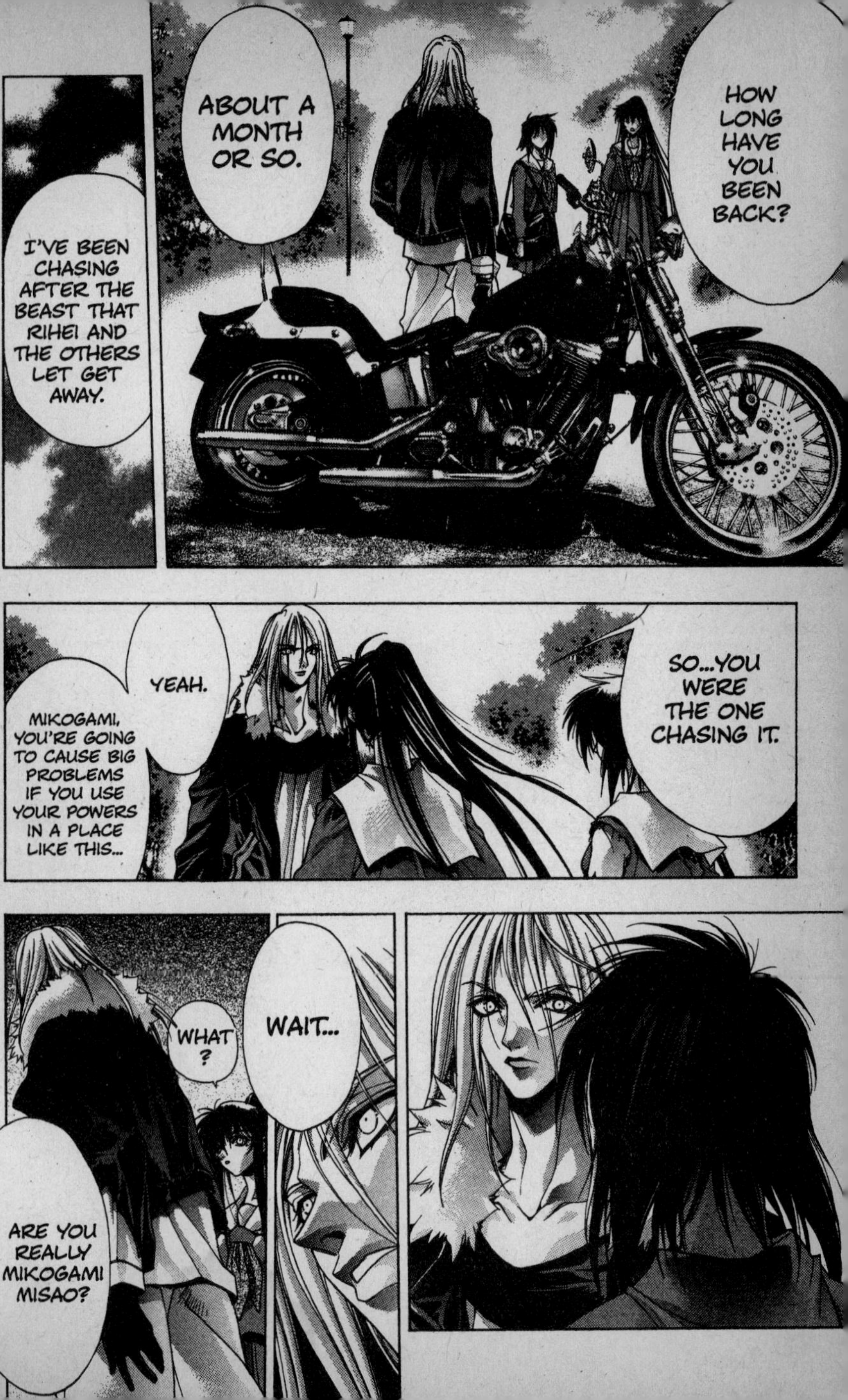
HOW LONG HAVE YOU BEEN BACK?
ABOUT A MONTH OR SO.
I'VE BEEN CHASING AFTER THE BEAST THAT RIHEI AND THE OTHERS LET GET AWAY.
SO...YOU WERE THE ONE CHASING IT.
YEAH.
MIKOGAMI, YOU'RE GOING TO CAUSE BIG PROBLEMS IF YOU USE YOUR POWERS IN A PLACE LIKE THIS...
WAIT...
WHAT?
ARE YOU REALLY MIKOGAMI MISAO?

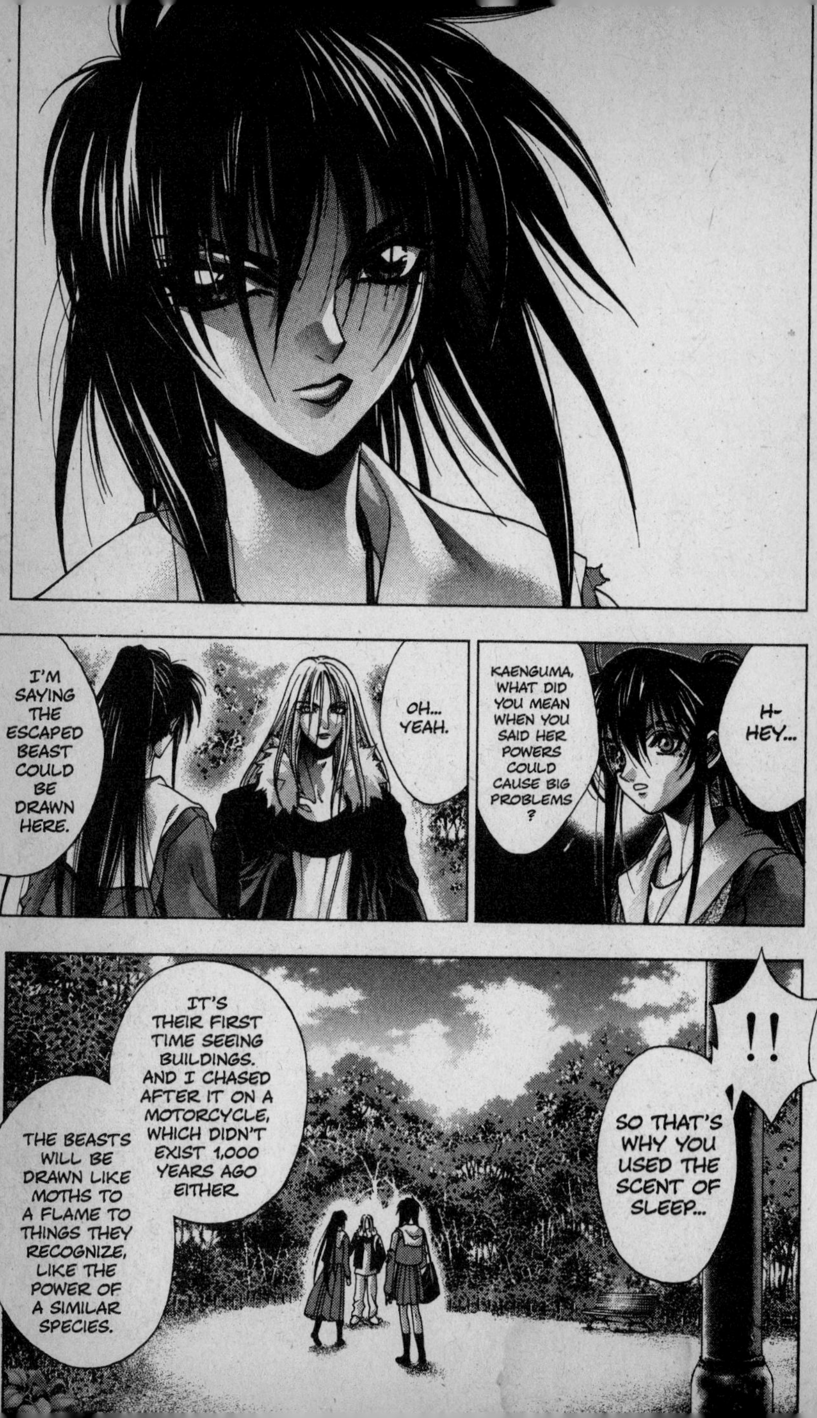
H-HEY...
KAENGUMA, WHAT DID YOU MEAN WHEN YOU SAID HER POWERS COULD CAUSE BIG PROBLEMS?
OH... YEAH.
I'M SAYING THE ESCAPED BEAST COULD BE DRAWN HERE.
!!
SO THAT'S WHY YOU USED THE SCENT OF SLEEP...
IT'S THEIR FIRST TIME SEEING BUILDINGS. AND I CHASED AFTER IT ON A MOTORCYCLE, WHICH DIDN'T EXIST 1,000 YEARS AGO EITHER.
THE BEASTS WILL BE DRAWN LIKE MOTHS TO A FLAME TO THINGS THEY RECOGNIZE, LIKE THE POWER OF A SIMILAR SPECIES.

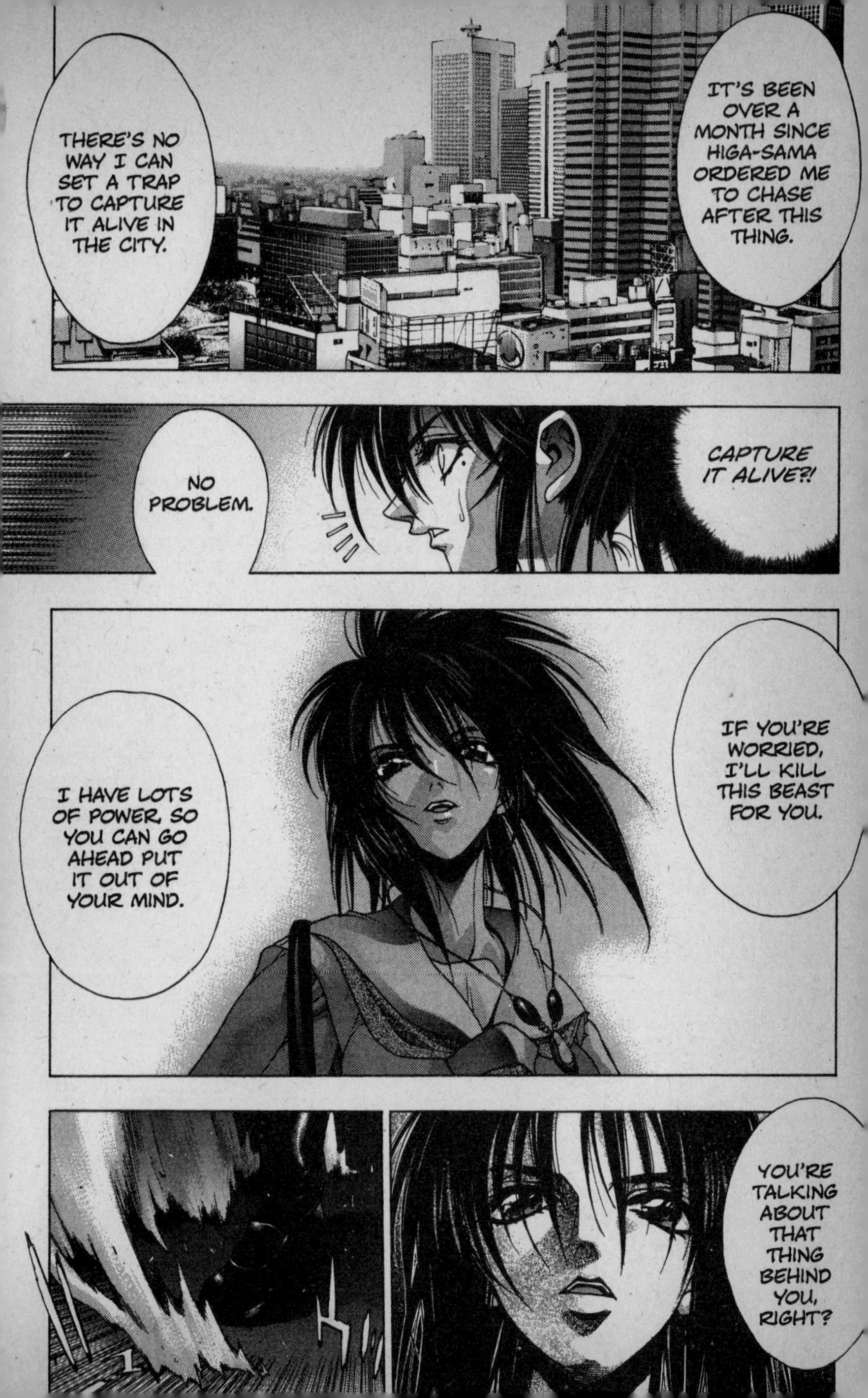
IT'S BEEN OVER A MONTH SINCE HIGA-SAMA ORDERED ME TO CHASE AFTER THIS THING.
THERE'S NO WAY I CAN SET A TRAP TO CAPTURE IT ALIVE IN THE CITY.
CAPTURE IT ALIVE?!
NO PROBLEM.
IF YOU'RE WORRIED, I'LL KILL THIS BEAST FOR YOU.
I HAVE LOTS OF POWER, SO YOU CAN GO AHEAD PUT IT OUT OF YOUR MIND.
YOU'RE TALKING ABOUT THAT THING BEHIND YOU, RIGHT?

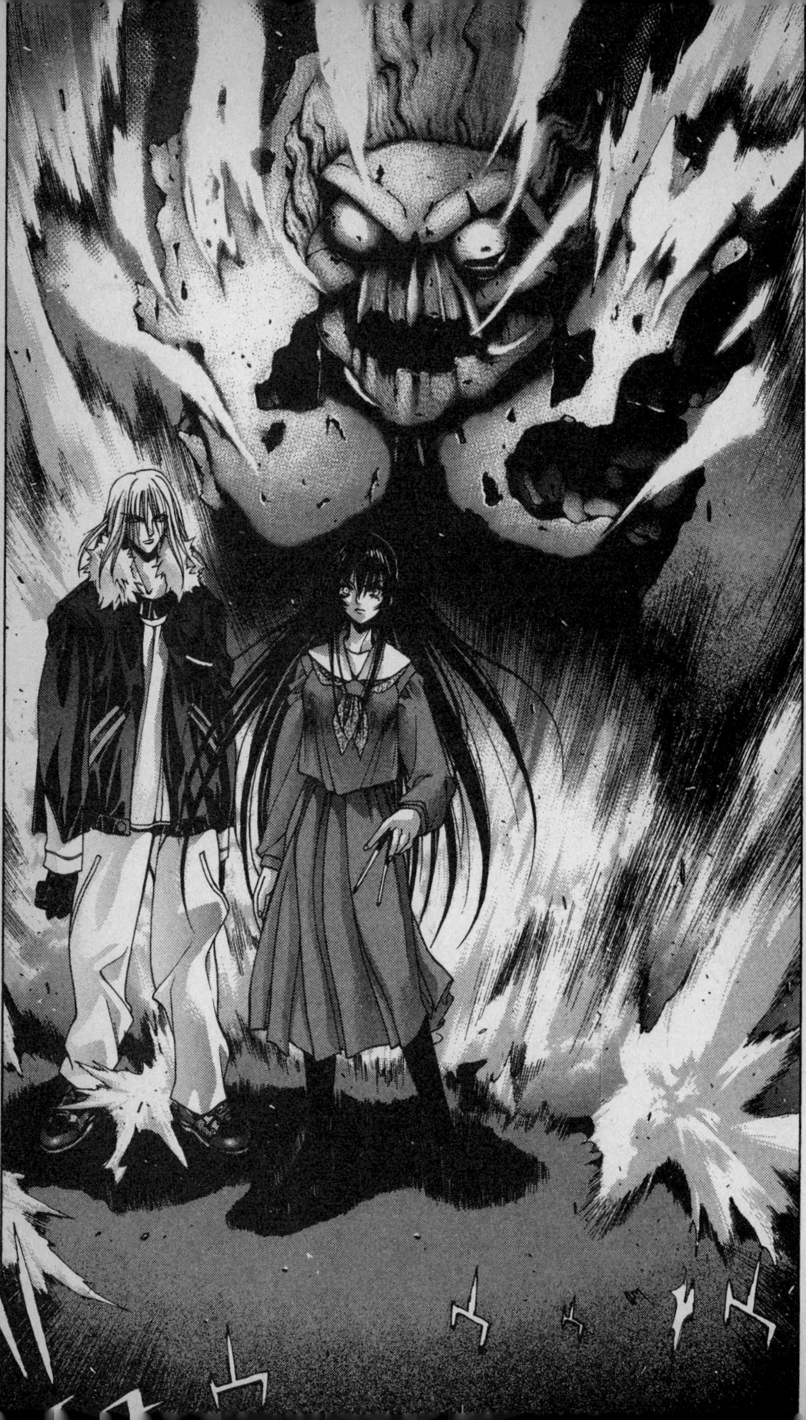

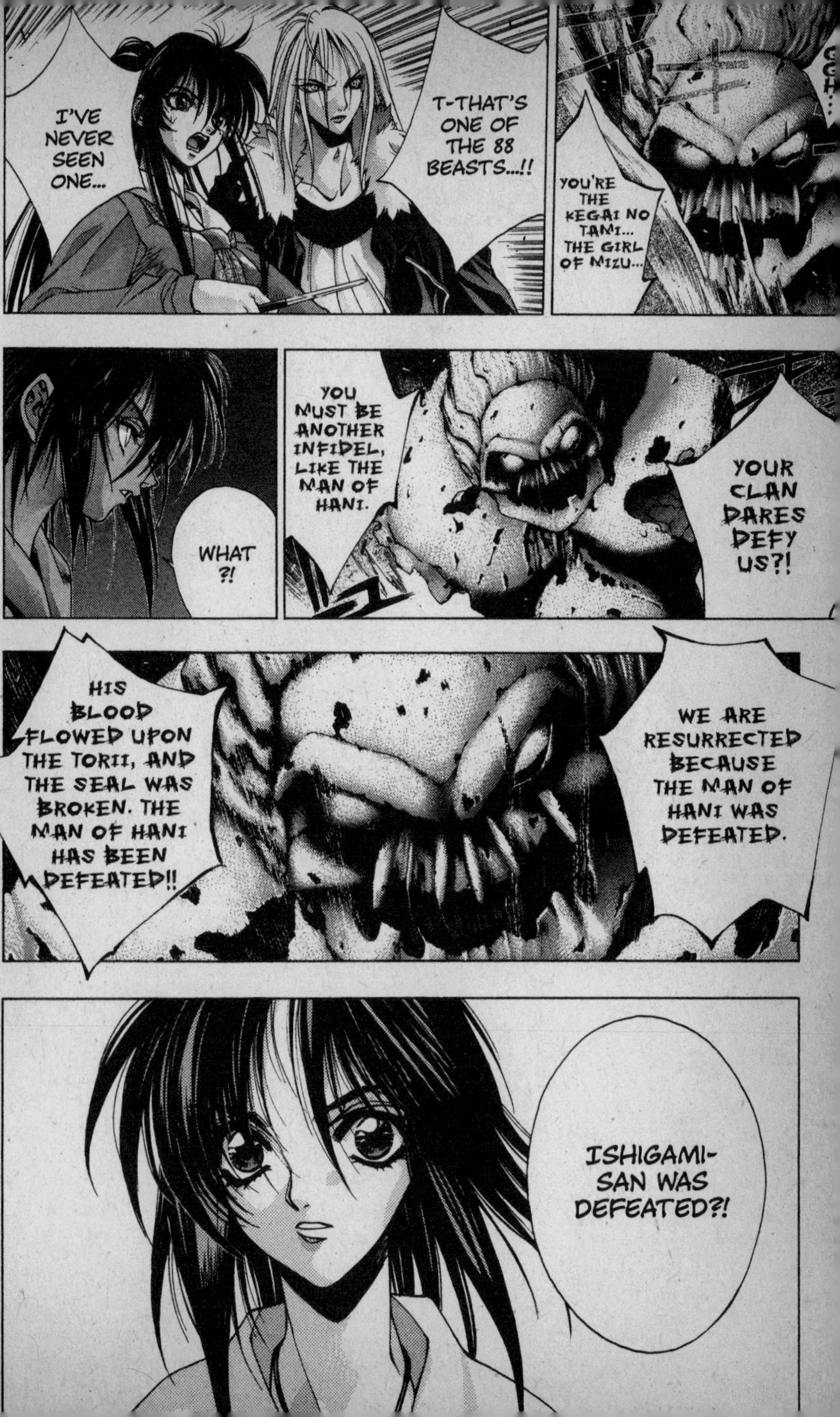
UGH...
YOU'RE THE KEGAI NO TAMI... THE GIRL OF MIZU...
T-THAT'S ONE OF THE 88 BEASTS...!!
I'VE NEVER SEEN ONE...
YOUR CLAN DARES DEFY US?!
YOU MUST BE ANOTHER INFIDEL, LIKE THE MAN OF HANI.
WHAT ?!
WE ARE RESURRECTED BECAUSE THE MAN OF HANI WAS DEFEATED.
HIS BLOOD FLOWED UPON THE TORII, AND THE SEAL WAS BROKEN. THE MAN OF HANI HAS BEEN DEFEATED!!
ISHIGAMI-SAN WAS DEFEATED?!

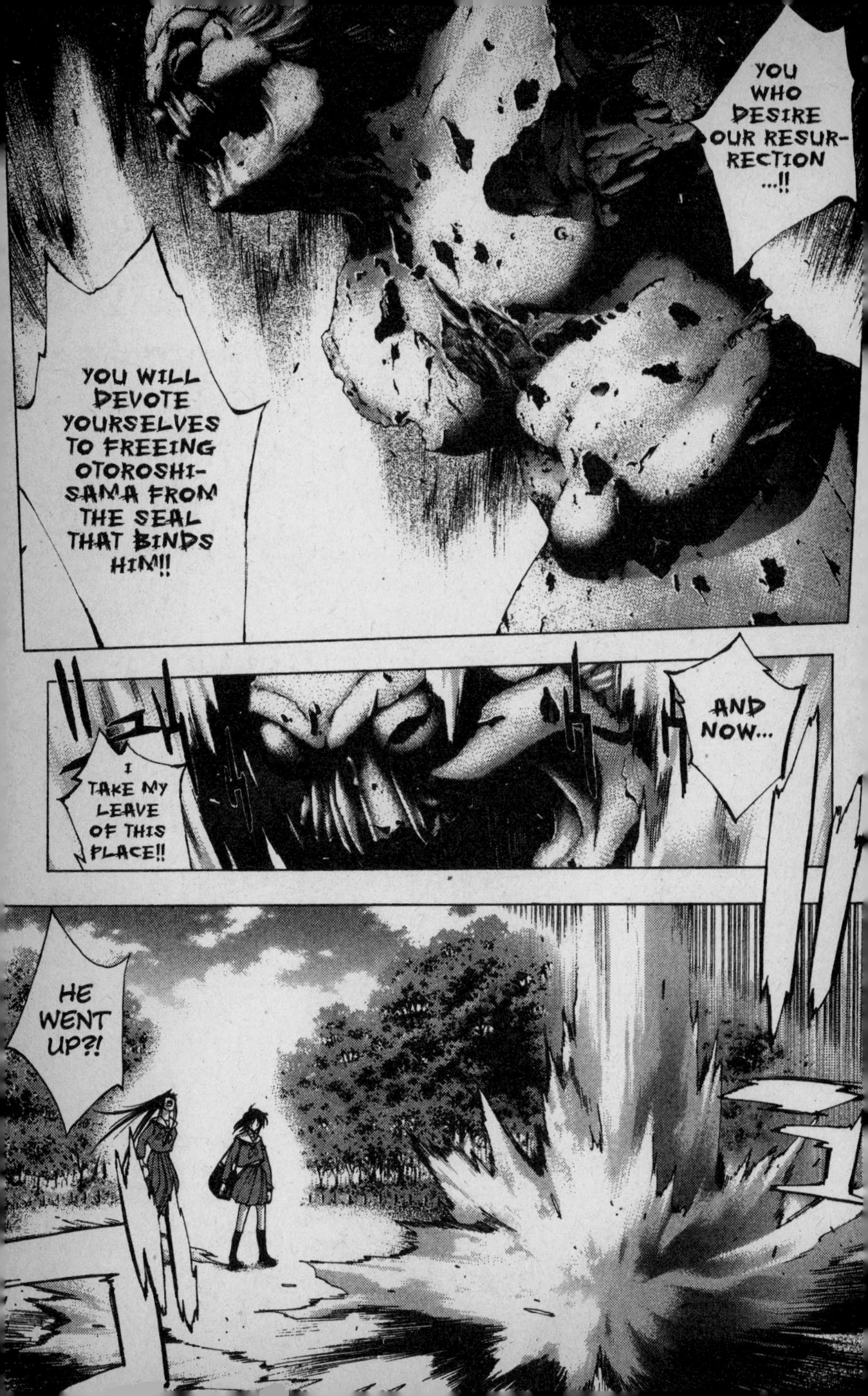
YOU WHO DESIRE OUR RESURRECTION ...!!
YOU WILL DEVOTE YOURSELVES TO FREEING OTOROSHI-SAMA FROM THE SEAL THAT BINDS HIM!!
AND NOW...
I TAKE MY LEAVE OF THIS PLACE!!
HE WENT UP?!

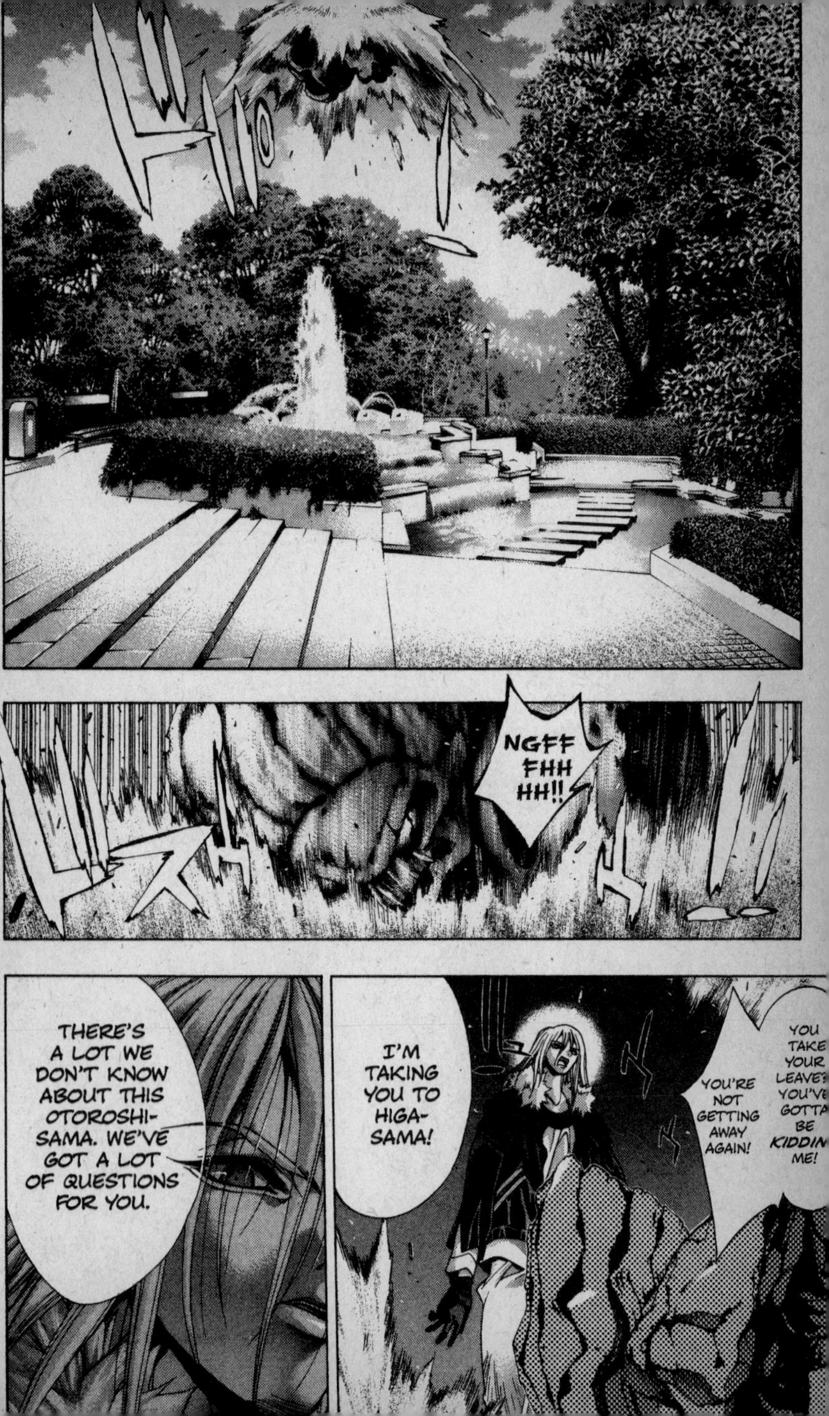
NGFFFHHHH!!
YOU TAKE YOUR LEAVE? YOU'VE GOTTA BE *KIDDING* ME!
YOU'RE NOT GETTING AWAY AGAIN!
I'M TAKING YOU TO HIGA-SAMA!
THERE'S A LOT WE DON'T KNOW ABOUT THIS OTOROSHI-SAMA. WE'VE GOT A LOT OF QUESTIONS FOR YOU.

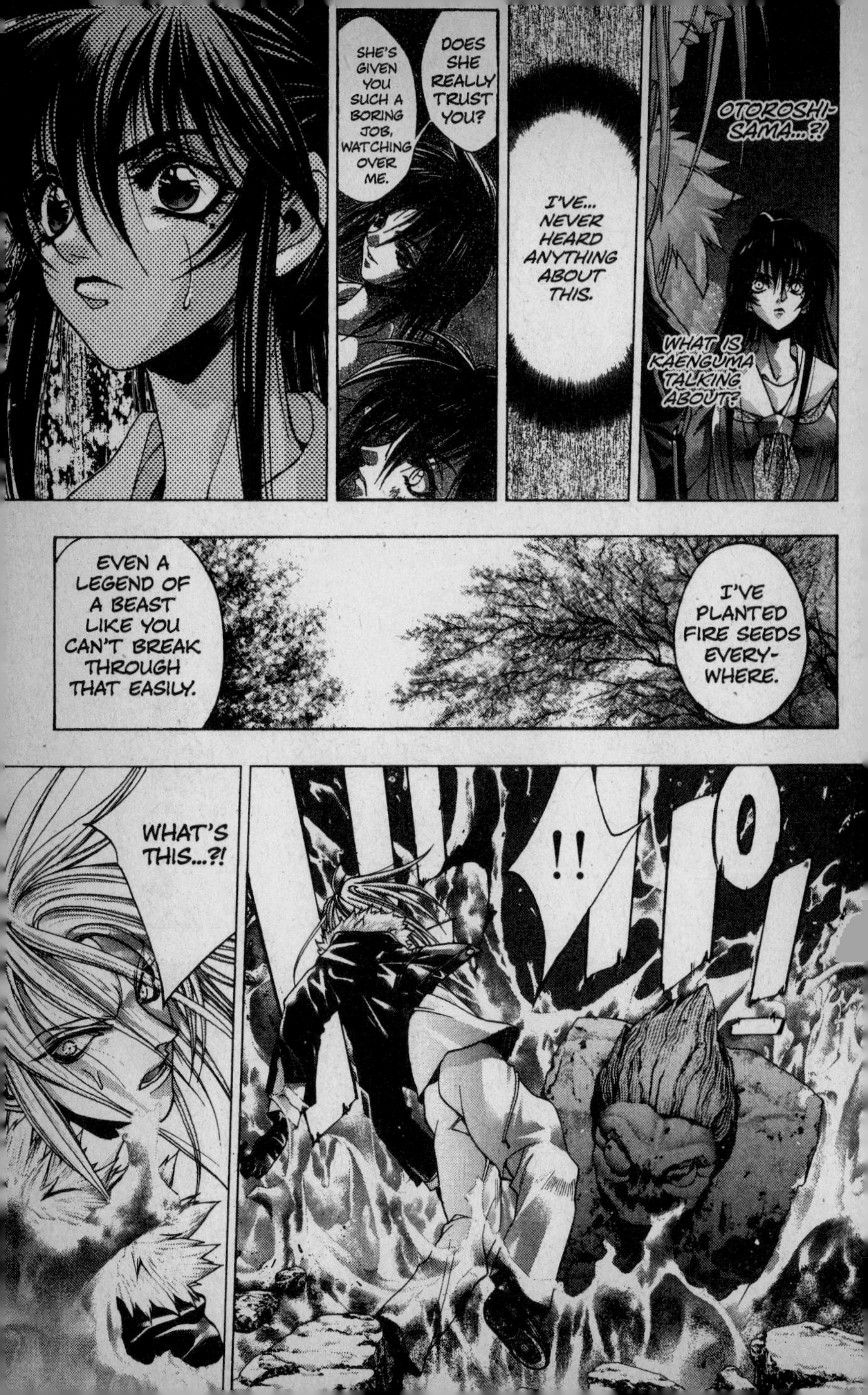
OTOROSHI-SAMA...?!
WHAT IS KAENGUMA TALKING ABOUT?
I'VE... NEVER HEARD ANYTHING ABOUT THIS.
DOES SHE REALLY TRUST YOU?
SHE'S GIVEN YOU SUCH A BORING JOB, WATCHING OVER ME.
I'VE PLANTED FIRE SEEDS EVERY-WHERE.
EVEN A LEGEND OF A BEAST LIKE YOU CAN'T BREAK THROUGH THAT EASILY.
!!
WHAT'S THIS...?!

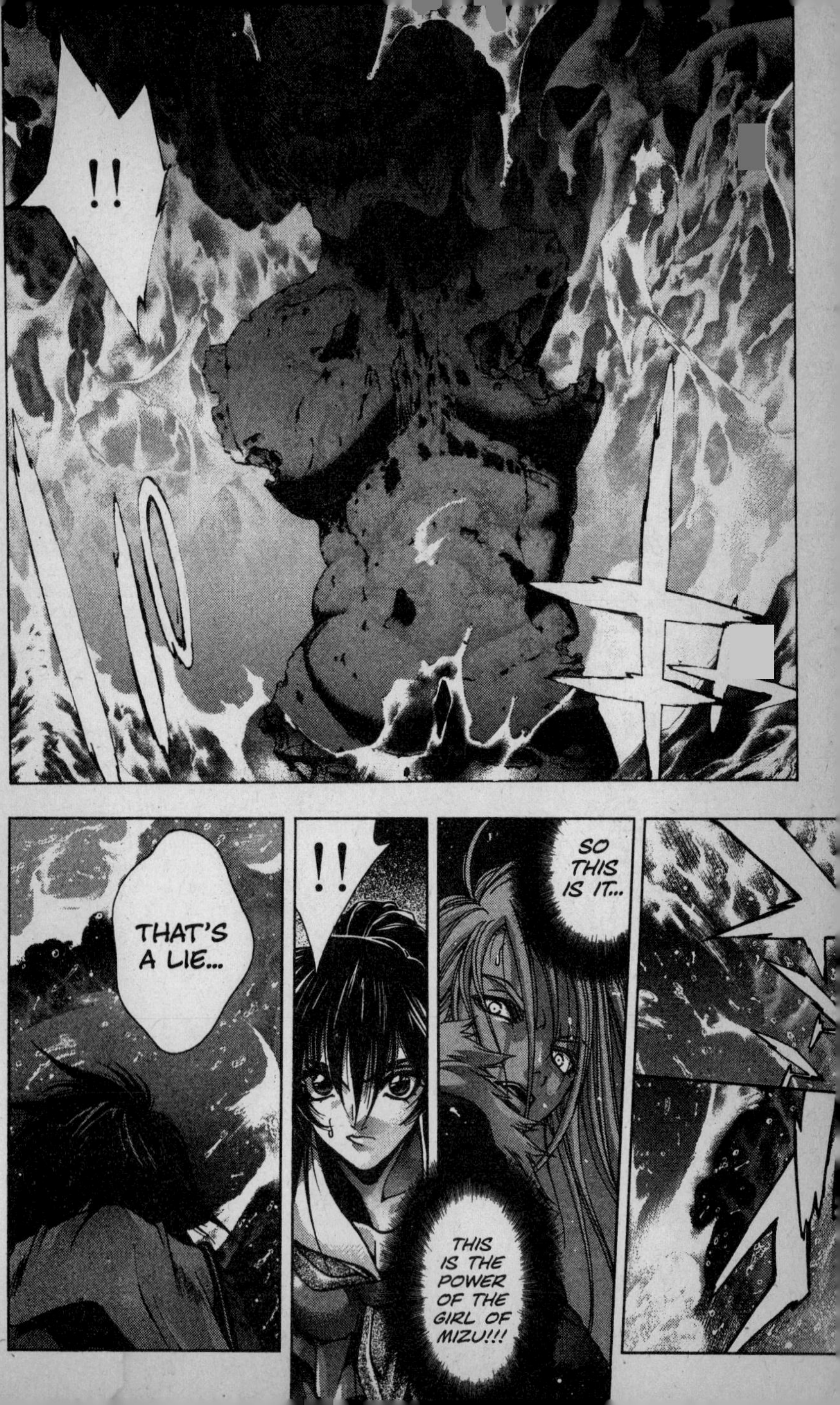
!!
SO THIS IS IT...
THIS IS THE POWER OF THE GIRL OF MIZU!!!
!!
THAT'S A LIE...

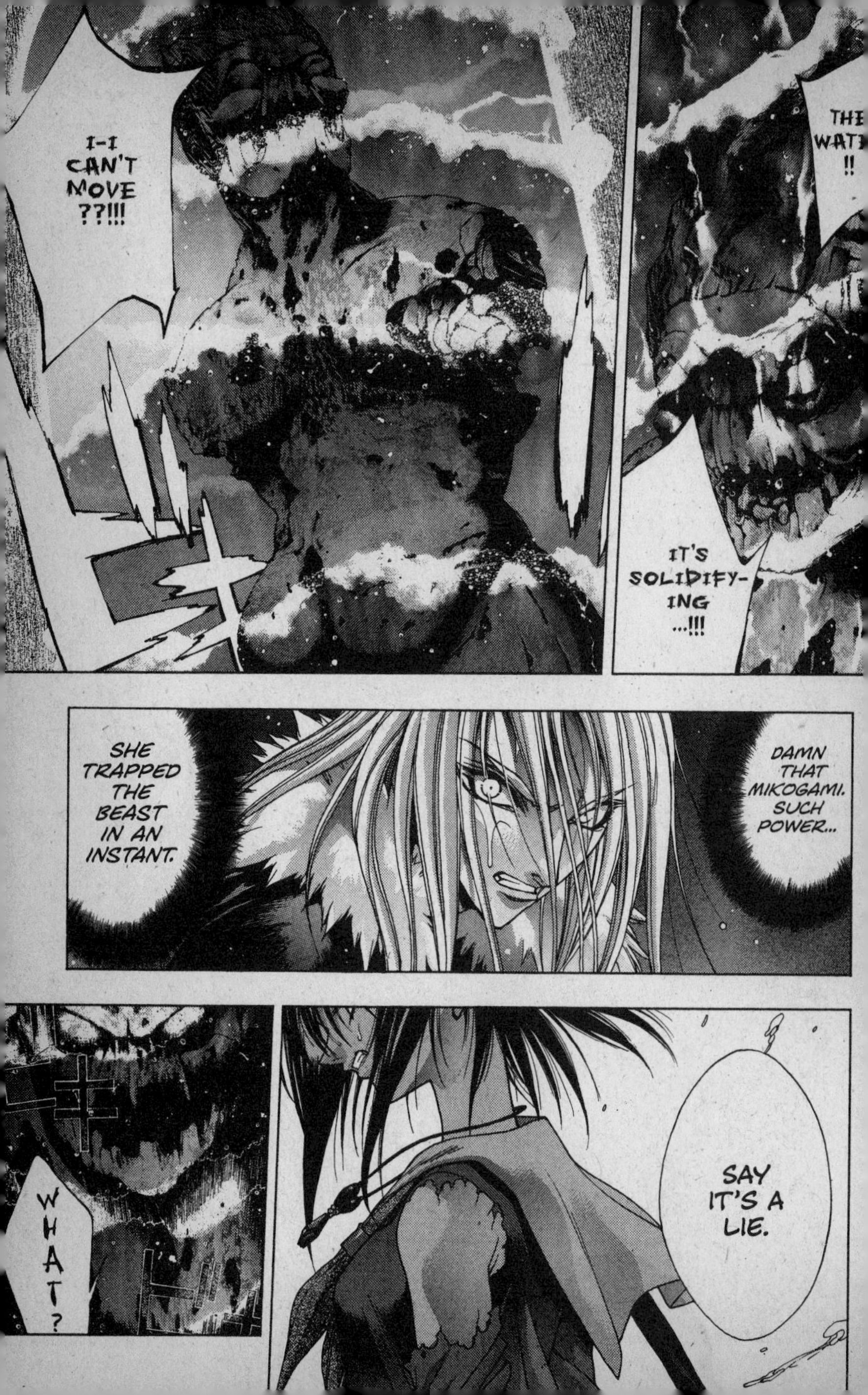
THE WAT
!!
IT'S SOLIDIFY-ING ...!!!
I-I CAN'T MOVE ??!!!
DAMN THAT MIKOGAMI. SUCH POWER...
SHE TRAPPED THE BEAST IN AN INSTANT.
SAY IT'S A LIE.
WHAT?

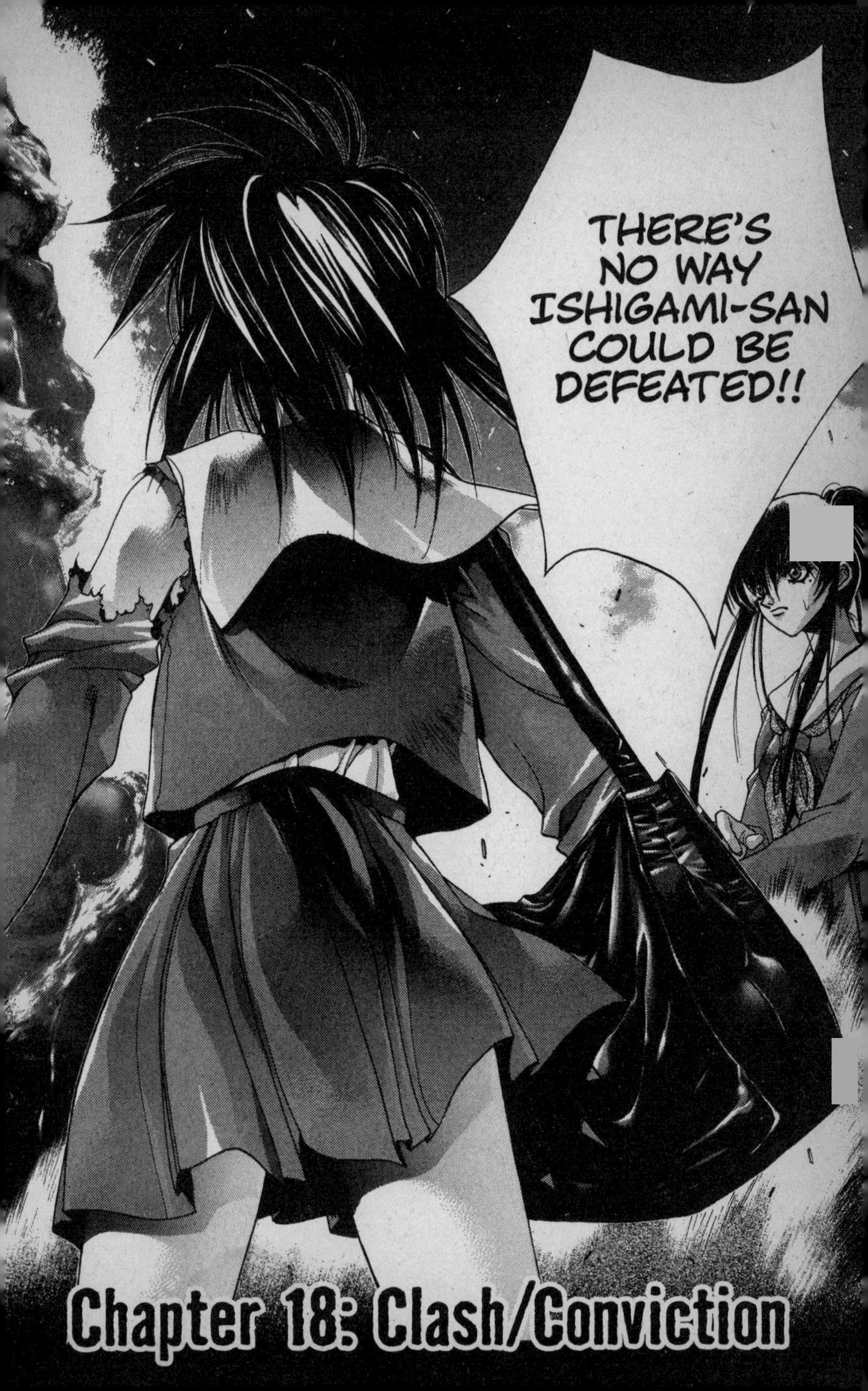
THERE'S NO WAY ISHIGAMI-SAN COULD BE DEFEATED!!
Chapter 18: Clash/Conviction

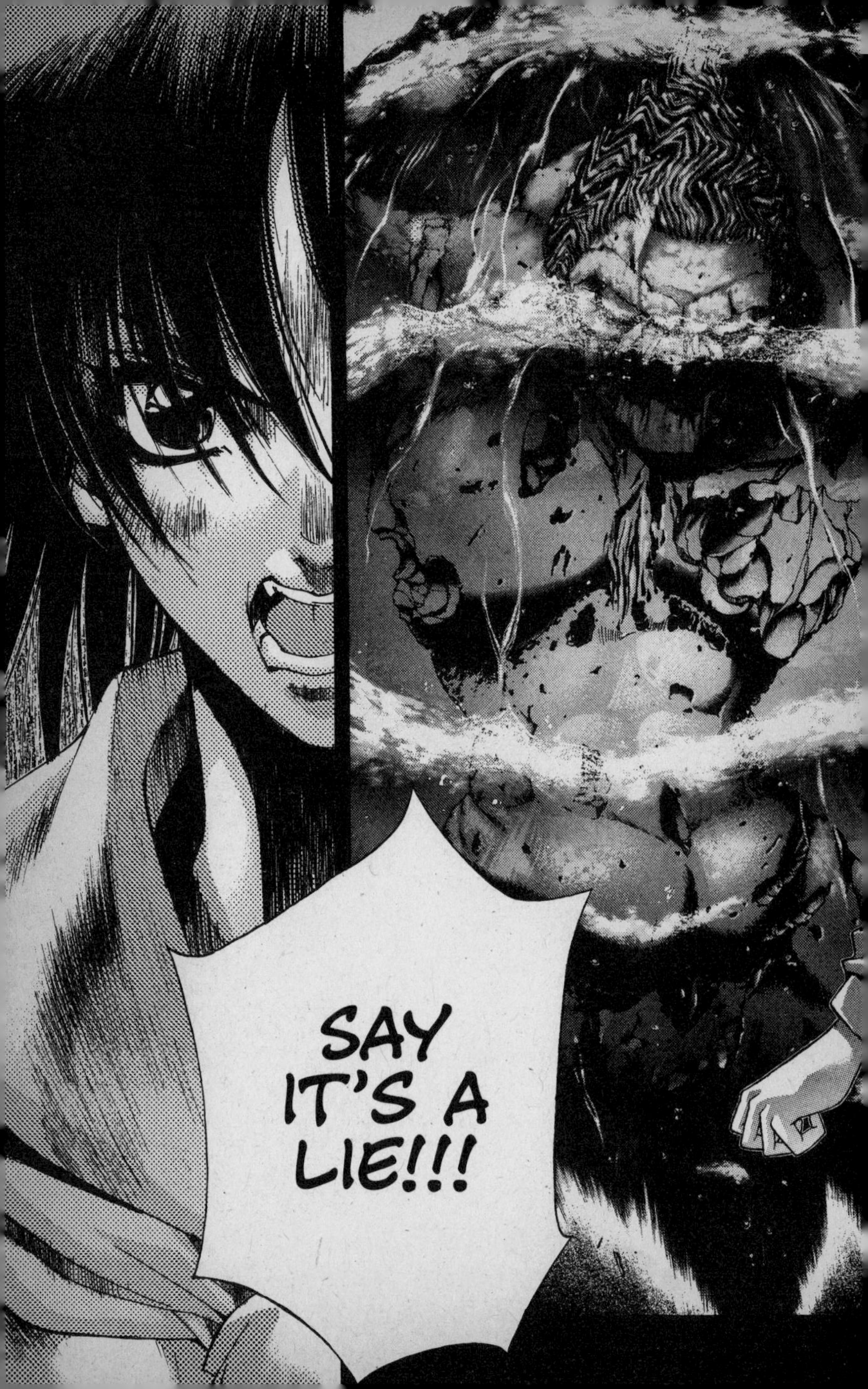
SAY IT'S A LIE!!!

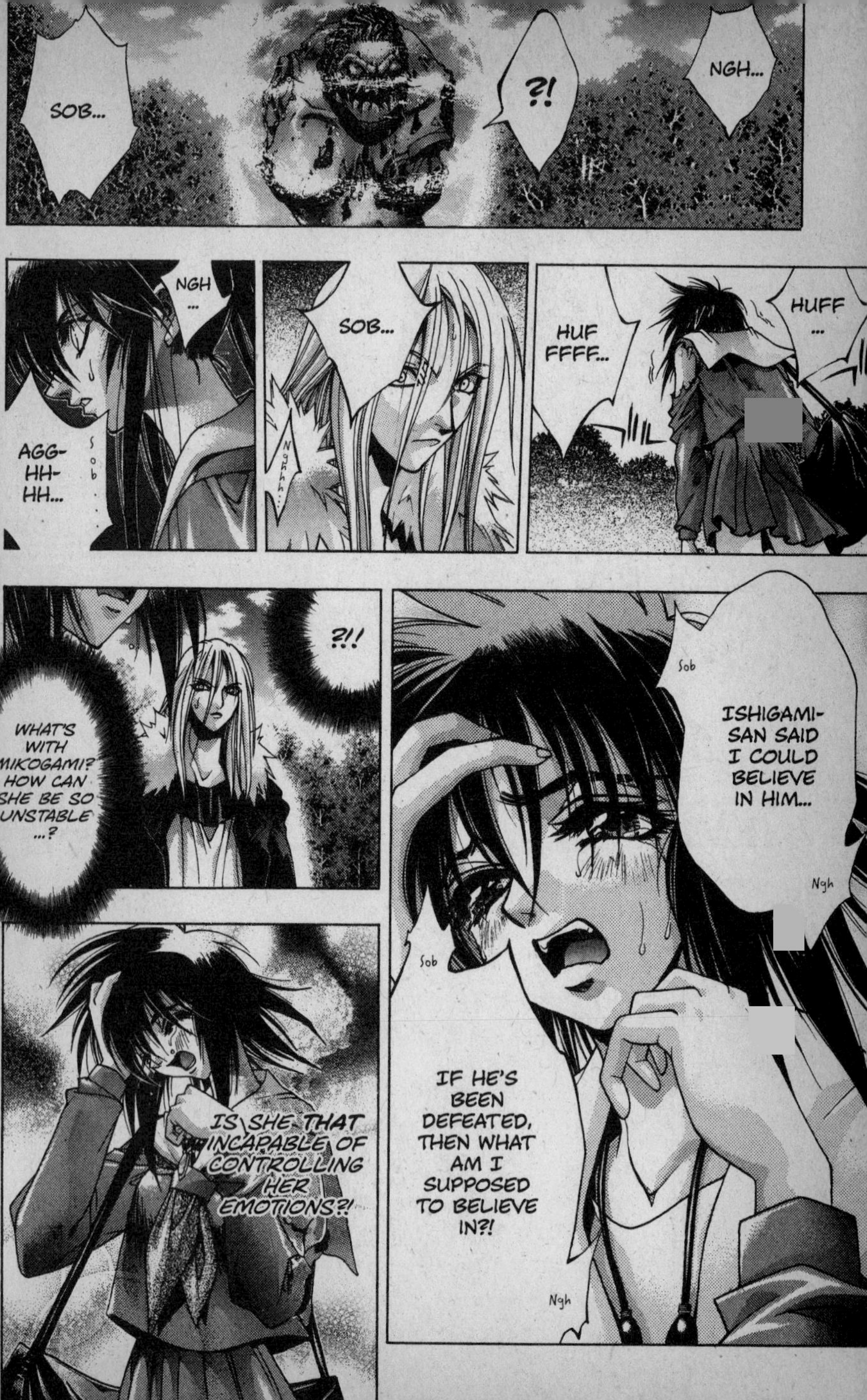
NGH...
?!
SOB...
HUFF...
HUF FFFF...
SOB...
Nghhh...
NGH...
AGG-HH-HH...
Sob...
Sob
ISHIGAMI-SAN SAID I COULD BELIEVE IN HIM...
Ngh
Sob
IF HE'S BEEN DEFEATED, THEN WHAT AM I SUPPOSED TO BELIEVE IN?!
Ngh
?!!
WHAT'S WITH MIKOGAMI? HOW CAN SHE BE SO UNSTABLE...?
IS SHE THAT INCAPABLE OF CONTROLLING HER EMOTIONS?!

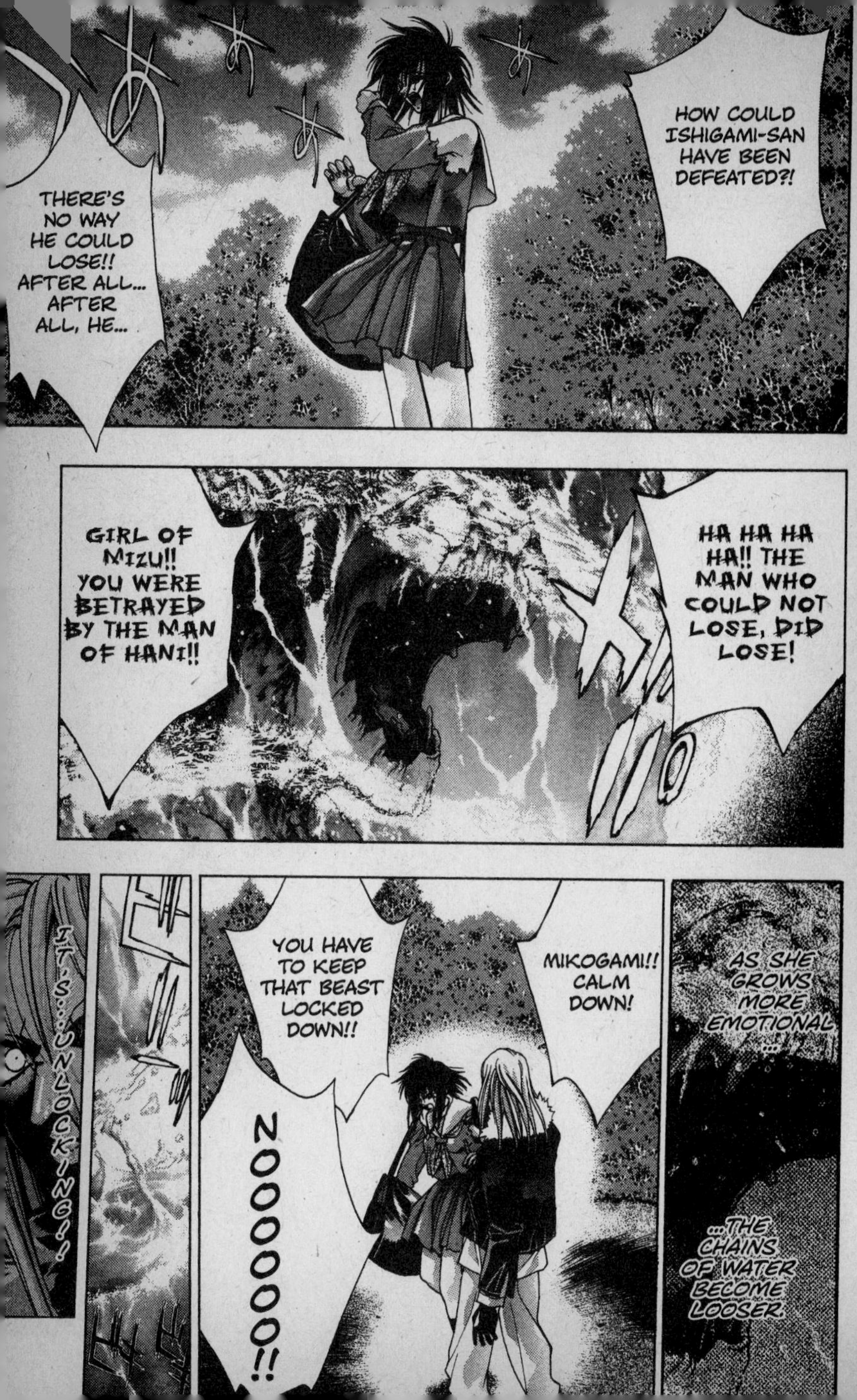
HOW COULD ISHIGAMI-SAN HAVE BEEN DEFEATED?!
THERE'S NO WAY HE COULD LOSE!! AFTER ALL... AFTER ALL, HE...
HA HA HA HA!! THE MAN WHO COULD NOT LOSE, DID LOSE!
GIRL OF MIZU!! YOU WERE BETRAYED BY THE MAN OF HANI!!
AS SHE GROWS MORE EMOTIONAL...
...THE CHAINS OF WATER BECOME LOOSER
MIKOGAMI!! CALM DOWN!
YOU HAVE TO KEEP THAT BEAST LOCKED DOWN!!
NOOOOOOO!!
IT'S...UNLOCKING!!

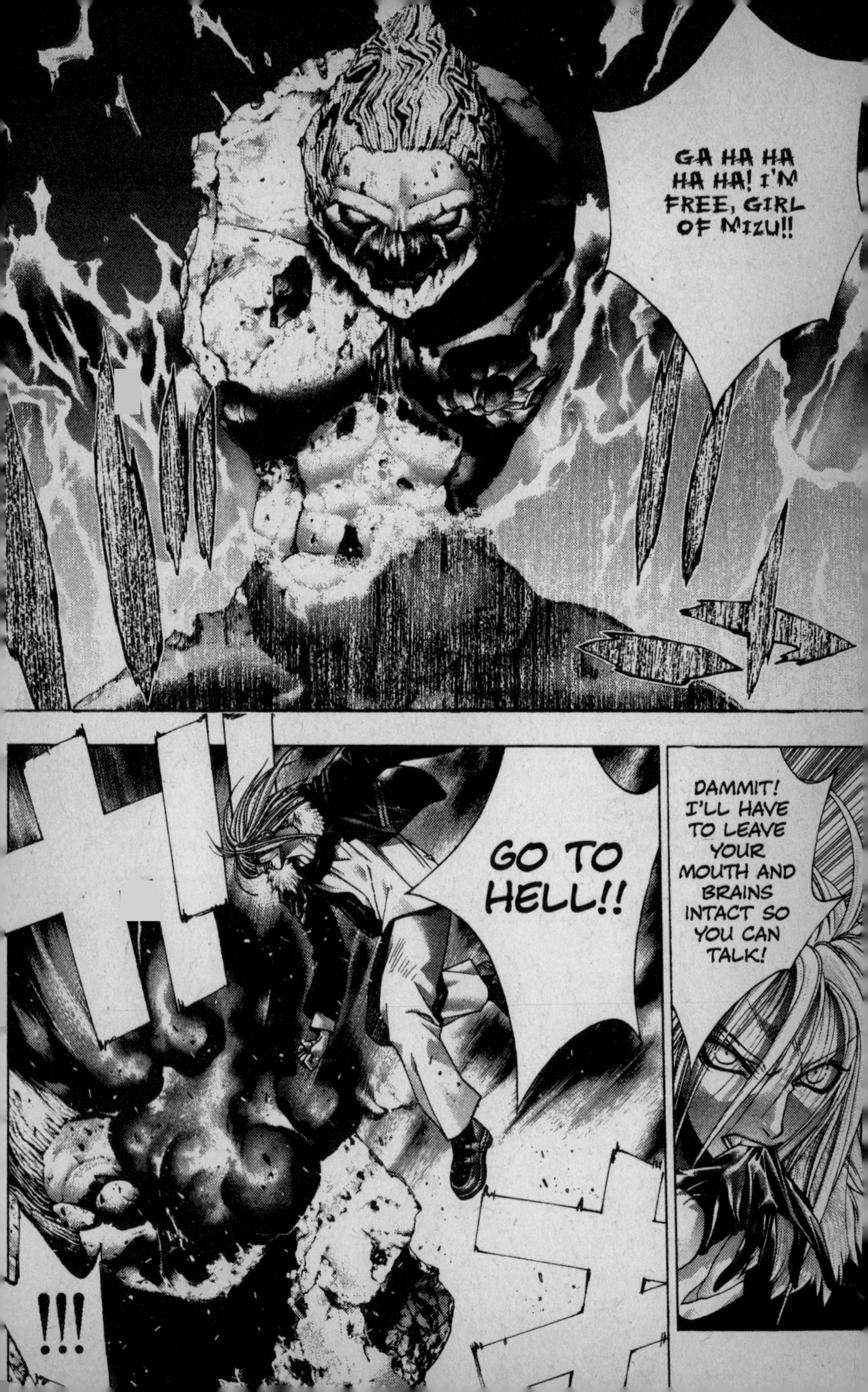
GA HA HA HA HA! I'M FREE, GIRL OF MIZU!!
DAMMIT! I'LL HAVE TO LEAVE YOUR MOUTH AND BRAINS INTACT SO YOU CAN TALK!
GO TO HELL!!
!!!

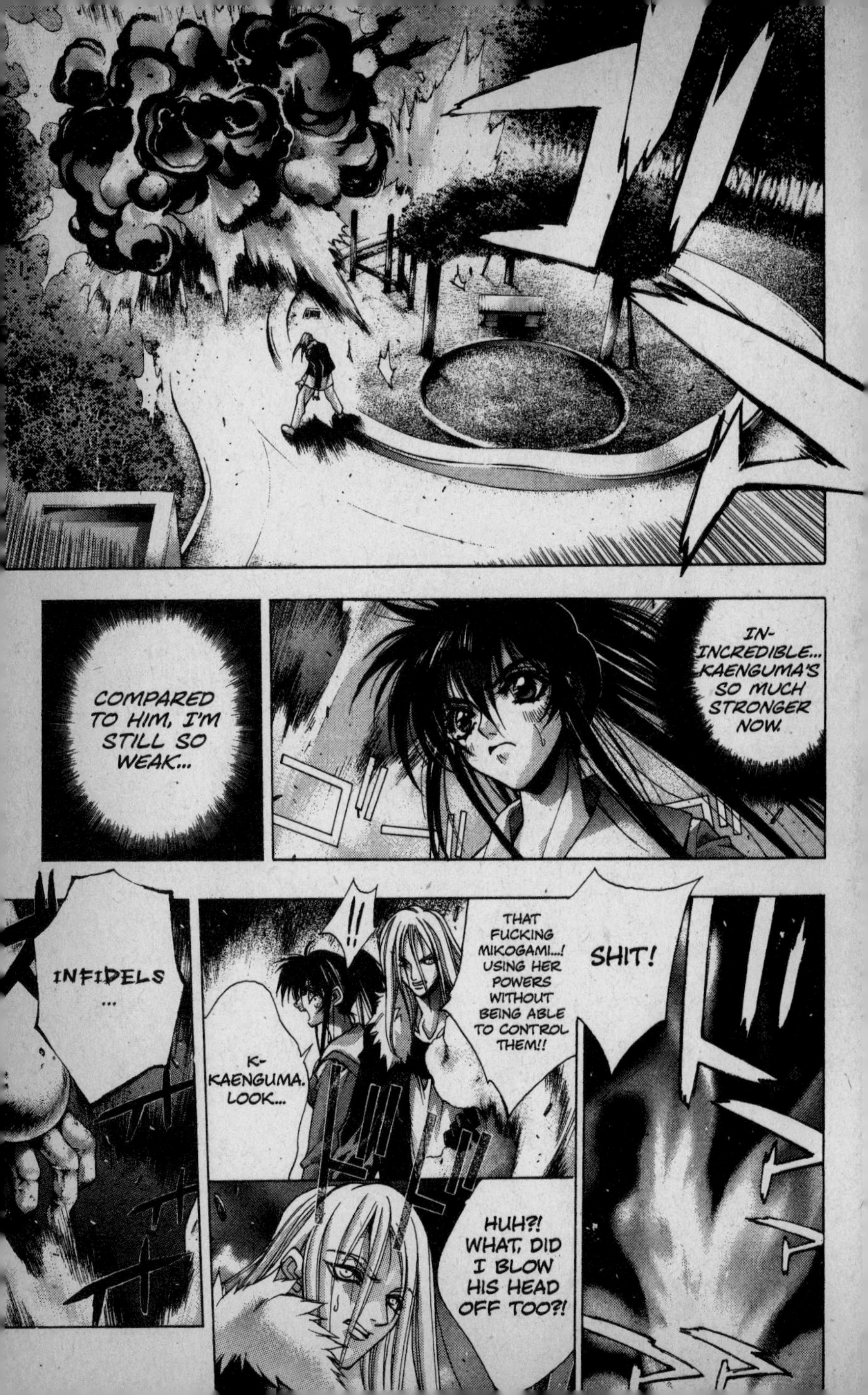
IN- INCREDIBLE... KAENGUMA'S SO MUCH STRONGER NOW.
COMPARED TO HIM, I'M STILL SO WEAK...
SHIT!
THAT FUCKING MIKOGAMI...! USING HER POWERS WITHOUT BEING ABLE TO CONTROL THEM!!
!!
K-KAENGUMA. LOOK...
HUH?! WHAT, DID I BLOW HIS HEAD OFF TOO?!
INFIDELS ...

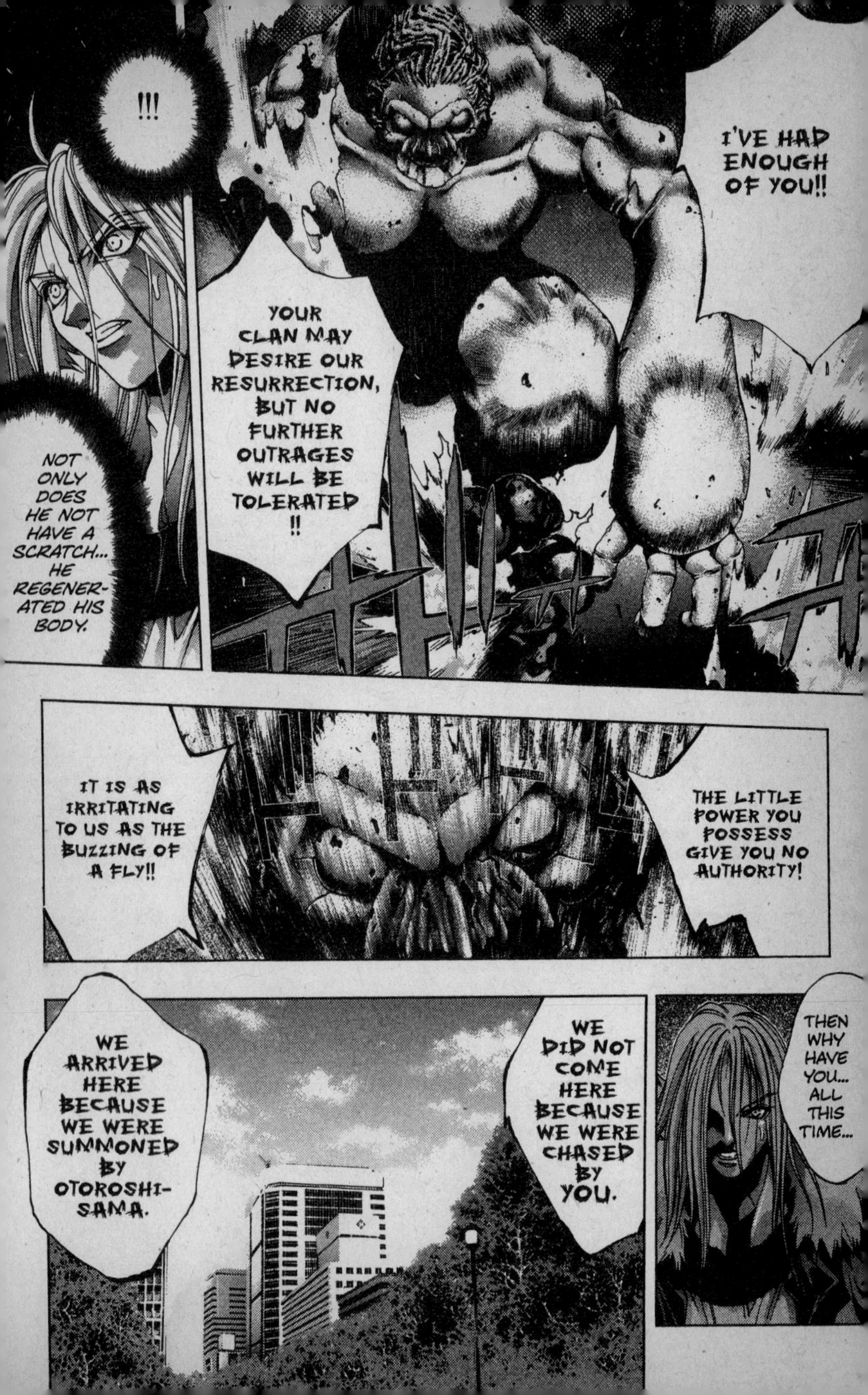
I'VE HAD ENOUGH OF YOU!!
YOUR CLAN MAY DESIRE OUR RESURRECTION, BUT NO FURTHER OUTRAGES WILL BE TOLERATED!!
!!!
NOT ONLY DOES HE NOT HAVE A SCRATCH... HE REGENERATED HIS BODY.
THE LITTLE POWER YOU POSSESS GIVE YOU NO AUTHORITY!
IT IS AS IRRITATING TO US AS THE BUZZING OF A FLY!!
THEN WHY HAVE YOU... ALL THIS TIME...
WE DID NOT COME HERE BECAUSE WE WERE CHASED BY YOU.
WE ARRIVED HERE BECAUSE WE WERE SUMMONED BY OTOROSHI-SAMA.

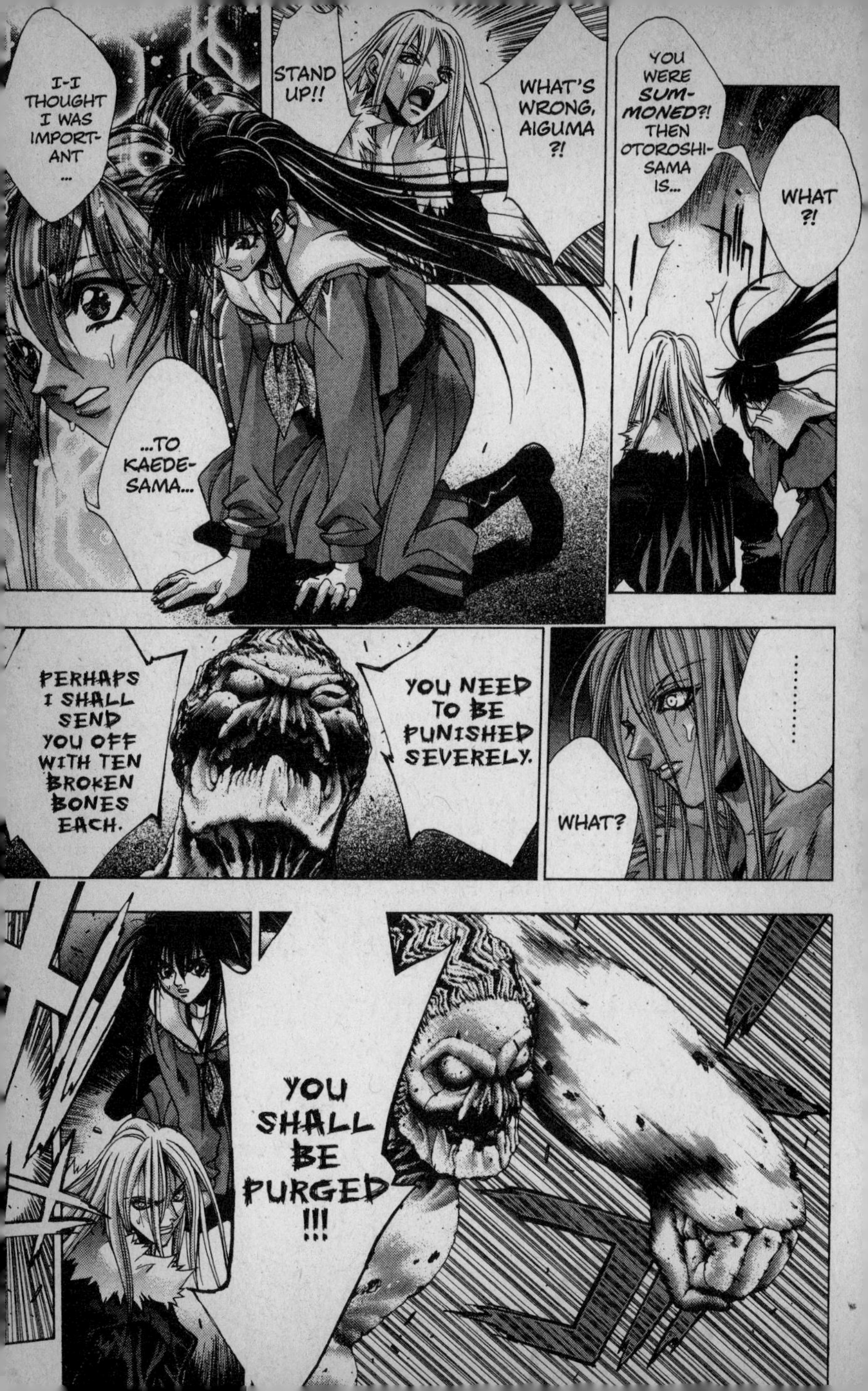
YOU WERE SUMMONED?! THEN OTOROSHI-SAMA IS...
WHAT?!
WHAT'S WRONG, AIGUMA?!
STAND UP!!
I-I THOUGHT I WAS IMPORTANT...
...TO KAEDE-SAMA...
......
WHAT?
YOU NEED TO BE PUNISHED SEVERELY.
PERHAPS I SHALL SEND YOU OFF WITH TEN BROKEN BONES EACH.
YOU SHALL BE PURGED!!!

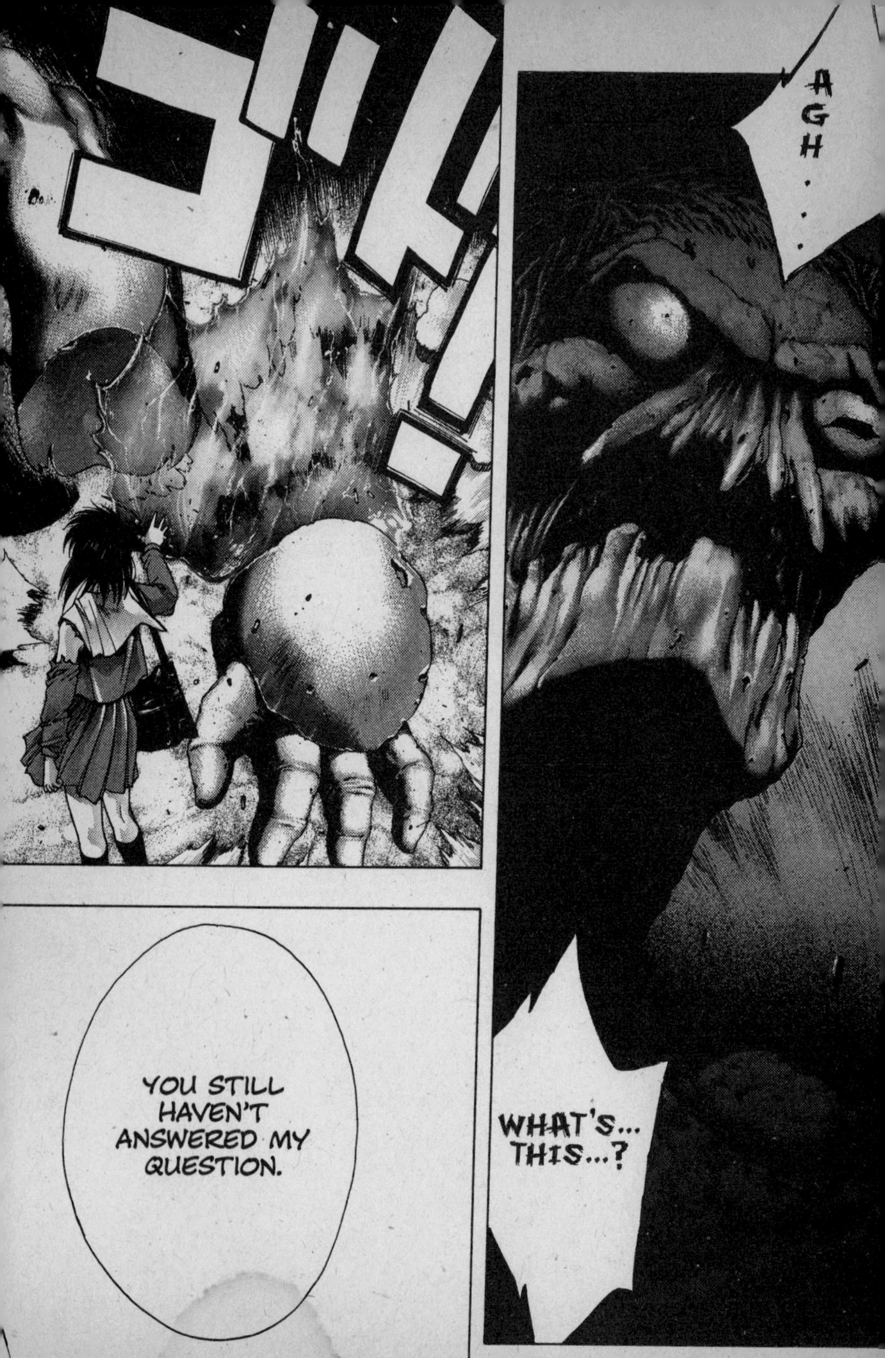
AGH...
WHAT'S... THIS...?
YOU STILL HAVEN'T ANSWERED MY QUESTION.

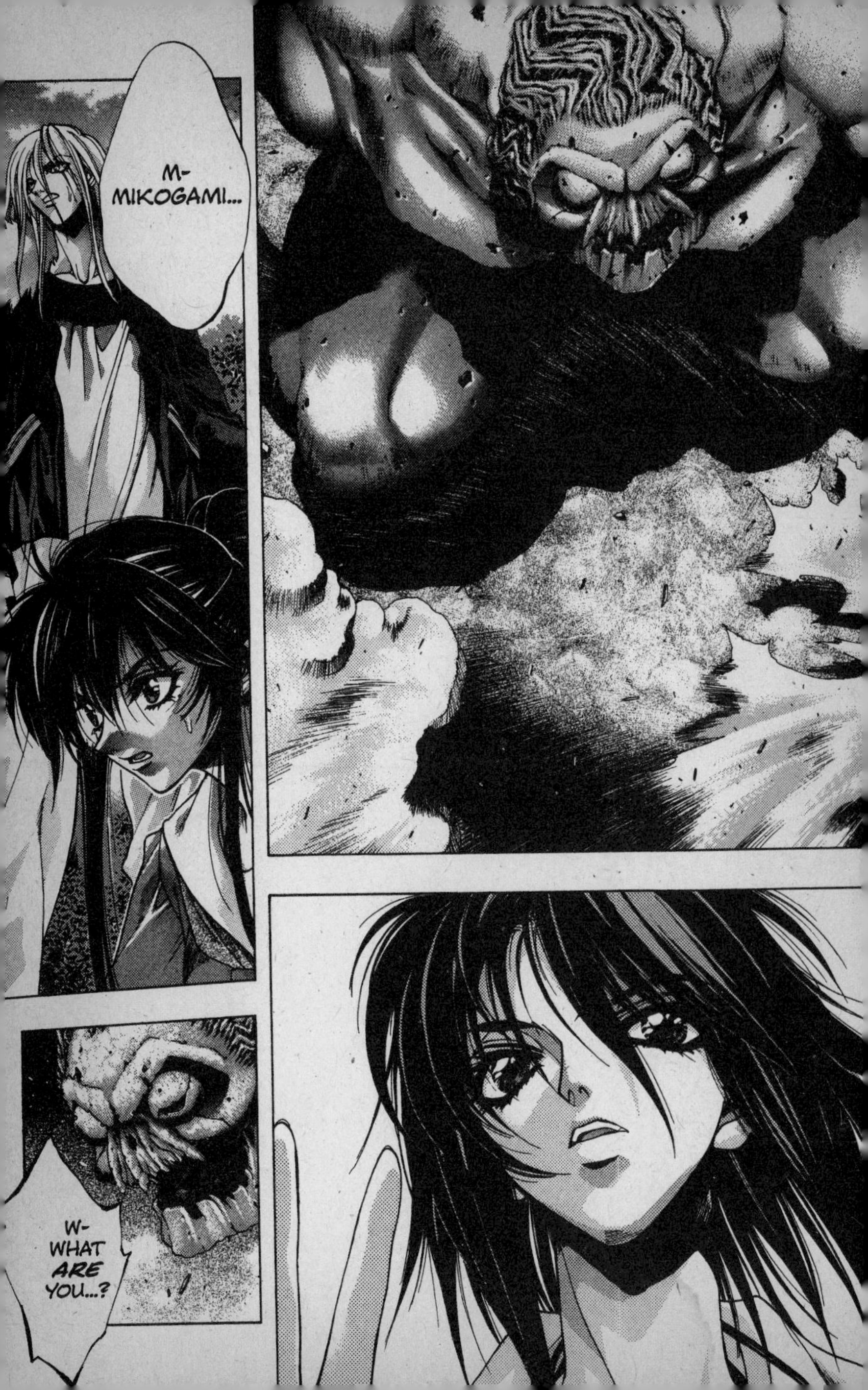
M-MIKOGAMI...
W-WHAT ARE YOU...?

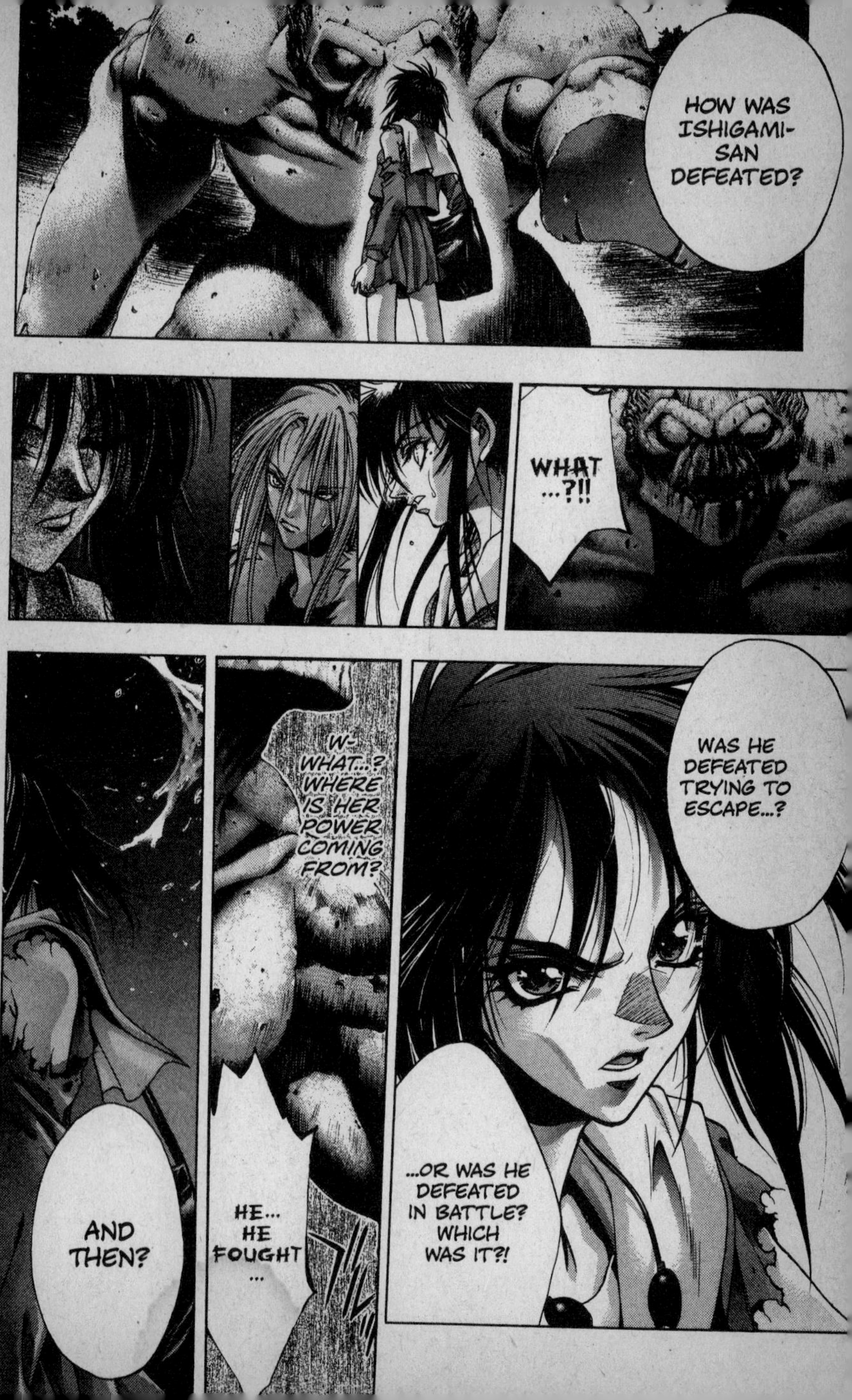
HOW WAS ISHIGAMI-SAN DEFEATED?
WHAT ...?!!
WAS HE DEFEATED TRYING TO ESCAPE...?
...OR WAS HE DEFEATED IN BATTLE? WHICH WAS IT?!
W-WHAT...? WHERE IS HER POWER COMING FROM?
HE... HE FOUGHT...
AND THEN?

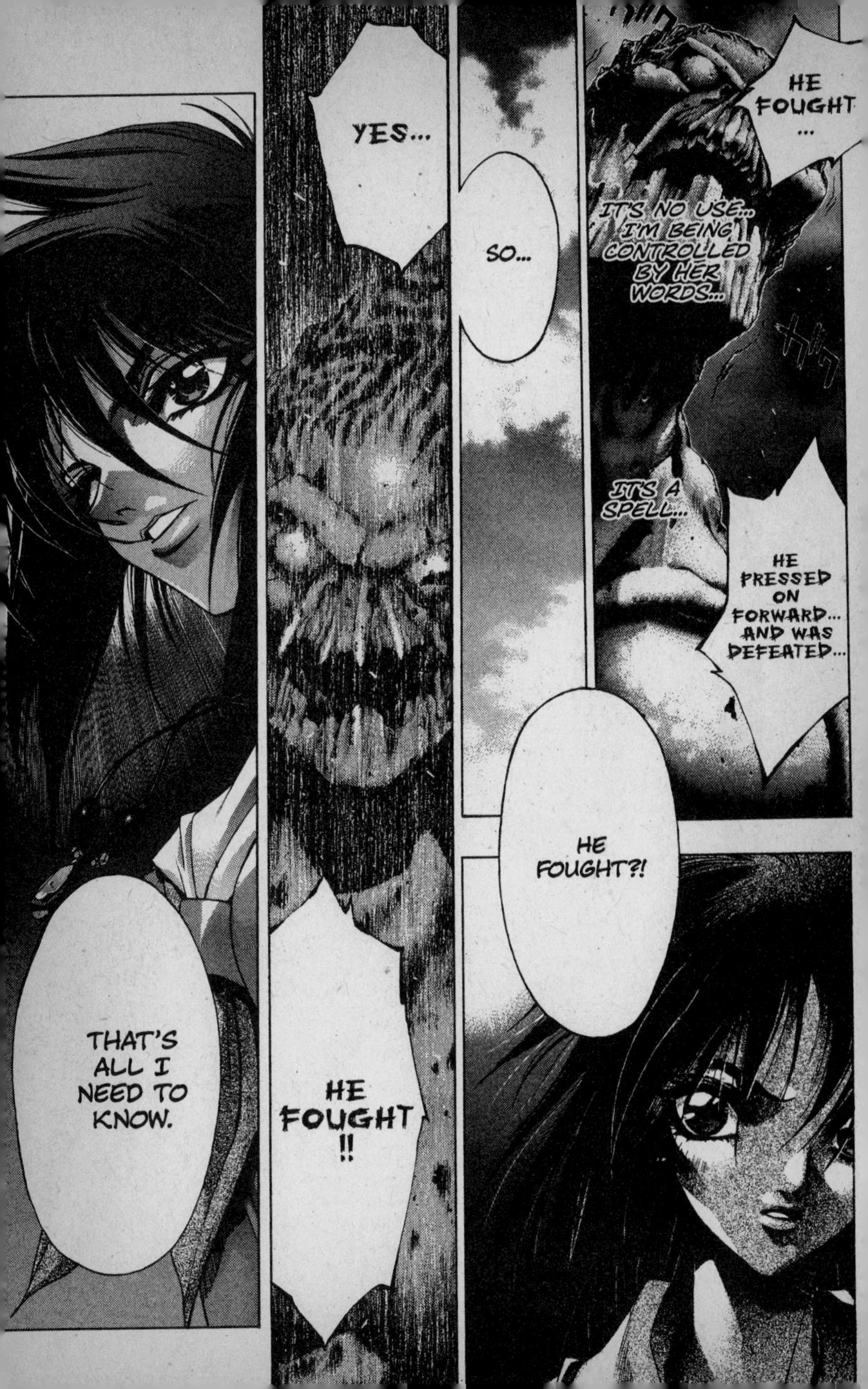
HE FOUGHT ...
IT'S NO USE... I'M BEING CONTROLLED BY HER WORDS...
IT'S A SPELL...
HE PRESSED ON FORWARD... AND WAS DEFEATED...
SO...
HE FOUGHT?!
YES...
HE FOUGHT !!
THAT'S ALL I NEED TO KNOW.

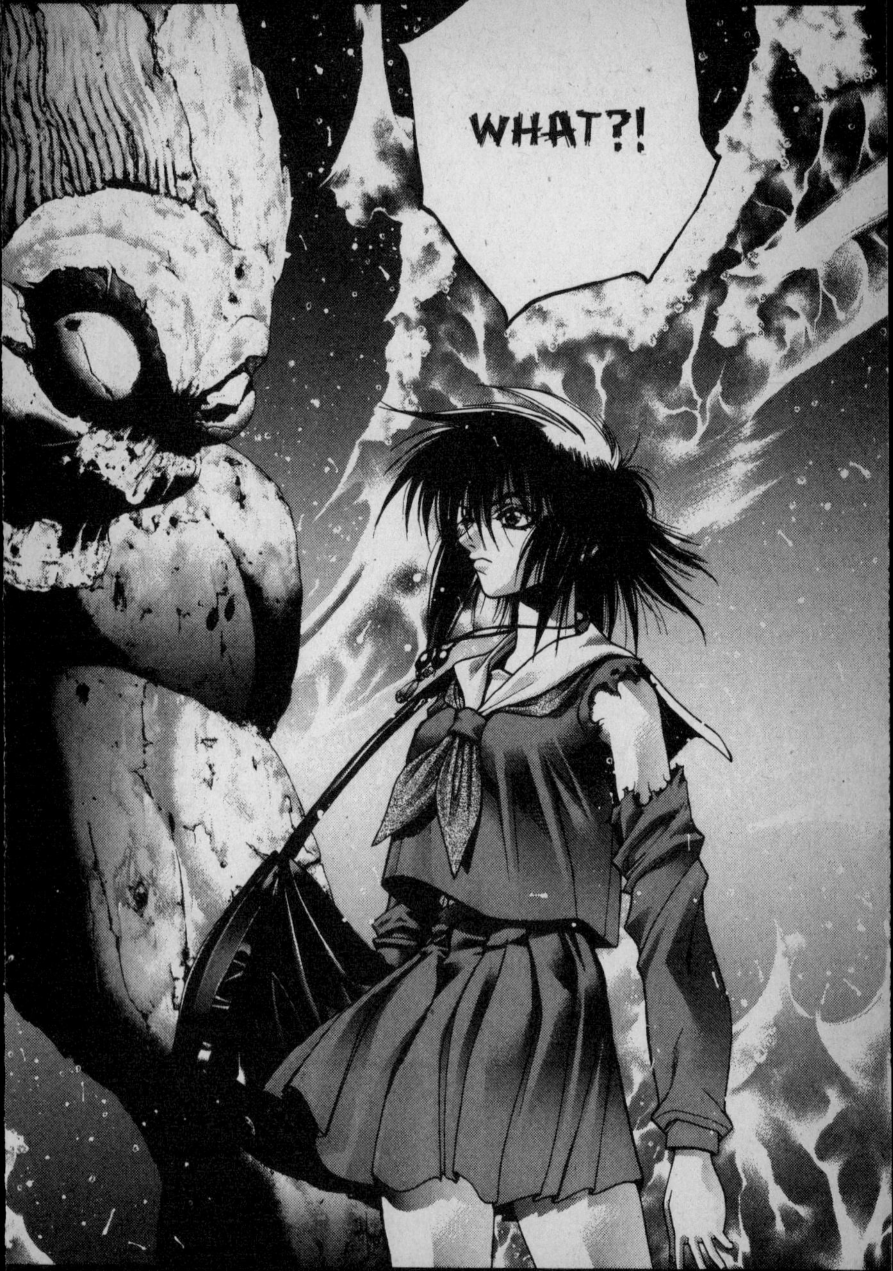
WHAT?!

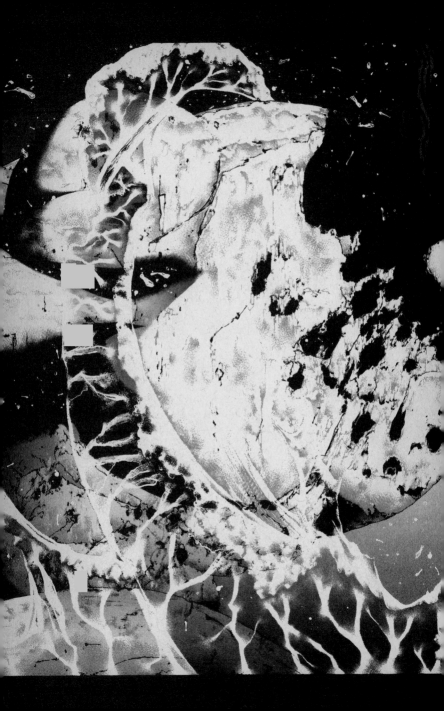

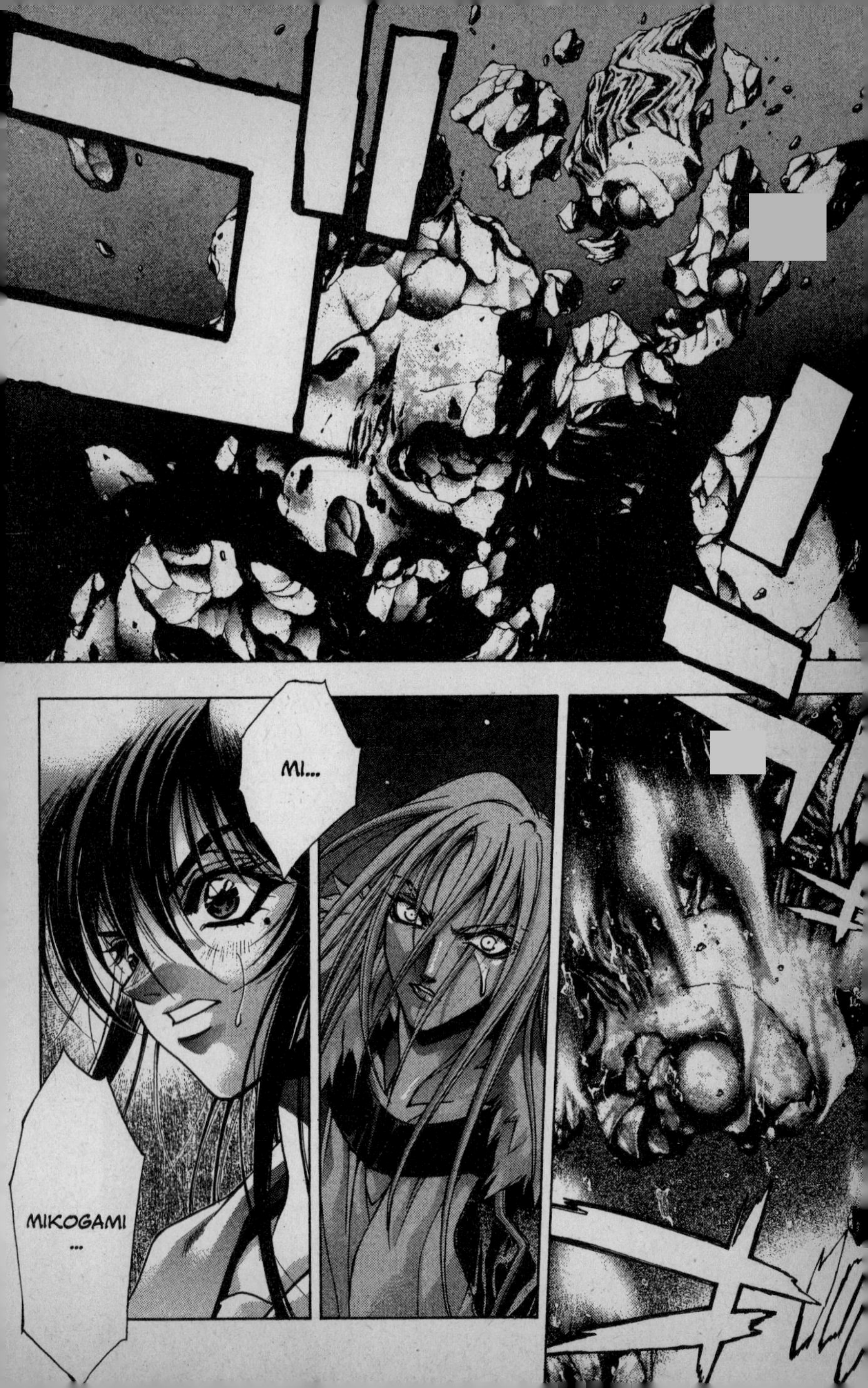
MI...
MIKOGAMI
...

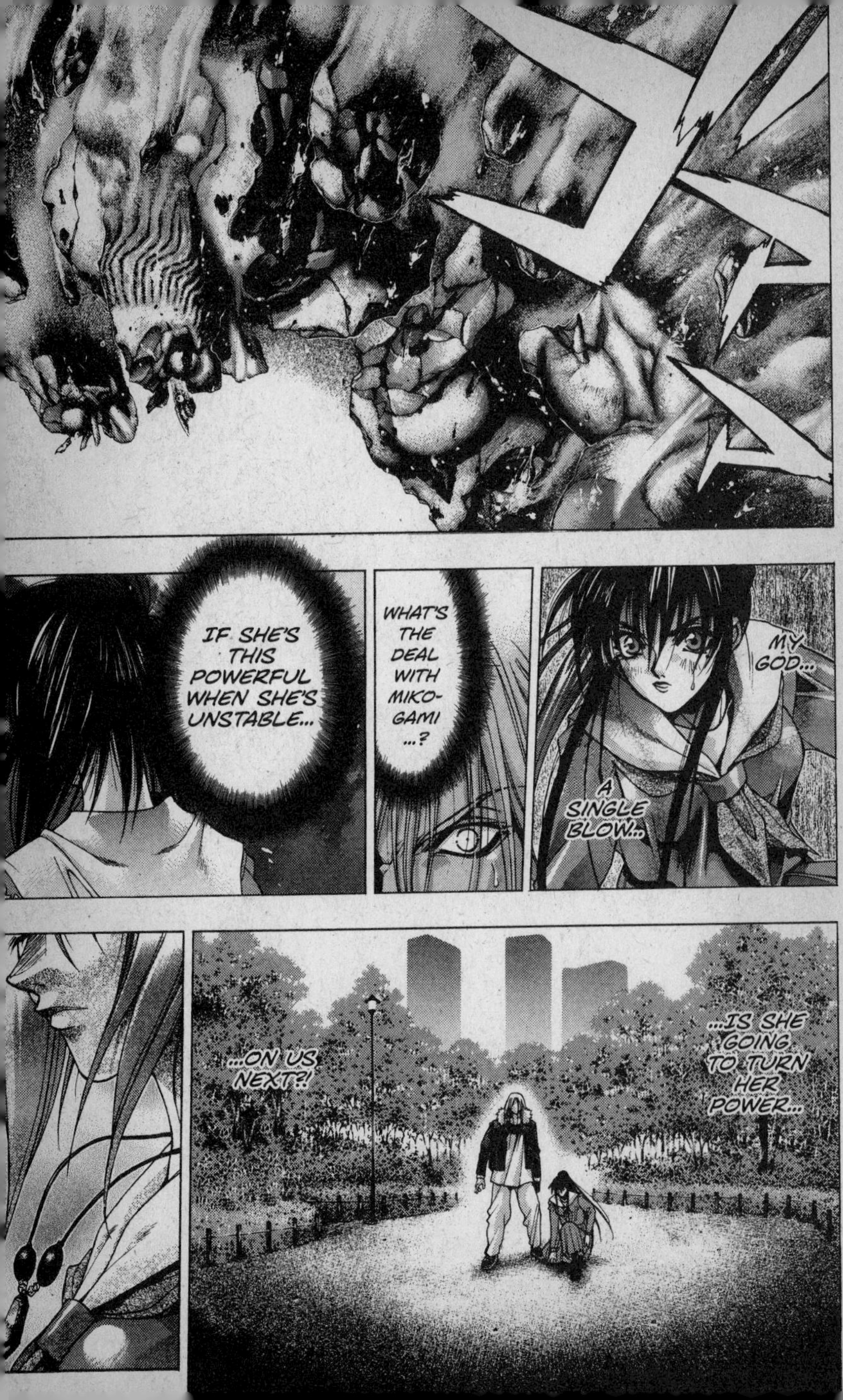
MY GOD...
A SINGLE BLOW...
WHAT'S THE DEAL WITH MIKO-GAMI ...?
IF SHE'S THIS POWERFUL WHEN SHE'S UNSTABLE...
...IS SHE GOING TO TURN HER POWER...
...ON US NEXT?!

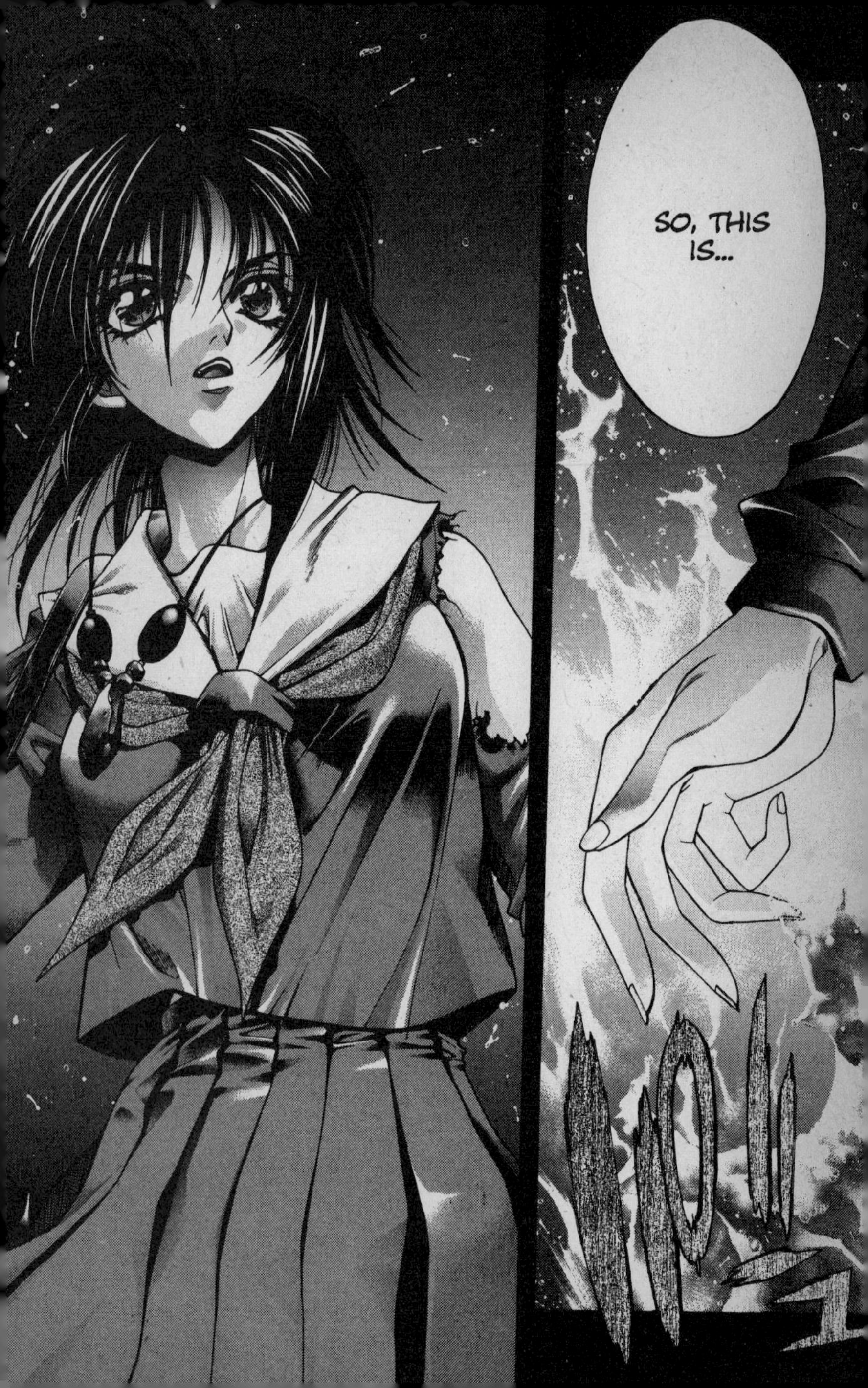
SO, THIS IS...

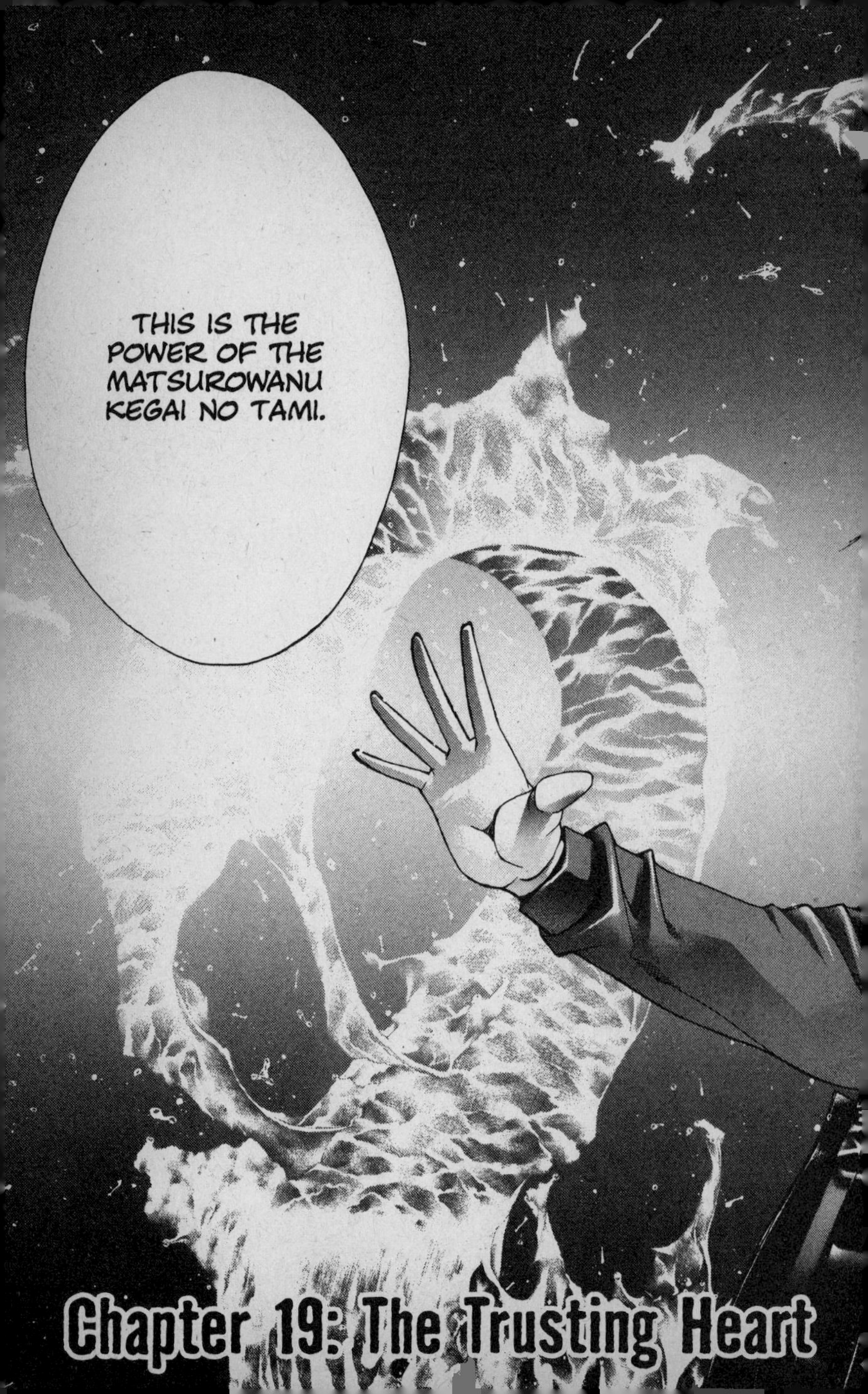
THIS IS THE POWER OF THE MATSUROWANU KEGAI NO TAMI.
Chapter 19: The Trusting Heart

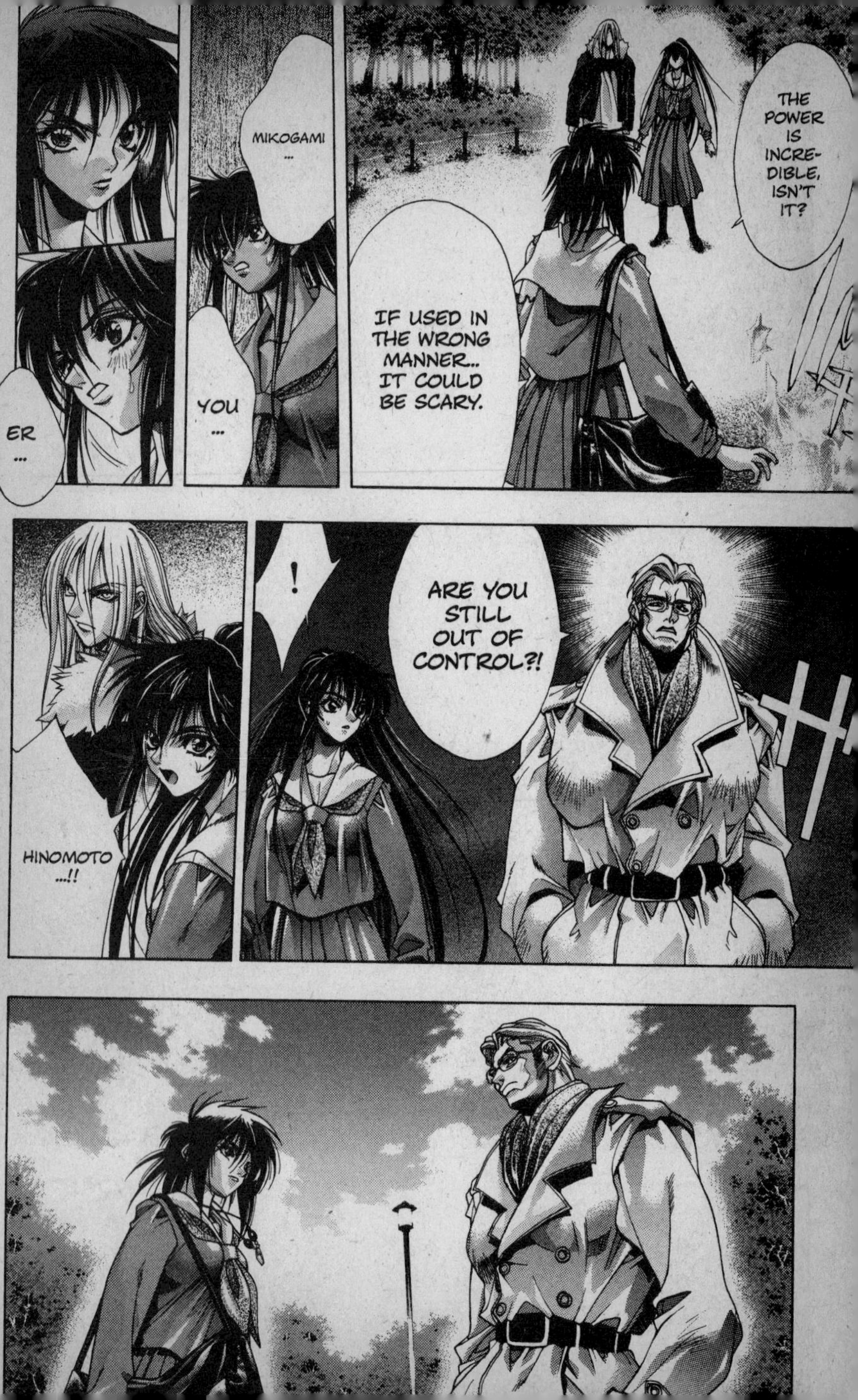
THE POWER IS INCRE-DIBLE, ISN'T IT?
IF USED IN THE WRONG MANNER... IT COULD BE SCARY.
MIKOGAMI ...
YOU ...
ER ...
ARE YOU STILL OUT OF CONTROL?!
!
HINOMOTO ...!!

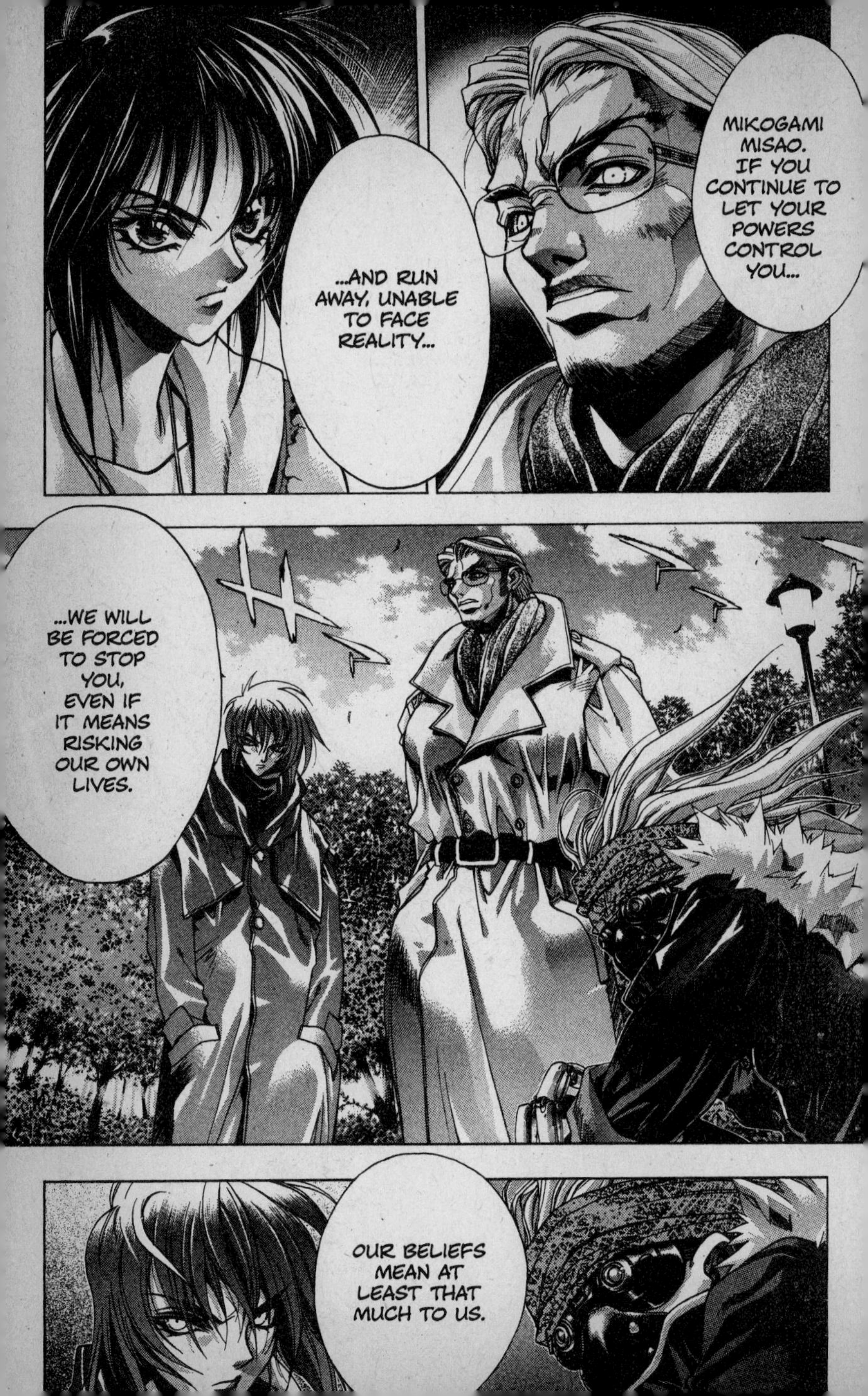
MIKOGAMI MISAO. IF YOU CONTINUE TO LET YOUR POWERS CONTROL YOU...
...AND RUN AWAY, UNABLE TO FACE REALITY...
...WE WILL BE FORCED TO STOP YOU, EVEN IF IT MEANS RISKING OUR OWN LIVES.
OUR BELIEFS MEAN AT LEAST THAT MUCH TO US.

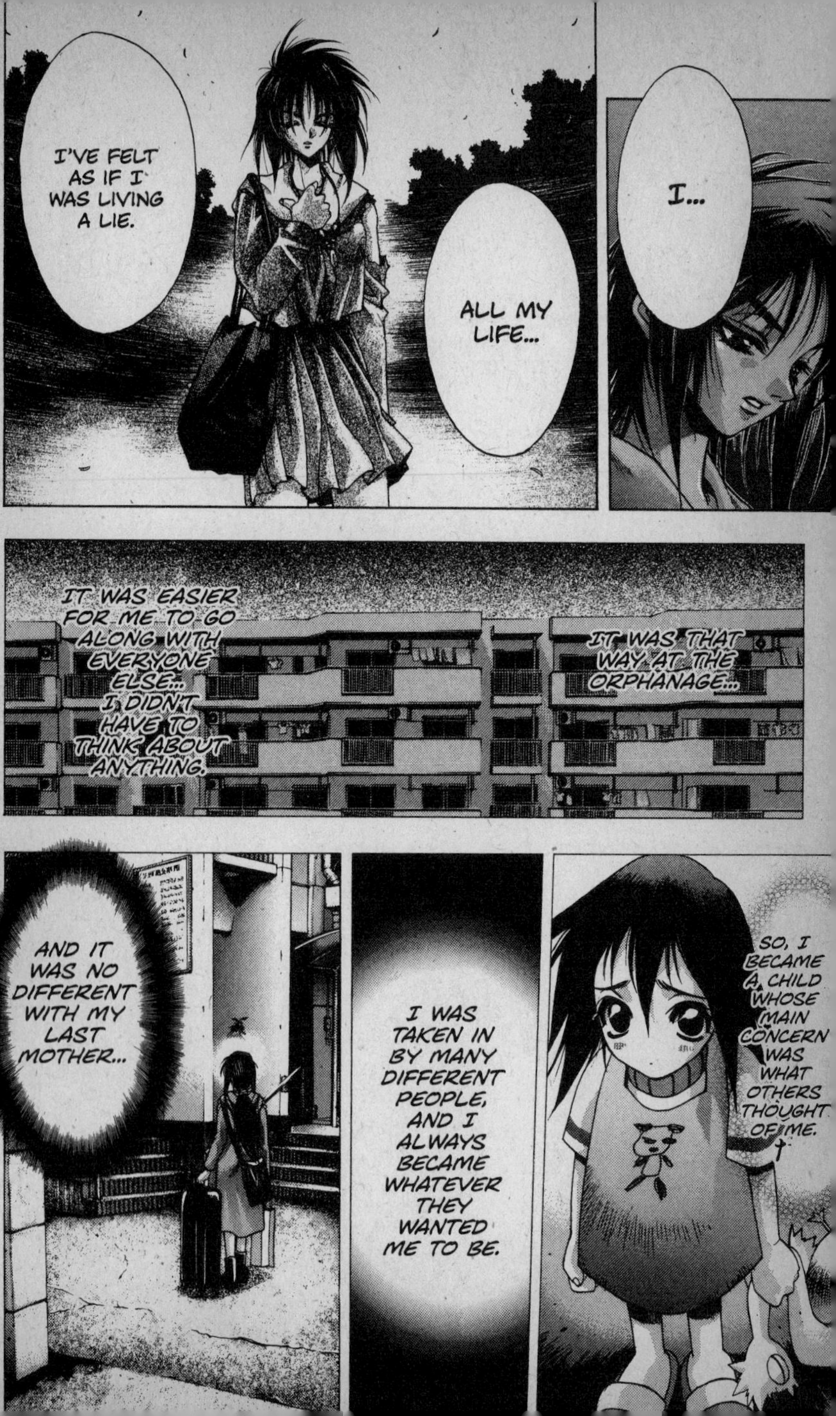
I...
ALL MY LIFE...
I'VE FELT AS IF I WAS LIVING A LIE.
IT WAS THAT WAY AT THE ORPHANAGE...
IT WAS EASIER FOR ME TO GO ALONG WITH EVERYONE ELSE... I DIDN'T HAVE TO THINK ABOUT ANYTHING.
SO, I BECAME A CHILD WHOSE MAIN CONCERN WAS WHAT OTHERS THOUGHT OF ME.
I WAS TAKEN IN BY MANY DIFFERENT PEOPLE, AND I ALWAYS BECAME WHATEVER THEY WANTED ME TO BE.
AND IT WAS NO DIFFERENT WITH MY LAST MOTHER...

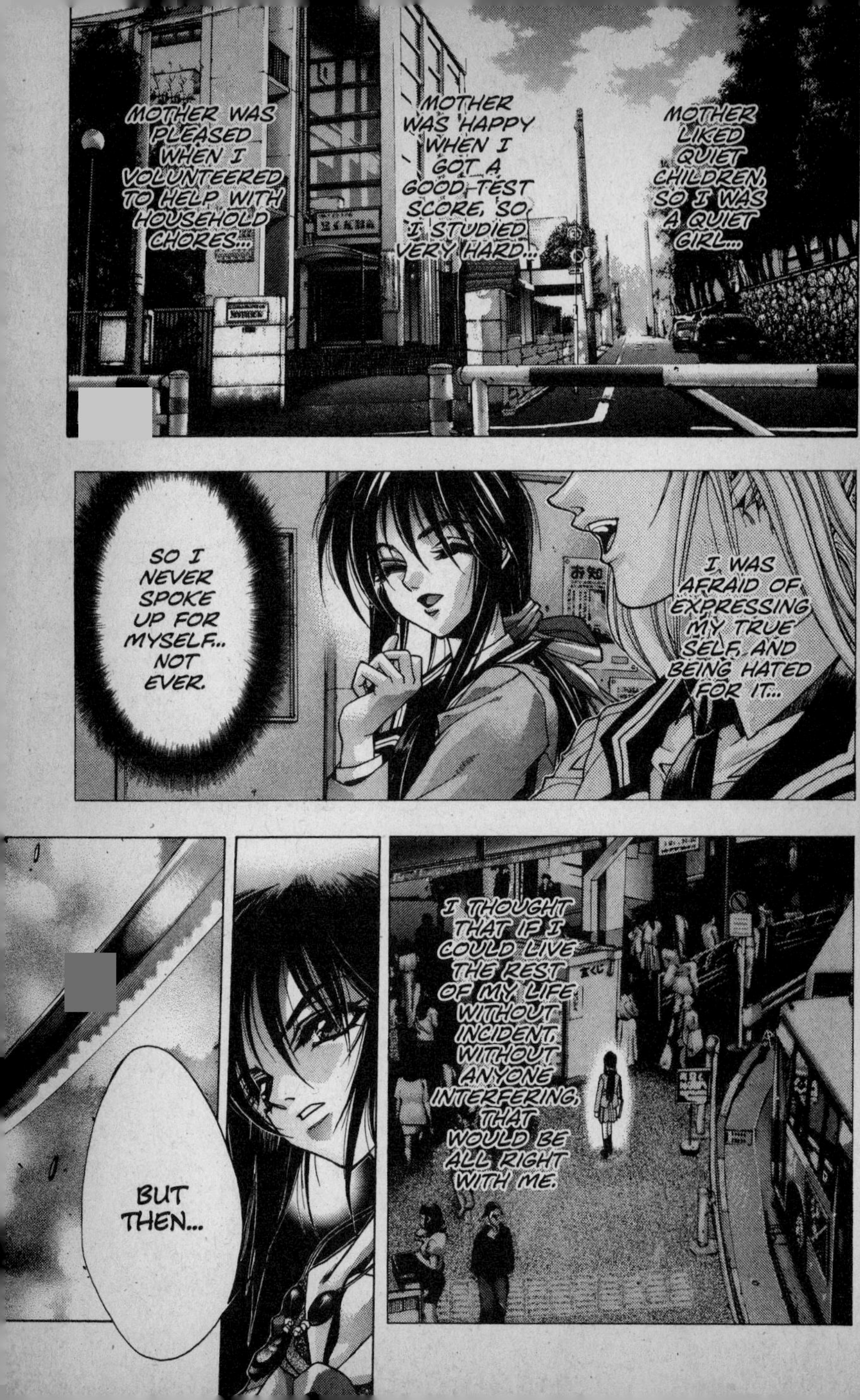
MOTHER LIKED QUIET CHILDREN, SO I WAS A QUIET GIRL...
MOTHER WAS HAPPY WHEN I GOT A GOOD TEST SCORE, SO I STUDIED VERY HARD...
MOTHER WAS PLEASED WHEN I VOLUNTEERED TO HELP WITH HOUSEHOLD CHORES...
I WAS AFRAID OF EXPRESSING MY TRUE SELF, AND BEING HATED FOR IT...
SO I NEVER SPOKE UP FOR MYSELF... NOT EVER.
I THOUGHT THAT IF I COULD LIVE THE REST OF MY LIFE WITHOUT INCIDENT, WITHOUT ANYONE INTERFERING, THAT WOULD BE ALL RIGHT WITH ME.
BUT THEN...

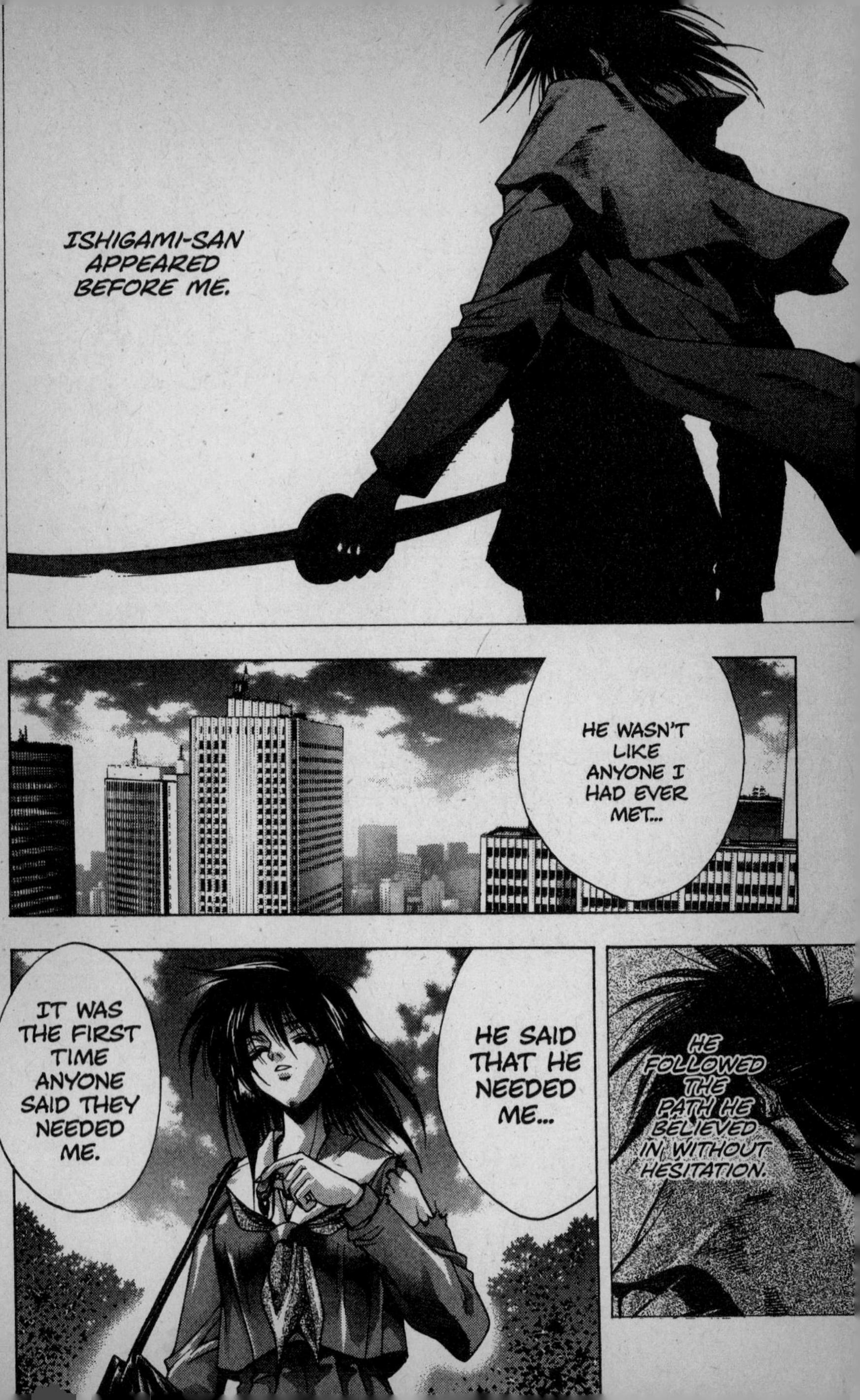
ISHIGAMI-SAN APPEARED BEFORE ME.
HE WASN'T LIKE ANYONE I HAD EVER MET...
HE FOLLOWED THE PATH HE BELIEVED IN WITHOUT HESITATION.
HE SAID THAT HE NEEDED ME...
IT WAS THE FIRST TIME ANYONE SAID THEY NEEDED ME.

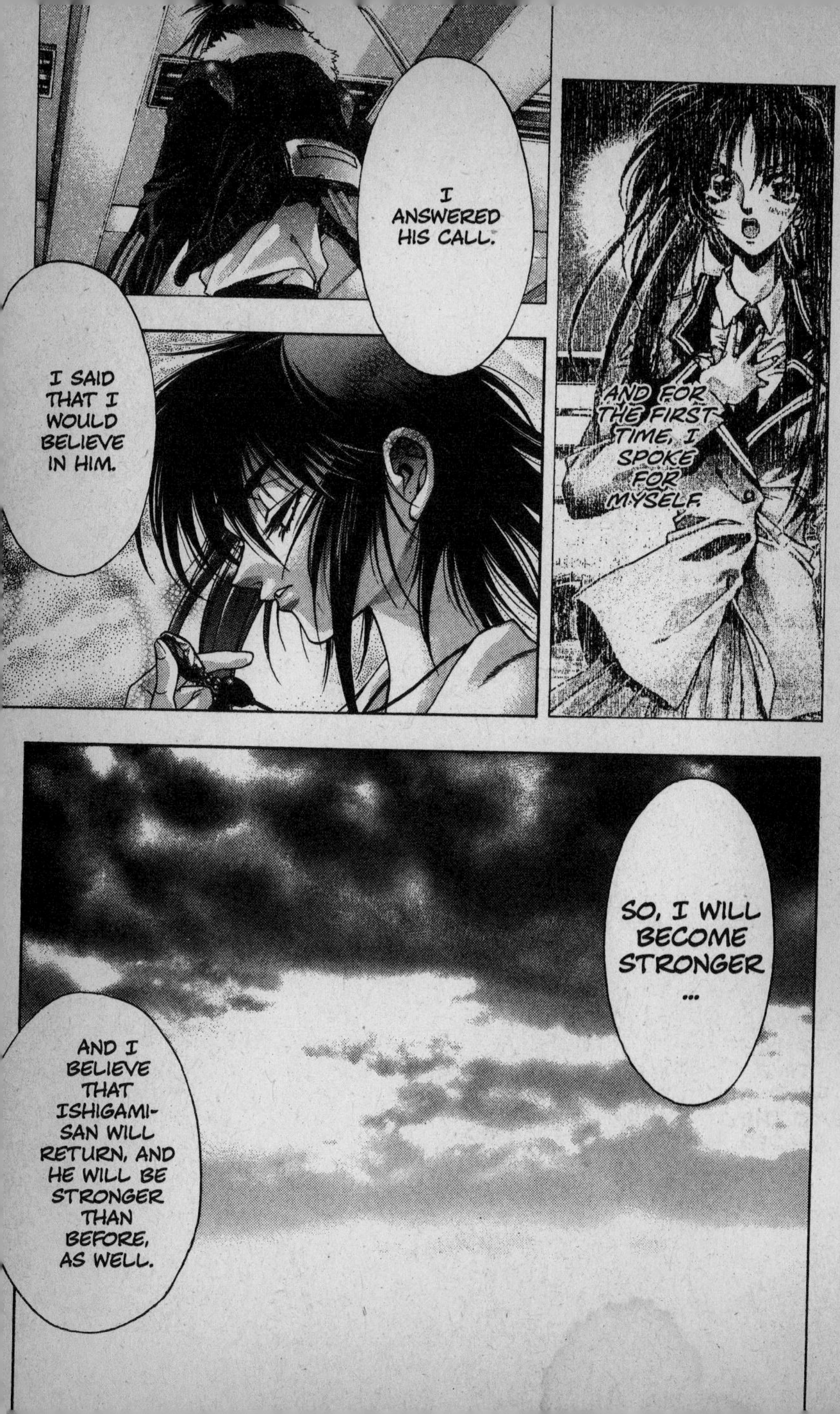
AND FOR THE FIRST TIME, I SPOKE FOR MYSELF.
I ANSWERED HIS CALL.
I SAID THAT I WOULD BELIEVE IN HIM.
SO, I WILL BECOME STRONGER ...
AND I BELIEVE THAT ISHIGAMI-SAN WILL RETURN, AND HE WILL BE STRONGER THAN BEFORE, AS WELL.

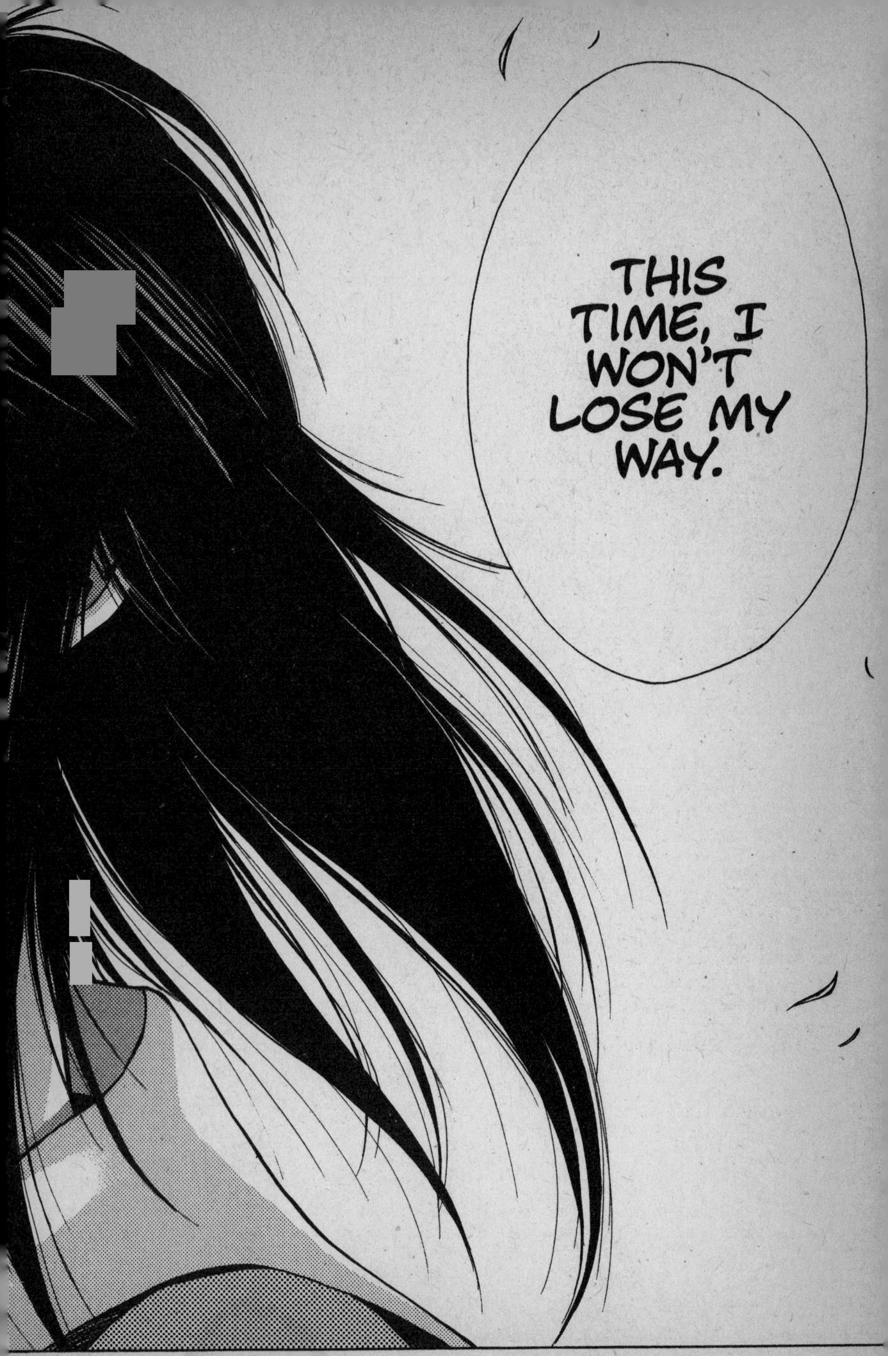
THIS TIME, I WON'T LOSE MY WAY.

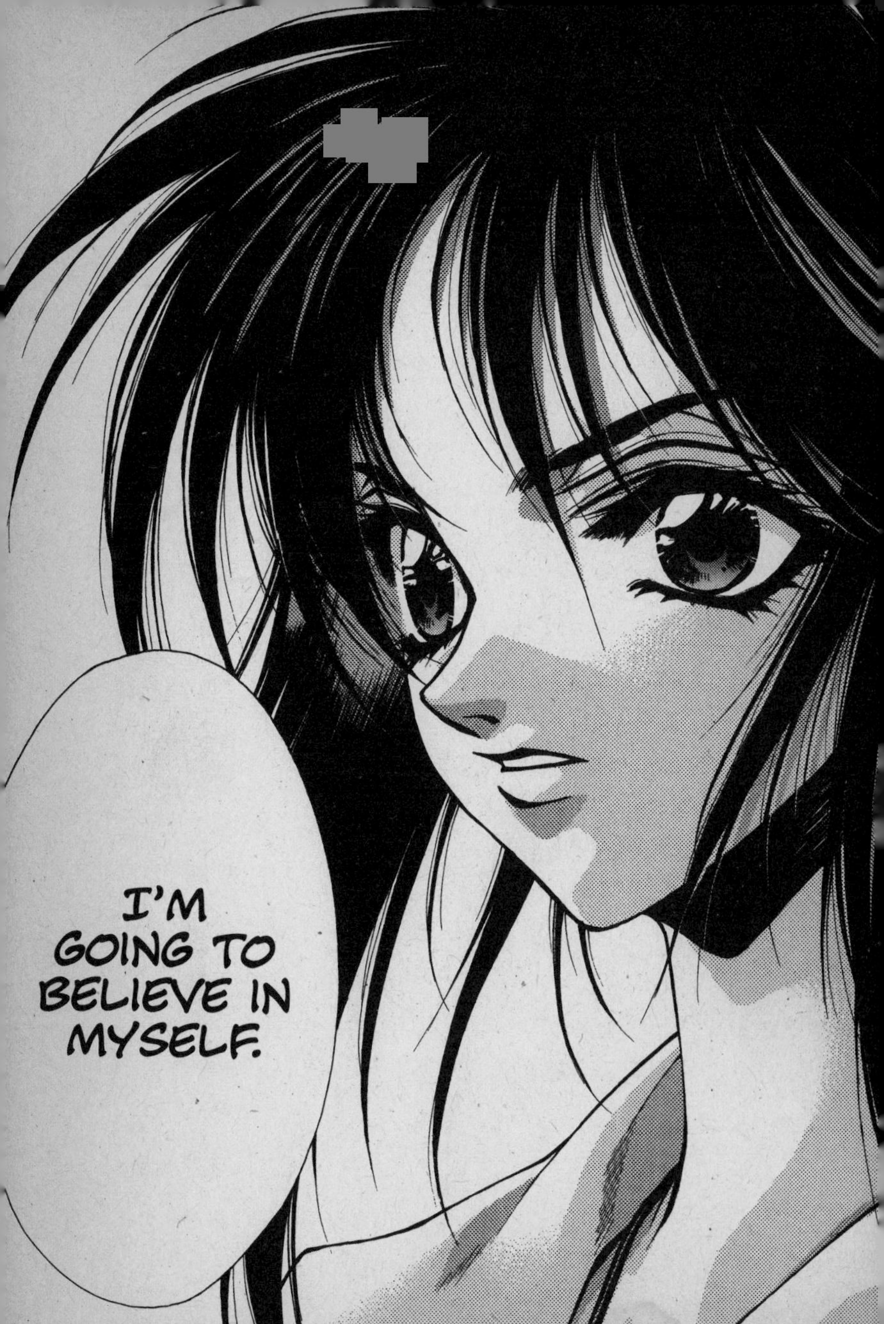
I'M GOING TO BELIEVE IN MYSELF.

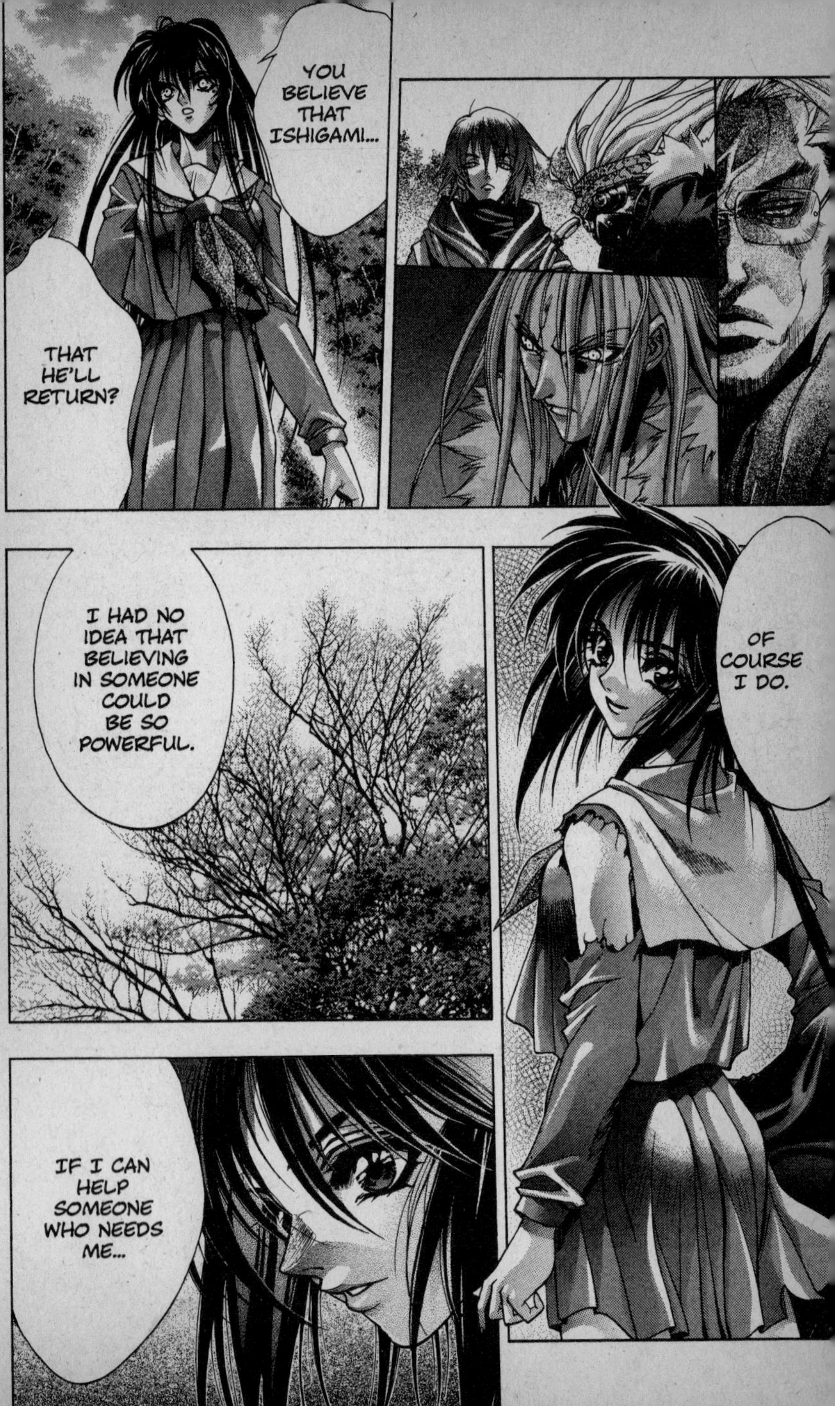
YOU BELIEVE THAT ISHIGAMI...
THAT HE'LL RETURN?
OF COURSE I DO.
I HAD NO IDEA THAT BELIEVING IN SOMEONE COULD BE SO POWERFUL.
IF I CAN HELP SOMEONE WHO NEEDS ME...

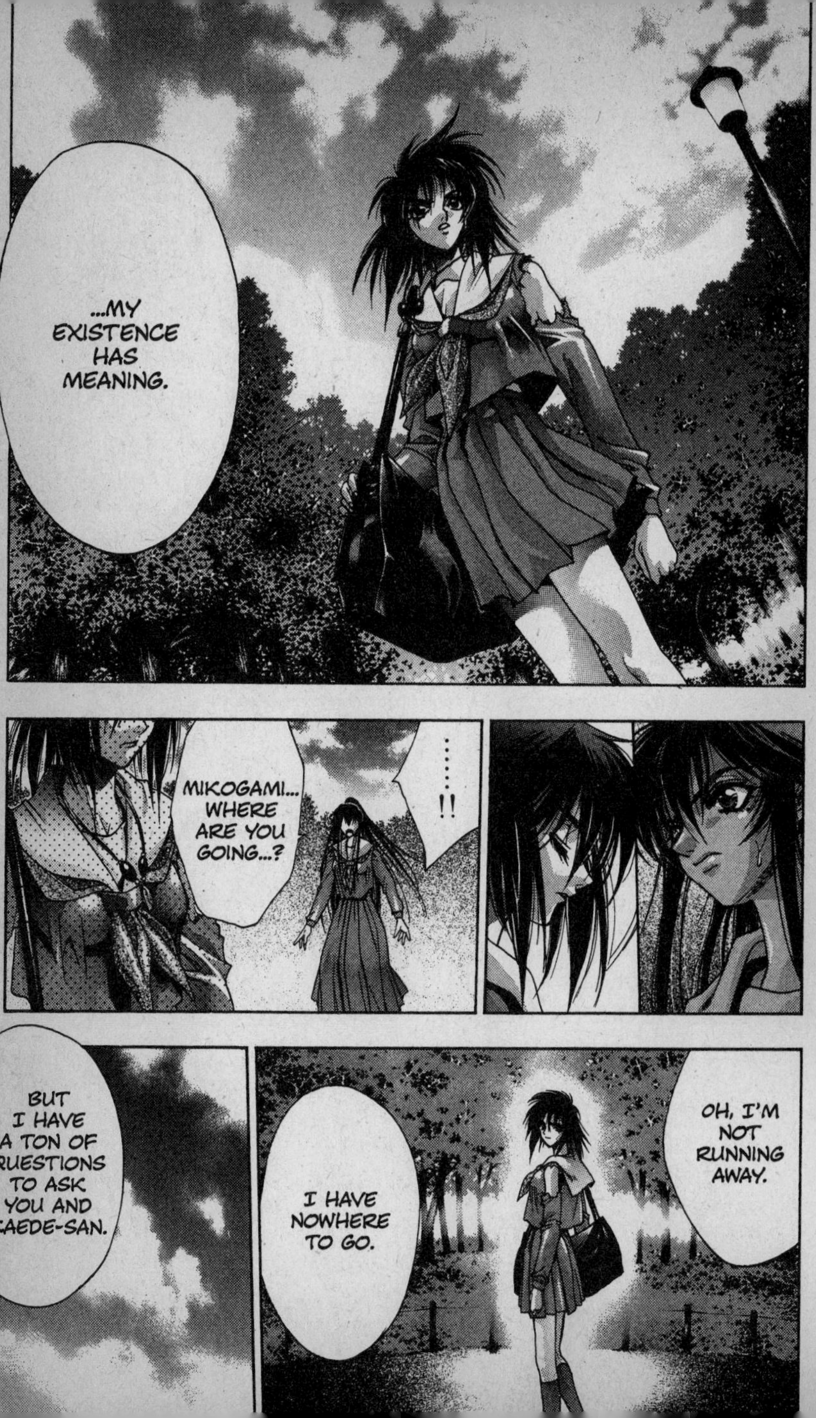
...MY EXISTENCE HAS MEANING.
......!!
MIKOGAMI... WHERE ARE YOU GOING...?
OH, I'M NOT RUNNING AWAY.
I HAVE NOWHERE TO GO.
BUT I HAVE A TON OF QUESTIONS TO ASK YOU AND KAEDE-SAN.

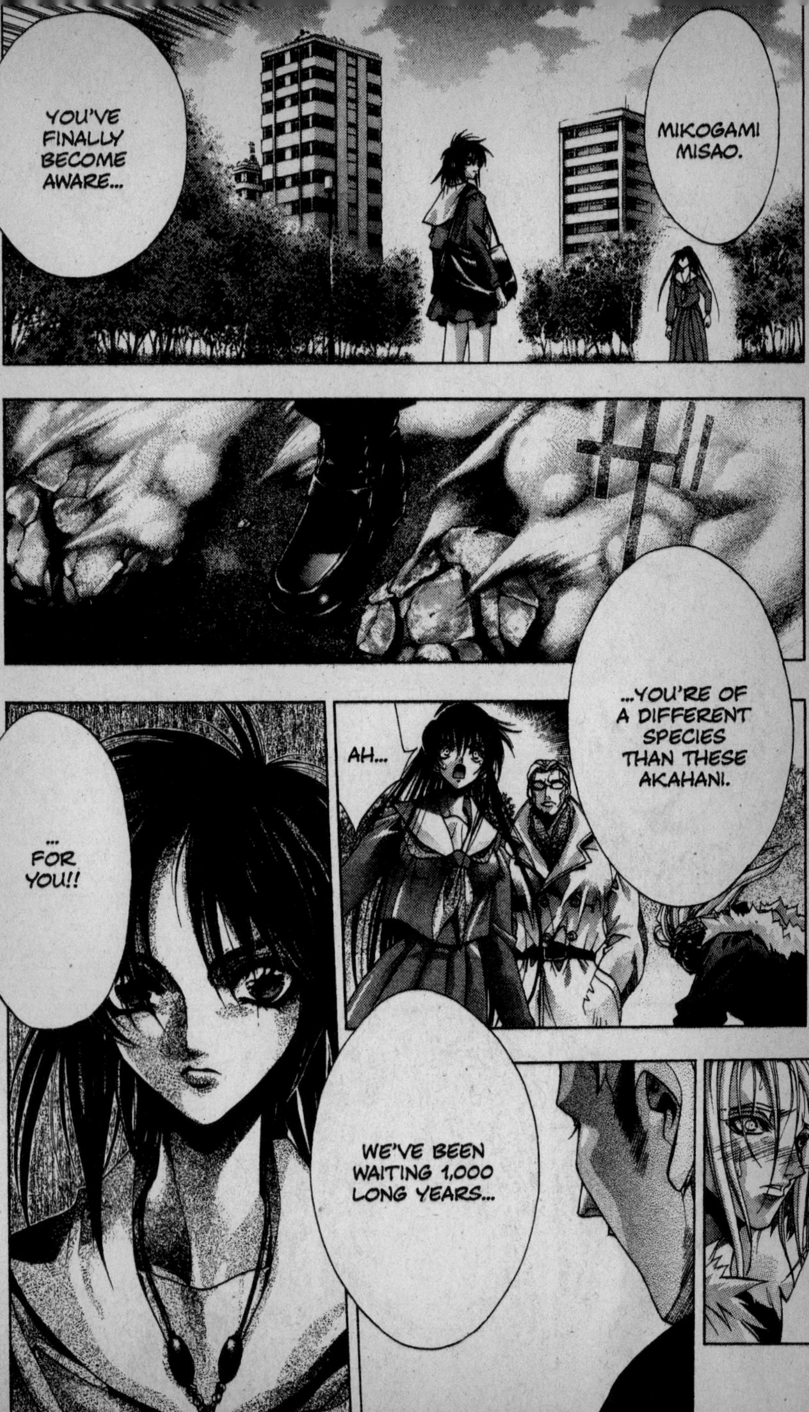
MIKOGAMI MISAO.
YOU'VE FINALLY BECOME AWARE...
...YOU'RE OF A DIFFERENT SPECIES THAN THESE AKAHANI.
AH...
WE'VE BEEN WAITING 1,000 LONG YEARS...
... FOR YOU!!

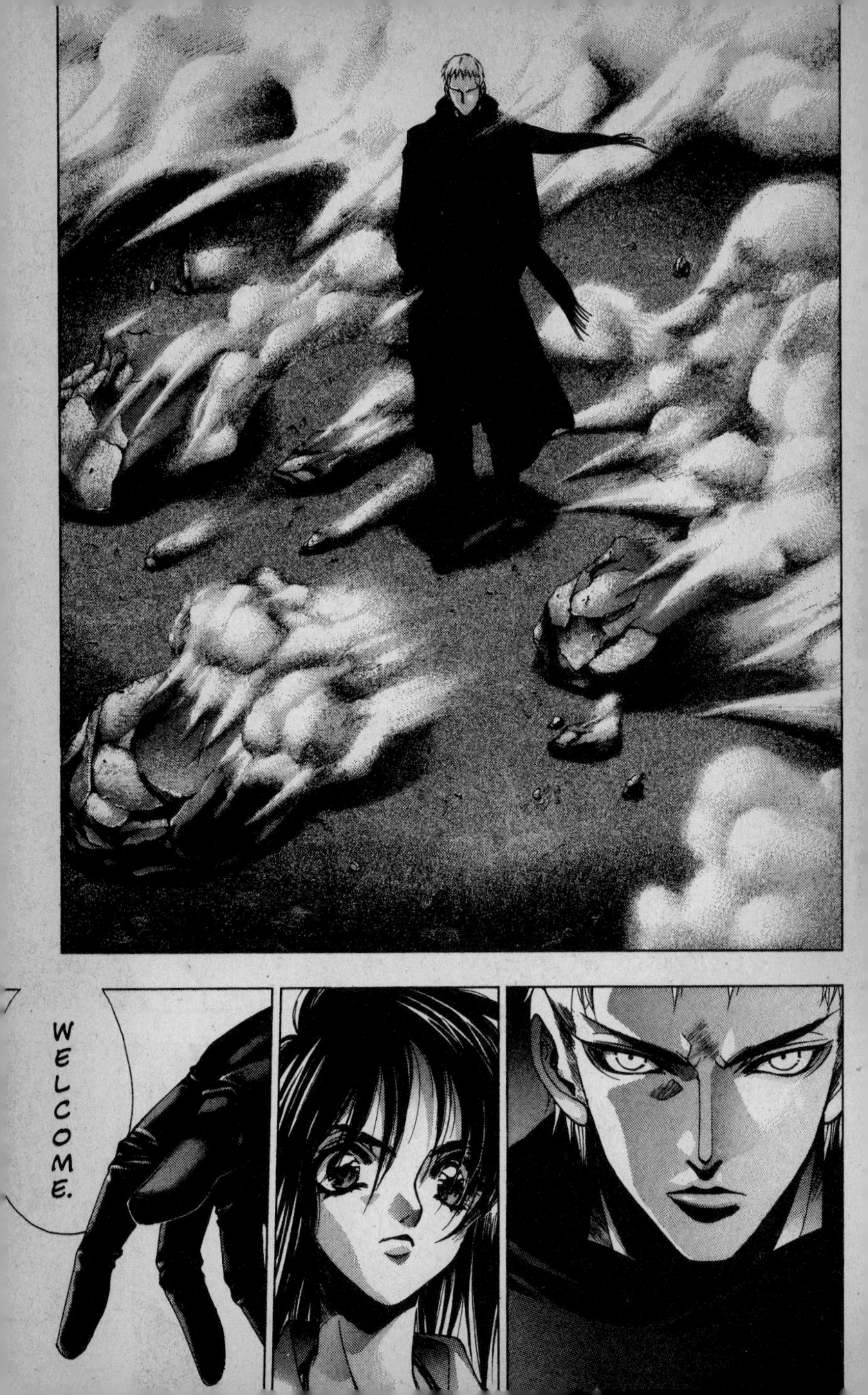
WELCOME.

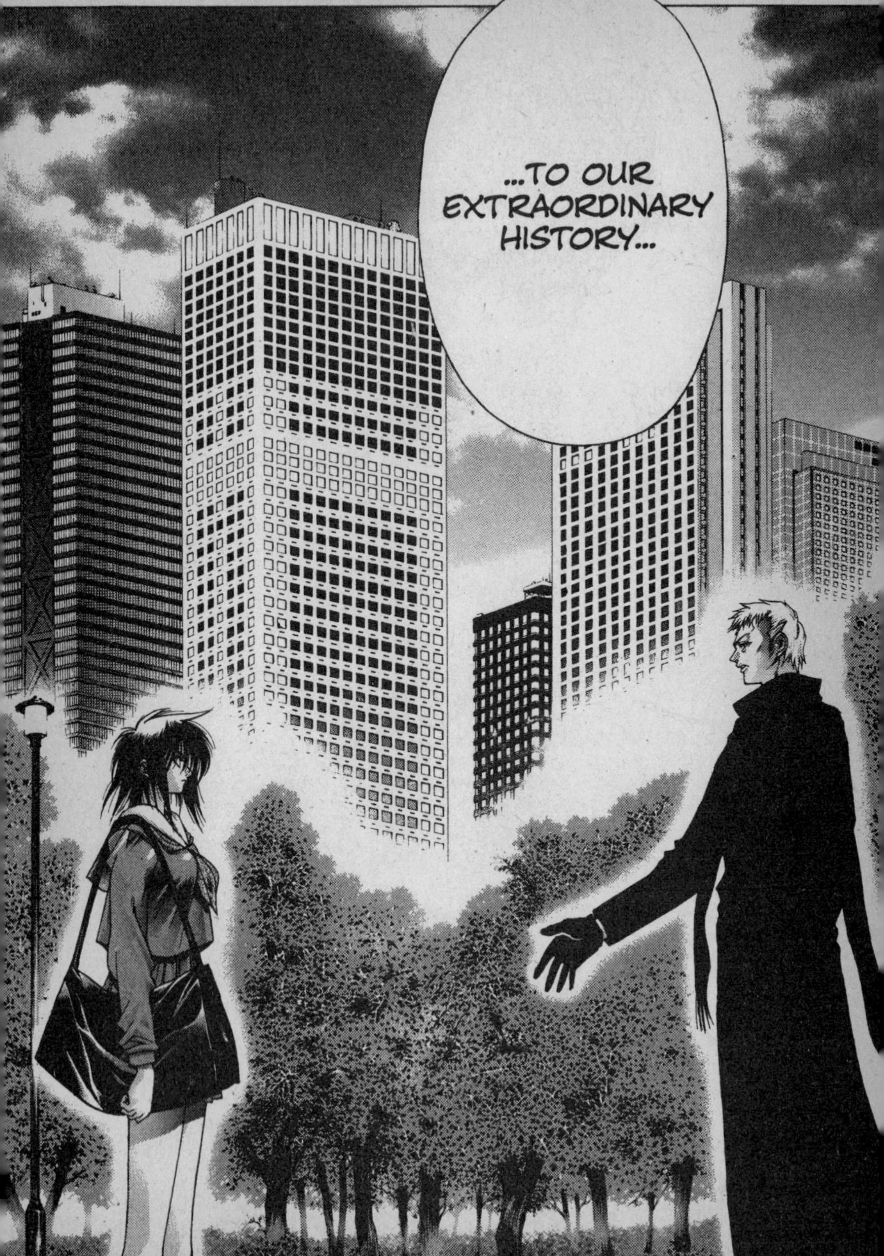
...TO OUR EXTRAORDINARY HISTORY...

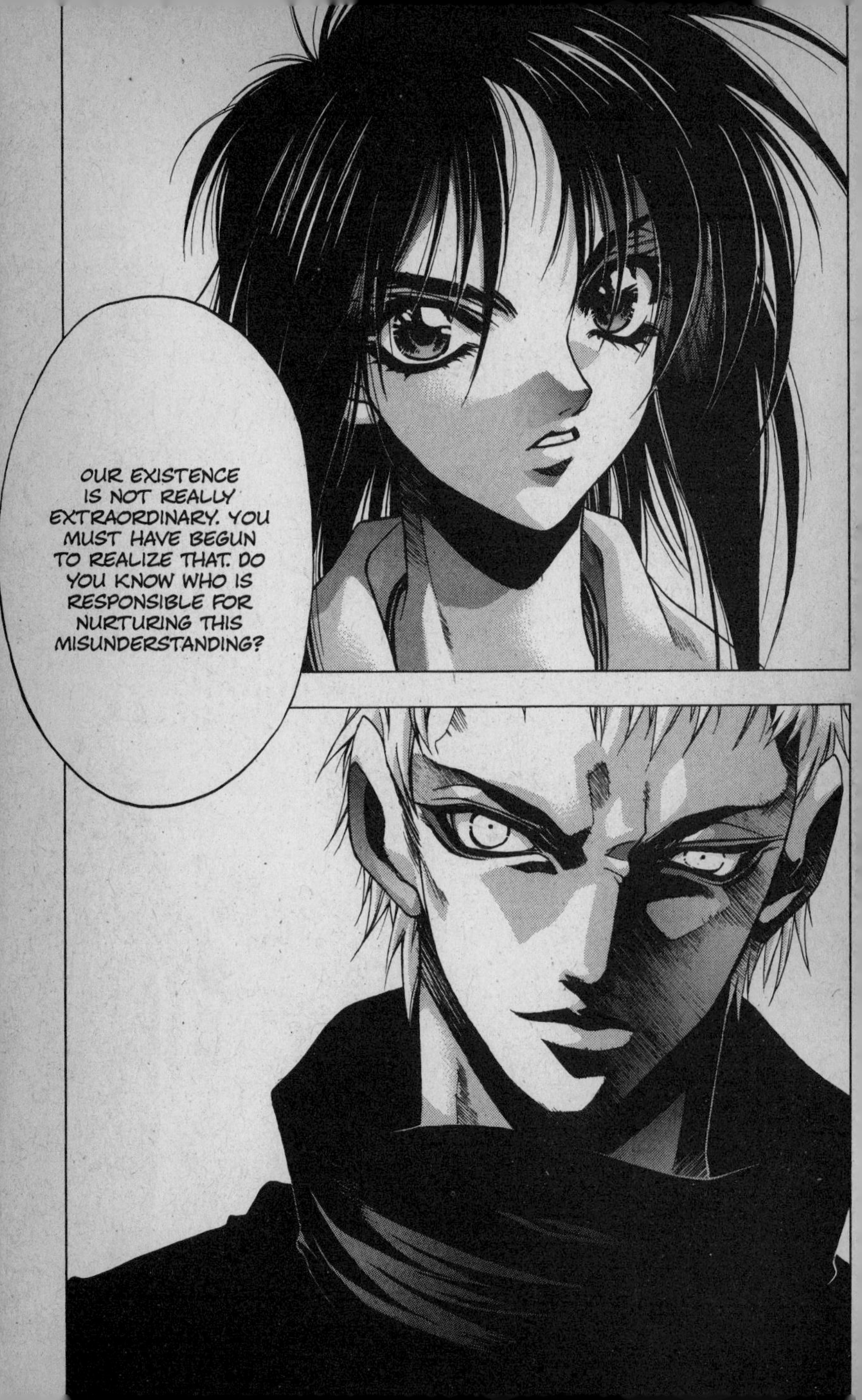
OUR EXISTENCE IS NOT REALLY EXTRAORDINARY. YOU MUST HAVE BEGUN TO REALIZE THAT. DO YOU KNOW WHO IS RESPONSIBLE FOR NURTURING THIS MISUNDERSTANDING?

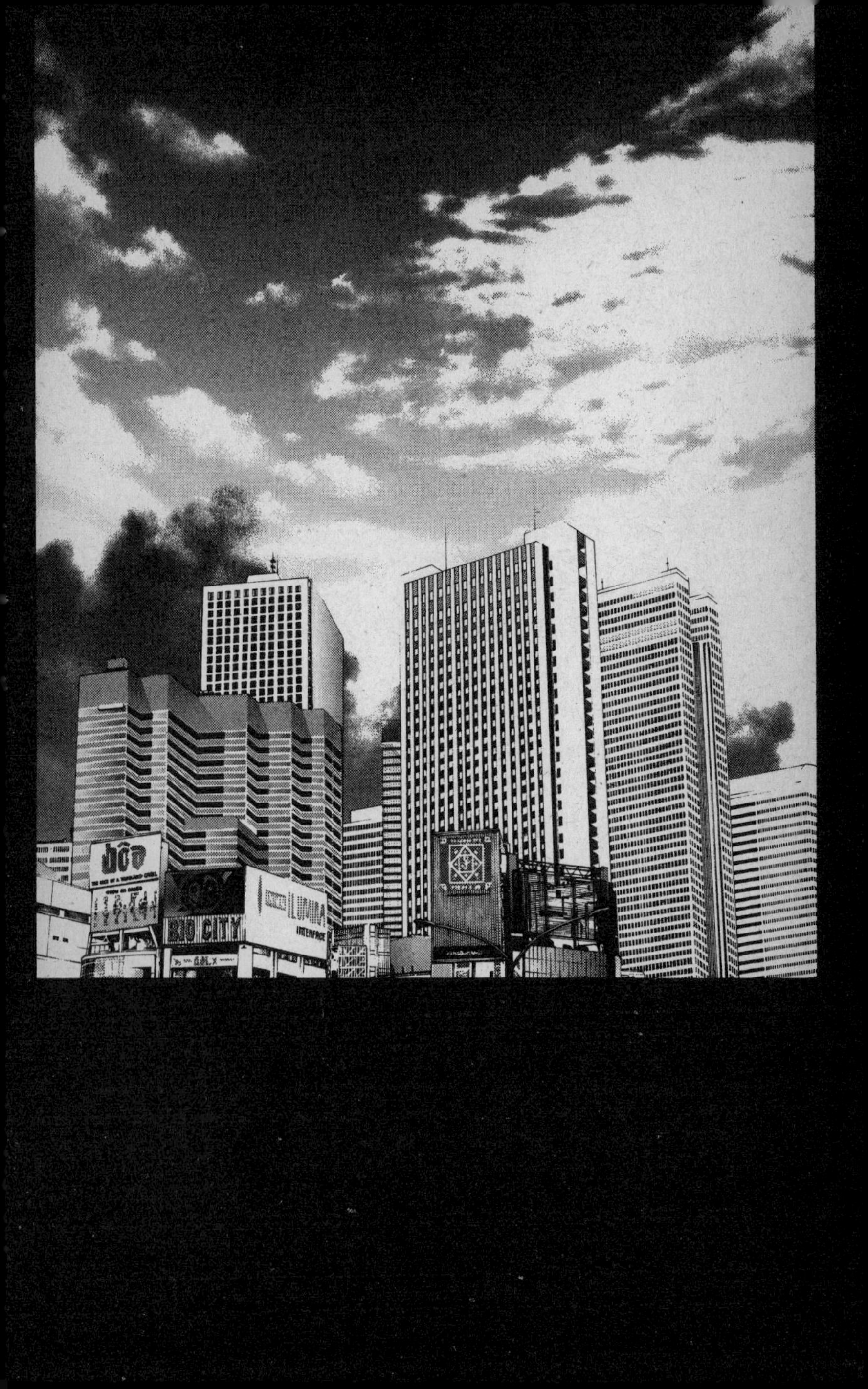
BIG CITY
INTERFACE

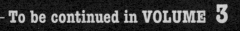
To be continued in VOLUME 3

STAFF

Masahiro Uchida
Hideaki Amano
Masao Yamagishi

•

Hirofumi Sugimoto
Ryo Sugino

•

Naoki Hirose
Masanobu Takahashi

•

Wrench Studio
Shiki Satoshi

In the next VOLUME of

Without any clue as to where Ishigami could have gone, Mikogami continues her life at high school. But when a Kegai no Tami hunter shows up, it threatens the mission to recaptured the now escaped 88 beasts. And when Kikunosuke tries to discover more about the mysterious Kegai no Tami hunter, he is faced with the mystery of his past. And Mikogami's disappearance again sends everyone on another desperate search.

TOKYOPOP SHOP

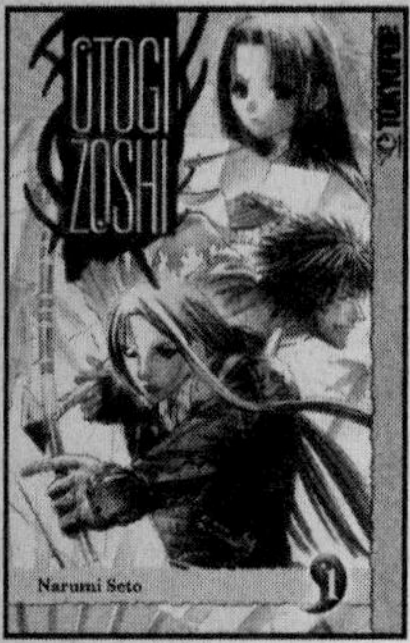
OTOGI ZOSHI
Narumi Seto
1

© NARUMI SETO. © IG/VAP/NTV.

OTOGI ZOSHI

BY NARUMI SETO

An all-out samurai battle to retrieve the Magatama, the legendary gem that is said to hold the power to save the world!

ACTION

T TEEN AGE 13+

Hot new prequel to the hit anime!

STRAWBERRY MARSHMALLOW

BY BARASUI

Cute girls do cute things...in *very* cute ways.

A sweet slice of delight that launched the delicious anime series!

COMEDY

T TEEN AGE 13+

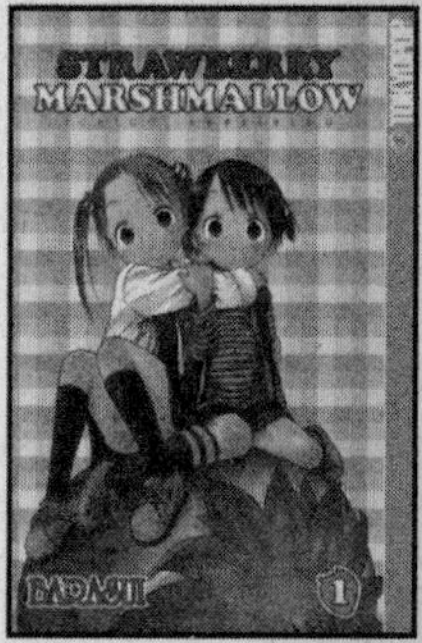
STRAWBERRY
MARSHMALLOW
1

© Barasui.

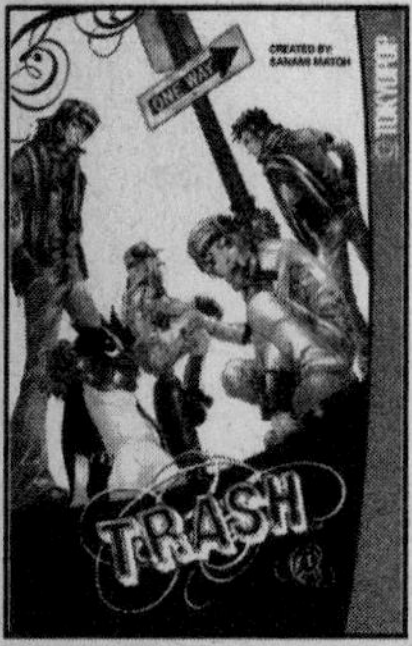
ONE WAY
TRASH

© SANAMI MATOH.

TRASH

BY SANAMI MATOH

When your uncle is the biggest mob boss in New York, it's hard to stay out of the family business!

COMEDY

OT OLDER TEEN AGE 16+

From the creator of the fan-favorite *Fake!*

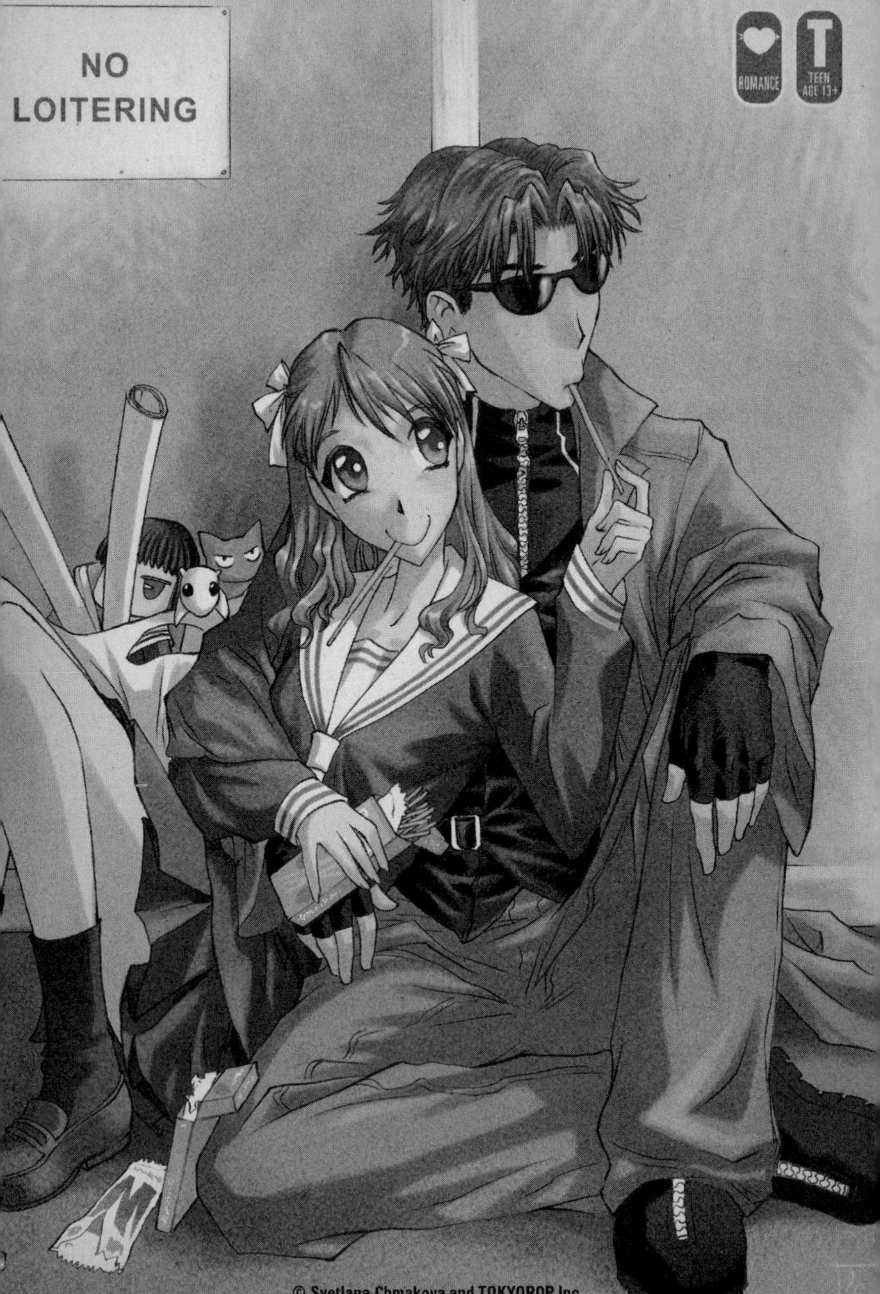
NO
LOITERING
ROMANCE
T
TEEN
AGE 13+

Sometimes even two's a crowd.

When Christie settles in the Artist Alley of her first-ever
anime convention, she only sees it as an opportunity to
promote the comic she has started with her boyfriend.
But conventions are never what you expect, and soon a
whirlwind of events sweeps Christie off her feet and
changes her life. Who is the mysterious cosplayer who
won't even take off his sunglasses indoors? What do you
do when you fall in love with a guy who is going to be miles
away from you in just a couple of days?

STOP!

This is the back of the book.
You wouldn't want to spoil a great ending!

This book is printed "manga-style," in the authentic Japanese right-to-left format. Since none of the artwork has been flipped or altered, readers get to experience the story just as the creator intended. You've been asking for it, so TOKYOPOP® delivered: authentic, hot-off-the-press, and far more fun!

DIRECTIONS

If this is your first time reading manga-style, here's a quick guide to help you understand how it works.

It's easy... just start in the top right panel and follow the numbers. Have fun, and look for more 100% authentic manga from TOKYOPOP®!